D1778888

THE SOVIET LEGAL SYSTEM

PARKER SCHOOL STUDIES
IN FOREIGN AND COMPARATIVE LAW

THE SOVIET LEGAL SYSTEM

Selected Contemporary Legislation and Documents

Compiled and Translated
by
WILLIAM E. BUTLER

Published for the
PARKER SCHOOL OF FOREIGN AND COMPARATIVE LAW
COLUMBIA UNIVERSITY IN THE CITY OF NEW YORK

BY

OCEANA PUBLICATIONS, INC.
DOBBS FERRY, NEW YORK
1978

Library of Congress Cataloging in Publication Data

Soviet legal system: fundamental principles and historical commentary. III. Series: Columbia University. Parker School of Foreign and Comparative Law. Parker School studies in foreign and comparative law.
Law 340'.0947 78-2419
ISBN 0-379-00791-6

Manufactured in the United States of America

THE PARKER SCHOOL
OF FOREIGN AND COMPARATIVE LAW

The Parker School of Foreign and Comparative Law is dedicated exclusively to the study and teaching of foreign and comparative law. The School owes its existence to the beneficence of Judge Edwin B. Parker, who left the bulk of his estate for the founding and support of a school which would prepare young persons "to render practical service of a high order to the government of the United States in its foreign relations or to financial and industrial institutions engaged in foreign trade or commerce."

The present mission of the Parker School is threefold. The School is required by the University Statutes to provide "the educational needs of the School of Law and the School of International Affairs with respect to instruction in the laws of foreign countries." To this end, the School offers five courses and five seminars. The School also has a research and publication program of its own and to date has published more than a dozen books on various aspects of foreign law. Lastly, the School offers each June a concentrated four weeks program in foreign law for lawyers interested in international problems. To date, more than five hundred lawyers have attended the program. They have come from all of the United States, and from Canada, Latin America, Western Europe, Japan, and the Middle East.

In 1978 the School marked its forty-seventh year of affiliation with Columbia University in the City of New York.

TABLE OF CONTENTS

CHAPTER VIII
NATURAL RESOURCES AND ENVIRONMENT LAW

CHAPTER IX ADMINISTRATIVE LAW

CHAPTER X FINANCE LAW

CHAPTER XI LABOR LAW

CHAPTER XII PUBLIC HEALTH

CHAPTER XIII PUBLIC EDUCATION

CHAPTER XIV
CRIMINAL LAW, CRIMINAL PROCEDURE, AND PENOLOGY

PREFACE

The present volume is a new addition to *The Soviet Legal System*. It contains the full texts of most legislation and other documents referred to or excerpted in *The Soviet Legal System; Fundamental Principles and Historical Commentary, 3rd ed.*, as well as a great deal of additional material of interest to the student, scholar, practitioner, or government legal adviser. Of special note are the full set of Fundamental Principles of all-union legislation as amended, the complete text of the 1936 USSR Constitution in its final *redaction*, the draft 1977 USSR Constitution, and the economic legislation.

All materials in this volume have been translated anew, and except for the 1936 USSR Constitution and 1977 Draft Constitution, all documents included are in force as amended to December 31, 1977. Certain changes are imminent in Soviet legislation as a consequence of the adoption of the new USSR Constitution in 1977. The expression "soviet of working people's deputies" has been replaced in the new Constitution by "soviet of people's deputies." The process of substitution in each act must occur through an express amendment, and three sets of Fundamental Principles already had been amended to this effect in 1977. In addition, the USSR Council of Ministers is preparing new Laws for submission to the USSR Supreme Soviet including: a Law on the USSR Council of Ministers; a Law on People's Control in the USSR; and a Law on State Arbitrazh in the USSR.

W.E.B.

ABBREVIATIONS

Biulleten'	Biulleten' normativnykh aktov ministerstv i vedomstv SSSR
CPSU	Communist Party of the Soviet Union
MVD	Ministry of Internal Affairs
SP RSFSR	Sobranie postanovlenii Pravitel'stva RSFSR
SP SSSR	Sobranie postanovlenii Pravitel'stva SSSR
SU RSFSR	Sobranie uzakonenii i rasporiazhenii Raboche-Krest'ianskogo Pravitel'stva RSFSR
Vedomosti RSFSR	Vedomosti verkhovnogo soveta RSFSR
Vedomosti SSSR	Vedomosti verkhovnogo soveta SSSR
VLKSM	All-Union Leninist Communist Youth League
VTsSPS	All-Union Central Trade Union Council

CHAPTER I

THE STATE SYSTEM

CONSTITUTION (BASIC LAW) OF THE UNION OF SOVIET SOCIALIST REPUBLICS

[Adopted by the USSR Supreme Soviet, Law of October 7, 1977; entered into force October 7, 1977. Izvestia, October 8, 1977, pp. 3-6]

*The Great October Socialist Revolution, performed by the workers and peasants of Russia under the leadership of the Communist Party headed by V.I. Lenin, overthrew the power of the capitalists and landowners, broke the fetters of oppression, *established the dictatorship of the proletariat*, and created the Soviet state, a state of a new type, the principal instrument for the defense of revolutionary conquests and for the construction of socialism and communism. *The worldwide historical turning of mankind from capitalism toward socialism had begun.*

**Having gained victory in the civil war and having repulsed imperialist intervention, Soviet power has carried out the most profound socio-economic transformations, ended forever the exploitation of man by man, class antagonism, and national enmity. The unification of the soviet republics into the USSR augmented the forces and possibilities of the peoples of the country in the construction of socialism. Social ownership of the means of production and genuine democracy for the toiling masses were confirmed. For the first time in the history of mankind a socialist society was created.

The unfading exploit of the Soviet people and its Armed Forces, who secured an historic victory in the Great Fatherland War, became a clear manifestation of the power of socialism. This triumph strengthened the international position of the USSR and opened new favorable possibilities for the growth of the forces of socialism, national liberation, democracy, and peace in the entire world.

*In continuing their creative activity, *the working people of the Soviet Union* have ensured the rapid and all-round development of the country and the improvement of the socialist system. The alliance of the working class, collective farm peasantry, and people's intelligentsia, and the friendship of nations and peoples of the USSR have been consolidated. The socio-political unity of Soviet society has been formed, the leading force of which is the working class. Having fulfilled the tasks of the dictatorship of the proletariat, the Soviet state has become an all-people's state. The leading role of the Communist Party, vanguard of the whole people, has grown.

A developed socialist society has been built in the USSR. At this stage, when socialism already is developing on its own basis, the creative forces of the new society and the advantages of the socialist way of life are being revealed more fully and the fruits of the great revolutionary conquests being enjoyed more extensively.

---

*Asterisked paragraphs or Articles contain new language, which appears in italics.

**Indicates language in the Draft has been deleted from the final version.

***Indicates a new Article which did not appear in the Draft.

Article 16 of the Draft was deleted from the final redaction.

*This is a society in which powerful productive forces have been created and an advanced science and culture, in which the well-being of the people is constantly growing and more favorable conditions for the all-round development of the individual are being formed.

*This is a society of mature socialist social relations in which a new historical community of people, the Soviet people, has been formed on the basis of the coming together of all classes and social strata and the legal and actual equality of all nations and peoples, and their fraternal cooperation.

This is a society of high organization, ideological commitment, and consciousness of the working people, who are patriots and internationalists.

*This is a society whose law of life is the concern of all for the good of each and the concern of each for the good of all.

*This is a society of genuine democracy, whose political system ensures the efficient administration of all public affairs, the more active participation of the working people in state life, and the combining of real rights and freedoms of citizens with their duties and responsibility to society.

The developed socialist society is an objectively necessary stage on the path to communism.

*The ultimate purpose of the Soviet state is the building of a classless communist society in which social communist self-administration is being developed. The principal tasks of the socialist all-people's state are: creation of the material-technical base of communism; improvement of socialist social relations and their transformation into communist, bring up the man of a communist society, raise the material and cultural level of the life of the working people, ensure the security of the country, and further the strengthening of peace and the development of international cooperation.

The Soviet people,

being guided by the ideas of scientific communism and observing fidelity to their revolutionary traditions,

resting on the great socio-economic and political conquests of socialism,

striving toward the further development of socialist democracy,

taking into account the international position of the USSR as an integral part of the world system of socialism and being conscious of its international responsibility,

*preserving the succession of the ideas and principles of the first Soviet constitution of 1918, the 1924 USSR Constitution, and the 1936 USSR Constitution,

*consolidate the bases of the social system and policy of the USSR, establish the rights, freedoms, and duties of citizens and the principles for the organization and the purposes of the socialist all-people's state and proclaim them in the present Constitution.

I. Bases of the Socio-Political and Economic Structure

Chapter 1. Political System

Article 1. The Union of Soviet Socialist Republics is a socialist all-people's state, expressing the will and interests of the workers, peasants and intelligentsia, and working people of all nations and peoples of the country.

*Article 2. All power in the USSR shall belong to the people.

The people shall exercise state power through soviets of people's deputies, which shall constitute the political foundation of the USSR.

All other state agencies shall be under the control of and accountable to the soviet of people's deputies.

Article 3. The organization and activity of the Soviet state shall be structured in accordance with the principle of democratic centralism: the electivity of all agencies of state power from bottom to top, their accountability to the people, and the binding nature of decisions of superior agencies for inferior. Democratic centralism shall combine unified direction with initiative and creative activity on the spot and with the responsibility of each state agency and official for the matter entrusted.

*Article 4. The Soviet state and all its agencies shall operate on the basis of socialist legality and ensure the protection of the legal order, and the rights and freedoms of citizens.

**State and social organizations and officials shall be obliged to observe the USSR Constitution and Soviet laws.

Article 5. The most important questions of state life shall be submitted for discussion by the whole people, and also to a vote by the whole people (referendum).

**Article 6. The Communist Party of the Soviet Union shall be the guiding and directing force of Soviet society and the nucleus of its political system and state and social organizations. The CPSU shall exist for the people and shall serve the people.

Armed with Marxist-Leninist teaching, the Communist Party shall determine the general perspective of the development of society and the internal and foreign policy line of the USSR, direct the great creative activity of the Soviet people, and impart a planned, scientifically well-founded character to its struggle for the triumph of communism.

*All party organizations shall operate within the framework of the USSR Constitution.

**Article 7. Trade unions, the All-Union Leninist Communist Youth League, cooperative, and other social organizations shall, in accordance with their charter tasks, take part in the administration of state and social affairs and in deciding political, economic, and socio-cultural questions.

***Article 8. Labor collectives shall participate in the discussion and deciding of state and social affairs, in the planning of production and social development, in the training and placing of cadres, and in the discussion and deciding of questions of the management of enterprises and institutions, the improvement of labor and domestic conditions, the use of assets earmarked for production development, and also for socio-cultural measures and material incentive.

Labor collectives shall develop socialist competition, promote the dissemination of progressive work methods and the strengthening of labor discipline, nurture their members in the spirit of communist morality, and be concerned for raising their political consciousness, culture, and professional qualifications.

*Article 9. The further unfolding of socialist democracy shall be the basic orientation of the development of the political system of Soviet society: more extensive participation of citizens in the administration of the affairs of society and the state, improvement of the state apparatus, increasing the activeness of social organizations, intensifying people's control, strengthening the legal basis of state and social life, expanding publicity, and constantly taking account of public opinion.

Chapter 2. Economic System

*Article 10. Socialist ownership of the means of production in the form of state (all-people's) and collective farm-cooperative ownership shall constitute the basis of the economic system of the USSR.

The property of trade union and other social organizations needed by them to carry out charter tasks also shall be socialist ownership.

The state shall protect socialist ownership and create the conditions for its increase.

No one shall have the right to use socialist ownership for the purposes of personal gain and other mercenary purposes.

*Article 11. State ownership shall be the common property of the whole Soviet people, the basic form of socialist ownership.

There shall be in the exclusive ownership of the state: land, its minerals, water, forests. The basic means of production in industry, construction, and agriculture, means of transport and communications, banks, property of trade, municipal, and other enterprises organized by the state, the basic city housing fund, and also other property needed to carry out the tasks of the state, shall belong to the state.

*Article 12. The means of production and other property needed for them to carry out charter tasks shall be the ownership of collective farms and other cooperative organizations and their associations.

Land occupied by collective farms shall be allocated to them free of charge and in perpetuity.

The state shall promote the development of collective-farm-cooperative ownership and its coming together with state ownership.

Collective farms, just as other land users, shall be obliged to use land efficiently, to treat it carefully, and to increase its fertility.

*Article 13. Labor incomes shall comprise the basis of personal ownership of citizens of the USSR. Articles of everyday use, personal consumption, convenience, and subsidiary household husbandry, a dwelling house, and labor savings may be in personal ownership. The personal ownership of citizens and the right to inherit it shall be protected by the state.

Land parcels granted in the procedure established by law for subsidiary husbandry (including the maintenance of livestock and poultry), gardening, and vegetable growing, and also for individual housing construction, may be in the use of citizens. Citizens shall be obliged to use rationally the land plots granted to them. The state and collective farms shall render assistance to citizens in the conduct of subsidiary husbandry.

Property in the personal ownership or use of citizens should not serve to derive nonlabor income nor be used to the prejudice of the interests of society.

*Article 14. The labor of the Soviet people, free from exploitation, shall be the source for the growth of social wealth and the well-being of the people and every Soviet person.

In accordance with the principle of socialism: "From each according to his ability, to each according to his labor", the state shall exercise control over the measure of labor and consumption. It shall determine the amount of tax on incomes subject to taxation.

Socially useful labor and its results shall determine the status of a person in society. The state shall, by combining material and moral incentives, encouraging innovation and a creative attitude toward work, promote the transformation of labor into the primary vital requirement of every Soviet person.

*Article 15. The ultimate aim of social production under socialism shall be the fullest satisfaction of the growing material and spiritual needs of people.

Relying on the creative activeness of the working people, socialist competition, and the achievements of scientific-technical progress, and improving the forms and methods for direction of the economy, the state shall ensure the growth of labor productivity and increase of production efficiency and work quality, and the dynamic, planned, and proportional development of the national economy.

*Article 16. The economy of the USSR shall constitute a single national economic complex embracing all links of social production, distribution, and exchange on the territory of the country.

The direction of the economy shall be carried out on the basis of state plans for economic and social development, taking into account branch and territorial principles and combining centralized management with economic independence and initiative of enterprises, associations, and other organizations. Economic accountability, profit, cost of production, and other economic levers and stimuli shall be used actively in this connection.

*Article 17. In the USSR individual labor activity shall be permitted in accordance with the law in the sphere of handicrafts, agriculture, domestic servicing of the populace, and also other forms of activity based exclusively on the personal labor of citizens and members of their families. The state shall regulate individual labor activity, ensuring its use in the interests of society.

*Article 18. In the interests of present and future generations in the USSR necessary measures shall be taken for the protection and scientifically well-founded, rational use of land and its minerals, water resources, flora and fauna, for the preservation of air and water purity, for ensuring the reproduction of natural wealth, and improvement of the human environment.

Chapter 3. Social Development and Culture

*Article 19. The indissoluble alliance of workers, peasants, and intelligentsia constitutes the social basis of the USSR.

The state shall promote the intensification of the social homogeneity of society: the eradication of essential differences between town and countryside, intellectual and physical labor, and the all-round development and coming together of all nations and peoples of the USSR.

**Article 20. In accordance with the communist ideal: "Free development for each is the condition of the free development of all", the state shall pursue the aim of expanding the real possibilities for the application by citizens of their creative forces, abilities, and talents, for the all-round development of the individual.

*Article 21. The state shall be concerned for the improvement of conditions and protection of labor, its scientific organization, and for the reduction and, in future, the complete abolition of arduous physical labor on the basis of the complex mechanization and automation of production processes in all branches of the national economy.

*Article 22. In the USSR the program for successively transforming agricultural labor into a variety of industrial; expanding the network of institutions for public education, culture, public health, trade and public dining, domestic servicing, and municipal economy in rural localities; and transformation of villages and towns into comfortable rural settlements shall be implemented.

*Article 23. On the basis of the growth of labor productivity, the state shall steadfastly pursue the course of raising the level of payment for labor and the real incomes of the working people.

Social consumption funds shall be created with a view to the fullest satisfaction of the requirements of the Soviet people. With the broad participation of social organizations and labor collectives, the state shall ensure the growth and just distribution of these funds.

*Article 24. State systems for public health, social security, trade and public dining, domestic servicing, and municipal economy shall operate and be developed in the USSR.

The state shall encourage the activity of cooperative and other social organizations in all spheres of services for the populace. It shall promote the development of mass physical culture and sport.

*Article 25. A uniform system of public education which provides the general education and professional training of citizens, serves communist upbringing, the spiritual and physical development of youth, and prepares them for labor and social activity.

Article 26. In accordance with the requirements of society, the state shall ensure the planned development of science and the training of scientific cadres and organize the introduction of the results of scientific research into the national economy and other spheres of life.

*Article 27. The state shall be concerned for the protection, increase, and extensive use of the spiritual requirements of society for the moral and aesthetic nurturing of Soviet people and for raising their cultural level.

The development of professional art and people's artistic activity shall be encouraged in the USSR in every possible way.

Chapter 4. Foreign Policy

*Article 28. The USSR shall steadfastly carry on the Leninist policy of peace and favor the consolidation of the security of peoples and extensive international cooperation.

The foreign policy of the USSR is aimed at ensuring favorable international conditions for the building of communism in the USSR, the protection of state interests of the Soviet Union, strengthening the position of world socialism, supporting the struggle of peoples for national liberation and social progress, preventing aggressive wars, achieving general and complete disarmament, and consistently implementing the principle of peaceful coexistence of states with a different social system.

**War propaganda shall be prohibited in the USSR.

Article 29. Relations of the USSR with other states shall be built on the basis of observing the principles of mutual renunciation of sovereign equality; mutual renunciation of the use or threat of force; inviolability of frontiers; territorial integrity of states; peaceful settlement of disputes; non-interference in internal affairs; respect for human rights and basic freedoms; equality and the right of peoples to decide their own destiny; cooperation between states; good-faith fulfillment of obligations arising from generally recognized principles and norms of international law and from international treaties concluded by the USSR.

Article 30. As an integral part of the world system of socialism and socialist commonwealth, the Soviet Union shall develop and strengthen friendship and cooperation, comradely mutual assistance with the countries of socialism on the basis of socialist internationalism and shall participate actively in economic integration and in the international socialist division of labor.

Chapter 5. Defense of the Socialist Fatherland

*Article 31. Defense of the socialist Fatherland is regarded as among the most important functions of the state and is the cause of the whole people.

**The Armed Forces of the USSR have been created and universal military service established for the purpose of defending socialist conquests, the peaceful labor of the Soviet people, and the sovereignty and territorial integrity of the state.

The duty of the USSR Armed Forces to the people shall be to reliably defend the socialist Fatherland, to be in constant combat readiness, guaranteeing the immediate rebuff to any aggressor.

*Article 32. The state shall ensure the security and defense capability of the country and equip the USSR Armed Forces with everything necessary.

The duties of state agencies, social organizations, officials, and citizens in ensuring the security of the country and strengthening its defense capability shall be determined by USSR legislation.

II. The State and The Individual

Chapter 6. Citizenship of the USSR. Equality of Citizens

*Article 33. A single union citizenship has been established in the USSR. Each citizen of a union republic shall be a citizen of the USSR.

The bases and procedure for the acquisition and loss of Soviet citizenship shall be determined by a Law on Citizenship of the USSR.

Citizens of the USSR abroad shall enjoy the defense and protection of the Soviet state.

Article 34. Citizens of the USSR shall be equal before the law irrespective of origin, social and property status, racial and national affiliation, sex, education, language, attitude toward religion, type and nature of occupation, place of residence, and other circumstances.

The equality of citizens of the USSR shall be ensured in all areas of economic, political, social, and cultural life.

*Article 35. Women and men shall have equal rights in the USSR.

The realization of these rights shall be ensured by granting women opportunities equal to men to receive an education and professional training, labor, remuneration therefor and advancement in work, socio-political and cultural activity, and also special measures for the protection of the labor and health of women; the creation of conditions allowing women to combine labor with motherhood; legal protection and material and moral support for motherhood and children, including the granting of paid leaves and other privileges for pregnant women and mothers, and a gradual reduction of work hours for women who have small children.

Article 36. Soviet citizens of different races and nationalities shall have equal rights.

The realization of these rights shall be ensured by the policy of the all-round development and coming together of all nations and peoples of the USSR, the nurturing of citizens in the spirit of Soviet patriotism and socialist internationalism, and the possibility to use the native language and the languages of other peoples of the USSR.

Any direct or indirect limitation of the rights whatever or the establishment of direct or indirect privileges for citizens on grounds of race or nationality, and equally any advocacy of racial or national exclusivity, animosity, or contempt, shall be punished by law.

Article 37. Foreign citizens and stateless persons in the USSR shall be guaranteed the rights and freedoms provided by law, including the right to have recourse to a court and other state agencies in order to defend personal, property, family, and other rights belonging to them.

Foreign citizens and stateless persons on the territory of the USSR shall be obliged to respect the USSR Constitution and to observe Soviet laws.

Article 38. The USSR shall grant the right of asylum to foreigners who are persecuted for defending the interests of the working people and the cause of peace, for participating in the revolutionary and national liberation movement, and for progressive socio-political, scientific, or other creative activity.

Chapter 7. Basic Rights, Freedoms, and Duties of Citizens of the USSR

Article 39. Citizens of the USSR shall possess in their entirety the socio-economic, political, and personal rights and freedoms proclaimed and guaranteed by the USSR Constitution and Soviet laws. The socialist system shall ensure the expansion of rights and freedoms, the uninterrupted improvement of the conditions of life of citizens through the fulfillment of programs for socio-economic and cultural development.

The use by citizens of rights and freedoms should not harm the interests of society and the state nor the rights of other citizens.

*Article 40. Citizens of the USSR shall have the right to labor, that is, to receive guaranteed work with payment for labor in accordance with its quantity and quality and not lower than the minimum amount established by the state, including the right to choose a profession, type of occupation, and work in accordance with their vocation, abilities, professional training, education, and taking into account social requirements.

This right shall be ensured by the socialist system of economy, steady growth of the productive forces of society, free professional training, raising labor qualifications, the study of new specialties, and the development of systems of professional orientation and arrangement of employment.

*Article 41. Citizens of the USSR shall have the right to leisure.

This right shall be ensured by the establishment for workers and employees of a work week not exceeding 41 hours, a reduced work day for a number of professions and trades and a reduced work period at night; by granting annual paid leaves. weekly days of leisure, and also expanding the network of cultural-enlightenment and therapeutic institutions, the development of mass sport, physical culture, and tourism; the creation of favorable possibilities for leisure at the place of residence and other conditions for the rational use of free time.

The duration of work time and leisure for collective farmers shall be regulated by the collective farms.

*Article 42. Citizens of the USSR shall have the right to health protection.

This right shall be ensured by free qualified medical assistance rendered by state public health institutions; expansion of the network of institutions for care and for strengthening the health of citizens; the development and improvement of safety techniques and production sanitation; the implementation of extensive or preventive measures; measures for improving the environment; special concern for the health of the rising generation, including the prohibition of child labor not connected with study and labor upbringing; the development of scientific research directed toward preventing and reducing the incidence of disease and ensuring a long active life for citizens.

*Article 43. Citizens of the USSR shall have the right to material security in old age, in the event of illness, and also in the event of complete or partial loss of the capacity to work or of loss of breadwinner.

This right shall be guaranteed by social insurance for workers, employees, and collective farmers, and benefits for temporary loss of capacity to work; by payment from the state and collective farms of pensions for age, disability, and loss of breadwinner; arranging employment of citizens who have partially lost the capacity to work; concern for elderly citizens and disabled persons; other forms of social security.

*Article 44. Citizens of the USSR shall have the right to housing.

This right shall be ensured by the development and protection of a state and social housing fund, the promotion of cooperative and individual housing construction, the just distribution of housing premises under social control granted in effectuation of the construction program for well-built dwellings, and also by low apartment rent and municipal services. Citizens of the USSR should treat carefully the housing granted to them.

**Article 45. Citizens of the USSR shall have the right to education.

This right shall be ensured by free education of all types, universal compulsory secondary education for youth, the extensive development of professional-technical, secondary specialized, and higher education on the basis of linking study with life, with production; the development of correspondence and evening education; the granting of state stipends and benefits to pupils and students; the issuance of school textbooks free of charge; the possibility of studying in school in the native language, and the creation of conditions for self-education.

*Article 46. Citizens of the USSR shall have the right to use the achievements of culture.

This right shall be ensured through public accessibility to the valuables of fatherland and world culture in state and social funds; the development and equitable siting of cultural-enlightenment institutions on the territory of the country; the development of television and radio, book publishing and the periodical press, and a network of free libraries; and the expansion of cultural exchange with foreign states.

*Article 47. Citizens of the USSR shall, in accordance with the aims of communist construction, be guaranteed the freedom of scientific, technical, and artistic creativity. It shall be ensured by the extensive development of scientific research, invention and rationalization activity, and the development of literature and art. The state shall create the material conditions necessary therefor and render support to voluntary societies and creative unions, and organize the introduction of inventions and rationalization proposals into the national economy and other spheres of life.

The rights of authors, inventors, and rationalizers shall be protected by the state.

*Article 48. Citizens of the USSR shall have the right to participate in the administration of state and social affairs and in the discussion and adoption of laws and decisions of general-state and local significance.

This right shall be ensured by the opportunity to elect and to be elected to soviets of people's deputies and other elective state agencies, take part in all-people's discussions and voting, people's control, the work of state agencies, social organizations, and public initiative agencies, and in meetings of labor collectives and at their place of residence.

*Article 49. Each citizen of the USSR shall have the right to submit proposals to state agencies and social organizations concerning the improvement of their activity and to criticize shortcomings in work.

Officials shall be obliged within the established periods to consider proposals and applications of citizens, to reply to them, and to take necessary measures.

Persecution for criticism shall be prohibited. Persons who persecute for criticism shall be brought to responsibility.

Article 50. In accordance with the interests of the working people and with a view to strengthening the socialist system, citizens of the USSR shall be guaranteed the freedom of: speech, press, assembly, meetings, street processions, and demonstrations.

The realization of these political freedoms shall be ensured by granting public buildings, streets and squares, extensive dissemination of information, and the possibility of using the press, television, and radio to the working people and their organizations.

Article 51. In accordance with the aims of communist construction, citizens of the USSR shall have the right to unite in social organizations which further the development of political activeness and initiative and the satisfaction of their diverse interests.

Social organizations shall be guaranteed conditions for the successful fulfillment of their charter tasks.

*Article 52. Freedom of conscience, that is, the right to confess any religion or not to confess such, to perform religious cults, or to carry on atheistic propaganda shall be guaranteed to citizens of the USSR. Incitement of animosity and hatred in connection with religious beliefs shall be prohibited.

The church in the USSR shall be separated from the state, and the school from the church.

*Article 53. The family shall be under the protection of the state.

Marriage shall be based upon the voluntary consent of a woman and a man; spouses shall be completely equal in family relations.

The state shall manifest concern for the family through the creation and development of an extensive network of children's institutions, organizations, and the improvement of domestic and public dining services, the payment of an allowance for the birth of a child, granting benefits and privileges to families with many children, and also other types of benefits and assistance to the family.

*Article 54. Citizens of the USSR shall be guaranteed inviolability of the person. No one may be subjected to arrest other than on the basis of a judicial decision or with the sanction of a procurator.

Article 55. Citizens of the USSR shall be guaranteed inviolability of the home. No one shall have the right to enter a home without legal grounds against the will of the persons residing therein.

Article 56. The personal life of citizens, secrecy of correspondence, telephone conversations, and telegraph communications shall be protected by law.

*Article 57. Respect for the individual and the protection of the rights and freedoms of citizens shall be the duty of all state agencies, social organizations, and officials.

Citizens of the USSR shall have the right to judicial protection against infringements against honor and dignity, life and health, and personal freedom and property.

*Article 58. Citizens of the USSR shall have the right to appeal the actions of officials and of state and social agencies. Appeals should be considered in the procedure and within the periods established by law.

The actions of officials committed in violation of law, in excess of their powers, and impinging upon the rights of citizens may be appealed to a court in the procedure established by law.

**Citizens of the USSR shall have the right to compensation for damage caused by the illegal actions of state and social organizations, and also of officials during the execution of their official duties.

Article 59. The realization of rights and freedoms shall be inseparable from the execution by a citizen of his duties.

A citizen of the USSR shall be obliged to observe the USSR Constitution, Soviet laws, respect the rules of socialist community life, and bear with dignity the high calling of citizen of the USSR.

*Article 60. The duty and matter of honor for every citizen of the USSR capable of labor shall be conscientious labor in the domain of socially useful activity which he has chosen and observance of labor discipline. Avoidance of socially useful labor is incompatible with the principles of a socialist society.

*Article 61. A citizen of the USSR shall be obliged to care for and reinforce socialist ownership. The duty of a citizen of the USSR shall be to struggle against stealing and dissipation of state and social property and to treat the public weal carefully.

Persons who infringe socialist ownership shall be punished according to law.

Article 62. A citizen of the USSR shall be obliged to safeguard the interests of the Soviet state and to further the strengthening of its might and authority.

Protection of the socialist Fatherland shall be the sacred duty of each citizen of the USSR.

Treason shall be the gravest crime against the people.

Article 63. Military service in the ranks of the USSR Armed Forces shall be the honorable duty of Soviet citizens.

Article 64. The duty of every citizen of the USSR shall be to respect the national dignity of other citizens and to strengthen friendship of nations and peoples of the Soviet multinational state.

Article 65. A citizen of the USSR shall be obliged to respect the rights and legal interests of other persons, to be intolerant of antisocial offenses, and to promote in every possible way the protection of public order.

*Article 66. Citizens of the USSR shall be obliged to be concerned about the upbringing of children, to prepare them for socially useful labor, and to raise worthy members of socialist society. Children shall be obliged to be concerned about parents and to render them assistance.

***Article 67. Citizens of the USSR shall be obliged to care for nature and to protect its wealth.

***Article 68. Concern for the preservation of historical monuments and other cultural valuables shall be a duty and responsibility of citizens of the USSR.

Article 69. The internationalist duty of a citizen of the USSR shall be to further the development of friendship and cooperation with the peoples of other countries and the maintenance and strengthening of world peace.

III. The National and State Structure of the USSR

Chapter 8. The USSR: A Union State

*Article 70. The Union of Soviet Socialist Republics shall be a single union multinational state formed on the basis of the principle of socialist federalism as a result of the free self-determination of nations and the voluntary association of equal Soviet Socialist Republics.

The USSR shall personify the state unity of the Soviet people and unite all nations and peoples for the purpose of the joint construction of communism.

*Article 71. There shall be associated in the Union of Soviet Socialist Republics:

Russian Soviet Federated Socialist Republic,

Ukrainian Soviet Socialist Republic,

Belorussian Soviet Socialist Republic,

Uzbek Soviet Socialist Republic,

Kazakh Soviet Socialist Republic,

Georgian Soviet Socialist Republic,

Azerbaidzhan Soviet Socialist Republic,

Lithuanian Soviet Socialist Republic,

Moldavian Soviet Socialist Republic,

Latvian Soviet Socialist Republic,

Kirgiz Soviet Socialist Republic,

Tadzhik Soviet Socialist Republic,

Armenian Soviet Socialist Republic,

Turkmen Soviet Socialist Republic,

Estonian Soviet Socialist Republic.

Article 72. The right of free secession from the USSR shall be preserved for each union republic.

*Article 73. There shall be subject to the jurisdiction of the Union of Soviet Socialist Republics in the person of its highest agencies of state power and administration:

(1) admission of new republics into the USSR; confirmation of the formation of new autonomous republics and autonomous regions within union republics;

(2) determination of the state frontier of the USSR and confirmation of changes of frontiers between union republics;

(3) establishment of general principles for the organization and activity of republic and local agencies of state power and administration;

(4) ensuring the unity of legislative regulation throughout the territory of the USSR, the establishment of fundamental principles of legislation of the USSR and union republics;

(5) implementation of a uniform socio-economic policy, direction of the economy of the country; determination of the basic orientations of scientific and technical progress and general measures for the rational use and protection of natural resources; the working out and confirmation of plans for the development of the national economy and for socio-cultural development of the USSR, confirmation of reports concerning their fulfillment;

(6) working out and confirmation of a uniform state budget of the USSR, confirmation of the report concerning its execution; direction of a single monetary and credit system; establishment of taxes and revenues received for the formation of the USSR state budget; determination of the policy in the domain of prices and payment for labor;

**(7) direction of branches of the national economy and associations and enterprises of all-union subordination; general direction of branches of union republic subordination;

(8) questions of peace and war, defense of sovereignty, protection of the state frontiers and territory of the USSR, organization of defense, and direction of the Armed Forces;

(9) ensuring state security;

(10) representation of the USSR in international relations; links of the USSR with foreign states and international organizations; establishment of the general procedure for and coordination of relations of union republics with foreign states and international organizations; foreign trade and other types of foreign economic activity on the basis of the state monopoly;

(11) control over the observance of the USSR Constitution and ensuring the conformity of the union republic constitutions to the USSR Constitution;

(12) deciding other questions of all-union significance.

Article 74. Laws of the USSR shall have the same force on the territory of all union republics. In the event of a divergence between a union republic law and an all-union law, the law of the USSR shall prevail.

Article 75. The territory of the Union of Soviet Socialist Republics shall be integral and shall include the territories of the union republics.

The sovereignty of the USSR shall extend throughout all of its territory.

Chapter 9. The Union Soviet Socialist Republic

*Article 76. The union republic shall be a sovereign soviet socialist state which has combined with other Soviet republics into the Union of Soviet Socialist Republics.

Beyond the limits specified in Article 73 of the USSR Constitution, a union republic shall exercise state power independently on its territory.

A union republic shall have its own Constitution which corresponds to the USSR Constitution and takes into account the peculiarities of the republic.

*Article 77. A union republic shall take part in deciding questions relegated to the jurisdiction of the USSR in the USSR Supreme Soviet, the Presidium of the USSR Supreme Soviet, the Government of the USSR, and other agencies of the USSR.

A union republic shall ensure integrated economic and social development on its territory, further the effectuation on this territory of the powers of the USSR, and implement the decisions of the highest agencies of state power and administration of the USSR.

In regard to questions relegated to its jurisdiction, a union republic shall coordinate and control the activity of enterprises, institutions, and organizations of union subordination.

Article 78. The territory of a union republic may not be changed without its consent. Frontiers between union republics may be changed by mutual agreement of the respective republics, which shall be subject to confirmation by the USSR.

Article 79. A union republic shall determine its own territorial, regional, national area, and district division and decide other questions of administrative and territorial structure.

Article 80. A union republic shall have the right to enter into relations with foreign states, conclude treaties with them, and exchange diplomatic and consular representatives, and to participate in the activity of international organizations.

Article 81. The sovereign rights of union republics shall be protected by the USSR.

Chapter 10. The Autonomous Soviet Socialist Republic

Article 82. An autonomous republic shall be a part of a union republic.

Beyond the limits of the rights of the USSR and the union republic, an autonomous republic shall independently decide questions relegated to its jurisdiction.

An autonomous republic shall have its own Constitution which corresponds to the USSR Constitution and union republic constitution and takes into account the peculiarities of the autonomous republic.

*Article 83. An autonomous republic shall participate in deciding questions relegated to the jurisdiction of the USSR and union republic through the highest agencies of state power and administration respectively of the USSR and union republic.

An autonomous republic shall ensure integrated economic and social development on its territory, further the effectuation on this territory of the powers of the USSR and union republic, and implement the decisions of the highest agencies of state power and administration of the USSR and union republic.

In regard to questions relegated to its jurisdiction, an autonomous republic shall coordinate and control the activity of enterprises, institutions, and organizations of union and republic (union republic) subordination.

Article 84. The territory of an autonomous republic may not be changed without its consent.

Article 85. The Russian Soviet Federated Socialist Republic shall consist of the autonomous soviet socialist republics: Bashkir, Buriat, Dagestan, Kabardino-Balkarskaia, Kalmytskaia, Karelia, Komi, Mariiskaia, Mordovia, North Osetian, Tatar, Tuva, Udmurt, Checheno-Ingush, Chuvash, Iakut.

In the Uzbek Soviet Socialist Republic shall be the Karakalpak Autonomous Soviet Socialist Republic.

In the Georgian Soviet Socialist Republic shall be the Abkhazian and Adzharian Autonomous Soviet Socialist Republics.

In the Azerbaidzhan Soviet Socialist Republic shall be the Nakhichevan Autonomous Soviet Socialist Republic.

Chapter 11. The Autonomous Region and Autonomous National Area

*Article 86. An autonomous region shall be a part of a union republic or territory. A law concerning an autonomous region shall be adopted by the union republic supreme soviet upon the recommendation of the soviet of people's deputies of the autonomous region.

Article 87. In the Russian Soviet Federated Socialist Republic shall be the autonomous regions: Adygei, Gorno-Altai, Jewish, Karachaevo-Cherkesskaia, Khakasskaia.

In the Georgian Soviet Socialist Republic shall be the Nagorno-Karabakhskaia Autonomous Region.

In the Tadzhik Soviet Socialist Republic shall be the Gorno-Badakhshan Autonomous Region.

*Article 88. An autonomous national area shall be a part of a territory or region. A law on autonomous national areas shall be confirmed by the union republic supreme soviet.

IV. Soviets of People's Deputies and the Procedure for Electing Them

Chapter 12. System and Principles of Activity of Soviets of People's Deputies

Article 89. Soviets of people's deputies -- the USSR Supreme Soviet, union republic supreme soviets, autonomous republic supreme soviets, territory and regional soviets of people's deputies, autonomous region and autonomous national area soviets of people's deputies, district, city, district in city, settlement, and rural soviets of people's deputies -- shall constitute a unified system of agencies of state power.

*Article 90. The term of powers of the USSR Supreme Soviet, union republic supreme soviets, and autonomous republic supreme soviets shall be for five years.

The term of powers of local soviets of people's deputies shall be two and one-half years.

Elections for soviets of people's deputies shall be designated at least two months before the expiry of the period of powers of the respective soviets.

*Article 91. The most important questions relegated to the jurisdiction of the respective soviets of people's deputies shall be considered and decided at their sessions.

Soviets of people's deputies shall elect permanent commissions and create executive and administrative and also other agencies accountable to them.

**Article 92. Soviets of people's deputies shall form people's control agencies, combining state control with social control of the working people at enterprises, collective farms, institutions, and organizations.

People's control agencies shall control the fulfillment of state plans and planning tasks, conduct a struggle against violations of state discipline, manifestations of localism, a departmental approach to matters, mismanagement, wastefulness, red tape, and bureaucratism, and promote the improvement of the work of the state apparatus.

Article 93. Soviets of people's deputies shall, directly and through agencies they have created, direct all branches of state, economic and socio-cultural construction, adopt decisions, ensure their execution, and exercise control over the implementation of decisions.

*Article 94. The activity of soviets of people's deputies shall be built on the basis of collective, free, and business-like discussion and deciding of questions, publicity, and regular accountability of executive and administrative agencies and other agencies created by soviets to the soviets and the populace and on the extensive involvement of citizens in their work.

Soviets of people's deputies and agencies they have created shall systematically inform the populace about their work and decisions adopted.

Chapter 13. The Electoral System

Article 95. Deputies to all soviets of people's deputies shall be elected on the basis of universal, equal, and direct suffrage by secret ballot.

*Article 96. Elections of deputies shall be universal: all citizens of the USSR who have attained 18 years of age shall have the right to elect and to be elected, except for persons deemed insane in the procedure established by law.

A citizen of the USSR who has attained 21 years of age may be elected a deputy of the USSR Supreme Soviet.

Article 97. Elections of deputies shall be equal: each elector shall have one vote; all electors shall participate in elections on an equal basis.

Article 98. Elections of deputies shall be direct: deputies of all soviets of people's deputies shall be elected by citizens directly.

Article 99. Voting during elections of deputies shall be secret: control over the expression of the will of electors shall be excluded.

*Article 100. The right to nominate candidates for deputy shall belong to organizations of the Communist Party of the Soviet Union, trade unions, the All-Union Leninist Communist Youth League, cooperative and other social organizations, labor collectives, and also meetings of military servicemen in military units.

Citizens of the USSR and social organizations shall be guaranteed free and all-round discussion of political, professional, and personal qualities of candidates for deputy, and also the right of agitation at meetings, in the press, and on television and radio.

Expenses connected with holding elections to soviets of people's deputies shall be at the expense of the state.

*Article 101. Deputies to soviets of people's deputies shall be elected by electoral districts.

A citizen of the USSR may not, as a rule, be elected to more than two soviets of people's deputies.

Electoral commissions shall ensure the holding of elections for soviets, which shall be formed from representatives of social organizations, labor collectives, and meetings of military servicemen at military units.

The procedure for holding elections to soviets of people's deputies shall be determined by laws of the USSR and union and autonomous republics.

***Article 102. The electors shall give mandates to their deputies.

The respective soviets of people's deputies shall consider the mandates of electors, take them into account when working out the plans for economic and social development and when drawing up the budget, organize the fulfillment of the mandates, and inform citizens about their realization.

Chapter 14. The People's Deputy

Article 103. Deputies shall be the authorized representatives of the people in soviets of people's deputies.

In participating in the work of soviets, deputies shall decide questions of state, economic, and socio-cultural construction, organize the implementation of decisions of the soviet, and exercise control over the work of state agencies, enterprises, institutions, and organizations.

A deputy shall be guided in his activity by the interests of the state as a whole, shall take account of the inquiries of the populace of the electoral district, and shall endeavor to implement mandates of the electors.

*Article 104. A deputy shall exercise his powers without discontinuing production or employment activity.

During the sessions of the soviet, and also in order to exercise the powers of a deputy in other instances provided by law, a deputy shall be relieved from fulfilling production or employment duties while retaining his average earnings at the place of permanent work.

**Article 105. A deputy shall have the right of inquiry to the respective state agencies and officials, who shall be obliged to reply to the inquiry at a session of the soviet.

A deputy shall have the right to turn to all state and social agencies, enterprises, institutions, and organizations in regard to questions of deputy activity and take part in the consideration of questions raised by them. Directors of the respective state and social agencies, enterprises, institutions, and organizations shall be obliged without delay to receive a deputy and consider his proposals within the established periods.

Article 106. A deputy shall be provided with conditions for the unhindered and efficient exercise of his rights and duties.

The inviolability of deputies, and also other guarantees of deputy activity, shall be established by the Law on the Status of Deputies and other legislation of the USSR and union and autonomous republics.

*Article 107. A deputy shall be obliged to report on his work and the work of the soviet to the electors, and also to collectives and social organizations who nominated him as a candidate for deputy.

A deputy who has not justified the trust of the electors may be recalled at any time by decision of the majority of electors in the procedure established by law.

V. Highest Agencies of State Power and Administration of the USSR

Chapter 15. The USSR Supreme Soviet

*Article 108. The USSR Supreme Soviet shall be the highest agency of state power of the USSR.

The USSR Supreme Soviet shall be empowered to decide all questions relegated by the present Constitution to the jurisdiction of the USSR.

The adoption of the USSR Constitution and making changes therein; the admission of new republics to the USSR and the confirmation of the formation of new autonomous republics and autonomous regions; the confirmation of state plans for economic and social development of the USSR, the USSR state budget and reports concerning their fulfillment; the formation of USSR agencies accountable to it shall be carried out exclusively by the USSR Supreme Soviet.

Laws of the USSR shall be adopted by the USSR Supreme Soviet or an all-people's vote (referendum) held by decision of the USSR Supreme Soviet.

Article 109. The USSR Supreme Soviet shall consist of two chambers: the Soviet of the Union and the Soviet of Nationalities.

The chambers of the USSR Supreme Soviet shall be equal.

Article 110. The Soviet of the Union and the Soviet of Nationalities shall consist of an equal number of deputies.

The Soviet of the Union shall be elected by electoral districts with an equal number of the populace.

The Soviet of Nationalities shall be elected according to the norm: 32 deputies from each union republic, 11 deputies from each autonomous republic, 5 deputies from each autonomous region, and one deputy from each autonomous national area.

The Soviet of the Union and the Soviet of Nationalities shall, upon the recommendation of credentials commissions which they elect, adopt a decision recognizing the powers of deputies, and in the event of a violation of election legislation, recognizing the elections of individual deputies deputies to be void.

**Article 111. Each chamber of the USSR Supreme Soviet shall elect a chairman of the chamber and four deputies.

The chairmen of the Soviet of the Union and of the Soviet of Nationalities shall preside over sessions of the respective chambers and conduct their internal proceedings.

The chairmen of the Soviet of the Union and the Soviet of Nationalities shall conduct alternately the joint sessions of the chambers of the USSR Supreme Soviet.

*Article 112. Sessions of the USSR Supreme Soviet shall be convoked twice a year.

Extraordinary sessions shall be convoked by the Presidium of the USSR Supreme Soviet at its initiative, and also upon the proposal of a union republic or at least one-third of the deputies of one of the chambers.

A session of the USSR Supreme Soviet shall consist of separate and joint sessions of the chambers, and also sessions of the permanent commissions or commissions of the USSR Supreme Soviet held in the interval between them. The sessions shall be opened and closed at separate or joint sessions of the chambers.

*Article 113. The right of legislative initiative in the USSR Supreme Soviet shall belong to the Soviet of the Union and the Soviet of Nationalities, the Presidium of the USSR Supreme Soviet, the USSR Council of Ministers, the union republics in the person of their highest agencies of state power, commissions of the USSR Supreme Soviet and permanent commissions of its chambers, deputies of the USSR Supreme Soviet and permanent commissions of its chambers, deputies of the USSR Supreme Soviet, the USSR Supreme Court, and the USSR Procurator General.

**Social organizations in the person of their all-union agencies also shall enjoy the right of legislative initiative.

***Article 114. Draft laws and other questions submitted for consideration of the USSR Supreme Soviet shall be discussed by the chambers at their separate or joint sessions. If necessary, a draft law or respective question may be transferred for preliminary or additional consideration to one or several commissions.

A law of the USSR shall be considered to be adopted if a majority of the total number of deputies of a chamber have voted for it in each of the chambers of the USSR Supreme Soviet. Decrees and other acts of the USSR Supreme Soviet shall be adopted by a majority of the total number of deputies of the USSR Supreme Soviet.

Draft laws and other most important questions of state life may, by decision of the USSR Supreme Soviet or the Presidium of the USSR Supreme Soviet adopted at their initiative or upon the proposal of a union republic, be submitted for all-people's discussion.

*Article 115. In the event of disagreement between the Soviet of the Union and the Soviet of Nationalities, the question shall be transferred for settlement by a conciliation commission formed by the chambers on an equal basis, after which the question shall be considered for a second time by the Soviet of the Union and the Soviet of Nationalities at a joint session. If agreement also is not reached in this event, the question shall be carried over for discussion at the next session of the USSR Supreme Soviet or transferred for an all-people's vote (referendum).

Article 116. Laws of the USSR, decrees, and other acts of the USSR Supreme Soviet shall be published in the languages of the union republics over the signatures of the Chairman and Secretary of the Presidium of the USSR Supreme Soviet.

*Article 117. A deputy of the USSR Supreme Soviet shall have the right to address an inquiry to the USSR Council of Ministers and to ministers and directors of other agencies formed by the USSR Supreme Soviet. The USSR Council of Ministers or official to whom the inquiry is addressed shall be obliged to make an oral or written reply at the given session of the USSR Supreme Soviet within not more than three days.

Article 118. A deputy of the USSR Supreme Soviet may not be brought to criminal responsibility, arrested, or subjected to measures of administrative sanction imposed in a judicial proceeding without the consent of the USSR Supreme Soviet, and in the interval between sessions, without the consent of the Presidium of the USSR Supreme Soviet.

*Article 119. The USSR Supreme Soviet shall elect the Presidium of the USSR Supreme Soviet, the permanently functioning agency of the USSR Supreme Soviet accountable to it in all its activity, at a joint session of the chambers, and exercising the functions of the highest agency of state power of the USSR in the interval between its sessions within the limits provided for by the Constitution.

Article 120. The Presidium of the USSR Supreme Soviet shall be elected from among the deputies and shall consist of: the Chairman of the Presidium of the Supreme Soviet, the first deputy chairman, fifteen deputy chairmen -- one from each union republic, the Secretary of the Presidium, and twenty one members of the Presidium of the USSR Supreme Soviet.

*Article 121. The Presidium of the USSR Supreme Soviet shall:

(1) designate elections to the USSR Supreme Soviet;

(2) convoke sessions of the USSR Supreme Soviet;

(3) coordinate the activity of permanent commissions of chambers of the USSR Supreme Soviet;

(4) exercise control over the observance of the USSR Constitution and ensure the conformity of the union republic constitutions and laws to the USSR Constitution and laws;

(5) give an interpretation of laws of the USSR;

(6) ratify and denounce international treaties of the USSR;

(7) repeal decrees and regulations of the USSR Council of Ministers and union republic councils of ministers in the event they fail to conform to the law;

(8) establish military ranks, diplomatic ranks, and other special ranks; confer the highest military ranks, diplomatic ranks, and other special ranks;

(9) institute orders and medals of the USSR; establish honorary titles of the USSR, award orders and medals of the USSR; confer honorary titles of the USSR;

(10) admit to citizenship of the USSR, decide questions of withdrawal from USSR citizenship and deprivation of USSR citizenship, and on granting asylum;

(11) issue all-union acts concerning amnesty and grant pardons;

(12) appoint and recall plenipotentiary representatives of the USSR to foreign states and international organizations;

(13) accept credentials and letters of recall of diplomatic representatives of foreign states accredited to it;

(14) form the Defense Council of the USSR and confirm its membership, and appoint and remove the supreme command of the USSR Armed Forces;

(15) declare martial law in the interests of the defense of the USSR in individual localities or throughout the country;

(16) declare a general or partial mobilization;

(17) declare, in the interval between sessions of the USSR Supreme Soviet, a state of war in the event of a military attack on the USSR or in the event of the need to fulfill international treaty obligations for mutual defense from aggression;

(18) exercise other powers established by the Constitution and laws of the USSR.

*Article 122. The Presidium of the USSR Supreme Soviet, in the interval between sessions of the Supreme Soviet with subsequent submission for confirmation at a regular session, shall:

(1) make changes, when necessary, in prevailing legislative acts of the USSR;

(2) confirm changes of frontiers between union republics;

(3) form and abolish, upon the recommendation of the USSR Council of Ministers, ministries of the USSR and state committees of the USSR;

(4) relieve from office and appoint individual persons to membership of the USSR Council of Ministers upon the recommendation of the Chairman of the USSR Council of Ministers.

Article 123. The Presidium of the USSR Supreme Soviet shall issue edicts and adopt decrees.

Article 124. Upon the expiry of the powers of a USSR Supreme Soviet, the Presidium of the USSR Supreme Soviet shall retain its powers until the formation of the newly elected Presidium by the newly elected USSR Supreme Soviet.

The newly elected USSR Supreme Soviet shall be convoked by the outgoing Presidium of the USSR Supreme Soviet not later than two months after the elections.

*Article 125. The Soviet of the Union and the Soviet of Nationalities shall elect permanent commissions from among the deputies for the preliminary consideration and preparation of questions relegated to the jurisdiction of the USSR Supreme Soviet, and also for furthering the implementation of laws of the USSR and other decisions of the USSR Supreme Soviet and its Presidium, and for control over the activity of state agencies and organizations. The chambers of the USSR Supreme Soviet may create joint commissions on the basis of equality.

The USSR Supreme Soviet shall create, when it considers this necessary, investigative, audit, and other commissions on any question.

All state and social agencies, organizations, and officials shall be obliged to fulfill requests of commissions of the USSR Supreme Soviet and commissions of its chambers and to submit necessary materials and documents to them.

The recommendations of commissions shall be subject to obligatory consideration by state and social agencies, institutions, and organizations. The results of the consideration and measures taken should be notified to the commissions within the established period.

Article 126. The USSR Supreme Soviet shall exercise control over the activity of all state agencies accountable to it.

The USSR Supreme Soviet shall form the USSR People's Control Committee heading the system of people's control agencies.

*Article 127. The procedure for the activity of the USSR Supreme Soviet and its agencies shall be determined by the Reglament of the USSR Supreme Soviet and other laws of the USSR issued on the basis of the USSR Constitution.

Chapter 16. The USSR Council of Ministers

Article 128. The USSR Council of Ministers -- the Government of the USSR -- shall be the highest executive and administrative agency of state power of the USSR.

*Article 129. The USSR Council of Ministers shall be formed by the USSR Supreme Soviet at a joint session of the Soviet of the Union and the Soviet of Nationalities and shall consist of the Chairman of the USSR Council of Ministers, the first deputy and deputy chairmen, ministers of the USSR, and chairmen of the USSR state committees.

The chairmen of the union republic councils of ministers shall be ex officio members of the USSR Council of Ministers.

Upon the recommendation of the Chairman of the USSR Council of Ministers, the USSR Supreme Soviet may include in the Government of the USSR the directors of other agencies and organizations of the USSR.

The USSR Council of Ministers shall lay aside its powers to a newly elected Supreme Soviet of the USSR at its first session.

Article 130. The USSR Council of Ministers shall be responsible to the USSR Supreme Soviet and accountable thereto, and in the interval between sessions of the USSR Supreme Soviet, to the Presidium of the USSR Supreme Soviet, to which it shall be accountable.

The USSR Council of Ministers shall report regularly on its work to the USSR Supreme Soviet.

*Article 131. The USSR Council of Ministers shall be empowered to decide all questions of state administration relegated to the jurisdiction of the USSR insofar as they are not, according to the Constitution, within the competence of the USSR Supreme Soviet and the Presidium of the USSR Supreme Soviet.

Within the limits of its powers, the USSR Council of Ministers shall:

(1) ensure the direction of the national economy and socio-cultural construction; work out and effectuate measures ensuring the growth of the well-being and culture of the people and the development of science and technology and the rational use and protection of natural resources, and strengthening the monetary and credit system, implementing a uniform price policy, payment of labor, social security, organization of state insurance, and a uniform system for records and statistics; organize the management of industrial, construction, and agricultural enterprises and associations, transport and communications enterprises, banks, and also other organizations and institutions of union subordination;

(2) work out and submit to the USSR Supreme Soviet current and long-term state plans for economic and social development of the USSR and the state budget of the USSR; take measures for the effectuation of state plans and the budget; submit reports on the fulfillment of the plan and execution of the budget to the USSR Supreme Soviet;

(3) effectuate measures to defend the interests of the state, protect socialist ownership and public order, and ensure and protect the rights of citizens;

(4) take measures to ensure state security;

(5) exercise general direction over the construction of the USSR Armed Forces and determine the annual quotas of citizens subject to being called to active military service;

(6) exercise general direction in the domain of relations with foreign states, foreign trade, economic, scientific-technical, and cultural cooperation of the USSR with foreign countries; take measures to ensure the fulfillment of international treaties of the USSR; confirm and denounce intergovernmental international treaties;

(7) form committees, chief administrations, and other departments, when necessary, attached to the USSR Council of Ministers for matters of economic, socio-cultural, and defense construction.

**Article 132. The Presidium of the USSR Council of Ministers, consisting of the Chairman of the USSR Council of Ministers and the first deputy and deputy chairmen, shall operate as a permanent agency of the USSR Council of Ministers in order to decide questions connected with ensuring direction of the national economy and other questions of state administration.

*Article 133. The USSR Council of Ministers shall, on the basis of and in execution of laws of the USSR and other decisions of the USSR Supreme Soviet and its Presidium, issue decrees and regulations and verify their execution. Decrees and regulations of the USSR Council of Ministers shall be binding for execution on the entire territory of the USSR.

*Article 134. The USSR Council of Ministers shall have the right to suspend the execution of decrees and regulations of the union republic councils of ministers on questions relegated to the jurisdiction of the USSR, and also to repeal acts of USSR ministries, USSR state committees, and other agencies within its jurisdiction.

*Article 135. The USSR Council of Ministers shall coordinate and direct the work of all-union and union republic ministries and state committees of the USSR and other agencies within its jurisdiction.

All-union ministries and state committees of the USSR shall direct branches of administration entrusted to them or carry out interbranch administration throughout the entire territory of the USSR directly or through agencies they have created.

Union republic ministries and state committees of the USSR shall direct branches of administration entrusted to them or carry out interbranch administration, as a rule, through the respective ministries, state committees, and other union republic agencies and, directly administer enterprises and associations of union subordination. The procedure for the transfer of enterprises and associations from republic and local subordination to union shall be determined by the Presidium of the USSR Supreme Soviet.

USSR ministries and state committees shall bear responsibility for the state and the development of spheres of administration entrusted to them; within the limits of their competence shall issue acts on the basis of and in execution of laws of the USSR, other decisions of the USSR Supreme Soviet and its Presidium, decrees and regulations of the USSR Council of Ministers; organize and verify their execution.

*Article 136. The competence of the USSR Council of Ministers and its Presidium, the procedure for their activity, relations of the Council of Ministers with other state agencies, and also a list of all-union and union republic ministries and state committees of the USSR shall be determined on the basis of the Constitution by a Law on the USSR Council of Ministers.

VI. Bases of the Structure of Agencies of State Power and Administration in the Union Republics

Chapter 17. Highest Union Republic Agencies of State Power and Administration

*Article 137. The union republic supreme soviet shall be the highest union republic agency of state power.

A union republic supreme soviet shall be empowered to decide all questions relegated to union republic jurisdiction by the USSR Constitution and the union republic constitution.

The adoption of a union republic constitution and making changes therein; confirmation of state plans for economic and social development and the union republic state budget and reports concerning its fulfillment; the formation of agencies accountable to it shall be carried out exclusively by the union republic supreme soviet.

Union republic laws shall be adopted by the union republic supreme soviet or by a popular vote (referendum) held by decision of the union republic supreme soviet.

Article 138. A union republic supreme soviet shall elect the Presidium of the supreme soviet, a permanently functioning agency of the union republic supreme soviet accountable to it in all its activity. The membership and powers of the union republic supreme soviet shall be determined by the union republic constitution.

Article 139. A union republic supreme soviet shall form the union republic council of ministers -- the Government of the union republic -- which is the highest executive and administrative agency of union republic state power.

A union republic council of ministers shall be responsible to the union republic supreme soviet and accountable thereto, and in the interval between sessions of the supreme soviet, to the Presidium of the union republic supreme soviet, to which it is accountable.

Article 140. A union republic council of ministers shall issue decrees and regulations on the basis of and in execution of laws of the USSR and union republic and decrees and regulations of the USSR Council of Ministers, and shall organize and verify their execution.

*Article 141. A union republic council of ministers shall have the right to suspend the execution of decrees and regulations of autonomous republic councils of ministers and to repeal decisions and regulations of executive committees of territory, regional, city (or cities of republic subordination) soviets of people's deputies, autonomous region soviets of people's deputies, and in union republics not divided into regions, of executive committees of district and respective city soviets of people's deputies.

*Article 142. A union republic council of ministers shall coordinate and direct the work of union republic and republic ministries, union republic state committees, and other agencies within its jurisdiction.

Union republic ministries and union republic state committees shall direct the branches of administration entrusted to them or carry out interbranch administration, being subordinate both to the union republic council of ministers and to the respective union republic ministry of the USSR or state committee of the USSR.

Republic ministries and state committees shall direct branches of administration entrusted to them or carry out interbranch administration, being subordinate to the union republic council of ministers.

Chapter 18. Highest Autonomous Republic Agencies of State Power and Administration

*Article 143. An autonomous republic supreme soviet shall be the highest autonomous republic agency of state power.

The adoption of an autonomous republic constitution and making changes therein; confirmation of state plans for economic and social development, and also the autonomous republic state budget; the formation of agencies accountable thereto shall be carried out exclusively by the autonomous republic supreme soviet.

**Laws of an autonomous republic shall be adopted by the autonomous republic supreme soviet.

Article 144. An autonomous republic supreme soviet shall elect the Presidium of the autonomous republic supreme soviet and shall form the autonomous republic council of ministers, the Government of the autonomous republic.

Chapter 19. Local Agencies of State Power and Administration

Article 145. Agencies of state power in territories, regions, autonomous regions, autonomous national areas, districts, cities, districts in cities, settlements, and rural population centers shall be the respective soviets of people's deputies.

*Article 146. Local soviets of people's deputies shall decide all questions of local significance, proceeding from the interests of the whole state and the interests of the citizens who reside on the territory of the soviet, implement decisions of superior state agencies, direct the activity of inferior soviets of people's deputies, participate in the discussion of questions of republic and all-union significance and submit proposals in regard to them.

Local soviets of people's deputies shall direct state, economic, and socio-cultural construction on their territory; confirm plans for economic and social development and the local budget; exercise direction over state agencies, enterprises, institutions, and organizations subordinate to them; ensure the observance of laws and the protection of state and public order and of the rights of citizens; further the strengthening of the defense capability of the country.

*Article 147. Within the limits of their powers, local soviets of people's deputies shall ensure integrated economic and social development on their territory; exercise control over the observance of legislation by enterprises, institutions, and organizations of superior subordination which are situated on this territory; coordinate and control their activity in the domain of land use, nature conservation, construction, use of labor resources, production of consumer goods, and socio-cultural, domestic, and other servicing of the populace.

*Article 148. Local soviets of people's deputies shall adopt decisions within the limits of the powers granted them by legislation of the USSR and union and autonomous republics. Decisions of local soviets shall be binding for execution by all enterprises, institutions, and organizations, and also by officials and citizens, situate on the territory of the soviet.

*Article 149. Executive committees elected from among the deputies shall be the executive and administrative agencies of local soviets of people's deputies.

Executive committees shall report at least once a year to the soviets which elected them, and also to meetings of labor collectives and the place of residence of citizens.

Article 150. Executive committees of local soviets of people's deputies shall be accountable directly to both the soviet which elected them and to the superior executive and administrative agency.

VII. Justice, Arbitrazh, and Procuracy Supervision

Chapter 20. Court and Arbitrazh

Article 151. Justice in the USSR shall be carried out only by a court.

The USSR Supreme Court, union republic supreme courts, autonomous republic supreme courts, territory, regional, and city courts, autonomous region courts, autonomous national area courts, district (or city) people's courts, and also military tribunals in the Armed Forces, shall operate in the USSR.

*Article 152. All courts in the USSR shall be formed on the principle of electivity of judges and people's assessors.

People's judges of district (or city) people's courts shall be elected by the citizens of the district (or city) on the basis of universal, equal, and direct suffrage by secret ballot for a term of five years. People's assessors of district (or city) people's courts shall be elected at meetings of working people at their place of work or residence by open ballot for a term of two and one half years.

Superior courts shall be elected by the respective soviets of people's deputies for a term of five years.

Judges of military tribunals shall be elected by the Presidium of the USSR Supreme Soviet for a term of five years, and people's assessors, by meetings of military servicemen for a term of two and one half years.

Judges and people's assessors shall be responsible to the electors or to the agencies which elected them and be accountable to them <u>and may be recalled by them in the procedure established by law</u>.

**<u>Article 153.</u> The USSR Supreme Court shall be the highest judicial agency of the USSR and shall exercise supervision over the judicial activity of courts of the USSR, and also of union republic courts, within the limits established by law.

The USSR Supreme Court shall be elected by the USSR Supreme Soviet and composed of a chairman, his deputies, members, and people's assessors. The chairmen of the union republic supreme courts shall be members of the USSR Supreme Court ex officio.

The organization and procedure for the activity of the USSR Supreme Court shall be determined by a Law on the USSR Supreme Court.

<u>Article 154.</u> Consideration of civil and criminal cases in all courts shall be carried out collegially, and in a court of first instance, with the participation of people's assessors. When carrying out justice, people's assessors shall enjoy all the rights of judges.

<u>Article 155.</u> Judges and people's assessors shall be independent and subordinate only to law.

<u>Article 156.</u> Justice in the USSR shall be carried out on the principle of equality of citizens before the law and the court.

<u>Article 157.</u> Examination of cases in all courts shall be open. The hearing of cases in a closed session of a court shall be permitted only in the instances established by law, with observance of all rules of procedure.

<u>Article 158.</u> An accused shall be ensured the right of defense.

<u>Article 159.</u> A court proceeding shall be conducted in the language of the union or autonomous republic, autonomous region, autonomous national area, or in the language of the majority of the populace of a particular locality. Those persons participating in a case who do not command the language in which the court proceeding is conducted shall be ensured the right to completely familiarize themselves with the materials of the case, to participate in the judicial actions through an interpreter, and the right to speak in court in their native language.

**<u>Article 160.</u> No one may be deemed guilty of committing a crime and subjected to criminal punishment other than by judgment of a court and in accordance with the law.

*<u>Article 161.</u> Colleges of advocates shall operate in order to render legal assistance to citizens and organizations. Legal assistance shall be rendered to citizens free of charge in the instances provided by <u>legislation</u>.

The organization and procedure for activity of the advocates shall be determined by USSR and union republic legislation.

Article 162. The participation of representatives of social organizations and labor collectives shall be permitted in a court proceeding relating to civil and criminal cases.

*Article 163. The settlement of economic disputes between enterprises, institutions, and organizations shall be carried out by state arbitrazh agencies within the limits of their competence.

The organization and procedure for the activity of state arbitrazh agencies shall be determined by a Law on State Arbitrazh in the USSR.

Chapter 21. Procuracy

Article 164. Supreme supervision over the precise and uniform execution of the laws by all ministries, state committees and departments, enterprises, institutions, and organizations, executive and administrative agencies of local soviets of people's deputies, collective farms, cooperative, and other social organizations, officials, and also citizens, shall be entrusted to the USSR Procurator General and procurators subordinate to him.

Article 165. The USSR Procurator General shall be appointed by the USSR Supreme Soviet and shall be responsible to it and accountable to it, and in the interval between sessions of the Supreme Soviet, to the Presidium of the USSR Supreme Soviet, to which he is accountable.

Article 166. Procurators of union republics, autonomous republics, territories, regions, and autonomous regions shall be appointed by the USSR Procurator General. Procurators of autonomous national areas, and district and city procurators, shall be appointed by union republic procurators and confirmed by the USSR Procurator General.

Article 167. The term of powers of the USSR Procurator General and all inferior procurators shall be five years.

*Article 168. Procuracy agencies shall exercise their powers independently of any local agencies whatever, being subordinate only to the USSR Procurator General.

The organization and procedure for the activity of procuracy agencies shall be determined by the Law on the Procuracy of the USSR.

VIII. Arms, Flag, Anthem, and Capital of the USSR

*Article 169. The state arms of the Union of Soviet Socialist Republics shall depict a sickle and hammer against a globe in the rays of the sun and framed by ears of grain, with the inscription in the languages of the union republics: "Proletarians of All Countries, Unite!" In the upper portion of the arms shall be a five-pointed star.

Article 170. The state flag of the Union of Soviet Socialist Republics shall consist of a red rectangular cloth depicting in the upper corner near the flagstaff a gold sickle and hammer and above them a red five-pointed star bordered in gold. The proportion of the breadth of the flag to its length shall be 1:2.

Article 171. The state anthem of the Union of Soviet Socialist Republics shall be confirmed by the Presidium of the USSR Supreme Soviet.

Article 172. The city of Moscow shall be the capital of the Union of Soviet Socialist Republics.

IX. Procedure for the Effect of and Changes in the USSR Constitution

**Article 173. The USSR Constitution shall possess the highest juridical force. All laws and other acts of state agencies shall be issued on the basis of and in accordance with the USSR Constitution.

Article 174. The USSR Constitution shall be changed by decision of the USSR Supreme Soviet, adopted by a majority of not less than two thirds of the total number of deputies of each of its chambers.

DRAFT CONSTITUTION (BASIC LAW) OF THE UNION OF SOVIET SOCIALIST REPUBLICS

[Approved by the Presidium of the USSR Supreme Soviet, Edict of May 27, 1977, and published for discussion on June 4, 1977. Vedomosti SSSR (1977), no. 22, item 351. Izvestia, June 4, 1977, p. 1]

The Great October Socialist Revolution, performed by the workers and peasants of Russia under the guidance of the Communist Party headed by V.I. Lenin, overthrew the power of the capitalists and landowners, broke the fetters of oppression, and created the Soviet state, a state of a new type, the principal instrument for the defense of revolutionary conquests and for the construction of socialism and communism.

Soviet power has carried out the most profound socio-economic transformations, ended forever the exploitation of man by man, class antagonism, and national enmity, and confirmed social ownership of the means of production and genuine democracy for the toiling masses. For the first time in the history of mankind a socialist society was created.

The unfading exploit of the Soviet people and its Armed Forces, who secured an historic victory in the Great Fatherland War, became a clear manifestation of the power of socialism. This triumph strengthened the international position of the USSR and opened new favorable possibilities for the growth of the forces of socialism, national liberation, democracy, and peace in the entire world.

In continuing their creative activity, the Soviet people have ensured the rapid and all-round development of the country and the improvement of the socialist system. The alliance of the working class, collective farm peasantry, and people's intelligentsia, and the friendship of nations and peoples of the USSR have been consolidated. The socio-political unity of Soviet society has been formed, the leading force of which is the working class. Having fulfilled the tasks of the dictatorship of the proletariat, the Soviet state has become an all-people's state. The leading role of the Communist Party, vanguard of the whole people, has grown.

A developed socialist society has been built in the USSR. At this stage, when socialism already is developing on its own basis, the creative forces of the new society and the advantages of the socialist way of life are being revealed more fully and the fruits of the great revolutionary conquests being enjoyed more extensively.

This is a society in which mighty productive forces have been created, and an advanced science and culture, in which the well-being of the people is constantly growing and more favorable conditions for the all-round development of the individual are being formed.

This is a society of mature socialist social relations in which a new historical community of people, the Soviet people, has arisen on the basis of the coming together of all social strata and the legal and actual equality of all nations and peoples.

This is a society well-organized, with a high ideological commitment and consciousness of the working people, who are patriots and internationalists.

This is a society whose law of life is the concern of all for the welfare of each and the concern of each for the welfare of all.

This is a society of genuine democracy, whose political system ensures the efficient administration of all public affairs, the more active participation of the working people in state life, and the combining of real human rights and freedoms with civic responsibility.

The developed socialist society is an objectively necessary stage on the path to communism.

The ultimate purpose of the Soviet state is the building of a classless communist society. The principal tasks of the state are: creation of the material-technical base of communism; improvement of socialist social relations and their transformation into communist, bringing up the man of a communist society, raising the material and cultural level of the life of the working people, ensuring the security of the country, and furthering the strengthening of peace and the development of international cooperation.

The Soviet people,

being guided by the ideas of scientific communism and being faithful to their revolutionary traditions,

resting on the great socio-economic and political conquests of socialism;

striving toward the further development of socialist democracy,

taking into account the international position of the USSR as an integral part of the world system of socialism and being conscious of its internationalist responsibility,

preserving the succession of the ideas and principles of the 1918 RSFSR Constitution, the 1924 USSR Constitution, and the 1936 USSR Constitution,

proclaim the aims and principles and establish the foundation for the organization of an all-people's socialist state and consolidate them in the present Constitution.

I. Bases of the Socio-Political and Economic Structure

Chapter 1. Political System

Article 1. The Union of Soviet Socialist Republics is a socialist all-people's state expressing the will and interests of the working class, peasantry, and intelligentsia and of all nations and peoples of the country.

Article 2. All power in the USSR shall belong to the people.

The people shall exercise state power through soviets of people's deputies, which shall constitute the political foundation of the USSR.

All other state agencies shall be under the control of and accountable to the soviets.

Article 3. The organization and activity of the Soviet state shall be structured in accordance with the principle of democratic centralism: the electivity of all agencies of state power from bottom to top, their accountability to the people, and the binding nature of decisions of superior agencies for inferior. Democratic centralism shall combine unified direction with initiative and creative activity on the spot and with the responsibility of each state agency and official for the matter entrusted.

Article 4. The Soviet state and all its agencies shall operate on the basis of socialist legality and ensure the protection of the legal order, the interests of society, and the rights of citizens. State institutions, social organizations, and officials shall be obliged to observe the USSR Constitution and Soviet laws.

Article 5. The most important questions of state life shall be submitted for discussion by the whole people, and also to a vote by the whole people (referendum).

Article 6. The Communist Party of the Soviet Union shall be the guiding and directing force of Soviet society and the nucleus of its political system and all state and social organizations. The CPSU shall exist for the people and shall serve the people.

Armed with Marxist-Leninist teaching, the Communist Party shall determine the general perspective of the development of society and the internal and foreign policy line of the USSR, direct the great creative activity of the Soviet people, and impart a planned, scientifically well-founded character to its struggle for the triumph of communism.

Article 7. Trade unions, the All-Union Leninist Communist Youth League, cooperative, and other mass social organizations shall, in accordance with their charter tasks, take part in the administration of state and social affairs and in deciding political, economic and socio-cultural questions.

Article 8. The further unfolding of socialist democracy shall be the basic orientation of the development of the political system of Soviet society: more extensive participation of the working people in the administration of the affairs of society and the state, improvement of the state apparatus, increasing the activeness of social organizations, intensifying people's control, strengthening the legal basis of state and social life, expanding publicity, and constantly taking account of public opinion.

Chapter 2. Economic System

Article 9. Socialist ownership of the means of production shall constitute the basis of the economic system of the USSR. Social ownership shall include: state (all-people's) ownership; ownership of collective farms and other cooperative organizations (collective farm-cooperative); ownership of trade unions and other social organizations.

The State shall protect socialist ownership and create the conditions for its increase.

No one shall have the right to use socialist ownership for the purposes of personal gain.

Article 10. State ownership shall be the common property of the whole Soviet people, the basic form of socialist ownership.

There shall be in the exclusive ownership of the state: land, its minerals, water, and forests. The basic means of production shall belong to the state: industrial, construction, and agricultural enterprises, means of transport and communications, and also banks, trade and socio-domestic enterprises, and the basic city housing fund.

Article 11. The means of production and other property which serve the realization of their charter tasks shall be the ownership of collective farms and other cooperative organizations and their associations. Land occupied by collective farms shall be allocated to them free of charge and in perpetuity.

The state shall promote the development of collective farm-cooperative ownership and its coming together with state ownership.

The property necessary for them to realize their charter tasks shall be the ownership of trade union and other social organizations.

Article 12. Labor incomes and savings, a dwelling house and subsidiary husbandry, and articles of everyday use and of personal consumption and convenience may be in the personal ownership of citizens of the USSR. The right of personal ownership of citizens, and equally the right to inherit it, shall be protected by law.

Land parcels granted by the state or collective farms in the procedure established by law for subsidiary husbandry (including the maintenance of livestock and poultry), gardening, and vegetable growing, and also for individual housing construction, may be in the use of citizens.

Property in the personal ownership and use of citizens may not serve to derive nonlabor income nor be used to the detriment of society.

Article 13. The free labor of the Soviet people shall be the source for the growth of social wealth and the well-being of the people and every Soviet person.

In accordance with the principle: "From each according to his ability, to each according to his labor", the state shall exercise control over the amount of labor and consumption. It shall determine the amount of income tax and establish the wage level exempted from taxes.

Socially useful labor and its results shall determine the status of a person in society. The state shall, by combining material and moral incentives, promote the transformation of labor into the primary vital requirement of every Soviet person.

Article 14. The ultimate aim of social production under socialism shall be the fullest satisfaction of the growing material and spiritual needs of people.

Relying on the creative activeness of the working people, socialist competition, and the achievements of scientific-technical progress, the state shall ensure the growth of labor productivity, and increase of production efficiency and work quality, and the dynamic and proportional development of the national economy.

Article 15. The economy of the USSR shall constitute a single national economic complex embracing all links of social production, distribution, and exchange on the territory of the country.

The direction of the economy shall be carried out on the basis of state plans for the development of the national economy and socio-cultural construction, taking into account branch and territorial principles and combining centralized direction with economic independence and initiative of enterprises, associations, and other organizations. Economic accountability, profit, and cost of production shall be used actively in this connection.

Article 16. Collectives of working people and social organizations shall participate in the management of enterprises and associations and in deciding questions of the organization of labor and everyday life, the use of assets earmarked for production development, and also for socio-cultural needs and material incentive.

Article 17. In the USSR individual labor activity shall be permitted in accordance with the law in the sphere of handicrafts, agriculture, domestic servicing of the populace, and also other forms of labor activity based exclusively on the personal labor of citizens and members of their families.

Article 18. In the interests of present and future generations in the USSR necessary measures shall be taken for the protection and scientifically well-founded, rational use of land and its minerals and flora and fauna, for the preservation of air and water purity, for ensuring the reproduction of natural wealth, and for improvement of the human environment.

Chapter 3. Social Development and Culture

Article 19. The Soviet state shall promote the intensification of the social homogeneity of society, the eradication of essential differences between town and countryside, intellectual and physical labor, and the further development and coming together of all nations and peoples of the USSR.

Article 20. In accordance with the communist ideal: "Free development for each is the condition of the free development of all", the Soviet state shall pursue the aim of expanding the real possibilities for the development and application by citizens of their creative forces, abilities, and talents and for the all-round development of the individual.

Article 21. The state shall be concerned for the improvement of labor conditions and for the reduction and, in future, the complete abolition of arduous manual labor on the basis of the complex mechanization and automation of production.

Article 22. In the USSR the program for successively transforming agricultural labor into a variety of industrial, for expanding the network of institutions for public education, culture, public health, domestic servicing, trade, and municipal economy in rural localities, and for transforming villages and towns into comfortable rural settlements, shall be implemented.

Article 23. The state shall steadfastly pursue the course of raising the level of payment for labor and the real income of the working people in accordance with the growth of labor productivity.

Social consumption funds shall be created with a view to the fullest satisfaction of the requirements of the members of society. With the broad participation of social organizations and labor collectives, the state shall ensure the growth and just distribution of these funds.

Article 24. State systems for public health, social security, domestic servicing, public dining, and municipal economy shall operate and be developed in the USSR.

The state shall encourage the activity of cooperative and other social organizations in the domain of services for the populace.

Article 25. A uniform system of education shall exist in the USSR which serves communist upbringing, the spiritual and physical development of youth, and preparation for labor and social activity. Education in the USSR shall be free of charge.

Article 26. In accordance with the requirements of society, the state shall ensure the planned development of science and the training of scientific cadres and shall organize the introduction of the results of scientific research into the national economy and other spheres of life.

Article 27. The state shall be concerned for the protection and increase of the spiritual requirements of society and their extensive use for raising the cultural level of the Soviet people.

The development of professional art and of people's artistic activity shall be encouraged in the USSR in every possible way.

Chapter 4. Foreign Policy

Article 28. The Soviet state shall consistently carry on the Leninist policy of peace and favor the consolidation of the security of peoples and extensive international cooperation.

The foreign policy of the USSR is aimed at ensuring favorable international conditions for the building of communism in the USSR, strengthening the position of world socialism, supporting the struggle of peoples for national liberation and social progress, preventing aggressive wars, and consistently implementing the principles of peaceful coexistence of states with a different social system.

War propaganda shall be prohibited by law in the USSR.

Article 29. Relations of the USSR with other states shall be built on the basis of observing the principles of mutual renunciation of the use or threat of force; sovereign equality; inviolability of frontiers; territorial integrity of states; peaceful settlement of disputes; non-interference in internal affairs, respect for human rights and basic freedoms, equality, and the right of peoples to decide their own destiny; cooperation between states; good-faith fulfillment of obligations arising from generally recognized principles and norms of international law and international treaties concluded by the USSR.

Article 30. As an integral part of the world system of socialism and socialist commonwealth, the Soviet Union shall develop and strengthen friendship and cooperation, and comradely mutual assistance with the countries of socialism on the basis of socialist internationalism, and shall participate actively in economic integration and in the international socialist division of labor.

Chapter 5. Defense of the Socialist Fatherland

Article 31. Defense of the socialist Fatherland is the most important function of the state, the cause of the whole people.

Armed Forces have been created in the USSR and universal military services established for the purpose of defending socialist conquests, the peaceful labor of the Soviet people, and the sovereignty and territorial integrity of the state.

The duty of the USSR Armed Forces to the people shall be to reliably defend the socialist Fatherland and to be in constant combat readiness, guaranteeing an immediate rebuff to any aggressor.

Article 32. The state shall ensure the security and defense capability of the country and equip the USSR Armed Forces with everything necessary.

The duties of state agencies, social organizations, officials, and citizens in ensuring the security of the country and strengthening its defense capability shall be determined by law.

II. The State and The Individual

Chapter 6. Citizenship of the USSR, Equality of Citizens

Article 33. Soviet citizenship shall be uniform for the entire USSR. Each citizen of a union republic shall be a citizen of the USSR.

The bases of and procedure for the acquisition and loss of Soviet citizenship shall be established by a law of the USSR.

Citizens of the USSR abroad shall enjoy the defense and protection of the Soviet state.

Article 34. Citizens of the USSR shall be equal before the law irrespective of origin, social and property status, national and racial affiliation, sex, education, language, attitude toward religion, type and nature of occupation, place of residence, and other circumstances.

The equality of citizens of the USSR shall be ensured in all areas of economic, political, social, and cultural life.

Article 35. A woman in the USSR shall have equal rights with a man.

The realization of these rights shall be ensured by granting women equal opportunities to receive an education and professional training, labor, remuneration therefor and advancement in work, socio-political and cultural activity, and also by special measures for the protection of the labor and health of women; legal protection and material and moral support for motherhood and childhood, including the granting of paid leaves and other privileges for pregnant women and mothers; state assistance to unmarried mothers.

Article 36. Soviet citizens of different nationalities and races shall have equal rights.

The realization of these rights shall be ensured by the policy of the all-round development and coming together of all nations and peoples of the USSR, the nurturing of citizens in the spirit of Soviet patriotism and socialist internationalism, and the possibility to use the native language and the languages of other peoples of the USSR.

Any direct or indirect limitation of the rights whatever or the establishment of direct or indirect privileges for citizens on grounds of race or nationality, and equally any advocacy of racial or national exclusivity, animosity, or contempt, shall be punished by law.

Article 37. Foreign citizens and stateless persons in the USSR shall be guaranteed the rights and freedoms provided by law, including the right to have recourse to a court and other state agencies in order to defend personal, property, family, and other rights belonging to them by law.

Foreign citizens and stateless persons on the territory of the USSR shall be obliged to respect the USSR Constitution and to observe Soviet laws.

Article 38. The USSR shall grant the right of asylum to foreigners who are persecuted for defending the interests of the working people and the cause of peace, for participating in the revolutionary and national liberation movement, and for progressive socio-political, scientific, or other creative activity.

Chapter 7. Basic Rights, Freedoms, and Duties of Citizens of the USSR

Article 39. Citizens of the USSR shall possess in their entirety the socio-economic, political, and personal rights and freedoms proclaimed and guaranteed by the USSR Constitution and Soviet laws. The socialist system shall ensure the expansion of rights and freedoms, the continuous improvement of the conditions of life of citizens through the fulfillment of programs for socio-economic and cultural development.

The use by citizens of rights and freedoms should not harm the interests of society and the state nor the rights of other citizens.

Article 40. Citizens of the USSR shall have the right to labor, that is, to receive guaranteed work with payment for labor in accordance with its quantity and quality, including the right to choose a profession, type of occupation, and work in accordance with their vocation, abilities, professional training, education, and taking into account social requirements.

This right shall be ensured by the socialist system of economy, steady growth of the productive forces of society, free professional training, raising of labor qualifications, and study of new specializations.

Article 41. Citizens of the USSR shall have the right to leisure.

This right shall be ensured by a 41-hour work week for workers and employees and a reduced work day for a number of professions and trades and a reduced work period at night; by granting annual paid leaves, weekly days of leisure, and also expanding the network of cultural-enlightenment and therapeutic institutions, the development of mass sport, physical culture, and tourism; the creation of favorable possibilities for leisure at the place of residence and other conditions for the rational use of free time.

The duration of work time and leisure for collective farmers shall be regulated by collective farm charters.

Article 42. Citizens of the USSR shall have the right to health protection.

This right shall be ensured by free qualified medical assistance rendered by state public health institutions; the development and improvement of safety techniques and production sanitation; expansion of the network of institutions for care and for strengthening the health of citizens; the implementation of extensive preventive measures; measures for improving the environment; special concern for the health of the rising generation and prohibition of child labor; the development of scientific research directed toward preventing and reducing the incidence of disease and ensuring a long active life for citizens.

Article 43. Citizens of the USSR shall have the right to material security in old age, in the event of illness, and also in the event of complete or partial loss of the capacity to work or of loss of breadwinner.

This right shall be guaranteed by social insurance for workers, employees, and collective farmers; pensions for old age, disability, and loss of breadwinner, benefits for temporary loss of capacity to work; arranging the employment of citizens who have partially lost the capacity to work; and concern for elderly citizens who are alone and for disabled persons.

Article 44. Citizens of the USSR shall have the right to housing.

This right shall be ensured by the development and protection of a state and social housing fund, the promotion of cooperative and individual housing construction, the just distribution of housing premises under social control granted in effectuation of the housing construction program, and also by low apartment rent.

Article 45. Citizens of the USSR shall have the right to education.

This right shall be ensured by free education of all types, universal compulsory secondary education for youth, the extensive development of professional-technical, secondary specialized, and higher education on the basis of linking study with life, with production; the development of correspondence and evening education; the granting of state stipends and other benefits to pupils and students; the issuance of school textbooks free of charge; the possibility of studying in school in the native language; and the development of a system of professional orientation and the creation of conditions for the self-education of the working people.

Article 46. Citizens of the USSR shall have the right to use the achievements of culture.

This right shall be ensured through public accessibility to the valuables of fatherland and world culture in state and social funds; the development and equitable siting of cultural-enlightenment institutions on the territory of the country; and the expansion of cultural exchange with foreign states.

Article 47. Citizens of the USSR shall, in accordance with the aims of communist construction, be guaranteed the freedom of scientific, technical, and artistic creativity. It shall be ensured by the extensive development of scientific research, invention and rationalization activity, and the development of art. The state shall create the material conditions necessary therefor and render support to voluntary societies and creative unions.

The rights of authors, inventors, and rationalizers shall be protected by law.

Article 48. Citizens of the USSR shall have the right to participate in the administration of state and social affairs.

Citizens of the USSR shall elect and may be elected to soviets of people's deputies, shall take part in the discussion and working out of draft laws and decisions of all-state and local significance, in the work of state agencies, cooperative, and other social organizations, in control over their activity, in the management of production and the affairs of labor collectives, and in meetings at their place of residence.

Article 49. Each citizen of the USSR shall have the right to submit proposals to state agencies and social organizations concerning the improvement of their activity and to criticize shortcomings in work.

Officials shall be obliged within the periods established by law to consider proposals and applications of citizens, to reply to them, and to take necessary measures.

Persecution for criticism shall be prohibited.

Article 50. In accordance with the interests of the working people and with a view to strengthening the socialist system, citizens of the USSR shall be guaranteed freedom of speech, press, assembly, meetings, street processions, and demonstrations. The realization of these political freedoms shall be ensured by granting public buildings, streets and squares, extensive dissemination of information, and the possibility of using the press, television, and radio to the working people and their organizations.

Article 51. In accordance with the aims of communist construction, citizens of the USSR shall have the right to unite in social organizations which further the development of political activeness and initiative and the satisfaction of their diverse interests.

Social organizations shall be guaranteed conditions for the successful fulfillment of their charter tasks.

Article 52. Freedom of conscience, that is, the right to confess any religion, to perform religious cults, or not to confess any religion, and to carry on atheistic propaganda shall be recognized for citizens of the USSR. Incitement of animosity and hatred in connection with religious beliefs shall be prohibited.

The church in the USSR shall be separated from the state, and the school from the church.

Article 53. The family shall be under the protection of the state.

Marriage shall be concluded upon the voluntary consent of a woman and a man; spouses shall be completely equal in family relations.

The state shall render assistance to the family through the creation and development of an extensive network of children's institutions and organizations, the improvement of domestic and public dining services, granting benefits and privileges to families with many children, and the payment of an allowance for the birth of a child.

Article 54. Citizens of the USSR shall be guaranteed inviolability of the person. No one may be subjected to arrest other than by decree of a court or with the sanction of a procurator.

Article 55. Citizens of the USSR shall be guaranteed inviolability of the home. No one shall have the right to enter a home without legal grounds against the will of the persons residing therein.

Article 56. The personal life of citizens and the secrecy of correspondence, telephone conversations, and telegraph communications shall be protected by law.

Article 57. Respect for the individual and the protection of the rights and freedoms of the Soviet person shall be the duty of all state agencies, social organizations, and officials.

Citizens of the USSR shall have the right to judicial protection against infringements on life and health, property and personal freedom, and honor and dignity.

Article 58. Citizens of the USSR shall have the right to appeal against the actions of officials and state agencies and social organizations. Such appeals should be considered in the procedure and within the periods established by law.

The actions of officials committed in violation of law, in excess of their powers, and impinging upon the rights of citizens may be appealed to a court in the procedure established by law.

Citizens of the USSR shall have the right to compensation for damage caused by the illegal actions of state institutions and social organizations, and also of officials during the execution of their official duties, in the procedure and within the limits established by law.

Article 59. The realization of rights and freedoms shall be inseparable from the execution by a citizen of his duties.

A citizen of the USSR shall be obliged to observe the USSR Constitution and Soviet laws, respect the rules of socialist community life, and bear with dignity the high calling of citizen of the USSR.

Article 60. The duty and matter of honor for every citizen of the USSR capable of labor shall be conscientious labor in the domain of socially useful activity which he has chosen and strict observance of labor and production discipline.

Article 61. A citizen of the USSR shall be obliged to care for and reinforce socialist ownership. The duty of a citizen of the USSR shall be to struggle against stealing and dissipation of state and social property.

Persons who infringe socialist ownership shall be punished according to law.

Article 62. A citizen of the USSR shall be obliged to safeguard the interests of the Soviet state and to further the strengthening of its might and authority.

Protection of the socialist Fatherland shall be the sacred duty of each citizen of the USSR.

Treason shall be the gravest crime against the people.

Article 63. Military service in the ranks of the USSR Armed Forces shall be the honorable duty of Soviet citizens.

Article 64. The duty of every citizen of the USSR shall be to respect the national dignity of other citizens and to strengthen friendship of nations and peoples of the Soviet multinational state.

Article 65. A citizen of the USSR shall be obliged to respect the rights and legal interests of other persons, to be intolerant of anti-social offenses, and to promote in every possible way the protection of public order.

Article 66. Citizens of the USSR shall be obliged to be concerned about the upbringing of children, to prepare them for socially useful labor, and to raise worthy members of socialist society.

Article 67. Citizens of the USSR shall be obliged to care for nature and to protect its wealth.

Concern for the preservation of historical monuments and other cultural valuables shall be a duty of citizens of the USSR.

Article 68. The internationalist duty of a citizen of the USSR shall be to further the development of friendship and cooperation with the peoples of other countries and the maintenance and strengthening of world peace.

III. The National and State Structure of the USSR

Chapter 8. The USSR: A Union State

Article 69. The Union of Soviet Socialist Republics shall be a single union multinational state formed as a result of the free self-determination of nations and the voluntary association of equal Soviet socialist republics.

The USSR shall personify the state unity of the Soviet people and unite all nations and peoples for the purpose of the joint construction of communism.

Article 70. There shall be associated in the USSR:

Russian Soviet Federated Socialist Republic,

Ukrainian Soviet Socialist Republic,

Belorussian Soviet Socialist Republic,

Uzbek Soviet Socialist Republic,

Kazakh Soviet Socialist Republic,

Georgian Soviet Socialist Republic,

Azerbaidzhan Soviet Socialist Republic,

Lithuanian Soviet Socialist Republic,

Moldavian Soviet Socialist Republic,

Latvian Soviet Socialist Republic,

Kirgiz Soviet Socialist Republic,

Tadzhik Soviet Socialist Republic,

Armenian Soviet Socialist Republic,

Turkmen Soviet Socialist Republic,

Estonian Soviet Socialist Republic.

Article 71. The right of free secession from the USSR shall be preserved for each union republic.

Article 72. There shall be subject to the jurisdiction of the Union of Soviet Socialist Republics in the person of its highest agencies of state power and administration:

(1) admission of new republics into the USSR; confirmation of the formation of new autonomous republics and autonomous regions within union republics;

(2) determination of the state frontier of the USSR and confirmation of changes of frontiers between union republics;

(3) establishment of general principles for the organization and activity of republic and local agencies of state power and administration;

(4) ensuring the unity of legislative regulation throughout the territory of the USSR, the establishment of fundamental principles of legislation of the USSR and union republics;

(5) implementation of a uniform socio-economic policy and direction of the economy of the country; determination of the basic orientations of scientific and technical progress; the working out and confirmation of plans for the development of the national economy and for socio-cultural construction of the USSR, confirmation of reports concerning their fulfillment;

(6) working out and confirmation of a uniform state budget of the USSR and confirmation of the report concerning its execution; direction of a single monetary and credit system; establishment of taxes and revenues received for the formation of union, republic, and local budgets; determination of policy in the domain of prices and payment for labor;

(7) direction of branches of the national economy and associations and enterprises of all-union subordination; general direction of branches, associations, and enterprises of union republic subordination;

(8) questions of peace and war, defense of sovereignty, protection of the state frontiers and territory of the USSR, organization of defense, and direction of the Armed Forces;

(9) ensuring state security;

(10) representation of the USSR in international relations; links of the USSR with foreign states and international organizations; establishment of the general procedure for and coordination of relations of union republics with foreign states and international organizations; foreign trade on the basis of the state monopoly;

(11) control over the observance of the USSR Constitution and ensuring the conformity of the union republic constitutions to the USSR Constitution;

(12) deciding other questions of all-union significance.

Article 73. Laws of the USSR shall have the same force on the territory of all union republics. In the event of a divergence between a union republic law and an all-union law, the law of the USSR shall prevail.

Article 74. The territory of the Union of Soviet Socialist Republics shall be integral and shall include the territories of the union republics.

The sovereignty of the USSR shall extend throughout all of its territory.

Chapter 9. The Union Soviet Socialist Republic

Article 75. The union republic shall be a soviet socialist state which has combined with other Soviet republics into the Union of Soviet Socialist Republics.

Beyond the limits specified in Article 72 of the USSR Constitution, a union republic shall exercise state power independently on its territory.

A union republic shall have its own Constitution which corresponds to the USSR Constitution and takes into account the peculiarities of the republic.

Article 76. A union republic shall take part in deciding questions relegated to the jurisdiction of the USSR in the USSR Supreme Soviet, the

Presidium of the USSR Supreme Soviet, the Government of the USSR, and other agencies of the USSR.

A union republic shall further the effectuation of the powers of the USSR on its territory and implement the decision of agencies of state power and administration of the USSR.

Article 77. The territory of a union republic can not be changed without its consent. Frontiers between union republics may be changed by mutual agreement of the respective republics, which shall be subject to confirmation by the USSR.

Article 78. A union republic shall determine its own territorial, regional, national area, and district divisions and decide other questions of administrative and territorial structure.

Article 79. A union republic shall have the right to enter into relations with foreign states, conclude treaties with them, and exchange diplomatic and consular representatives, and to participate in the activity of international organizations.

Article 80. The sovereign rights of union republics shall be protected by the USSR.

Chapter 10. The Autonomous Soviet Socialist Republic

Article 81. An autonomous republic shall be a part of a union republic.

Beyond the limits of the rights of the USSR and the union republic, an autonomous republic shall independently decide questions relegated to its jurisdiction.

An autonomous republic shall have its own Constitution which corresponds to the USSR Constitution and union republic constitution and takes into account the peculiarities of the autonomous republic.

Article 82. An autonomous republic shall participate in deciding questions relegated to the jurisdiction of the USSR and union republic through the highest agencies of state power and administration respectively of the USSR and union republic.

An autonomous republic shall further the effectuation of the powers of the USSR and union republic on its territory and implement the decisions of agencies of state power and administration of the USSR and union republic.

Article 83. The territory of an autonomous republic may not be changed without its consent.

Article 84. In the Russian Soviet Federated Socialist Republic shall be the autonomous soviet socialist republics: Bashkir, Buriat, Dagestan, Kabardino-Balkarskaia, Kalmyk, Karelia, Komi, Mari, Mordovia, North Osetian, Tatar, Tuva, Udmurt, Checheno-Ingush, Chuvash, Iakut.

In the Uzbek Soviet Socialist Republic shall be the Karakalpak Autonomous Soviet Socialist Republic.

In the Georgian Soviet Socialist Republic shall be the Abkhazian and Adzharian Autonomous Soviet Socialist Republics.

In the Azerbaidzhan Soviet Socialist Republic shall be the Nakhichevan Autonomous Soviet Socialist Republic.

Chapter 11. The Autonomous Region and Autonomous National Area

Article 85. An autonomous region shall be a part of a union republic. A law concerning an autonomous region shall be adopted by the union republic supreme soviet upon the recommendation of the soviet of people's deputies of the autonomous region.

Article 86. In the Russian Soviet Federated Socialist Republic shall be the autonomous regions: Adygei, Gorno-Altai, Jewish, Karachaevo-Cherkesskaia, Khakasskaia.

In the Georgian Soviet Socialist Republic shall be the South Osetian Autonomous Region.

In the Azerbaidzhan Soviet Socialist Republic shall be the Nagorno-Karabakhskaia Autonomous Region.

In the Tadzhik Soviet Socialist Republic shall be the Gorno-Badakhshan Autonomous Region.

Article 87. An autonomous national area shall be a part of a territory or region. A statute on autonomous national areas shall be confirmed by the union republic supreme soviet.

IV. Soviets of People's Deputies and the Procedure for Electing Them

Chapter 12. System and Principles of Activity of Soviets of People's Deputies

Article 88. Soviets of people's deputies -- the USSR Supreme Soviet, union republic supreme soviets, autonomous republic supreme soviets, territory and regional soviets of people's deputies, autonomous region and autonomous national area soviets of people's deputies, city, district, district in city, settlement, and rural soviets of people's deputies -- shall constitute a unified system of agencies of state power.

Article 89. The term of powers of the USSR Supreme Soviet, union republic supreme soviets, and autonomous republic supreme soviets shall be for five years.

The term of powers of territory and regional soviets of people's deputies, autonomous region and autonomous national area soviets of people's deputies, city, district, district in city, settlement, and rural soviets of people's deputies shall be two and one-half years.

Elections for soviets of people's deputies shall be designated at least two months before the expiry of the period of powers of the respective soviets.

Article 90. The most important questions relegated to the jurisdiction of the respective soviets of people's deputies shall be considered and decided at their sessions.

Soviets of people's deputies shall create executive and administrative, and also other agencies accountable to them, and elect permanent commissions.

Article 91. Soviets of people's deputies shall form people's control agencies, combining state control with social control of the working people at enterprises, collective farms, institutions, and organizations.

People's control agencies shall control the fulfillment of state plans and planning tasks, wage a struggle against violations of state discipline, manifestations of localism, a departmental approach to matters, mismanagement, wastefulness, red tape, and bureaucratism, and promote the improvement of the work of the state apparatus.

The procedure for the organization and activity of people's control agencies shall be determined by law.

Article 92. Soviets of people's deputies shall, directly and through agencies they have created, direct all branches of state, economic, and socio-cultural construction, adopt decisions, ensure their execution, and exercise control over the implementation of decisions.

Article 93. The activity of soviets of people's deputies shall be built on the basis of collective, free, and business-like discussion and deciding of questions, publicity, and regular accountability of executive and administrative agencies and other agencies created by soviets to the soviets and the populace, and the extensive involvement of citizens in their work.

Chapter 13. The Electoral System

Article 94. Deputies to all soviets of people's deputies shall be elected on the basis of universal, equal, and direct suffrage by secret ballot.

Article 95. Elections of deputies shall be universal: all citizens of the USSR who have attained 18 years of age shall have the right to elect and to be elected, except for persons deemed insane in the procedure established by law.

Article 96. Elections of deputies shall be equal: each elector shall have one vote; all electors shall participate in elections on an equal basis.

Article 97. Elections of deputies shall be direct: deputies of all soviets of people's deputies shall be elected by citizens directly.

Article 98. Voting during elections of deputies shall be secret; control over the expression of the will of electors shall be excluded.

Article 99. The right to nominate candidates for deputy shall belong to organizations of the Communist Party of the Soviet Union, trade unions, the All-Union Leninist Communist Youth League, cooperative and other social organizations, and labor collectives.

Citizens of the USSR and social organizations shall be guaranteed free and all-round discussion of political, professional, and personal qualities of candidates for deputy, and also the right of agitation at meetings, in the press, and on television and radio.

Article 100. Deputies to soviets of people's deputies shall be elected by electoral districts. Electoral commissions shall ensure the holding of elections for soviets, which shall be formed from representatives of social organizations and labor collectives.

The procedure for holding elections to soviets of people's deputies shall be determined by law.

Chapter 14. The People's Deputy

Article 101. Deputies shall be the authorized representatives of the people in soviets of people's deputies.

In participating in the work of soviets, deputies shall decide questions of state, economic, and socio-cultural construction, organize the implementation of decisions of the soviet, and exercise control over the work of state agencies, enterprises, institutions, and organizations.

A deputy shall be guided in his activity by the interests of the state as a whole, shall take account of the inquiries of the populace of the electoral district, and shall endeavor to implement mandates of the electors.

Article 102. A deputy shall exercise his powers without discontinuing production or employment activity.

During the sessions of the soviet, and also in order to fulfill the powers of a deputy in other instances provided by law, a deputy shall be relieved from fulfilling production or employment duties while retaining his average earnings at the place of permanent work.

Article 103. A deputy shall have the right of inquiry to the respective state agencies and officials, who shall be obliged to reply to the inquiry at a session of the soviet.

A deputy shall have the right to turn to all state and social agencies, enterprises, institutions, and organizations in regard to questions of deputy activity and take part in the consideration of questions raised by them. Directors of the respective state and social agencies, enterprises, institutions, and organizations shall be obliged without delay to receive a deputy and consider his proposals within the periods established by law.

Article 104. A deputy shall be provided with conditions for the unhindered and efficient exercise of his rights and duties.

The inviolability of deputies, and also other guarantees of deputy activity, shall be established by the Law on the Status of Deputies and other legislation of the USSR and the union and autonomous republics.

Article 105. A deputy shall be obliged to report to the electors on his work and the work of the soviet.

A deputy who has not justified the trust of the electors may be recalled at any time by decision of the majority of electors in the procedure established by law.

V. Highest Agencies of State Power and Administration of the USSR

Chapter 15. The USSR Supreme Soviet

Article 106. The USSR Supreme Soviet shall be the highest agency of state power of the USSR.

The USSR Supreme Soviet shall be empowered to decide all questions relegated by the present Constitution to the jurisdiction of the USSR.

The adoption of the USSR Constitution and making changes therein; the admission of new republics to the USSR and the confirmation of the formation of new autonomous republics and autonomous regions; the confirmation of state plans for the development of the national economy and socio-cultural construction of the USSR, the USSR state budget and reports concerning their execution; the formation of USSR agencies accountable to it shall be carried out exclusively by the USSR Supreme Soviet.

Laws of the USSR shall be adopted only by the USSR Supreme Soviet.

Article 107. The USSR Supreme Soviet shall consist of two chambers: the Soviet of the Union and the Soviet of Nationalities.

The chambers of the USSR Supreme Soviet shall be equal.

Article 108. The Soviet of the Union and the Soviet of Nationalities shall consist of an equal number of deputies.

The Soviet of the Union shall be elected by electoral districts with an equal number of the populace.

The Soviet of Nationalities shall be elected according to the norm: 32 deputies from each union republic, 11 deputies from each autonomous republic, 5 deputies from each autonomous region, and one deputy from each autonomous national area.

The Soviet of the Union and the Soviet of Nationalities shall, upon the recommendation of credentials commissions which they elect, adopt a decision recognizing the powers of deputies, and in the event of a violation of election legislation, recognizing the elections of individual deputies to be void.

Article 109. Each chamber of the USSR Supreme Soviet shall elect a chairman of the chamber and four deputies.

The chairmen of the Soviet of the Union and of the Soviet of Nationalities shall preside over sessions of the respective chambers and conduct their internal proceedings.

The chairmen of the Soviet of the Union and the Soviet of Nationalities shall conduct alternately the joint plenary sessions of the chambers of the USSR Supreme Soviet.

Article 110. Sessions of the USSR Supreme Soviet shall be convoked twice a year.

Extraordinary sessions shall be convoked by the Presidium of the USSR Supreme Soviet at its initiative or upon the proposal of at least one-third of the deputies of one of the chambers, and also upon the request of one of the union republics.

A session of the USSR Supreme Soviet shall consist of separate and joint plenary sessions of the chambers, and also sessions of the permanent commissions of the USSR Supreme Soviet held during the session. The session shall be opened and closed at plenary sessions of the chambers.

The sessions of the Soviet of the Union and the Soviet of Nationalities shall commence and end simultaneously.

Article 111. Legislative initiative in the USSR Supreme Soviet shall belong to the Soviet of the Union and the Soviet of Nationalities, the Presidium of the USSR Supreme Soviet, the USSR Council of Ministers, the union republics in the person of their highest agencies of state power, commissions of the USSR Supreme Soviet and permanent commissions of its chambers, deputies of the USSR Supreme Soviet, the USSR Supreme Court, and the USSR Procurator General.

Mass social organizations in the person of their all-union agencies also shall enjoy the right of legislative initiative.

Article 112. After discussion of a draft law at sessions of the chambers, it may be transferred for consideration to one or several commissions. The chambers shall have the right to discuss and vote on a draft law also without transferring it to a commission.

Laws of the USSR, decrees, and other acts of the USSR Supreme Soviet shall be adopted at separate or joint sessions of the chambers.

A law of the USSR shall be considered adopted if a majority of the total number of deputies of a chamber have voted for it at each of the chambers of the USSR Supreme Soviet.

Draft laws of the USSR may, by decision of the USSR Supreme Soviet or the Presidium of the USSR Supreme Soviet adopted at their initiative or upon the proposal of one of the union republics, be transferred for discussion by the whole people, and also for a vote by the whole people (referendum).

Article 113. In the event of disagreement between the Soviet of the Union and the Soviet of Nationalities, the question shall be transferred for settlement by a conciliation commission formed by the chambers on an equal basis, after which the question shall be considered for a second time by the Soviet of the Union and the Soviet of Nationalities at a joint session.

Article 114. Laws of the USSR, decrees, and other acts of the USSR Supreme Soviet shall be published in the languages of the union republics over the signatures of the Chairman and Secretary of the Presidium of the USSR Supreme Soviet.

Article 115. A deputy of the USSR Supreme Soviet shall have the right to address an inquiry to the USSR Council of Ministers and to ministers and directors of other agencies formed by the USSR Supreme Soviet. The USSR Council of Ministers or official to whom the inquiry is addressed shall be obliged to make an oral or written reply at the session of the USSR Supreme Soviet within not more than three days.

Article 116. A deputy of the USSR Supreme Soviet may not be brought to criminal responsibility, arrested, or subjected to measures of administrative sanction imposed in a judicial proceeding without the consent of the USSR Supreme Soviet, and in the interval between sessions, without the consent of the Presidium of the USSR Supreme Soviet.

Article 117. The USSR Supreme Soviet shall elect the Presidium of the USSR Supreme Soviet, the permanently functioning agency of the USSR Supreme Soviet accountable to it in all its activity, at a joint session of the chambers.

Article 118. The Presidium of the USSR Supreme Soviet shall be elected from among the deputies and shall consist of: the Chairman of the Presidium of the Supreme Soviet, the first deputy chairman, fifteen deputy chairmen -- one from each union republic, the Secretary of the Presidium, and twenty one members of the Presidium of the USSR Supreme Soviet.

Article 119. The Presidium of the USSR Supreme Soviet shall:

(1) convoke sessions of the USSR Supreme Soviet;

(2) coordinate the activity of permanent commissions of chambers of the USSR Supreme Soviet;

planning of the issuance of this product by the enterprises not within its system and shall work out questions connected with the improvement of the technical level of the said product.

(3) exercise control over the observance of the USSR Constitution and ensure the conformity of the union republic constitutions to the USSR Constitution;

(4) give an interpretation of laws of the USSR;

(5) ratify and denounce international treaties of the USSR;

(6) repeal decrees and regulations of the USSR Council of Ministers and union republic councils of ministers in the event they fail to conform to the law;

(7) establish military ranks, diplomatic ranks, and other special ranks; confer the highest military ranks, diplomatic ranks, and other special ranks;

(8) institute orders and medals of the USSR; establish honorary titles of the USSR, award orders and medals of the USSR; confer honorary titles of the USSR;

(9) admit to citizenship of the USSR, decide questions of withdrawal from USSR citizenship and deprivation of USSR citizenship, and of granting asylum;

(10) issue all-union acts concerning amnesty and grant pardons;

(11) appoint and recall plenipotentiary representatives of the USSR to foreign states and international organizations;

(12) accept credentials and letters of recall of diplomatic representatives of foreign states accredited to it;

(13) form the Defense Council of the USSR and confirm its membership, and appoint and remove the supreme command of the USSR Armed Forces;

(14) declare martial law in the interests of the defense of the USSR in individual localities or throughout the country;

(15) declare a general or partial mobilization;

(16) declare, in the interval between sessions of the USSR Supreme Soviet, a state of war in the event of a military attack on the USSR or in the event of the need to fulfill international treaty obligations for mutual defense from aggression.

Article 120. The Presidium of the USSR Supreme Soviet, in the interval between sessions of the Supreme Soviet with subsequent submission for confirmation at a regular session, shall:

(1) make changes, when necessary, in prevailing USSR legislation;

(2) confirm changes of frontiers between union republics;

(3) form and abolish, upon the recommendation of the USSR Council of Ministers, ministries of the USSR and state committees of the USSR;

(4) relieve from office and appoint individual members of the USSR Council of Ministers upon the recommendation of the Chairman of the USSR Council of Ministers.

Article 121. The Presidium of the USSR Supreme Soviet shall issue edicts and adopt decrees.

Article 122. Upon the expiry of the powers of a USSR Supreme Soviet, the Presidium of the USSR Supreme Soviet shall retain its powers until the formation of the new Presidium by the newly elected USSR Supreme Soviet.

The newly elected USSR Supreme Soviet shall be convoked by the outgoing Presidium of the USSR Supreme Soviet not later than two months after the elections.

Article 123. The Soviet of the Union and the Soviet of Nationalities shall elect permanent commissions from among the deputies for the preliminary consideration and preparation of questions relegated to the jurisdiction of the USSR Supreme Soviet, and also for furthering the implementation of laws of the USSR and other decisions of the USSR Supreme Soviet and its Presidium, and for control over the activity of state agencies and organizations.

The chambers of the USSR Supreme Soviet may create joint commissions on the basis of equality.

Article 124. The USSR Supreme Soviet shall exercise control over the activity of all state agencies accountable to it.

The USSR Supreme Soviet shall form the USSR People's Control Committee, heading the system of people's control agencies.

Article 125. The USSR Supreme Soviet shall create, when it is considered necessary, investigative, auditing, and other commissions for any question. All state agencies, institutions, and officials shall be obliged to fulfill the requirements of these commissions and to submit necessary materials and documents to them.

Article 126. The procedure for the activity of the USSR Supreme Soviet and its agencies shall be determined by the Reglament of the USSR Supreme Soviet and laws of the USSR issued on the basis of the USSR Constitution.

Chapter 16. The USSR Council of Ministers

Article 127. The USSR Council of Ministers -- the Government of the USSR -- shall be the highest executive and administrative agency of state power of the USSR.

Article 128. The USSR Council of Ministers shall be formed by the USSR Supreme Soviet at a joint session of the Soviet of the Union and the Soviet of Nationalities and shall consist of: the Chairman of the USSR Council of Ministers, the first deputy and deputy chairmen of the USSR Council of Ministers, ministers of the USSR, and chairmen of USSR state committees.

The chairmen of the union republic councils of ministers shall be members *ex officio* of the USSR Council of Ministers.

Upon the recommendation of the Chairman of the USSR Council of Ministers, the USSR Supreme Soviet may include in the Government of the USSR the directors of other agencies and organizations of the USSR.

Article 129. The USSR Council of Ministers shall be responsible to the USSR Supreme Soviet and accountable thereto, and in the interval between sessions of the USSR Supreme Soviet, to the Presidium of the USSR Supreme Soviet, to which it shall be accountable.

The USSR Council of Ministers shall report regularly on its work to the USSR Supreme Soviet.

Article 130. The USSR Council of Ministers shall be empowered to decide all questions of state administration relegated to the jurisdiction of the USSR insofar as they are not, by virtue of the Constitution, within the competence of the USSR Supreme Soviet and the Presidium of the USSR Supreme Soviet.

Within the limits of its powers, the USSR Council of Ministers shall:

(1) ensure the direction of the national economy and socio-cultural construction and carry out a uniform policy in the domain of science and technology; work out and effectuate measures ensuring the growth of the well-being and culture of the people, strengthening a uniform monetary and credit system, implementing a uniform price policy, and organizing state insurance and a uniform system for records and statistics; organize the management of industrial, construction, and agricultural enterprises and associations, transport and communications enterprises, banks, and also other organizations and institutions of all-union subordination;

(2) work out and submit to the USSR Supreme Soviet current and long-term state plans for the development of the national economy and socio-cultural construction of the USSR and the state budget of the USSR; take measures for the effectuation of the state plan and budget; submit reports on the fulfillment of the plan and execution of the budget to the USSR Supreme Soviet;

(3) effectuate measures to defend the interests of the state, protect socialist ownership and public order, and ensure and protect the rights of citizens;

(4) take measures to ensure state security;

(5) exercise general direction over the construction of the USSR Armed Forces and determine the annual quotas of citizens subject to being called to active military service;

(6) exercise general direction in the domain of relations with foreign states, foreign trade, economic, scientific-technical, and cultural cooperation of the USSR with foreign countries; take measures to ensure the fulfillment of international treaties of the USSR; confirm and denounce inter-governmental international treaties.

Article 131. The Presidium of the USSR Council of Ministers, consisting of the Chairman of the USSR Council of Ministers and the first deputy and deputy chairmen of the USSR Council of Ministers, shall operate as a permanent agency of the USSR Council of Ministers in order to decide questions connected with ensuring direction of the national economy and other questions of state administration.

When necessary, the USSR Council of Ministers shall form committees, chief administrations, and other departments attached to the USSR Council of Ministers for matters of economic, social, cultural, and defense construction.

Article 132. The USSR Council of Ministers shall, on the basis of and in execution of the laws of the USSR and edicts of the Presidium of the USSR Supreme Soviet, issue decrees and regulations and verify their execution. Decrees and regulations of the USSR Council of Ministers shall be binding for execution on the entire territory of the USSR.

Article 133. The USSR Council of Ministers shall have the right to suspend, on questions relegated to the jurisdiction of the USSR, decrees and regulations of the union republic councils of ministers and to repeal acts of USSR ministries, USSR state committees, and also of other agencies within its jurisdiction.

Article 134. The USSR Council of Ministers shall coordinate and direct the work of all-union and union republic USSR ministries, USSR state committees, and other agencies within its jurisdiction.

All-union ministries and state committees of the USSR shall direct the branches of administration entrusted to them throughout the entire territory of the USSR directly or through agencies they have created.

Union republic ministries of the USSR and state committees of the USSR shall direct branches of administration entrusted to them through, as a rule, the respective union republic ministries and state committees directly administering enterprises and associations according to a list confirmed by the Presidium of the USSR Supreme Soviet.

USSR ministries and USSR state committees shall bear responsibility for the state and the development of branches of administration entrusted to them and within the limits of their competence shall issue acts on the basis of and in execution of laws of the USSR, edicts of the Presidium of the USSR Supreme Soviet, decrees and regulations of the USSR Council of Ministers, and shall organize and verify their execution.

Article 135. The competence of the USSR Council of Ministers and its Presidium, the procedure for their activity, mutual relations of the USSR Council of Ministers with USSR ministries and USSR state committees, and also the list of all-union and union republic ministries of the USSR and state committees of the USSR, shall be defined by a Law on the USSR Council of Ministers.

VI. Bases of the Structure of Agencies of State Power and Administration in the Union Republics

Chapter 17. Highest Union Republic Agencies of State Power and Administration

Article 136. The union republic supreme soviet shall be the highest union republic agency of state power.

A union republic supreme soviet shall be empowered to decide all questions relegated to union republic jurisdiction by the USSR Constitution and the union republic constitution.

The adoption of a union republic constitution, making changes therein, confirmation of state plans for the development of the national economy and socio-cultural construction, and also of the union republic state budget, and the formation of agencies accountable to it shall be carried out exclusively by the union republic supreme soviet.

Union republic laws shall be adopted only by a union republic supreme soviet.

Article 137. A union republic supreme soviet shall elect the Presidium of the supreme soviet, a permanently functioning agency of the union republic supreme soviet accountable to it in all its activity. The membership and powers of the union republic supreme soviet shall be determined by the union republic constitution.

Article 138. A union republic supreme soviet shall form the union republic council of ministers -- the Government of the union republic --

which is the highest executive and administrative agency of union republic state power.

A union republic council of ministers shall be responsible to the union republic supreme soviet and accountable thereto, and in the interval between sessions of the supreme soviet, to the Presidium of the union republic supreme soviet, to which it is accountable.

Article 139. A union republic council of ministers shall issue decrees and regulations on the basis of and in execution of laws of the USSR and union republic and decrees and regulations of the USSR Council of Ministers, and shall organize and verify their execution.

Article 140. A union republic council of ministers shall have the right to suspend decrees and regulations of autonomous republic councils of ministers and to repeal decisions and regulations of executive committees of territory, regional, city (or cities of republic subordination) soviets of people's deputies, autonomous region soviets of people's deputies, and in union republics not divided into regions, of executive committees of district and respective city soviets of people's deputies.

Article 141. A union republic council of ministers shall coordinate and direct the work of union republic and republic ministries and union republic state committees.

Union republic ministries and union republic state committees shall direct the branches of administration entrusted to them, being subordinate both to the union republic council of ministers and to the respective union republic ministry of the USSR or state committee of the USSR.

Republic ministries and state committees shall direct branches of administration entrusted to them, being subordinate to the union republic council of ministers.

Chapter 18. Highest Autonomous Republic Agencies of State Power and Administration

Article 142. An autonomous republic supreme soviet shall be the highest autonomous republic agency of state power.

The adoption of an autonomous republic constitution, making changes therein, confirmation of state plans for the development of the national economy and socio-cultural construction, and also the autonomous republic state budget, and the formation of agencies accountable thereto, shall be carried out exclusively by the autonomous republic supreme soviet.

Laws of an autonomous republic shall be adopted only by the autonomous republic supreme soviet.

Article 143. An autonomous republic supreme soviet shall elect the Presidium of the autonomous republic supreme soviet and shall form the autonomous republic council of ministers, the Government of the autonomous republic.

Chapter 19. Local Agencies of State Power and Administration

Article 144. Agencies of state power in territories, regions, autonomous regions, autonomous national areas, cities, districts, districts in cities, settlements, and rural population centers shall be the respective soviets of people's districts.

Article 145. Local soviets of people's deputies shall decide all questions of local significance, proceeding from the interests of the whole state and the interests of the citizens who reside on the territory of the soviet, shall implement decisions of superior state agencies, and also shall participate in the discussion of questions of republic and all-union significance and submit proposals in regard to them.

Soviets of people's deputies shall direct state, economic, and socio-cultural construction on their territory; confirm plans for economic and socio-cultural development and the local budget; exercise direction over the activity of state agencies, enterprises, institutions, and organizations subordinate to them; ensure observance of the laws; protection of state and public order and of the rights of citizens; further the strengthening of the defense capability of the country.

Article 146. Within the limits of their powers, local soviets of people's deputies shall exercise control over the observance of legislation by enterprises, institutions, and organizations of superior subordination which are situated on their territory, coordinate and control their activity in the domain of land use, nature conservation, construction, production of consumer goods, and socio-cultural, domestic, and other servicing of the populace.

Article 147. Local soviets of people's deputies shall take decisions within the limits of the rights granted them by laws of the USSR and union and autonomous republics. Decisions of local soviets shall be binding for execution by all enterprises, institutions, and organizations, and also by officials and citizens, situate on the territory of the soviet.

Article 148. Executive committees elected from among the deputies shall be the executive and administrative agencies of local soviets of people's deputies.

Executive committees shall report at least once a year to the soviets which elected them.

Article 149. Executive committees of local soviets of people's deputies shall be accountable directly to both the soviet which elected them and to the superior executive and administrative agency.

VII. Justice, Arbitrazh, and Procuracy Supervision

Chapter 20. Court and Arbitrazh

Article 150. Justice in the USSR shall be carried out only by a court.

The USSR Supreme Court, union republic supreme courts, autonomous republic supreme courts, territory, regional, and city courts, autonomous region courts, autonomous national area courts, district (or city) people's courts, and also military tribunals in the Armed Forces, shall operate in the USSR.

Article 151. All courts in the USSR shall be formed on the principle of electivity of judges and people's assessors.

People's judges of district (or city) people's courts shall be elected by the citizens of the district (or city) on the basis of universal, equal, and direct suffrage by secret ballot for a term of five years. People's assessors of district (or city) people's courts shall be elected at meetings of working people at their place of work or residence by open ballot for a term of two and one half years.

Superior courts shall be elected by the respective soviets of people's deputies for a term of five years.

Judges of military tribunals shall be elected by the Presidium of the USSR Supreme Soviet for a term of five years, and people's assessors, by meetings of military servicemen for a term of two and one half years.

Judges and people's assessors shall be responsible to the electors or to the agencies which elected them and accountable to them.

Article 152. The USSR Supreme Court shall be the highest judicial agency of the USSR and shall exercise supervision over the judicial activity of courts of the USSR, and also of union republic courts, within the limits established by law.

The USSR Supreme Court shall be elected by the USSR Supreme Soviet and composed of: a chairman, his deputies, members, and people's assessors, for a term of five years. The chairmen of the union republic supreme courts shall be *ex officio* members of the USSR Supreme Court.

The procedure for the organization and activity of the USSR Supreme Court shall be determined by a Law on the USSR Supreme Court.

Article 153. Consideration of civil and criminal cases in all courts shall be carried out collegially, and in a court of first instance, with the participation of people's assessors. When carrying out justice, people's assessors shall enjoy all the rights of judges.

Article 154. Judges and people's assessors shall be independent and subordinate only to law.

Article 155. Justice in the USSR shall be carried out on the principle of equality of citizens before the law and the court.

Article 156. Examination of cases in all courts shall be open. The hearing of cases in a closed session of a court shall be permitted only in the instances established by law, with observance of all rules of procedure.

Article 157. An accused shall be ensured the right of defense.

Article 158. A court proceeding shall be conducted in the language of the union or autonomous republic, autonomous region, autonomous national area, or in the language of the majority of the populace of a particular locality. Those persons participating in a case who do not command the language in which the court proceeding is conducted shall be ensured the right to completely familiarize themselves with the materials of the case, to participate in the judicial actions through an interpreter, and the right to speak in court in their native language.

Article 159. No one may be deemed guilty of committing a crime and subjected to criminal punishment other than by judgment of a court and in accordance with a criminal law.

Article 160. Colleges of advocates shall operate in order to render legal assistance to citizens and organizations. Legal assistance shall be rendered to citizens free of charge in the instances provided by law.

Article 161. The participation of representatives of social organizations and labor collectives shall be permitted in a court proceeding relating to civil and criminal cases.

Article 162. The settlement of economic disputes between organizations, institutions, and enterprises shall be carried out by state arbitrazh agencies. The procedure for the organization and activity of state arbitrazh agencies shall be determined by law.

The direction of the activity of all arbitrazh agencies and supervision over it shall be carried out by State Arbitrazh of the USSR. The Chief Arbitrator of State Arbitrazh of the USSR shall be appointed by the USSR Supreme Soviet for a term of five years.

Chapter 21. Procuracy

Article 163. Supreme supervision over the precise and uniform execution of the laws by all ministries, state committees and departments, enterprises, institutions, and organizations, executive and administrative agencies of local soviets of people's deputies, collective farms, cooperative, and other social organizations, officials, and also citizens, shall be entrusted to the USSR Procurator General and procurators subordinate to him.

Article 164. The USSR Procurator General shall be appointed by the USSR Supreme Soviet and shall be responsible to it and accountable to it, and in the interval between sessions of the Supreme Soviet, to the Presidium of the USSR Supreme Soviet, to which it is accountable.

Article 165. Procurators of union republics, autonomous republics, territories, regions, and autonomous regions shall be appointed by the USSR Procurator General. Procurators of autonomous national areas, and district and city procurators, shall be appointed by union republic procurators and confirmed by the USSR Procurator General.

Article 166. The term of powers of the USSR Procurator General and all inferior procurators shall be five years.

Article 167. Procuracy agencies shall exercise their powers independently of any local agencies whatever, being subordinate only to the USSR Procurator General.

The procedure for the organization and activity of agencies of the Procuracy of the USSR shall be determined by a Law on Procuracy Supervision in the USSR.

VIII. Arms, Flag, Anthem, and Capital of the USSR

Article 168. The state arms of the Union of Soviet Socialist Republics shall depict a sickle and hammer against a globe in the rays of the sun and framed by ears of grain, with the inscription in the languages of the union republics: "Proletarians of All Countries, Unite!" At the top of the arms shall be a five-pointed star.

Article 169. The state flag of the Union of Soviet Socialist Republics shall consist of a red rectangular cloth depicting in the upper corner near the flagstaff a gold sickle and hammer and above them a red five-pointed star bordered in gold. The proportion of the breadth of the flag to its length shall be 1:2.

Article 170. The state anthem of the Union of Soviet Socialist Republics shall be confirmed by the Presidium of the USSR Supreme Soviet.

Article 171. The city of Moscow shall be the capital of the Union of Soviet Socialist Republics.

IX. Procedure for the Effect of and Changes in the USSR Constitution

Article 172. The USSR Constitution shall possess the highest juridical force. All laws and other acts of state agencies shall be issued on the basis of and in accordance with the USSR Constitution.

The USSR Constitution shall be effective from the time of its adoption.

Article 173. The USSR Constitution shall be changed by decision of the USSR Supreme Soviet, adopted by a majority of not less than two thirds of the total number of deputies of each of its chambers.

CONSTITUTION (BASIC LAW) OF THE UNION OF SOVIET SOCIALIST REPUBLICS

[Confirmed by Decree of the Extraordinary VIII Congress of Soviets of the USSR, December 5, 1936, as amended to October 7, 1977; lost effect October 7, 1977]

Chapter I

The Social Structure

Article 1. The Union of Soviet Socialist Republics is a socialist state of workers and peasants.

Article 2. Soviets of working people's deputies which grew and became strong as a result of the overthrow of the landlords and capitalists and the victory of the dictatorship of the proletariat shall constitute the political foundation of the USSR.

Article 3. All power in the USSR shall belong to the working people of the city and country in the person of soviets of working people's deputies.

Article 4. The socialist system of economy and socialist ownership of the instruments and means of production confirmed as a result of the liquidation of the capitalist system of economy. the abolition of private ownership of the instruments and means of production, and the elimination of the exploitation of man by man shall constitute the economic foundation of the USSR.

Article 5. Socialist ownership in the USSR shall have either the form of state ownership (the whole people's wealth) or the form of cooperative and collective farm ownership (ownership of individual collective farms, ownership of cooperative combines).

Article 6. The land, its minerals, waters, forests, plants, factories, mines, quarries, rail, water, and air transport, banks, means of communications, large agricultural enterprises organized by the state (state farms, machine-tractor stations, etc.), as well as municipal enterprises and the basic housing fund in cities and industrial centers shall be in state ownership, that is, the wealth of the whole people.

Article 7. Social enterprises on collective farms and cooperative organizations with their livestock and implements, the output produced by collective farms and cooperative organizations, and also their social buildings, shall constitute social, socialist ownership of collective farms and cooperative organizations.

Each collective farm household shall, in addition to the basic income from the social collective farm economy, have for personal use a small plot of land and in personal ownership a subsidiary husbandry on the household plot, a dwelling house, productive livestock, poultry, and minor agricultural implements, according to the charter of the agricultural artel.

Article 8. Land occupied by collective farms shall be allotted for them free of charge and for unlimited time of use, that is, in perpetuity.

Article 9. Alongside the socialist system of economy, which shall be the predominant form of economy in the USSR, small-scale private economy of individual peasants and artisans based on personal labor and precluding the use of another's labor shall be permitted by law.

Article 10. The right of personal ownership of citizens in their labor income and savings, dwelling house, and subsidiary household economy, and in household articles, and in articles of personal consumption and convenience, as well as the right to inherit the personal ownership of citizens, shall be protected by law.

Article 11. The economic life of the USSR shall be determined and directed by the state national economic plan in the interests of increasing social wealth, a steady rise in the material and cultural level of the working people, strengthening the independence of the USSR, and intensifying its defense capability.

Article 12. Labor in the USSR shall be a duty and a matter of honor for every citizen able to work according to the principle: "He who does not work, neither shall he eat."

In the USSR the principle of socialism shall be carried out: "From each according to his ability, to each according to his labor."

Chapter II

The State Structure

Article 13. The Union of Soviet Socialist Republics is a union state formed on the basis of a voluntary combination of equal Soviet Socialist Republics:

Russian Soviet Federated Socialist Republic,

Ukrainian Soviet Socialist Republic,

Belorussian Soviet Socialist Republic,

Uzbek Soviet Socialist Republic,

Kazakh Soviet Socialist Republic,

Georgian Soviet Socialist Republic,

Azerbaidzhan Soviet Socialist Republic,

Lithuanian Soviet Socialist Republic,

Moldavian Soviet Socialist Republic,

Latvian Soviet Socialist Republic,

Kirgiz Soviet Socialist Republic,

Tadzhik Soviet Socialist Republic,

Armenian Soviet Socialist Republic,

Turkmen Soviet Socialist Republic,

Estonian Soviet Socialist Republic.

Article 14. There shall be subject to the jurisdiction of the Union of Soviet Socialist Republics in the person of its highest agencies of state power and agencies of state administration:

(a) representation of the USSR in international relations; the concluding, ratification, and denunciation of USSR treaties with other states, the establishment of a general procedure in mutual relations of union republics with foreign states;

(b) questions of war and peace;

(c) admission of new republics into the USSR;

(d) control over the observance of the Constitution of the USSR and ensuring the conformity of the union republic Constitutions with the Constitution of the USSR;

(e) confirmation of changes of boundaries between union republics;

(f) confirmation of the formation of new autonomous republics and autonomous regions within union republics;

(g) organization of the defense of the USSR, direction of all Armed Forces of the USSR, the establishment of guiding basic principles for the organization of union republic military formations;

(h) foreign trade on the basis of a state monopoly;

(i) protection of state security;

(j) establishment of national economic plans of the USSR;

(k) confirmation of a unified state budget of the USSR and the report on its execution, the establishment of taxes and revenues which go to the formation of union, republic, and local budgets;

(l) administration of banks, industrial and agricultural institutions and enterprises, as well as trade enterprises, of all-union subordination; general direction of industry and construction of union republic subordination;

(m) administration of transport and communications of all-union significance;

(n) direction of the monetary and credit system;

(o) organization of state insurance;

(p) concluding and granting of loans;

(q) establishment of basic principles of land use, as well as the use of minerals, forests, and waters;

(r) establishment of basic principles in the domain of enlightenment and public health;

(s) organization of a unified system of national economic accounting;

(t) establishment of fundamental principles of legislation on labor;

(u) establishment of fundamental principles of legislation on court organization and procedure, and fundamental principles of civil, criminal, and correctional labor legislation;

(v) legislation on union citizenship; legislation on the rights of aliens;

(w) establishment of fundamental principles of legislation on marriage and the family;

(x) promulgation of all-union acts on amnesty;

Article 15. The sovereignty of the union republics shall be restricted only within the limits specified in Article 14 of the USSR Constitution. Beyond such limits each union republic shall exercise state power independently. The USSR shall protect the sovereign rights of the union republics.

Article 16. Each union republic shall have its own Constitution, which shall take into account the peculiarities of the republic and which shall be drawn up in full accordance with the USSR Constitution.

Article 17. The right of free secession from the USSR shall be preserved for each union republic.

Article 18. The territory of a union republic may not be changed without its consent.

Article 18a. Each union republic shall have the right to enter into direct relations with foreign states, to conclude agreements with them, and to exchange diplomatic and consular representatives.

Article 18b. Each union republic shall have its own republic military formations.

Article 19. Laws of the USSR shall have the same force on the territory of all union republics.

Article 20. In the event a law of a union republic diverges from an all-union law, the all-union law shall be valid.

Article 21. A single union citizenship shall be established for citizens of the USSR.

Each citizen of a union republic shall be a citizen of the USSR.

Article 22. In the Russian Soviet Federated Socialist Republic shall be the autonomous soviet socialist republics: Bashkir, Buriat, Dagestan, Kabardino-Balkarskaia, Kalmyk, Karelia, Komi, Mari, Mordovia, North Osetian, Tatar, Tuva, Udmurt, Checheno-Ingush, Chuvash, Iakut; autonomous regions: Adygei, Gorno-Altai, Jewish, Karachaevo-Cherkess, Khakass.

Article 23. Repealed.

Article 24. In the Azerbaidzhan Soviet Socialist Republic shall be the Nakhichevan Autonomous Soviet Socialist Republic and the Nagorno-Karabakh Autonomous Region.

Article 25. In the Georgian Soviet Socialist Republic shall be the Abkhazian and Adzharian autonomous soviet socialist republics and the South Osetian Autonomous Region.

Article 26. In the Uzbek Soviet Socialist Republic shall be the Karakalpak Autonomous Soviet Socialist Republic.

Article 27. In the Tadzhik Soviet Socialist Republic shall be the Gorno-Badakhshan Autonomous Region.

Article 28. The resolution of questions concerning regional or territory administrative and territorial structure of union republics shall be relegated to the jurisdiction of the union republics.

Article 29. Repealed.

Chapter III

Highest Agencies of State Power of the Union of Soviet Socialist Republics

Article 30. The Supreme Soviet of the USSR shall be the highest agency of state power of the USSR.

Article 31. The USSR Supreme Soviet shall exercise all rights conferred on the Union of Soviet Socialist Republics according to Article 14 of the Constitution insofar as they do not, by virtue of the Constitution, come within the competence of USSR agencies which are accountable to the USSR Supreme Soviet: the Presidium of the USSR Supreme Soviet, the USSR Council of Ministers, and Ministries of the USSR.

Article 32. The legislative power of the USSR shall be exercised exclusively by the USSR Supreme Soviet.

Article 33. The USSR Supreme Soviet shall consist of two chambers: the Soviet of the Union and the Soviet of Nationalities.

Article 34. The Soviet of the Union shall be elected by citizens of the USSR by electoral areas according to the norm of: one deputy per 300,000 of population.

Article 35. The Soviet of Nationalities shall be elected by citizens of the USSR by union and autonomous republics, autonomous regions, and national areas according to the norm of: 32 deputies from each Union Republic, 11 deputies from each autonomous republic, 5 deputies from each autonomous region, and one deputy from each national area.

Article 36. The USSR Supreme Soviet shall be elected for a term of four years.

Article 37. Both chambers of the USSR Supreme Soviet, the Soviet of the Union and the Soviet of Nationalities, shall have equal rights.

Article 38. Legislative initiative shall belong in equal measure to the Soviet of the Union and the Soviet of Nationalities.

Article 39. A law shall be considered confirmed if it is adopted by both chambers of the USSR Supreme Soviet by a simple majority of votes of each chamber.

Article 40. Laws adopted by the USSR Supreme Soviet shall be published in the languages of the union republics over the signatures of the Chairman and the Secretary of the Presidium of the USSR Supreme Soviet.

Article 41. Sessions of the Soviet of the Union and of the Soviet of Nationalities shall commence and end simultaneously.

Article 42. The Soviet of the Union shall elect a Chairman of the Soviet of the Union and four of his deputies.

Article 43. The Soviet of Nationalities shall elect a Chairman of the Soviet of Nationalities and four of his deputies.

Article 44. The Chairmen of the Soviet of the Union and of the Soviet of Nationalities shall direct the sessions of the respective chambers and shall be in charge of their internal procedure.

Article 45. Joint sessions of both chambers of the USSR Supreme Soviet shall be conducted alternately by the chairmen of the Soviet of the Union and of the Soviet of Nationalities.

Article 46. Sessions of the USSR Supreme Soviet shall be convoked by the Presidium of the USSR Supreme Soviet twice a year.

Special sessions shall be convoked by the Presidium of the USSR Supreme Soviet at its discretion or at the demand of one of the union republics.

Article 47. In the event of disagreement between the Soviet of the Union and the Soviet of Nationalities, the question shall be transferred for settlement to a conciliation commission formed by the chambers on the basis of parity. If a conciliation commission does not come to an agreed decision or if its decision does not satisfy one of the chambers, the question shall be considered a second time in the chambers. In the absence of an agreed decision of both chambers, the Presidium of the USSR Supreme Soviet shall dissolve the USSR Supreme Soviet and designate new elections.

Article 48. The USSR Supreme Soviet shall, at a joint session of both chambers, elect the Presidium of the USSR Supreme Soviet, composed of: the Chairman of the Presidium of the USSR Supreme Soviet, fifteen deputy chairmen -- one from each union republic -- the Secretary of the Presidium, and twelve members of the Presidium of the USSR Supreme Soviet.

The Presidium of the USSR Supreme Soviet shall be accountable to the USSR Supreme Soviet in all its activity.

Article 49. The Presidium of the USSR Supreme Soviet shall:

(a) convoke sessions of the USSR Supreme Soviet;

(b) issue edicts;

(c) give an interpretation of prevailing USSR laws;

(d) dissolve the USSR Supreme Soviet on the basis of Article 47 of the USSR Constitution and designate new elections;

(e) conduct a referendum of the whole people at its own initiative or the demand of one of the union republics;

(f) repeal decrees and regulations of the USSR Council of Ministers and of the union republic councils of ministers in the event they fail to conform to the law;

(g) in the interval between sessions of the USSR Supreme Soviet, remove from office and appoint individual Ministers of the USSR upon the representation of the Chairman of the USSR Council of Ministers, with subsequent submission for confirmation of the USSR Supreme Soviet;

(h) institute orders and medals of the USSR and establish honorary titles of the USSR;

(i) award orders and medals of the USSR and confer honorary titles of the USSR;

(j) exercise the right of pardon;

(k) establish military ranks, diplomatic ranks, and other special ranks;

(l) appoint and remove the high command of the USSR Armed Forces;

(m) in the interval between sessions of the USSR Supreme Soviet, declare a state of war in the event of a military attack on the USSR or in the event of the need to fulfill international treaty obligations relating to mutual defense from aggression;

(n) declare a general or partial mobilization;

(o) ratify and denounce international treaties of the USSR;

(p) appoint and recall plenipotentiary representatives of the USSR in foreign states;

(q) accept credentials and letters of recall of diplomatic representatives of foreign states accredited to it;

(r) declare martial law in individual localities or throughout the USSR in the interests of the defense of the USSR or of securing public order and state security.

Article 50. The Soviet of the Union and the Soviet of Nationalities shall elect credentials commissions which shall verify the powers of the deputies of each chamber.

Upon the representation of credentials commissions, the chambers shall decide either to recognize the powers or to annul the elections of individual deputies.

Article 51. The USSR Supreme Soviet shall appoint, when it considers this necessary, investigative or inspection commissions on any question.

All institutions and officials shall be obliged to fulfill the demands of these commissions and to submit necessary materials and documents to them.

Article 52. A deputy of the USSR Supreme Soviet may not be brought to judicial responsibility or arrested without the consent of the USSR Supreme Soviet, and in the interval between sessions of the USSR Supreme Soviet, without the consent of the Presidium of the USSR Supreme Soviet.

Article 53. Upon the expiry of the powers or after the dissolution before time of the USSR Supreme Soviet, the Presidium of the USSR Supreme Soviet shall retain its powers until the formation of a new Presidium of the USSR Supreme Soviet by the newly elected USSR Supreme Soviet.

Article 54. Upon the expiry of the powers or in the event of the dissolution before time of the USSR Supreme Soviet, the Presidium of the USSR Supreme Soviet shall designate new elections within a period of not more than two months from the expiry of the powers or the dissolution of the USSR Supreme Soviet.

Article 55. The newly elected USSR Supreme Soviet shall be convoked by the Presidium of the USSR Supreme Soviet of the previous membership not later than three months after the elections.

Article 56. The USSR Supreme Soviet shall form the USSR Council of Ministers -- the Government of the USSR -- at a joint session of both chambers.

Chapter IV

Highest Agencies of State Power of Union Republics

Article 57. The Supreme Soviet of a union republic shall be the highest agency of state power of a union republic.

Article 58. The Supreme Soviet of a union republic shall be elected by the citizens of the republic for a term of four years.

Article 59. The Supreme Soviet of a union republic shall be the sole legislative agency of the republic.

Article 60. The Supreme Soviet of a republic shall:

(a) adopt the Constitution of the republic and make changes therein in accordance with Article 16 of the USSR Constitution;

(b) confirm the Constitutions of the constituent autonomous republics and determine the boundaries of their territories;

(c) confirm the national economic plan and budget of the republic;

(d) enjoy the right of amnesty and pardon of citizens sentenced by judicial agencies of the union republic;

(e) establish the representation of the union republic in international relations;

(f) establish the procedure for the formation of republic military formations.

Article 61. A union republic Supreme Soviet shall elect a Presidium of the union republic Supreme Soviet composed of: the Chairman of the Presidium of the union republic Supreme Soviet, his deputies, the Secretary of the Presidium, and members of the Presidium of the union republic Supreme Soviet.

The powers of the Presidium of the union republic Supreme Soviet shall be determined by the Constitution of the union republic.

Article 62. In order to conduct sessions, a union republic Supreme Soviet shall elect a Chairman of the union republic Supreme Soviet and his deputies.

Article 63. The union republic Supreme Soviet shall form the Government of the union republic, the union republic Council of Ministers.

Chapter V

Agencies of State Administration of the Union of Soviet Socialist Republics

Article 64. The USSR Council of Ministers shall be the highest executive and administrative agency of state power of the Union of Soviet Socialist Republics.

Article 65. The USSR Council of Ministers shall be responsible to the USSR Supreme Soviet and accountable to it, and in the interval between sessions of the Supreme Soviet, to the Presidium of the USSR Supreme Soviet, to which it shall be accountable.

Article 66. The USSR Council of Ministers shall issue decrees and regulations on the basis of and in execution of prevailing laws and shall verify execution.

Article 67. Decrees and regulations of the USSR Council of Ministers shall be binding for execution throughout the entire territory of the USSR.

Article 68. The USSR Council of Ministers shall:

(a) coordinate and direct the work of all-union and union republic Ministries of the USSR, State Committees of the USSR Council of Ministers, and other institutions subordinate to it;

(b) take measures to carry out the national economic plan and the state budget, and to strengthen the credit and monetary system;

(c) take measures to secure public order, defend the interests of the state, and protect the rights of citizens;

(d) exercise general direction in the domain of relations with foreign states;

(e) determine the annual contingents of citizens subject to being called to active military service and direct the general construction of the Armed Forces of the country;

(f) form the State Committees of the USSR, as well as, when necessary, special Committees and Chief Administrations attached to the USSR Council of Ministers for economic, cultural, and defense construction.

Article 69. The USSR Council of Ministers shall have the right, in regard to branches of administration and economy relegated to the competence of the USSR, to suspend decrees and regulations of the union republic councils of ministers and to repeal orders and instructions of Ministers of the USSR, as well as acts of other institutions subordinate to it.

Article 70. The USSR Council of Ministers shall be formed by the USSR Supreme Soviet, composed of:

Chairman of the USSR Council of Ministers;

First Deputy Chairmen of the USSR Council of Ministers;

Deputy Chairmen of the USSR Council of Ministers;

Ministers of the USSR;

Chairman of the State Planning Committee of the USSR Council of Ministers;

Chairman of the State Committee of the USSR Council of Ministers for Construction;

Chairman of the State Committee of the USSR Council of Ministers for Material-Technical Supply;

Chairman of the Committee of People's Control of the USSR;

Chairman of the State Committee of the USSR Council of Ministers for Labor and Social Questions;

Chairman of the State Committee of the USSR Council of Ministers for Science and Technology;

Chairman of the State Committee of the USSR Council of Ministers for Inventions and Discoveries;

Chairman of the State Committee for Prices of the USSR Council of Ministers;

Chairman of the State Committee for Standards of the USSR Council of Ministers;

Chairman of the State Committee of the USSR Council of Ministers for Professional-Technical Education;

Chairman of the State Committee of the USSR Council of Ministers for Television and Radio;

Chairman of the State Committee of the USSR Council of Ministers for Cinematography;

Chairman of the State Committee of the USSR Council of Ministers for Publishing Houses, Printing, and the Book Trade;

Chairman of the State Committee for Forestry of the USSR Council of Ministers;

Chairman of the State Committee of the USSR Council of Ministers for Foreign Economic Relations;

Chairman of the Committee of State Security attached to the USSR Council of Ministers;

Chairman of the All-Union Combine "Soiuzsel'khoztekhnika" of the USSR Council of Ministers;

Chairman of the Board of the USSR State Bank;

Head of the Central Statistical Administration attached to the USSR Council of Ministers.

The Chairmen of union republic councils of ministers shall be members ex officio of the USSR Council of Ministers.

Article 71. The Government of the USSR or the Minister of the USSR to whom a question of a deputy of the USSR Supreme Soviet is addressed shall be obliged within not more than three days to give an oral or written reply in the respective chamber.

Article 72. Ministers of the USSR shall direct branches of state administration which are within the competence of the USSR.

Article 73. Ministers of the USSR shall issue, within the limits of the competence of the respective ministries, orders and instructions on the basis of and in execution of prevailing laws, as well as of decrees and regulations of the USSR Council of Ministers and shall verify their execution.

Article 74. Ministries of the USSR shall be either all-union or union republic.

Article 75. All-union ministries shall direct the branches of state administration entrusted to them throughout the territory of the USSR either directly or through agencies designated by them.

Article 76. Union republic ministries shall direct the branch of state administration entrusted to them through, as a rule, union republic ministries of the same name and shall administer directly only a certain limited number of enterprises according to a list confirmed by the Presidium of the USSR Supreme Soviet.

Article 77. To all-union Ministries shall be relegated the Ministries of:

Aviation Industry;

Automobile Industry;

Foreign Trade;

Gas Industry;

Civil Aviation;

Machine-building;

Machine-building for Animal Husbandry and Fodder Production;

Machine-building for Light and Food Industry and for Household Instruments;

Medical Industry;

Maritime Fleet;

Petroleum Industry;

Defense Industry;

General Machine-building;

Instrument-making, Means of Automation, and Control Systems;

Industry for Means of Communications;

Transport;

Radio Industry;

Medium Machine-building;

Machine-tool and Instrument Industry;

Construction, Highway, and Municipal Machine-building;

Construction of Enterprises of the Petroleum and Gas Industry;

Ship-building Industry;

Tractor and Agricultural Machine-building;

Transport Construction;

Heavy and Transport Machine-building;

Chemical and Petroleum Machine-building;

Chemical Industry;

Cellulose-Paper Industry;

Electronics Industry;

Electrical Engineering Industry;

Power Machine-building.

Article 78. To union republic ministries shall be relegated the Ministries of:

Internal Affairs;

Higher and Secondary Specialized Education;

Geology;

Procurements;

Public Health;

Foreign Affairs;

Culture;

Light Industry;

Timber and Wood-processing Industry;

Soil and Water Conservation;

Assembly and Special Construction Works;

Meat and Milk Industry;

Oil Refining and Petrochemical Industry;

Defense;

Food Industry;

Industrial Construction;

Industry of Construction Materials;

Enlightenment;

Fisheries;

Communications;

Rural Construction;

Agriculture;

Construction;

Construction of Enterprises of Heavy Industry;

Trade;

Coal Industry;

Finances;

Non-ferrous Metallurgy;

Ferrous Metallurgy;

Power and Electrification;

Justice.

Chapter VI

Agencies of State Administration of Union Republics

Article 79. The union republic council of ministers shall be the highest executive and administrative agency of state power of the union republic.

Article 80. The union republic council of ministers shall be responsible to the union republic Supreme Soviet and shall be accountable to it, and in the interval between sessions of the union republic Supreme Soviet, to the Presidium of the union republic Supreme Soviet, to which it is accountable.

Article 81. The union republic council of ministers shall issue decrees and regulations on the basis of and in execution of prevailing laws of the USSR and union republic and decrees and regulations of the USSR Council of Ministers, and shall verify their execution.

Article 82. A union republic Council of Ministers shall have the right to suspend decrees and regulations of autonomous republic councils of ministers, and repeal decisions and regulations of executive committees of soviets of working people's deputies of territories, regions, and autonomous regions.

Article 83. The union republic Council of Ministers shall be formed by the union republic Supreme Soviet, composed of:

Chairman of the union republic Council of Ministers;

Deputy Chairmen of the Council of Ministers;

Ministers;

Chairmen of state committees, commissions, and directors of other departments of the Council of Ministers formed by the union republic Supreme Soviet in accordance with the union republic Constitution.

Article 84. The union republic Ministers shall direct the branches of state administration within the competence of the union republic.

Article 85. Ministers of a union republic shall issue, within the limits of the competence of the respective ministries, orders and instructions on the basis of and in execution of the laws of the USSR and the union republic, decrees and regulations of the USSR and union republic Council of Ministers, and orders and instructions of union republic Ministries of the USSR.

Article 86. Ministries of a union republic shall be union republic or republic.

Article 87. Union republic ministries shall direct the branch of state administration entrusted to them, being subordinate to both the union republic Council of Ministers and to the respective union republic Ministry of the USSR.

Article 88. Republic ministries shall direct the branch of state administration entrusted to them, being subordinate directly to the union republic Council of Ministers.

Chapter VII

Highest Agencies of State Power of Autonomous Soviet Socialist Republics

Article 89. The Supreme Soviet of an ASSR shall be the highest agency of state power of an autonomous republic.

Article 90. An autonomous republic supreme soviet shall be elected by citizens of the republic for a term of four years according to the norms of representation established by the autonomous republic Constitution.

Article 91. The autonomous republic Supreme Soviet shall be the sole legislative agency of the ASSR.

Article 92. Each autonomous republic shall have its own Constitution, taking into account the peculiarities of the autonomous republic and constructed in full conformity with the union republic Constitution.

Article 93. An autonomous republic Supreme Soviet shall elect the Presidium of the autonomous republic Supreme Soviet and shall form the autonomous republic Council of Ministers according to their own Constitution.

Chapter VIII

Local Agencies of State Power

Article 94. Soviets of working people's deputies shall be the agencies of state power in territories, regions, autonomous regions, national areas, districts, cities, and rural localities (stanitsas, villages, hamlets, kishlaks, auls).

Article 95. Territory, regional, autonomous region, national area, district, city, and rural (stanitsas, villages, hamlets, kishlaks, auls) soviets of working people's deputies shall be elected respectively by the working people of the territory, region, autonomous region, national area, district, city, or rural locality for a term of two years.

Article 96. Norms of representation in soviets of working people's deputies shall be determined by the union republic Constitutions.

Article 97. Soviets of working people's deputies shall direct the activity of agencies of administration subordinate to them, ensure the protection of the state order and the observance of the laws and protection of the rights of citizens, direct local economic and cultural construction, and establish the local budget.

Article 98. Soviets of working people's deputies shall adopt decisions and issue regulations within the limits of the rights granted to them by USSR and union republic laws.

Article 99. The executive and administrative agencies of territory, regional, autonomous region, national area, district, city, and rural soviets of working people's deputies shall be the executive committees elected by them, composed of: chairman, his deputies, secretary, and members.

Article 100. The executive and administrative agencies of soviets of working people's deputies in small settlements shall, in accordance with the union republic Constitutions, be the chairman, deputy chairman, and secretary elected by the soviets of working people's deputies.

Article 101. The executive agencies of soviets of working people's deputies shall be accountable directly both to the soviet of working people's deputies which elected them and to the executive agency of the superior soviet of working people's deputies.

Chapter IX

The Court and the Procuracy

Article 102. Justice in the USSR shall be carried out by the USSR Supreme Court, the union republic supreme courts, territory and regional courts, autonomous republic and autonomous region courts, national area courts, special USSR courts created by decree of the USSR Supreme Soviet, and people's courts.

Article 103. The consideration of cases in all courts shall be carried out with the participation of people's assessors except for instances specially provided for by law.

Article 104. The USSR Supreme Court shall be the highest judicial agency. To the USSR Supreme Court shall be entrusted supervision over the judicial activity of USSR judicial agencies, as well as judicial agencies of union republics within the limits established by law.

Article 105. The USSR Supreme Court shall be elected by the USSR Supreme Soviet for a term of five years.

The presidents of the union republic supreme courts shall be members *ex officio* of the USSR Supreme Court.

Article 106. The union republic supreme courts shall be elected by the union republic Supreme Soviets for a term of five years.

Article 107. The autonomous republic supreme courts shall be elected by the autonomous republic supreme soviets for a term of five years.

Article 108. Territory and regional courts, autonomous region courts, and national area courts shall be elected by territory, regional, or national area soviets of working people's deputies or by autonomous region soviets of working people's deputies for a term of five years.

Article 109. People's judges of district (or city) people's courts shall be elected by citizens of the district (or city) on the basis of universal, equal, and direct suffrage by secret ballot for a term of five years.

People's assessors of district (or city) people's courts shall be elected at general meetings of workers, employees, and peasants at their place of work or residence, and of military servicemen, at military units, for a term of two years.

Article 110. Judicial proceedings shall be conducted in the language of the union or autonomous republic or autonomous region, ensuring for persons not knowing this language complete familiarization with the materials of the case through an interpreter, as well as the right to speak in court in the native language.

Article 111. Examination of cases in all courts of the USSR shall be open, insofar as exceptions are not provided for by law, securing the accused the right to defense.

Article 112. Judges shall be independent and subordinate only to law.

Article 113. Supreme supervision over the precise execution of the laws by all ministries and institutions subordinate to them, and equally by individual officials, as well as by citizens of the USSR, shall be entrusted to the USSR Procurator General.

Article 114. The USSR Procurator General shall be appointed by the USSR Supreme Soviet for a term of seven years.

Article 115. Republic, territory, and regional procurators, as well as autonomous republic and autonomous region procurators, shall be appointed by the USSR Procurator General for a term of five years.

Article 116. National area, district, and city procurators shall be appointed by union republic procurators for a term of five years, confirmed by the USSR Procurator General.

Article 117. Agencies of the procuracy shall carry out their functions independently of any local agencies whatever, being subordinate only to the USSR Procurator General.

Chapter X

Fundamental Rights and Duties of Citizens

Article 118. Citizens of the USSR shall have the right to labor, that is, the right to receive a guaranteed job with payment for their labor in accordance with its quantity and quality.

The right to labor shall be guaranteed by the socialist organization of the national economy, the steady growth of the productive forces of Soviet society, the eradication of the possibility of economic crises, and the liquidation of unemployment.

Article 119. Citizens of the USSR shall have the right to leisure.

The right to leisure shall be secured by the establishment for workers and employees of a seven-hour working day and a reduction of the working day to six hours for a number of professions with arduous working conditions, and to four hours in shops with especially arduous working conditions; the establishment of annual vacations for workers and employees with retention of wages; by providing a network of sanatoriums, rest homes, and clubs serving working people.

Article 120. Citizens of the USSR shall have the right to financial security in old age, as well as in the event of illness or loss of the capacity to labor.

This right shall be secured by the extensive development of social insurance of workers and employees at the expense of the state, medical aid free of charge for working people, and an extensive network of resorts provided for the use of working people.

Article 121. Citizens of the USSR shall have the right to education.

This right shall be secured by universal, compulsory eight-year education, the extensive development of secondary general polytechnic education, professional-technical education, and secondary specialized and higher education on the basis of the bond of study with life, with production, with every possible development of evening and correspondence education, by all types of education being free of charge, by a system of state stipends, by study at schools in the native language, by the organization at plants, state farms, and collective farms of production, technical, and agronomy study for working people free of charge.

Article 122. Women in the USSR shall be granted equal rights with men in all domains of economic, state, cultural, and socio-political life.

The possibility of exercising these rights of women shall be secured by granting women an equal right with men to labor, payment for labor, rest, social insurance, and education, by state protection of the interests of mother and child, by state aid to mothers with many children and to unmarried mothers, by granting women pregnancy leaves with retention of maintenance, and by an extensive network of maternity homes, children's nurseries, and kindergartens.

Article 123. The equality of rights of citizens of the USSR, irrespective of their nationality and race, in all domains of economic, state, cultural, and socio-political life shall be an unalterable law.

Any direct or indirect limitation of rights whatever or, conversely, the establishment of direct or indirect privileges for citizens depending on their racial or national affiliation, or any advocacy of racial or national exclusiveness or of hatred or contempt shall be chastised by law.

Article 124. With a view to securing for citizens the freedom of conscience, the church in the USSR shall be separated from the state, and the school from the church. Freedom of religious worship and the freedom of anti-religious propaganda shall be recognized for all citizens.

Article 125. In accordance with the interests of the working people and with a view to strengthening the socialist system, citizens of the USSR shall be guaranteed by law:

(a) freedom of speech;

(b) freedom of the press;

(c) freedom of assembly and meetings;

(d) freedom of street processions and demonstrations.

These rights of citizens shall be secured by granting working people and their organizations printing presses, supplies of paper, public buildings, streets, means of communication, and other material conditions necessary for their exercise.

Article 126. In accordance with the interests of the working people and with a view to developing the organizational initiative and political activism of the popular masses, citizens of the USSR shall be secured the right to unite in social organizations: trade unions, cooperative associations, youth organizations, sport and defense organizations, cultural, technical, and scientific societies, and the most active and conscientious citizens from the ranks of the working class, the toiling peasantry, and the laboring intelligentsia shall be voluntarily united in the Communist Party of the Soviet Union, which is the vanguard of the working people in their struggle to build a communist society and is the leading core of all organizations of working people, both social and state.

Article 127. Citizens of the USSR shall be secured the inviolability of the person. No one may be subjected to arrest other than by decree of a court or with the sanction of the procurator.

Article 128. The inviolability of the dwelling of citizens and the secrecy of correspondence shall be protected by law.

Article 129. The USSR shall grant the right of asylum to foreign citizens persecuted for defending the interests of the working people, or for scientific activity, or for national-liberation struggle.

Article 130. Each citizen of the USSR shall be obliged to observe the Constitution of the Union of Soviet Socialist Republics, to execute the laws, to maintain labor discipline, to be honorably concerned with his social duty, and to respect the rules of socialist community life.

Article 131. Each citizen of the USSR shall be obliged to safeguard and strengthen social, socialist ownership as the sacred and inviolable basis of the Soviet system, as the source of the wealth and might of the motherland, as the source of the prosperous and cultural life of all working people.

Persons who commit offenses against social, socialist ownership shall be enemies of the people.

Article 132. Universal military obligation shall be a law.

Military service in the ranks of the USSR Armed Forces shall be the honorable duty of citizens of the USSR.

Article 133. Defense of the fatherland is the sacred duty of every citizen of the USSR. Treason: violation of the oath of allegiance, crossing over to the side of the enemy, infliction of damage to the military might of the state, espionage -- shall be chastised with all the severity of the law as the gravest evil crime.

Chapter XI

The Electoral System

Article 134. Deputies to all soviets of working people's deputies, the USSR Supreme Soviet, union republic supreme soviets, territory and regional soviets of working people's deputies, autonomous republic supreme soviets, autonomous region soviets of working people's deputies, national area, district, city, and rural (stanitsa, village, hamlet, kishlak, aula) soviets of working people's deputies shall be elected on the basis of universal, equal, and direct suffrage by secret ballot.

Article 135. Elections of deputies shall be universal: all citizens of the USSR who have attained 18 years of age irrespective of racial and national affiliation, sex, religious confession, educational qualification, domicile, social origin, property status, or past activity shall have the right to participate in the elections of deputies, except for persons who have been deemed insane in the procedure established by law.

Each citizen of the USSR who has attained 23 years of age, irrespective of racial and national affiliation, sex, religious confession, educational qualification, domicile, social origin, financial status, and past activity may be elected a deputy of the USSR Supreme Soviet.

Article 136. Elections of deputies shall be equal: each citizen shall have one vote; all citizens shall participate in elections on an equal basis.

Article 137. Women shall enjoy the right to elect and to be elected equally with men.

Article 138. Citizens in the ranks of the USSR Armed Forces shall enjoy the right to elect and to be elected equally with all citizens.

Article 139. Elections of deputies shall be direct: all soviets of working people's deputies, from rural and city soviets of working people's deputies to the USSR Supreme Soviet, shall be elected by citizens directly by means of direct elections.

Article 140. Voting in elections of deputies shall be secret.

Article 141. Candidates in elections shall be nominated by electoral districts.

The right to nominate candidates shall be secured for social organizations and societies of working people: communist party organizations, trade unions, cooperatives, youth organizations, and cultural societies.

Article 142. Each deputy shall be obliged to account to the electors for his own work and for the work of the soviet of working people's deputies and may be recalled at any time by decision of a majority of electors in the procedure established by law.

Chapter XII

Arms, Flag, Capital

Article 143. The State Arms of the Union of Soviet Socialist Republics shall consist of a sickle and hammer against a globe depicted in the rays of the sun and framed by ears of grain, with the inscription in the language of the union republics: "Proletarians of All Countries, Unite!" At the top of the arms shall be a five-pointed star.

Article 144. The State Flag of the Union of Soviet Socialist Republics shall consist of a red cloth depicting in the upper corner near the flagstaff a gold sickle and hammer and above them a red five-pointed star bordered in gold. The proportion of breadth to length shall be 1:2.

Article 145. The city of Moscow shall be the capital of the Union of Soviet Socialist Republics.

Chapter XIII

Procedure for Amending the Constitution

Article 146. The Constitution of the USSR shall be amended only by decision of the USSR Supreme Soviet adopted by a majority of not less than 2/3 of the votes in each of its chambers.

GENERAL STATUTE ON USSR MINISTRIES

[Confirmed by Decree of the USSR Council of Ministers, July 10, 1967. _SP SSSR_ (1967), no. 17, item 116]

Principal Tasks and Basic Questions of the Organization of the Work of a USSR Ministry

1. A USSR ministry shall be the central agency of state administration exercising direction of a respective branch of the national economy.

A USSR ministry shall bear responsibility to the party, state, and people for the state of and the further development of the branch, for scientific and technical progress and the technical level of production, for the quality of products issued and for the fullest satisfaction of the requirements of the country in all types of products of the branch.

2. The principal tasks of a USSR ministry shall be to:

ensure the development by every possible means of the branch entrusted to it as a constituent part of the national economy of the country, the high tempos of the development of production and the growth of labor productivity on the basis of scientific technical progress with a view to the fullest satisfaction of the requirements of the national economy and the defense of the country for all types of products;

fulfill the planning tasks of the state plan and ensure the strict observance of state discipline;

ensure the production of high-quality products with minimal losses of social labor, increase production efficiency, improve the use of basic funds and of labor, material, and financial resources;

carry on a unified technology policy in the branch, introduce the newest achievements of science and technology and progressive experience, and ensure high technical and economic production indicators;

use capital investments rationally and increase their efficiency, reduce the cost and lower the periods for construction, for the timely introduction into operation of production capacities and basic funds, as well as for mastering production capacities quickly;

introduce the scientific organization of labor and administration, provide enterprises, organizations, and institutions of the system of the ministry with qualified cadres, create the conditions for the best use of the knowledge and experience of workers, and promote to executive work young, well-recommended specialists;

improve the housing and cultural and everyday conditions of workers and employees and create safe labor conditions for production.

3. A USSR ministry shall carry out planned direction of a branch on a scientific basis, taking into account the requirements of the integrated development of the USSR national economy, of union republics, and of economic areas of the country.

4. A USSR ministry shall ensure the correct combining of economic and administrative methods of direction, the fullest use of such economic levers as profit, price, bonus, and credit, and the introduction of efficient systems of management, applying computer technology, and improving the structure and organizational forms of management.

5. A USSR ministry shall ensure the effectuation of the Leninist principles of selecting, promoting, and placing of leading economic, engineering, and scientific cadres, concentrate their attention on the verification and control of the execution by leading cadres of the directives and decisions of the Party and Government, carry on work with the participation of social organizations relating to the nurturing of cadres in a spirit of a communist attitude toward labor, strict observance of state interests and discipline, ensure the correct combining of material and moral stimuli for raising social production, and increasing the responsibility of each worker for the work entrusted to him and for the general results of the collective's work.

6. In accordance with the USSR Constitution, a USSR ministry shall be all-union or union republic and shall be formed by the USSR Supreme Soviet.

An all-union ministry shall direct the branch entrusted to it throughout the entire territory of the USSR directly or through agencies created by it.

A union republic ministry of the USSR shall direct the branch entrusted to it through, as a rule, union republic ministries of the same name and shall manage enterprises, organizations, and institutions of union subordination directly or through agencies which it has created.

7. A USSR ministry, union republic ministries of the same name, and enterprises, organizations, and institutions subordinate to them shall constitute the unified system of the respective ministry.

Union republic ministries of union republics shall be subordinate to the council of ministers of the respective union republics and to union republic ministries of the USSR of the same name. Statutes concerning union republic ministries of union republics and the structure and number of workers of the central apparatus of these ministries shall be confirmed by the union republic councils of ministers by agreement with the union republic ministry of the USSR of the same name.

8. A USSR ministry shall decide all questions by branches within the limits of the rights granted to it and may entrust the decision of individual questions within its competence to union republic ministries of the same name, as well as to enterprises, organizations, and institutions of union subordination.

A USSR ministry shall be obliged to strictly observe the rights of union republic ministries of the same name, as well as the rights of enterprises, organizations, and institutions of the system of the ministry provided for by the Statute on the Socialist State Production Enterprise and other acts of prevailing legislation, and to promote in every possible way the development of their economic independence and initiative.

A USSR ministry shall in its activity effectuate contacts and professional cooperation with other ministries and departments in working out and deciding inter-branch questions.

9. A USSR ministry which is in charge in the production of products issued by enterprises of several ministries shall participate in the

10. A USSR ministry shall ensure the protection of socialist state ownership at enterprises, organizations, and institutions of the system of the ministry and an attitude of care toward it.

11. A USSR ministry shall ensure the development of democratic principles in management, create conditions for the manifestation of initiative and the active participation of the working people and their social organizations in work relating to the improvement of production and the elimination of shortcomings in the activity of ministries and of enterprises, organizations, and institutions within their jurisdiction.

Questions of labor and the daily life of workers and employees shall be decided by the ministry, taking into account the proposals of Soviet and trade union agencies, and in instances provided for by prevailing legislation, jointly or by agreement with such agencies.

12. A USSR ministry shall be guided in its activity by laws of the USSR, edicts of the Presidium of the USSR Supreme Soviet, decrees and regulations of the Government of the USSR, and other normative acts, the present General Statute, as well as by the Statute concerning the particular ministry, confirmed by the USSR Council of Ministers, and shall ensure the correct application of prevailing legislation at enterprises, organizations, and institutions of the system of the ministry.

A USSR ministry shall summarize the practice of the application of legislation in the branch entrusted to it, shall work out proposals regarding its improvement, and shall submit them for consideration of the USSR Council of Ministers.

13. A USSR ministry shall organize its work on the basis of combining collegiality and one-man leadership in the discussion and resolution of all questions relating to directing the branch, establishing the precise responsibility of officials for the state of affairs at the entrusted sector of work and for the fulfillment of specific planning tasks.

14. A USSR ministry shall be headed by a minister appointed in accordance with the USSR Constitution by the USSR Supreme Soviet, and in the interval between sessions, by the Presidium of the USSR Supreme Soviet with subsequent submission for confirmation of the USSR Supreme Soviet.

A minister of the USSR shall have deputies appointed by the USSR Council of Ministers. The distribution of duties between the deputy ministers shall be by the minister.

15. A college shall be formed in a USSR ministry composed of the minister (chairman) and deputy ministers *ex officio*, as well as other executive workers of the ministry.

Members of the college of the ministry shall be confirmed by the USSR Council of Ministers.

16. A minister of the USSR shall bear personal responsibility for the fulfillment of tasks and duties entrusted to the ministry, and shall establish the extent of responsibility of deputy ministers, heads of chief administrations, and directors of other subdivisions of the ministry for the activity of enterprises, organizations, and institutions of the system of the ministry.

17. A minister of the USSR shall, within the limits of the competence of the ministry, issue on the basis of and in execution of prevailing laws, as well as of decrees and regulations of the USSR Council of Ministers,

orders and instructions and shall issue ukazaniia binding for execution by union republic ministries of the same name, enterprises, organizations, and institutions of the system of the ministry and shall verify their execution.

Ministers of the USSR shall, when necessary, issue joint orders and instructions.

18. The college of a USSR ministry shall consider at its regularly held sessions the basic questions of the development of the branch and other questions of the activity of the ministry, discuss questions of the practical direction by enterprises, organizations, and institutions, the verifications of execution, the selection and use of cadres, drafts of the most important orders and instructions, and shall hear reports of minister of union republic ministries of the same name, reports of chief administrations, administrations, and sections of the ministry, enterprises, organizations, and institutions of the system of the ministry.

Decisions of the college shall be implemented, as a rule, by orders of the minister. In the event of disagreement between the minister and the college, the minister shall carry out his own decisions, reporting the disagreements which arose to the USSR Council of Ministers, and members of the college, in their turn, may communicate their view to the USSR Council of Ministers.

19. In order to consider proposals relating to the basic directions of the development of science and technology, determine the scientific well-foundedness of a unified technological policy in the branch, work out the recommendations for the use of and introduction into production of the most modern achievements of domestic and foreign science, technology, and progressive experience, a scientific-technical (or scientific) council shall be created in a ministry of the USSR composed of: well-known scholars, highly qualified specialists, production innovators, as well as representatives of scientific and technical societies and other organizations.

The membership of the scientific-technical (or scientific) council and the statute concerning it shall be confirmed by the minister.

20. A USSR ministry shall create, reorganize, and liquidate an enterprise, organization, and institution of union subordination within the limits of the labor plan (budget appropriations) established for it.

Decisions concerning the creation, reorganization, and liquidation of enterprises, organizations, and institutions shall be adopted by a union republic ministry of the USSR after a preliminary consideration, when necessary, of such questions with the council of ministers of the respective union republics.

A USSR ministry shall confirm the charters of enterprises and the statutes (or charters) of organizations and institutions of union subordination.

21. A USSR ministry shall form an arbitrazh for the consideration of economic disputes between enterprises, organizations, and institutions of the system of the ministry. The right to issue orders for compulsory execution of decisions rendered by it shall be granted to the arbitrazh of the ministry. The statute on the arbitrazh shall be confirmed by the minister.

22. The structure and number of workers of the central apparatus of a USSR ministry shall be confirmed by the USSR Council of Ministers.

The personnel establishment of the central apparatus of a ministry, as well as statutes on chief administrations, administrations, and sections of the ministry shall be confirmed by the minister. In statutes on chief administrations, administrations, and sections their powers within the limits of the competence of the ministry shall be defined.

Chief administrations, administrations, and sections of a ministry may be transferred by a minister to economic accountability.

23. A USSR ministry shall convoke, in the established procedure, meetings of the _aktiv_ with the participation of social organizations at which reports concerning measures relating to the fulfillment of decisions of the Party and the Government, the most important problems of the development of the branch, shall be heard and discussed, and also questions connected with the improvement of the activity of the ministry and enterprises, organizations, and institutions within its jurisdiction shall be discussed on the basis of the unfolding criticism and self-criticism.

24. A USSR ministry shall organize the timely and attentive consideration of the letters (applications and complaints) of the working people, while reaching the correct decision of questions raised in such letters, as well as take measures to eliminate the shortcomings in the activity of enterprises, organizations, and institutions of the system of the ministry communicated in letters of the working people.

The Functions of a USSR Ministry

In the domain of planning a USSR ministry shall:

25. study the requirements of the national economy for products of the branch and carry out the planning of the development of the branch, according to the system of the ministry and by territory, in accordance with the tasks for the development of the entire national economy of the country and the economy of union republics and economic districts, taking into account the specialization and cooperation of production.

work out schemes for the development and allocation of industry of the branch, send them to union republic councils of ministers, and consider proposals received from them in regard to such schemes.

26. ensure the rational use and replacement of natural resources, taking into account the interests of other branches and the national economy as a whole in their use, carry out the necessary measures in regard to the protection of air, soil, and water reservoirs from pollution by industrial and household effluents, sewage, radioactive substances, and production wastes and to the preservation of the plant and animal world.

27. determine, proceeding from control figures for the development of the national economy of the USSR, and bring to the information of union republic ministries of the same name, enterprises, organizations, and institutions of union subordination, control figures for long-term and annual plans.

work out on the basis of control figures for the development of the USSR national economy and draft plans submitted by union republic ministries of the same name, enterprises, organizations, and institutions of union subordination, taking into account the proposals of the union republic councils of ministers, the drafts of long-term and annual plans relating to the system of the ministry and by territory and submit them to the USSR Council of Ministers and to Gosplan SSSR.

consider with the participation of union republic ministries of the same name, enterprises, organizations, and institutions of union subordination and confirm for them long-term and annual plans in accordance with established indicators corresponding to planning tasks of the national economic plan, ensuring the coordination of all sections and indicators of these plans.

A USSR ministry shall communicate to union republic councils of ministers the control figures, draft plans, and confirmed plans relating to union republic ministries of the same name, enterprises, organizations, and institutions, and institutions of union subordination (except indicators regarding the production of defense products).

28. work out and effectuate measures connected with the realization by enterprises of the system of the ministry of products which they produced.

determine, taking into account the proposals of interested agencies, the volume of production by enterprises of the system of the ministry of products by nomenklatura not provided for in the national economic plan.

take measures for the development of rational economic links of enterprises, organizations, and institutions of the system of the ministry.

29. Organize the work relating to the drawing up of long-term and annual plans by enterprises, organizations, and institutions of the system of the ministry, work out methods instructions relating to the preparation of drafts of such plans, and confirm the forms for the technical-industrial-financial plans of enterprises.

30. Ensure the fulfillment of established plans by all enterprises, organizations, and institutions of the system of the ministry.

31. Work out and confirm in the established procedure the technical and economic norms, norms for the expenditure and reserves of raw materials, fuel, materials, and norms for the expenditure of electrical power for production and use needs; establish the list of standards and norms confirmed by union republic ministries of the same name, enterprises, organizations, and institutions of the system of the ministry; ensure the introduction of confirmed standards and norms.

32. Confirm or submit for confirmation in accordance with prevailing legislation the prices and tariffs for products and services of enterprises and organizations of the system of the ministry; exercise control over the correct application of prices and tariffs by enterprises, organizations, and institutions of the system of the ministry.

33. Organize the primary accounting at enterprises, organizations, and institutions of the system of the ministry, confirm primary accounting forms for them; receive statistical and bookkeeping reports in the established procedure; carry out measures relating to the centralization of accounting work and the introduction of progressive accounting methods.

<u>In the domain of science and technology a USSR ministry shall</u>:

34. Conduct systematic work to evaluate the technical and economic level of production achieved and of products of the branch issued, determine the ways of the most efficient use of scientific and technical

achievement, and ensure a high technical level of the development of the branch on the basis of the achievements of domestic and foreign science and technology.

35. Ensure the working out of scientific and technical problems in the branch from scientific inquiry to introduction of the results obtained into production, as well as fulfill the work connected with the resolution of inter-branch scientific and technical questions.

36. Direct the activity of scientific research institutions and of drafting and design organizations of the system of the ministry and effectuate measures to improve planning and the organization of scientific research and experimental design works and increase their efficiency.

37. Provide scientific research institutions and drafting and design organizations with the requisite experimental production base of the appropriate modern technological standard.

38. Ensure the working out and introduction into production of new types of products corresponding to modern achievements of science and technology and the requirements of the national economy, as well as the working out and introduction of highly efficient technological processes and methods for the organization of production and carry out measures for the integrated mechanization and automation of production and the use of the most economical materials and raw materials.

Decide by agreement with the respective USSR ministries and departments questions concerning the removal of obsolete products from production.

Study the experience of the exploitation and use of products issued and work out and take measures to eliminate uncovered design and production defects of products, and increase the dependability and the service periods of manufactures.

39. Work out and submit for confirmation the drafts of state standards; ensure the introduction of state standards and modern means and methods of measurement and testing the quality of products, as well as control the observance of standards and the state of measuring and testing means.

Confirm normative technological documentation of branch significance for individual types of products for which there are no state standards.

40. Organize scientific and scientific-technical information and ensure the preparation and publication in the established procedure of scientific and scientific-technical literature regarding the branch.

41. Direct the development of invention and rationalization; work out long-term and current topical plans relating to invention and rationalization; ensure the introduction of inventions and rationalization proposals. The ministry shall conduct work relating to the development of inventions and rationalization jointly with the trade union central committee and the Central Committee of the All-Union Society of Inventions and Rationalizers.

42. Ensure the broad study and use of domestic and foreign patent materials when working out new and when improving existing techniques and technology and the patentability of machines, instruments, equipment, and other products, as well as technological processes; ensure the submission in the established procedure by enterprises, scientific research, and other organizations of applications for the issuance of authors'

certificates in the USSR and, when advisable, for the patenting of inventions abroad.

43. Work out and submit in the established procedure proposals concerning the purchase abroad of licenses for the most progressive machines, equipment, materials, and technological processes, technologically and economically, and ensure the most rapid mastery of the production of products under licenses purchased.

<u>In the domain of capital construction a USSR ministry shall</u>:

44. Carry out capital construction in the system of the ministry, ensure the efficient use of capital investments, the rational allocation of new construction, priority development of progressive production of branches, priority channeling of capital investments for the technical re-equipping of operating enterprises, improvement of inter-branch and intra-branch proportions, concentration of capital investments on construction sites being started, and a reduction of incomplete construction.

Capital construction shall be carried out, as a rule, by sub-contract.

45. Work out and confirm in the established procedure technical and economic standards and indicators, optimal capacities for newly constructed, reconstructed, or enlarged enterprises of the branch, and norms for technological drafting.

Ensure the working out and confirmation of technical and economic criteria and planning tasks for the design of construction of new, reconstruction, and expansion of operating enterprises, buildings, and installations of the branch.

46. Work out and confirm in the established procedure itemized lists of construction sites, as well as itemized lists of design and survey work for construction of future years.

Ensure the timely working out, confirmation, and issuance of the necessary design and estimate documentation to construction sites.

Exercise control over the quality of design and estimate documentation and observance of the confirmed estimated price of construction, as well as technical supervision over the quality of construction and assembly work and of equipment delivered for objects being built; organize designers' supervision over construction.

47. Ensure the financing of construction sites and the supply of equipment, materials, and manufactures whose delivery is the duty of the customer.

Exercise control over the allocation of orders by subordinate enterprises and organizations for capital construction equipment in accordance with the funds allotted and appropriations for its acquisition.

Work out measures relating to the mobilization of internal resources for construction and exercise control over their fulfillment.

48. Ensure the timely introduction into operation of production capacities and basic funds, as well as the mastery of production capacities rapidly.

Appoint within the limits of its competence state commissions for the acceptance into use of enterprises, buildings, and installations whose construction has been completed and confirm acts accepting them and take decisions to close the overall estimate and financial accounts.

49. Organize capital repair of basic funds ensuring the modernization, and raising of the technical standard and the productivity of equipment, as well as improving the technical and operational condition of buildings and installations; carry out measures to increase the quality of repair and reduce its cost.

In the domain of material-technical supply a USSR ministry shall:

50. Determine the requirements of the enterprises, organizations, and institutions of the system of the ministry for raw materials, fuel, equipment, and other material resources, dispose of material resources allotted to the ministry and bear responsibility for the material-technical supply of such enterprises, organizations, and institutions.

51. Distribute the funds allotted to the ministry for raw material, fuel, equipment, and other material resources among union republic ministries of the same name and enterprises, organizations, and institutions of union subordination, as well as redistribute when necessary the said funds taking into account the fulfillment and over-fulfillment of the production program and capital construction plan.

52. Work out and confirm plans for intra-branch cooperative deliveries of products taking into account the ensuring of delivery of products to users of other branches.

53. Exercise control over the realization of funds for raw materials, fuel, equipment, and other material resources, as well as over the timely conclusion by enterprises, organizations, and institutions of the system of the ministry of contracts for the delivery of products and the fulfillment of contractual obligations.

54. Ensure the correct storage and use by enterprises, organizations, and institutions of the system of the ministry of raw materials, fuel, equipment, and other material resources and take measures for the realization of surplus and unused material resources.

55. Work out and carry out measures relating to the economical expenditure of materials, raw materials, and fuel, the reduction of production loss, the use of production wastes and secondary raw materials, and other measures aimed at the efficient use of material resources.

In the domain of finances and credit a USSR ministry shall:

56. Carry out measures relating to the strengthening of economic accountability, increasing the profitability and maximizing the accumulations of enterprises and organizations of the system of the ministry, the effective use of basic funds, circulating assets, and bank credits.

Finance in the established procedure enterprises, organizations, and institutions of union subordination and direct their financial activity.

Exercise control over the use of financial resources in the system of the ministry.

57. Ensure the fulfillment by union republic ministries of the same name, enterprises, and organizations of union subordination of financial plans, preservation of its own circulating assets, timely accounts with workers and employees, the budget, suppliers, sub-contractors, banks, as well as the transfer by enterprises and organizations of its own assets designated for financing capital construction and capital repair and for other purposes provided for by the financial plan.

58. Form in the established procedure a fund for the mastery of new technology, a fund for bonuses for the creation and introduction of new technology and other centralized funds, as well as reserves for rendering financial assistance to enterprises and organizations of union subordination.

59. Organize jointly with banking institutions the introduction of the most economical and progressive forms of accounts enabling the acceleration of payments, the liquidity of circulating assets, and the strengthening of payment discipline; participate in the organization and conducting of offsets of mutual indebtedness of enterprises, organizations, and institutions of the system of the ministry.

60. Open accounts in banks for the redistribution among enterprises and organizations of union subordination its own circulating assets, profits, amounts for forming a fund for the mastery of new technology, and other assets, as well as individual accounts for keeping reserve assets to render financial assistance to enterprises and organizations and reserve assets for amortization deductions for capital repair.

61. Consider the overall reports and balances of union republic ministries of the same name, confirm accounts and balances of chief administrations, administrations, and sections of the ministry, enterprises, organizations, and institutions of union subordination; draw up overall accounts and balances by types of activity of the ministry.

62. Organize control and inspection work in the system of the ministry; ensure in accordance with prevailing legislation concerning departmental control the regular holding of inspections, the comprehensive analysis of the state of economic activity, the verification of the safekeeping of cash assets and material valuables, and observance of the regime of economic activity; exercise control over the correct handling and reliability of accounts and reporting in the system of the ministry, as well as measures relating to the protection of state property and the compensation of material damage caused.

In the domain of cadres, labor, and wages a USSR ministry shall:

63. Provide enterprises, organizations, and enterprises of the system of the ministry with qualified cadres of workers, organize the training of cadres and raise their qualifications; study cadres in the system of the ministry, ensure the combining of older experienced cadres and young capable workers, create conditions for the promotion to executive work of politically mature specialists who know their work well and who enjoy authority and trust in the collective; take measures for the rational use of young specialists and carry out measures aimed at creating permanent cadres in the system of the ministry.

64. Work out the basic directions of improving the scientific organization of labor in the branch and direct the work relating to the introduction of the scientific organization of labor and management at enterprises, organizations, and institutions of the system of the ministry; ensure the implementation of measures relating to the further improvement of labor conditions and to making them healthy and to strict observance of technical safety rules and requirements of production sanitation.

65. Work out and introduce in the established procedure at enterprises, organizations, and institutions of the system of the ministry uniform and model output norms (or service) and standards for the number of workers, and tariff-qualification manuals.

Organize jointly with the trade union central committee work relating to the review of output norms (or service) at enterprises and organizations of the system of the ministry and carry out other measures relating to the improvement of normatization of labor.

66. Confirm model structures and model personnel establishments for enterprises, organizations, and institutions of the system of the ministry.

67. Ensure the correct application of prevailing conditions for payment of labor and bonuses, as well as the correct co-relation between the growth of labor productivity and the growth of wages; exercise control over the expenditure of wage funds and incentive funds.

68. Establish and modify post salaries for workers of the central apparatus of the ministry, observing the scheme for post salaries and within the limits of the wage fund calculated on the basis of average post salaries.

69. Work out and confirm by agreement with the trade union central committee or submit for confirmation branch norms for labor protection and technical safety and production sanitation rules.

70. Determine jointly with the trade union central committee the basic directions of collective contracts, taking into account the specific tasks of development of the branch, direct the conclusion of collective contracts, and exercise control over their fulfillment.

71. Ensure with the participation of the trade union the improvement of housing, cultural, and everyday conditions for workers of enterprises, organizations, and institutions of the system of the ministry, as well as the implementation of health measures.

72. Organize, jointly with the trade union committee, the socialist competition, confirm the conditions for the all-union competition in the system of the ministry, confirm in the established procedure the challenge Red Banners with cash bonuses, promote the development of the movement for communist labor and for a high degree of culture in production.

Total jointly with the trade union central committee the results of the socialist competition and award the challenge Red Banners and cash bonuses to the victorious collectives, confer the titles of collectives of enterprises and organizations of communist labor, organize the study, summary, and dissemination of progressive methods of labor and progressive experience.

In the domain of economic, scientific-technical, and cultural links with foreign countries a USSR ministry shall:

73. Effectuate in the established procedure economic, scientific-technical, and cultural links with foreign countries and ensure the fulfillment of obligations of the USSR arising from treaties and agreements concluded with foreign states which relate to the branch.

74. Work out measures relating to the long-term development of economic and scientific-technical cooperation in the domain of the corresponding branch of the economy of the USSR and socialist countries on the principles of mutual advantage and comradely mutual assistance.

Prepare proposals relating to the coordination of plans for the development of the branch with plans for the development of analogous branches of member countries of the Council of Mutual Economic Assistance and other interested socialist countries, as well as proposals relating to the development of economically efficient and stable inter-state specialization and cooperation by branch.

75. Ensure the fulfillment of planning tasks relating to the production of products for export which correspond to the requirements of the foreign market, take measures to expand the production of goods for export whose realization has a high foreign currency efficiency, take part in working out and implementing measures relating to questions of the export of products of the branch, as well as questions of the import of goods, the demand for which it is economically advisable to satisfy by means of purchase abroad.

76. The present General Statute shall, insofar as it pertains to mutual relations of a USSR ministry with union republic ministries of the same name, also relate to chief administrations of the same name, administrations, union republic combines, and other union republic agencies of the republic which are part of the system of the USSR ministry.

77. A USSR ministry shall have a seal depicting the State Arms of the USSR and its own name.

STATUTE ON THE STATE COMMITTEE OF THE USSR COUNCIL OF MINISTERS FOR THE PRESS

[Confirmed by Decree of the USSR Council of Ministers, September 22, 1964. _SP SSSR_ (1964), no. 18, pp. 413-421. On August 1, 1972, the name of the State Committee was changed to: State Committee of the USSR Council of Ministers for Publishing Houses, Printing, and the Book Trade. _Vedomosti SSSR_ (1972), no. 32, item 277.]

1. The State Committee of the USSR Council of Ministers for the Press shall be a union republic agency.

2. The basic tasks of the State Committee of the USSR Council of Ministers for the Press shall be:

(a) direction of the publishing industry, printing, and book trade in the country;

(b) control on an all-state scale over the content and orientation of the publication of literature in all its forms and control over the fulfillment of decisions of the Party and Government in the publishing industry, printing, book trade, and protection of military and state secrets in the press;

(c) implementation of a unified technological policy in the printing machine-building industry;

(d) keeping state statistics of printed publications;

(e) carrying out international links in the domain of the press.

3. The State Committee of the USSR Council of Ministers for the Press shall, in accordance with the tasks entrusted to it:

(a) organize and direct the publishing industry; ensure a high ideological and theoretical level of printed publications and high quality of artistic design and printing of publications and their timely issuance; eliminate parallelism and duplication of publications and not allow the issuance of books of slight content; ensure the improvement of the editorial and publishing process; direct republic, territory, and regional newspaper and journal publishing houses in the established procedure; submit in the established procedure proposals concerning the creation, transformation, or abolition of publishing houses, or editorial and publishing sections of ministries, state committees, departments, and other organizations and concerning the granting of the right to publish to institutions and organizations of union subordination (except for scientific and technical information agencies); hold competitions for the best printed publications, their artistic design and printing, paying prize money in the established procedure; organize exhibitions of Soviet literature in the USSR and abroad; promote the development of social principles in the publishing industry; publish the journals _V mire knig_, _Novye knigi_, _Poligrafiia_, and _Knizhnaia torgovlia_;

(b) work out and effectuate measures relating to the development of printing on the basis of the most modern achievements of science and technology, increase production capacities, effectuate specialization and cooperation of printing; work out with the participation of interested organizations and confirm technological reglaments for all new processes and production, and also for the mass production of printing products; work out and confirm in the established procedure standards for the expenditure of basic materials, raw materials, fuel, labor, and technical and economic work indicators and confirm price lists of wholesale prices for the products of printing enterprises; work out requirements for closely related branches of industry with regard to the assortment, quality, and quantity of printing equipment and materials; exercise control over the observance of technological processes by enterprises when manufacturing printing equipment and take the necessary operative measures to eliminate violations uncovered; submit proposals in the established procedure regarding paper production plans for the press;

(c) coordinate the work of book trade organizations irrespective of their departmental subordination; ensure the correct determination of the print order for books in the country; organize the dissemination of republic and local publications in the country; work out and effectuate measures for the development of new, progressive book trade forms and promote the development of social principles for the dissemination of books; consider the conditions and procedure, submitted for agreement, for holding book lotteries; hold book fairs within the country in the established procedure; organize propaganda and advertising for printed products, as well as information concerning them;

(d) prepare plans for the issuance of books in the country and coordinate plans for the issuance of literature by all publishing houses and editorial and publishing sections within the jurisdiction of ministries, state committees, departments, social, and other organizations; confirm plans, upon the recommendation of ministries, state committees, and departments, for the issuance of literature regarding questions of the respective branch of the national economy and culture, except for plans for publications of scientific and technical information; confirm annual and long-term plans for the issuance of literature by publishing houses directly subordinate to the Committee and for publishing houses under dual subordination, jointly with the respective organizations; work out draft plans, taking into account the suggestions of state committees of union republic councils of ministers for the press, and interested ministries, state committees, departments, and other organizations, for the development of the printing industry and book trade and submit them in the established procedure for inclusion in the draft national economic plan; consider draft plans submitted by union republics for the development of printing machine-building, the introduction of new technology, and scientific research and experimental work in this branch; prepare proposals jointly with councils of national economy for increasing production capacities, specialization, and cooperation of printing machine-building enterprises and consider draft plans for the issuance of printing machine-building products; work out and confirm plans in the established procedure for scientific research, construction design, technological, and design work in the publishing industry, printing, the book trade, and printing machine-building for organizations and enterprises directly subordinate to the Committee;

(e) work out draft plans for production, capital construction, material-technical supply, and draft labor plans, revenue and expenditures balances of the Committee, and submit in the established procedure the said draft plans for confirmation and carry out measures regarding the fulfillment of the confirmed plans;

(f) determine the requirement for cadres of specialists having a higher or secondary specialized education in the publishing industry, printing, and book trade; carry out measures for training and for raising the qualifications of cadres of the publishing industry, printing, and book trade; work out and submit for confirmation in the established procedure draft plans to train cadres for enterprises and organizations directly subordinate to the Committee; work out draft plans jointly with the union republic councils of ministers and the USSR Ministry of Higher and Secondary Specialized Education for the training of engineering and technical cadres for printing machine-building;

(g) ascertain the requirement of publishing houses for a printing base and distribute the production capacities of printing enterprises directly subordinate to the Committee; coordinate the work load of the printing base of ministries, state committees, departments, and other organizations, except for the printing base of scientific and technical information agencies; distribute paper for printing, printing equipment (including imported), and printing materials in the established procedure to state committees of union republic councils of ministers for the press, ministries, state committees, departments, and other organizations;

(h) submit proposals to the Government concerning the procedure for the publication of materials having important state significance and concerning a list of institutions and organizations having the right to receive control copies of printed publications free of charge, establish the procedure for the delivery of control copies of printed publications (free of charge or with a charge), and exercise control over the observance of this procedure by printing enterprises irrespective of their departmental subordination;

(i) work out and confirm in the established procedure technical conditions, model prices, and standards for all types of printed publications, royalty rates, and prices for artistic and graphic works for publication; confirm a price list for retail prices for published products; work out and submit for confirmation in the established procedure rates for royalties for all types of literary works;

(j) direct the implementation of scientific research, construction design, and design work in the publishing industry, printing, book trade, and printing machine-building; work out and effectuate in the established procedure measures for the creation and introduction into production of new production machines, equipment, automated systems, and technological processes for the printing industry, book trade, and publishing industry; prepare draft state standards; form a commission by agreement with interested organizations for the acceptance of new models of equipment and materials and confirm programs to test them; confirm by agreement with the USSR State Planning Committee the types of the most important printing machines which are subject to being worked out, improved, and introduced into series production; consider and confirm jointly with interested organizations the technical planning tasks for the design and projects of the most important new printing machine-building; work out and submit in the established procedure plans for scientific research and experimental work relating to the most important complex and inter-branch scientific and technical problems in the publishing industry, printing, and book trade; submit proposals in the established procedure concerning the fulfillment by organizations of other ministries and departments of scientific research, construction design, technological, and design work in the printing and printing machine-building industry;

(k) organize the working out of designs for the technical part of constructing a printing house, publishing house, and objects of the book trade, and also model designs for printing enterprises and book trade enterprises, submit proposals relating to the designing and construction of the said objects, work out and confirm product lists, designs, and estimates in the established procedure for the construction of these objects, and work out and effectuate measures for the reconstruction of existing and the construction of new enterprises directly subordinate to the Committee;

(l) distribute financial and material resources allocated for the fulfillment of plans for new technology, as well as finance scientific research, experimental construction design, and experimental work being fulfilled for the printing industry, publishing houses, and enterprises and organizations of the book trade irrespective of their departmental subordination within the limits of budget appropriations provided for these purposes and exercise control over the fulfillment of such work;

(m) effectuate the material-technical supply of enterprises, organizations, and institutions directly subordinate to the Committee, provide financing for such enterprises, organizations, and institutions, consider and confirm their bookkeeping reports and balances, exercise control over the observance of financial, budget, and estimate discipline, conduct documentary audits of their activity; direct work relating to the revision and observance of processing norms and the implementation of measures for the scientific organization of labor and its regulation, observance of labor legislation, technical safety rules and labor protection rules at the said enterprises, organizations, and institutions; draw up composite, periodic, and annual reports and balances for all types of production, financial, and economic activity of the Committee; verify the funds of the retail and wholesale book trade network directly subordinate and, when necessary, reduce the prices or write off obsolete publications;

(n) work out, taking into account progressive experience and the application of computer technology, the basic principles for the organization of labor and production at publishing houses, printing industry enterprises, printing machine-building, and the book trade; direct the development of inventions and rationalization proposals and the dissemination of progressive experience; carry out measures to raise labor productivity, for strict observance of principles of economic accountability, and reduction of production costs;

(o) carry on, jointly with trade union agencies, work relating to the conclusion of collective agreements and the development of socialist competitions in the printing industry and book trade, work out its conditions, and reckon up the results of the socialist competition;

(p) carry out technical and economic information on questions of progressive production and scientific and technical experience, domestic and foreign, in the publishing industry, printing industry, printing machine-building, and book trade;

(q) effectuate cooperation in the established procedure with foreign countries in the publishing industry, printing industry, printing machine-building, and book trade, as well as the exchange of publications and information in regard to questions relegated to the competence of the Committee; participate in book fairs in the established procedure and exhibitions abroad; distribute the allocated quotas for the fulfillment of printing work abroad; conclude on the basis of legal provisions on the monopoly of foreign trade legal transactions for the printing of Soviet orders abroad through the All-Union Combine Vneshtorgizdat;

(r) organize a primary record at enterprises, organizations, and institutions of the Committee, work out and confirm forms for the primary record on the basis of model forms of the USSR Central Statistical Administration, and exercise control over keeping them; carry out a unified state recording of publishing organizations, printing enterprises, and enterprises of the book trade network of the country, and also keep state statistics and a unified bibliographic registration of printed publications.

4. The State Committee of the USSR Council of Ministers for the Press shall be granted the right to:

(a) prohibit organizations and institutions from engaging in publishing activity to which such rights have not been granted in the established procedure; clarify the profile of the activity of publishing houses;

(b) authorize the opening of printing enterprises in the established procedure irrespective of their departmental subordination;

(c) receive information from ministries, state committees, departments, social, and other organizations needed by the Committee in order to fulfill the functions entrusted to it;

(d) enlist scientific research organizations, institutions of higher education, scientific workers, and specialists in the established procedure to work out individual questions, give advice, and conduct expert examinations;

(e) receive control copies of all printed publications issued on the territory of the country;

(f) confirm head scientific research and design institutes and construction design bureaus for the printing industry and printing machine-building.

5. The State Committee of the USSR Council of Ministers for the Press shall direct the publishing industry, printing, and book trade through the state committees of the union republic councils of ministers for the press and shall administer enterprises, institutions, and organizations directly subordinate to the Committee.

6. The State Committee of the USSR Council of Ministers for the Press shall be formed, comprised of: the Chairman of the Committee appointed by the USSR Supreme Soviet, deputy chairmen, and members of the Committee appointed by the USSR Council of Ministers.

The deputy chairman of the Committee dealing with questions of printing, capital construction, distribution of printing paper grades, and printing equipment shall be a member of the USSR State Planning Committee.

7. The chairman of the Committee shall head the State Committee of the USSR Council of Ministers for the Press.

The Chairman of the State Committee of the USSR Council of Ministers for the Press shall direct the activity of the Committee and enterprises, organizations, and institutions subordinate to it, issue orders and instructions within the limits of his competence and on the basis of and in execution of laws of the USSR, as well as decrees and regulations of the USSR Council of Ministers, and shall verify their execution; create, reorganize, and liquidate enterprises, organizations, and institutions in the established procedure, and also change their subordination when necessary; confirm model personnel establishments and the structure of enterprises, organizations, and institutions of the Committee in the established procedure; confirm statutes on the chief editorial boards, chief administrations, administration, and sections of the Committee, and also charters (or statutes) of directly subordinate enterprises, organizations, and institutions; appoint to office and relieve from office the leading workers of the central apparatus of the Committee and enterprises, organizations, and institutions directly subordinate to it.

8. The State Committee of the USSR Council of Ministers for the Press shall consider at its sessions the most important questions connected with the creation of printed publications having high ideals and high artistic merit, the further improvement of the direction of the publishing industry, printing, the book trade, the protection of military and state secrets in the press, carrying on a uniform technological policy in printing machine-building, verifying the execution, selection, placement, and education of cadres, and other questions relegated to the jurisdiction of the Committee. Decisions of the Committee shall be implemented by orders of the Chairman of the Committee.

9. Scientific publishing and scientific technical councils shall be attached to the State Committee of the USSR Council of Ministers for the Press with the rights of consultative agencies.

10. The structure and personnel establishment of the central apparatus of the State Committee of the USSR Council of Ministers for the Press shall be confirmed by the USSR Council of Ministers.

11. The State Committee of the USSR Council of Ministers for the Press shall have a seal depicting the State Arms of the USSR and its own name.

ON THE BASIC RIGHTS AND DUTIES OF CITY AND DISTRICT IN CITY SOVIETS OF WORKING PEOPLE'S DEPUTIES

[Edict of the Presidium of the USSR Supreme Soviet, adopted March 19, 1971. Vedomosti SSSR (1971), no. 12, item 133]

With a view to further raising the role of city and district in city soviets of working people's deputies in carrying out the tasks of state, economic, and socio-cultural construction, increasing their initiative and responsibility for deciding planning and financial questions, for the development of local industry, construction, housing, and municipal economy, improvement of domestic and socio-cultural services for the populace, strengthening of socialist legality, as well as with a view to the further development of the democratic principles of the activity of such soviets, the Presidium of the USSR Supreme Soviet decrees:

Article 1. A city or district in city soviet of working people's deputies shall, as an agency of state power in a city or city district, decide all questions of local significance within the limits of the rights granted by law, proceeding from the interests of the whole state and the interests of the working people of the city.

Article 2. A city soviet of working people's deputies shall direct state, economic, and socio-cultural construction on the territory of the city and the activity of agencies of administration subordinate to the soviet and enterprises, institutions, and organizations of city subordination.

Enterprises, institutions, and organizations servicing primarily the populace of the city shall be of city subordination. The procedure for transferring the said enterprises, institutions, and organizations to city subordination shall be established by USSR and union republic legislation.

Enterprises, institutions, and organizations of city subordination shall be directed by the executive committee of the city soviet of working people's deputies through its sections and administrations or directly. The sections and administrations of an executive committee of a city soviet, as well as the enterprises, institutions, and organizations which the executive committee directs shall be subordinate directly in their activity to both the city soviet and to its executive committee and also to the respective superior branch agency of state administration.

Article 3. A city soviet of working people's deputies shall coordinate and control the activity of all enterprises, institutions, and organizations situate on the territory of the city for housing, municipal construction, construction of socio-cultural and domestic objects, production of consumer goods, and local construction materials, for working out and implementing measures in the domain of public amenities, trade, and public dining, public education, public health, culture, and other domains connected with servicing the populace of the city; shall exercise control within the limits of rights granted to the soviet over the work of enterprises, institutions, and organizations of superior subordination situate on the territory of the city and over the observance of legislation by them.

A city soviet shall hear reports of the directors of enterprises, institutions, and organizations in regard to the questions specified in the present Article, shall take decisions in regard to them, and when necessary shall make proposals to the appropriate superior agencies.

Article 4. With a view to the more active participation of enterprises and organizations in the development of the city economy and to increasing the interest of city soviets of working people's deputies in the results of the work of enterprises and organizations, a part of the profits of enterprises and economic organizations of republic and regional (or territory) subordination which are situate on the territory of the respective cities shall be transferred to the city budgets.

The types and amounts of deductions specified in the present Article and the procedure for their entering city budgets shall be established by USSR and union republic legislation.

Article 5. The administration of the state housing fund and objects of municipal economy servicing the populace of cities, simultaneously strengthening the material and repair-construction base of executive committees of city soviets, shall be concentrated in the jurisdiction of city soviets of working people's deputies.

The conditions and periods for transferring the housing fund belonging to enterprises, institutions, and organizations to the cities, as well as objects of municipal economy servicing the populace of these cities, shall be established by the USSR Council of Ministers and union republic councils of ministers.

Article 6. The rights and duties of a city soviet of working people's deputies shall be determined by USSR, and by union and autonomous republic, legislation, depending on whether a city is relegated to the category of cities of republic (union or autonomous republic), territory, regional, or city subordination. A city shall be relegated to a category of subordination in the procedure established by union republic legislation, taking into account the population of the city and its political, economic, and cultural significance.

Article 7. A city soviet of working people's deputies of a city of republic, territory, or regional subordination shall:

(1) confirm composite long-term and annual plans for the development of the city economy and socio-cultural construction of the city, organize and control their fulfillment; confirm long-term and annual planning tasks of enterprises, institutions, and organizations of city subordination, and also plans for the siting, development, and specialization of the said enterprises, institutions, and organizations;

(2) consider plans for the siting, development, and specialization of enterprises of local industry, domestic services, trade, and public dining, organizations and institutions of culture, public education, and public health of superior subordination and, when necessary, submit proposals to the respective superior agencies;

(3) consider draft plans of enterprises, institutions, and organizations of superior subordination situate on the territory of the city in that part affecting the development of housing and the municipal economy, road construction, socio-cultural and domestic objects, production of consumer goods and local construction materials, public amenities, trade, public dining, public education, public health, culture, and other questions connected with servicing the populace and, when necessary, shall

submit its proposals to the appropriate superior agencies, and shall confirm on these questions composite planning indicators, including them in the plan for the development of the city economy and socio-cultural construction of the city;

(4) ensure the compilation of balances for the use of labor resources, local construction materials, and fuel, the revenue and expenditures balance for the populace, and other balances necessary to plan the integrated development of the city economy; exercise control over the rational use of mineral raw materials, forestry, water, and power resources;

(5) confirm the city budget and organize its execution; redistribute when necessary in the process of executing the budget the assets of the city budget from section to section, and also redistribute appropriations for wages within the limits of the confirmed wage fund; confirm the report concerning execution of the city budget;

(6) direct the revenues received additionally when executing the city budget, as well as amounts of revenue exceeding expenses at the end of the year as a result of the overfulfillment of revenues or economy in expenditures to the financing of the city economy and socio-cultural measures, including capital investments, for the construction of administrative buildings and the acquisition of means of transport for the executive committees of city, district in city, rural, and settlement soviets, to carry out the capital repair of buildings of executive committees, their sections and administrations, and judicial agencies, and to acquire inventory and equipment for them (removing the said assets from the city budget, except for appropriations not used in connection with the failure to fulfill the plan for centralized capital investments and the plan for the development of the network of socio-cultural institutions, shall not be permitted);

(7) direct the work relating to the computation and recovery of state and local taxes and fees; establish in the procedure provided by legislation additional exemptions for individual payers in accordance with Article 3 of the Edict of the Presidium of the USSR Supreme Soviet on the State Duty and Article 4 of the Edict of the Presidium of the USSR Supreme Soviet on the Income Tax from the populace;

(8) consider the quarterly cash plans for branches of the USSR State Bank and take measures to fulfill them; take decisions concerning the granting by institutions of the USSR State Bank and the USSR Construction Bank of cash loans for individual housing construction and repairs of houses which belong to citizens by right of personal ownership within the allocated limits; grant exemptions for compulsory state insurance to individual citizens in accordance with legislation;

(9) direct industrial enterprises of city subordination, confirm the results of their financial and economic activity and the distribution in the established procedure of profits received; distribute the products of industrial enterprises of city subordination made from local raw materials, wastes, and raw materials of the enterprises' own procurements;

(10) take measures for the development of the production of consumer goods and local construction materials on the base of local raw materials, using production wastes not distributed in a centralized procedure of enterprises situate on the territory of the city, and also for reprocessing agricultural products; decide questions concerning the use of additionally uncovered local raw material resources, fuel, industrial wastes, and agricultural production;

(11) render assistance to industrial enterprises of superior subordination situate on the territory of the city in raising the efficiency of production, using material, labor, and financial resources, raising labor productivity, and improving the socio-cultural and domestic servicing of workers and employees; give the proper compulsory consideration to opinions on questions connected with expanding the existing and constructing new industrial enterprises, buildings, and installations and submit when necessary proposals concerning the organization, reorganization, or liquidation of industrial enterprises of superior subordination on the territory of the city;

(12) organize the working out of a draft general city plan and a design for planning the suburban zone, consider these drafts and in the established procedure submit them to the appropriate superior agencies of state administration for confirmation; confirm drafts of detailed planning and designs for the building of districts, microdistricts, and other town-planning complexes and designs for engineering installations and city public amenities; exercise control over construction being carried on in the city territory; prohibit or suspend the construction of objects of civic housing being carried on with violations of the requirements of legislation;

(13) direct construction organizations of city subordination; organize housing, municipal, highway, cultural, and domestic construction and the construction of objects of public enlightenment, public health, trade, public dining, and other objects at the expense of assets allocated to local soviets; decide questions, with the consent of enterprises, institutions, and organizations situate on the territory of the city, concerning the joint use of their assets allocated for housing, municipal, highway, cultural, and domestic construction and the construction of objects of public enlightenment, public health, trade, and public dining, as well as, when necessary, concerning the combining of assets; act as the customer or determine the customer for these types of construction; appoint state acceptance commissions in the established procedure, consider and confirm acts relating to the acceptance for use of civil housing objects whose construction is completed, and also take part in accepting for use other objects situate on the territory of the city whose construction is completed;

(14) manage all lands within the limits of the city boundary; grant and withdraw land plots and settle land disputes in the instances and in the procedure established by USSR and union republic legislation; exercise state control over the use of land; issue a permit for the working of minerals in general use; control the observance of nature conservation legislation;

(15) manage water objects on the territory of the city within the limits and in the procedure established by legislation and exercise state control over the use and conservation of waters;

(16) direct the housing and municipal economy, and also the public amenities of the city; exercise control over the state of and the proper use of the housing fund, municipal enterprises and installations belonging to enterprises, institutions, and organizations; enlist enterprises, institutions, and organizations of superior subordination in the established procedure to take part in the work relating to public amenities of the city and the construction of roads; exercise control over public amenities on the territory of all enterprises and organizations situate on the territory of the city;

(17) distribute the housing fund which belongs to the soviet; control the correctness of the distribution of dwelling premises, and also confirm joint decisions of the administration and of factory, plant, and local trade union councils concerning the granting of dwelling premises in house of state, cooperative, and other social organizations, except for instances provided for by legislation; take decisions concerning the organization of housing construction and other cooperatives and exercise control over their activity; issue uniform warrants to citizens to occupy dwelling premises;

(18) direct city transport; exercise control over the activity of transport enterprises and organizations of superior subordination and communications enterprises and organizations servicing the populace of the city;

(19) direct state and cooperative trade, as well as public dining on the territory of the city, by trade and public dining enterprises and organizations of city subordination; exercise control over the work of trade and public dining enterprises and organizations of superior subordination; confirm planning tasks for goods turnover by trade and public dining enterprises and organizations of city subordination; direct collective farm markets on the territory of the city; establish, in the procedure and within the limits determined by legislation, the amounts of retail charges and rates of pay for services rendered at collective farm markets;

(20) direct the domestic servicing of the populace by enterprises and organizations for domestic services of city subordination, confirm the results of their financial and economic activity and the distribution of profits received in the established procedure; exercise control over the work of enterprises and organizations for domestic services of superior subordination;

(21) direct public education and pre-school and extracurricular nurturing of children; provide universal compulsory education; exercise control over work of children's homes and children's pre-school and extracurricular institutions which are not on the city budget; decide questions, in the instances and in the procedure established by legislation, concerning the granting of allowances to citizens for the maintenance of children in boarding schools, boarding schools attached to schools, and also for the payment of food for children in schools (or groups) having an extended day; distribute the universal education fund in the established procedure; decide questions of adoption, and also of guardianship and curatorship over minors;

(22) direct cultural and enlightenment work and cultural and enlightenment organizations and institutions of city subordination and control the activity of other organizations and institutions of culture irrespective of their subordination; exercise control over the use of assets of cultural funds of enterprises, institutions, and organizations, and, when necessary, take measures agreed with them for the centralized use of the said assets; direct cinema services for the populace;

(23) direct public health in the city and public health institutions of city subordination; exercise control over the work of public health institutions of superior subordination; organize the protection of motherhood and childhood; carry out measures ensuring the observance of sanitary rules for the maintenance of dwelling and public buildings and the proper sanitary state of the city; ensure the implementation of measures to prevent the spreading of infectious diseases and also to liquidate these;

(24) exercise state control over the observance of rules for the protection of air, waters, soil, and the natural environment;

(25) direct physical culture and sport; confirm plans for siting sport buildings and installations on the territory of the city irrespective of subordination; take measures for the development of suburban mass leisure zones and for equipping them and providing public amenities, and exercise control over the use of these zones;

(26) keep a record and regulate the distribution of labor resources on the territory of the city and take measures for their rational use; confirm labor plans for youth who have completed general education schools and ensure they are fulfilled by all enterprises, institutions, and organizations; exercise control over the observance of labor legislation and rules for the protection and safety of labor at enterprises, institutions, and organizations; determine the time for beginning work by agreement with enterprises, institutions, and organizations situate on the territory of the city; establish work days and hours of enterprises and organizations connected with servicing the populace;

(27) direct social security; ensure the timely and correct assignment and payment of pensions and allowances established by legislation; decide questions of guardianship and curatorship over persons who have attained majority and who by reason of their state of health can not independently exercise their rights and fulfill their duties; exercise control over the work of agencies for medical and labor expertise;

(28) form a city committee of people's control and direct its activity; ensure the observance of the laws of the USSR and the union and autonomous republics and other acts of superior agencies of state power and agencies of state administration, the protection of the state and public order, socialist ownership, and the rights and interests of citizens, state institutions, enterprises, cooperative, and other social organizations which are protected by law; organize the explanation of legislation to the populace;

(29) repeal, when necessary, orders and regulations of directors of agencies of administration subordinate to the soviet, as well as of enterprises, institutions, and organizations of city subordination; suspend the execution of orders and regulations of directors of enterprises, institutions, and organizations of superior subordination which are contrary to legislation in regard to questions of housing, municipal, cultural, and domestic construction, public amenities, land use, building, nature conservation and monuments of culture, socio-cultural, and domestic servicing of the populace, and shall notify the respective superior agencies thereof;

(30) ensure the timely and correct consideration and settlement of proposals, applications, and complaints of citizens; verify the state of cases relating to the consideration of proposals, applications, and complaints of citizens at enterprises, institutions, and organizations situate on the territory of the city, and hear reports of their directors on these questions;

(31) adopt decisions in the instances and in the procedure determined by legislation which provide administrative responsibility for their violation within the established limits;

(32) ensure the observance of passport system rules;

(33) enlist enterprises, institutions, and organizations, as well as the populace, when necessary, in the struggle against natural disasters and the liquidation of their consequences;

(34) ensure the execution of the Law of the USSR on Universal Military Obligation by all officials and citizens, as well as by enterprises, institutions, and organizations; direct civil defense on the territory of the city;

(35) consider and initiate petitions concerning the awarding of orders and medals of the USSR, conferment of the honorary title "Mother-Heroine", as well as awarding badges of a union or autonomous republic.

Article 8. A city soviet of working people's deputies of district subordination shall confirm composite long-term and annual plans for the development of the city economy and socio-cultural construction of the city, organize and control their fulfillment, confirm the city budget and report on its execution, and also may exercise other rights and duties provided by Article 7 of the present Edict within the limits established by USSR and by union and autonomous republic legislation.

The activity of city soviets of working people's deputies of cities of district subordination shall be directed within the limits of the rights granted by law to the district soviet of working people's deputies.

Article 9. A district in city soviet of working people's deputies shall direct the state, economic, and socio-cultural construction on the territory of the district and the activity of agencies of administration subordinate to the soviet.

A district in city soviet shall confirm composite long-term and annual plans for the development of the district economy and for socio-cultural construction of the district, and shall organize and control their fulfillment, confirm the district budget and the report on its execution, direct the activity of enterprises and organizations for domestic services, trade, and public dining of district subordination, housing, municipal economy, and public amenities of the district, cultural-enlightenment work, public education, public health, social security, and protection of the state and public order.

A district in city soviet of working people's deputies shall coordinate and control the activity of all enterprises, institutions, and organizations situate on the territory of the district in regard to housing and municipal construction, the construction of socio-cultural and domestic objects, the production of consumer goods and local construction materials, in regard to working out and implementing measures in the domain of public amenities, trade, public dining, public education, public health, culture, and other domains connected with servicing the populace of the district; exercise, within the limits of rights granted to the soviet, control over the work of enterprises, institutions, and organizations of superior subordination situate on the territory of the district and over the observance of legislation by them.

A district in city soviet shall hear reports of directors of enterprises, institutions, and organizations in regard to the questions specified in paragraph three of the present Article, shall take decisions in regard to them, and shall submit proposals when necessary to the appropriate superior agencies.

A district in city soviet of working people's deputies may exercise other rights and duties provided for by Article 7 of the present Edict, except for those rights and duties which are exercised in accordance with legislation by a city soviet of working people's deputies for deciding questions of all-city significance and for ensuring unity in the development of the city economy.

Article 10. Within the limits of rights granted by law, a city soviet of working people's deputies shall direct the activity of district in city soviets of working people's deputies.

The direction of enterprises, institutions, and organizations of district subordination shall be exercised by the executive committee of a district in city soviet of working people's deputies through its sections and administrations or directly. Sections and administrations of an executive committee of a district in city soviet, as well as enterprises, institutions, and organizations which the executive committee directs directly, shall be subordinate in their activity to both the district in city soviet of working people's deputies and its executive committees and to the respective superior branch agency of state administration.

Article 11. Any question may be considered and decided at a session of a city or district in city soviet of working people's deputies which is relegated to the jurisdiction of the soviet, whereas only the following questions may be considered and decided at sessions:

recognition of the powers of deputies; relieving deputies of powers upon personal applications; election of the executive committee and changing its composition; the formation and election of permanent commissions and changing their composition; reports concerning the work of the executive committee and its permanent commissions;

formation of sections and administrations of the executive committee, confirmation and release of their directors from office; formation of city and district committee of people's control; formation of administrative and supervisory commissions, and commissions for cases of minors attached to the executive committee; election of the city court; confirmation of the chairman of the city (or district) people's court;

confirmation of composite long-term and annual plans for the development of the city or district economy and for socio-cultural construction;

confirmation of plans for measures relating to the fulfillment of mandates of the electorate;

adoption of decisions relating to inquiries of deputies;

confirmation of the city or district budget and the report on its execution; confirmation of decisions of the executive committee concerning the revenues additionally received when executing the city or district in city budget, as well as amounts of revenues exceeding expenditures formed at the end of the year as a result of the overfulfillment of revenues or economies in expenditures;

consideration of the draft general city plan and design for planning the suburban zone and submitting them for confirmation to the appropriate superior agencies of state administration.

Other questions considered and decided only at sessions of city and district in city soviets of working people's deputies also may be provided by union and autonomous republic legislation.

Article 12. The executive committee of a city or district in city soviet of working people's deputies shall consider and decide questions relegated to the jurisdiction of the soviet, except for those questions which should be considered and decided only at sessions of the soviet.

The executive committee of a city or district in city soviet of working people's deputies shall:

convoke sessions of the soviet and ensure their preparation; coordinate in the interval between sessions the work of permanent commissions of the soviet; render necessary assistance to deputies in their fulfillment of the duties of a deputy;

submit composite long-term and annual plans for the development of the city or district economy and socio-cultural construction, city or district budget, and the report on the execution of the budget for the confirmation of the soviet;

submit plans for measures relating to the fulfillment of mandates of the electorate for the confirmation of the soviet and organize their execution, and inform deputies and the populace about the fulfillment of mandates;

direct sections and administrations of the executive committee, enterprises, institutions, and organizations of city or district subordination;

appoint in the interval between sessions of the soviet, to be subsequently confirmed at the regular session, persons to execute duties and to dismiss directors of sections and administrations of the executive committees from the execution of duties;

appoint and relieve from office other leading workers of sections and administrations of the executive committee, directors of enterprises, institutions, and organizations of city or district subordination (according to a list of posts confirmed by the executive committee of the soviet by agreement with the superior agency of state administration).

An executive committee of a city or district in city soviet may accept for consideration questions relegated to the jurisdiction of its sections and administrations.

Article 13. The appointment and release from office of directors of enterprises and organizations for trade, public dining, and domestic services, housing and municipal economy agencies, and organizations and institutions for public health, social security, and culture which are in superior subordination, are situate on the territory of the city or district, and have important significance for servicing the populace of the particular city or district shall be only by agreement with the executive committee of the respective city or district in city soviet of working people's deputies.

Article 14. Sections and administrations of the executive committee of a city or district in city soviet of working people's deputies shall be formed in accordance with union or autonomous republic legislation and shall be on the budget or on economic accountability.

The competence of sections and administrations of executive committees of city or district in city soviets shall be defined by statutes confirmed by the union or autonomous republic councils of ministers.

Article 15. Decisions and regulations of a city or district in city soviet of working people's deputies and its executive committee adopted by them within the limits of the rights granted shall be binding for execution by all enterprises, institutions, and organizations situate on the territory of the city or district, and also by officials and citizens.

A city or district in city soviet and its executive committee shall, if the directors of enterprises, institutions, and organizations of superior subordination fail to fulfill their decisions, go to the respective superior agencies with representations concerning the imposition of disciplinary sanctions on these directors up to and including dismissal from the posts occupied. The results of the consideration of the representations should be notified to the city or district in city soviet or its executive committee within a month.

Article 16. A deputy of a city or district in city soviet of working people's deputies shall, during the session of the executive committee to which he has been elected, be released from the fulfillment of his production or official duties while retaining the average earnings (or wages) at his place of permanent work.

A deputy of a city or district in city soviet of working people's deputies shall, while exercising his duties, enjoy the right of transport free of charge on city transport (subway, bus, street car, trolley bus).

A deputy of a city or district in city soviet of working people's deputies may not be dismissed at the initiative of the administration from work at the enterprise, institutions or organization or excluded from a collective farm, and also may not be brought to criminal responsibility or arrested on the territory of the soviet without the consent of the city or district in city soviet, and in the interval between sessions, without the consent of its executive committee.

Article 17. The activity of a city or district in city soviet of working people's deputies shall be built on the basis of collective leadership, publicity, and regular accountability of deputies to the electorate and of the executive committee and its sections and administrations to the soviet and the populace, and on the extensive involvement of the working people in participating in the work of the soviet.

A city or district in city soviet shall work in close contact with city or district in city agencies of social organizations.

Article 18. A city or district in city soviet of working people's deputies shall organize the extensive participation of citizens in deciding questions of local and all-city significance.

A city or district in city soviet shall provide information to the populace abouts its activity, the work of the permanent commissions, the executive committee and its sections and administrations by means of regular speeches to working people's deputies of the soviet, workers of the executive committee and its sections and administrations, and also through the press, radio, and television.

A city or district in city soviet shall submit the most important questions of state, economic, and socio-cultural construction in the city or district for discussion at meetings of working people at enterprises, institutions, and organizations, and also at the place of residence of citizens.

A city or district in city soviet of working people's deputies shall direct the activity of city voluntary societies and the work of agencies for social amateur activity of the populace.

Article 19. A city or district in city soviet of working people's deputies shall, in addition to the rights and duties provided for by the present Edict, also exercise other rights and duties in accordance with USSR and union and autonomous republic legislation.

Article 20. A city or district in city soviet of working people's deputies shall, within the limits of the rights granted by law, direct the activity of rural and settlement soviets of working people's deputies whose territory is within the territory united by the city or district in city soviet of working people's deputies.

Article 21. The presidiums of the union republic supreme soviets shall be charged to bring union republic legislation on city and district in city soviets of working people's deputies into conformity with the present Edict.

Article 22. It shall be established that until prevailing USSR and union or autonomous republic legislation is brought into conformity with the present Edict, the acts regulating the activity of city and district in city soviets of working people's deputies shall be applied insofar as they are not contrary to the present Edict.

ON THE STATUS OF DEPUTIES OF SOVIETS OF WORKING PEOPLE'S DEPUTIES IN THE USSR

[Law of the USSR Supreme Soviet, September 20, 1972. Vedomosti SSSR (1972), no. 39, item 347]

The USSR Constitution consolidates the sovereignty of the working people of our country in the person of soviets of working people's deputies, which comprise the political basis of the USSR. Deputies have been empowered by the people to participate in the exercise of state power by the soviets, to reflect its will and interests.

To be a deputy is a high honor and great responsibility. The people entrust important state and social duties to deputies. The duty of deputies is to give all their powers and knowledge to the cause of the construction of communism, to further in every possible way the further strengthening of the alliance of the working class and the collective farm peasantry and friendship and fraternity of the peoples of the USSR, consolidation of the socio-political unity of Soviet society, the steady increase of the well-being and culture of the working people, and intensify the might of the socialist Motherland. Deputies have been called upon to transform into life the electoral platform of the indestructible bloc of communists and non-party members embodying the policy of the Communist Party and the interests of the people.

A deputy should justify the trust of the electorate in all his activity, and always be on the level of the requirements submitted to him by the people.

I. General Provisions

Article 1. Deputies -- Plenipotentiaries of the People in Soviets

Deputies shall be the plenipotentiaries of the people in agencies of state authority: the soviets of working people's deputies.

In accordance with the USSR Constitution, a deputy of the USSR Supreme Soviet, union republic supreme soviet, autonomous republic supreme soviet, territory and regional soviet of working people's deputies, autonomous region soviets of working people's deputies, national area, district, city, district in city, settlement, and rural soviet of working people's deputies shall receive his powers as a result of his being elected to a soviet on the basis of universal, equal, and direct suffrage by secret ballot.

Article 2. Participation of Deputies in the Exercise by Soviets of State Power

The exercise of state power by soviets shall be based on the active participation of each deputy in all the work of the soviet: deputies shall decide questions of state, economic, and socio-cultural construction, shall organize the implementation of soviet decisions, and shall take part in control over the work of state agencies, enterprises, institutions, and organizations and in carrying out other powers of the soviets.

A deputy shall be guided in his activity by the interests of the entire state, shall take into account questions of the populace of his electoral district, as well as the economic, cultural, national, and other peculiarities of the union or autonomous republic, autonomous region, and national area from which the deputy was elected or on the territory of which his electoral district is located.

A deputy shall build his work on the basis of legislation of the USSR or the union or autonomous republic, as well as decisions of the respective soviets of working people's deputies.

Article 3. Legislation on the Powers of Deputies

The powers of deputies of soviets of working people's deputies in the USSR shall be defined by the present Law, and also by:

legislation of the USSR: for deputies of the Soviet of the Union and the Soviet of Nationalities of the USSR Supreme Soviet;

legislation of the USSR and union republics: for deputies of the union republic supreme soviets;

legislation of the USSR and the union and autonomous republics: for deputies of autonomous republic supreme soviets;

legislation of the USSR and union republics, and in autonomous republics, also autonomous republic legislation: for deputies of territory and regional soviets of working people's deputies, autonomous region soviets of working people's deputies, national area, district, city, district in city, settlement, and rural soviets of working people's deputies.

Article 4. Term of Powers of a Deputy

The powers of a deputy shall commence from the day of his election to a soviet of working people's deputies. A credentials commission elected by the soviet shall verify the powers of deputies. Upon the recommendation of the credentials commission the soviet shall decide either to recognize the powers or to annul the elections of individual deputies.

The powers of a deputy shall end on the day of elections for a new convocation of the soviet.

Article 5. Combining Activity of a Deputy with the Fulfillment of Production and Official Duties

A deputy shall exercise his powers while continuing production and official activity. Powers of a deputy shall be exercised without compensation.

A deputy shall take part actively in production and socio-political life, serve as an example for the execution of Soviet laws, observance of labor discipline, and the rules of socialist community life.

Article 6. Link of a Deputy with the Electorate and his Accountability and Responsibility to Them

A deputy shall maintain a link with the electorate, with collectives of working people and social organizations which nominated him as a candidate for deputy, as well as with enterprises, institutions, organizations, and state agencies located on the territory of his electoral district.

A deputy shall be responsible to the electorate and accountable to them.

A deputy who has not justified the trust of the electorate or who has committed actions not worthy of the high rank of a deputy may be recalled at any time by decision of the majority of the electorate in the procedure established by law.

Article 7. Fulfillment of Mandates of the Electorate

A deputy shall take part in organizing the populace for the fulfillment of mandates of the electorate and in the control over their realization by enterprises, institutions, and organizations and shall strive to implement the mandates.

The respective soviet shall consider mandates approved by meetings of the electorate, confirm the plan for measures relating to fulfillment of the mandates, take them into account when working out plans for economic and socio-cultural construction and when drawing up the budget, organize the fulfillment of mandates of the electorate, and exercise control over their realization.

Article 8. Mutual Relations of a Deputy with the Soviet and its Agencies

A deputy, as a member of a collegial representative agency of state power, shall be obliged to take an active part in the activity of the soviet, the standing commissions and other agencies of the soviet, to the membership of which he is elected, and to fulfill the commissions of the soviet and its agencies.

A soviet may hear communications of deputies concerning the fulfillment of their duties as deputies and of decisions and commissions of the soviet and its agencies.

Presidiums of supreme soviets and executive committees of soviets shall render the necessary assistance to deputies of the respective soviets in their work, inform deputies concerning the activity of the soviet and its agencies, the course of fulfilling plans for economic and socio-cultural construction, the realization of mandates of the electorate, and measures adopted in regard to critical remarks and proposals of deputies, and shall facilitate the study of Soviet legislation and the work experience of soviets by deputies.

Article 9. Guarantee by the State of Conditions for a Deputy to Exercise his Powers

The Soviet state shall guarantee to each deputy the necessary conditions for the unhindered and efficient carrying out of his rights and duties.

Persons who obstruct a deputy in carrying out his duties or infringing the honor and dignity of a deputy as a representative of state power shall bear responsibility in accordance with the law.

Article 10. Termination of the Powers of a Deputy before Time

The powers of a deputy shall be terminated before time in the event the deputy is recalled by the electorate.

The powers of a deputy may be terminated before time by decision of the soviet adopted in connection with the personal statement of a deputy concerning his resignation of the powers of a deputy in view of circumstances preventing their fulfillment or in connection with a judicial judgment of guilt which has entered into legal force with respect to a person who is a deputy.

II. Activity of a Deputy in a Soviet

Article 11. Participation of a Deputy in Sessions of a Soviet

At sessions of a soviet, deputies shall discuss and decide collectively all basic questions relegated to the competence of the soviet.

A deputy shall be obliged to be present at each session of the soviet and actively take part in its work.

The Presidium of the USSR Supreme Soviet, the presidium of a union republic supreme soviet, the presidium of an autonomous republic supreme soviet, and the executive committee of a soviet shall notify a deputy in good time about the time of a convocation and the place of holding a session of the soviet and about questions submitted for consideration of a soviet and shall give him the necessary materials on these questions.

In the event it is impossible to be present at a session, a deputy shall notify respectively the Presidium of the supreme soviet or the executive committee of the soviet thereof.

Article 12. Rights of a Deputy at a Session of a Soviet

A deputy shall enjoy a casting vote in regard to all questions considered by a soviet at a session and shall have the right to elect and to be elected to agencies of the soviet.

A deputy shall have the right to suggest questions for consideration by the soviet, submit proposals for the session agenda and for the procedure for considering and the substance of questions being discussed, the personnel establishment of agencies created by the soviet and nominations of officials elected, appointed, or confirmed by the soviet, make inquiries, participate in debates, put forward questions, submit draft decisions and amendments thereto, speak in support of his proposals and reasons for voting, and give information.

A deputy shall have the right to submit proposals concerning a report heard at a session of the soviet or information of any agency or official accountable to or under the control of the soviet.

A deputy may transmit his proposals and comments in writing to the presiding officer in regard to a question being discussed at a session.

Article 13. Right of Legislative Initiative of a Deputy of Supreme Soviets

A deputy of the USSR Supreme Soviet, a deputy of a union republic supreme soviet, and a deputy of an autonomous republic supreme soviet shall possess the right of legislative initiative to the supreme soviet to which he has been elected.

Article 14. Inquiry of a Deputy

The discussion by soviets of inquiries of deputies is an efficacious means of control over the work of agencies of state administration and officials.

A deputy of the USSR Supreme Soviet, a deputy of a union republic supreme soviet, and a deputy of an autonomous republic supreme soviet shall have the right to resort with an inquiry respectively to the Government of the USSR, to union republic governments, to autonomous republic governments, or to ministers and directors of other agencies of state administration formed by the USSR Supreme Soviet or of a union or autonomous republic.

A deputy of a union republic supreme soviet and a deputy of an autonomous republic supreme soviet also shall have the right to resort with an inquiry to the directors of enterprises, institutions, and organizations of all-union subordination located on the territory of the respective republic in regard to questions relegated to the jurisdiction of the republic.

A deputy of a territory or regional soviet, an autonomous region soviet, or a national, district, city, district in city, settlement, or rural soviet shall have the right to resort with an inquiry to the executive committee, the directors of its sections and administrations, as well as to directors of enterprises, institutions, and organizations located on the territory of the soviet in regard to questions relegated to the competence of the said soviet.

An inquiry may be submitted by a deputy or by a group of deputies in writing or orally. An inquiry submitted in writing shall be subject to being made public at the session of the soviet. A state agency or official to which the inquiry is addressed shall be obliged to answer the inquiry within the period and in the procedure established by laws of the USSR or the union or autonomous republic.

Article 15. Procedure for Considering Proposals and Remarks of Deputies Submitted to a Session of a Soviet

Proposals and remarks expressed by deputies at a session of a soviet or transmitted in writing to the presiding officer at the session shall be considered by the soviet or sent by it for consideration of the appropriate state or social agencies and officials.

State and social agencies, as well as officials to whom the proposals and remarks of deputies submitted to a session of a soviet have been sent shall be obliged to consider these proposals and remarks within the established periods and to communicate the results directly to the deputy as well as respectively to the Presidium of the supreme soviet, the council of ministers, or the executive committee of the soviet.

Control over the consideration and realization of proposals and remarks of deputies shall be exercised respectively by the Presidium of the supreme soviet, the council of ministers, or the executive committee of the soviet.

Article 16. Participation of a Deputy in the Work of Agencies of a Soviet

A deputy elected to the Presidium of a supreme soviet, an executive committee, standing commissions, and other agencies of a soviet shall have the right to submit questions for consideration of the said agencies and participate in the preparation of questions for consideration, in the discussion of them and adoption of decisions regarding them, as well as in the organization of the implementation of decisions of a soviet and its agencies and in control over their fulfillment.

Article 17. Verifications by a Deputy of the Work of State Agencies, Enterprises, Institutions, and Organizations

Upon the commission of a soviet or its agencies, a deputy may verify the work of state agencies, enterprises, institutions, and organizations in regard to questions relegated to the jurisdiction of the soviet and familiarize himself with the necessary documents. The deputy shall inform the respective state agencies, enterprises, institutions, and organizations about the results of the verification and, when necessary, submit proposals concerning the improvement of their work, the elimination of shortcomings uncovered, and the bringing to responsibility of persons guilty of violating state discipline and legality.

A deputy shall have the right to raise at the soviet or its agencies the question of the need to verify the work of state agencies, enterprises, institutions, and organizations.

III. Activity of a Deputy in the Electoral District

Article 18. Work of a Deputy Among the Populace in the Electoral District

The active work of deputies in electoral districts is a necessary condition for the efficient activity of the soviet and of strengthening its links with the populace.

In maintaining a constant link with his electorate, a deputy shall inform them about the work of the soviet, the fulfillment of plans for economic and socio-cultural construction, decisions of the soviet, and mandates of the electorate, take part in organizing the execution of laws and decisions of the soviet and its agencies, study public opinion, inform the soviet and its agencies about the needs and requirements of the populace, take measures to satisfy them, submit proposals for the consideration of the appropriate agencies and officials regarding questions arising in connection with his activity as a deputy.

In his work in the electoral district a deputy shall rely upon the assistance and support of the _aktiv_ of the soviet, social organizations, social amateur agencies of the populace, collectives of enterprises, institutions, and organizations.

Article 19. Consideration by a Deputy of Proposals, Statements, and Complaints of the Electorate

A deputy shall consider proposals, statements, and complaints sent to him, take measures for their correct and timely resolution, receive citizens, study the reasons which give rise to complaints, and submit his proposals to the soviet, other state agencies, enterprises, institutions, as well as organizations.

A deputy shall have the right to exercise control over the consideration of proposals, statements, and complaints sent by him to state agencies, enterprises, institutions, and organizations located on the territory of the soviet and take part personally in the consideration of the said proposals, statements, and complaints.

Article 20. Reports of a Deputy to the Electorate

A deputy of the USSR Supreme Soviet, a union republic supreme soviet, and an autonomous republic supreme soviet periodically, but at least once a year, and a deputy of a territory or regional soviet, autonomous region soviet, national area, district, city, district in city, settlement, and rural soviet, at least twice a year, shall be obliged to report to the electorate on his work and the work of the soviet.

A report of a deputy may be made at any time upon the request of collectives of working people and social organizations which nominated him as a candidate for deputy or upon the request of meetings of the electorate at their place of residence.

A deputy shall inform the soviet about the report made and proposals received from the electorate.

Article 21. Assistance to a Deputy in Making Reports and Holding Meetings with the Electorate

The necessary conditions shall be provided to a deputy in his electoral district for making reports and holding meetings with the electorate. To this end the executive committee of the respective soviet, as well as the administration and social organizations of enterprises, institutions, and organizations shall allocate premises, notify the electorate of the time and place where the reports of the deputy will be made, of his meetings with the electorate, of the reception of the electorate by the deputy, and also take other measures relating to rendering the deputy assistance in his work in an electoral district.

At the request of the deputy, informational materials needed for reports and speeches to the electorate shall be given him respectively by the Presidium of the supreme soviet or the executive committee of that soviet of which he is a deputy, as well as by the executive committees of soviets located on the territory of the electoral district.

Article 22. Participation of a Deputy in the Work of Sessions of Lower Soviets and Meetings of Working People

A deputy shall, on the territory of the soviet of which he has been elected a member, have the right to participate with a consultative vote in the work of sessions of lower soviets.

In his electoral district a deputy may participate in meetings of the economic *aktiv*, collectives of working people, and citizens at their place of residence.

Article 23. Duties of State and Social Agencies and Officials Regarding the Consideration of Appeals of Deputies

A deputy shall have the right to appeal in regard to questions connected with the activity of the deputy to state and social agencies, enterprises, institutions, and organizations and officials, who shall be obliged to consider the question raised and give the deputy a reply within the period established by law.

Proposals of deputies in regard to the most important questions shall be subject to consideration respectively by the executive committees of soviets, colleges of ministries and departments, councils of ministers, and presidiums of supreme soviets. A deputy may take part in the discussions, in such agencies, of the questions he has raised. The deputy shall be notified in good time about the date of consideration.

Article 24. Right of a Deputy to being Received Urgently by Officials

In regard to questions of the activity of a deputy, a deputy shall enjoy the right of being received urgently by directors and other officials of state agencies, enterprises, institutions, and organizations subordinate to or under the control of the soviet.

Article 25. Right of a Deputy to Demand Elimination of Violations of Legality

A deputy shall be obliged to guard Soviet laws, actively participate in the struggle against violations of law, nurture the working people in the spirit of high consciousness, execution of civic duty, and undeviating observance of socialist legality.

If a violation of the rights and of the interests of citizens protected by law or other violation of legality is discovered, a deputy as the representative of Soviet power shall have the right to demand the cessation of such violations, and when necessary to turn to the appropriate agencies and officials with a demand to stop such violations.

Officials of state and social organizations, the administration of enterprises, institutions, and organizations, as well as police workers to whom the demand of the deputy is addressed, shall be obliged to take measures immediately to eliminate the violations and, if necessary, to bring the guilty persons to responsibility.

IV. Basic Guarantees of Activity of a Deputy

Article 26. Assistance to a Deputy in Carrying Out his Powers

State agencies, enterprises, institutions, organizations, and their officials shall be obliged to assist a deputy in carrying out his powers. If officials fail to fulfill duties in regard to rendering assistance to deputies in carrying out their powers, the soviet or its agencies may in the established procedure impose disciplinary sanctions on such officials or recommend to the appropriate agencies the imposition of disciplinary sanctions on the said persons up to and including being relieved of the post occupied.

Article 27. Relieving a Deputy from Production or Official Duties in Order to Fulfill the Powers of a Deputy

At the time of a session of a soviet, as well as in order to fulfill the powers of a deputy in other instances provided for by legislation, a deputy shall be relieved from fulfilling production or official duties while retaining average earnings (or wages) at his place of permanent work.

Article 28. Supplying a Deputy with Publications of a Soviet. Rendering Legal Assistance to a Deputy

The Presidium of the USSR Supreme Soviet, the Presidium of a union republic supreme soviet, the Presidium of an autonomous republic supreme soviet, and the executive committee of a soviet shall supply a deputy of the respective soviet with the official publications and informational materials of the soviet.

Executive committees of soviets, the administration of enterprises and organizations, as well as legal institutions, shall provide assistance to a deputy on legal questions arising in his activity as a deputy.

Article 29. Duty of Directors of Enterprises, Institutions, and Organizations to Grant Necessary Information to a Deputy

Directors of enterprises, institutions, and organizations located in an electoral district shall at the request of a deputy give him informational materials and other information necessary to carry out the activity of a deputy.

Article 30. Compensation to a Deputy of Expenses Connected with the Fulfillment of the Powers of a Deputy

In instances and in the procedure established by legislation, a deputy shall be compensated for expenses connected with the fulfillment of the powers of a deputy.

Article 31. Right of a Deputy to Free Transport

A deputy of the USSR Supreme Soviet on the territory of the USSR, a deputy of a union republic supreme soviet and a deputy of an autonomous republic supreme soviet on the territory of the respective republic shall enjoy the right of free transport on all railway, motor vehicle, water, and air internal routes and on all types of urban passenger transport (except taxis).

A deputy of a territory or regional soviet, an autonomous region soviet, national area, district, city, district in city, settlement, and rural soviet shall enjoy respectively on the territory of the territory [krai], region, national area, district, city, settlement, and rural soviet the right of free transport on motor vehicle and water transport of republic subordination and on all types of urban passenger transport (except taxis), and the deputy of a territory or regional soviet, autonomous region soviet, and national area or district soviet, also on railway transport.

The procedure for and conditions of free transport for deputies of union and autonomous republic supreme soviets and local soviets, and also the procedure for accounts connected therewith with transport organizations, shall be determined by the USSR Council of Ministers and union republic councils of ministers.

Article 32. Protection of Labor Rights of a Deputy

A deputy may not be dismissed at the initiative of the administration from work at an enterprise, institution, or organization, expelled from a collective farm, or transferred by way of disciplinary sanction to lower-paid work without the prior consent of the soviet, and in the interval between sessions, without the prior consent of the respective executive committee of the soviet or of the Presidium of the supreme soviet.

A deputy released from work as a consequence of being elected to an elective post in an agency of a soviet shall be given, after the expiry of his powers in the elective post, his former work (or post), and if such is lacking, other equivalent work (or post) at the same or, with his consent, at another enterprise, institution, or organization.

The work time of a deputy at an elective post in an agency of a soviet shall be counted in the labor experience record of that specialization in which the deputy worked before being elected to the elective post in the agency of the soviet.

Article 33. Inviolability of Deputies of Supreme Soviets

A deputy of the USSR Supreme Soviet and a deputy of a union republic supreme soviet may not be brought to criminal responsibility, arrested, or subjected to measures of administrative sanction imposed in a judicial procedure without the consent respectively of the USSR Supreme Soviet, union republic supreme soviet, and in the interval between sessions, without the consent of the Presidium of the supreme soviet.

A deputy of an autonomous republic supreme soviet may not, on the territory of the autonomous republic as well as on the entire territory of the union republic of which the autonomous republic is a member, be brought to criminal responsibility, arrested, or subjected to measures of administrative sanction imposed in a judicial procedure without the consent of the autonomous republic supreme soviet, and in the interval between sessions, without the consent of the Presidium of the autonomous republic supreme soviet.

Article 34. Inviolability of Deputies of Local Soviets

A deputy of a territory or regional soviet, autonomous region soviet, national area, district, city, district in city, settlement, and rural soviet of working people's deputies may not, on the territory of the respective soviet, be brought to criminal responsibility, arrested, or subjected to measures of administrative sanction imposed in a judicial proceeding without the consent of the respective soviet, and in the interval between sessions, without the consent of its executive committee.

A decision of a soviet or its executive committee regarding the question specified in paragraph one of the present Article may be vacated respectively by a superior soviet or its executive committee, the questions being transferred for a second consideration by the soviet. If the soviet confirms the initial decision, the question may be decided in substance by a regional or territory soviet of working people's deputies, the Presidium of an autonomous or union republic supreme soviet upon the representation respectively of the procurator of the region, territory, or republic.

Article 35. Certificate and Badge of a Deputy

A deputy shall have a certificate and badge of a deputy, which he shall enjoy during the period of his powers.

Patterns of certificates and badges for deputies, as well as the Statutes on Badges of Deputies shall be confirmed:

for deputies of the USSR Supreme Soviet: by the Presidium of the USSR Supreme Soviet;

for deputies of union and autonomous republic supreme soviets and deputies of local soviets: by presidiums of supreme soviets of the respective union and autonomous republics.

CHAPTER II

THE ADMINISTRATION OF THE NATIONAL ECONOMY

STATUTE ON THE STATE PLANNING COMMITTEE OF THE USSR COUNCIL OF MINISTERS (Gosplan SSSR)

[Confirmed by Decree of the USSR Council of Ministers, September 9, 1968, as amended October 3, 1977. SP SSSR (1968), no. 17, item 113; (1977), no. 26, item 170]

1. The State Planning Committee of the USSR Council of Ministers (Gosplan SSSR) shall be a union republic agency which carries out all-state planning for the development of the USSR national economy and control over the fulfillment of national economic plans.

2. The principal task of Gosplan SSSR shall be the working out of state national economic plans in accordance with the Program of the CPSU, Directives of the Central Committee of the CPSU, and decisions of the USSR Council of Ministers which ensure the proportional development of the USSR national economy, the uninterrupted growth and increased efficiency of social production with a view to creating the material-technical base of communism, a steady increase in the living standard of the people and the strengthening of the defense capability of the country.

State plans for the development of the USSR national economy should be optimal and based on the economic laws of socialism, modern achievements and long-term development of science and technology, the results of scientific research of economic and social problems of communist construction, the all-round study of social requirements, the correct combining of branch and territorial planning, as well as of the centralized planning with the economic independence of enterprises and organizations.

3. Gosplan SSSR should provide in plans for:

the steady rise of all branches of the national economy, the increased efficiency of social production, and high rates of growth of national income;

improvement of national economic proportions, prevention of the origin and eradication of bottlenecks in the development of individual branches, and the balanced coordination of all sections of the plan;

improvement of the structure of social production, the fullest use of basic funds and production capacities, and the correct use of natural and material resources;

the rational allocation of productive forces about the territory of the country, taking into account the specialization and cooperation of production, the integrated development of the economy of the union republics and economic districts, correctly combining their interests with the interests of the entire national economy; improving inter-republic, inter-district, and inter-branch links;

further technological progress and the most rapid utilization in the national economy of the achievements of science and technology;

the issuance of products with technically advanced qualitative indicators, the introduction of advanced technology, and the integrated mechanization and automation of production;

rational utilization of capital investments, increasing their efficiency, reducing the cost and increasing the quality of construction, accelerating the introduction into effect of basic funds and production capacities and mastering them in the shortest possible periods;

the uninterrupted growth of labor productivity, the correct use of labor resources of the country, and provision of the national economy with qualified workers and specialists having a higher or secondary specialized education;

increasing the profitability of production, reducing the cost of production and costs of turnover, increasing profits, and improving the use of financial resources;

the steady growth of real incomes for the population, increasing the production of consumer goods, improving their quality and expanding their assortment, developing branches of material production and the non-production sphere connected with servicing the population;

expansion of international economic cooperation and raising the efficiency of foreign trade;

accumulation of necessary material state resources;

measures to strengthen the defense capacity of the country.

4. There shall be entrusted to Gosplan SSSR:

(a) the preparation on the basis of proposals of ministries, departments, union republic councils of ministers, and the USSR Academy of Sciences of the basic trends for the development of the USSR national economy in the long-term;

(b) the working out with the participation of USSR ministries and departments, union republic councils of ministers, the USSR Academy of Sciences, and the VTsSPS:

of draft long-term state plans on the basis of the basic trends for the development of the USSR national economy and draft plans submitted by ministries and departments of the USSR and the union republic councils of ministers;

of draft annual state plans on the basis of proposals relating to the clarification of planning tasks of long-term plans for the forthcoming year submitted by USSR ministries and departments and union republic councils of ministers;

(c) the consideration with the participation of USSR ministries and departments and union republic councils of ministers of proposals concerning the development and allocation of production forces in the union republics and economic districts; the consideration of union republic indicators worked out by the councils of ministers for the integrated development of the union republic economies;

(d) the effectuation of methods direction over the work relating to national economic planning, the working out of methods instructions, indicators, and forms for the drawing up of state plans in branch and territorial segments, as well as the organization of the exchange of experience in the domain of planning;

(e) the preparation with the participation of USSR ministries and departments, union republic councils of ministers, the USSR Academy of Sciences, and the VTsSPS of proposals and the effectuation of measures relating to the improvement of planning and economic stimulation in the national economy;

(f) effectuation of the verification of the timely and correct notifying by USSR ministries and departments and union republic councils of ministers of planning tasks of the national economic plan to enterprises, construction sites, and organizations;

(g) the preparation and submission of opinions relating to drafts of the USSR State Budget and of credit and cash plans;

(h) the consideration of proposals concerning the improvement of price formation prepared by the State Committee for Prices attached to Gosplan SSSR;

(i) the preparation with the participation of USSR ministries and departments and union republic councils of ministers of proposals concerning the development of foreign economic ties of the USSR, the improvement of inter-state specialization and cooperation of production, the coordination of plans for the development of the USSR national economy with the national economic plans of other member countries of the Council of Mutual Economic Assistance;

(j) the working out with the participation of the Ministry of Foreign Trade, the State Committee of the USSR Council of Ministers for Foreign Economic Relations, USSR ministries and departments, and union republic councils of ministers on the basis of draft plans compiled by them, draft plans for the import and export of goods, as well as draft plans for the delivery of equipment and materials for objects being built abroad with the technical assistance of the Soviet Union;

(k) the drawing up jointly with the USSR Ministry of Finances on the basis of draft currency plans submitted by USSR ministries and departments and by union republic councils of ministers of draft composite annual currency plans (or payment balances), as well as reports concerning the fulfillment of such plans;

(l) the implementation of the planning of works relating to the introduction into the national economy of mathematical economic methods, computer technology, and automated systems for the planning, management, and processing of information and control over the fulfillment of these works.

5. Gosplan SSSR shall:

(a) confirm plans for construction and assembly work fulfilled by independent-contract and economic means, plans for design and survey work and the work of design organizations, as well as other sections and planning tasks of plans and technical-economic norms in the established procedure;

(b) confirm balances and plans for the distribution of products according to the established nomenclature, planning tasks for the reduction of norms for the expenditure of material resources, as well as confirm norms in the established procedure for the expenditure of materials for individual needs and types of work, carry out scientific and methods direction of work relating to regulation of expenditures of material-technical resources and, jointly with Gossnab SSSR, to regulation of stocks of material-technical resources in the national economy, and determine the types of fuel for newly built, enlarged or reconstructed enterprises;

(c) consider itemized lists of construction sites and itemized lists of design and survey works for construction in future years submitted in the established procedure for agreement, as well as plans for design and survey works relating to the drawing up of technical and economic bases for the development of branches of the national economy and confirm itemized lists of newly begun constructions sites and objects carried out under foreign licenses and on the basis of sets of imported equipment;

(d) consider with the participation of Gosstroi SSSR, the union republic councils of ministers, and USSR ministries and departments, and determine, the procedure and principles for the selection of districts and points for the construction of new industrial enterprises, cities, and settlements;

(e) work out balances for labor resources on the basis of proposals of USSR ministries and departments and union republic councils of ministers and effectuate planning of the distribution and redistribution of the work force among branches of the national economy and union republics, with the participation of the State Committee of the USSR Council of Ministers for Labor and Social Questions;

(f) make changes in the planning tasks of the national economic plan arising out of individual decisions of the Government of the USSR, as well as in connection with the introduction in the established procedure of new prices not taken into account in the confirmed plans and consider proposals submitted for agreement by ministries and departments of the USSR and by union republic councils of ministers concerning changes of planning tasks of national economic plans in accordance with the rights granted to them;

(g) organize scientific research jointly with the USSR Academy of Sciences relating to general economic problems for the development of the national economy.

6. Gosplan SSSR shall bear responsibility for raising the scientific level of state planning, for the economic well-foundedness of draft plans worked out for the development of the national economy and their being in balance, for proportionality in the development of the national economy, and for the correct allocation of productive forces.

7. Gosplan SSSR shall exercise control over the fulfillment by ministries, departments, union republics, enterprises, and organizations of national economic plans, uncover reserves for the future growth of production and more efficient use of productive funds, capacities, and material resources, raise the profitability and improve other economic indicators of the development of branches of the USSR national economy, systematically inform the Government of the USSR about the fulfillment of plans, work out measures relating to the prevention and elimination of disproportions in the development of the national economy, and make appropriate proposals to the USSR Council of Ministers.

8. Gosplan SSSR shall be guided in its activity by the laws of the USSR, edicts of the Presidium of the USSR Supreme Soviet, decrees and regulations of the Government of the USSR, and other normative acts, as well as by the present Statute, and ensure the correct application of legislation in organizations and institutions within the jurisdiction of Gosplan SSSR.

Gosplan SSSR shall summarize the practice of the application of legislation relating to questions within its competence, work out proposals regarding the improvement of such legislation, and submit them to the USSR Council of Ministers for consideration.

9. Gosplan SSSR shall be granted the right to:

(a) enlist the USSR Academy of Sciences, the union republic academies of sciences, branch academies of science, scientific research and design institutes, structural design and other organizations and institutions, as well as individual scholars, specialists, and production peredoviki to work out draft plans and particular national economic problems;

(b) hear reports of directors of ministries, departments, scientific research, and other organizations relating to questions within its competence;

(c) receive from:

The USSR Central Statistical Administration statistical data necessary to work out national economic plans and verify their fulfillment;

USSR ministries and departments, as well as directly from enterprises, construction sites, scientific research, design, and other organizations and institutions, irrespective of their departmental subordination, all materials necessary to work out and verify the fulfillment of state plans, including statistical materials from ministries having departmental statistics and other informational materials;

(d) commission USSR ministries and departments to work out individual problems connected with the development of branches of the national economy;

(e) form interdepartmental commissions and councils relating to the working out and consideration of individual national economic problems, as well as convoke, in the established procedure, meetings relating to questions within its competence.

10. A State Expert Commission of scholars and highly qualified specialists shall be formed in Gosplan SSSR for expert opinion on the most important national economic problems, general schemes for the development of branches of the national economy, and the allocation of enterprises, specialization, and integrated development of the economy of economic areas and designs of large-scale integrated construction sites.

11. Gosplan SSSR shall be formed with a membership of the Chairman of the Committee appointed in accordance with the USSR Constitution by the USSR Supreme Soviet, deputy chairmen, and members of Gosplan SSSR personally appointed by the USSR Council of Ministers.

A College shall be formed in Gosplan SSSR composed of the Chairman of Gosplan SSSR (chairman of the college), deputy chairmen of Gosplan SSSR ex officio, as well as other leading workers who are members of Gosplan SSSR. Members of the college of Gosplan SSSR shall be confirmed by the USSR Council of Ministers.

Gosplan SSSR shall issue within the limits of its competence decrees, which are binding for execution by all ministries, departments, and other organizations.

The chairman of Gosplan SSSR shall issue orders and give instructions binding for execution by organizations and institutions of the system of Gosplan SSSR.

12. Gosplan SSSR shall direct the activity of organizations within it.

Union republic gosplans shall be subordinate to the councils of ministers of the respective union republic and to Gosplan SSSR.

13. The structure and number of workers of the central apparatus of Gosplan SSSR shall be confirmed by the USSR Council of Ministers.

The personnel establishment of the central apparatus of Gosplan SSSR shall be confirmed by the Chairman of Gosplan SSSR.

14. Gosplan SSSR shall have a seal depicting the State Arms of the USSR and its own name.

STATUTE ON THE STATE COMMITTEE OF THE USSR COUNCIL OF MINISTERS FOR SCIENCE AND TECHNOLOGY

[Confirmed by Decree of the USSR Council of Ministers, October 1, 1966. SP SSSR (1966), no. 21, item 193]

1. The State Committee of the USSR Council of Ministers for Science and Technology shall be an all-union agency called on to ensure the implementation in accordance with the directives of the Party and the Government of a unified state policy in the domain of scientific and technological progress and every possible use of the achievements of science and technology in the national economy.

2. The principal tasks of the State Committee of the USSR Council of Ministers for Science and Technology shall be:

determination of the basic directions of the development of science and technology in the country;

organization of the working out of inter-branch scientific and technological problems;

increasing the efficiency of scientific research and ensuring the rapid introduction of the achievements of science and technology in the national economy with a view to obtaining the most economical effect with minimal losses;

organization of scientific and technological information in the country;

control over the introduction of the achievements of science and technology in the national economy;

effectuation of links with foreign countries relating to questions of scientific and technological cooperation.

3. The State Committee of the USSR Council of Ministers for Science and Technology, in accordance with the tasks entrusted to it, shall:

(a) carry out a technical and economic evaluation of the level of the development of science and technology in branches of the national economy, work out and implement jointly with the USSR Academy of Sciences, USSR ministries and departments, and the union republic councils of ministers measures for the acceleration of scientific and technological progress and the development of scientific methods for the organization of labor to increase on this basis the efficiency of social production;

(b) work out jointly with the USSR Academy of Sciences, with the participation of Gosstroi SSSR (in the domain of construction and architecture), the USSR Ministry of Public Health (in the domain of public health), the USSR Ministry of Agriculture (in the domain of agriculture), USSR ministries and departments, and union republic councils of ministers, proposals concerning the basic directions for the development of science and technology in the country over a long-term period and submit them to the USSR Council of Ministers; work out on the basis of draft plans of

USSR ministries and departments and the union republic councils of ministers and submit to the USSR Council of Ministers draft long term plans for works relating to the resolution of basic scientific and technological problems;

(c) work out on the basis of materials of the USSR Academy of Sciences, the USSR ministries and departments, and the union republic councils of ministers, and submit proposals in good time, before the drawing up of long-term and annual national economic plans, to the USSR Council of Ministers and to Gosplan SSSR concerning the use in the national economy of scientific and technological achievements and results of scientific research work completed which has important national economic significance;

(d) select jointly with the USSR Academy of Sciences and ministries and departments the most fundamental long-term research fulfilled by scientific institutions of the USSR Academy of Sciences, union republic academies of sciences, and higher educational institutions, with a view to organizing their further working out in institutions and design bureaus of ministries and departments; determine the domain of application of the results of such research and organize their introduction into the national economy, thereby ensuring the link of the USSR Academy of Sciences, union republic academies of sciences, and higher educational institutions with branches of the national economy;

(e) work out on the basis of proposals of the USSR Academy of Sciences, USSR ministries and departments, and union republic councils of ministers, and confirm work plans relating to the resolution of individual major inter-branch scientific and technological problems, beginning from the implementation of scientific research up to the introduction of their results into the national economy, as well as exercise control over the course of the said work and adopt measures jointly with ministries and departments needed to ensure the most rapid fulfillment and application of the results of these works in the national economy;

(f) make known, jointly with the USSR Academy of Sciences and the Committee for Inventions and Discoveries attached to the USSR Council of Ministers, the most important discoveries, inventions, and results of inquiries, the practical utilization of which at present has not been prepared but which in the long-term are of great interest, and organize the working out jointly with ministries and departments the necessary measures to ensure the use in future of these discoveries, inventions, and research results;

(g) work out on the basis of draft plans of USSR ministries and departments and union republic councils of ministers and submit to the USSR Council of Ministers draft plans for financing scientific research work agreed with Gosplan SSSR and the USSR Ministry of Finances; participate in the consideration by Gosplan SSSR of proposals of the USSR Academy of Sciences, USSR ministries and departments, and union republic councils of ministers concerning the total amounts of capital investments for the development of science;

(h) work out jointly with Gosplan SSSR and the State Committee of the USSR Council of Ministers for Material-Technical Supply measures for the further improvement of the material-technical base of scientific institutions and for the organization of providing them with domestic and foreign unique equipment, apparatus, instruments, and special materials needed for scientific research; take part in the consideration by Gosplan SSSR of proposals of ministries, departments, and union republics concerning the amounts of appropriations for the purchase of equipment, instruments, and materials for import for scientific institutions and in the distribution of such appropriations among USSR ministries and departments and union republics;

(i) exercise general state control over the technical level of development of individual branches of the national economy, the fulfillment of the most important scientific research work according to the basic directions for the development of science and technology, as well as for the introduction into production of scientific and technological achievements having great national economic significance;

(j) work out and effectuate, jointly with ministries and departments, measures for the improvement of the organization of scientific research, for increasing their efficiency and improving the network of scientific institutions; consider proposals submitted for agreement concerning the organization of new scientific research institutions irrespective of their departmental subordination; take part in the preparation of proposals for the improvement of the wage and bonus systems for workers of scientific research and design organizations;

(k) work out jointly with the USSR Academy of Sciences, Gosplan SSSR, and the USSR Ministry of Higher and Secondary Specialized Education on the basis of draft plans of USSR ministries and departments and union republic councils of ministers, and submit to the USSR Council of Ministers draft long-term and annual plans for the training of scientific cadres, and work out measures to improve the training and use of scientific cadres;

(l) direct the study, dissemination, and propaganda of the achievements of domestic and foreign science and technology and progressive production and technological experience and effectuate methods guidance in the established procedure over the activity of scientific and technical information and propaganda agencies, irrespective of their departmental subordination;

(m) direct the activity of the Exhibition of Achievements of the National Economy of the USSR and the work of organizations and enterprises within the jurisdiction of the Committee;

(n) exercise coordination of scientific and technological links of USSR ministries and departments and union republics with foreign countries and international organizations.

4. The State Committee of the USSR Council of Ministers for Science and Technology shall be granted the right to:

(a) verify in ministries and departments, scientific research institutions, drafting and design organizations, and industrial enterprises the technical level of development of branches of the national economy and scientific research work and introduce their results into production, the conformity of annual scientific research work plans confirmed by ministries and departments to the basic directions for the development of science and technology in the country, work in the domain of scientific and technical cooperation with foreign countries, the training of scientific cadres in scientific institutions, the use of appropriations allotted for the development of science, as well as work for scientific and technical information agencies; hear reports and communications on these questions of directors of ministries and departments, as well as by agreement with them the reports and communications of directors of enterprises, scientific research, and drafting and design organizations and adopt decisions binding for execution relating to the results of the verifications;

(b) establish additional planning tasks for ministries and departments by agreement with them for carrying out with the efforts of scientific research, drafting and design organizations and enterprises subordinate to them of scientific research and experimental industrial work, the necessity for carrying out of which arises during the year and for deciding the most important inter-branch scientific and technological problems;

(c) have at its disposal reserve appropriations from the state budget for scientific research work and wage reserves by number and fund for workers of scientific research institutions and use these reserves for carrying on major scientific research work, the necessity for which arises during the year;

(d) consider lists of installations of scientific research organizations and their experimental industrial base which are subject to being constructed;

(e) conduct jointly with the Chief Committee of the Exhibition of Achievements of the National Economy of the USSR competitions to decide major scientific and technological problems and award, by agreement with ministries and departments, collectives of scientific institutions, higher educational institutions, experimental design organizations, enterprises, individual scholars, and specialists who win these competitions with diplomas, medals, and bonuses at the expense of appropriations allotted for expenditures connected with awards for participants of the Exhibition of Achievements of the National Economy of the USSR;

(f) take part in the distribution by Gosplan SSSR and the State Committee of the USSR Council of Ministers for Material-Technical Supply of special apparatus, precision instruments, new especially pure materials and chemical reagents, needed to carry out major scientific research;

(g) organize and carry out, when necessary, scientific expert examination relating to questions connected with the implementation of scientific research work and the introduction of the achievements of science and technology into the national economy which is of especially important significance for the economy of the country;

(h) create scientific councils for the major inter-branch problems of science and technology, scientific technical commissions, and expert groups, and enlist scholars and specialists to take part in their work;

(i) receive reports and materials needed to fulfill the tasks entrusted to the Committee from USSR ministries and departments, the USSR Academy of Sciences, and union republic councils of ministers, as well as from the Central Statistical Administration of the USSR:

(j) issue to ministries, departments, and organizations binding ukazaniia concerning the cessation of scientific research and experimental design work unjustifiably duplicating or not having theoretical and practical significance, and concerning the termination of financing it, as well as adding the funds released in this connection to the reserve of the Committee, notifying the USSR Ministry of Finances thereof; take decisions with the participation of ministries and departments concerning the closure of inefficient scientific institutions and their subdivisions or modifying the profile of their work;

(k) consider and adopt decisions regarding questions in dispute within the competence of the Committee which arose between ministries and departments in the process of carrying on major scientific research work;

(l) adopt decrees binding upon ministries and departments on questions relegated to the competence of the Committee;

(m) convoke in the established procedure conferences and meetings to discuss problems of the development of science and technology.

5. The State Committee of the USSR Council of Ministers for Science and Technology shall enlist scientific and technical societies and the All-Union Society of Inventors and Rationalizers to work out the basic directions for the development of science and technology in the country, to supervise the introduction of the achievements of science and technology into the national economy, to take part in the work of scientific councils, commissions, and groups of experts, and to organize scientific and technical information and propaganda of the achievements of science and technology and progressive production and technical work.

6. The State Committee of the USSR Council of Ministers for Science and Technology shall be formed comprising the Chairman of the Committee appointed by the USSR Supreme Soviet, and deputy chairmen and members of the Committee appointed by the USSR Council of Ministers, including as Committee members leading scholars and directors of industry who are not in the personnel establishment of the Committee apparatus.

The State Committee of the USSR Council of Ministers for Science and Technology shall have a college whose membership shall be confirmed by the USSR Council of Ministers.

7. The Chairman of the State Committee of the USSR Council of Ministers for Science and Technology shall direct all activity of the Committee and institutions and organizations subordinate to it, shall issue within the limits of the competence of the Committee orders and instructions on the basis of and in execution of laws, as well as of decrees and regulations of the USSR Council of Ministers, and shall verify their fulfillment; shall create in the established procedure, liquidate, and reorganize institutions, enterprises, and organizations; shall confirm statutes on scientific councils for major inter-branch problems of science and technology and on administrations and sections of the Committee and charters (or statutes) of institutions, enterprises, and organizations directly subordinate to them; shall appoint and relieve from office the leading workers of the central apparatus of the Committee and of institutions, enterprises, and organizations directly subordinate to it.

8. The structure and personnel establishment of the central apparatus of the State Committee of the USSR Council of Ministers for Science and Technology shall be confirmed by the USSR Council of Ministers.

9. The State Committee of the USSR Council of Ministers for Science and Technology shall have a seal depicting the State Arms of the USSR and its own name.

STATUTE ON THE PRODUCTION ASSOCIATION (OR COMBINE)

[Confirmed by Decree of the USSR Council of Ministers, March 27, 1974, No. 212. SP SSSR (1974), no. 8, item 38]

I. General Provisions

1. A production association (or combine) shall be a single production and economic complex composed of factories, plants, scientific research, construction design, design, and technological organizations and other production entities.

Production entities comprising the production association (or combine) shall not be juridical persons and the effect of the Statute on the Socialist State Production Enterprise shall not extend to them.

The production association (or combine) shall be the basic (primary) link of industry; its activity shall be built on a combination of centralized direction with economic independence and the initiative of the association itself.

2. The production association (or combine), using the state property allocated to its operative management or use, shall carry out its activity with the efforts of the collective of the association under the direction of a superior agency in accordance with a national economic plan on the basis of economic accountability, shall fulfill the duties entrusted to it and enjoy the rights connected with such activity, shall have an independent balance, and shall be a juridical person.

3. The present Statute shall extend to production associations (or combines) of industry irrespective of their departmental affiliation.

4. The principal tasks of a production association (or combine) shall be:

the development and improvement of production with a view to the fullest satisfaction of the requirements of the national economy and the populace for the respective types of products;

working out optimal plans, fulfillment of planning tasks for the production of products, profits, and other state plan indicators, fulfillment of the plan for payments to the budget, and the timeliness of accounts with banks and suppliers;

the extensive use of the achievements of science, technology, and progressive experience and reduction of the periods for introducing them into production, ensuring the high quality of experimental construction design and technological work fulfilled, the novelty and forward looking nature of research and scientific-technical workings being carried on, and the economic efficiency of their use;

the rational use of technical means of railway, water, air, and automotive transport, the systematic improvement of the organization of loading and unloading and transport work, the mechanization of such work and carrying out measures to reduce demurrage of means of transport when loading or unloading;

the issuance of high quality products, mastery of the production of new products conforming in their technical and economic indicators to the highest achievements of domestic and foreign technology;

raising labor productivity in every possible way and the efficiency of production on the basis of the concentration, specialization, cooperation, and combining of production, the maximal use of internal reserves, all possible intensification of production, and also the integrated use of raw materials, introduction of progressive technological processes and systems of managing them, and systematically reducing the cost of production and increasing the profitability of production;

strengthening labor discipline and creating conditions for assigning personnel and improving the forms and systems for the payment of labor and for material and moral incentives;

the rational use and increased effectiveness of capital investments, reduction of the periods for and reducing the cost of construction, ensuring the timely fulfillment of planning tasks for capital construction, introduction into effect of basic funds and production capacities and the full use of production capacities;

fulfillment of obligations for deliveries of products in the quantity, periods, and nomenclature (assortment) in conformity with contracts concluded (or allocation orders accepted for execution) and orders-allocation orders of foreign trade organizations;

improvement of planning, management, and economic accountability, the introduction of the scientific organization of labor and production; increasing the role of economic and mathematical methods and a more extensive use of computer technology and communications in production management;

all possible development of socialist competitions, ensuring the broad participation of the working people in production management, and carrying out measures for the social development of the collective of the association;

improvement of the cultural, domestic, and housing conditions for workers and the creation of more favorable and safe labor conditions;

the implementation of all necessary measures for the protection of air, soil, and waters from pollution by industrial or household effluents, sewage waters, and production wastes, and also for the struggle against noise and radio interference.

5. The production association (or combine) shall be formed, depending on its subordination, by a ministry (or department) of the USSR or by a union republic council of ministers in accordance with USSR and union republic legislation.

When forming an association, the technological community of production processes and the territorial location of the enterprises and organizations being combined, the homogeneity of the products which they issue, the existence of stable cooperation links, and the need for combined production, integrated processing of raw materials, complete or partial centralization for the fulfillment of production and economic functions with a view to increasing production efficiency shall be taken into account.

A production entity of an association shall be created by an agency superior to the association upon the recommendation of the director general (or director) of the association.

6. When necessary, by decision of the respective ministry (or department) of the USSR or the union republic council of ministers, individual independent enterprises and organizations enjoying the rights provided for by the Statute on the Socialist State Production Enterprise may be subordinated to a production association (or combine).

An association to which independent enterprises and organizations are subordinate shall act as a superior agency with respect to them. In such instances the association may centralize wholly or in part the fulfillment of individual production and economic functions of the said enterprises and organizations.

7. A production association (or combine) shall be liable for its obligations with that property allocated to it upon which execution may be levied according to USSR and union republic legislation.

The liability of an association for obligations of a superior agency and of independent enterprises and organizations subordinated to the association, as well as the liability of a superior agency and of independent enterprises and organizations subordinate to the association for the obligations of the association shall arise only in the instances provided for by USSR and union republic legislation or by contract.

The state shall not be liable for the obligations of an association, and an association shall not be liable for the obligations of the state.

8. A production association (or combine) shall have a charter confirmed by a superior agency.

The charter of an association should contain:

the name (or number) of the association, its location (postal address), and the numbers for bank accounts of the association;

the name of the agency to which the association is directly subordinate (superior agency);

the object and purpose of the activity of the association;

an indication as to whether the association has a charter fund;

an indication as to whether the association operates on the basis of the present Statute and is a juridical person;

the name of the official heading the association (director general, director);

the list of production entities which are a part of the association, indicating the location of each, the name of the head production entity, and if they have bank accounts, the numbers of these accounts.

Other provisions not contrary to law and relating to peculiarities of the activity of the enterprise also may be included in the charter.

An association shall acquire rights and duties connected with its activity and shall be a juridical person from the date its charter is confirmed.

9. The rights and duties of a production entity of a production association (or combine) shall be determined by prevailing legislation, by the present Statute, and by the statute on the particular production entity.

The statute on the production entity shall be confirmed by the director general (or director) of the association; statutes on its structural subdivisions (shops, sections, services, sectors, and others) shall be confirmed by the director (or head) of the production entity.

The director general (or director) of an association shall have the right to grant additional rights to a production entity within the limits of the competence of the association, except for rights transferred to the association by a superior agency.

10. A production entity shall have its own name, in which should be also specified the name of the production association (or combine) of which it is a part.

11. A production entity shall:

dispose of basic and circulating assets and labor and material resources allocated to it and carry out its activity on the principles of economic accountability within the limits of the rights established by legislation, and also the rights transferred to it by the production association (or combine);

conclude economic contracts in the name of the association, for which the association shall bear liability. A list and the types of such contracts shall be determined by the association.

A production entity situated outside the location of the association shall have a current account at the USSR State Bank and may have an account for the financing of capital investments at the USSR Construction Bank.

With the authorization of the director general (or director) of an association agreed with the USSR State Bank in which the checking account of the association is located, a current account also may be opened for a production entity situated where the association is located.

12. The procedure for carrying out intra-economic relations within the production association (or combine), the consequences of a violation by production entities of their duties, and also the procedure for the settlement of intra-economic disputes in the association, shall be determined by the association.

13. Planning tasks and ukazaniia connected with the activity of a production association (or combine), its production entities, and independent enterprises and organizations subordinate to the association may be given by superior agencies only to the association, except for instances provided for by prevailing legislation.

14. A production association (or combine) shall exercise the right of possession, use and disposition of property in its operative management and the right to use lands allotted to it within the limits established by law and in accordance with the purposes of the activity of the association, with planning tasks, and with the purpose of the property.

15. A production association (or combine) shall be obliged to observe socialist legality and state discipline in its activity. The rights granted to an association, as well as its production entities, should be used in the interests of the entire national economy, the association, and its production entities.

The superior agency should ensure the strict observance of the rights of the association and its production entities, as well as control over the fulfillment by the association of its duties and the proper use of the rights granted to it.

II. Management of a Production Association (or Combine)

16. A production association (or combine) shall be managed on the basis of the proper combination of one-man-leadership and collegiality in the discussion and decision of all questions relating to directing the activity of the association.

Social organizations and collectives of workers of the association and its production entities shall take extensive part in the preparation of draft plans of the production and economic activity of the association (or production entities), in the working out and effectuation of measures relating to ensuring the fulfillment of such plans, the development and improvement of the activity of the association, and improvement of the labor conditions and life of its workers.

17. A production association (or combine) shall be directed by the administrative apparatus of the head plant, head factory (or head production entity). In individual instances, with the authorization of the USSR Government, an association may be directed by a special administrative apparatus.

A director general (or director), acting on the basis of one-man-leadership, shall head an association.

The director general (or director) shall be appointed to and relieved from office in the procedure determined respectively by the ministry (or department) of the USSR or the union republic council of ministers.

18. The director general (or director) of a production association (or combine) shall organize all its work and bear full responsibility for the activity of the association.

The director general (or director) shall act in the name of the association without a power of attorney, represent it at all enterprises, institutions, and organizations, dispose of the property of the association in accordance with prevailing legislation and the present Statute, conclude contracts, issue powers of attorney (including with a right to transfer the power of attorney), and open checking and other accounts of the association at the bank.

Within the limits of his competence, the director general (or director) shall issue orders, hire and dismiss workers in accordance with labor legislation within the limits of the established nomenclature, take incentive measures, and impose sanctions on workers of the association.

The director general (or director) shall repeal orders of the directors of production entities or give *ukazaniia* binding for execution in modification of such orders if they are contrary to prevailing legislation, the present Statute, or other normative acts.

19. Deputies of the director general (or director), the chief bookkeeper, head of the legal section (or head of the legal bureau, senior jurisconsult, jurisconsult) and head of the technical control section of a production association (or combine) shall be appointed to and relieved from office by the superior agency upon the representation of the director general (or director) of the association.

20. The competence of deputies of the director general (or director) and other leading workers of a production association (or combine) shall be established by the director general (or director) of the association.

Deputies of the director general (or director) shall act in the name of the association within the limits of their competence, represent it in other institutions and organizations, may perform economic operations and conclude contracts without a power of attorney, and also issue powers of attorney to workers of the association.

21. A production entity shall be headed by a director (or head).

The director (or head) of a production entity shall be appointed to and relieved from office by the director general (or director) of the association.

Directors (or heads) of leading scientific research, construction design, and other large production entities shall be appointed to and relieved from office in the procedure determined respectively by ministries (or departments) of the USSR or by union republic councils of ministers.

22. The director (or head) of a production entity shall organize all its work and bear responsibility for the activity of the production entity.

23. Within the limits of the competence of a production entity, the director (or head) shall act in the name of the production entity without a power of attorney, dispose of property in accordance with prevailing legislation, the present Statute, and the statute on the particular enterprise which has allotted to it, issue orders, open a current account at the bank and, in the instances established by the USSR State Bank and the USSR Construction Bank, other accounts for the production entity, conclude economic contracts in the name of the association, and hire and dismiss workers in accordance with labor legislation. The director (or head) of a production entity shall take incentive measures in the established procedure and impose sanctions on workers of the production entity.

24. Workers may not be dismissed at the initiative of the administration of a production association (or combine) or of a production entity without the prior consent of the respective trade union committee, except for instances provided for by USSR legislation.

25. With a view to combining the interests of production entities with the interests of the production association (or combine), and also of raising the responsibility of production entities for the results of the economic activity of the association as a whole, an association council shall be created in the association. The director general (or director) of the association, his deputies, the directors (or heads) of production entities, as well as representatives of social organizations of the association, shall be on the council.

In those instances when individual independent enterprises and organizations are subordinate to an association, the directors of such enterprises and organizations shall be on the council.

The director general (or director) of the association shall be the chairman of the council.

When necessary, specialists and leading workers of the association, production peredoviki, and also representatives of other enterprises, organizations, and institutions shall be enlisted to take part in the work of the council.

26. The council of a production association (or combine) shall consider:

draft long-term and current plans for the development of the association, its production entities, and also draft plans for the development of independent enterprises and organizations subordinate to the association, having in view the adoption of optimal plans and maximal use of production reserves;

reports concerning the production and economic activity of the association, its production entities, and also independent enterprises and organizations subordinate to the association;

questions of the conclusion and execution of economic contracts;

questions of ensuring technical progress, raising the scientific and technological level of scientific research and design work being fulfilled, using the results of such work in production, raising the quality of products, and also of introducing standards;

questions of increasing the efficiency of capital investments, reducing periods and costs of construction, accelerating the mastery of design capabilities;

draft prices for the most important types of products and questions of observing state price discipline;

draft plans for organizational and technical measures directed toward ensuring specialization and cooperation of production entities and of independent enterprises and organizations subordinated to the association, the most efficient use of production capacities and material, labor, and financial resources, and improving the organizational structure of the association;

questions of the scientific organization of labor and production, improvement of management and economic accountability, labor norms, forms and systems for payment of labor, and material and moral incentives;

questions of the organization and development of socialist competition, the study and dissemination of progressive experience, and the introduction of progressive forms and methods for raising the creative activity of the working people;

questions of the selection and use of cadres;

questions of carrying out intra-economic relations, the consequences of the violation by production entities of their duties, and the procedure for the settlement of intra-economic disputes;

questions of the amounts of assets for the material incentive fund and the fund for socio-cultural measures and housing construction of the association which are transferred to the disposal of production entities, as well as draft standards for deductions for these funds, questions of determining the portion of the fund for the production development in instances of its being transferred to production entities; questions of the use of the economic incentive funds and other funds of the association;

questions of the distribution of the consumer goods fund between the production entities if such a fund is formed at the enterprise;

the state of labor conditions and safety techniques at the association;

questions of the social development of collectives of the association and its production entities, as well as collectives of independent enterprises and organizations subordinate to the association;

other questions of the activity of the association.

27. Decisions of the council of the production association (or combine) shall be implemented, as a rule, by orders of the director general (or director) of the association.

When there are disagreements between the director general (or director) and the association council relating to questions discussed at a session of the council, the director general (or director) shall implement his decision.

28. A technical-economic council may be created from highly qualified specialists, production innovators, and representatives of scientific research and other organizations in order to consider the technical and economic problems of the development of the production association (or combine), the working out of recommendations for the use and introduction into production of the newest achievements of domestic and foreign science and technology, large-scale inventions and results of scientific discoveries, scientific organization of labor, and progressive experience at the association.

The membership of the technical-economic council and a statute concerning it shall be confirmed by the director general (or director) of the association.

29. Collective contracts in production associations (or combines) and production entities therein shall be concluded in the procedure determined by the All-Union Central Trade Union Council and the State Committee of the USSR Council of Ministers for Labor and Wages.

30. Rules for internal labor discipline shall be established in accordance with branch rules for the administration of a production association (or combine) by agreement with the respective trade union agency or by their decision with the administration and the trade union committee of a production entity.

31. The administration of a production association (or combine) and, in the instances provided for by the present Statute, the administration of a production entity, shall distribute jointly with the respective trade union agency in the established procedure housing premises in association houses, and also housing premises placed at the disposal of the association (or production entity) in other houses.

32. The administration of a production association (or combine) and of a production entity shall, jointly with the respective trade union agency, organize the socialist competition, total its results, determine the winners in the competition, and decide questions of incentives for the outstanding collectives and workers.

33. The administration of a production association (or combine) and of a production entity shall report to sessions of the respective trade union agency about draft plans, the results of production and economic activity, the fulfillment of plans and obligations under the collective contract, measures provided for by the social development plans of collectives, and measures taken to eliminate shortcomings in work.

34. Permanently functioning production meetings, carrying out their activity on the basis of a Statute confirmed by the USSR Council of Ministers and the All-Union Central Trade Union Council, shall be organized in order to extensively involve workers and employees in deciding production questions in production entities and their structural subdivisions and, when necessary, also in the production association (or combine) as a whole.

The administration of an association, production entities, and their structural subdivisions shall further in every possible way the successful work of the permanently functioning production meetings and organize the fulfillment of their decisions.

35. Meetings (or conferences) of workers of a production association (or combine) and production entities shall discuss draft production plans upon the reports of the administration, the results of fulfilling plans, plans for the social development of collectives and the fulfillment of measures provided therein, draft collective contracts and the fulfillment of obligations pursuant to them, questions of production, the use of the economic incentive fund, and the consumer goods fund, and also questions of the state of labor and production discipline and the observance of internal labor discipline in production. The administration shall report to the meeting (or conference) about measures being carried out in execution of decisions of previously held meetings (or conferences), as well as the results of considering the critical remarks and proposals expressed at meetings (or conferences).

36. People's control groups and posts shall be created in a production association (or combine) and production entities, to which the administration of the association and production entities shall be obliged to render all possible assistance in work, consider their proposals and recommendations, and take the necessary measures to eliminate shortcomings uncovered.

37. The production and financial-economic activity of a production association (or combine) shall be audited by the superior agency, enlisting the interested organizations together once annually.

The activity of an association shall be verified by the superior agency and people's control agencies, and also may be carried out by other state agencies in accordance with the control functions over the activity of enterprises and organizations entrusted to them by prevailing legislation.

An association shall verify the production and financial and economic activity of its own production entities.

III. Property of a Production Association (or Combine)

38. The property of a production association (or combine) shall consist of the basic and circulating assets forming its charter fund, and also of the funds and other property allocated to the association.

Property allocated to an association shall be reflected in its independent balance sheet.

If independent enterprises and organizations are subordinate to the association, their property shall be reflected in the independent balances of these enterprises and organizations. In such instances the association shall draw up a composite balance sheet.

39. The following funds shall be created in a production association (or combine):

production development fund;

material incentive fund;

fund for socio-cultural measures and housing construction;

fund for amortization deductions earmarked for capital repairs;

bonus fund for the creation and introduction of new technology;

fund for promoting the introduction of inventions and rationalization proposals;

other funds in accordance with USSR legislation.

The procedure for forming and spending funds shall be determined by prevailing legislation and the present Statute.

40. A production association (or combine) shall allocate part of the basic and part of the circulating assets of an association needed to fulfill the production program to a production entity. Circulating assets shall be allocated in accordance with the established norms (or standards).

A production entity shall have part of the material incentive fund and part of the fund for socio-cultural measures and housing construction at its disposal, and also may have part of the production development fund determined by the combine.

If a consumer goods fund is created at an association, the production entities participating in the production of consumer goods and production articles from production wastes shall have at their disposal part of the assets of the consumer goods fund earmarked for bonuses for workers and improving their cultural and domestic servicing. The amount of assets transferred by an association shall be determined by the director general (or director) by agreement with the respective trade union agency in proportional participation shares for each production entity producing the said goods and manufactures.

An association also may transfer to the disposal of individual production entities in amounts determined by the director general (or director) a part of the assets of the consumer goods fund earmarked for expanding production and improving the quality of consumer goods, and manufacturing equipment to issue them and prepare new models of such goods, as well as for the construction and repair of dwelling houses.

A production entity may have a separate balance sheet.

41. Circulating assets allocated to a production entity may be withdrawn from it by a production association (or combine) when the norms (or standards) of circulating assets are changed in the established procedure.

An association shall have the right, and upon the proposal of a production entity shall be obliged, to withdraw surplus material valuables from it which relate to the basic and circulating assets.

42. The total amount (or standards) of the circulating assets of a production association (or combine) and their growth or reduction shall be confirmed in the established procedure, proceeding from planning tasks and in accordance with norms for the expenditure and reserves of goods and material valuables.

Circulating assets allocated to an association within the limits of the standard may not be withdrawn from it by a superior agency.

Surplus circulating assets (in excess of the standard) may be withdrawn from the combine by a superior agency only by way of redistributing pursuant to the annual report of the association or if the standard of its circulating assets are changed in connection with a change of the production plan of the association.

43. Buildings, installations, operating equipment, and other basic assets allocated to a production association (or combine) may be transferred to other enterprises or organizations in the procedure established by USSR and union republic legislation.

44. Temporarily unused buildings and installations, production, warehouse, and other premises, equipment, means of transport, and other objects relating to basic funds may be leased by a production association to other enterprises and organizations. The rental for a building, installation, or premises shall be recovered at the rates prevailing in the locality where they are situate, and for other objects relating to basic funds, in an amount not exceeding the amortization deductions and payment for funds for the particular type of property.

45. Surplus unused equipment, means of transport, tools, instruments, inventory, raw materials, materials, and fuel may be sold by a production association (or combine) to other enterprises and organizations on condition of observing the following procedure.

As regards the existence of surplus material valuables, the funds for which were allotted to the association by a superior agency, this agency should be notified, and with respect to surplus material valuables distributed by territorial agencies of material-technical supply, the respective territorial agency.

If the superior agency refuses to redistribute the surplus or a reply is not received from it within two weeks from the day notification is sent, the association shall notify the respective territorial agency of material-technical supply about these surpluses.

If the territorial agency of material-technical supply refuses to realize the surplus or a reply is not received from it within a month from the day notification is sent, the association shall realize the surplus independently.

Materials, instruments, and other material valuables acquired by the association by way of local procurements shall be realized by it independently.

The amounts received as a result of the sale of material valuables relating to circulating assets shall remain at the disposal of the association as its circulating assets.

The amounts obtained from the sale of material valuables which are basic assets shall remain at the disposal of the association and shall be sent by it to the production development fund.

46. A production association (or combine) and a production entity shall grant for use free of charge to the appropriate trade union agency of the association (or production entity) buildings, premises, installations, gardens, and parks on the balance of the association (or production entity) or leased by it which are earmarked for carrying on cultural, enlightenment, therapeutic, physical culture, and sport work among the workers of the association (or production entity) and members of their families, pioneer camps, and also buildings, premises, and installations earmarked for carrying on technical propaganda.

The maintenance, repair, heating, lighting, cleaning, protection, and equipping of the said objects shall be at the expense of the association (or production entity). In instances when workers of other enterprises and organizations also use them, these enterprises and organizations shall share in the said expenditures.

An association (or production entity) shall grant free of charge to the respective trade union agency and other social organizations of the association (or production entity) the premises needed for their work and to hold meetings of workers and employees, provide equipment, heating, lighting, protection, and cleaning for such premises, and also grant means of transport and communications to the said organizations free of charge.

47. A production association (or production entity) shall transfer from the balance without compensation to the balance of the trade union and other social organizations of the association (or production entity) cultural, domestic, and sport inventory acquired at the expense of the association (or production entity) which may be used in accordance with prevailing legislation to acquire this type of property.

48. A production association (or combine) and a production entity shall grant free of charge to:

public health institutions attached to them or their structural subdivisions: premises, providing heating, lighting, water supply, protection, cleaning, and repair of such premises;

lunch rooms and other public dining organizations on the balance sheet of the association (or production entity) or situate on the territory of the association (or production entity) and servicing the collective of its workers: premises, providing heating, lighting, and water supply of such premises.

49. A production association (or combine) and a production entity may grant without compensation to:

a secondary general education evening (or shift) or correspondence school, an evening (or shift) professional-technical high school, courses, and study and training combines for raising qualifications in which their workers study, and a plant higher technical school or technical school attached to the association: premises for training purposes, necessary equipment, tools, instruments, and materials for training laboratories and cabinets, providing repairs and servicing for the premises, including the supply of electrical power and fuel;

higher and secondary specialized educational institutions and institutes for raising qualifications: models of machines, machine tools, tools, and equipment, as well as exhibits taken from exhibition demonstrations which might be used for training purposes.

An association may transfer equipment and materials to general education schools without compensation, as well as pay for construction, repairs, and equipment of such schools at the expense of accumulations in excess of the plans.

50. A production association (or combine) shall make amortization deductions for capital repairs and complete replacement of basic funds.

Amortization deductions earmarked for financing capital repairs shall comprise a special fund of the association and shall be expended by it both for capital repairs and for modernization of basic funds, and also for the acquisition of components and assemblies needed to fulfill such work and for the replacement of worn out components and assemblies.

Expenditures for the acquisition of new equipment in place of obsolete equipment whose capital repair is economically inadvisable also may be carried out at the expense of assets of the said fund.

Part of the amortization deductions earmarked for financing capital repairs shall be transferred in the established amount to the superior agency for the creation of a reserve for rendering assistance to those enterprises and organizations who have insufficient assets of their own to carry out capital repairs.

Amortization deductions earmarked for the complete replacement of basic funds shall remain in the established amounts at the disposal of the association and shall be included in the production development fund. The remaining part of amortization deductions earmarked for the complete restoration of basic funds shall be directed in accordance with prevailing legislation to finance centralized capital investments.

51. The amounts of the material incentive fund and fund for socio-cultural measures and housing construction, and also the standards for deductions from profits for such funds and for the production development fund shall be determined for the production association (or combine) as a whole in the established procedure by a superior agency by agreement with the appropriate trade union agency.

The amounts of assets of the material incentive fund and fund for socio-cultural measures and housing construction transferred to the disposal of production entities, and also the standards for deductions from such assets, shall be determined by the association by agreement with the appropriate trade union agency according to indicators of the activity of each production entity. An association may retain at its own disposal the undistributed portion of such funds.

The assets of the material incentive fund and fund for socio-cultural measures and housing construction transferred to the disposal of a production entity shall be used along the lines established by prevailing legislation concerning such funds in accordance with the estimates confirmed by the administration of the production entity jointly with the trade union committee. The unused remnants of assets of these funds shall be carried over to the following year and shall not be subject to withdrawal from the production entity.

The assets of a production development fund transferred by an association to a production entity shall be used along the lines determined by the association in accordance with prevailing legislation concerning this fund.

Assets of the material incentive fund retained by an association for its own disposal shall be used for bonuses for workers of the association for the fulfillment of specially important planning tasks, to augment assets of the material incentive fund transferred to the disposal of individual production entities in connection with a temporary reduction of economic indicators for their activity for reasons not dependent on them, and for bonuses for winners in the socialist competition of the association.

Assets of the material incentive fund retained at the disposal of the association whose direction is effectuated by a special administrative apparatus also may be expended for bonuses for workers of this apparatus according to the established bonus systems to pay compensation for annual work results and to render one-time assistance to them.

Assets of the fund for socio-cultural measures and housing construction retained by an association at its own disposal shall be used to augment assets of the fund for socio-cultural measures and housing construction transferred to the disposal of individual production entities in connection with a temporary reduction of economic indicators for their activity for reasons not dependent on them, and also for the construction of dwelling houses and cultural and domestic objects for workers of the association.

Assets of the fund for socio-cultural measures and housing construction retained at the disposal of the association whose direction is effectuated by a special administrative apparatus also shall be expended to improve the cultural and domestic servicing of workers of this apparatus.

Estimates of expenditures of assets of the material incentive fund and the fund for socio-cultural measures and housing construction left at the disposal of an association shall be confirmed by the administration of the association jointly with the respective trade union agency.

Withdrawal and redistribution of assets of the economic incentive fund of the association by a superior agency shall not be permitted except for instances determined by the USSR Council of Ministers. The unused remnants of such funds shall remain at the disposal of the association and shall be carried over to the following year.

52. All dwelling space built at the expense of assets of the fund for socio-cultural measures and housing construction, the consumer goods fund, and other assets of a production association (or combine) which may be directed toward housing construction in accordance with legislation shall be inhabited by persons according to a list confirmed by joint decision of the administration of the association and the respective trade union agency, subsequently notifying the executive committee of the soviet of working people's deputies.

All dwelling space built at the expense of assets of the fund for socio-cultural measures and housing construction and the consumer goods fund which were transferred to the disposal of a production entity shall be inhabited by persons according to a list confirmed by joint decision of the administration of the production entity and trade union committee, subsequently notifying the executive committee of the soviet of working people's deputies.

The siting in houses built at the expense of the said assets of trade, public dining, and domestic servicing enterprises may be only with the consent of the administration of the association (or production entity) and respective trade union agency.

53. Workers of a production association (or combine) shall be obliged to be careful of state property, properly use buildings, installations, and equipment, and observe strict economy in the expenditure of material and monetary assets. Persons guilty of spoiling state property and causing material damage to the state shall bear responsibility in the established procedure.

IV. Rights and Duties of a Production Association (or Combine)

54. The rights appertaining to a production association (or combine) and duties entrusted to it which are connected with its activity shall be carried out by the director general (or director) and the duties according to an established distribution by his deputies and other officials,

and in other instances provided by the present Statute and other normative acts, jointly by agreement or with the participation of the respective trade union agency.

55. A production association (or combine) may be allotted additional rights by a superior agency (in the domain of planning, scientific and technical progress, capital construction, material-technical supply, and others) within the limits of the competence of this agency.

Rights and Duties in the Domain of Planning

56. A production association (or combine) shall, with the participation of trade union and other social organizations and the collective of workers of the association, work out draft five year and annual plans for all types of its activity, and also proposals for draft plans for a longer period proceeding from planning tasks of the superior agency, the need to satisfy the requirements of the national economy and the populace for products issued by the association, the achievements of scientific and technical progress, economic links formed with customers and supply and sale and trading organizations, and the need for the future development of such links.

A mutual interlinking of all sections of the plans should be ensured in the draft plans worked out by the association and the complete use of internal reserves should be provided.

57. The superior agency shall consider, involving the production association (or combine), and shall confirm the five year and annual planning tasks according to the established system of indicators and shall supply the association with the appropriate material, technical, and financial resources and wage fund needed to fulfill these planning tasks.

All remaining indicators of the plans of the association shall not be confirmed, but shall be worked out by the association and use by planning agencies as account materials in justification of the plans.

Plan indicators confirmed by an association, depending on the peculiarities of its work, may be reckoned according to an ukazanie of the ministry (or department), proceeding from the production volume, to be computed by taking into account and without taking into account internal turnover.

58. All planning tasks shall be communicated to a production association (or combine) only by a superior agency, and to production entities only by the association.

59. A production association (or combine) which has production entities in other regions, territories, and republics shall work out plans not only in a branch but also in a territorial profile according to the respective indicators.

60. A production association (or combine) shall, in accordance with the indicators confirmed by it, work out a five year plan, distributing the most important planning tasks by year, which shall be the principal form of planning for the production and economic activity of the association.

An association shall work out the annual technical, industrial, and financial plan and quarterly and monthly plans for production and economic activity in accordance with planning tasks confirmed and contracts concluded.

A five year plan, annual technical, industrial and financial plan, and quarterly and monthly plans of an association shall be confirmed by the director general (or director).

An association shall establish basic indicators of the five year, annual, quarterly, and monthly plans for production entities which are a part thereof, ensuring the fulfillment of the planning tasks confirmed by the association with the greatest economic efficiency.

A production entity shall work out plans for production and economic activity on the basis of indicators established by the association for the production entity as a whole and for its structural subdivisions.

61. The periods for working out and confirming five year and annual plans of a production association (or combine) shall be determined by a ministry (or department) of the USSR or a union republic council of ministers.

62. Planning tasks confirmed for a production association (or combine) should be stable and may be changed by a superior agency only in exceptional instances after preliminary discussion of such changes with the administration of the association in the procedure and within the periods established by the USSR Council of Ministers.

When planning tasks for an association are changed by a superior agency, the respective changes should be made simultaneously to all interconnected planning indicators, including with the budget, without modifying the mutual relationship of the superior agency with the budget.

Amendments in the production plan for consumer goods caused by justified change in orders of trading or sale organizations may be made within the established periods during the year by the association itself within the limits of the planning tasks confirmed for the volume of consumer goods realized, and for profits and allotted resources and materials. In instances when orders of trading or sale organizations decline and it is necessary to reduce payments to the budget or the additional allocation of raw materials and materials, the amendments shall be made by the association by agreement with the superior agency at the expense of reserves which this agency has so as not to allow a reduction on the goods resources and revenues of the state.

An association shall notify the superior agency and respective executive committee of the soviet of working people's deputies or the autonomous republic council of ministers about changes made in the consumer goods production plan.

63. A production association (or combine) may manufacture a product in excess of the established plan only on condition that the sale of this product is guaranteed.

64. A production association (or combine) shall have the right, taking into account the prevailing system for the distribution of products in excess of plan, to accept orders from other enterprises and organizations for the production of work and the manufacture of a product in excess of plan from raw materials and materials of the customer or from its own materials and production wastes unless this would cause damage to the fulfillment of the state plan established for it and obligations under contracts.

65. A production association (or combine) shall direct the organization of planning work in production entities, ensuring the qualitative

and timely working out of plans, their stability, and also exercise day-to-day control over the fulfillment of plans and take necessary measures to do so.

Rights and Duties in the Domain of Scientific and Technical Progress

66. A production association (or combine) shall take part in working out scientific and technical forecasts regarding the most important problems of production development in the branch (or sub-branch). Taking into account such forecasts, the association shall work out long-term programs for the development of the association (including the determination of the structure and amounts of the new product to be issued), and also measures relating to the improvement of technology, means of mechanizing and automating production, management systems, and reducing expenditures relating to production.

An association shall take part in working out draft long-term and annual plans for scientific research work and for using the achievements of science and technology in production.

67. A production association (or combine) may conclude contracts with other enterprises and organizations for the association to carry out complex works and individual scientific research and design, for the delivery of new types of manufactures, rendering necessary services connected with the installation and use of such manufactures.

Technical planning tasks to carry on scientific research, experimental, design, construction design, and technological work having as its purpose the creation of new scientific and technical directions in the branch shall be obligatorily submitted by the association for the opinion of the organization coordinating the respective work.

Expenditures on the said work shall be at the expense of assets which the association has for such purposes, and also at the expense of bank credit.

An association may fulfill complex works and individual scientific research and design, the delivery of new types of manufactures, render necessary services connected with the installations and use of such manufactures in accordance with the profile of the particular association by contracts with other enterprises and organizations.

68. A production association (or combine) shall take measures to raise the quality of products issued, systematically analyzing its technical level by studying the achievements of domestic and foreign science and technology, patent materials, recommendations for the standardization of and standards of international organizations, and summaries of use experience of the products issued, and also shall ensure the mastery of production of the new product which meets the highest achievements of domestic and foreign technology in its technical and economic indicators.

An association shall be obliged to make proposals for the consideration of the appropriate agencies concerning the removal from production and replacement of morally obsolete products which are not in demand according to the nomenclature allocated for the association, and in instances provided for by legislation shall independently remove such products from production and replace them with a new product meeting the requirements of the national economy and populace.

69. With a view to issuing a high quality product, a production association (or combine) shall ensure the timely discovery of defects in a manufactured product through the technical control service section of the association and shall prevent the issuance (or delivery) of a product not conforming to standards, technical conditions, drawings, confirmed models (or standards), and conditions of delivery.

70. A production association (or combine) shall confirm technical conditions by agreement with the customer for individual product types for which there are no standards and technical conditions confirmed by appropriate agencies, having in view to ensure the issuance of a product at the highest technical level.

An association shall have the right to issue a product of a higher quality in comparison with prevailing standards and technical conditions for this product by agreement with the customer. Additional expenditures connected therewith shall be paid to the association in the established procedure, taking into account the economic efficiency of the higher quality product.

71. A production association (or combine) shall carry out measures to prepare a product issued for quality certification.

72. A production association (or combine) shall work out draft standards and technical conditions for a product according to the nomenclature allocated for it or shall participate in their working out, shall submit these drafts for confirmation in the established procedure, shall ensure the introduction and observance of confirmed standards and technical conditions, and also the application of modern means and methods for measuring and testing the product during production and control over the state of such means and observance of the procedure established for their use.

73. A production association (or combine) shall:

(a) work out technical and economic standards, norms for the expenditure and stocks of raw materials, fuel, materials, and norms for the expenditure of heat and electric power for production and use needs in accordance with prevailing legislation;

(b) confirm norms and standards according to a list established by the superior agency within the limits of its competence;

(c) and may establish a list of norms and standards to be confirmed by production entities.

74. A production association (or combine) shall carry out systematic work to evaluate the level of standardization and product unification of the association which has been achieved, and also the raw materials, materials, and other resources which it requires.

An association shall carry out measures to ensure a high quality of standardization and unification of a newly developed product.

75. A production association (or combine) shall ensure an uninterrupted increase in the technical level of production, the improvement of technological processes applied in production and management systems, and the integrated mechanization and automation of basic and auxiliary production processes.

An association shall work out and confirm in the established procedure long-term and annual plans for the introduction of new technology, providing therein for the use of inventions and rationalization proposals.

76. A production association (or combine) shall confirm technological production processes for production entities unless these processes are confirmed by an agency which carries out a uniform technological policy in the particular branch of production.

When necessary, an association shall have the right to change technological processes confirmed by the respective agencies which carry out a uniform technological policy in the particular branch of production if such changes improve product quality (increase reliability and durability) or, without lowering quality or violating standards and technical conditions, reduce its cost of production or produce another positive effect, except for technological processes whose modification without the consent of the agencies which confirmed them is prohibited. The observance of rules and norms for labor protection, safety technique, and production sanitation should be ensured in this connection.

The agency which confirmed a technological process should be notified at once about its modification.

77. A production association (or combine) shall organize work for invention and rationalization on the basis of long-term and current thematic plans and ensure the timely use of inventions and rationalization proposals as well as the payment in the established procedure of compensation for the use of inventions and rationalization proposals and bonuses for promoting an invention and rationalization.

An association shall organize the exchange of experience, hold competitions, contests, and showings relating to invention and rationalization jointly with the appropriate trade union agency and organization of the All-Union Society for Inventors and Rationalizers.

An association shall ensure the timely revelation of inventions created by workers of the association, in the established procedure, in connection with the fulfillment of their employment tasks and the formalization and filing of applications for the issuance of authors' certificates in the USSR and for obtaining patents abroad when necessary.

78. With a view to developing the creative initiative of the working people, a production association (or combine) shall promote in every possible way the activity of primary organizations of the Scientific-Technical Society and the All-Union Society of Inventors and Rationalizers and involve them in working out specific tasks for the technical development of production and renovation of products issued, draft long-term and current plans for the introduction of new technology, inventions, and rationalization proposals, and also in the fulfillment of such plans.

An association shall provide the said primary organizations, and also social design, technological, and patent bureaus, standards bureau, councils of innovators, social scientific research institutes and laboratories, bureaus and groups for economic analysis, technical information bureau, councils for the scientific organization of labor, and other creative associations with premises, equipment, tools, inventory, and technical and informational literature.

With a view to involving engineering and technical workers and innovative workers more extensively in the technical improvement of production, an association may by agreement with the respective trade union agency and council of the primary organization of the Scientific-Technical Society transfer to this council the effectuation of the functions of the technical and economic council of the production association (or combine).

79. The administration of a production association (or combine) shall, jointly with the respective trade union agency and councils of the primary organizations of the Scientific and Technical Society and the All-Union Society for Inventors and Rationalizers, regularly hold conferences and meetings of engineering, technical, and scientific workers, peredoviki, and innovators of production in order to discuss questions of technical progress, the economic development of the association and the working out of recommendations and proposals directed toward the future improvement of production technique, technology, and management, and ensure the timely implementation of such recommendations and proposals.

80. A production association (or combine) shall carry out, in accordance with confirmed plans, work connected with scientific, technical, and production cooperation with foreign countries.

81. A production association (or combine) shall submit proposals in the established procedure for the sale and purchase of licenses for inventions and other scientific and technical achievements.

An association shall bear responsibility for the timely mastery of the production of a product pursuant to licenses purchased.

Rights and Duties in the Domain of Capital Construction

82. A production association (or combine) shall carry out capital construction, ensure the most efficient use of capital investments and their being directed as a priority toward the technical rearmament and reconstruction of basic funds, the improvement of proportions within the association, the concentration of assets on vacant building sites and objects, and a reduction in the amount of incomplete construction.

83. A production association (or combine) shall take measures to reduce the periods for, raise the quality of, and lower the cost of construction, and also ensure the observance of established norms for construction continuity and periods for the introduction into operation of production capacities and basic funds; master newly introduced production capacities within the periods provided by norms for the duration of mastering them.

84. A production association (or combine) shall carry out capital construction and reconstruction of basic funds by independent work contracts concluded with construction and assembly organizations. In instances when the performance of capital construction work by independent contract means is economically inadvisable, such work may be fulfilled by the plant.

85. A production association (or combine) shall conclude contracts for the working out of design and estimate documentation with design organizations. When necessary, the association shall involve design and construction design subdivisions which are part of the association in working out such documentation, in the established procedure.

86. A production association (or combine) shall confirm:

design and estimate documentation, title lists of production designated construction sites being carried out at the expense of centralized capital investments, and title lists of design and prospecting work for construction of future years in the procedure established by the ministry (or department) of the USSR or a union republic council of ministers within the limits of their competence;

design and estimate documentation and title lists for the expansion (or reconstruction) of operating production designated objects being carried out at the expense of assets of the production development fund irrespective of the estimated cost of the work;

design and estimate documentation and title lists for construction and expansion (or reconstruction) of objects being carried out at the expense of assets of the fund for socio-cultural measures and housing construction, the consumer goods fund, and other noncentralized sources for financing irrespective of the estimated cost of the work;

title lists for the construction of dwelling houses and designated cultural, domestic, and municipal economy objects being carried out at the expense of centralized capital investments, except for title lists of newly begun construction of theaters, cinemas, circuses, and concert, film, exhibition, and sport halls, palaces of culture and sport, houses of culture and clubs, stadiums, swimming pools, rinks and tracks with artificial ice and other analogous objects, as well as sanatoriums, rest homes, and boarding houses;

title lists for work to ensure labor protection, safety technique, and production sanitation;

intrabuilding-site title lists by agreement with the independent contractor.

Title lists for the construction of dwelling houses and designated cultural and domestic objects at the expense of the fund for socio-cultural measures and housing construction and the consumer goods fund, and also title lists for work to ensure labor protection, safety technique, and production sanitation shall be confirmed by the association by agreement with the respective trade union agency.

87. A production association (or combine) shall have the right to transfer to independent work organizations by contracts, with their consent, the fulfillment of construction and assembly work and, in connection therewith, the respective wage fund and funds for material resources and materials, subsequently notifying the superior agency thereof.

88. A production association (or combine) shall have the right to confirm by agreement with the independent work organization individual prices for work the need for which arises in the course of construction unless the prices for such work have been confirmed in the established procedure.

89. Work plans for capital repairs and the corresponding estimate and financial accounts shall be confirmed by the director general (or director) of a production association (or combine). Capital repair work shall be carried out by both plant and independent work means.

If an association transfers an amount of capital repair work to an independent work organization, the association shall have the right to also transfer to the independent work organization the respective wage funds and funds for material resources and materials, subsequently notifying the superior agency thereof.

90. A production association (or combine) shall have the right to use part of the assets allocated to it in a centralized procedure for housing construction in order to construct children's preschool institutions. A decision concerning such use of the assets shall be taken by the director general (or director) jointly with the respective trade union agency.

91. A production association (or combine) may carry out the construction of dwelling houses, the construction and expansion of municipal economy objects, medical and children's preschool institutions, pioneer camps, and other designated cultural and domestic objects, jointly (by shares) with other enterprises and organizations at the expense of capital investments provided by the association by the plan respectively for such purposes.

Rights and Duties in the Domain of Material-Technical Supply and Sale

92. A production association (or combine) shall organize and ensure the material-technical supply of the association and the sale of products which it produces, taking into account the general state system of supply and sale operating in the country.

93. A production association (or combine) shall establish standards for stocks of material valuables for production entities, and also allocate limits (or funds) for material resources and redistribute them in the established procedure, taking into account changes in the production program.

A production entity situated outside the place where the association is located shall receive funds: from the association, for material resources distributed by the agency superior to the association; and from territorial agencies of material-technical supply where the production entity is located, for material resources distributed by these agencies. The said production entity shall realize the funds in the established procedure.

94. A production association (or combine) shall carry out the realization of funds allotted to it and the sale or products manufactured on the basis of economic contracts, ensure the fulfillment of planning tasks and obligations for deliveries of products according to quantity, nomenclature (assortment), quality, periods, and other delivery conditions, and also bear responsibility for the efficient use and proper storage of material resources.

The failure of an association to fulfill planning tasks and obligations for deliveries of products shall be a flagrant violation of state discipline and shall entail responsibility of the guilty officials in the established procedure.

Products not distributed by way of plan, and also products not sold by way of allocation order shall be realized by the association independently in the procedure established by prevailing legislation.

95. A production association (or combine) shall carry out measures for the expansion of economically advisable direct protracted links and to this end shall make proposals to agencies which attach buyers to suppliers regarding the forming of such links and on the basis of attachment plans shall conclude long-term economic contracts with other enterprises and organizations.

A change of direct protracted economic links which have been formed between suppliers and buyers for deliveries shall be permitted when necessary with observance of the procedure established by prevailing legislation.

96. A production association (or combine) may conclude long-term contracts with territorial material-technical supply agencies for organizing

the supply of the association which provide for a guaranteed integrated provision of products (allotted either by funds or by way of non-fund supply), the preparation of products for production consumption, centralized delivery of materials and manufactures according to agreed schedules, the realization of surplus and unused material valuables, and the rendering of other services.

An association which has concluded the said contract shall have the right to transfer its stocks of material resources in agreed amounts to the territorial material-technical supply agency.

97. A production association (or combine) may acquire without funds a product from other enterprises and organizations which is realized without allocation orders, surplus material valuables, and also buy necessary articles of material-technical supply by way of wholesale or retail trade in accordance with prevailing legislation.

98. A production association (or combine) shall have the right to transfer funds to other enterprises and organizations and to give them materials from their own resources and sets of equipment according to established norms for the manufacture by contract of a product needed by the association.

99. A production association (or combine) shall have the right to transfer work to specialized organizations on the basis of contracts concluded with them relating to the study of long-term demand and advertising of a new product, and also to render other types of services for the active introduction of progressive types of materials and manufactures into the national economy.

100. A production association (or combine) shall have the right by agreement with the buyer (or customer) to change, when necessary, in the established procedure the assortment, periods, and other delivery conditions provided in the contract and to make a delivery before time within the limits of the year from a product whose receipt has been refused by a customer, on condition that obligations for deliveries to other customers are fulfilled.

An association shall notify the appropriate agency about a change in the assortment of a product provided for in a planning task.

An association shall have the right to refuse wholly or in part a product allotted to it and to conclude a contract, notifying such refusal to the supplier, fund holder, and agency which issued the allocation order within a period of not more than 10 days after receiving notification of the product allotted to it or after receiving the allocation order.

An association shall have the right also to refuse, by agreement with the supplier, to receive a product provided for by a contract, notifying the fund holder and the agency which issued the allocation order thereof within a 5 day period.

101. A production association (or combine) shall have the right to assign, with payment in the established procedure to organizations which fulfill scientific research and experimental construction design work for it, raw materials, materials, semi-finished products, and finished articles within the limits of funds allotted to it which are needed to carry on such work.

102. A production association (or combine) shall have the right to assign production wastes in excess of the plan for the transfer and processing of them by the association to other enterprises and organizations

which are necessary for their production and economic activity, unless otherwise established by prevailing legislation.

Rights and Duties in the Domain of Cadres, Labor, and Wages

103. A production association (or combine) shall select and place leading cadres in the nomenclature of the association, determine the current and long-term demand for labor resources according to standards, including specialists with a higher and specialized secondary education and qualified workers, take measures for the rational use of young specialists and graduates of professional-technical schools, and carry out measures directed toward the creation of permanent cadres of the association.

104. A production association (or combine) shall constantly improve its structure, achieving maximum reduction of expenditures for production management on the basis of applying optimal management schemes, standards for numbers of engineering and technical workers and employees, using the experience of associations which have the most economical management apparatus, and modern computer technology, mechanization and automation of engineering and technical and management work.

105. A production association (or combine) shall carry out and constantly improve the organization of labor and steadfastly raise the level of its normative standards; systematically verify prevailing labor norms and standards, introduce inter-branch and branch time norms in the established procedure and servicing and other standards whose application is mandatory, create conditions for high work productivity, achieving the constant growth of labor productivity; ensure observance of labor legislation and rules and norms for labor protection, safety technique, production sanitation, state social insurance, carry out therapeutic measures, and ensure observance of labor discipline.

Each member of the collective of an association should strictly observe the rules for internal labor discipline.

106. A production association (or combine) shall carry out measures to improve the organization of wages of workers and employees with a view to intensifying the material interest of workers both in the results of their personal labor and in the overall results of the work of production entities and the association as a whole, ensure the proper co-relation between the growth of labor productivity and the growth of wages, the economical and rational expenditure of the wage fund and the material incentive fund, and also timely accounts with workers and employees.

107. A production association (or combine) shall create a training materials base for the training of cadres directly at production and in accordance with USSR and union republic legislation shall ensure the training of new cadres, taking into account the requirements of scientific and technical progress, the training of workers in new professions, and systematically raising the production qualifications of workers. To these ends, besides individual and brigade apprenticeship, production-technical courses and schools for the study of progressive labor methods shall be organized in the association.

An association shall create the necessary conditions for workers who are studying in educational institutions without interruption from production to combine study with work and shall grant them the privileges provided for by prevailing legislation.

108. A production association (or combine) shall render all possible assistance to secondary general education evening (or shift) and correspondence schools, an evening (or shift) professional-technical high school, courses, and study and training combines for raising qualifications in which workers of the association study; ensure the necessary conditions for production training of pupils of secondary general education schools and students of higher and pupils of secondary specialized educational institutions; organize in accordance with prevailing legislation and carry out probationary training for graduates of higher educational institutions; grant work places and posts to higher and secondary specialized educational institutions and professional-technical high schools for placing their students (or pupils) during their production practice.

109. A production association (or combine) and production entities shall be given incentives for the successful fulfillment of the tasks before them in accordance with prevailing legislation and conditions of the socialist competition.

Incentives provided for by prevailing legislation, rules for internal labor discipline, and discipline charters shall be given to workers and employees of an association for achievements in work and for displaying initiative.

Workers and employees of an association shall be recommended in the established procedure for the awarding of orders and medals of the USSR and the conferment of honorary titles and the title Hero of Socialist Labor for especially outstanding innovative activity in the domain of economic construction and high production indicators.

110. A production association (or combine) shall ensure the systematic improvement of housing and cultural and domestic conditions of workers, organize the construction of dwelling houses, children's preschool institutions, hospitals, and designated cultural and domestic objects, and promote cooperative and individual housing construction.

111. A production association (or combine) shall:

(a) establish piece rates, time rates, or job rates for the labor of individual groups of workers, and in instances provided by prevailing legislation for engineering and technical workers and employees;

(b) work out and confirm in accordance with prevailing legislation statutes concerning bonuses in regard to the association as a whole, with a view to intensifying the material interest of workers of the association in the fulfillment and overfulfillment of production plans, the growth of labor productivity, the improvement of product quality, and also raising the efficiency and profitability of production. Indicators, conditions, and amounts of bonuses for leading workers of production entities (except head), and also for workers and engineering and technical workers and employees of a head production entity (if there is a special administrative apparatus, for engineering and technical workers and employees of this apparatus) shall be established by the director general (or director of the association. The indicators, conditions, and amounts of bonuses for workers, engineering and technical workers, and employees of other production entities shall be established by the directors of these production entities in accordance with the statutes concerning bonuses for workers of the association;

(c) work out and confirm a statute on the payment of remuneration for annual work results in regard to the association as a whole, on the basis of which directors of production entities shall confirm the procedure and conditions for the payment of remuneration to workers of such entities;

(d) determine the list of professions of workers for whom piece work rates shall be applied to time rates, and also individual professions of workers for whom monthly salaries shall replace time rates in accordance with a list confirmed in the established procedure. Piece work rates may be applied to time-rate workers on condition that their work is according to branch and other technical well-founded norms for labor expenditures (planning task, service, and personnel number standards);

(e) determine lists of professions of workers and of work paid according to rates established for workers engaged in heavy or harmful labor conditions, and especially heavy or especially harmful labor conditions, in accordance with prevailing model lists for such professions and work by branches of production;

(f) establish work grades and confer work grades in accordance with rates and qualification manuals;

(g) establish post duties and qualification requirements for directors, specialists, and technical performers in accordance with the qualifications manual for posts of employees and certify in the established procedure executive, engineering, and technical workers and other specialists of the association. When necessary, post instructions shall be worked out on the basis of the qualifications manual for individual categories of engineering and technical workers and employees;

(h) relegate production entities, and also shops, sectors, and other structural subdivisions of production entities to the appropriate group (or category) for the payment of labor of executive, engineering, and technical workers and employees, and also transfer them from one group (or category) to another in connection with a change of production volume, being guided by indicators confirmed in the established procedure (except for instances when a special procedure has been established for payment of labor for relegated groups (or categories);

(i) establish for workers with an unregulated working day the duration of additional leave in accordance with labor legislation and a list of posts of workers with an unregulated working day confirmed in the established procedure;

(j) introduce a summarized record of the working time of workers and employees of individual production entities or their subdivisions where because of the production (or work) conditions the daily or weekly duration of working time can not be observed for the particular category of workers and employees;

(k) confirm new and review prevailing norms for processing, servicing, numbers of workers, and other standards for labor expenditures in the established procedure, raising the specific gravity of technically well-founded norms;

(l) confirm a list of production units at which a short working day can not be established for workers by virtue of the nature of the work on the day before the day off (if there is a six day work week) or on days before holidays but who should be granted an additional day of leisure by accumulating overtime.

The measures specified in subpoints (a)-(l) of the present point shall be carried out by the director general (or director) of an association (and in the instances provided by subpoints (b) and (c), also by the director of a production entity) within the limits of the wage fund and the material incentive fund of the association (or production entity) and by agreement with the respective trade union agency;

(m) establish lists, by agreement with the respective trade union agency on the basis of branch norms confirmed in the procedure determined by the USSR Council of Ministers, of work and professions giving workers and employees the right to receive special clothing, footwear, and protective appliances free of charge, and also lists of work and professions giving workers and employees the right to receive milk in connection with harmful labor conditions and to receive special soap.

112. A production association (or combine) may, by agreement with the respective trade union agency when reviewing norms on the basis of introducing organizational and technical measures, use part of the assets received from economies in connection therewith for additional payment for the labor of workers during the period for the mastery of new processing and servicing norms of 3 to 6 months. The foreman and other engineering and technical workers of production sectors who have taken direct part in working out and introducing the said organizational and technical measures also may receive bonuses at the expense of assets from these economies.

113. A production association (or combine) shall have the right to establish wage increments for highly qualified foreman and other engineering and technical workers in an amount of up to 30 percent of the post salary within the limits of the planned wage fund, using for this purpose up to 0.3 percent of the planned wage fund of the association. The said increments shall not be taken into account when determining the amount of the average wage for the personnel establishment schedule.

114. A production association (or combine) shall have the right by agreement with the respective trade union agency to:

(a) establish lower processing norms for young workers who have begun work upon completing general education schools or professional-technical educational institutions and courses, and also training directly in production in the instances provided for by legislation and in the amounts and the periods determined for them;

(b) authorize, if advisable, the combining of professions (or posts), the expansion of servicing zones, or an increase of the amount of work fulfilled and establish appropriate supplemental payment in an amount of up to 30 percent of the rate or salary for workers, engineering and technical workers, and employees. Supplemental payments to rates or salaries may be reduced or completely eliminated when implementing measures for the introduction of new technology, improvement of the organization of labor and management of production, and introducing new standards for number of workers, servicing, and labor expenditures in connection therewith;

(c) establish supplemental payments in an amount of up to 30 percent of salary for heads of shops and their deputies, heads of shifts (or sectors), senior foremen, foremen, and other engineering and technical workers who work directly in shops which as a result of effectuating organizational and technical measures worked out have secured an increase in labor productivity in comparison with the plan by reducing the number of personnel in the sectors served. The maximum appropriations for maintenance of the management apparatus established for the association shall be increased with the authorization of the respective superior agency to the amount of the said supplemental payments. When reducing the level of labor productivity attained or increasing the number of personnel (except for instances when this is caused by a change of natural or mining and geological conditions), the supplemental payments to salaries may be lowered or eliminated;

(d) pay lump-sum remuneration to workers, leading and engineering and technical workers for working out and effectuating measures ensuring a reduction in the number of workers and raising labor productivity in comparison with the plan. The amount of remuneration shall be established depending on the level of increased labor productivity attained and the actual economies in the wage fund received from introducing the said measures.

The supplemental payments and remuneration provided for in subpoints (b), (c), and (d) of the present point shall be paid at the expense of economies in the wage fund obtained from freeing numbers of workers in comparison with inter-branch and branch standards for numbers of workers, servicing, and other standards for labor expenditures.

(e) make a supplemental payment to time-rate workers who are temporarily fulfilling the duties of absent workers together with their own work (in the event of illness, leave, business trip, and other reasons). The specific amount of supplemental payment for the fulfillment of the duties of an absent worker shall be determined by taking into account the actual amount of work fulfilled so that the total amount of supplemental payment, irrespective of the number of workers among whom it is distributed, did not exceed 50 percent of the rate (or salary) of the absent worker (except for instances when a higher amount of supplemental payment is provided for by decisions of the USSR Council of Ministers);

(f) establish a supplemental payment for brigade leaders from among the workers not released from basic work in the amounts provided for by prevailing legislation for directing a brigade consisting of more than 5 persons on condition that the brigade fulfills the established monthly planning task norms.

115. A production association (or combine) may preserve the average earnings in individual instances for qualified workers and engineering and technical workers of an association if they are transferred to production entities or shops newly introduced into operation for the period for mastery of production, but not more than 6 months if the earnings at the new place of work are lower than their earnings received at the previous place of work.

116. A production association (or combine) may use economies in the wage fund obtained in the preceding quarters and months, recalculated in accordance with the percentage of plan fulfillment (taking into account the prevailing standard) for the payment of wages and bonuses in subsequent quarters and months of the same year.

An overexpenditure of the wage fund shall be subject to reimbursement in the subsequent months. The unreplaced portion of the amount of the overexpenditure of the wage fund may be on the books of the enterprise for not longer than until July 1st of the following fiscal year. Bonuses deducted for leading workers of an association shall, in the event of a relative overexpenditure of the wage fund for the association as a whole, be reduced in the amount of the overexpenditure permitted, but not more than 50 percent of the bonuses calculated for the period until the overexpenditure is reimbursed. If an association reimburses the overexpenditure of the wage fund permitted within a period of up to six months, the said workers shall be paid 50 percent of the portion of the bonus which was not paid in the preceding period in connection with the overexpenditure of the wage fund.

Bonuses shall be paid in the said procedure in the event of the overexpenditure of the wage fund by executive workers of production entities and their structural subdivisions. The overexpenditure of the wage fund shall be taken into account only for the respective production entity (or subdivision).

If there is no overexpenditure of the wage fund for an association as a whole, the association may write off the unreimbursed overexpenditure of the wage fund for the preceding period for individual production entities.

If there are economies for the wage fund of the association as a whole, the association shall have the right to authorize the payment of bonuses in full amount also to the leading workers of production entities which improved their work but did not reimburse the overexpenditure of the wage fund permitted in the preceding period.

The procedure for writing off unreimbursed overexpenditure of the wage fund permitted by individual structural subdivisions of a production entity and for payment of bonuses to leading workers if there are wage fund economies for the production entity as a whole shall be determined by the director general (or director).

117. A production association (or combine) shall, within the limits of the total wage fund and appropriations for the maintenance of the management apparatus and in accordance with the list of production entities provided for by the association charter, work out the structure and personnel establishment of the association in conformity with model structures, personnel establishments, and standards for the number of engineering and technical workers and employees. The structure and personnel establishment of an association shall be confirmed by the director general (or director).

On the basis of prevailing legislation, the director general (or director) of an association shall establish and modify the post salaries for engineering and technical workers and employees in accordance with the scheme for post salaries and within the limits of the wage fund, computed by the average salaries for the post salary scheme.

A director (or head) of a production entity shall establish and modify post salaries for engineering and technical workers and employees in accordance with the scheme for post salaries and within the limits of the wage fund of a production entity, computed by the post salaries provided in its personnel establishment schedule confirmed by the director general (or director).

The director general (or director) shall confirm the expenditure estimate for the maintenance of the management apparatus of an association within the limits of the appropriations established for this purpose by the superior agency.

The personnel establishment, salaries, and expenditure estimate for the maintenance of the management apparatus which are confirmed by the director general (or director) shall not be subject to registration in financial agencies.

118. The director general (or director) may authorize business trips for workers of the association to factories, plants, scientific research organizations, and other production entities, independent enterprises, and organizations subordinate to the association, and also to other enterprises and organizations in accordance with prevailing legislation.

119. A production association (or combine) may, in exceptional instances, issue non-plan advance payments to individual workers at the expense of the wage fund in an amount of not more than a month's earnings.

120. A production association (or combine) shall have the right to send executive workers and employees, at their wish, for study at an institution of higher education or a technical school and to pay them higher stipends in accordance with prevailing legislation on condition that these workers make an obligation, upon completing the educational institution, to return to the enterprise which sent them to the institution of higher education. Candidates being sent for study at an institution of higher education or technical school for whom higher stipends have been established shall be nominated jointly with social organizations of the association.

121. A production association (or combine) may grant short-term leave without pay to workers at their request for family obligations and other justifiable reasons.

122. The measures specified in subpoints (a), (f), and (k) of point 111, subpoints (b), (d), and (f) of point 114, and points 119 and 121 may be carried out by a production entity in the procedure established by the director general (or director) by agreement with the respective trade union agency.

Rights and Duties in the Domain of Finances, Credit, Records, and Reports

123. A production association (or combine) shall organize and carry out work relating to financial planning, work out and implement measures relating to the fulfillment of financial plan planning tasks, the strengthening of economic accountability, planning and financial discipline, increasing profitability, ensure the safe keeping and the special and efficient use of circulating assets and accelerate their turnover, the fulfillment of the annual and quarterly planning tasks for payments to the budget established by the superior agency, timely accounts with the banks, suppliers, independent work contractors, superior organizations, and workers and employees for wages and obligations arising out of the financial plan and contracts.

When working out the financial plan, an association shall ensure the maximal mobilization of internal reserves, reduce production and circulation expenses, and increase accumulations on this basis.

124. Accounts with the budget, suppliers and buyers, independent work contractors, superior organization, credit relations, and also control on the part of banks over the expenditure of the wage fund and economic and financial activity shall be carried out for the production association (or combine) as a whole irrespective of the place where its production entities are situated.

A production entity which has a current account in the USSR State Bank and an account for financing capital investments in the USSR Construction Bank shall carry out accounts with suppliers, buyers, and independent work organizations in the procedure established respectively by the USSR State Bank and the USSR Construction Bank.

For associations to which independent enterprises and organizations enjoying the rights provided for by the Statute on the Socialist State Production Enterprise are subordinate, accounts with the budget for payments from profits shall be made by the enterprises and organizations themselves or may be made by the association centrally in the procedure established by the USSR Ministry of Finances by agreement with the ministry (or department) in whose system the association is.

125. A production association (or combine) shall open a checking account and other accounts at banks in the established procedure and perform the appropriate operations in regard to them.

126. A production association (or combine) may use bank credit and bear responsibility for its special use and timely return.

Applications for credits needed for the association shall be submitted by it in the established procedure to the USSR State Bank or the USSR Construction Bank, and also to the superior agency.

127. A production association (or combine) shall determine the standards for circulating assets according to the elements within the general standard, and also shall establish standards for the circulating assets of production entities.

128. A production association (or combine) shall fill in shortages of circulating assets formed as a result of the failure to fulfill the profit plan or carry out expenditures in excess of plan to be financed from profits, at the expense of the fulfillment of planning tasks established by the superior agency for receiving an additional profit from carrying out organization and technical measures, and also at the expense of part of the profit in excess of plan subject to being sent for this purpose in the established procedure, and of reducing deductions from profits to the economic incentive fund in an amount of up to 30 per cent within more than three years.

The procedure for filling in shortages of circulating assets formed at individual production entities as a result of their failure to fulfill the profit plan or carry out expenses in excess of plan to be financed from profits (if the general standard for circulating assets established for the association as a whole is preserved) shall be determined by the association, taking into account that this shortage should be filled in as a priority at the expense of the production entity from which it was formed, including at the expense of reducing the amount of assets of the economic incentive fund within limits of up to 30 percent allotted to the production entity.

129. A production association (or combine) shall, in accordance with prevailing legislation, confirm the prices (or tariffs) or work out and submit for confirmation in the established procedure prices (or tariffs) for the product (or work, services) issued and shall bear responsibility for observing state price discipline.

130. A production association (or combine) shall work out estimate and financial accounts and accounts for made up expenditures for carrying out measures within the limits established by prevailing legislation:

for the creation and introduction of new technology, new materials, the mechanization and automation of production, modernization of equipment, improvement of production technology, and rationalization and intensification of production processes;

for the organization and expansion of the production of consumer goods and improvement of their quality.

The said accounts shall be confirmed by the director general (or director) of the association.

131. A production association (or combine) shall have the right to write off from the balance sheet obsolete, worn out, and unsuitable equipment for further use, means of transport, inventory, and instruments when restoration of such property is impossible or economically inadvisable and it can not be realized.

An association also shall have the right to write off from the balance sheet buildings and installations demolished in connection with the construction of new objects or reconstruction, and also which have fallen into a dilapidated state.

132. A production association (or combine) shall have the right to write off as losses, notifying the superior agency thereof:

debts for which the period of limitation has expired;

judgment debts for which writs of execution have been returned with an act confirmed by a court concerning the insolvency of the defendant and the impossibility of levying execution on his property;

other debts deemed hopeless for collection by the association.

133. A production association (or combine) shall have the right to write off from its balance, notifying the superior agency, in each individual instance within the limits of up to 100 rubles:

shortages of valuables in excess of norms for natural loss, and also loss of goods, materials, and products from spoilage in instances when the specific guilty persons have not been ascertained;

debts relating to shortages of goods and material valuables, the recovery of which is refused by a court as a consequence of the groundlessness of the suit.

134. A production association (or combine) may write off losses from the balance provided for by points 132 and 133 of the present Statute only after a careful verification, with the participation of social organizations, of the causes of the losses, the exposure of the persons at fault, and after taking the necessary measures to recover from them the amounts expended in connection with the losses.

135. A production association (or combine) shall work out and confirm revenue plans and expenditure estimates for housing and municipal economy, expenditure estimates for the plant maintenance of buildings, premises, installations, gardens, parks, and pioneer camps transferred to trade union organizations free of charge.

136. A production association (or combine) shall keep bookkeeping, operational, and statistical records; draw up and submit a report in the established procedure to the appropriate agencies concerning all types of production and economic activity of the association in the confirmed forms and within the established periods and bear responsibility for its accuracy; carry out the centralization and mechanization of computer record work and introduce progressive record methods.

An association in which there are production entities situated on the territory of other districts, cities, regions, territories, and republics shall ensure the submission of reports to statistical agencies for the basic work indicators of each production entity in the procedure established by the USSR Central Statistical Administration.

137. An association archive shall be created at the production association (or combine) to keep documents of all production entities. Archives may be created at production entities situated beyond the place where the association is situated in order to serve them directly.

V. Reorganization and Liquidation of a Production Association (or Combine)

138. A production association (or combine) shall be reorganized (merged, joined, separated, and divided) or liquidated by decision of the agency which is empowered to form the respective association.

139. In the event a production association (or combine) is merged with another association (or enterprise, organization), all property rights and duties of each of them shall pass to the association which arose as a result of the merger.

If an association is joined to another association (or enterprise, organization), all property rights and duties of the joined association (or enterprise, organization) shall pass to it.

140. In the event a production association (or combine) is separated, the property rights and duties of the reorganized association shall pass to the new associations (or enterprises, organizations) which arose as a result of this separation according to the separation act in the respective portions.

If a new association (or enterprise, organization) is detached from an association, the property rights and duties of the reorganized association shall pass to it according to the separation act in the respective portions.

141. The procedure and period for liquidation of a production association (or combine) shall be established by the agency which adopted the decision concerning liquidation of the association. The question of the procedure for executing contracts concluded should be settled by the same agency without damage to the fulfillment of the state plan.

The period for creditors to file their claims against the association being liquidated shall be established by the agency by whose decision the liquidation is being done but may not be less than one month.

142. The liquidation of a production association (or combine) shall be carried out either by a liquidation commission appointed by the superior agency or, upon the commission of this agency, by the director general (or director) of the association being liquidated.

143. The liquidation commission or in proper instances the director general (or director) of the production association (or combine) being liquidated shall place an announcement in the official regional, territory, or republic press organ at the place where the association is situate concerning the liquidation of the association and the period for creditors to file claims. Irrespective thereof, the liquidation commission or the director general (or director) of the association being liquidated shall be

obliged to elucidate from available materials all claims of creditors of the enterprise and to notify them of its liquidation.

Claims against the association being liquidated shall be satisfied from its property against which according to law execution may be levied.

Claims uncovered or filed after expiry of the period established for creditors to file their claims shall be satisfied from the said property remaining after satisfying the claims uncovered, and also claims filed within the established period.

Claims not uncovered nor filed during the period of liquidation, and also claims not satisfied because the property of the enterprise being liquidated is insufficient, shall be considered extinguished. Claims not recognized by the liquidation commission (or director general, or director of the association being liquidated) also shall be considered extinguished in whole or respective part unless the creditors file a suit for satisfaction of the claim within two weeks from the date of receiving notification of their whole or partial nonrecognition.

144. The payment of periodic payments due from the production association (or combine) being liquidated in connection with the causing of mutilation or other harm to the health or of death shall be secured in the procedure established by prevailing legislation.

Claims and suits of citizens concerning compensation of harm connected with injury to health or of death, and also other claims and suits of citizens not filed for justifiable reasons before the completion of the liquidation, may be filed subsequently in the ordinary procedure against the agency superior to the association being liquidated. This agency may entrust satisfaction of the claims recognized by it or satisfied by a court to the association (or enterprise, organization) subordinate to it which has received the property of the liquidated enterprise.

* *
*

145. A production association (or combine) shall have a seal depicting the State Arms of the USSR (or union republic state arms) and its own name.

A production entity shall have a seal with its own name.

STATUTE ON THE SOCIALIST STATE PRODUCTION ENTERPRISE

[Confirmed by Decree of the USSR Council of Ministers, October 4, 1965. SP SSSR (1965), nos. 19-20, item 155]

I. General Provisions

1. The socialist state production enterprise shall be the basic link of the national economy of the USSR. Its activity shall be built on a combination of centralized direction with economic independence and initiative of the enterprise.

2. The socialist state production enterprise, using the state property allocated to its operative management or use, shall carry out its production and economic activity (manufacture of products, fulfillment of work, rendering of services) with the efforts of its collective under the direction of a superior agency in accordance with a national economic plan on the basis of economic accountability, shall fulfill its duties, and shall enjoy the rights connected with such activity, shall have an independent balance, and shall be a juridical person.

3. The present Statute shall extend to state industrial, construction, and agricultural enterprises, transport, and communications enterprises.

The peculiarities of applying the present Statute to construction and agricultural enterprises and transport and communications enterprises shall be established respectively by union republic councils of ministers or USSR ministries and departments on the basis of prevailing legislation for enterprises of the respective branch of the national economy.

4. An enterprise shall be managed on the basis of one-man-leadership. Social organizations and the entire collective of workers of the enterprise shall take an extensive part in the discussion and effectuation of measures to ensure the fulfillment of the state plan, the development and improvement of production and economic activity of the enterprise, and improvement of the labor and living conditions of its workers.

5. An enterprise shall be obliged in all its activity to observe socialist legality and state discipline. The rights granted to an enterprise should be used in the interests of the entire national economy and collective of workers of the enterprise.

Agencies of economic direction should ensure the strict observance of the rights of the enterprise and control over the fulfillment by the enterprise of its duties.

6. An enterprise shall be formed by order (or decision) of a superior agency in accordance with USSR or union republic legislation.

7. An enterprise shall have a charter confirmed by the agency which adopted the decision to form the enterprise, and in instances provided for by USSR or union republic legislation shall function on the basis of a general statute concerning enterprises of the particular type.

The charter of an enterprise should contain:

the name (or number) of the enterprise and its location (postal address);

name of the agency to which the enterprise is directly subordinate (superior agency);

the object and purpose of the activity of the enterprise;

an indication as to whether the enterprise has a charter fund;

an indication as to whether the enterprise operates on the basis of the present Statute and is a juridical person;

the name of the official heading the enterprise (director, manager, head).

If the enterprise consists of several production entities (point 10), a special indication to that effect shall be made in the charter of the enterprise and the production entities shall be enumerated.

Other provisions not contrary to law and connected with the peculiarities of the activity of the enterprise also may be included in the charter.

An enterprise shall acquire rights and duties connected with its production and economic activity and shall be a juridical person from the date its charter is confirmed, and in instances when it functions on the basis of a general statute on enterprises of the particular type, from the date the respective agency adopts the decision to form it.

8. An enterprise shall exercise the right of possession, use, and disposition of property under its operative management and the right to use the land allotted to it within the limits established by law in accordance with the purposes of the activity of the enterprise, planning tasks, and purpose of the property.

9. An enterprise shall be liable for its obligations with that property allocated to it upon which execution may be levied according to USSR and union republic legislation.

An enterprise shall not be liable for obligations of the organization to which it is subordinate nor for the obligations of other enterprises and organizations. The organization to which the enterprise is subordinate shall not be liable for its obligations. Exceptions to these rules shall be allowed in instances provided by USSR and union republic legislation.

The state shall not be liable for the obligations of an enterprise, and an enterprise shall not be liable for the obligations of the state.

10. A combine, trust, firm, or other economic organization which includes production entities which are not independent enterprises shall operate in accordance with the present Statute as a production enterprise.

A combine, trust, or other economic organization to which independent enterprises are subordinate shall operate with respect to them as an agency of economic administration.

A combine, trust, firm, or other economic organization that includes production entities which are not independent enterprises and to which at the same time independent enterprises are subordinate shall exercise with respect to the former and with respect to the production activity fulfilled directly by the organization itself the rights and duties of a production enterprise in accordance with the present Statute, and shall operate as an agency of economic administration with respect to independent enterprises subordinate to it.

II. Property and Assets of the Enterprise

11. The basic and circulating assets allocated to an enterprise shall form its charter fund, the amount of which shall be reflected in the balance of the enterprise.

12. The total amount (or normative standard) of its own circulating assets shall be established for the enterprise upon its recommendation by the superior agency and may be changed during the year only in connection with a change in the production plan of the enterprise.

Circulating assets allocated to an enterprise within the limits of the normative standard may not be withdrawn from it by a superior agency.

Surplus circulating assets (in excess of the normative standard) may be withdrawn from an enterprise by a superior agency only by way of redistribution pursuant to the annual report of the enterprise or when changing the normative standard of its circulating assets in connection with a change in the production plan of the enterprise.

13. An enterprise shall make amortization deductions for capital repairs and for complete renewal of basic funds.

Amortization deductions designated for capital repairs shall constitute a special fund of the enterprise and shall be expended by it both for capital repairs and for modernization of the basic funds, and also for the acquisition of components and assemblies to fulfill such work and replace worn components and assemblies.

In those instances when it is economically advisable, an enterprise may, instead of capital repairs, acquire new equipment at the expense of amortization deductions designated for capital repairs.

With a view to the most rational use of amortization deduction assets designated for capital repairs, an enterprise shall transfer up to 10% of the total amount of such deductions to the superior agency in order to create a reserve for rendering assistance to those enterprises whose own assets are inadequate to carry out capital repairs.

Amortization deductions designated for the complete renewal of basic funds shall be assigned for the financing of capital investments in accordance with prevailing legislation.

14. The profit of an enterprise (and for an enterprise whose plan does not provide for obtaining a profit, economies from reducing production costs) shall be distributed in accordance with its balance of revenues and expenditures (financial plan) and in the procedure established by the USSR Council of Ministers.

With a view to increasing the material interest of the collective of an enterprise in the fulfillment of the plan and of ensuring the profitability of production, deductions shall be made from profits received and at the disposal of the enterprise (or economies from reducing production costs), which shall form the enterprise fund for improving the cultural and domestic conditions of workers and for improving production (enterprise fund). The amount of the deductions from profit (or economies from reducing production costs) and the procedure for forming and using the enterprise fund shall be determined for enterprises of various branches of production by statutes on the enterprise fund confirmed by the USSR Council of Ministers.

Assets from the enterprise fund shall be expended on the implementation of measures for new technology, for modernizing equipment, for expanding production, for repairs of the housing fund, for housing and cultural and domestic construction, for individual bonuses, for improvement of cultural, domestic, and medical services for workers, for the acquisition of medicines for medical and sanitary institutions of the enterprise, for passes to rest homes and sanatoriums, and for rendering assistance to workers with extraordinary aid.

The withdrawal and redistribution of assets of the enterprise fund by a superior agency shall not be permitted.

The profit obtained from the realization of consumer goods and manufactures made from production wastes shall remain wholly at the disposal of the enterprise (enterprise fund) and shall be used in the procedure established by the USSR Council of Ministers.

Living premises in houses built at the expense of assets of the enterprise fund and consumer goods fund shall be occupied completely by persons on a list confirmed by joint decision of the administration of the enterprise and the factory, plant, and local trade union committee, the executive committee of the soviet of working people's deputies being subsequently notified.

15. An enterprise shall deduct assets in the established procedure for bonuses to workers for work relating to the creation and introduction of new technology and to form a fund for the mastery of new technology.

16. An enterprise may lease to other enterprises and organizations, at rental rates prevailing in the particular locality, buildings and installations, as well as production, warehouse, and other premises allocated for the enterprise, which are temporarily not being used.

An enterprise also may lease to other enterprises and organizations equipment and means of transport temporarily not being used. Payment for the use of equipment and means of transport leased shall be exacted in the amount of the amortization deductions for the particular type of property.

Means of transport which belong to transport enterprises and are temporarily not being used shall be leased with the authorization of the superior agency.

17. An enterprise shall grant for use free of charge to the factory, plant, and local trade union committee buildings, premises, installations, gardens, and parks which are on the balance of the enterprise or are leased by it and are designated for cultural, enlightenment, therapeutic, physical culture, and sport work among the workers of the enterprise and members of their families, pioneer camps, and also buildings, premises, and installations designated for technical propaganda.

The economic maintenance, repair, heating, lighting, cleaning, guarding, and equipping of the said facilities shall be at the expense of the enterprise. In instances when workers of other enterprises and organizations use them, these enterprises and organizations shall participate in a share of the said expenditures.

An enterprise shall grant to the factory, plant, and local trade union committee and other social organizations the use free of charge of premises necessary for their work and holding meetings of workers and employees, shall provide equipment, heating, lighting, guarding, and cleaning of these premises, and also shall grant to the said organizations the use, free of charge, of means of transport and of communication.

An enterprise shall transfer without compensation, from balance sheet to balance sheet, to the trade union and other social organizations of the enterprise the cultural, domestic, and sport inventory acquired by the enterprise at the expense of the enterprise fund, the consumer goods fund, and amounts for bonuses for the socialist competition.

18. An enterprise shall grant free of charge to:

its medical and sanitary institution (or center): premises, with heating, lighting, water supply, guarding, cleaning, and repair of the premises;

lunchroom and other public dining organizations on its territory or calculated in the balance sheet of the enterprises and servicing the collective of its workers: premises, with heating, lighting, and water supply for the premises.

19. An enterprise may grant without compensation to:

a school for working (or rural) youth, an evening (or shift) professional-technical school and courses for raising qualifications in which workers of the enterprise study and a plant higher technical school and secondary school attached to it: premises for study purposes, necessary equipment, tools, instruments, and materials for study laboratories and rooms, providing the repair and servicing of the premises, including the supply of electric power and fuel;

a higher or secondary specialized educational institution: models of machines, machine tools, instruments, and equipment, as well as items displayed at exhibitions which may be used for study purposes.

20. Buildings, installations, functioning equipment, and other basic assets allocated to an enterprise may be transferred to other enterprises and organizations in the procedure established by USSR and union republic legislation.

21. Surplus equipment, means of transport, tools, instruments, inventory, raw materials, materials, fuel, draft and productive livestock, seed, and fodder not being used at an enterprise may be sold by the enterprise to other enterprises and organizations on condition that the superior agency refuses to redistribute the surpluses, and also if no reply has been received within a month after sending notification of the existence of surpluses.

Materials, instruments, and other material valuables acquired by an enterprise by way of local procurements shall be realized by the enterprise independently.

Amounts received as a result of the sale of material valuables which are circulating assets shall remain at the disposal of the enterprises as its circulating assets.

Amounts received from the sale of material valuables which are basic assets shall remain at the disposal of the enterprise and shall be assigned by it for capital investments in excess of the established annual plan.

22. Workers of the enterprise shall be obliged to be careful with state property, properly use the buildings, installations, and equipment, and observe strict economy in the expenditure of material and cash assets. Persons guilty of damaging state property and causing material harm to the state shall bear responsibility in the established procedure.

III. Production and Economic Activity of the Enterprise

23. An enterprise shall, when carrying out production and economic activity on the basis of economic accountability in accordance with the plan, ensure in the interests of the national economy the achievement of the best results with the least expenditures of labor, material, and financial resources, maximally use production capacities, internal reserves, and land and other natural resources granted for its use, introduce the latest achievements of science, technology, and progressive experience, and also progressive norms for the expenditure of raw materials, materials, fuel, electric power, reduce production costs for products (or work, services), and raise the profitability of production. An enterprise shall use as fully as possible the local sources of raw materials and materials, as well as production wastes.

The production and economic activity of shops, sectors, divisions, and other internal links of the enterprise shall be carried out, as a rule, on the basis of internal economic accountability.

24. An enterprise shall ensure high quality, reliability, and durability of products produced (or work or services fulfilled) in accordance with state standards, technical conditions, models, conditions, norms, and rules.

An enterprise shall constantly improve the products produced by it (or work or services fulfilled) on the basis of the achievements of science, technology, progressive experience, and taking into account the demands of the national economy, the needs of the populace, and the aesthetic requirements of Soviet society.

To this end, an enterprise shall be obliged to submit proposals for the consideration of the appropriate agencies concerning the removal from production and replacement of obsolete machines, mechanisms, and other items which do not meet the needs of consumers, and proposals concerning the improvement of state standards, technical conditions, and other norms determining the quality of products (or work or services), and for consumer goods, to remove obsolete products from production and replace them with new products in demand by the populace.

25. An enterprise shall carry out the construction, reconstruction, and also the capital repair of basic funds in accordance with confirmed plans, itemized lists of construction projects, and design and estimate documentation, and shall ensure the timely mastery of new production capacities and most rapid introduction of acquired equipment into operation.

26. An enterprise shall organize work relating to inventions, shall ensure the timely consideration and introduction of inventions and rationalization proposals and timely payment of the establishment rewards to inventors and rationalizers, and support and encourage innovators in production.

An enterprise shall ensure the extensive use of the achievements of domestic and foreign science and technology and patent materials when working out new and improving existing technology, and also the protection of the priority of Soviet inventions by filing applications for the issuance of author's certificates in the USSR and obtaining, when necessary, patents abroad in the established procedure.

27. An enterprise shall make rational use of technical means of railway, water, air, and automotive transport, systematically improve the organization of loading and unloading and transport work, and carry out the mechanization of such work and measures to reduce the demurrage of means of transport when loading and unloading.

28. An enterprise shall carry out operative activity regarding the material-technical provision for production. To this end, the enterprise shall, proceeding from established normative standards, submit timely and well-founded applications for material resources distributed by way of planning which are needed to fulfill the basic program to carry out experimental work, to fulfill the plan for organizational and technical measures and for repair and operational needs, realize material resources allotted by funds, and also independently acquire other material resources needed for the enterprise.

An enterprise should have reserves of raw materials, materials, fuel, and other resources in accordance with the established normative standards which ensure the continuous and rhythmic work without allowing the formation of reserves in excess of the plan.

29. In accordance with confirmed plans and concluded contracts, an enterprise shall produce and deliver products while observing the nomenclature, assortment, and proper quality and completeness and ensuring priority of delivery for all-union needs.

The failure of an enterprise to fulfill plans and planning tasks for deliveries of products shall be a flagrant violation of state discipline and shall entail responsibility of the guilty officials in the established procedure.

An enterprise may manufacture a product in excess of the established plan only on condition that the sale of this product is ensured.

30. An enterprise should expand and strengthen in every possible way the direct economic links with enterprises and consumer organizations with a view to better providing the consumers of products with the proper quality and the nomenclature and assortment which they need.

A change in direct links that have formed between suppliers and customers in regard to deliveries shall be permitted, when necessary, with observance of the procedure established by prevailing legislation.

An enterprise producing consumer goods shall organize the production of these goods on the basis of orders from trading organizations and contracts concluded with them.

31. An enterprise shall dispose of its own financial resources, ensuring the maximum economies in the expenditure of assets and the purpose of their use, and also the timely accounts with the state budget, bank institutions, suppliers, independent contractors, and other organizations.

32. An enterprise shall keep bookkeeping, operative, and statistical records, introduce progressive methods and forms of records and computer work, draw up reports according to the confirmed forms, and submit them to the appropriate agencies within the established periods.

33. An enterprise shall constantly improve its structure, achieving maximum reduction of expenditures for the management of production on the basis of applying the most progressive management schemes and introducing modern computer technology, mechanization, and automation of engineering, technical, and administrative work.

34. An enterprise shall carry out and constantly improve the organization and rate-fixing of labor, create conditions for highly productive work, achieving constant growth in labor productivity, ensure the observance of labor legislation, rules and norms for labor protection, technical safety, production sanitation, and state social insurance, carry out therapeutic measures, and ensure the observance of labor discipline.

Each member of the collective of an enterprise should strictly observe the rules for internal labor discipline.

35. An enterprise shall carry out measures to improve the organization of wages for workers and employees with a view to intensifying the material interest of workers both in the results of their personal labor and in the total results of the work of the enterprise and shall ensure the proper co-relation between the growth of labor productivity and the growth of wages, the economical and rational expenditure of the wage fund, and timely accounts with workers and employees.

36. An enterprise shall, in accordance with USSR and union republic legislation, ensure the training of new cadres of workers directly on the production line and the teaching of new professions to workers and systematically raise the production qualifications of workers. To this end, in addition to individual and brigade apprenticeships, production and technical courses, schools for the study of progressive labor methods shall be organized at the enterprise.

An enterprise shall create the necessary conditions for workers studying at educational institutions without interrupting work to combine study with work and grant them the exceptions provided by prevailing legislation.

37. An enterprise shall render all possible assistance to the school for working (or rural) youth, the evening (or shift) professional-technical school, and the courses for raising qualifications at which workers of the enterprise are studying; ensure the necessary conditions for the production training of pupils from secondary general education schools and students of higher and pupils of secondary specialized educational institutions; grant to higher, secondary specialized educational institutions, and professional-technical schools, in accordance with prevailing legislation, the work places and posts to place their students (or pupils).

38. An enterprise shall ensure the systematic improvement of housing, cultural, and domestic conditions for workers, organize the construction of dwelling houses, preschool children's institutions, hospitals, and cultural and domestic objects, and promote cooperative and individual housing construction.

39. An enterprise shall be rewarded for successfully fulfilling its tasks in accordance with prevailing legislation and the conditions of socialist competition.

Workers and employees of an enterprise shall be rewarded with honorary certificates and bonuses for achievements in work and for displaying initiative; honorary titles may be conferred on them.

Workers and employees of an enterprise shall be recommended for the awarding of orders and medals of the USSR and the conferment of the title Hero of Socialist Labor in the established procedure for especially outstanding innovations in economic construction and high production indicators.

40. The activity of an enterprise should not violate the normal work conditions of other enterprises and organizations nor worsen the living conditions of citizens.

An enterprise shall carry out all necessary measures to protect the air, soil, and bodies of water from pollution by industrial and economic refuse, sewage waters, and production wastes, as well as to struggle against noise and radio interference.

IV. Rights of an Enterprise

41. The rights belonging to an enterprise which are connected with its production and economic activity shall be exercised by the director (or manager, head) and according to the established distribution of duties, by other officials of the enterprise, and in instances provided for by prevailing legislation, jointly by agreement with or with the participation of the factory, plant, and local trade union committee.

42. Individual important enterprises may, in the procedure determined by the USSR Council of Ministers, be endowed by superior agencies of economic direction with the additional rights granted to such agencies.

Rights in the Domain of Planning

43. An enterprise shall, proceeding from control figures, work out with the extensive participation of workers and employees and taking into account the need to provide the needs of the national economy, the economic links which have been formed with consumers, sale, and trading organizations, and the further development of such links, draft long-term and annual plans for all types of its activity in accordance with established indicators.

44. The superior agency shall consider, involving the enterprise, and shall confirm for it the long-term and annual planning tasks according to the established indicators.

All planned tasks shall be communicated to an enterprise only by the superior agency.

45. An enterprise shall, in accordance with indicators established for it by the plan and contracts concluded, work out an expanded annual technical-industrial-financial plan (or industrial-financial, construction-financial plan, and so forth) quarterly, and monthly plans for production and economic activity, which shall be confirmed by the director of the enterprise.

An enterprise shall establish independently the quantitative and qualitative plan indicators for shops, sections, services, sectors, production, and other structural subdivisions, ensuring the fulfillment of the planning tasks established for it with the greatest economic efficiency.

46. Planning tasks established for an enterprise should be mutually coordinated and should provide for the full use of production capacities.

The superior agency shall provide an enterprise with the appropriate material-technical and financial resources and the wage fund needed to fulfill the planning task.

47. Planning tasks confirmed for an enterprise may be changed by the superior agency only in exceptional instances, with a preliminary discussion of these questions with the administration of the enterprise in the procedure and within the periods established by the USSR Council of Ministers.

When planning tasks for an enterprise are changed by a superior agency, the necessary changes in all inter-related planning indicators, as well as in the accounts of the enterprise with the budget, should be made simultaneously.

48. An enterprise shall have the right to accept orders from other enterprises and organizations for performing work and manufacturing products in excess of the plan from raw materials and materials of the customer or from their own materials and production wastes unless harm would be caused to the fulfillment of the state plan established for it and to contractual obligations.

Rights in the Domain of Capital Construction and Capital Repair

49. An enterprise shall carry out capital construction and the reconstruction of basic funds under independent-work contracts concluded with construction and assembly organizations. In instances when the performance of capital construction work by independent-work means is economically inadvisable, the fulfillment of such work may be carried out by economic means.

50. An enterprise shall conclude contracts with design organizations to work out design and estimate documentation. Design and estimate documentation shall be confirmed in the procedure established by the USSR Council of Ministers.

There shall be confirmed by the director of an enterprise:

title lists for construction of all objects being carried out at the expense of assets of the enterprise fund and consumer goods fund;

title lists for the construction of dwelling houses and cultural and domestic objects and municipal economy being carried out at the expense of centralized capital investments, except for title lists for the construction of clubs in cities, palaces of culture, and sport, stadiums, and swimming pools;

title lists for work to ensure labor protection, technical safety, and production sanitation;

title lists of interior building by agreement with an independent contractor.

Title lists for the construction of objects at the expense of assets of the enterprise fund and consumer goods fund, and also title lists for work to ensure labor protection, technical safety, and production sanitation, shall be confirmed by the director of an enterprise by agreement with the factory, plant, and local trade union committee.

51. An enterprise shall have the right to transfer by contracts with independent-work organizations with their consent the fulfillment of construction and assembly work and the respective quotas for labor, funds,

and materials in connection therewith, subsequently notifying the superior agency.

52. Capital repair plans and the respective estimate and financial accounts shall be confirmed by the director of an enterprise. Capital repairs of basic assets shall be carried out by both economic and independent-work means.

If an enterprise transfers an amount of capital repair work to an independent work organization to be fulfilled by independent-work means, the enterprise shall have the right to transfer to the independent work organization the appropriate quotas for labor, funds, and materials, subsequently notifying the superior agency thereof.

53. An enterprise shall have the right to confirm, by agreement with the independent-work organization, individual prices for work the requirement for which arises in the course of construction unless prices for such work have been confirmed in the established procedure.

54. An enterprise shall have the right to enlist its own specialists to draw up designs for the reconstruction of shops, sectors, divisions, farms, or changes of technological processes and to fulfill work relating to the adaptation of model designs, and paying for the labor of the enlisted specialists in the procedure established for the respective categories of workers of design organizations.

55. An enterprise shall have the right to use part of the assets allotted to it in a centralized procedure for housing construction in order to build preschool children's institutions. These assets shall be used by decision adopted by the director of the enterprise jointly with the factory, plant, and local trade union committee.

56. An enterprise shall have the right to combine with other enterprises and organizations assets of the enterprise fund and other special assets at its disposal, for the joint (by way of shares) construction of dwelling houses, medical, and preschool children's institutions, pioneer camps, and other cultural and domestic objects.

Rights in the Domain of Improving Technology and Production Technology

57. An enterprise shall confirm the technological processes of production insofar as they have not been established by an agency which effectuates a uniform technological policy in the particular branch of production.

When necessary, an enterprise shall have the right to modify technological processes established by the respective agencies which effectuate a uniform technological policy in the particular branch of production if such modifications improve the quality (increase durability or reliability) of their product or, without worsening its quality nor violating state standards and technical conditions, reduce its production cost or give another positive result, except for technological processes whose modification without the consent of the agencies which confirmed them is prohibited. The agency which confirmed it should be notified immediately about the modification of the technological process.

Agricultural enterprises shall establish systems for carrying on agriculture and its individual branches; the pattern of arable land use; periods for sowing, and other technological processes of agricultural production.

The procedure for confirming and changing technological processes for the work of transport and communications enterprises shall be established by the respective ministry (or department).

58. An enterprise shall confirm technical conditions by agreement with the customers for individual product types for which there are no state standards and technical conditions have not been established by the appropriate agencies, having in view the issuance of products of a high technical level.

An enterprise shall have the right to issue by agreement with the customer a product of higher quality by comparison with the requirements of state standards or technical conditions. The additional expenditures connected therewith shall be reimbursed by the enterprise in the established procedure, taking into account the economic efficiency of the higher quality products.

59. An enterprise shall confirm norms for the expenditure of raw materials, materials, fuel, electric power, seed, fodder, and fertilizer unless the confirmation of such norms is relegated to the jurisdiction of superior agencies.

60. An enterprise shall, in accordance with prevailing legislation, have the right to conclude contracts with scientific research, design, and construction design organizations and institutions of higher education for the working out of new technology and production technology, designs for the reconstruction of the enterprise, and its shops, sectors, divisions, and farms, the modernization of equipment, mechanization and automation of production processes, and the organization of labor and production.

Expenditures for the said works shall be at the expense of assets of the enterprise, and also at the expense of a bank credit.

Rights in the Domain of Material-Technical Supply and Sale

61. An enterprise shall acquire the equipment, raw materials, materials, fuel, and other material valuables necessary for its production and economic activity by contracts for delivery concluded on the basis of planning acts for the distribution of products (allocation orders, fund notifications, and others).

The said material valuables also may be acquired on the basis of allocation orders accepted for execution (or documents replacing them) which contain all the data needed to effectuate the delivery unless agreement on any additional condition is required.

An enterprise may acquire necessary articles of material-technical supply from state and cooperative organizations by concluding contracts with them for a product realized without allocation orders, and also by purchases from small, specialized depots and retail trade stores in the procedure established by prevailing legislation.

62. An enterprise shall have the right when concluding a contract for delivery to refuse a superfluous or unnecessary product allocated to it, notifying such refusal to the supplier, fundholder, and the agency which issued the allocation order within ten days after receiving the allocation order.

An enterprise shall have the right also to refuse by agreement with the supplier to receive a product provided for by a contract in the event its requirements change, notifying the fundholder and agency which issued the allocation order thereof within fifteen days.

63. An enterprise shall have the right to transfer funds to other enterprises and organizations or to issue them resources of materials and sets of equipment according to the established norms for manufacture by contract of a product needed by the particular enterprise.

64. An enterprise shall have the right to commission by contracts the realization of funds for materials, raw materials, and equipment to other enterprises and organizations with payment of the expenses connected therewith according to the established norms.

65. An enterprise may conclude contracts for delivery to it of equipment, machines, and other material valuables which are subject to being relegated to basic funds of the enterprise within the limits of assets available therefor or at the expense of a bank credit.

An enterprise shall have the right to acquire special equipment, tools, and materials for carrying on scientific research and experimental design work within the limits of appropriations allocated for the production of such work.

66. An enterprise shall effectuate the sale of products by contracts for delivery, except for instances when another procedure has been established by USSR and union republic legislation.

Contracts for the delivery of a product distributed by a superior agency or sold by an organization shall be concluded on the basis of distribution acts (or allocation orders) issued by this agency or organization.

Contracts for the realization of products which are not distributed in the said procedure shall be concluded by an enterprise independently by agreement with the respective buyer organization (or customer).

67. An enterprise shall have the right by agreement with the buyer (or customer) to modify when necessary the assortment, periods, and other conditions for delivery established in the contract and to make delivery before time at the expense of overfulfilling the production plan or at the expense of products not chosen by other consumers.

An enterprise shall notify the respective agencies about modifying the assortment of the product established by the planning task.

68. An enterprise shall have the right to realize to other state and cooperative enterprises and organizations without funds, including collective farms, a product which is not sold by allocation orders.

69. An enterprise shall have the right to release, with payment in the established procedure, raw materials, semifinished items, and finished manufactures, the demand for which arises in the process of the fulfillment of scientific research and experimental design work, to scientific institutions.

70. An enterprise shall have the right to release in the established procedure to other enterprises and organizations the production wastes needed for their production and economic activity which are in excess of the plan for their delivery to and processing by the particular enterprise.

Rights in the Domain of Finances

71. An enterprise shall determine the normative standards for its own circulating assets by elements within the limits of the total normative standard established by the superior agency, proceeding from planning tasks and in accordance with norms for the expenditure and reserves of goods and material valuables.

Normative standards worked out by an enterprise for its own circulating assets should further the most rational and efficient use of material and financial resources and accelerate the turnover of circulating assets.

72. An enterprise may use a bank credit and shall bear responsibility for its use and its timely repayment.

73. An enterprise shall work out estimate and financial accounts and accounts for the recoupment of expenditures for carrying out measures, within the limits established by prevailing legislation, for:

the creation and introduction of new technology and new materials, for the mechanization and automation of production, the modernization of equipment, the improvement of production technology and the rationalization and intensification of production processes;

the organization and expansion of production of consumer goods and improvement of their quality.

The said accounts shall be confirmed by the director of the enterprise.

74. An enterprise shall establish prices and tariffs in accordance with prevailing legislation for individual types of products (or work, services) and prices and tariffs which are not subject to confirmation by superior agencies. Prices for a product and the amount of payment for work and services (except those designated for internal needs of the enterprise) shall be established by agreement with the customer enterprise.

75. An enterprise shall have the right to write off from the balance sheet obsolete, worn out, and unsuitable equipment for further use, means of transport, inventory, and instruments when restoration of such property is impossible or economically inadvisable and it can not be realized.

An enterprise also shall have the right to write off from the balance buildings and installations demolished in connection with the construction of new objects and also which have fallen into a dilapidated state.

76. An enterprise shall have the right to write off as losses, notifying the superior agency thereof:

debts for which the period of limitations has expired;

judgment debts for which writs of execution have been returned with an act confirmed by a court concerning the insolvency of the defendant and the impossibility of levying execution on his property;

other debts deemed hopeless for collection by the enterprise.

77. An enterprise shall have the right to write off from its balance sheet, notifying the superior agency, in each individual instance within the limits of up to 100 rubles:

shortages of valuables in excess of norms for natural loss, and also loss of goods, materials, and products from spoilage in instances when the specific guilty persons have not been ascertained;

debts relating to shortages of goods and material valuables, the recovery of which is refused by a court as a consequence of the groundlessness of the suit.

78. An enterprise may write off losses from the balance provided for by points 76 and 77 of the present Statute only after a careful verification, with the participation of social organizations, of the causes of the losses, the exposure of the persons at fault, and after taking the necessary measures to recover from them the amounts expended in connection with the losses.

79. An enterprise shall work out an estimate for administrative and management expenditures, proceeding from the need for every possible economy of assets, within the limits of the total wage fund and appropriations for administrative and management expenditures confirmed by the superior agency for the enterprise.

The estimate for administrative and management expenditures shall be confirmed and changed by the director of the enterprise.

80. An enterprise may allocate its production and economic units to a separate balance; liability for obligations connected with the activity of these production and economic units shall be borne by the enterprise. Assets and liabilities of the balances of the said production and economic units shall be included in the general balance of the enterprise.

Rights in the Domain of Labor and Wages

81. The right shall be granted to an enterprise:

(a) to establish piece rates, time rates, or job rates for the labor of individual groups of workers;

(b) to determine a list of professions of workers for which piece work rates shall be applied to time rates and for which monthly salaries shall replace time rates;

(c) to determine lists of professions of workers and of work paid according to rates established for workers engaged in hot or heavy work, work with harmful labor conditions, and work with especially heavy and harmful labor conditions in accordance with prevailing model lists for such professions and work by branches of production;

(d) to establish indicators and conditions of bonuses for workers on the basis of model statutes;

(e) to establish work grades and to confer work grades in accordance with rates and qualification manuals. Workers of new professions shall be rated according to the characteristics of analogous work contained in the manuals, informing the superior agency;

(f) to establish the indicators, conditions, and amounts of bonuses for engineering and technical workers and employees of individual production shops, sectors, and services, taking into account the specific tasks of the respective subdivisions of the enterprise and being guided by the conditions for bonuses and the amounts of bonuses established by model statutes;

(g) to relegate the shops, sectors, divisions, farms, and other internal links of an enterprise to the appropriate group for the payment of labor of leading and engineering and technical workers and employees, and also to transfer them from one group to another in connection with a change of production volume, being guided by indicators confirmed in the established procedure;

(h) to establish for workers with an unregulated working day the duration of additional leave in accordance with labor legislation and a list of posts of workers with an unregulated working day confirmed by the superior agency;

(i) to introduce a summarized record of the working time of workers and employees of individual production units, shops, sectors, and divisions where it is impossible to establish a working day of normal duration; to change, in agricultural enterprises at the interval of intense work (sowing, crop cultivation, laying in of fodder, harvesting, autumn ploughing), the duration of the working day within the limits of the normal work time for the record period, paying for the work actually fulfilled according to existing norms and prices.

The procedure for adding up the working time at agricultural enterprises shall be established by the USSR Council of Ministers;

(j) to confirm new and to revise prevailing norms for processing and services in the established procedure;

(k) to confirm a list of production units at which a short working day can not be established for workers by virtue of the nature of the work on holidays and days before holidays but who should be granted an additional day of leisure by accumulating overtime;

(l) to authorize, when advisable, workers to combine professions with payment in the established procedure.

The measures specified in subpoints (a)-(l) of the present point shall be carried out by the director of the enterprise within the limits of the wage fund of the particular enterprise and by agreement with the factory, plant, and local trade union committee;

(m) to establish lists, by agreement with the factory, plant, and local trade union committee on the basis of branch norms confirmed in the procedure determined by the USSR Council of Ministers, of work and professions giving workers and employees the right to receive special clothing, footwear, and protective appliances free of charge, and also lists of work and professions giving workers and employees the right to receive milk in connection with harmful labor conditions and to receive special soap.

82. An enterprise shall work out the structure and personnel establishments of the enterprise according to model structures and personnel establishments confirmed by the superior agency in the established procedure. The structure and personnel establishment of the enterprise shall be confirmed by the director.

The director of an enterprise shall confirm and change, on the basis of prevailing legislation, the wages of engineering and technical workers and employees in accordance with the scheme for posts within the limits of the wage fund, and also the average wage according to the personnel establishment schedule.

The personnel establishment, salaries, and also the estimate for administrative and management expenditures confirmed by the director of an enterprise shall not be subject to registration in financial agencies.

83. An enterprise shall have the right to establish increments in wages of up to 30 per cent of the post salary within the limits of the planned wage fund for highly qualified skilled workers and other engineering and technical workers, using for this purpose with the authorization of the superior agency of economic direction up to 0.3 per cent of the planned wage fund of the enterprise. The said increments shall not be taken into account when determining the amount of the average wage for the personnel establishment schedule.

84. An enterprise may use economies in the wage fund obtained in the preceding quarters and months, recalculated in accordance with the percentage of plan fulfillment, for the payment of wages and bonuses in subsequent quarters and months of the same year.

An overexpenditure of the wage fund shall be subject to reimbursement in the subsequent months, and leading workers of the enterprise who allowed the overexpenditure of the wage fund shall be deprived of a bonus for the period before its reimbursement. The unreplaced portion of the amount of the overexpenditure of the wage fund may be on the books of the enterprise for not longer than until July 1st of the following fiscal year.

If an enterprise repays in full the overexpenditure from the wage fund within the period (six months) or before time, the leading workers who allowed the overexpenditure shall be paid 50 per cent of the bonus due them which was not paid in the preceding period in connection with the overexpenditure from the wage fund.

Bonuses shall be paid in the same procedure in the event of an overexpenditure of the wage fund in shops, divisions, farms, and services of an enterprise. In this event the overexpenditure of the wage fund shall be taken into account only for the respective structural subdivision of the enterprise.

If there is no overexpenditure of the wage fund for the enterprise as a whole, the enterprise may write off the unreimbursed overexpenditure of the wage fund for the preceding period which individual shops, sectors, and other links of the enterprise had.

85. An enterprise shall have the right to establish a wage fund, above and beyond the confirmed wage fund, for workers engaged in construction and assembly work being carried out at the expense of noncentralized sources of finance (enterprise fund, consumer goods fund, loans of the USSR State Bank and the USSR Construction Bank, socialist competition bonuses, and other sources provided for by legislation), proceeding from the indicators agreed with the superior agency.

86. An enterprise may in exceptional instances issue non-plan advance payments to individual workers at the expense of the wage fund in an amount of not more than a month's earnings.

87. An enterprise may grant, when necessary, short periods of leave without wages to workers at their request.

88. An enterprise shall have the right to send distinguished workers and employees, at their wish, for study at an institution of higher education or a technical school and to pay them higher stipends in accordance with prevailing legislation on condition that these workers make an obligation, upon completing the educational institution, to return to the enterprise which sent them to the institution of higher education. Candidates being sent for study at an institution of higher education or technical school for whom higher stipends have been established shall be nominated jointly with social organizations of the enterprise.

V. Administration of the Enterprise

89. The director (or head, manager) shall head an enterprise.

The director of an enterprise shall be appointed to or relieved from the post by the superior agency.

90. The director shall organize all work of the enterprise and bear full responsibility for its state and activity.

The director of an enterprise shall act in the name of an enterprise without a power of attorney, represent it in all institutions and organizations, dispose of the property and assets of the enterprise in accordance with law, conclude contracts, issue powers of attorney (including those with the right of a further power of attorney), and open checking accounts and other accounts of the enterprise at banks.

Within the limits of his competence, a director shall issue orders relating to the enterprise; shall hire and dismiss workers in accordance with labor legislation; and shall apply incentives and impose sanctions on enterprise workers.

Workers shall be dismissed at the initiative of the administration with the consent of the factory, plant, and local trade union committee.

92. The competence of deputy directors and other leading workers of an enterprise shall be established by the director of the enterprise in accordance with USSR and union republic legislation.

93. Shops, sections, services, sectors, production units, economic units, farms, and other structural subdivisions of the enterprise shall operate in accordance with statutes confirmed by the director of the enterprise.

94. The foreman (or senior foreman, sector head, brigadier, farm manager, work superintendent, senior work superintendent) shall be a fully authorized leader and the direct organizer of production and labor and shall bear responsibility for the fulfillment of the production plan in his sector and for the product quality. All instructions at work places shall be given by the foreman.

The foreman shall be directly subordinate to the head of the shop or other respective subdivision of the enterprise.

A foreman shall be appointed, transferred, or dismissed from work by order of the director of the enterprise.

95. The administration of an enterprise in the person of the director shall conclude a collective contract with the factory, plant, and local trade union committee as the representative of the workers and employees of the enterprise and shall ensure the timely fulfillment of the obligations assumed.

96. The administration of an enterprise, jointly with the factory, plant, and local trade union committee, shall:

establish rules for internal labor discipline in accordance with the model rules;

confirm the estimate for use of the assets of the enterprise fund and other incentive funds for workers and employees, and shall issue bonuses and one-time assistance from the said funds;

distribute living premises in houses of the enterprise, as well as living premises placed at the disposal of the enterprise in other houses.

97. The administration of an enterprise shall, jointly with the factory, plant, and local trade union committee, organize the socialist competition, total the results and determine the victors of the competition, and decide questions of rewarding the leading collectives and workers.

98. The administration of an enterprise shall report to sessions of the factory, plant, and local trade union committee about draft plans, the results of production and economic activity, the fulfillment of plans and obligations under the collective contract, measures to improve the organization and conditions of labor, material and cultural services for workers and employees, and the elimination of shortcomings in work.

99. Production conferences shall be held in order to extensively involve workers and employees in participating in the decision of production questions of the enterprise and in large shops, divisions, and farms. These conferences shall work on the basis of a Statute on the Standing Production Conference, confirmed by the USSR Council of Ministers and the All-Union Central Trade Union Council.

The administration of an enterprise shall further in every possible way the successful work of production conferences and shall organize the fulfillment of their decisions.

100. With a view to developing the creative initiative of the working people, an enterprise shall involve the primary organizations of the All-Union Society of Inventors and Rationalizers in the working out of long-term and current plans for introducing new technology and production technology. The enterprise shall create the necessary conditions for the successful activity of these primary organizations, and also for social construction design, technology, and standard bureaus, councils of innovators, scientific research laboratories, bureaus and groups for economic analysis, supplying them with premises, equipment, instruments, inventory, and technical and informational literature.

101. The administration of an enterprise shall, jointly with the factory, plant, and local trade union committee, regularly convene production, technical, and economic conferences, meetings of production workers at which questions of technical progress and the economic development of the enterprise shall be discussed and measures to eliminate shortcomings in the activity of the enterprise and its individual shops shall be worked out.

102. Meetings of enterprise workers shall discuss, upon the reports of the administration, draft production plans, the results of fulfilling the plans, draft collective contracts and the fulfillment of obligations under them, and production questions, the domestic and cultural services for workers, and the use of the enterprise fund (or consumer goods fund). The administration of the enterprise shall report to the meeting about measures being carried out in execution of the decisions of meetings previously held.

103. Groups and posts for the promotion of party-state control shall be created at enterprises, to which the administration of the enterprise shall be obliged to render every possible assistance in the work which they are carrying on, to consider their suggestions, and to take necessary measures for the elimination of shortcomings uncovered.

104. The activity of an enterprise shall be verified by the superior agency and agencies of party-state control.

The production and financial and economic activity of the enterprise shall be audited by the superior agency with the involvement of interested organizations on an integrated basis once a year.

VI. Reorganization and Liquidation of an Enterprise

105. An enterprise shall be reorganized or liquidated by decision of the agency which is empowered to form the respective enterprise.

106. In the event an enterprise is merged with another enterprise, all property rights and duties of each of them shall pass to the enterprise which arose as a result of the merger.

In the event one enterprise is joined to another, all property rights and duties of the joined enterprise shall pass to the latter.

107. In the event an enterprise is separated, the property rights and duties of the reorganized enterprise shall pass to the new enterprise which arose as a result of this separation according to the separation act in the respective portions.

If one or several new enterprises are separated from an enterprise, the property rights and duties of the reorganized enterprise shall pass to each of them according to the separation act in the respective portions.

108. The liquidation of an enterprise shall be carried out either by a liquidation commission appointed by the superior agency or, upon the commission of this agency, by the director of the enterprise being liquidated.

109. The procedure and period for liquidation of the enterprise shall be established by the superior agency. The question of the procedure for executing contracts concluded should be settled by the same agency without damage to the fulfillment of the state plan.

The period for creditors to file their claims against the enterprise being liquidated shall be established by the agency by whose decision the liquidation is being done but may not be less than one month.

110. The liquidation commission or in proper instances the director of the enterprise being liquidated shall place an announcement in the official regional, territory, or republic press organ at the place where the enterprise is situate concerning the liquidation of the enterprise and the period for creditors to file claims. Irrespective thereof, the liquidation commission or the director of the enterprise being liquidated shall be obliged to elucidate from available materials all claims of creditors of the enterprise and to notify them of its liquidation.

Claims against the enterprise being liquidated shall be satisfied from its property against which according to law execution may be levied.

Claims uncovered or filed after expiry of the period established for creditors to file their claims shall be satisfied from the said property remaining after satisfying the claims uncovered, and also claims filed within the established period.

Claims not uncovered nor filed during the period of liquidation, and also claims not satisfied because the property of the enterprise being liquidated is insufficient, shall be considered extinguished. Claims not recognized by the liquidation commission (or director of the enterprise being liquidated) also shall be considered extinguished in whole or respective part unless the creditors file a suit for satisfaction of the claim within two weeks from the date of receiving notification of their whole or partial nonrecognition.

111. The payment of periodic payment due from the enterprise being liquidated in connection with the causing of mutilation or other harm to the health or of death shall be secured in the procedure established by prevailing legislation.

Claims and suits of citizens concerning compensation of harm connected with injury to health or of death, and also other claims and suits of citizens not filed for justifiable reasons before the completion of the liquidation, may be filed subsequently in the ordinary procedure against the agency superior to the enterprise being liquidated. This agency may entrust satisfaction of the claims recognized by it or satisfied by a court to the enterprise subordinate to it which has received the property of the liquidated enterprise.

MODEL CHARTER OF A DACHA CONSTRUCTION COOPERATIVE

[Confirmed by Decree of the RSFSR Council of Ministers, September 24, 1958. SP RSFSR (1958), no. 13, item 154]

Procedure for Organizing a Cooperative

1. A dacha construction cooperative shall be organized upon the petition of an enterprise, institution, or organization attached to the executive committee of a city (or settlement) soviet of working people's deputies (at the place where the enterprise, institution, or organization is located) on the basis of its decision.

2. An association of not less than 10 citizens is required to form a cooperative. The question of organizing a cooperative shall be initiated by the working people before the enterprise, institution, or organization, which shall hold a general meeting of citizens desiring to join a dacha construction cooperative. The meeting shall adopt a decision concerning the organization of the cooperative.

3. Upon the receipt by the enterprise, institution, or organization of the decision of the executive committee of the local soviet of working people's deputies concerning the organizing of a cooperative, a general meeting of the citizens desiring to join the cooperative shall be convoked in order to adopt a charter. The charter adopted by the meeting shall be registered at the executive committee of the local soviet of working people's deputies which rendered the decision concerning the organizing of the cooperative.

4. After the charter is registered, the cooperative members shall convoke a general meeting in order to elect the cooperative board and auditing commission.

Note. Workers and employees of several small enterprises, institutions, or organizations, and also pensioners, may unite into a single dacha construction cooperative.

Purpose, Rights, and Duties of a Cooperative

5. The dacha construction cooperative under the name . . . shall be founded with a view to satisfying the cooperative members with dacha premises at . . . (precise name of the locality) by erecting dacha buildings from the assets of the cooperative, and also for the subsequent use and management of such dachas.

6. Cooperative members may be citizens of the USSR who have attained 18 years of age and who do not have dachas by right of personal ownership.

State institutions, enterprises, and social organizations may not be cooperative members nor take part in the construction of cooperative dachas with their own assets.

7. From the moment of the registration of its charter at the executive committee of a local soviet of working people's deputies, a cooperative shall acquire the rights of a juridical person.

A cooperative shall use a seal designating its own name.

8. The number of cooperative members may not exceed the number of dachas or separate dacha premises erected by the cooperative according to the construction plan.

9. A dacha construction cooperative shall use the dachas built by right of cooperative ownership and on the principle of paying its own way, without state subsidy.

10. A cooperative shall have the right to:

(a) receive land plots for use in perpetuity in order to erect dachas and auxiliary structures on them;

(b) carry out construction by way of independent work means in the procedure provided by the decree of the USSR Council of Ministers of March 20, 1958, "On Housing Construction and Dacha Construction Cooperatives" with the assets deposited by the cooperative in the bank for the entire amount of the cost of the construction.

The estimated construction cost of the dachas shall be determined by taking into account the expenditures for design, amenities, landscaping, and laying of communications. The cost of construction materials, construction components, instruments, semifinished products, and hardware for which retail prices have been established shall be determined by proceeding from the distribution conditions according to retail prices; the cost of the said goods if retail prices have not been established for them shall be according to wholesale prices;

(c) conclude a contract for the construction of dachas with an independent work organization and effectuate accounts for the fulfillment of work, and also conclude other contracts connected with the construction and use of dachas;

(d) organize the cultural and domestic servicing of cooperative members (lunchroom, laundry, clubs, libraries, and so forth).

11. A dacha construction cooperative shall construct dachas according to model designs and, as an exception, according to individual designs at the wish of cooperative members which have been confirmed in the established procedure.

12. Dachas may be constructed by a cooperative after confirmation of the designs in the established procedure and the receipt of a construction permit. The size and the periods for beginning and completing construction shall be specified in the act for the use in perpetuity of the land plot.

13. Dacha structures erected by a cooperative shall belong to it by right of cooperative ownership and may not be sold or transferred either as a whole or in parts (dachas, rooms) to organizations or individual persons except for a transfer made when the cooperative is liquidated.

14. A cooperative shall be liable for its obligations with all the property which belongs to it.

Assets of a Cooperative

15. The assets of a cooperative shall consist of:

(a) entry contributions of cooperative members;

(b) share contributions;

(c) contributions for the maintenance and use of the dachas;

(d) other receipts.

16. By decree of the general meeting, a cooperative may form special funds to be expended for purposes corresponding to the tasks of the cooperative provided in the charter. The procedure for forming and spending the special funds shall be determined by the general meeting of the cooperative.

Rights and Duties of Cooperative Members

17. A separate dacha premise or dacha living space of not more than 60 square meters shall be granted for permanent use to each cooperative member in accordance with the amount of his share and the number of his family members.

18. Cooperative members shall be obliged to deposit monies in an amount of the entire share before construction begins. The amount of the share of each cooperative member should correspond to the cost of one dacha or a separate dacha premise.

If a cooperative member or members of his family personally take part in the construction of the dacha, the amount of their labor expenditures and the procedure for reckoning the value of such labor expenditures into the account of the share shall be established by the cooperative board by agreement with the independent work construction organization.

19. A member of a dacha construction cooperative may not simultaneously be a member of another dacha construction cooperative.

20. A cooperative member shall have the right to:

(a) live with his family in the cooperative dacha premise granted to him during the entire time the cooperative exists;

(b) voluntarily, at his application, withdraw from the cooperative at any time of its existence, both before the beginning and during the construction of the dacha, and also after it is completed;

(c) transfer, with the consent of the general meeting of cooperative members, his share and right of use of the premises granted to him, to parents, spouse, or children if these persons had previously used the said premise jointly with the cooperative member.

21. A cooperative member may be expelled from the cooperative in instances of insubordination to the charter, the failure to fulfill obligations established by the general meeting, destruction and damage to the dacha, or conduct making it impossible for other persons to live together with him.

A cooperative member expelled from a cooperative shall be subject to eviction in a judicial proceeding from the dacha premises of the cooperative with all the persons living with him, without being granted another dacha premise.

If a cooperative member is expelled because it is impossible to live with him, the dacha premise shall remain in the use of the family of the expelled person on condition that one of the family members joins the cooperative.

22. The share of a cooperative member who has withdrawn from the cooperative shall be returned to him at the balance sheet value, and the

dacha premise released shall be granted to another person admitted as a cooperative member by decision of the general meeting.

The amount of the share of the newly admitted cooperative member may not be less than the balance sheet value of the share.

The share of the cooperative member who has withdrawn shall be returned not later than three months after the confirmation by the general meeting of the annual report for the operations year during which the shareholder withdrew from the cooperative.

23. The share of a deceased cooperative member shall pass to his heirs. Family members of the deceased who used the dacha premises granted to him jointly with him shall have a preferential right to the future use of this premise on condition that one of the family members joins the cooperative.

Heirs who have not used the premises during the testator's life or who have renounced future use shall be paid the value of the share or portion thereof which he inherited.

24. A person admitted to membership of the cooperative in place of the cooperative member who withdrew shall be liable for his obligations to the cooperative.

25. A cooperative member shall be obliged to bear all expenses for the management and use of the dacha in the amount determined by the general meeting of cooperative members.

Management Agencies of a Cooperative

26. The management agencies of a cooperative shall be: the general meeting of cooperative members and the cooperative board.

27. The general meeting shall be the highest agency of the cooperative and shall decide the following questions:

(a) the admission and expulsion of cooperative members;

(b) the confirmation of the construction plan and estimate, and also the annual economic and financial plan and report concerning its fulfillment;

(c) the distribution of dacha premises among cooperative members, and also the authorization for a cooperative member to transfer his share to family members living together with him.

All questions of granting premises in cooperative dachas shall be subject to obligatory agreement with the executive committee of the city (or settlement) soviet of working people's deputies;

(d) the establishment of the amounts of entry and share contributions, and also contributions for the maintenance and use of the dachas;

(e) the formation of special funds of the cooperative;

(f) the election of the board and auditing commission;

(g) consideration of complaints against the board and auditing commissions

(h) liquidation of the cooperative.

28. The general meeting shall be convoked by the board at least twice a year.

Extraordinary general meetings shall be convoked within six days at the request of 1/3 of the cooperative members, and also at the request of the auditing commission or the executive committee of the local soviet of working people's deputies which registered the cooperative charter.

29. The general meeting shall be deemed to have a quorum when not less than 2/3 of the total number of cooperative members or persons empowered by cooperative members take part in it.

Decisions shall be adopted at the general meeting by a simple majority of votes of the cooperative members or empowered persons present.

Decisions of a general meeting concerning the amounts of share contributions and contributions for the maintenance and use of a dacha (or dachas), the expulsion of cooperative members from the cooperative, and liquidation of the cooperative shall be adopted by a majority of 2/3 of the votes.

30. The cooperative board, of not less than three members, shall be elected by the general meeting for a term of two years.

The board shall elect a chairman of the board and his deputy (or deputies) from its membership.

31. The board shall be the executive agency of the cooperative, accountable to the general meeting. The duties of the board shall be:

(a) the receipt of the entry and share contributions established by the general meeting from cooperative members;

(b) the drawing up of plans, estimates, and reports;

(c) management of the dachas;

(d) the hiring and dismissal of workers and employees to service the dachas;

(e) the conclusion of contracts and the performance of other legal transactions in the name of the cooperative;

(f) representation of the cooperative in all judicial and administrative institutions;

(g) keeping a list of cooperative members and keeping the accounts and files of the cooperative;

(h) fulfillment of other duties arising from the present charter.

32. The cooperative board shall have the right to dispose of the cash assets of the dacha construction cooperative in the current bank account, in accordance with the financial plan confirmed by the general meeting of cooperative members.

33. An auditing commission composed of three members shall be elected by the meeting of cooperative members for a term of two years and shall be the agency which controls and audits the activity of the board.

The auditing commission shall elect the chairman of the commission from its own membership.

34. Spouses, parents, children, grandchildren, natural brothers and sisters and their spouses may not be simultaneously a member of the board and of the auditing commission.

35. A cooperative shall carry out its activity under the observation and control of the executive committee of the local soviet of working people's deputies which registered its charter.

36. The civil law disputes between the cooperative and its members shall be subject to settlement in a judicial proceeding.

Termination of the Activity of a Cooperative and Liquidation of its Affairs

37. The activity of a dacha construction cooperative shall terminate with the liquidation of its affairs and property by a decision of the general meeting of cooperative members in instances of:

(a) the cooperative being deemed insolvent by a court;

(b) the cooperative being deemed by a court decision to have deviated from the purposes specified in the charter.

The activity of a cooperative shall terminate also in the event the general meeting of the cooperative deems its liquidation to be necessary. The decision of a general meeting of cooperative members concerning the liquidation of the cooperative shall be subject to confirmation by the executive committee of the city (or settlement) soviet of working people's deputies.

38. The affairs of a cooperative shall be liquidated in accordance with laws on the procedure for terminating the activity of cooperative organizations, with the obligatory participation of a representative of the executive committee of the local soviet of working people's deputies which registered the cooperative charter.

39. The cooperative property left after the satisfaction of all claims filed against the cooperative, the fulfillment of obligations assumed by it, and the payment of share contributions to cooperative members, and also all the files and documents of the cooperative, shall be transferred to the executive committee of the local soviet of working people's deputies which registered the cooperative charter.

MODEL COLLECTIVE FARM CHARTER

[Adopted by the Third All-Union Congress of Collective Farmers and Confirmed by Decree of the Central Committee of the Communist Party of the Soviet Union and the USSR Council of Ministers, November 28, 1969. Resheniia partii i pravitel'stva po sel'skomu khoziaistvu (1965-1971gg.). (Moscow, 1971), pp. 419-436]

The collective farm system is an integral part of Soviet socialist society; this path of gradual transition to communism selected by V. I. Lenin has proved its worth historically and corresponds to the peculiarities and interests of the peasantry.

Social ownership of the means of production, the advantages of a large-scale collective farm, the day-to-day concern and assistance of the party and state have allowed enormous socio-economic transformations to be achieved in the countryside. Thanks to the selfless labor of the collective farm peasantry, the efforts of the working class and of the entire Soviet people, collective farms have been transformed into large-scale mechanized agricultural enterprises, have increased their social wealth immeasurably, and have gradually overcome the differences between city and country.

As a social form of socialist economy, the collective farm fully meets the tasks of the future development of productive forces in the countryside, ensures the management of production by the collective farm masses themselves on the basis of collective farm democracy, and allows the proper combination of the personal interests of collective farmers with social interests of the whole people. The collective farm is a school of communism for the peasantry.

Under the guidance of the Communist Party, the collective farm peasantry, in close and indissoluble alliance with the working class, actively takes part in the construction of communism in our country.

I. Purposes and Tasks

1. Collective farm . . . . (name of collective farm) . . . . district . . . . national area . . . . region (or territory) . . . . republic shall be a cooperative organization voluntarily uniting peasants to jointly carry on large-scale socialist agricultural production on the basis of social means of production and collective labor.

2. A collective farm shall have as its basic tasks to:

strengthen and develop in every possible way the social economy and steadfastly raise labor productivity and the efficiency of social production;

increase the production and sale to the state of agricultural products through the intensification and future technological rearmament of collective farm production, the introduction of integrated mechanization and electrification, and the extensive implementation of the chemicalization and improvement of land;

carry on work, under the guidance of the party organization, for the communist nurturing of collective farmers, involving them in social life and developing socialist competitions;

satisfy more fully the growing material and cultural requirements of collective farmers, improve the domestic conditions of their life, and gradually transform village and rural settlement into settlements with public amenities.

II. Membership in a Collective Farm, the Rights and Duties of Collective Farm Members

3. Citizens who have attained 16 years of age and manifested a desire by their labor to take part in the social economy of a collective farm may be collective farm members.

Members of a collective farm shall be admitted by the general meeting of collective farmers upon the recommendation of the collective farm board in the presence of the person who submitted the application.

An application for admission to collective farm membership shall be considered by the collective farm board within a month.

A standard form "Labor Book for a Collective Farmer" shall be kept for each collective farm member.

4. A collective farm member shall have the right to:

receive work in the social economy of a collective farm with a guaranteed payment in accordance with the quantity and quality of labor entrusted to him;

take part in the management of the affairs of the collective farm, elect and be elected to its administrative agencies; make proposals to improve the activity of a collective farm and eliminate shortcomings in the work of the board and officials;

receive assistance from the collective farm in raising production qualifications and acquiring a specialization;

use a personal land plot to carry on subsidiary husbandry, for the construction of a dwelling house and farm structures, and also collective farm pastures and social working livestock and transport for personal needs in the procedure established at the collective farm;

social security, cultural and domestic servicing and assistance of the collective farm in the construction and repair of the dwelling house and provision of fuel.

5. A collective farm member shall be obliged to:

observe the collective farm charter and the rules for internal discipline, fulfill the decrees of general meetings and decisions of the collective farm board;

labor conscientiously in the social economy, observe labor discipline, and master progressive methods and means of work;

participate actively in the management of the affairs of the collective farm, care for, protect, and strengthen state and collective farm ownership, not allow waste and a careless attitude toward the social goods, and rationally and properly use lands of the social use and personal plot fund.

6. Membership in a collective farm shall be preserved for persons who have temporarily left the collective farm in instances of:

active military service;

being elected to an elective post in soviet, social, or cooperative organizations;

commencing studies while continuing to work;

being sent to work at inter-collective farm organizations or departing to work in industry or other branch of the national economy for a period established by the collective farm board.

Collective farm membership also shall be preserved for collective farmers who have ceased work by reason of age or disability if they continue to reside on the territory of the collective farm.

7. An application of a collective farmer to withdraw from the collective farm should be considered by the board and general meeting of collective farm members within three months from the date the application is filed.

The collective farm board shall settle accounts with a former collective farmer at the end of the farm year not later than a month after confirmation of the collective farm annual report.

III. Land and its Use

8. In accordance with the USSR Constitution, land occupied by a collective farm shall be allocated to it for free and perpetual use, that is, in perpetuity.

Land allocated to a collective farm shall be state ownership, that is, the property of the whole people, and may not be the object of purchase-sale, lease, or other legal transactions.

A state act for the right of land use in which the dimensions and precise boundaries of the land allocated to the collective farm are specified shall be issued to each collective farm by the executive committee of the district (or city) soviet of working people's deputies.

Lands allocated to the collective farm shall be subdivided into social use and personal plot lands. Personal plot lands shall be demarcated in kind from social use lands.

9. The collective farm shall be obliged to: fully and properly use and constantly improve the land allocated to it and raise its fertility; bring unused lands into agricultural production; carry out measures to irrigate and drain lands, struggle against soil erosion, create shelterbelt forests; care for and strictly protect collective farm lands from squandering; observe the established rules for the protection of nature, use of forests, water sources, and useful minerals (sand, clay, stones, peat, and so forth).

The board, directors, and specialists of the collective farm shall be responsible for the high productive use of land.

10. The areas of collective farm lands shall be reduced or the boundaries of collective farm land use changed because of state or social needs shall be only with the consent of the general meeting of collective farmers by decisions of the respective state agencies. The granting for non-agricultural needs of irrigated or drained lands, pastures or

land plots occupied by established orchards and vineyards shall, as a rule, not be permitted.

The collective farm shall have the right to compensation for losses connected with a reduction of the area of collective farm lands or their temporary occupation. Losses shall be compensated in accordance with the procedure established by prevailing legislation.

IV. Social Ownership of a Collective Farm

11. The social ownership of a collective farm shall be the economic basis of a collective farm, together with state ownership of the land.

Social ownership of the collective farm shall constitute the enterprises, buildings, installations, tractors, combines, and other machines, equipment, means of transport, working and productive livestock, established plantings, land improvement and irrigation installations, production produce, cash, and other collective farm property. The property and assets of inter-collective farm and state-collective farm organizations and enterprises also shall be social property of a collective farm in accordance with its share participation.

12. A collective farm shall create, use productively and in a planned manner, and augment basic and circulating production funds in order to carry on its activity and the future growth of the social economy. These funds shall be indivisible (their assets shall not be subject to distribution among collective farm members) and shall be used only for their special purpose.

Designated basic non-production funds also shall be indivisible.

13. The right to dispose of collective farm property and cash shall belong only to the collective farm itself and its administrative agencies. The collective farm shall not permit the diversion of assets for purposes not connected with its activity.

The acquisition, sale, rejection, and writing off of basic assets and other material valuables shall be in the procedure established by the general meeting of collective farm members and on the basis of prevailing legislation.

Collective farm members who have allowed the destruction, spoilage, or loss of collective farm property and also who are guilty of the arbitrary use of tractors, motor vehicles, agricultural machines, working livestock, or have caused material damage to the collective farm, shall be obliged to compensate the collective farm.

The amount of actual damage shall be determined by the collective farm board. The damage shall be recovered in the amount of actual damage, but not exceeding 1/3 the basic monthly earnings of a collective farm member if the damage was caused by negligence at work. If damage is intentionally caused, and also in instances provided by legislation, collective farm members shall bear material responsibility in an increased or the entire amount. The damage shall be recovered by the collective farm board, and in the event of a dispute, through the people's court.

V. Production, Economic, and Financial Activity of a Collective Farm

14. A collective farm shall carry on its economy according to a plan confirmed by the general meeting of collective farmers, applying the most progressive, scientifically well-founded forms and methods of organizing production, ensuring the maximal receipt of high quality products with the least expenditure of labor and assets.

When working out plans, a collective farm shall proceed from the need for expanded reproduction of the social economy, fulfillment of the state procurements plan, procurement contracts for agricultural produce and the sale of grain and other products needed by the state in excess of plan, and the satisfaction of material and cultural requirements of collective farmers.

15. Production and financial activity of a collective farm shall be carried out on the basis of economic accountability and the extensive application of moral and material stimuli directed toward the development of production and increasing the profitability of the farm.

16. The board and all collective farm members shall be obliged to ensure:

the rational conduct of agricultural production through its intensification and specialization and the preferential development of those branches for which there are the best natural and economic conditions;

increasing the yield of agricultural crops on the basis of increasing cultivation of the crop, observance of crop rotation, improvement of seed-growing, application of fertilizer systems and the effectuation of other measures;

the introduction of new technology and progressive technology into production, integrated mechanization, electrification, and the achievements of science and progressive experience; carrying out land improvement and chemicalization;

the efficient use and preservation of tractors, combines, motor vehicles, and other machines, working and productive livestock, buildings, and installations;

the construction of production buildings and designated cultural and domestic objects, dwelling houses, and children's institutions, roads, water conservancy, and other installations in accordance with plans for the development of the economy and the building of population centers.

17. With a view to the fullest and equal use of labor resources and local sources of raw materials, and to raising the revenues of the social economy of the collective farm, a collective farm shall create and develop subsidiary enterprises, not to the detriment of agricultural production, and also various trades; may enter into contractual relations with industrial enterprises and trading organizations for the creation on the collective farm of branches (or shops) for the production of various manufactures and goods by the efforts of collective farmers during the periods free from agricultural work.

18. A collective farm may take part on a voluntary basis in the activity of inter-collective farm and state-collective farm enterprises and organizations and join associations or unions.

19. By decision of the general meeting of collective farmers, a collective farm may combine part of its assets with the assets of local soviets of working people's deputies, state farms, and other state and cooperative enterprises and organizations for the construction of cultural and domestic objects on the basis of shares, public amenities, and other measures directed toward the development of collective farm production and the improvement of cultural and domestic servicing of collective farmers.

20. A collective farm shall conclude contracts with state, cooperative, and social organizations for the sale of agricultural produce, the purchase of machines, materials, livestock, and other property, the sale of semifinished and manufactured articles of subsidiary enterprises and trades, for the fulfillment of various work and rendering of services, and also enter into other contractual relations which correspond to the purposes of its activity.

21. A collective farm shall open an account in the USSR State Bank to account for and keep cash and perform all cash and account operations in accordance with the established rules.

The transfer or drawing of cash from collective farm accounts in the USSR State Bank shall be by order of the collective farm board.

A collective farm may use state short-term and long-term credits.

The orders of a collective farm board to transfer or draw cash from the collective farm accounts, and also obligations of the collective farm for credits, shall be valid if the signatures of the chairman and chief bookkeeper of the collective farm are present.

22. A collective farm shall keep bookkeeping, operational, and statistical records, introduce progressive methods and forms of records, draw up reports according to the confirmed forms and submit them to the appropriate agencies within the established periods.

23. A collective farm shall not be liable for obligations and debts of collective farm members. Collective farm members shall not be liable with their property for the obligations and debts of the collective farm.

VI. Organization, Payment, and Discipline of Labor

24. All work in the social economy of a collective farm shall be fulfilled by the personal labor of collective farmers.

The hiring of specialists and other workers from outside for work shall be permitted only in those instances when there are no corresponding specialists on the collective farm or when agricultural and other work can not be fulfilled within the necessary periods by the efforts of the collective farmers.

A collective farm shall introduce the scientific organization of labor and manifest concern for the fullest and most rational use of the work force in social production.

25. The duration and discipline of the work day in a collective farm, the procedure for granting days off and annual paid leave, and also the minimum labor participation in the social economy of able-bodied collective farmers, shall be regulated by rules for internal discipline of the collective farm.

26. The forms for organizing production and labor -- sectors, farms, brigades, links, and other production subdivisions -- shall be established

and applied by the collective farm depending on the specific conditions of the farm and the level of mechanization, specialization, and production technology.

Collective farmers shall be chosen as members of production subdivisions proceeding from the interests of developing the social economy and taking into account the qualifications, work experience, skills, place of residence, and personal wishes.

Land plots, tractors, machines, inventory, working and productive livestock, necessary structures and other means of production shall be allocated to production subdivisions of the collective farm. The activity of production subdivisions of a collective farm shall be carried out on the basis of intra-farm accountability.

27. The social economy of a collective farm shall be the basic source of income for collective farmers. Labor on the collective farm shall be paid in accordance with the quantity and quality of labor entrusted to each collective farmer in the social economy according to the principle: the highest payment for the best labor and for the best results. The growth of the payment for the labor of collective farm members should be on the basis of the outstripped growth of labor productivity.

Piece work and job rate payment of labor for the amount of work fulfilled and produce produced and time or time-bonus and other systems for the payment of labor shall be applied on the collective farm. Poor quality work fulfilled by the fault of the collective farmer shall not be paid or the amount of payment shall be correspondingly reduced.

Processing and price norms for agricultural and other work shall be worked out and, when necessary, reviewed with the extensive participation of the collective farmers and specialists, proceeding from model processing norms and taking into account the specific conditions of the farm, and shall be confirmed by the collective farm board.

28. A collective farm shall establish a guaranteed payment for the labor of collective farm members for work in social production.

With a view to increasing the material interest of collective farmers in increasing the production of agricultural produce, improving quality, and reducing its cost of production, supplemental payment and other forms of material incentive shall be applied together with the basic payment for labor.

Collective farm members who have not fulfilled the established minimum of labor participation in the social economy without justifiable reasons, and also have allowed shirking, may be wholly or partially deprived of the supplemental payment and other forms of material incentive by decision of the collective farm board.

29. In order to satisfy the needs of the collective farmers for agricultural products on the collective farm, a natural fund shall be created to which shall be allotted a specific part of the gross yield of grain and other products, as well as feed. These products and feed shall be issued as payment for labor or sold to collective farmers in the quantity and in the procedure established by the general meeting of collective farm members.

30. A collective farm board shall ensure the timely payment of earnings due to collective farmers. Money shall be paid at least once a month, and natural produce shall be issued as it is received.

The final accounting with collective farmers shall be not later than a month after confirmation of the annual collective farm report.

31. The collective farm board, being guided by the present Charter, shall work out rules for internal discipline, statutes on the payment of labor and on intra-farm accountability, which shall be confirmed by the general meeting of collective farmers.

32. All work on a collective farm shall be carried out with observance of the established rules for safety technique and requirements of production sanitation.

A collective farm shall allot the necessary means to carry out measures relating to safety technique and production sanitation, the acquisition of special clothing, special footwear, and protective appliances for issue or sale to collective farmers according to the established norms.

33. Female members of a collective farm shall have the right to pregnancy and birth leave; pregnant women shall be given easier work; the necessary conditions for the timely feeding of children shall be created for women who have nursing children and they may be granted additional leave.

A collective farm shall establish a short work day and other exemptions for adolescents.

34. For achieving high production results, working out and introducing rationalization proposals and economies in social assets, for long years of irreproachable work in collective farm production, and for other services to a collective farm, the general meeting of collective farm members or the board may apply the following incentive measures for collective farmers:

announcement of gratitude;

give a bonus or award a valuable gift;

award a certificate of honor;

being entered on a Board of Honor or in a Book of Honor;

conferment of the title "Merited Collective Farmer" or "Honored Collective Farmer".

Other incentive measures also may be established at the discretion of the general meeting of collective farm members.

The titles "Merited Collective Farmer" and "Honored Collective Farmer" shall be conferred by decision of the general meeting of collective farm members according to a statute confirmed by the collective farm.

35. For violation of labor discipline, the collective farm charter, or the rules of internal discipline, the following sanctions may be imposed on the guilty persons by the general meeting of collective farmers or the collective farm board:

warning;

reprimand;

strict reprimand;

transfer to lower paid work;

release from the post occupied;

warning of expulsion from collective farm membership.

Expulsion from collective farm membership may be allowed as an extreme measure only with respect to persons who have systematically violated labor discipline or the collective farm charter after applying other sanctions to such persons. A decree of a general meeting of collective farmers concerning the expulsion from collective farm membership may be appealed to the executive committee of a district (or city) soviet of working people's deputies.

Persons expelled from collective farm membership shall be deprived of the rights of collective farm membership established by the present Charter.

A sanction may be imposed by the general meeting of collective farmers on the chairman of the collective farm and chairman of the auditing commission, board members, and auditing commission members, and by the general meeting or the collective farm board on the chief (or senior) specialists, chief bookkeeper, and directors of production subdivisions.

The procedure for imposing and removing sanctions shall be determined by the collective farm rules for internal discipline.

VII. Distribution of Gross Produce and Revenues of a Collective Farm

36. The proper combining of accumulation and consumption, the constant growth of production, insurance, cultural, and domestic social funds, and the raising of the living standard of collective farmers should be ensured when distributing revenues.

Material expenditures for production (amortization, basic funds, expenditures for seed, feed, fertilizer, oil products, current repairs, and others) shall be compensated from the gross produce produced by the collective farm.

A collective farm shall form a labor payment fund from the gross revenues received.

Net income of the collective farm shall be used for:

payment of taxes and making cash payment to the state;

increasing the basic and circulating funds;

creating the cultural and domestic fund and fund for social security and material assistance to collective farmers;

material incentives for collective farmers and specialists;

forming and augmenting the reserve fund and for other purposes.

Deductions to increase the basic and circulating funds shall be obligatory; the amounts of deductions shall be established annually, taking into account the requirements for assets to ensure the future uninterrupted growth of social production.

37. From the plant-growing and livestock produced in kind by a collective farm shall be:

created a seed fund for the entire requirements;

fulfilled a plan for the sale of agricultural products to the state, repaid loans in kind, created a grain fund in kind and other products to be issued as payment for labor or sold to collective farmers and, if possible, grain and other produce needed by the state shall be sold in excess of the plan;

allotted feed for the number of social livestock and poultry for the annual requirements, and also for issuance or sale to collective farmers;

formed insurance and transition funds: seed, forage, and provision;

allotted products for public dining, the maintenance of children's institutions and orphans and a portion of the products and feed to assist pensioners, disabled persons, and needy members of the collective farm.

A collective farm shall realize the remaining produce through a consumer cooperative or collective farm market or use it for other needs at its discretion.

38. Monies received from the realization of produce and other sources the collective farm shall use in priority for accounts with collective farmers for labor, to cover other production expenditures, to make payments to the state and repay cash loans, and to form or augment social funds of the collective farm.

VIII. Social Security of Collective Farmers

39. In accordance with prevailing legislation, collective farm members shall receive pensions for old age, disability, loss of breadwinner, and, in addition, allowances for pregnancy and birth for women, at the expense of the centralized union social security fund.

40. Collective farm members shall receive, in accordance with the established procedure at the expense of the centralized social security fund, allowances for temporary inability to work, passes to a sanatorium or rest home, and other types of social insurance also shall be granted to them.

By decision of the general meeting, a collective farm may make supplemental payments for all types of pensions established for collective farmers and establish personal pensions for veterans of collective farm construction and persons of special merit in developing the social economy of a collective farm.

A collective farm shall render material assistance from its own assets to collective farm members not capable of working and who do not receive pensions or allowances. By decision of the general meeting of collective farmers, a collective farm may allot assets for the construction of collective farm and inter-collective farm sanatoriums, rest homes, pioneer camps, and homes for the aged and disabled.

A collective farm shall make deductions in the established procedure from assets for the centralized union social security fund for collective farmers and the centralized union social insurance fund for collective farmers.

IX. Culture, Domestic Life, Public Amenities

41. A collective farm shall take measures to improve the cultural and domestic conditions of the life of collective farmers and manifest day-to-day concern for strengthening the health and physical nurturing of collective farm members and their families.

For this purpose a collective farm shall:

build and equip collective farm clubs, libraries, and other cultural and enlightenment institutions and sport installations, promote the development of physical culture and sport, and create kindergartens and nurseries;

promote the proper nurturing of children by parents and in school, maintain a close link with school, render assistance to public education agencies in the production training of children, grant land plots to schools and technology, seeds, fertilizer, and transport, and ensure the arrangement of work for graduates of schools on the collective farm;

organize public dining for collective farmers when necessary;

render assistance to public health agencies in carrying out medicinal and preventive measures on the collective farm and grant transport to collective farmers free of charge and as a matter of urgency to deliver ill persons to medical institutions;

provide public amenities, electrification, and radio for population centers of the collective farm and houses of collective farmers and promote the organization of domestic services for collective farm members; render assistance in the procedure established on the collective farm to collective farmers in the construction and repair of dwelling houses, and grant living space to specialists who work on the collective farm and require it.

A collective farm shall be concerned to raise the production qualifications and the cultural and technical level of collective farm members; send collective farmers in the established procedure for study at higher and secondary specialized educational institutions, professional-technical high schools and schools, and courses for the raising of qualifications; grant exemptions provided by prevailing legislation to collective farmers who successfully are studying at correspondence and evening general education and special educational institutions and who are conscientiously working on the collective farm.

Collective farmers sent by the collective farm who have graduated from educational institutions shall be obliged to return for work on this collective farm in their specialization.

X. Subsidiary Husbandry of the Family of a Collective Farmer (Collective Farm Household)

42. The family of a collective farmer (or collective farm household) may have in ownership a dwelling house, farm buildings, productive livestock, poultry, bees, and minor agricultural implements for work on the personal plot.

A personal land plot shall be granted for use to the family of a collective farmer (or collective farm household) for a kitchen garden, garden, and other needs up to one-half hectare in size, including the land occupied by buildings, and on irrigated lands, up to one-fifth hectare.

The size of a personal plot shall be determined by the collective farm charter within the limits of established norms. The size of existing personal plots established in accordance with the agricultural artel charter which previously prevailed may be retained.

A personal plot shall be granted to the family of a collective farmer (or collective farm household) by decision of the general meeting of collective farm members, and its size shall be established taking into account the number of family members of the collective farmer (or collective farm household) and their labor participation in the social economy of the collective farm.

When building compact rural population centers, a collective farm shall allot personal plots to collective farmers around their dwelling houses (or apartments) in a smaller size, granting them the remaining portion of the land plot beyond the limits of the dwelling zone of the population center. The common land area allotted for the use of a family of a collective farmer (or collective farm household) should not exceed the size of the personal plot provided by the collective farm charter.

The use of personal plots in the sizes established by the collective farm shall be preserved for the families of collective farmers (or collective farm household) if all family members (or collective farm household) is by reason of age or disability not able to work, if the sole able-bodied family member (or collective farm household) is called to active military service, is elected to an elective post, or has commenced study, or has been temporarily transferred to other work with the consent of the collective farm, or if only minors remain in the family (or collective farm household). In all other instances the question of retaining the personal plot shall be decided by the general meeting of collective farm members.

A personal plot may not be transferred to the use of other persons or worked with the use of hired labor.

The collective farm board shall render assistance to collective farmers in the procedure established by the collective farm in working the personal plots; such assistance shall be rendered in priority to families in which there are no able-bodied persons.

The collective farm board shall be obliged to systematically control the observance of the established sizes of personal plots. In the event of an arbitrary increase in the sizes of personal plots, the surpluses above the established norms shall be confiscated by the board, transferring the crop harvested therefrom to the collective farm without reimbursing expenditures made for the period of illegal use.

43. The family of a collective farmer (or collective farm household) may have one cow with issue up to one year and one head of younger horned livestock up to two years of age, one sow with issue up to three months of age, or two pigs being fattened, up to 10 sheep and goats together, bee swarms, poultry, and rabbits.

An increase in the norms for keeping livestock in the personal ownership of the family of a collective farmer (or collective farm household) and the substitution of one species of livestock by others in individual areas, taking into account the national peculiarities and local conditions, shall be permitted by decision of the union republic council of ministers.

The number and types of livestock which the family of a collective farmer (or collective farm household) may have shall be determined by the collective farm charter within the limits of the established norms.

A collective farm board shall render assistance to collective farmers in paraphenalia for livestock, veterinary services, and also in providing livestock with feed and pasture.

Keeping livestock above the norms established by the charter shall be prohibited.

44. By decision of the general meeting of collective farmers, a collective farm shall grant personal land plots to teachers, doctors, and other specialists who work in a rural locality and reside on the territory of the collective farm. By decision of the general meeting of collective farmers, personal plots may be granted to workers, employees, pensioners, and disabled persons who reside on the territory of the collective farm if there are free personal plots.

A collective farm also may authorize the said persons to use pastures for their livestock in the established procedure.

XI. Administrative Agencies and Auditing Commission of a Collective Farm

45. The administration of the affairs of a collective farm shall be carried out on the basis of broad democracy and the active participation of collective farmers in deciding all questions of collective farm life.

The general meeting of collective farm members shall manage the affairs of the collective farm, and in the interval between meetings, the collective farm board.

46. The general meeting of collective farm members shall be the highest collective farm agency of administration.

The general meeting shall:

adopt the collective farm charter and make changes in and additions to it;

elect the board, chairman of the collective farm, and collective farm auditing commission;

decide questions concerning the admission or expulsion of collective farm members;

adopt the rules for internal discipline of the collective farm and statutes concerning the payment of labor and intra-farm accountability;

confirm the organizational, economic, long-term, and annual production and finance plans of the collective farm;

hear reports of the board and auditing commission of the collective farm concerning their activity;

confirm the annual report and the amounts of natural and cash funds of the collective farm;

confirm decisions of the collective farm board concerning the appointment or release of chief (or senior) specialists and the chief bookkeeper of the collective farm;

decide questions concerning the participation of the collective farm in inter-collective farm and state-collective farm enterprises and organizations, and its joining associations or unions, and concerning the amalgamation or breaking up of the collective farm;

consider questions concerning a modification of the size of collective farm land and its boundaries of land use.

In regard to the aforesaid questions, decisions of the collective farm board shall be void without their being confirmed by the general meeting of collective farmers.

The general meeting of collective farmers shall also consider other questions of collective farm activity.

47. The general meeting of collective farm members shall be convoked by the collective farm board at least four times a year. The collective farm board shall be obliged also to convoke a general meeting of collective farmers if at least 1/3 of the collective farm members or the auditing commission requests this.

The general meeting shall be empowered to decide questions if there are at least 2/3 of all collective farm members present at the meeting.

Decisions shall be adopted by a simple majority of votes at a general meeting of collective farmers.

The collective farm board shall notify collective farmers about the convocation of a general meeting at least seven days before the meeting.

48. In large collective farms where it is difficult to convoke general meetings of collective farm members, a meeting of authorized representatives may be convoked to decide questions relegated to the jurisdiction of the general meeting.

Authorized representatives shall be elected at meetings of collective farmers in brigades and other collective farm subdivisions. Norms of representation and the procedure for electing authorized representatives shall be determined by the collective farm board. Questions relegated to the competence of a meeting of authorized representatives shall be discussed in advance at brigade meetings of collective farmers (or subdivisions). Authorized representatives shall report to brigade (or subdivision) meetings about decisions adopted by the meeting of authorized representatives.

49. A collective farm board shall be the executive and administrative agency responsible to the general meeting of collective farm members and shall direct all the organizational, production, financial, cultural, domestic, and educational activity of the collective farm.

The collective farm board shall organize the fulfillment of plans for production and for the sale of agricultural produce to the state, ensure the rational use of land, carefully and economically spend material and cash assets, and take measures to strengthen production and labor discipline.

The collective farm board shall constantly rely in its activity on the broad collective farm aktiv, develop and support the creative initiative of collective farm members to improve the organization of social production and raise labor productivity, display constant concern for the improvement of labor conditions and the life of collective farmers, and sympathetically and attentively consider their requests and suggestions.

A collective farm board shall be elected for a term of three years. The collective farm board shall annually account for its activity to the general meeting of collective farmers.

Sessions of a collective farm board shall be convoked as necessary, but at least once a month; the board shall be empowered to decide questions if at least 3/4 of the board members are present at the session. Decisions of the board shall be adopted by a single majority of votes.

50. The general meeting of collective farmers shall elect the chairman of the collective farm for a term of three years, who shall be simultaneously the chairman of the collective farm board.

The collective farm chairman shall carry on the day-to-day direction of the collective farm activity, ensure the fulfillment of decisions of the general meeting and board, and represent the collective farm in relations with state agencies and other institutions and organizations.

The collective farm board shall elect one or two deputy chairmen of the collective farm from its own membership.

51. A collective farm board shall appoint a chief bookkeeper from among the collective farm members or hire him under a labor contract.

The chief bookkeeper shall organize the records and accounts in the collective farm, exercise day-to-day control over the preservation and proper expenditure of cash assets and material valuables. The chief bookkeeper shall sign, together with the collective farm chairman, the annual collective farm report and documents relating to the receipt or disbursement of cash assets and material valuables.

52. The board shall appoint from among collective farm members or hire under a labor contract specialists to direct individual branches of collective farm activity.

The chief (or senior) specialists shall bear responsibility for the state of the branch which they direct and organize the fulfillment of the production and financial plan. The <u>ukazaniia</u> of chief (or senior) specialists on questions relegated to their jurisdiction shall be binding on collective farm members, and also officials of the collective farm.

53. Meetings of collective farmers shall be convoked in brigades and other collective farm production subdivisions so that collective farm members take part extensively in the management of social production.

A meeting of a brigade (or subdivision) of collective farmers shall:

elect the brigadier (or director of the subdivision), he being subsequently confirmed by the collective farm board;

consider the planning task, reports of the brigadier (or director of the subdivision) concerning the work and other questions of production activity;

discuss measures to strengthen labor discipline and submit proposals to the collective farm board concerning incentive measures and sanctions.

The meeting shall be convoked by the director of the production subdivison, the board, or the collective farm chairman.

A bridade (or subdivision) council shall be elected at the meeting. The director of the respective subdivision shall be the chairman of the council. The rights and duties of the council shall be determined by the collective farm board.

Regulations of the brigadier (or director of a subdivision) connected with production activity shall be binding on all collective farmers working in the particular subdivision. The brigadier (or subdivision director) shall be subordinate in his work to the board and collective farm chairman, and in regard to specialized questions, also to the chief (or senior) specialists.

54. An auditing commission shall be elected for a term of three years to control the economic and financial activity of the collective farm board and officials. The auditing commission shall elect a chairman from its own membership.

The auditing commission shall be guided by the collective farm charter and prevailing legislation, accountable to the general meeting of collective farm members, and exercise control over the observance of the collective farm charter, the preservation of collective farm property, the legality of contracts and economic operations, the expenditure of cash assets and material valuables, the correctness of records, reports, and accounts with collective farmers, and also the timely consideration by the collective farm board and officials of complaints and applications of collective farmers.

The auditing commission shall carry on annually at least two audits of the economic and financial activity of the collective farm, periodically verify the economic activity of brigades and other production subdivisions, and give its own opinion on the annual report of the collective farm. Auditing acts shall be subject to confirmation by the general meetin of collective farmers.

55. The auditing commission shall have the right to:

verify the correctness of the use and preservation of agricultural produce, seeds and forage, material-technical and cash assets, working and productive livestock, buildings, installations, and other property;

demand the necessary documents for verification from officials and collective farm members;

make proposals for the consideration of the collective farm general meeting and board relating to the results of verifications and audits.

Proposals of the auditing commission shall be considered at a regular general meeting, and those submitted to the collective farm board, within 10 days.

56. The elections for the collective board and chairman and the audit ing commission shall be held by open or secret ballot at the discretion of the general meeting of collective farmers.

The number of members of the board and auditing commission shall be determined by the general meeting of collective farm members.

The collective farm chairman, board members, chairman and members of the auditing commission who have not justified the trust of the collective farmers may be recalled before time by decision of the general meeting of collective farm members.

57. A collective farm shall create the necessary conditions for the successful activity of social organizations.

58. An economic council or economic analysis bureau, cultural, domestic, and other commissions working on social principles, and also a mutual assistance benefit fund, may be created on a collective farm.

XII. Adoption and Registration of the Collective Farm Charter

59. The collective farm charter adopted by the general meeting of col lective farm members on the basis of the Model Charter shall be submitted

for registration to the executive committee of a district (or city) soviet of working people's deputies. Subsequent changes in and additions to the collective farm charter shall be submitted in the same procedure.

60. The registered collective farm charter shall be kept at the collective farm board, district agricultural agency, and executive committee of the district (or city) soviet of working people's deputies.

61. A collective farm shall be guided in its activity by the collective farm charter and prevailing legislation.

A collective farm shall be a socialist agricultural enterprise, enjoy the rights of a juridical person, and have a seal and banner.

CHAPTER III

THE ADMINISTRATION OF SOCIALIST LEGALITY

FUNDAMENTAL PRINCIPLES OF LEGISLATION ON COURT ORGANIZATION OF THE USSR AND OF THE UNION AND AUTONOMOUS REPUBLICS

[Law of December 25, 1958, as amended August 12, 1971. Vedomosti SSSR (1959), no. 1, item 12; (1971), no. 33, item 332]

Article 1. Judicial System. In accordance with Article 102 of the USSR Constitution, justice in the USSR shall be realized by the USSR Supreme Court, by union republic supreme courts, by autonomous republic supreme courts, by region, territory, and city courts, by autonomous region and national area courts, and by district (or city) people's courts, as well as by military tribunals.

Article 2. Goals of Justice. Justice in the USSR shall be called on to protect from any infringements:

a) the social and state system of the USSR secured by the USSR Constitution, and by union and autonomous republic constitutions, the socialist system of economy, and socialist ownership;

b) political, labor, housing, and other personal and property rights and interests of citizens guaranteed by the USSR Constitution and by union and autonomous republic constitutions;

c) rights and legally protected interests of state institutions, enterprises, collective farms, cooperative and other social organizations.

Justice in the USSR shall have as its task the securing of the strict and undeviating execution of the laws by all institutions, organizations, officials, and citizens of the USSR.

Article 3. Tasks of the Court. By all its activity a court shall nurture citizens of the USSR in the spirit of loyalty to the Motherland and to the cause of communism, and in the spirit of strict and undeviating execution of Soviet laws, of an attitude of care toward socialist ownership, of observance of labor discipline, of an honorable attitude toward state and social duty, and of respect for the rights, honor, and dignity of citizens and for the rules of socialist community life.

In applying measures of criminal punishment a court not only chastises criminals, but also has as its purpose their correction and re-education.

Article 4. Realization of Justice through Judicial Consideration of Civil and Criminal Cases. Justice in the USSR shall be realized through:

a) consideration and resolution in judicial sessions of civil cases concerning disputes affecting the rights and legal interests of citizens, state enterprises, institutions, collective farms, cooperative and other social organizations;

b) consideration in judicial sessions of criminal cases and either the application of measures of punishment established by law to persons guilty of committing a crime or the acquittal of the innocent.

Article 5. Equality of Citizens before Law and Court. Justice in the USSR shall be realized on the basis of equality of citizens before the law and court, irrespective of their social, property, or occupational status, national or racial affiliation, or religious confession.

Article 6. Realization of Justice in Strict Accordance with the Law. Justice in the USSR shall be realized in strict accordance with legislation of the USSR and legislation of the union and autonomous republics.

Article 7. Formation of All Courts on the Basis of Election. In accordance with Articles 105-109 of the USSR Constitution, all courts in the USSR shall be formed on the basis of election.

Article 8. Collegial Consideration of Cases in All Courts. Cases in courts shall be considered collegially.

Consideration of cases in all courts of first instance shall be by a judge and two people's assessors.

Cases on cassational appeal or on protest shall be considered in judicial divisions of higher courts by benches of three members of the respective court.

Cases regarding protests against decisions, judgments, rulings, or decrees of courts which have entered into legal force shall be considered in judicial divisions of the USSR Supreme Court and union republic supreme courts, in benches of three members of the court.

The presidium of the court shall consider cases when a majority of the presidium members is present.

The plenum of the court shall consider cases in the presence of not less than two-thirds of its bench.

Article 9. Independence of Judges and their Subordination Only to Law. In realizing justice, judges and people's assessors shall be independent and subordinate only to law.

Article 10. Language in which Judicial Proceedings Shall be Conducted In accordance with Article 110 of the USSR Constitution, judicial proceedings in the USSR shall be conducted in the language of the union or autonomous republic, or autonomous region, but in instances provided by union and autonomous republic constitutions, in the language of the national area or in the language of the majority of the population of the district, persons not having command of that language being secured a full acquaintance with materials of the case through an interpreter and also the right to speak in court in their native language.

Article 11. Open Examination of Cases in All Courts. In accordance with Article 111 of the USSR Constitution, examination of cases in all courts of the USSR and union republics shall be open, insofar as an exception is not provided by law.

Article 12. Guaranteeing an Accused the Right to Defense. In accordance with Article 111 of the USSR Constitution, an accused shall be guaranteed the right to defense.

Article 13. Colleges of Advocates. Colleges of advocates shall operate for the purpose of providing defense in court and also for rendering other legal assistance to citizens, enterprises, institutions, and organizations.

Colleges of advocates shall be voluntary societies of persons engaged in advocacy, and they shall operate on the basis of a statute confirmed by the union republic supreme soviet.

General direction of the advocates shall be effectuated by the USSR Ministry of Justice, by union and autonomous republic ministries of justice, and by justice sections of the executive committees of region, territory, and city soviets of working people's deputies within the limits and in the procedure established by USSR and union republic legislation.

Article 14. Participation of Procurator in Court. The USSR Procurator General and procurators subordinate to him shall participate, on the basis of and in the procedure established by USSR and union republic legislation, in administrative sessions and in judicial sessions during the consideration of criminal and civil cases, shall support the state accusation in court, shall present and support suits in court, and shall exercise supervision over the legality and well-foundedness of judgments, decisions, rulings, and decrees rendered by judicial agencies, as well as over the execution of court judgments.

Article 15. Social Accusers and Social Defense Counsel. Social accusation and defense in court may be carried out by representatives of social organizations in the procedure established by USSR and union republic legislation.

In instances provided for by USSR and union republic legislation, an accusation also may be supported by victims of a crime.

Article 16. Courts of the USSR and of Union Republics. Courts of the USSR and union republic courts shall operate in the Union of Soviet Socialist Republics.

Article 17. Courts of the USSR. The USSR Supreme Court and military tribunals shall be courts of the USSR.

Article 18. Union Republic Courts. Union republic courts shall be: the union republic supreme court, autonomous republic supreme courts, region, territory, and city courts, autonomous region and national area courts, and district (or city) courts.

Article 19. Procedure for Election of District (or City) People's Courts. People's judges of district (or city) people's courts shall be elected by citizens of the district (or city) on the basis of universal, equal, and direct suffrage by secret ballot for a term of five years.

People's assessors of district (or city) people's courts shall be elected at general meetings of workers, employees, and peasants at their place of work or residence, and at general meetings of military servicemen in their military units, for a term of two years.

The procedure for elections of people's judges and people's assessors shall be established by union republic legislation.

Article 20. Procedure for Election of Region, Territory, and City Courts, Autonomous Region and National Area Courts. Region, territory, and city courts, autonomous region and national area courts shall be elected by the respective soviets of working people's deputies for a term of five years.

Article 21. Composition of Region, Territory, and City Court, Autonomous Region and National Area Court. Region, territory, and city courts, and autonomous region and national area courts shall consist of a chairman, deputy chairman, members of the court, and people's assessors, and shall operate in the form of:

a) judicial division for civil cases;

b) judicial division for criminal cases;

c) presidium of the court.

Article 22. Election Procedure and Powers of Autonomous Republic Supreme Court. An autonomous republic supreme court shall be the highest judicial agency of an autonomous republic.

An autonomous republic supreme court shall be charged with supervision over the judicial activity of all judicial agencies of the autonomous republic in the procedure established by USSR and union republic legislation.

An autonomous republic supreme court shall be elected by the autonomous republic supreme soviet for a term of five years.

Article 23. Composition of autonomous republic supreme court. An autonomous republic supreme court shall consist of a chairman, deputy chairman, members of the supreme court, and people's assessors, and shall operate in the form of:

a) judicial division for civil cases;

b) judicial division for criminal cases;

c) presidium of the supreme court.

Article 24. Election Procedure and Powers of Union Republic Supreme Court. A union republic supreme court shall be the highest judicial agency of a union republic.

A union republic supreme court shall be charged with supervision over the judicial activity of all union republic judicial agencies in the procedure established by USSR and union republic legislation.

A union republic supreme court shall be elected by the union republic supreme soviet for a term of five years.

Article 25. Composition of Union Republic Supreme Court. A union republic supreme court shall consist of a chairman, deputy chairman, members of the supreme court, and people's assessors, and shall operate in the form of:

a) judicial division for civil cases;

b) judicial division for criminal cases;

c) plenum of the supreme court.

In accordance with union republic legislation, presidiums may be formed in union republic supreme courts.

The competence of presidiums and plenums of union republic supreme courts shall be established by union republic legislation.

Article 26. Election Procedure and Powers of USSR Supreme Court. The USSR Supreme Court shall be the highest judicial agency of the Union of Soviet Socialist Republics.

The USSR Supreme Court shall be charged with supervision over the judicial activity of USSR judicial agencies, as well as union republic judicial agencies, within the limits established by the Statute on the USSR Supreme Court.

The USSR Supreme Court shall be elected by the USSR Supreme Soviet for a term of five years.

Article 27. Composition of the USSR Supreme Court. The USSR Supreme Court shall consist of a chairman, deputy chairman, members of the USSR Supreme Court, and people's assessors elected by the USSR Supreme Soviet, as well as chairmen of union republic supreme courts who are members of the USSR Supreme Court *ex officio*.

The USSR Supreme Court shall operate in the form of:

a) Judicial Division for Civil Cases;

b) Judicial Division for Criminal Cases;

c) Military Division;

d) Plenum of the USSR Supreme Court.

Article 28. Military Tribunals. The system and competence, and also the election procedure, of military tribunals shall be defined by the Statute on Military Tribunals.

Article 29. Requirements for Candidates for Judges and People's Assessors. Citizens of the USSR possessing the right of suffrage and who have attained twenty-five years of age on election day may be elected judges and people's assessors.

Article 30. Equal Rights of People's Assessors and Judges While Realizing Justice. During the execution of their duties in court, people's assessors shall enjoy all the rights of a judge.

Article 31. Term for Which People's Assessors Are Called Upon to Perform Duties in Court. People's assessors shall be called upon to perform their duties in courts in their regular term for not more than two weeks a year, except for instances when it is necessary to prolong this term in order to finish the consideration of a judicial case begun with their participation.

Article 32. Retention of Wages for People's Assessors During Their Execution of Duties in Court. Wages shall be retained for people's assessors from among workers and employees during their execution of duties in court.

People's assessors who are not workers or employees shall be compensated for expenses connected with the performance of their duties in court. The procedure and amounts of reimbursement shall be established by union republic legislation.

Article 33. Reports of People's Judges to Voters. People's judges shall report systematically to the voters about their work and the work of the people's court.

Article 34. Accountability of Courts to Agencies Which Elect Them. Region, territory, and city courts, and autonomous region and national area courts shall be accountable to the respective soviets of working people's deputies.

Union and autonomous republic supreme courts shall be accountable respectively to the union and autonomous republic supreme soviets, and in the interval between sessions, to the presidiums of union and autonomous republic supreme soviets.

The USSR Supreme Court shall be accountable to the USSR Supreme Soviet, and in the interval between sessions, to the Presidium of the USSR Supreme Soviet.

Article 35. Early Recall of Judges and People's Assessors. Judges and people's assessors may be prematurely deprived of their powers only by recall of the voters or the agency which elected them or by virtue of a court judgment passed on them.

The procedure for early recall of judges and people's assessors of USSR and union republic courts shall be determined respectively by USSR and union republic legislation.

Article 36. Procedure for Bringing Judges and People's Assessors to Criminal Responsibility. Judges may not be brought to criminal responsibility nor removed from office in such connection nor subjected to arrest:

a) people's judges, chairmen, deputy chairmen, and members of region, territory, and city courts, autonomous region and national area courts, and autonomous republic supreme courts: without the consent of the presidium of the union republic supreme soviet;

b) chairmen, deputy chairmen, and members of union republic supreme courts, as well as people's assessors of such courts: without the consent of the union republic supreme soviet, and in the interval between sessions, of the presidium of the union republic supreme soviet;

c) chairman, deputy chairmen, and members of the USSR Supreme Court, and also people's assessors of the USSR Supreme Court: without the consent of the USSR Supreme Soviet, and in the interval between sessions, of the Presidium of the USSR Supreme Soviet;

d) chairmen, deputy chairmen, and members of military tribunals: without the consent of the Presidium of the USSR Supreme Soviet.

Article 37. Disciplinary Responsibility of Judges. Judges shall bear disciplinary responsibility in the procedure established by USSR legislation for judges of USSR courts and by union republic legislation for judges of union republic courts.

Article 38. Execution of decisions, rulings, and decrees of courts. Execution of decisions, rulings, and decrees in civil cases, as well as the execution of judgments, rulings, and decrees in criminal cases to the extent that they involve levying against property, shall be performed by sheriffs who are attached to courts and who are appointed by the heads of justice sections of executive committees of region, territory, and city soviets of working people's deputies, by autonomous republic ministers of justice, and by union republic ministers of justice for republics not divided into regions.

Article 38-1. Organizational Direction of Courts. Organizational direction of courts within the limits and in the procedure provided by legislation of the USSR and of the union and autonomous republics shall be carried out by:

the USSR Ministry of Justice, with respect to union republic courts and military tribunals;

union republic ministries of justice, with respect to autonomous region and national area courts, and district (or city) people's courts;

autonomous republic ministries of justice and justice sections of executive committees of region, territory, and city soviets of working people's deputies, with respect to district (or city) people's courts.

The USSR Ministry of Justice shall:

a) work out proposals on questions of the organization of judicial agencies and the holding of elections for judges and people's assessors;

b) direct work with cadres of judicial agencies;

c) verify the organization of the work of judicial agencies;

d) study and generalize judicial practice, coordinating this activity with the USSR Supreme Court;

e) organize the work of keeping judicial statistics.

The USSR Minister of Justice shall have the right to introduce in the Plenum of the USSR Supreme Court proposals concerning the issuance to courts of guiding explanations on questions of the application of legislation.

The USSR Ministry of Justice, union and autonomous republic ministries of justice, and the justice sections of executive committees of region, territory, and city soviets of working people's deputies shall be called on to facilitate in every possible way the realization of the purposes of justice and the tasks of the court, strictly observing the principle of the independence of judges and their subordination only to law.

Article 39. Promulgation by Union Republics of Laws on Union Republic Court Organization. On the basis of Article 14(u) of the USSR Constitution and in accordance with the present Fundamental Principles, union republic supreme soviets shall promulgate laws on union republic court organization.

STATUTE ON THE SUPREME COURT OF THE USSR

[Confirmed by a Law of the USSR Supreme Soviet, February 12, 1957, as amended September 30, 1967, and August 12, 1971. Vedomosti SSSR (1957), no. 4, item 84; (1967), no. 40, item 526; (1971), no. 33, item 332]

Article 1. In accordance with Article 104 of the USSR Constitution, the USSR Supreme Court shall be the highest judicial agency of the Union of Soviet Socialist Republics.

The USSR Supreme Court shall be charged with supervision over the judicial activity of USSR judicial agencies, as well as of union republic judicial agencies within the limits established by the present statute. The USSR Supreme Court shall study the practice of the application by courts of legislation and shall issue guiding explanations to courts in regard to questions of its application.

The USSR Supreme Court, in instances and in the procedure provided by law, shall decide questions arising from legal assistance treaties concluded by the USSR with other states.

The USSR Supreme Court shall have the right of legislative initiative.

Article 2. The USSR Supreme Court shall be responsible to the USSR Supreme Soviet and, in the interval between sessions of the USSR Supreme Soviet, to the Presidium of the USSR Supreme Soviet.

In realizing justice, members of the USSR Supreme Court and people's assessors of the USSR Supreme Court shall be independent and subordinate only to law.

Article 3. The USSR Supreme Court shall consist of a chairman of the USSR Supreme Court, deputy chairmen of the USSR Supreme Court, members of the USSR Supreme Court, and people's assessors elected by the USSR Supreme Soviet, as well as of the chairmen of the union republic supreme courts, who shall be members of the USSR Supreme Court *ex officio.*

The numerical composition of the USSR Supreme Court shall be established by the USSR Supreme Soviet at the time of election of the USSR Supreme Court.

Article 4. In accordance with Article 105 of the USSR Constitution, the USSR Supreme Court shall be elected for a term of five years.

Article 5. The USSR Supreme Court shall be governed in its activity by all-union laws as well as by union republic laws.

Article 6. The USSR Supreme Court shall include the:

(a) Plenum of the USSR Supreme Court;

(b) Judicial Division for Civil Cases;

(c) Judicial Division for Criminal Cases;

(d) Military Division.

Article 7. The Plenum of the USSR Supreme Court shall consist of the chairman of the USSR Supreme Court, the deputy chairmen of the USSR Supreme Court, and the members of the USSR Supreme Court.

Participation of the USSR Procurator General in sessions of the Plenum shall be obligatory.

The USSR Minister of Justice shall participate in sessions of the plenum.

Article 8. The Plenum of the USSR Supreme Court shall be convoked by the President of the USSR Supreme Court at least once every three months.

A session of the plenum shall be considered empowered if not less than two-thirds of its membership is present.

Decrees of the plenums shall be adopted by a simple majority of the votes of the members of the Plenum of the USSR Supreme Court participating in the session.

Article 9. The Plenum of the USSR Supreme Court shall:

(a) consider protests of the chairman of the USSR Supreme Court and of the USSR Procurator General against decisions, judgments, and rulings of the USSR Supreme Court;

(b) consider protests of the chairman of the USSR Supreme Court and of the USSR Procurator General against decrees of the union republic supreme courts in the event that such decrees are contrary to all-union legislation or violate the interests of other union republics;

(c) consider materials summarizing judicial practice and judicial statistics and issue guiding explanations to courts concerning questions of the application of legislation in connection with the consideration of judicial cases;

(d) make representations to the Presidium of the USSR Supreme Soviet concerning questions which are subject to resolution by legislation and concerning questions of the interpretation of USSR laws;

(e) settle disputes among union republic judicial agencies;

(f) hear reports of chairmen of judicial divisions of the Supreme Court concerning the activity of the divisions and reports of chairmen of union republic supreme courts concerning judicial practice in the application of all-union legislation, as well as of decrees of the Plenum of the USSR Supreme Court.

Article 10. Judicial divisions shall be appointed by the Plenum of the USSR Supreme Court from among the members of the USSR Supreme Court.

The chairman of the USSR Supreme Court shall be granted the right to make changes when necessary in the composition of divisions, with subsequent submission for confirmation by the Plenum of the USSR Supreme Court.

Members of military tribunals of branches of the armed forces, areas, military groups, and fleets may be allowed, when necessary, to serve as reserve judges for the consideration of cases in the Military Division of the USSR Supreme Court.

Article 11. The Judicial Division for Civil Cases and the Judicial Division for Criminal Cases of the USSR Supreme Court shall:

(a) consider as a court of first instance civil and criminal cases, respectively, of exceptional importance relegated by law to their jurisdiction;

(b) consider by way of judicial supervision protests of the chairman of the USSR Supreme Court, the USSR Procurator General, and their deputies against decisions and judgments of the union republic supreme courts in civil and criminal cases in the event that such decisions or judgments are contrary to all-union legislation or violate the interests of other union republics.

Article 12. The Military Division of the USSR Supreme Court shall:

(a) consider as a court of first instance criminal cases of exceptional importance relegated by law to its jurisdiction;

(b) consider cassational appeals and protests against judgments, decisions, and rulings of military tribunals of branches of the armed forces, areas, military groups, fleets, and separate armies in instances provided by law;

(c) consider by way of judicial supervision protests of the chairman of the USSR Supreme Court, the USSR Procurator General, and his deputies, as well as protests of the chairman of the Military Division of the USSR Supreme Court and the Chief Military Procurator, against judgments, decisions, and rulings of military tribunals of branches of the armed forces, areas, military groups, fleets, and separate armies.

Article 13. Divisions of the USSR Supreme Court shall consider cases as a court of first instance composed of a presiding member of the USSR Supreme Court and two people's assessors.

Cassational appeals and protests, as well as protests by way of judicial supervision, shall be considered by a bench of three members of the USSR Supreme Court.

Article 14. Decisions of the Judicial Division for Civil Cases and judgments of the Judicial Division for Criminal Cases and the Military Division of the USSR Supreme Court shall be rendered in the name of the Union of Soviet Socialist Republics.

Article 15. The chairman of the USSR Supreme Court shall:

(a) submit to the USSR Supreme Court, in accordance with the present statute, protests against decisions, judgments, and rulings of judicial divisions of the USSR Supreme Court, against decisions, judgments, and decrees of union republic supreme courts, and against judgments, and rulings of military tribunals of branches of the armed forces, areas, military groups, fleets, and separate armies;

submit to presidiums and plenums of union republic supreme courts, in accordance with the competence of presidiums and plenums determined by union republic legislation, protests against decisions, judgments, and decrees of union republic supreme courts, and against judgments, decisions and rulings of military tribunals of branches of the armed forces, areas, military groups, fleets, and separate armies;

(b) preside at sessions of the Plenum of the USSR Supreme Court and, if he wishes, assume the chairmanship at judicial sessions of divisions of the USSR Supreme Court during the consideration of any case;

(c) exercise general organizational direction over the work of the divisions of the USSR Supreme Court;

(d) secure the preparation of materials on questions subject to consideration at a plenum of the USSR Supreme Court;

(e) [Repealed]

(f) direct the work of the staff of the USSR Supreme Court.

In the absence of the chairman of the USSR Supreme Court, a deputy chairman of the USSR Supreme Court shall exercise all his rights and duties.

Article 15-1. Deputy chairman of the USSR Supreme Court shall:

(a) submit to the USSR Supreme Court, in accordance with the present statute, protests against decisions and judgments of union republic supreme courts, as well as protests against judgments, decisions, and rulings of military tribunals of branches of the armed forces, areas, military groups, fleets, and separate armies;

(b) submit to presidiums and plenums of union republic supreme courts, in accordance with the competence of presidiums determined by union republic legislation, protests against decisions, judgments, and decrees of union republic supreme courts in the event that they are contrary to all-union legislation or violate the interests of other union republics;

(c) assume, if he wishes, the chairmanship at judicial sessions of divisions of the USSR Supreme Court during the consideration of cases.

Article 16. Chairman of divisions of the USSR Supreme Court shall:

(a) exercise direction over the work of the respective divisions;

(b) preside at preparatory and judicial sessions of divisions;

(c) form benches for judicial sessions of divisions from among the members of the respective divisions and the people's assessors;

(d) present to the Plenum of the USSR Supreme Court reports of the activity of the divisons.

Article 17. The chairman, deputy chairmen, and members of the USSR Supreme Court, as well as people's assessors of the USSR Supreme Court, may not be brought to responsibility in court or arrested without the consent of the USSR Supreme Soviet and, in the interval between sessions, of the Presidium of the USSR Supreme Soviet.

Article 18. The chairman, deputy chairmen, and members of the USSR Supreme Court, as well as people's assessors of the USSR Supreme Court, may be relieved of their duties before expiry of their term of office only by decree of the USSR Supreme Soviet and, in the interval between sessions, by decree of the Presidium of the USSR Supreme Soviet with subsequent confirmation by the USSR Supreme Soviet.

Article 19. The personnel establishment of the staff of the USSR Supreme Court shall be confirmed by the Presidium of the USSR Supreme Soviet.

Article 20. The USSR Supreme Court shall publish a Bulletin of the Supreme Court of the USSR.

STATUTE ON MILITARY TRIBUNALS

[Confirmed by a Law of the USSR of December 25, 1958, as amended February 21, 1968, July 6, 1970, August 12, 1971, and November 26, 1973. Vedomosti SSSR (1959), no. 1, item 14; (1968), no. 9, item 64; (1970), no. 28, item 250; (1971), no. 33, item 332; (1973), no. 48, item 679]

Chapter I. General Provisions

Article 1. In accordance with Article 102 of the USSR Constitution, military tribunals shall be courts of the USSR and shall be a part of the unified judicial system of the USSR.

Judgments and decisions rendered by military tribunals shall be proclaimed in the name of the Union of Soviet Socialist Republics.

Article 2. Military tribunals, in carrying out the tasks of socialist justice, shall be called upon to wage a struggle against infringements on the security of the USSR, the battle capacity of its armed forces, military discipline, and the procedure established in the USSR armed forces for performing military service.

Article 3. The consideration of cases in military tribunals shall be carried out on the principles of collegiality.

As a court of first instances, military tribunals shall consider cases with a chairman, deputy chairman, or member of the military tribunal presiding and two people's assessors.

Cases relating to cassational or private appeals and protests, as well as cases relating to protests by way of judicial supervision, shall be considered by a bench of three members of the military tribunal.

Article 4. Citizens of the USSR who are on active military service and who on election day have attained twenty-five years of age may be elected chairmen, deputy chairmen, or members of military tribunals.

Chairmen, deputy chairmen, and members of military tribunals shall be elected by the Presidium of the USSR Supreme Soviet for a term of five years.

Article 5. Any citizen of the USSR who is on active military service may be elected a people's assessor of a military tribunal.

People's assessors of military tribunals shall be elected by open ballot at general meetings of servicemen of a military unit (or institution) for a term of two years.

During the performance of their duties in court, people's assessors shall have the rights of a judge.

Article 6. In realizing justice, the chairmen, deputy chairmen, and members of military tribunals, as well as people's assessors of military tribunals, shall be independent and subordinate only to law.

Article 7. Military tribunals shall be guided in their activity by legislation of the USSR and by union republic legislation.

Article 8. Military tribunals shall be organized and shall operate in areas, force groups, fleets, armies, flotillas, military formations, and garrisons.

Chapter II. Jurisdiction of Military Tribunals

Article 9. Military tribunals shall have jurisdiction over:

(a) cases concerning all crimes committed by servicemen, as well as by reservists during their training periods;

(b) cases concerning all crimes committed by officers, ensigns, warrant officers, sergeants, master sergeants, soldiers, sailors, and enlisted personnel of agencies of state security;

(c) cases concerning crimes against the established procedure for performing service committed by persons of the command staff of correctional labor institutions;

(d) all cases concerning espionage;

(e) cases concerning crimes committed by persons with regard to whom there is a special reference in USSR legislation.

Article 10. In localities where by virtue of exceptional circumstances ordinary courts do not operate, military tribunals shall consider all criminal and civil cases.

Article 11. Military tribunals shall consider, jointly with criminal cases, civil suits of military units (or institutions), state and social enterprises, institutions, and organizations, as well as individual citizens, concerning compensation for material damage caused to them by crime.

Article 12. When one person or group of persons is accused of committing several crimes, if the case of one of the crimes is within the jurisdiction of a military tribunal and the others within any other court, the case concerning all the crimes shall be considered by a military tribunal.

When a group of persons is accused of committing one or several crimes if the case with regard to one of the accused is within the jurisdiction of a military tribunal and to the remaining persons within any other court, the cases in regard to all the accused shall be considered by a military tribunal.

Article 13. Cases concerning crimes committed by persons specified in Article 9(1), (b), and (c) of the present statute during the period of their service, but who are discharged at the time the case is considered in court, shall be considered by military tribunals.

Cases concerning crimes committed by persons prior to their being called for military service or prior to entering the service of agencies of state security, but who at the time the case is considered are on military service or in service in agencies of state security, shall be considered by ordinary courts.

Article 14. Cases concerning crimes of persons who hold military ranks up to lieutenant colonel or second captain inclusive, as well as all civil cases in the instances provided by Article 10 of the present statute, shall be within the jurisdiction of military tribunals of armies, flotillas, military formations, and garrisons.

Article 15. Military tribunals of branches of the armed forces, areas, force groups, fleets, and individual armies shall have jurisdiction over:

(a) cases concerning crimes of persons holding the military ranks of colonel or first captain;

(b) cases concerning crimes of persons occupying the post of field commander, second warship commander, or higher, and of persons equal to them in service status;

(c) cases concerning all crimes for which in peacetime the death penalty is provided by law.

Article 16. The Military Division of the USSR Supreme Court shall have jurisdiction over criminal cases of exceptional importance, cases concerning crimes of servicemen holding the military rank of general (or admiral), as well as servicemen holding the post of formation commander or higher, and of persons equal to them.

Article 17. The question of transferring a case from military tribunals of one area, fleet (or force group, individual army) to military tribunals of another area, fleet (or force group, individual army) shall be resolved by the Military Division of the USSR Supreme Court.

Within the limits of a military area, force group, or fleet, the question of transferring a case from one military tribunal to another shall be resolved by the military tribunal of the area, force group, or fleet.

Article 18. A superior military tribunal or the Military Division of the USSR Supreme Court shall have the right to take jurisdiction as a court of first instance over any case within the jurisdiction of an inferior military tribunal.

Chapter III. Supervision over Judicial Activity of Military Tribunals

Article 19. The USSR Supreme Court shall exercise supervision over the judicial activity of military tribunals.

Article 20. The Military Division of the USSR Supreme Court shall:

(a) consider cases regarding cassational or private appeals and protests against judgments, decisions, and rulings of military tribunals of areas, force groups, fleets, and individual armies;

(b) consider by way of judicial supervision cases regarding protests of the chairman of the USSR Supreme Court, the USSR Procurator General, their deputies, the chairman of the Military Division of the USSR Supreme Court, and the Chief Military Procurator against judgments, decisions, and rulings of military tribunals of areas, force groups, fleets, and individual armies.

Article 21. Military tribunals of areas, force groups, and fleets shall:

(a) consider cases regarding cassational and private appeals and protests against judgments, decisions, and rulings of military tribunals of armies, flotillas, military formations, and garrisons;

(b) consider by way of judicial supervision cases regarding protests of the chairman of the USSR Supreme Court, the USSR Procurator General, their deputies, the chairman of the Military Division of the USSR Supreme Court, the Chief Military Procurator, the chairmen of military tribunals, and military procurators of areas, force groups, and fleets against judgments, decisions, and rulings of military tribunals of armies, flotillas, military formations, and garrisons.

Chapter IV. Organizational Direction of Military Tribunals

Article 22. The structure and personnel of military tribunals and of the Administration of Military Tribunals of the USSR Ministry of Justice shall be determined by the USSR Ministry of Justice jointly with the USSR Ministry of Defense.

The personnel of military tribunals, of the Administration of Military Tribunals of the USSR Ministry of Justice, and of the Military Division of the USSR Supreme Court shall be part of the personnel strength of the USSR armed forces and shall be provided with all types of allowances on an equal basis with the personnel of military units and institutions of the USSR Ministry of Defense.

A list of staff posts for the judges of military tribunals and the Military Division of the USSR Supreme Court and the military ranks corresponding to these posts shall be confirmed by the Presidium of the USSR Supreme Soviet: for military tribunals, upon the joint representation of the USSR Minister of Justice and the USSR Minister of Defense; for the Military Division of the USSR Supreme Court, upon the joint representation of the Chairman of the USSR Supreme Court and the USSR Minister of Defense.

Article 23. Officers and noncommissioned officers, ensigns, and warrant officers of military tribunals, of the Administration of Military Tribunals of the USSR Ministry of Justice, and the Military Divison of the USSR Supreme Court shall be on active military service, and the statutes on performance of military service, military status, and orders of the USSR Minister of Defense defining the procedure for performing service shall extend to them.

The conferment of military ranks of junior and senior officers shall be performed in the procedure established by the USSR Council of Ministers: on servicemen of military tribunals and the Administration of Military Tribunals of the USSR Ministry of Justice, upon the representation of the head of the Administration of Military Tribunals of the USSR Ministry of Justice and the chairman of military tribunals of branches of the armed forces, areas, force groups, and fleets; on servicemen of the Military Division of the USSR Supreme Court, upon the representation of the chairman of the Military Division of the USSR Supreme Court.

Military ranks of generals shall be conferred on servicemen of military tribunals and of the Administration of Military Tribunals of the USSR Ministry of Justice by the USSR Council of Ministers upon the joint representation of the USSR Minister of Justice and the USSR Minister of Defense; and servicemen of the Military Division of the USSR Supreme Court, upon the joint representation of the chairman of the USSR Supreme Court and the USSR Minister of Defense.

Article 24. The USSR Ministry of Justice and its Administration of Military Tribunals shall carry out:

(a) the verification of the organization of the work of military tribunals;

(b) the study and generalization of judicial practice of military tribunals, coordinating this activity with the USSR Supreme Court, as well as the organization of work for the keeping of judicial statistics;

(c) the preparation jointly with the USSR Ministry of Defense of proposals on questions of the organization of military tribunals.

The USSR Minister of Justice and the head of the Administration of Military Tribunals of the USSR Ministry of Justice shall promulgate orders relating to the organization of the work of military tribunals.

Article 25. The chairmen of military tribunals of areas, force groups, and fleets shall:

(a) organize the verification of the activity of inferior military tribunals;

(b) direct the study of judicial practice of inferior military tribunals and the keeping of judicial statistics;

(c) give instructions concerning the organization of the work of inferior military tribunals;

(d) determine by agreement with the respective military soviets the number of people's assessors for the military tribunals.

Article 26. Appointment and dismissal of employees of military tribunals shall be performed by the chairman of the respective military tribunal.

Article 27. The head of the Administration of Military Tribunals of the USSR Ministry of Justice and the chairman of the Military Division of the USSR Supreme Court shall, within the limits of their competence, inform the USSR Minister of Defense and the head of the Chief Political Administration of the Soviet Army and Navy about questions arising out of the activity of military tribunals.

Chairmen of military tribunals of areas, force groups, fleets, armies, and flotillas shall inform the respective military soviets about questions arising out of the activity of military tribunals, and the chairmen of military tribunals of military formations and garrisons, the respective military command and political organs.

Article 28. Material and technical supply, financing, providing transport and means of communication, and keeping the archives of military tribunals shall be entrusted to the respective institutions of the USSR Ministry of Defense.

Protection of the official premises of military tribunals shall be carried out by military units of the formations and garrisons for which the military tribunals operate.

Escorting persons arrested to military tribunals and protecting them shall be performed by the military units for formations and garrisons for which the military tribunals operate, as well as by units of the escort guard of the USSR Ministry of Internal Affairs.

Chapter V. Responsibility of Members of Military Tribunals

Article 29. Chairmen, deputy chairmen, and members of military tribunals shall bear disciplinary responsibility in the procedure established by USSR legislation concerning disciplinary responsibility of judges for violation of military discipline and for service offenses.

Article 30. Chairmen, deputy chairmen, and members of military tribunals may not be brought to criminal responsibility, removed from office, or subjected to arrest without the consent of the Presidium of the USSR Supreme Soviet.

STATUTE ON THE MINISTRY OF JUSTICE OF THE USSR

[Confirmed by Decree of the USSR Council of Ministers, March 21, 1972, No. 194, as amended April 28, 1976. SP SSSR (1972), No. 6, item 32; (1976), no. 7, item 38]

1. In conformity with the USSR Constitution, the USSR Ministry of Justice shall be a union republic ministry.

The USSR Ministry of Justice shall exercise organizational direction over union republic courts and over military tribunals, shall carry on work in regard to systematization and shall prepare proposals concerning the codification of legislation, shall exercise methods direction over legal work in the national economy, methods direction over and coordination of the work of state agencies and social organizations in regard to the propagandizing of legal knowledge and explaining legislation to the populace, direction over the notariat and forensic examination institutions, as well as general direction over the activity of agencies of the Registry of Acts of Civil Status and the advocates, and shall effectuate in the established procedure international ties in regard to legal questions.

The USSR Ministry of Justice shall bear responsibility before the Party, the state, and the people for the organizational state of the work of judicial agencies, for the activity of agencies and institutions of justice, and for the strengthening of the legal order and socialist legality.

2. The principal tasks of the Ministry of Justice shall be:

the strengthening of socialist legality in every possible way, protection of the rights and legal interests of state, cooperative, and social organizations and citizens; the improvement, jointly with other state agencies, of activity in regard to the struggle against crime and elimination of the reasons and conditions facilitating the commission of crimes and other breaches of law;

securing organizational direction over courts, increasing the standard of such work, assisting in every possible way the implementation of the purposes or goals of justice and the tasks of the court, while strictly observing the principle of the independence of judges and their subordination only to law;

the systematization and preparation of proposals concerning the codification of legislation, all possible assistance in raising the level of codification work being carried on by USSR ministries and departments, and the improvement of legislation in conformity with the tasks of communist construction;

improving the activity of the notariat, agencies of the Registry of Acts of Civil Status, the advocates, and forensic examination and other organizations and institutions of justice within its jurisdiction;

improving legal work in the national economy with a view to intensifying its influence in increasing the economic efficiency of social production, protection of socialist ownership, further strengthening of state and labor discipline, and strict observance of the rights and legal interests of enterprises, organizations, institutions, and citizens;

organizing the propaganda of legal knowledge and explaining legislation to the populace;

promoting the development of legal science and the use of its achievements in state, economic, and cultural construction;

providing institutions and organizations of the system of the ministry and judicial agencies with qualified personnel, retraining and raising the qualifications of the personnel of these organizations, institutions, and agencies, combining senior experienced personnel and young capable workers, creating conditions for the best use of the knowledge and experience of workers, promoting young, well-recommended workers to supervisory work.

3. The USSR Ministry of Justice shall direct the branch of state administration entrusted to it, as a rule, through the union republic ministries of justice and shall administer institutions and organizations directly subordinate to it.

4. The USSR Ministry of Justice, the ministries of justice of the union and autonomous republics, the justice sections of the executive committees of territory, regional, and city soviets of working people's deputies, the notariat, scientific research institutions, institutions of higher education, and other institutions and organizations within their jurisdiction shall comprise the unified system of the USSR Ministry of Justice.

5. The USSR Ministry of Justice shall be guided in its activity by the laws of the USSR, by edicts of the Presidium of the USSR Supreme Soviet, by decrees and regulations of the government of the USSR, and by other normative acts, by the General Statute on Ministries of the USSR, as well as by the present statute, and shall ensure the correct application of prevailing legislation and institutions and organizations of the system of the ministry.

The USSR Ministry of Justice shall summarize the practice of applying legislation on questions relating to the organization and activity of agencies and institutions of the system of the ministry and courts, shall work out proposals relating to the improvement of this legislation, and shall submit these for the consideration of the USSR Council of Ministers.

6. Together with carrying out the functions provided by the General Statute on Ministries of the USSR, the USSR Ministry of Justice shall:

(a) work out proposals relating to the organization of union republic courts and to military tribunals (distribution, structure, posts); hold elections of judges and people's assessors; direct the organization of reports by judges to the electors;

(b) verify the organization of the work of judicial agencies of the union republics and of military tribunals, hear reports on these questions by the chairmen of courts and military tribunals, and take measures to improve it; study and disseminate positive experience; ensure the creation of proper conditions for the carrying out of justice;

(c) with a view to the further improvement of the activity of courts, study and summarize judicial practice, coordinating this work with the USSR Supreme Court, and use the results of the summary to eliminate shortcomings uncovered in organizing the work of the courts;

(d) verify the organization of the work of the courts in regard to consideration of materials concerning administrative responsibility and take measures to improve this work;

(e) organize the work of keeping judicial statistics and use the data to improve the organization and activity of union republic courts and military tribunals in carrying out justice and to prepare proposals for the improvement of legislation;

(f) organize sociological research with a view to working out measures in regard to the struggle against crime and strengthening socialist legality, coordinating this work with the USSR Procuracy, the USSR Supreme Court, the USSR Ministry of Internal Affairs, and other concerned institutions and organizations;

(g) exercise direction and control over the work relating to the execution of decisions, rulings, and decrees of courts in civil cases and of the judgments, rulings, and decrees of courts in criminal cases, in that part relating to exactions of property;

(h) render legal aid to comrades' courts, voluntary people's patrols, and other social organizations struggling against breaches of the law;

(i) carry on work, with the participation of USSR ministries and departments, relating to the systematization and codification of legislation of the USSR and prepare proposals relating to making changes therein;

compile and publish a Collection of Legislation in Force of the USSR;

(j) prepare on behalf of superior agencies or at their own initiative draft legislative acts and draft decrees of the USSR Council of Ministers, and give legal opinions on drafts of important normative acts submitted for the consideration of the government of the USSR;

prepare, taking into account the proposals of USSR ministries and departments, draft work plans for the improvement of economic legislation, coordinate the working out by USSR ministries and departments of draft legislative and other normative acts provided by the plans, render methods assistance to them, take part in such work in accordance with the plans, and exercise control over the fulfillment of the said work by ministries and departments;

(k) exercise methods direction over legal work in the national economy, acquaint themselves with the state of such work in ministries, departments, enterprises, organizations, and institutions, as well as in the executive committees of local soviets of working people's deputies, and shall hear communications from representatives of ministries and departments concerning the state of legal work; work out and give methods instructions and recommendations relating to the improvement of legal work;

study and summarize the practice of organizing legal work, disseminate positive experience of the work of legal sections and jurisconsults, and take measures to raise the qualifications of workers of these sections (or of jurisconsults);

(l) direct the work with personnel of judicial agencies and organizations and institutions of justice within its jurisdiction, organize the retraining and raising of the qualifications of the said personnel; in the established procedure award workers of these agencies, institutions, and organizations with chest badges and certificates of honor, and apply other forms of incentive;

(m) participate in working out drafts of state plans for the training of legal personnel in the country and plans for distributing young specialists who have completed legal institutions of higher education;

(n) take part in working out teaching plans and syllabi relating to legal disciplines for legal institutes and law faculties of state universities, as well as of other higher institutions of learning, secondary specialized and professional-technical institutions of higher education, and general education schools;

(o) participate in the working out of plans for the publication of textbooks and teaching aids for legal institutions of higher education, as well as codes, collections of normative acts, legal scientific and popular and other juridical literature, and take measures to provide courts and organizations and institutions within their jurisdiction with legislative materials;

(p) organize scientific research in the domain of improving legislation and forensic expertise;

coordinate, jointly with the USSR Academy of Sciences and appropriate USSR ministries and departments, the activity of legal scientific research institutions; organize scientific conferences, meetings, and symposia on questions of developing legal science;

(q) exercise methods direction over and coordination of the work of state agencies and social organizations in regard to the propagandizing of legal knowledge and explaining legislation to the populace, acquaint themselves with the state of such work in ministries, departments, and social organizations, coordinate their plans for work in regard to legal propaganda, and give the necessary methods instructions and recommendations;

(r) carry out general direction over the advocates within the limits and in the procedure established by prevailing legislation;

establish the procedure for organizing legal aid rendered by advocates to the populace, enterprises, institutions, collective farms, state farms, and other organizations, and by agreement with the State Committee of the USSR Council of Ministers for Labor and Wages, the VTsSPS, and the USSR Ministry of Finances, the procedure for payment for legal aid and the terms for payment for the work of advocates;

(s) organize the work of institutions of the notariat, verify their activity, and give instructions to improve it;

(t) work out and effectuate measures to improve the activity of agencies of the Registry of Acts of Civil Status, verify their work, and give instructions to improve such work;

(u) effectuate in the established procedure international ties relating to legal questions; participate in the preparation of international treaties and agreements;

organize the fulfillment of treaties on rendering legal assistance, concluded by the USSR with other states, as well as conventions and agreements relating to questions within the competence of the ministry.

7. In accordance with Article 38-1 of the Fundamental Principles of Court Organization of the USSR, Union Republics, and Autonomous Republics, the USSR Minister of Justice shall have the right to submit proposals to the Plenum of the USSR Supreme Court on giving guiding explanations to courts in regard to questions of applying legislation.

8. The USSR Ministry of Justice shall have the right to receive, when necessary, from ministries and departments of the USSR and union republics, as well as from scientific research institutions and institutions of higher education, opinions relating to draft legislative acts, decrees of the government of the USSR, and other documents worked out by the ministry, as well as to enlist, by agreement with the directors of the appropriate ministries, departments, institutions, and organizations, the specialists of ministries, departments, scientific research institutions, and institutions of higher education to participate in the work connected with the improvement of legislation.

9. The USSR Ministry of Justice shall be headed by a minister appointed in conformity with the USSR Constitution by the USSR Supreme Soviet, and in the interval between sessions, by the Presidium of the USSR Supreme Soviet, with a subsequent submission for the confirmation of the USSR Supreme Soviet.

The USSR Minister of Justice shall have deputies appointed by the USSR Council of Ministers. The distribution of duties among deputy ministers shall be made by the USSR Minister of Justice.

The members of the collegium of the ministry shall be confirmed by the USSR Council of Ministers.

11. The USSR Minister of Justice shall bear personal responsibility for the fulfillment of tasks and duties entrusted to the ministry and shall establish the degree of responsibility for deputy ministers, heads of administrations, and directors of other subdivisions of the ministry over the direction of particular areas of activity of the ministry and over the work of institutions and organizations of the system of the ministry.

12. Within the limits of the competence of the ministry, the USSR Minister of Justice shall promulgate the prevailing laws, orders, and instructions on the basis of and in execution of the decrees and regulations of the USSR Council of Ministers and shall give directives which are binding for execution by union and autonomous republic ministries of justice, by sections of justice of executive committees of territory, regional, and city soviets of working people's deputies, by agencies of the Registry of Acts of Civil Status, the advocates, institutions of forensic expertise, the notariat, and other institutions of justice and organizations within the jurisdiction of the ministry, and in regard to the organization of work, by union republic judicial agencies and military tribunals; shall verify the execution of such orders, instructions, and directives.

Instructions and directives of the USSR Minister of Justice in regard to the performance of notarial actions and the Registry of Acts of Civil Status shall be binding on ministries, departments, executive committees of local soviets of working people's deputies, enterprises, organizations, and institutions.

The USSR Minister of Justice, when necessary, shall promulgate joint orders and instructions with the directors of other USSR ministries and departments.

13. The Collegium of the USSR Ministry of Justice shall consider at its regularly held sessions basic questions of the ministry's activity,

shall hear reports of ministers of justice of union and autonomous republics, of heads of sections of justice of executive committees of territory, regional, and city soviets of working people's deputies, directors of agencies of the Registry of Acts of Civil Status, the notariat, the advocates, scientific research institutions, institutions of higher education, and other institutions and organizations within its jurisdiction, reports of the chairmen of supreme courts of union and autonomous republics, territory, regional, city, and district people's courts and military tribunals in regard to the organization of the work of courts, reports of administrations and sections of the ministry, questions of the verification of the performance, selection, and upbringing of personnel, shall discuss drafts of important legislative acts and decrees of the government of the USSR worked out by the ministry, opinions relating to draft normative acts, questions of the systematization of legislation, and drafts of the most important orders and instructions.

Decisions of the collegium shall be implemented, as a rule, by orders of the minister. In the event of disagreements between the minister and the collegium, the minister shall implement his own decision, reporting to the USSR Council of Ministers about the disagreements which have arisen and the collegium members, in turn, may communicate their view to the USSR Council of Ministers.

14. The USSR Ministry of Justice shall convene in the established procedure meetings of the aktiv, with the participation of social organizations, at which reports concerning measures relating to the fulfillment of decisions of the Party and government, the most important problems of organizing the activity of courts, the improvement of legislation and strengthening of legality shall be heard and discussed, and there also shall be discussed on the basis of developing criticism and self-criticism questions connected with the improvement of the activity of the ministry and of institutions and organizations within its jurisdiction.

15. A scientific advisory council attached to the USSR Ministry of Justice, composed of well-known scholars and highly qualified specialists, shall be created to consider scientific recommendations and other proposals for the improvement of the organization and activity of institutions of justice and for other questions.

A coordinating and methods council attached to the USSR Ministry of Justice, in which representatives of appropriate ministries, departments, and organizations participate, shall be created with a view to working out questions connected with the methods direction over and coordination of the activity of state agencies and social organizations in regard to the propagandizing of legal knowledge and explaining legislation to the populace.

The composition of the scientific advisory council and the coordinating and methods council, as well as statutes therefor, shall be confirmed by the USSR Minister of Justice.

16. The structure and numerical strength of workers of the central apparatus of the USSR Ministry of Justice shall be confirmed by the USSR Council of Ministers.

The staffing schedule of the central apparatus of the ministry, as well as statutes on administrations and sections of the ministry, shall be confirmed by the USSR Minister of Justice.

17. The USSR Ministry of Justice shall have a seal depicting the State Arms of the USSR and its own name.

STATUTE ON PROCURACY SUPERVISION IN THE USSR

[Confirmed by Edict of the Presidium of the USSR Supreme Soviet, May 24, 1955, as amended February 27, 1959, March 3, 1960, February 14, 1964, and December 14, 1966. Vedomosti SSSR (1955), no. 9, item 222; (1959), no. 9, item 67; (1960), no. 10, item 65; (1964), no 8, item 100; (1966), no. 50, item 1021]

Chapter I. General Provisions

Article 1. In accordance with Article 113 of the USSR Constitution, the USSR Procurator General shall be charged with supreme supervision over strict execution of the laws by all ministries and their subordinate institutions and by individual officials, as well as by citizens of the USSR.

Article 2. The task of supreme supervision over strict execution of the laws shall be to strengthen socialist legality in the USSR and to protect from any infringements:

(1) the social and state system of the USSR secured by the USSR Constitution and by the union and autonomous republic constitutions, the socialist system of economy, and socialist ownership;

(2) the political, labor, housing, and other personal and property rights and legally protected interests of citizens of the USSR guaranteed by the USSR Constitution and by the union and autonomous republic constitutions;

(3) the rights and legally protected interests of state institutions and enterprises, collective farms, and cooperative and other social organizations.

The USSR Procurator General and procurators subordinate to him shall be obliged to watch over the proper and uniform application of the laws of the USSR and of the union and autonomous republics, notwithstanding any local differences and despite any local influences.

Article 3. The USSR Procurator General and procurators subordinate to him shall carry out the tasks with which they are charged through:

(1) supervision over strict execution of the laws by all ministries and departments and their subordinate institutions and enterprises, by executive and administrative agencies of local soviets of working people's deputies, and by cooperative and other social organizations, and also supervision over strict observance of the laws by officials and citizens;

(2) bringing to criminal responsibility persons who are guilty of committing crimes;

(3) supervision over observance of legality in the activity of agencies of inquiry and preliminary investigation;

(4) supervision over the legality and justification of judgments, decisions, rulings, and decrees of judicial agencies;

(5) supervision over the legality of execution of judgments;

(6) supervision over the observance of the legality of the keeping of persons confined in places of deprivation of freedom.

Article 4. The USSR Procurator General and procurators subordinate to him shall, in exercising supervision over legality on behalf of the state, be obliged to take prompt measures to eliminate any violations of the laws, regardless of who has committed such violations.

Article 5. Procuratorial agencies in the USSR shall constitute a single centralized system headed by the USSR Procurator General with the subordination of inferior procurators to superiors.

Article 7. The USSR Procurator General shall be responsible to the USSR Supreme Soviet and accountable thereto, and in the interval between sessions of the USSR Supreme Soviet, to the Presidium of the USSR Supreme Soviet, to which it also shall be accountable.

Article 8. The USSR Procurator General, on the basis of and in execution of the laws in force, shall issue orders and instructions which shall be binding on all agencies of the procuracy.

Orders and instructions of the USSR Procurator General may be annulled by the Presidium of the USSR Supreme Soviet if they do not conform to law.

Article 9. The USSR Procurator General may make recommendations to the Presidium of the USSR Supreme Soviet concerning questions which are subject to resolution by legislation or which require interpretation of the law under Article 49(c) of the USSR Constitution.

Chapter II. Supervision over Execution of the Laws by Institutions, Organizations, Officials, and Citizens of the USSR

Article 10. The USSR Procurator General and procurators subordinate to him, within the limits of their jurisdiction, shall exercise supervision over:

(1) the strict conformity of acts issued by ministries and departments and their subordinate institutions and enterprises, as well as by executive and administrative agencies of local soviets of working people's deputies and by cooperative and other social organizations, to the Constitution and laws of the USSR, to the constitutions and laws of union and autonomous republics, and to decrees of the USSR Council of Ministers and the union and autonomous republic councils of ministers;

(2) strict execution of the laws by officials and citizens of the USSR

Article 11. The USSR Procurator General, procurators of union and autonomous republics, procurators of territories, regions, autonomous regions, national areas, districts, and cities, as well as military procurators, within the limits of their jurisdiction, shall have the right to:

(1) demand orders, instructions, decisions, regulations, decrees, and other acts issued by ministries and departments and their subordinate institutions and enterprises, as well as by executive and administrative agencies of local soviets of working people's deputies, by cooperative and other social organizations, and by officials, in order to verify the conformity of such acts to the law;

(2) require from directors of ministries, departments, institutions, enterprises, executive and administrative agencies of local soviets of working people's deputies, cooperative and other social organizations, and officials the presentation of necessary documents and information;

(3) perform on-the-spot verifications of the execution of laws in connection with petitions, complaints, and other information concerning violations of the law;

(4) require, in connection with available data concerning violations of the law, from directors of ministries, departments, institutions, enterprises, executive and administrative agencies of local soviets of working people's deputies, cooperative and other social organizations, and officials the performance of verifications and reviews of the activity of their subordinate institutions, enterprises, and organizations and their subordinate officials;

(5) require personal explanations concerning violations of the law from officials and citizens.

Article 12. Ministries, departments, institutions, enterprises, executive and administrative agencies of local soviets of working people's deputies, cooperative and other social organizations, as well as officials, shall be obliged upon demand of a procurator to send him orders, instructions, decisions, regulations, decrees, and other documents, as well as to present necessary information and explanations.

Article 13. The USSR Procurator General and procurators subordinate to him shall protest orders, instructions, decisions, regulations, decrees, and other acts which are contrary to law, to the agency which issued the relevant act or to the superior agency.

A procurator's protest must be considered within ten days. The procurator who lodged the protest shall be notified of the decision adopted with regard to the protest.

The lodging of a protest by a procurator against a decree to bring a person to administrative responsibility issued by an authorized agency shall suspend execution of the administrative sanction until consideration of the protest by the respective agency.

Article 14. A procurator shall be obliged to accept and consider petitions and complaints of citizens concerning a violation of a law, to verify such petitions and complaints within the time periods established by law, and to take measures to restore rights which have been violated and to defend the legal interests of citizens.

Article 15. In regard to officials or citizens who have violated the law, a procurator, depending on the nature of the violation, shall either bring the guilty person to criminal responsibility or shall take measures to bring the offender to administrative or disciplinary responsibility.

When necessary, a procurator shall take measures to ensure compensation for material damage caused by a violation of the law.

Article 16. The USSR Procurator General and procurators subordinate to him shall have the right to submit recommendations to state agencies and to social organizations for eliminating violations of a law and the causes which make violation of the law possible.

A state agency or social organization shall be obliged within one month to consider the recommendation of a procurator and to take necessary measures to eliminate violations of the law and the causes which make violation of the law possible.

Chapter III. Supervision over Execution of the Laws in the Activity of Agencies of Inquiry and Preliminary Investigation

Article 17. The USSR Procurator General and procurators subordinate to him, in exercising supervision over strict execution of the laws in the activity of agencies of inquiry and preliminary investigation, shall be obliged to:

(1) bring to criminal responsibility the persons guilty of committing crimes, take measures to the end that not a single crime should remain unsolved and that not a single criminal should evade responsibility;

(2) watch closely that no citizen should be subjected to being brought illegally or without justification to criminal responsibility or to any other illegal limitation of his rights;

(3) watch over the undeviating observance by agencies of inquiry and preliminary investigation of the procedure established by law for investigation of crimes.

Article 18. A procurator shall exercise supervision to the end that no one should be arrested without a court decree or the sanction of a procurator.

In deciding the question of sanctioning an arrest, a procurator shall be obliged to familiarize himself thoroughly with all materials which form the basis for the necessity of arrest and, when necessary, personally to question the person subject to arrest.

Article 19. A procurator, in exercising supervision over the investigation of crimes, shall have the right to:

(1) give instructions to agencies of inquiry and of preliminary investigation concerning the investigation of crimes, the selection, modification, or annulment of measures of restraint with respect to an accused person, as well as the searching for criminals in hiding;

(2) demand from agencies of inquiry and of preliminary investigation the files of criminal cases, documents, materials, and other information concerning crimes which have been committed, in order to verify them;

(3) participate in performing the preliminary investigation or inquiry in criminal cases and, when necessary, personally to investigate any type of case;

(4) return criminal cases to agencies of inquiry or of preliminary investigation with his directives concerning the performing of additional investigation;

(5) annul illegal or unjustified decrees of agencies of inquiry or of preliminary investigation;

(6) remove an investigator or person performing an inquiry in a case from further conduct of the investigation or inquiry if such persons have allowed a violation of the law in the investigation of the case;

(7) withdraw any case from an agency of inquiry and transfer it to an agency of preliminary investigation, as well as transfer a case from

one agency of preliminary investigation to another, with the aim of ensuring the fullest and most objective possible investigation of the case;

(8) commission agencies of inquiry to perform individual investigative acts in cases being handled by investigators of agencies of the procuracy, in particular the detention, appearance, or arrest of an accused person, to perform a search or seizure, or search for criminals in hiding;

(9) terminate criminal cases on the grounds specified in the law.

Article 20. Directives of a procurator to agencies of inquiry and of preliminary investigation in connection with the investigation by them of criminal cases and given in the procedure provided by the procedural law shall be binding on such agencies.

Article 21. A procurator shall be obliged, within the time periods established by law, to consider complaints addressed to him or received by him against actions of agencies of inquiry or of preliminary investigation and to inform complainants of decisions with respect to complaints.

Chapter IV. Supervision over the Legality and Grounds for Judgments, Decisions, Rulings, and Decrees of Judicial Agencies

Article 22. The Procurator General of the USSR and procurators subordinate thereto shall be obliged to exercise supervision over the legality and the grounds for judgments, decisions, rulings, and decrees rendered by judicial agencies.

Article 23. The USSR Procurator General and procurators subordinate thereto shall:

(1) participate in administrative sessions of a court;

(2) participate in the consideration of criminal and civil cases in judicial sessions and give opinions on questions arising during judicial consideration;

(3) support the state accusation in court during consideration of criminal cases;

(4) present suits by way of a civil proceeding or civil suit in a criminal proceeding and support the suits in court if such is required for the protection of state or social interests or of the rights or legal interests of citizens;

(5) lodge protests, in the procedure established by law, against illegal or unfounded judgments, decisions, rulings, or decrees of judicial agencies;

(6) give opinions with regard to criminal and civil cases being considered by a superior court on appeal or on protest;

(7) exercise supervision over the execution of court judgments.

Article 24. The USSR Procurator General and all procurators subordinate thereto shall have the right, within the limits of their jurisdiction, to demand by way of supervision the file of any civil or criminal case from judicial agencies for verification.

Article 25. The right of lodging protests against judgments, decisions, rulings, and decrees of a court which have entered into legal force shall appertain to:

the USSR Procurator General and his deputies: with regard to judgments, decisions, rulings, and decrees of any court of the USSR or of the union or autonomous republics;

the union republic procurator and his deputies: with regard to judgments, decisions, rulings, and decrees of union republic courts and of autonomous republics forming part thereof, except for decrees of the presidium of the union republic supreme court;

the autonomous republic procurator: with regard to judgments, decrees decisions, and rulings of autonomous republic people's courts, as well as the rulings of judicial divisions of the autonomous republic supreme court as a court of second instance;

the procurator of a territory, region, or autonomous region: with regard to judgments, decisions, and rulings of people's courts, as well as rulings of judicial divisions of the territorial or regional court, or court of the autonomous region, respectively, as a court of second instanc

the Chief Military Procurator: with regard to judgments and rulings of any military tribunal;

the military procurator of a military area (or fleet): with regard to judgments and rulings of inferior military tribunals.

Article 26. A protest against a judgment, decision, ruling, or decree of a court may be revoked by the procurator who lodged the protest or by a superior procurator, prior to the consideration of the protest by a court.

Article 27. The USSR Procurator General and his deputies shall have the right to suspend execution of a protested judgment, decision, ruling, or decree of any court of the USSR or of a union or autonomous republic prior to resolution of the case by way of supervision.

Article 28. Participation of the USSR Procurator General in sessions of the Plenum of the USSR Supreme Court shall be obligatory.

Article 29. In the event that the USSR Procurator General perceives that a decree of the Plenum of the USSR Supreme Court does not conform to law, he shall be obliged to make a representation to the Presidium of the USSR Supreme Soviet with respect to this question.

Article 30. The USSR Procurator General shall have the right to submit representations for consideration by the Plenum of the USSR Supreme Court concerning guiding explanations to be given to judicial agencies on questions of judicial practice.

Article 31. Procurators of union and autonomous republics, territorie regions, and autonomous regions shall participate in the consideration of criminal and civil cases by the presidiums of union or autonomous republic supreme courts, of territory or region courts, or of autonomous region courts.

Chapter V. Supervision over Observance of Legality in Places of Deprivation of Freedom

Article 32. The USSR Procurator General and procurators subordinate thereto, within the limits of their jurisdiction, shall be obliged to exercise supervision to the end that only persons confined under guard with the sanction of a procurator or by a court decree should be kept in places of deprivation of freedom, as well as over the observance of rules established by law for the keeping of confined persons.

Procuratorial agencies shall be charged with responsibility for observance of socialist legality in places of deprivation of freedom.

Article 33. A procurator shall be obliged to visit regularly places of deprivation of freedom to familiarize himself at first hand with the activity of their administration, to suspend execution of orders or regulations of the administration of places of deprivation of freedom which are contrary to law and to protest them in the established procedure, as well as to take measures to bring to criminal or disciplinary responsibility persons guilty of a violation of legality in places of deprivation of freedom.

Article 35. In exercising supervision over the legality of keeping persons confined in places of deprivation of freedom, the USSR Procurator General and procurators subordinate thereto, within the limits of their jurisdiction, shall have the right to:

(1) visit, with the aim of verifying observance of the procedure established by law for the keeping of persons confined under guard, places of deprivation of freedom at any time, with unobstructed access to all buildings;

(2) familiarize himself with the documents on the basis of which persons have been subjected to deprivation of freedom;

(3) personally question confined persons;

(4) verify the conformity to law of orders and regulations of the administration of places of deprivation of freedom which determine the conditions and regime for the keeping of confined persons;

(5) require personal explanations of representatives of the administration of places of deprivation of freedom concerning violations of the legality of keeping of confined persons.

Article 36. The administration of a place of deprivation of freedom shall be obliged within twenty-four hours to send to a procurator a complaint addressed to him or a petition of a confined person.

A procurator who has received a complaint or petition of a confined person shall be obliged to consider it within the time periods established by law, to take necessary measures, and to inform the complainant of his decision.

A procurator shall be obliged to see that complaints and petitions of confined persons are dispatched without delay by the administration of places of deprivation of freedom to those agencies or those officials to whom they are addressed.

Article 37. The administration of a place of deprivation of freedom shall be obliged to carry out proposals of a procurator regarding observance of the rules established by law for the keeping of confined persons.

Chapter VI. Structure of Agencies of the Procuracy, Procedure for Appointment and Service of Procuracy Personnel

Article 38. The USSR Procuracy shall be headed by the USSR Procurator General.

The USSR Procurator General, in accordance with Article 114 of the USSR Constitution, shall be appointed for a term of seven years by the USSR Supreme Soviet.

Article 39. The USSR Procurator General shall direct the activity of procuratorial agencies and shall exercise supervision over the work of the procurators subordinate to him.

There shall be formed in the USSR Procuracy a College composed of the USSR Procurator General (as president) and leading personnel of the procuracy.

College members shall be appointed by the Presidium of the USSR Supreme Soviet upon the representation of the USSR Procurator General.

At its sessions, the College shall consider, with the participation when necessary of personnel of local procuratorial agencies, the most important questions of effectuating procuratorial supervision over legality in practice, verifying execution, and selecting and preparing procuratorial and investigative cadres and the drafts of major orders and instructions, and shall hear reports by chiefs of administrations and sections of the USSR Procuracy, of union republic procurators, and of other procuracy personnel.

College decisions shall be carried out by orders of the USSR Procurator General. In the event of disagreement between the USSR Procurator General and the College, the USSR Procurator General shall carry out his own decision, reporting to the Presidium of the USSR Supreme Soviet about the disagreements which arose. College members may also contact the Presidium of the USSR Supreme Soviet.

Article 40. The USSR Procurator General shall have deputies, who shall be appointed upon his representation by the Presidium of the USSR Supreme Soviet.

Article 41. Within the USSR Procuracy there shall be formed administrations and sections, as well as a Chief Military Procuracy.

Chiefs of administrations and sections of the USSR Procuracy shall be senior assistants and assistants to the USSR Procurator General.

Within administrations and sections there shall be procurators of the administrations and sections.

The Chief Military Procuracy shall be headed by a Chief Military Procurator.

Sections may be created within the Chief Military Procuracy.

Article 42. The table of organization of the central staff of the USSR Procuracy shall be confirmed by the Presidium of the USSR Supreme Soviet.

Article 43. Procuracies shall be formed in union republics, in autonomous republics, in territories, in regions, in autonomous regions, in national areas, in cities of republic, territory, and region rank, and in districts.

By decision of the USSR Procurator General a single procuracy may be created for several administrative districts.

Article 44. Military procurators of military areas, fleets, formations, and garrisons shall be formed in the Soviet Army and Navy.

Article 45. In rail and water transport independent procuracies may be created when necessary by decision of the USSR Procurator General, with the rights of district procuracies and subordinate to the appropriate territory procuracies.

Article 46. Union republic procuracies shall be headed by union republic procurators.

Union republic procurators shall be appointed for a term of five years by the USSR Procurator General.

In union republic procuracies there shall be formed colleges composed of the union republic procurator (as president) and leading personnel of the republic procuracy.

College members shall be appointed by the USSR Procurator General upon the representation of the union republic procurator.

Colleges in union republic procuracies shall consider in their sessions questions of verifying the organization of the execution of orders of the USSR Procurator General with regard to the exercise of supervision over legality, shall hear reports of session chiefs, of procurators of autonomous republics, territories, and regions, and of other republic procuratorial personnel, and also shall consider questions of selecting and training procuratorial and investigative cadres, and drafts of major orders and instructions.

College decisions shall be carried out by orders of the union republic procurator. In the event of disagreement between the union republic procurator and the college, the union republic procurator shall carry out his own decision, reporting to the USSR Procurator General about disagreements which arose. College members also may contact the USSR Procurator General.

Union republic procurators shall have deputies, senior assistants, and assistants.

In union republic procuracies there shall be formed sections whose chiefs shall be senior assistants or assistants of union republic procurators.

Article 47. Autonomous republic procuracies shall be headed by autonomous republic procurators.

Autonomous republic procurators shall be appointed for a term of five years by the USSR Procurator General.

Autonomous republic procurators shall have deputies, senior assistants, and assistants.

In autonomous republic procuracies there may be formed sections whose chiefs shall be senior assistants or assistants of autonomous republic procurators.

Article 48. Procuracies of territories, regions, and autonomous regions shall be headed by procurators of territories, regions, or autonomous regions.

Procurators of territories, regions, and autonomous regions shall be appointed for a term of five years by the USSR Procurator General.

Procurators of territories, regions, and autonomous regions shall have deputies, senior assistants, and assistants.

In procuracies of territories, regions, and autonomous regions there may be formed sections whose chiefs shall be senior assistants or assistants of procurators of territories, regions, or autonomous regions.

Article 49. Procuracies of areas, districts, and cities shall be headed by procurators of areas, districts, or cities.

Procurators of areas, districts, and cities shall be appointed for a term of five years by procurators of union republics, with confirmation by the USSR Procurator General.

Procurators of areas, districts, and cities shall have deputies and assistants.

Article 50. Investigators shall be attached to the USSR Procurator General, to union republic procurators, and to the Chief Military Procurator, for especially important cases.

In procuracies of autonomous republics, territories, regions, and autonomous republics there shall be senior investigators.

In procuracies of areas, cities, and districts there shall be senior investigators and investigators.

Article 51. The table of organization and the staff of procuratorial agencies shall be established by the USSR Procurator General within the confirmed numerical limits for workers and for the wage fund.

Article 52. To the post of procurator and investigator shall be appointed persons having a higher legal education.

In individual instances persons not having a higher legal education may be appointed to the post of procurator or investigator only with the authorization of the USSR Procurator General.

Persons who have completed institutions of higher legal education shall be appointed to the post of procurator or investigator only after passing a one-year probationary period as investigator of a district (or city) procuracy or assistant to a district (or city) procurator.

Except for academic work and teaching, it shall not be permitted to serve in procuratorial agencies and simultaneously work in other institutions.

Article 53. Persons not younger than twenty-five years of age may be appointed procurators of territories, regions, autonomous regions, areas, cities, and districts, as well as military procurators.

Article 54. The procedure for appointing personnel to the post of procurator or investigator and for relieving them from such post, except for personnel the procedure of whose appointment is specified in Articles 40, 46, 47, 48, and 49, shall be established by the USSR Procurator General.

Article 55. The procedure for disciplinary responsibility of procurators and investigators shall be established by the Presidium of the USSR Supreme Soviet upon the representation of the USSR Procurator General.

Article 56. Established grade ranks shall be conferred on personnel of agencies of the USSR Procuracy in accordance with posts occupied by them

The grade rank of Actual State Councillor of Justice shall be conferred by the Presidium of the USSR Supreme Soviet.

The grade ranks of State Councillor of Justice, grades I, II, and III, shall be conferred by the Presidium of the USSR Supreme Soviet upon the representation of the USSR Procurator General.

Other grade ranks shall be conferred by order of the USSR Procurator General, and the grade ranks of Jurist, I, II, and III classes, and of Junior Jurist, also by orders of union republic procurators.

Article 57. Procuratorial and investigative personnel holding grade ranks shall wear uniforms and established insignia of distinction when executing official duties.

STATUTE ON STATE ARBITRAZH ATTACHED TO THE USSR COUNCIL OF MINISTERS

[Confirmed by Decree of the USSR Council of Ministers, January 18, 1974. SP SSSR (1974), no. 4, item 19]

1. State Arbitrazh attached to the USSR Council of Ministers (Gosarbitrazh USSR) shall be a union republic agency.

Gosarbitrazh USSR shall exercise direction over state arbitrazh agencies, ensure the uniform and correct application of legislation in the settlement of economic disputes by all state arbitrazhes and by arbitrazhes of ministries and departments, and also supervision over the correctness of decisions of state arbitrazhes, settle the biggest and most important economic disputes among state, cooperative, and other social enterprises, organizations, and institutions of union subordination or of various union republics in accordance with the competence established.

Gosarbitrazh USSR shall bear responsibility for the organization, state, and improvement of the activity of state arbitrazh agencies.

2. The principal tasks of Gosarbitrazh USSR shall be:

ensuring the protection of the property rights and legal interests of enterprises, organizations, and institutions in the settlement of economic disputes;

furthering the increased efficiency of social production, strengthening economic accountability, developing rational economic links between enterprises, organizations, and institutions, strengthening the role of contract in their relations, and developing cooperation among them in the fulfillment of the national economic plan;

giving active assistance in the settlement of economic disputes at enterprises, organizations, and institutions in the cause of their observing socialist legality and state discipline in the fulfillment of plan assignments and contractual obligations; struggle against manifestations of localism and departmentalism;

exercising direction over state arbitrazh agencies, ensuring that socialist legality is strictly observed in their activity and that legislation is uniformly and correctly applied in the settlement of economic disputes by all state arbitrazhes and by arbitrazhes of ministries and departments;

studying systematically and summarizing arbitrazh practice and the working out of proposals on this basis aimed at improving economic relations, as well as eliminating shortcomings in the activity of enterprises, organizations, and institutions.

3. Gosarbitrazh USSR, state arbitrazhes attached to union and autonomous republic councils of ministers, and state arbitrazhes attached to the executive committees of territory, region, and city soviets of working people's deputies shall constitute the unified system of Gosarbitrazh USSR.

State arbitrazhes attached to union republic councils of ministers shall be subordinate to the councils of ministers of the corresponding union republics and to Gosarbitrazh USSR.

Statutes on state arbitrazhes attached to union republic councils of ministers, as well as general statutes on state arbitrazhes attached to autonomous republic councils of ministers and attached to executive committees of territory, region, and city soviets of working people's deputies shall be confirmed by union republic councils of ministers by agreement with Gosarbitrazh USSR.

Gosarbitrazh USSR shall direct state arbitrazh agencies, as a rule, through state arbitrazhes attached to union republic councils of ministers

4. Gosarbitrazh USSR shall be guided in its activity by laws of the USSR, edicts of the Presidium of the USSR Supreme Soviet, decrees and regulations of the USSR government, other normative acts, and the present statute.

5. Gosarbitrazh USSR shall:

a) ensure the correct and timely settlement of economic disputes and the undeviating application when considering such disputes of property sanctions to enterprises, organizations, and institutions which do not fulfill plan assignments and contractual obligations;

b) organize the work of state arbitrazh agencies relating to the study and summary of materials of economic disputes by individual categories and by branches of the economy; study the reasons that disputes arise; work out and effectuate necessary measures for the purpose of preventing them and ensuring the strict observance of the procedure for prearbitrazh settlement of disputes;

c) summarize the materials of disputes considered by arbitrazh agencies and the practice of applying economic legislation; work out proposals for its improvement and when necessary submit them for the consideration of the USSR Council of Ministers; carry on the propaganda of economic legislation;

d) notify directors or superior agencies, as well as social organizations, about material shortcomings in the economic activity of enterprises, organizations, and institutions uncovered when considering disputes so that appropriate measures are taken; transfer materials when necessary to the respective agency for consideration of the question of imposing a disciplinary sanction or effecting a monetary deduction against the guilty persons or of bringing them to criminal responsibility in the established procedure;

e) report to the USSR Council of Ministers about the most serious violations of socialist legality and state discipline permitted by enterprises, organizations, and institutions when they fulfill plan assignments and contractual obligations;

f) carry on systematically the verification of the activity of state arbitrazhes; study the experience of arbitrazhes of ministries and departments of the USSR; instruct arbitrazhes on questions of the practice of settling disputes.

Instructive regulations of Gosarbitrazh USSR on questions of the practice of settling economic disputes shall be binding on state arbitrazh agencies and on arbitrazhes of ministries and departments;

g) ensure the retraining and raise the qualifications of arbitrazh personnel, the creation of conditions for the best use of the knowledge and experience of workers, and the promotion to managerial work of young, well-recommended specialists; award honorary certificates to state arbitrazh workers in the established procedure and apply other types of incentive;

h) organize the work of keeping arbitrazh statistics and use the data for improving the activity of state arbitrazh agencies, as well as to prepare proposals for the improvement of economic legislation; instruct state arbitrazhes on keeping statistics;

i) organize the conducting of scientific research work on legal problems for the organization and activity of state arbitrazh agencies and of intensifying its influence on increasing the efficiency of social production and eliminating the reasons and conditions giving rise to economic disputes;

j) effectuate in the established procedure international ties with state arbitrazh agencies of socialist countries.

6. Gosarbitrazh USSR shall confirm:

special conditions for the delivery of particular types of consumer goods;

special conditions for the delivery of particular types of products of production-technical designation (jointly with Gossnab USSR);

instructions on the procedure for accepting products of production-technical designations and consumer goods in terms of quantity and quality;

rules for the consideration of economic disputes by state arbitrazhes (by agreement with union republic councils of ministers);

a statute on an arbitration court for the settlement of economic disputes among enterprises, organizations, and institutions.

7. Gosarbitrazh USSR shall give explanations to ministries and departments regarding the application of:

statutes on the deliveries of products of production-technical designation (by agreement with Gossnab USSR) and statutes on the deliveries of consumer goods;

conditions for the delivery of goods for export (by agreement with the Ministry of Foreign Trade and the State Committee of the USSR Council of Ministers for Economic Relations);

conditions for the fulfillment by all-union foreign trade combines of orders of Soviet organizations for the import of goods (with the involvement of the Ministry of Foreign Trade and the State Committee of the USSR Council of Ministers for Economic Relations);

statutes on the procedure for submitting and considering claims by enterprises, organizations, and institutions and for settling disagreements on economic contracts.

8. Gosarbitrazh USSR shall settle:

a) disputes arising in the conclusion of contracts for an amount exceeding 5 million rubles, as well as in the execution of contracts and for other reasons when the amount of the suit exceeds 50,000 rubles, if:

the parties or one party are enterprises, organizations, or institutions of union subordination;

the parties are enterprises, organizations or institutions of different union republics;

b) disputes arising in the conclusion of contracts for the exploitation of railway spurlines with a goods turnover exceeding 100 wagons per diem;

c) disputes transferred for the consideration of Gosarbitrazh USSR by the USSR Council of Ministers.

Gosarbitrazh USSR may charge state arbitrazhes in union republics with settling the disputes specified in subpoints (a) and (b) of the present point if the parties are situated on the territory of one union republic.

9. There shall not be subject to settlement in Gosarbitrazh USSR:

a) disputes between enterprises, organizations, and institutions of a single ministry, department, cooperative system, or other social organization;

b) disputes of collective farms, intercollective farm organizations, and state-collective farm enterprises and organizations with state, cooperative, or other social enterprises, organizations, and institutions, as well as between themselves;

c) disputes relating to tax and nontax payments recovered for the stat budget in accordance with the Statute on the Recovery of Taxes and Nontax Payments;

d) disputes relating to bank operations connected with the effectuation of financial control functions over the correct use by enterprises, organizations, and institutions of assets for capital investments (excluding disputes subject to consideration in arbitrazh agencies regarding payment for the cost of equipment, machinery, and other material valuables relating to the basic funds which are delivered under contract);

e) disputes arising when reaching agreement on standards and technical conditions;

f) disputes concerning the fixing of prices for a product subject to delivery, as well as concerning the fixing of tariffs for rendering services, unless such prices and tariffs are to be established by agreement of the parties according to prevailing legislation;

g) disputes arising in the conclusion of contracts which are not based on a plan assignment binding for both parties, unless provided otherwise by legislation or by agreement of the parties;

h) other disputes whose settlement has been relegated to the jurisdiction of other agencies by prevailing legislation.

10. Gosarbitrazh USSR shall consider disputes upon petitions of interested enterprises, organizations, and institutions or upon petitions of superior agencies submitted in the interests of enterprises, organizations, and institutions within their jurisdiction.

Gosarbitrazh USSR shall initiate cases upon its own initiative if it has information about violations of socialist legality or state discipline permitted by enterprises, organizations, and institutions in the fulfillment of plan assignments and contractual obligations. The forfeit exacted in such instances (fine, penalty) shall be applied in whole or in part to the revenues of the union budget or to the benefit of the enterprise, organization, or institution in whose interests the case was initiated.

11. Gosarbitrazh USSR shall declare void in whole or in specific part contracts which are contrary to laws and also to decrees and regulations of the USSR government or to state plans or plan assignments, and shall oblige the parties to make appropriate changes in the contracts concluded.

12. Disputes may be transferred for the consideration of Gosarbitrazh USSR only after the parties have taken measures to settle them directly. In the event of failure to submit evidence that such measures were taken, the petition to sue shall not be accepted for consideration and shall be returned to the plaintiff.

13. Disputes in Gosarbitrazh USSR shall be considered by a state arbiter and by representatives of the parties under the chairmanship of the state arbiter.

For the consideration of complex cases the Chief Arbiter may join the bench of arbitrazh in addition to the two state arbiters.

Representatives of the parties in Gosarbitrazh USSR shall be the directors or deputy directors of enterprises, organizations, or institutions or, upon their authority, other workers of these enterprises, organizations, or institutions, as well as officials of agencies which are superior to the parties in dispute.

14. At its own initiative or at the request of the parties, Gosarbitrazh USSR may deem the appearance of representatives at a session of state arbitrazh as not obligatory if the materials of the case permit the dispute to be decided in the absence of representatives of the parties.

15. Gosarbitrazh USSR shall have the right to terminate the case if the plaintiff without justifiable reasons, has not submitted requested materials which are necessary to settle the dispute, or the representative of the plaintiff has not answered the summons to the session and his failure to appear hinders the consideration of the case.

16. Gosarbitrazh USSR shall be granted the right to:

a) summon officials of the disputant superior to them, as well as officials of enterprises, organizations, and institutions who are not parties to the case, for the purpose of giving explanations in connection with the settlement of the dispute if their explanations would have material significance for settling the dispute;

b) demand the submission of documents, information, and opinions needed to settle the dispute from enterprises, organizations, and institutions;

c) designate expert examination;

d) acquaint itself at enterprises, organizations, and institutions with materials needed to settle the dispute.

When necessary, disputes may be considered directly at enterprises, organizations, and institutions which are parties to the case.

17. The decision of Gosarbitrazh USSR shall be made by the state arbiter and the representatives of the parties participating in the consideration of the case according to the results of the discussion of all circumstances of the case in the arbitrazh session.

The state arbiter shall further the attainment by representatives of the parties of agreement in the dispute. If the agreement of the parties does not conform to the requirements of the law or to the materials of the case, or if there are disagreements between the parties or the case has been considered without the participation of representatives of one or both parties, the decision shall be made by the state arbiter.

In the instances provided for by the second paragraph of point 13 of the present statute, the decision shall be made by the state arbiters by a majority vote.

The decision made shall be announced at the session after the consideration of the case. In specially complex cases, the state arbiter may postpone making a decision for a period not exceeding 3 days.

The decision in the case shall be signed by the state arbiter who presides at the session.

18. When rendering a decision with regard to a case, Gosarbitrazh USSR shall have the right to:

a) reduce, in exceptional instances, the amount of a forfeit (fine, penalty) which is subject to recovery from a party which has violated obligations;

b) recover from a party to a contract who has flagrantly violated its provisions a forfeit (fine, penalty) in an increased amount of up to 50 percent, this portion of the amounts recovered being applied to the union budget;

c) recover a forfeit (fine, penalty) at its personal initiative, applying it to the benefit of the party or to the income of the union budget, from an enterprise, organization, or institution which has not fulfilled plan assignments and contractual obligations if such demands concerning sanctions have not been presented by the plaintiff;

d) apply the recovered forfeit (fine, penalty) to the revenue of the union budget in whole or in part if it is established when settling the dispute that violations of legislation which do not diminish the liability of the defendant have been permitted by the plaintiff;

e) recover, when settling economic disputes, 2 percent of the amount of the suit, but not less than 10 rubles nor more than 1,000 rubles from enterprises, organizations, and institutions which have permitted violations of the established periods for presenting and considering claims, and apply it to the income of the union budget.

19. Decisions of Gosarbitrazh USSR relating to economic disputes shall be final and binding for execution by all state, cooperative, and other social enterprises, organizations, and institutions.

Decisions of state arbitrazh shall be executed on the basis of an order. Orders shall be issued to the recoveror, as a rule, at the same time as the decision. State arbitrazh shall have the right to send orders for the recovery of monetary sums directly to the bank where the payor is located.

An order of state arbitrazh shall have the force of a document of execution. Orders for the recovery of monetary sums from the accounts of enterprises, organizations, and institutions shall be executed in the established procedure through a bank. In the remaining instances, orders shall be executed through sheriffs.

An order may be submitted for execution within three months from the day the decision is rendered or the end of the period established by state arbitrazh when execution of a decision is postponed or deferred.

In the event execution of an order by a bank or sheriff is impossible and it is returned in this connection without execution, a new three-month period for execution of the decision shall be reckoned from the date the order is returned.

20. Gosarbitrazh USSR shall be headed by a Chief Arbiter appointed by the USSR Council of Ministers.

The Chief Arbiter of Gosarbitrazh USSR shall have deputies appointed by the USSR Council of Ministers.

The Chief Arbiter shall distribute duties among the deputies of the Chief Arbiter.

21. The Chief Arbiter of Gosarbitrazh USSR shall bear personal responsibility for the fulfillment of tasks and duties entrusted to Gosarbitrazh USSR and shall establish the degree of responsibility for deputies of the Chief Arbiter, for state arbiters, and for section directors for individual spheres of activity of Gosarbitrazh USSR.

22. The Chief Arbiter of Gosarbitrazh USSR shall, within the limits of the competence of Gosarbitrazh USSR, promulgate on the basis of and in execution of prevailing laws, as well as decrees and regulations of the USSR Council of Ministers, orders, instructions, and decrees which are binding for state arbitrazh agencies and shall verify their execution.

23. The Chief Arbiter of Gosarbitrazh USSR and the deputies of the Chief Arbiter shall:

a) verify, upon the application of the parties or at their own initiative, the correctness of decisions made by Gosarbitrazh USSR and decisions made by state arbitrazhes in union republics in regard to disputes being considered by them upon the commission of Gosarbitrazh USSR in accordance with point 8 of the present statute;

b) verify by way of supervision, upon the application of the parties or at their own initiative, the correctness of decisions made by chief arbiters and deputy chief arbiters of state arbitrazhes attached to union republic councils of ministers in regard to disputes within the jurisdiction of these arbitrazhes in which enterprises, organizations, and institutions of union subordination or of different union republics take part.

24. Applications concerning a review of decisions specified in point 23 of the present statute may be submitted by enterprises, organizations, and institutions which are parties to a case within a month from the day the decisions are rendered.

The submission of an application concerning the review of a decision shall not suspend execution of this decision.

25. The submission of Gosarbitrazh USSR of applications concerning the review of decisions specified in subpoint (b) of point 23 of the present statute by way of supervision shall not be permitted if the amount in dispute (in property disputes) is less than 500 rubles.

26. Upon the petitions of ministers or departments or at their own initiative, the Chief Arbiter of Gosarbitrazh USSR and the deputies of the Chief Arbiter shall have the right to verify the correctness of decisions made by chief arbiters and deputy chief arbiters of state arbitrazhes

attached to union republic councils of ministers in regard to disputes considered by state arbitrazhes attached to autonomous republic councils of ministers or to executive committees of territory, region, and city soviets of working people's deputies.

27. The Chief Arbiter of Gosarbitrazh USSR and the deputy chief arbiters may, in regard to the results of the verification of the correctness of a decision, leave the decision unchanged, modify or vacate it, make a new decision, transfer the file of the case for a new consideration by the same or by another state arbitrazh, or terminate the case.

A decision shall be subject to modification or being vacated if it is contrary to law or does not conform to the circumstances and materials of the case.

The Chief Arbiter of Gosarbitrazh USSR and the deputy chief arbiters shall, when necessary, have the right to suspend the execution of a decision.

Decisions of state arbitrazh may be reviewed not later than a year from the day they are rendered.

28. Colleges shall be formed in Gosarbitrazh USSR composed of the Chief Arbiter (chairman) and deputy chief arbiters *ex officio*, and also other managerial workers of state arbitrazh.

Members of the college of Gosarbitrazh USSR shall be confirmed by the USSR Council of Ministers.

29. At its regularly held sessions, the college of Gosarbitrazh USSR shall consider basic questions of the activity of state arbitrazhes and the practice of the application of economic legislation by them, shall discuss questions of the practical guidance by state arbitrazhes, the verification of execution, and the selection and use of personnel, shall hear reports of state arbiters and section heads of Gosarbitrazh USSR and chief arbiters of union republic state arbitrazhes and the results of the study of work experience by arbitrazhes of ministries and departments, and shall discuss the drafts of normative acts and drafts of the most important orders, instructions, and decrees worked out by Gosarbitrazh USSR.

Decisions of the college shall be implemented, as a rule, by orders of the Chief Arbiter. In the event of disagreement between the Chief Arbiter and the college, the Chief Arbiter shall implement his own decision, reporting on the disagreements which have arisen to the USSR Council of Ministers, and members of the college in turn may inform the USSR Council of Ministers of their opinion.

30. Gosarbitrazh USSR shall convoke, in the established procedure, meetings of workers of state arbitrazh agencies and arbitrazhes of ministries and departments of the USSR at which reports concerning measures in regard to the fulfillment of decisions of the Party and government shall be heard and discussed and questions of the application of prevailing legislation in settling economic disputes and other important issues of the practice of arbitrazh work shall be considered.

31. A scientific advisory council of well-known scholars and highly qualified specialists shall be created in Gosarbitrazh USSR to work out scientifically based recommendations in regard to questions of the organization and activity of arbitrazh agencies.

The composition of the scientific advisory council and a statute regarding it shall be confirmed by the Chief Arbiter of Gosarbitrazh USSR Council of Ministers.

32. The structure and establishment of workers of the central apparatus' of Gosarbitrazh USSR shall be confirmed by the USSR Council of Ministers.

The establishment of the apparatus of Gosarbitrazh USSR, and also statutes concerning sections, shall be confirmed by the Chief Arbiter of Gosarbitrazh USSR. The statutes concerning sections shall define their powers within the limits of the competence of Gosarbitrazh USSR.

33. Gosarbitrazh USSR shall have a seal depicting the State Seal of the USSR and its own name.

ON THE STATE NOTARIAT

[Law of the USSR Supreme Soviet, adopted July 19, 1973. Vedomosti SSSR (1973), no. 30, item 393]

Section I. General Provisions

Article 1. Tasks of the State Notariat. The tasks of the state notariat shall be the protection of socialist ownership, of the rights and legal interests of citizens, state institutions, enterprises, and organizations, collective farms, and other cooperative and social organizations; the strengthening of socialist legality and legal order; the prevention of violations of law through the certification of contracts and other transactions properly and in a timely manner, the formalization of inheritance rights, and the endorsement of documents of execution and other notarial activities.

Article 2. Legislation of the USSR and the Union Republics on the State Notariat. Legislation of the USSR and the union republics on the state notariat shall consist of the present law and other acts of USSR legislation promulgated in conformity therewith, laws on the state notariat, and other acts of union republic legislation.

Article 3. Agencies and Officials Who Perform Notarial Activities. State notarial offices shall be organized to perform notarial activities in the USSR.

In the capital of a union or autonomous republic or in a territorial or regional center, one of the state notarial offices shall be instituted as the principal state notarial office for the performance of the most complex notarial activities and the fulfillment of other functions in accordance with USSR and union republic legislation.

In the capital of a union or autonomous republic or in a territorial or regional center where one state notarial office is instituted, it shall be the principal state notarial office.

State notaries (senior state notaries, deputy senior state notaries, state notaries) shall perform notarial activities in state notarial offices.

In population centers where there are no state notarial offices, the notarial activities provided for by the present law and union republic legislation shall be performed by the executive committees of city, settlement, or rural soviets of working people's deputies. Taking local conditions into account, the performance of notarial activities also may be entrusted to the executive committee of district soviets of working people's deputies.

A list of officials of executive committees of city, settlement, or rural soviets of working people's deputies who perform notarial activities shall be established by union republic legislation.

The performance of notarial activities abroad shall be entrusted to consular institutions of the USSR. A list of consular officials who perform notarial activities shall be established by the Consular Statute of the USSR.

Wills and powers of attorney having the force of notarially certified documents also may be certified by the officials specified in Article 13 of the present law.

Article 4. Direction of the State Notariat. The state notariat shall be directed by the USSR Council of Ministers, union and autonomous republic councils of ministers, the executive committee of territory, region, national area, district, and city soviets of working people's deputies, the USSR Ministry of Justice, union and autonomous republic ministries of justice, as well as by other state agencies, in accordance with legislation of the USSR and of union and autonomous republics.

Article 5. Appointment to and Removal from the Office of State Notary. Citizens of the USSR who have a higher legal education shall be appointed to the office of state notary. In individual instances provided for by union republic legislation, persons who do not have a higher legal education may be appointed to the office of state notary.

The procedure for appointment to and removal from the office of state notary shall be established by USSR and union republic legislation.

State notaries may not be in the employ of other institutions, organizations, or enterprises. Exceptions may be made for state notaries who engage in pedagogical or scientific work.

Article 6. Performance of Notarial Activities on the Basis of Prevailing Legislation. State notaries and other officials who perform notarial activities shall be guided in their activity by USSR, union, and autonomous republic laws, edicts of the Presidium of the USSR Supreme Soviet and the union and autonomous republic presidiums of supreme soviets, decrees and regulations of the USSR Council of Ministers and the union and autonomous republic councils of ministers, orders and instructions of the USSR Ministry of Justice and the union and autonomous republic ministries of justice, as well as by acts promulgated by other agencies of state authority or agencies of state administration within the limits of their competence.

Article 7. Observance of the Secrecy of Notarial Activities Performed. State officials and other officials who perform notarial activities shall be obliged to observe the secrecy of notarial activities performed.

Information concerning notarial activities performed and documents shall be issued only to citizens, state institutions, enterprises, and organizations, collective farms, and other cooperative and social organizations upon whose commission or with regard to whom the notarial activities were performed.

At the request of a court, the procuracy, or agencies of investigation or inquiry, information concerning notarial activities performed or documents shall be issued in connection with proceedings in criminal or civil cases.

Information concerning wills shall be issued only after the death of the testator.

The rules concerning the observance of the secrecy of notarial activities also shall extend to persons who have become aware of the notarial activities performed in connection with the fulfillment of their official duties.

The persons specified in paragraphs one and five of the present article who are guilty of violating the secrecy of notarial activities performed shall bear responsibility in the procedure established by USSR and union republic legislation.

Article 8. Assistance to Citizens, Institutions, Enterprises, and Organizations in Exercising their Rights and Defending their Legal Interests. State notaries and other officials who perform notarial activities shall be obliged to render to citizens, state institutions, enterprises, and organizations, collective farms, and other cooperative and social organizations assistance in exercising their rights and defending their legal interests, explain their rights and duties, and anticipate the consequences of notarial activities performed so that lack of legal information and other similar circumstances can not be used to their detriment.

When necessary, state notaries and other officials who perform notarial activities at the request of citizens, state institutions, enterprises, and organizations, collective farms, and other cooperative and social organizations which have sought the performance of notarial activities should draw up draft transactions and applications, prepare copies or documents or extracts therefrom, and also give explanations relating to the performance of notarial activities.

Article 9. Language in Which Notarial Proceedings are Conducted. Notarial proceedings in state notarial offices and executive committees of city, settlement, and rural soviets of working people's deputies shall be conducted in that language in which court proceedings, in conformity with prevailing legislation, are conducted in the union or autonomous republic, autonomous region, or national area.

Notarial proceedings in consular institutions of the USSR shall be conducted in that language in which the proceedings of consular institutions of the USSR are conducted.

If a person who has sought the performance of notarial activities does not know the language in which proceedings are conducted, the texts of formalized documents should be translated for him by the state notary, or the official performing the notarial activity, or an interpreter who is known to the state notary, or the official performing the notarial activity.

Section II. Notarial Activities Performed by State Notarial Offices and Other Agencies

Article 10. Notarial Activities Performed by State Notarial Offices. State notarial offices shall perform the following notarial activities:

1) certify legal transactions (contracts, wills, powers of attorney, etc.);

2) take measures for the protection of inherited property;

3) issue certificates concerning the right to an inheritance;

4) issue certificates concerning the right of ownership in regard to a share in the common property of spouses;

5) impose prohibitions against alienation of a dwelling house;

6) witness the accuracy of copies of documents and extracts therefrom;

7) witness the authenticity of a signature on documents;

8) witness the accuracy of the translation of documents from one language to another;

9) certify the fact that a citizen is alive;

10) certify the fact that a citizen is in a particular place;

11) certify that a citizen is the same person who is depicted in a photograph;

12) certify the time at which documents are presented;

13) transfer applications of citizens, state institutions, enterprises, and organizations, collective farms, and other cooperative and social organizations to other citizens, state institutions, enterprises, and organizations, collective farms, and other cooperative and social organizations;

14) accept sums of money and securities for deposit;

15) endorse documents of execution;

16) protest promissory notes;

17) present checks for payment and certify nonpayment of checks;

18) accept documents for safekeeping;

19) perform maritime protests.

The performance of other notarial activities also may be entrusted to state notarial offices by USSR and union republic legislation.

Article 11. Notarial Activities Performed by Executive Committees of Soviets of Working People's Deputies. At population centers where there are no state notarial offices, the executive committees of city, settlement, and rural soviets of working people's deputies shall perform the following notarial activities:

1) certify wills;

2) certify other legal transactions (contracts, powers of attorney, etc.), except for contracts concerning the grant of land parcels in perpetuity for the construction of individual dwelling houses and transactions relating to property located abroad or rights which must be exercised abroad;

3) take measures for the protection of inherited property;

4) witness the accuracy of copies of documents and extracts therefrom;

5) witness the authenticity of a signature on documents;

6) transfer applications of citizens, state institutions, enterprises, and organizations, collective farms, and other cooperative and social organizations to other citizens, state institutions, enterprises, and organizations, collective farms, and other cooperative and social organizations.

The performance of the notarial activities provided by points 5, 9, 10, 12, 15, 18 and 19 of the present law may be entrusted by union republic legislation to the executive committees of city, settlement, and rural soviets of working people's deputies. When necessary, the performance of other notarial activities not provided for by Article 10 of the present law also may be entrusted by union republic legislation to the executive committees of city, settlement, and rural soviets of working people's deputies.

Article 12. Notarial Activities Performed by Consular Institutions of the USSR. Consular institutions of the USSR shall perform the following notarial activities:

1) certify legal transactions (contracts, wills, powers of attorney, etc.), except for contracts concerning the alienation or mortgage of dwelling houses located in the USSR;

2) take measures for the protection of inherited property;

3) issue certificates concerning the right to an inheritance;

4) issue certificates concerning the right of ownership in regard to a share in the common property of spouses;

5) witness the accuracy of copies of documents and extracts therefrom;

6) witness the authenticity of a signature on documents;

7) witness the accuracy of the translation of documents from one language to another;

8) certify the fact that a citizen is alive;

9) certify the fact that a citizen is in a particular place;

10) certify that a citizen is the same person who is depicted in a photograph;

11) certify the time at which documents are presented;

12) accept sums of money and securities for deposit;

13) endorse documents of execution;

14) accept documents for safekeeping;

15) safeguard evidence;

16) perform maritime protests.

Other notarial activities performed by consular institutions of the USSR also may be provided by USSR legislation.

Article 13. Certification by Officials of Wills and Powers of Attorney Which is Equivalent to Notarial Certification. There shall be equated to notarially certified documents:

wills of citizens who are in hospitals for treatment or in other inpatient preventive medical institutions and sanatoriums, or who reside in homes for the aged and disabled, which are certified by the chief doctors, their deputies for medical sections, or the duty doctors of these hospitals, therapeutic institutions, or sanatoriums, as well as by the directors or chief doctors of the said homes for the aged and disabled.

wills of citizens who are on a voyage on seagoing vessels or vessels of internal navigation sailing under the USSR flag, which have been certified by the masters of these vessels;

wills of citizens who are on exploratory, arctic, or other similar expeditions, which have been certified by the heads of these expeditions;

wills and powers of attorney of military servicemen and other persons who are in military hospitals, sanatoriums, and other military therapeutic institutions for treatment, which have been certified by the heads, their deputies for medical sections, or the senior and duty doctors of these military hospitals, sanatoriums, and other military therapeutic institutions;

wills and powers of attorney of military servicemen, and at points for the stationing of military units, formations, institutions, and military training institutions where there are no state notarial offices of other agencies which perform notarial activities, also the wills and powers of attorney of workers and employees, members of their families, and family members of military servicemen, which are certified by the commanders (or heads) of these units, formations, institutions, or establishments;

wills and powers of attorney of persons who are in places of deprivation of freedom, which are certified by the heads of places of deprivation of freedom.

The officials enumerated in the present article shall be obliged to transfer without delay one copy of wills they have certified for safekeeping to a state notarial office at the permanent place of residence of the testator.

The masters of seagoing vessels shall be obliged to transfer one copy of wills they have certified to the chief of a USSR port or to a USSR consul in a foreign port for subsequent transmission to a state notarial office at the place of residence of the testator.

If the testator had no permanent place of residence in the USSR or if the testator's place of residence is unknown, the will shall be sent to a state notarial office determined by the USSR Ministry of Justice.

A state notary shall be obliged to verify the legality of a will accepted for safekeeping, and if he establishes that it does not conform to law, to notify the testator thereof and the official who certified the will.

Wills and powers of attorney by the officials specified in the present article shall be certified, while observing the requirements of articles 6-8, 16, and 20 of the present law in the procedure established by the USSR Council of Ministers.

Section III. Basic Rules for the Performance of Notarial Activities

Article 14. Place of Performance of Notarial Activities. Notarial activities may be performed at any state notarial office or executive committee of a city, settlement, or rural soviet of working people's deputies throughout the entire territory of the USSR, except for instances when according to USSR or union republic legislation notarial activities must be performed in a particular state notarial office or executive committee of a particular soviet of working people's deputies.

Notarial activities shall be performed on the premises of a state notarial office or of the executive committee of a city, settlement, or rural soviet of working people's deputies. In particular instances provided for by union republic legislation, notarial activities may be performed outside the said premises.

The place for performing notarial activities by USSR consular institutions shall be defined by the Consular Statute of the USSR.

Article 15. Periods for Performing Notarial Activities. Notarial activities shall be performed on the day that all documents necessary therefor are presented and the state fee is paid.

The performance of notarial activities may be postponed when it is necessary to demand additional information or documents from the officials of state institutions, enterprises, and organizations, collective farms, and other cooperative and social organizations or to send documents for expert examination.

In the event notification is received from a court regarding the filing of an application by an interested person who disputes the right or fact which another interested person requests certification of, the performance of the notarial activity shall be suspended until the case is decided by the court.

Other grounds also may be established for the postponement or suspension of the performance of notarial activity by union republic legislation.

Article 16. Establishing the Identity and Verifying the Legal Capacity and Authenticity of Signatures of Persons Who Have Applied for the Performance of Notarial Activities. When performing notarial activities, the state notaries or other officials who perform notarial activities shall establish the identity of the citizens, their representatives, or the representatives of state institutions, enterprises, and organizations, collective farms, or other cooperative and social organizations who have applied for the performance of notarial activities.

When certifying transactions and performing certain other notarial activities in the instances provided for by USSR and union republic legislation, the authenticity of signatures of participants in transactions and other persons who have applied for the performance of notarial activities shall be verified.

When certifying transactions, the legal capacity of citizens shall be elucidated and the legal personality of juridical persons participating in the transactions shall be verified. When transactions are performed by a representative, his powers shall be verified.

Notarially certified transactions, as well as applications and other documents, shall be signed in the presence of the state notary or other official who performs notarial activities. If the transaction, application, or other document has been signed in the absence of the said officials, the signor must confirm in person that the document was signed by him.

Article 17. Demanding Information and Documents Needed to Perform Notarial Activities. State notaries and other officials who perform notarial activities shall have the right to demand from state institutions, enterprises, and organizations, collective farms, and other cooperative and social organizations information and documents needed to perform notarial activities. The respective information or documents must be submitted within the term specified by the state notary or other official who performs notarial activities. This period may not exceed one month.

Article 18. Limitations on the Right to Perform Notarial Activities. State notaries and officials of the executive committees of city, settlement, and rural soviets of working people's deputies who perform notarial activities shall not have the right to perform notarial activities in their own name or on their own behalf, in the name or on behalf of their spouses or relatives, as well as in the name or on behalf of workers of the particular state notarial office or the particular executive committee of the soviet of working people's deputies. Officials of the executive committees of city, settlement, or rural soviets of working people's deputies shall not have the right to perform notarial activities in the name or on behalf of the particular executive committee of the soviet of working people's deputies as well.

Notarial activities in the said instances shall be performed by another state notarial office or executive committee of another city, settlement, or rural soviet of working people's deputies in the procedure defined by union republic legislation.

A consular officer may not perform notarial activities in his own name or behalf or in the name or on behalf of his spouse or their blood relatives.

The officials enumerated in Article 13 of the present law shall not have the right to certify wills and powers of attorney in their own name or behalf, or that of their spouses, or their relatives.

Notarial activities, and those equivalent thereto, performed in violation of the rules established by the present article shall be void.

Article 19. Measures to be Taken by State Notaries or Other Officials Who Perform Notarial Activities When a Violation of the Law is Discovered. State notaries and other officials who perform notarial activities, having discovered a violation of legality by citizens or individual officials when performing notarial activities, shall notify the respective institution, enterprise, organization, or procurator thereof so that requisite measures are taken.

If doubt arises about the authenticity of a document presented, state notaries and other officials who perform notarial activities shall have the right to retain this document and send it for expert examination.

Article 20. Refusal to Perform Notarial Activities. State notaries and other officials who perform notarial activities:

shall refuse to perform a notarial activity if the performance of such activity is contrary to law;

shall not accept documents for the performance of notarial activities unless they conform to the requirements of legislation or contain information discrediting the honor and dignity of citizens.

State notaries and other officials who perform notarial activities must, at the request of the person to whom the performance of a notarial activity has been refused, set forth the reasons for the refusal in writing and explain the procedure for its appeal.

Other grounds for refusal to perform notarial activities by USSR consular institutions, as well as the procedure determined for such refusal, also may be established by the Consular Statute of the USSR.

Article 21. Appeal against Notarial Activities or Refusal to Perform Them. An interested person who considers the notarial activity performed or the refusal to perform a notarial activity to be incorrect shall have the right to submit an appeal in regard thereto to the district (or city) people's court at the place where the state notarial office or the executive committee of the city, settlement, or rural soviet of working people's deputies is located.

Appeals against the incorrect performance of a notarial activity or against the refusal to perform it by a consular officer shall be considered in the procedure established by the Consular Statute of the USSR.

Appeals against the incorrect certification of wills and powers of attorney or against the refusal to certify them by the officials enumerated in Article 13 of the present law shall be submitted to the court at the place where the respective hospital, other in-patient preventive medical institution, sanatorium, home for the aged and disabled, expedition, military hospital, military therapeutic institution, military unit, formation, institution, military training institution, or place of deprivation of freedom is located.

Appeals against the incorrect certification of a will or against the refusal to certify it by the master of a seagoing vessel or a vessel of internal navigation sailing under the USSR flag shall be submitted to a court at the port where the vessel is registered.

Article 22. The Procedure for Settling Disputes Concerning a Right Which is Based on Notarial Activity Performed. A dispute that has arisen between interested persons concerning a right based on a notarial activity performed shall be considered by a court or arbitrazh in conformity with USSR and union republic legislation in a contentious proceeding.

Article 23. Appeals Against State Notaries Not Connected With the Performance of Notarial Activities Thereby. Appeals against the activities of state notaries that do not relate to the substance of notarial activities which they have performed (violation of period for performing notarial activities, failure to observe established receiving hours, and so forth) shall be considered by the justice sections of executive committees of territory, region, and city soviets of working people's deputies, by union or autonomous republic ministries of justice, and by the USSR Ministry of Justice.

Article 24. Procedure for Performing Notarial Activities, Forms of Notarial Registers, Certificates, and Certified Endorsements. The procedure for performing notarial activities by state notarial offices and by executive committees of city, settlement, and rural soviets of working people's deputies shall be established by the present law and by other legislative acts of the USSR and union republics.

The procedure for performing notarial activities by USSR consular institutions shall be established by the present law, the Consular Statute of the USSR, and other legislative acts of the USSR.

The forms of registers for registering notarial activities, notarial certificates, certified endorsements on transactions, and witnessed documents shall be established in the procedure defined by the USSR Council of Ministers.

Article 25. State Fee. In conformity with prevailing legislation, a state fee shall be recovered from the interested persons for the performance of notarial activities by state notarial offices and by executive committees of city, settlement, and rural soviets of working people's deputies as well as for drawing up draft legal transactions or applications, for preparing copies of documents or extracts therefrom, and for issuing duplicate copies of documents.

When a state notary or official of an executive committee of a city, settlement, or rural soviet of working people's deputies travels to perform notarial activities, the interested persons shall reimburse actual transport expenses.

A consular fee shall be exacted from interested persons for the performance of notarial activities by USSR consular institutions; actual expenses connected with the performance of notarial activities shall be reimbursed by these same persons.

Section IV. Application of Legislation on the State Notariat to Foreigners and Stateless Persons. Application of Legislation of Foreign States. International Treaties and Agreements

Article 26. Notarial Activities for Foreigners, Stateless Persons, and for Foreign Enterprises and Organizations. Foreign citizens and stateless persons shall have the right on the same basis as Soviet citizens to apply to state notarial offices of the USSR and also to other agencies which perform notarial activities.

Foreign enterprises and organizations shall have the right to apply to state notarial offices and to USSR consular institutions.

Reciprocal limitations with regard to citizens, enterprises, and organizations of those states in which special limitations on the rights of Soviet citizens, institutions, enterprises, and organizations to apply to notarial agencies are admissible may be established by the USSR Council of Ministers.

Article 27. Application of Foreign Law. State notaries shall apply norms of foreign law in accordance with USSR and union republic legislation and international treaties and agreements in which the USSR or a union republic participates.

State notaries shall accept documents drawn up in accordance with the requirements of foreign law, as well as make certified endorsements in the form provided by foreign legislation, unless this is contrary to the fundamental principles of the Soviet system.

Article 28. Application of Soviet law in Connection with the Protection of Inherited Property or in Connection with the Issuance of Certificates Concerning the Right to an Inheritance. Powers of Attorney Intended for the Performance of Activities Abroad. Activities connected with the protection of property situated on the territory of the USSR remaining after the death of a foreign citizen or property due to a foreign citizen after the death of a Soviet citizen, as well as connected with the issuance of certificate concerning the right to an inheritance with regard to such property, shall be carried out in accordance with USSR and union republic legislation.

A power of attorney certified by a state notary and which is intended for the performance of activities abroad, but which does not contain an indication of the period of its validity, shall retain force until its revocation by the person who issued the power of attorney.

Article 29. Acceptance by USSR State Notarial Offices of Documents Drawn Up Abroad. Documents drawn up abroad with the participation of foreign authorities or emanating from them shall be accepted by USSR state notarial offices on condition they are legalized by agencies of the USSR Ministry of Foreign Affairs.

Without legalization, such documents shall be accepted by USSR state notarial offices in those instances when such has been provided for by USSR or union republic legislation or international treaties and agreements in which the USSR or union republic participates.

Article 30. Execution of Commissions of Foreign Organs of Justice and Application of USSR State Notarial Offices with Commissions to State Organs of Justice. State notarial offices of the USSR shall execute commissions of foreign organs of justice transferred to them in the established procedure for the performance of individual notarial activities, except for instances when:

1) the execution of a commission would be contrary to the sovereignty of the USSR or would threaten the security of the USSR;

2) the execution of the commission is not within the competence of USSR state notarial offices.

The execution of commissions of foreign organs of justice concerning the performance of particular notarial activities shall be performed on the basis of Soviet legislation.

USSR state notarial offices may apply to foreign organs of justice with commissions concerning the performance of particular notarial activities.

The procedure for relations of USSR state notarial offices with foreign organs of justice shall be determined by USSR and union republic legislation and by international treaties and agreements in which the USSR or union republic participates.

Article 31. Safeguarding Evidence Required for Conducting Cases in Organs of Foreign States. USSR state notarial offices shall safeguard evidence required for conducting cases in organs of foreign states.

Article 32. International Treaties and Agreements. If an international treaty or agreement in which the USSR or union republic participates has established other rules concerning notarial activities than those which are contained in USSR or union republic legislation, the rules of the international treaty or agreement shall be applied when performing notarial activities.

If an international treaty or agreement in which the USSR or union republic participates relegates to the competence of USSR state notarial offices the performance of notarial activities not provided for by USSR or union republic legislation, the USSR state notarial offices shall perform such notarial activity in the procedure established by the USSR Ministry of Justice.

If an international treaty or agreement in which the USSR or union republic participates provides for a notarial activity which in accordance with union republic legislation can be performed by the state notarial offices of several union republics or if union republic legislation does not define the competence of the state notarial office, the USSR Ministry of Justice shall establish which state notarial offices and in which union republic the said notarial activity should be performed.

STATUTE ON THE SECTION (OR BUREAU) FOR THE REGISTRY OF ACTS OF CIVIL STATUS OF THE EXECUTIVE COMMITTEE OF THE DISTRICT SOVIET OF WORKING PEOPLE'S DEPUTIES

[Confirmed by Decree of the RSFSR Council of Ministers, June 19, 1974, no. 363. SP RSFSR (1974), no. 17, item 94]

1. The Section (or Bureau) for the Registry of Acts of Civil Status of the executive committee of the district soviet of working people's deputies shall be formed by the district soviet of working people's deputies in accordance with RSFSR legislation and shall be subordinate in its activity both to the district soviet and its executive committee and to the section for the registry of acts of civil status of the executive committee of the superior soviet of working people's deputies.

2. The basic tasks of the section (or bureau) for the registry of acts of civil status of the executive committee of a district soviet of working people's deputies shall be:

the registration of acts of civil status in precise conformity with prevailing legislation on marriage and the family both in the interests of the state and society and also with a view to protecting the personal and property rights of citizens;

the introduction of new civil rites for the solemn registration of marriages and births.

3. The section (or bureau) for the registry of acts of civil status of an executive committee of a district soviet of working people's deputies shall be guided in its activity by the USSR Constitution and the RSFSR Constitution, by the RSFSR Law "On the District Soviet of Working People's Deputies of the RSFSR", by other USSR and RSFSR legislation, by decrees of the USSR Supreme Soviet and RSFSR Supreme Soviet, by edicts and decrees of the Presidium of the USSR Supreme Soviet and the Presidium of the RSFSR Supreme Soviet, by decrees and regulations of the USSR Council of Ministers and the RSFSR Council of Ministers, by decisions of the district and superior soviets of working people's deputies and their executive committees, by orders, instructions, and *ukazaniia* of the USSR Minister of Justice, orders and instructions of the RSFSR Minister of Justice, and orders of a superior agency for the registry of acts of civil status and the present Statute.

4. The section (or bureau) for the registry of acts of civil status of an executive committee of a district soviet of working people's deputies shall, in accordance with the tasks entrusted to it:

(a) perform the registration of a birth, the conclusion of a marriage, the dissolution of a marriage, adoption, the establishment of paternity, the change of surname, forename, and patronymic, and of death;

(b) ensure the solemn registration of birth, as well as the registration of marriages with the consent of persons entering into marriage;

(c) dissolve a marriage in the instances provided for by legislation;

(d) prepare materials and draw up opinions concerning a change of surname, forename, and patronymic by citizens of the USSR;

(e) correct, change, restore, and annul the registration of acts of civil status in accordance with prevailing legislation;

(f) prepare materials and draw up opinions regarding the correction of errors and the making of changes, as well as the restoration of lost registrations of acts of civil status and submit them for the confirmation of the executive committee of the district soviet of working people's deputies;

(g) study and summarize the practice of the application of prevailing legislation on marriage and the family when registering acts of civil status; disseminate progressive work experience;

(h) verify the observance of prevailing legislation by officials of executive committees of rural and settlement soviets of working people's deputies which have registered acts of civil status, render assistance to them in this work, and also in the organization of the solemn registration of marriages and births;

(i) accept second copies of registrations of acts of civil status from executive committees of rural and settlement soviets of working people's deputies and verify whether they have been correctly drawn up;

(j) keep a record of registrations of acts of civil status performed in the district, in the established procedure;

(k) submit reports in the established procedure to the section for the registry of acts of civil status of the superior soviet of working people's deputies concerning the registration of acts of civil status, and also send statistical reports to state statistics agencies;

(l) ensure the recording and keeping of books for the registration of acts of civil status and other documentation during the established periods; issue additional certificates for the registration of acts of civil status;

(m) explain prevailing legislation concerning marriage and the family and concerning the procedure for the registration of acts of civil status to the populace.

5. A section (or bureau) for the registry of acts of civil status of an executive committee of a district soviet of working people's deputies shall have the right to:

receive necessary materials and information affecting questions of the registration of acts of civil status from the executive committee of rural and settlement soviets of working people's deputies;

demand and obtain information and documents from enterprises, institutions, and organizations which are needed to prepare materials relating to the restoration of lost registrations of acts of civil status, and also to the change of surnames, forenames, and patronymics of citizens of the USSR.

6. The structure and personnel establishment of a section (or bureau) of a registry for acts of civil status of an executive committee of a district soviet of working people's deputies shall be confirmed, and the head of a section (or bureau) shall be confirmed or dismissed in or from office in accordance with the RSFSR Law on the District Soviet of Working People's Deputies.

7. A section (or bureau) for the registry of acts of civil status of an executive committee of a district soviet of working people's deputies shall report on its work to the district soviet and its executive committee, and also to meetings of working people at collective farms, state farms, enterprises, institutions, other organizations, and the place of residence of citizens.

8. The head of a section (or bureau) for the registry of acts of civil status of an executive committee of a district soviet of working people's deputies shall:

direct the activity of a section (or bureau) and ensure the fulfillment of the tasks before it;

issue orders within the limits of the competence of the section (or bureau);

submit draft decisions and regulations for the consideration of the district soviet of working people's deputies and its executive committee relating to questions within the competence of the section (or bureau);

exercise control over the fulfillment of decisions of the district soviet of working people's deputies, its executive committee, and also of superior state agencies, and of the mandates of the electorate relating to questions relegated to the activity of the section (or bureau) for the registry of acts of civil status; give replies within the established periods to inquiries of deputies; consider recommendations of permanent commissions of the district soviet; notify them about the results of the consideration and the measures taken; take part in or send a representative of the section (or bureau) to sessions of permanent commissions of the district soviet with a right of consultative vote;

reduce or increase the period, in accordance with prevailing legislation, upon whose expiry a marriage shall be registered;

bear responsibility for the proper storing, recording, and keeping of registration books for acts of civil status and other documentation, and also for the keeping, storing, and use of blanks for certificates for the registration of acts of civil status;

receive citizens; consider proposals, applications, and complaints of citizens; take necessary measures in regard to them;

dispose of credits and assets within the limits of the estimates and appropriations confirmed for the section (or bureau);

ensure the observance of financial and personnel establishment discipline and the safekeeping of monies and material valuables;

appoint and dismiss workers of the section (or bureau) from office in the established procedure;

carry out measures to raise the qualifications of workers of the section (or bureau) and instruction and seminars for officials of executive committees of rural, settlement, and city (or cities of district subordination) soviets which perform the registration of acts of civil status.

9. A section (or bureau) for the registry of acts of civil status of an executive committee of a district soviet of working people's deputies shall be maintained at the expense of the district budget.

10. A section (or bureau) for the registry of acts of civil status of the executive committee of a district soviet of working people's deputies shall be a juridical person and shall have a seal depicting the State Arms of the RSFSR and its own name.

STATUTE ON ADMINISTRATIVE COMMISSIONS ATTACHED TO EXECUTIVE COMMITTEES OF DISTRICT, CITY, RURAL, AND SETTLEMENT SOVIETS OF WORKING PEOPLE'S DEPUTES OF THE RSFSR AND ON THE PROCEDURE FOR CASES CONCERNING ADMINISTRATIVE VIOLATIONS

[Confirmed by Edict of the Presidium of the RSFSR Supreme Soviet, March 30, 1962, as amended September 22, 1965 and April 28, 1969. *Vedomosti RSFSR* (1962), no. 13, item 166; (1965), no. 23, item 934; (1969), no. 18, item 575]

I. Tasks of Administrative Commissions and Procedure for Their Organization

Article 1. Administrative commissions shall be attached to the executive committees of district or city soviets (in cities not divided into districts), and, when necessary with the authorization of the executive committee of the superior soviet, attached to executive committees of rural and settlement soviets of working people's deputies and shall be formed by the respective soviets of working people's deputies from among deputies of the soviets and representatives of social organizations, the membership consisting of a chairman (the deputy chairman, secretary, or member of the executive committee of the respective soviet), deputy chairman, secretary, and at least four members of the commission.

In the event several administrative commissions are formed attached to the executive committee of one district soviet of working people's deputies, they may be headed by deputies of the respective district soviet.

Administrative commissions shall rely in their activity on the broad *aktiv* of the public.

Article 2. The principal task of administrative commissions shall be the nurturing of citizens in the spirit of strict and undeviating execution of Soviet laws, of an attitude of care toward socialist ownership, of an honorable attitude toward state and social duty, of respect for the rights, honor, and dignity of citizens, and of observance of the rules of socialist community life.

Article 3. Administrative commissions shall consider cases concerning administrative violations, responsibility for which is provided expressly by acts of supreme agencies of state authority and state administration of the USSR, supreme agencies of state authority and state administration of the RSFSR, supreme agencies of state authority and state administration of autonomous republics, and decisions of local soviets of working people's deputies and their executive committees.

Article 4. Administrative commissions may apply one of the following sanctions to a person who has committed an administrative violation:

(a) warning;

(b) fine;

(c) another sanction which is provided for by the act establishing responsibility for the particular type of violation.

Article 5. A warning shall be applied as an independent measure of administrative sanction if it is provided for by the act establishing responsibility for the particular type of violation, or in place of imposing a fine on the offender.

Article 6. The amount of a fine shall be determined within the limits provided by the act establishing responsibility for the particular type of violation, taking into account the gravity of the violation committed and the personality and financial status of the guilty person.

Article 7. An administrative commission, as a rule, shall bring to the information of the public the imposition of an administrative sanction at the place of work, study, or residence of the offender.

Article 8. A decree of an administrative commission concerning the imposition of an administrative sanction may be annulled or modified by the administrative commission itself, as well as by the executive committee of the district, city, rural, or settlement soviet of working people's deputies to which the commission is attached.

Article 9. An administrative commission shall have the right to transfer the materials in respect of an offender, instead of imposing an administrative sanction, to a comrades' court or to social organizations at the place of work, study, or residence of the offender in order to apply measures of social pressure.

Article 10. An administrative commission shall have the right to demand necessary documents from institutions, enterprises, and organizations, as well as to summon officials and citizens in order to obtain information relating to questions being considered by the commission.

Article 11. If when considering a case concerning an administrative offense it is established that by its nature the violation falls under the indicia of a crime, the administrative commission shall send the materials with regard to the offender to police agencies or to the procuracy.

Article 12. Administrative commissions may consider cases concerning administrative violations at the offender's place of work, study, or residence.

Article 13. Direction and control over the activity of administrative commissions shall be effectuated by the executive committees of the corresponding district, city, rural, or settlement soviets of working people's deputies.

Article 14. Administrative commissions shall be responsible in all their activity to the corresponding soviets of working people's deputies and their executive committees.

Article 15. Secretarial and technical servicing of administrative commissions shall be entrusted to the executive committees of the district, city, rural, or settlement soviets of working people's deputies to which the administrative commissions are attached.

II. Procedure for Cases of Administrative Violations

Article 16. The tasks of proceedings in cases concerning administrative violations shall be to establish who is guilty and to ensure the proper application of legislation so that just measures of administrative pressure are applied to each person who has committed an administrative violation.

Article 17. A case concerning an administrative violation shall not be initiated, an administrative sanction not imposed, a sanction imposed shall not be executed, and a case shall be subject to termination if:

(a) at the moment a case concerning an administrative violation is initiated or considered, more than a month has passed since the day the administrative violation was committed;

(b) the three-month period of limitation established for execution of a decree imposing an administrative sanction has expired;

(c) at the moment a case concerning administrative responsibility is initiated or considered, the act establishing such responsibility was repealed;

(d) if the person who committed the administrative violation had not attained 16 years of age at the time the violation was committed.

Article 18. If a person who has been subjected to an administrative sanction does not commit a new administrative violation during the course of one year, then this person shall be considered as not having been subjected to an administrative sanction, except for instances when RSFSR legislation provides other periods.

Article 19. The fact of the commission of an administrative violation shall be established by the appropriate officials, representatives of social organizations (social controllers and inspectors, members of voluntary people's guard detachments, and others) to whom this right has been granted by USSR legislation or by RSFSR legislation.

Officials and representatives of social organizations must have appropriate documents or insignia of the established form which shall be presented on the demand of the person who has committed the administrative violation.

Article 20. A protocol (or act) in the established form must be drawn up concerning each administrative violation, except for instances when according to prevailing legislation the fine shall be recovered on the spot.

There must be specified in the protocol (or act) concerning an administrative violation: the date and place where the protocol was drawn up; the office, surname, forename, and patronymic of the person who drew up the protocol; the surname, forename, patronymic, age, occupation (for those employed, the amount of earnings), place of residence, family status of the offender, the time, place, and nature of administrative violation; name of the act providing responsibility for the particular type of violation; surname and addresses of witnesses (or eyewitnesses) and of the victim, if there are such.

If the offender has no documents certifying his identity, and there are no witnesses who can communicate the requisite data concerning the offender, he may be brought to a police department, executive committee of the rural or settlement soviet, or headquarters of a voluntary people's guard detachment in order to ascertain his identity and draw up the protocol (or act).

Article 21. The protocol (or act) must be signed by the official or representative of the social organization who has drawn it up and by the person who committed the administrative violation.

When witnesses and the victim are present, the protocol (or act) also may be signed by these persons.

If the offender refuses to sign the protocol (or act), a special notation certified by witnesses of investigative actions shall be made thereon.

A person who has committed an administrative violation may enter an explanation in his own hand on the protocol (or act) and remarks relating to the substantive content of the protocol (or act), the reasons he refused to sign it, and so forth.

Article 22. A protocol (or act) shall be sent to the respective administrative commission or to another agency or official on whom the right to impose an administrative sanction is granted.

If the violation is accompanied with the infliction of damage (forestry violation, illegal catching of fish, illegal hunting, and others), the protocol (or act) shall be drawn up in duplicate, one of which shall be attached to the petition to sue which is sent to a court.

Article 23. The protocol (or act) concerning an administrative violation committed by a military serviceman or enlisted man or officer of agencies of the Ministry of Internal Affairs which entails the imposition of a fine in an administrative proceeding shall be sent to the commander of the corresponding military unit or to the head of the institution.

Article 24. When a fine is exacted at the place of violation, a protocol (or act) shall not be drawn up. A receipt of the established type shall be issued concerning payment of the fine, for which purpose police workers and other officials who are granted the right to recover a fine on the spot shall be supplied with special receipt books with numbered sheets.

Article 25. In the event of refusal to pay the fine on the spot of the violation, the offender shall be obliged to indicate his address and to sign the receipt book concerning the imposition of a fine and to bring the fine within three days to the police department or other agency or official by whom the fine was imposed.

In the event of refusal to pay the fine on the spot or to sign the receipt book and indicate his address, and when there is doubt as to the correctness of the offender's address and surname and in the absence of witnesses who can communicate the requisite information about the offender, he may be brought to the police department, executive committee of a rural or settlement soviet, or headquarters of a voluntary people's guard detachment in order to ascertain his identity and draw up a protocol (or act).

III. Procedure for Considering Cases Concerning Administrative Violations by Administrative Commissions

Article 26. A protocol (or act) concerning an administrative violation drawn up by an official or representative of a social organization shall serve as the basis for considering cases concerning an administrative violation.

Article 27. A case concerning an administrative violation shall be considered by the administrative commission at the offender's place of residence within 10 days from receipt of the protocol (or act).

Cases concerning violations committed by officials of enterprises, institutions, or organizations in connection with their official activity shall be considered within the same period by an administrative commission at the place where these enterprises, institutions, or organizations are situated.

Article 28. An administrative commission shall consider cases in open sessions, which must as a rule take place during nonworking hours. The procurator shall be notified of the date of the commission session.

A commission session shall be considered empowered if not less than half of the commission membership take part therein.

Article 29. A case shall be considered with the participation of the person brought to administrative responsibility; he shall be guaranteed the right to familiarize himself with the act on the basis of which the case is initiated and other materials relating to the case, as well as the right to give explanations in regard to the nature of the violations and to submit petitions.

When necessary, before the consideration of a case an administrative commission shall charge a commission member or public representative to verify the substance of the case.

Consideration of a case without the offender may take place only when data are available concerning notification of the offender about the date and place of the commission session.

When necessary, witnesses may be summoned to a commission session, as well as representatives of state agencies and social organizations.

Article 30. An offender, witness, and other person shall be summoned to a commission session not later than three days before the commission session.

Article 31. The guilt of a person who committed an administrative violation shall be established on the basis of the data specified in the protocol (or act) concerning the commission of a violation and data obtained during consideration of the case at the commission session.

Article 32. There shall be specified in the protocol of the session of the administrative commission: date of the session; surname of those persons participating in the commission session; content of the case considered; and decision of the commission.

Article 33. The decree of a commission in regard to a case shall be rendered and announced immediately upon the conclusion of its consideration. The rendering of a decree shall be obligatory also when a person brought to responsibility has been deemed not guilty of committing an administrative violation or when a sanction is imposed.

Article 34. There must be specified in the decree of a commission concerning imposition of a sanction:

(a) the year, month, date, and place of rendering the decree;

(b) the name of the commission which considered the case;

(c) the surname, name, patronymic, age, place of work (or study), and residence of the offender;

(d) time, place, and nature of the violation;

(e) type of administrative sanction, and when a monetary fine is imposed, the amount and the term and procedure for payment;

(f) the period and procedure for appealing the decree.

Article 35. The decree of a commission shall be adopted by a simple majority vote and shall be signed by the commission chairman and members who took part in the consideration of the case.

Article 36. The decree of a commission concerning the imposition of a sanction must be handed to the offender, with a receipt acknowledged in writing, not later than five days from the day it was rendered.

IV. Procedure for Consideration by Other Agencies and Officials of Cases Concerning Administrative Violations

Article 37. Agencies and officials who have been granted the right to impose administrative sanctions shall, when considering cases concerning administrative violations and imposing sanctions, be guided by the rules established for the consideration of cases and the imposition of a sanction by administrative commissions (articles 3-7, 9-12, 17, 26, 27, 31, 33, 34, and 36 of the present statute), with the following exceptions:

(a) cases considered by the respective agency or official at the place where the violation is committed;

(b) notification of the person who committed the administrative violation about the day for considering the case shall be made only when necessary to obtain personal explanations from him.

Article 38. Agencies or officials who have been granted the right to impose an administrative sanction may transfer materials with regard to the offender to administrative commissions for the purpose of imposing an administrative sanction.

V. Procedure for Appealing Decrees Concerning Imposition of Administrative Sanctions

Article 39. The decree of an administrative commission or other agency or official having the right to impose administrative sanctions may be appealed by the offender within 10 days from the day this decree is handed to him.

Article 40. An appeal against a decree concerning the imposition of a fine shall be submitted to the district (or city) people's court at the offender's place of residence.

An appeal against a decree of an administrative commission concerning the imposition of another sanction shall be submitted to the executive committee of the respective district, city, rural, or settlement soviet of working people's deputies.

An appeal against the decree of another agency or official concerning the imposition of another sanction (not a fine) shall be submitted to the superior agency or official.

VI. Procedure for Executing a Decree Concerning the Imposition of Administrative Sanctions

Article 41. A decree concerning the imposition of a fine must be executed by the offender within 15 days from the day the decree is handed to him.

The fine shall be deposited in an institution of the USSR State Bank. A receipt for payment of the fine shall be presented at the administrative commission or agency which imposed the fine.

Article 42. If the fine is not paid within the 15-day period, the decree concerning the imposition of a fine shall be sent to the place of work of the person being fined so that the amount of the fine is withheld from his earnings in an uncontested proceeding.

If the person being fined has no earnings, the decree concerning imposition of a fine shall be sent to the sheriff at the fined persons's place of residence in order to levy execution against his property.

Article 43. Decrees concerning the imposition of other administrative sanctions shall be executed in the procedure determined by the normative act establishing responsibility for the particular type of violation.

STATUTE ON COMMISSIONS FOR CASES OF MINORS

[Confirmed by Edict of the Presidium of the RSFSR Supreme Soviet, June 3, 1967, as amended January 21, 1969, May 28, 1971, November 30, 1972, July 15, 1974, and March 11, 1977. Vedomosti RSFSR (1967), no. 23, item 536; (1969), no. 4, item 89; (1971), no. 22, item 433; (1972), no. 51, item 1209; (1974), no. 29, item 782; (1977), no. 12, item 259]

I. Tasks of Commissions for Cases of Minors and the Procedure for Organizing Them

Article 1. The principal tasks of commissions for cases of minors shall be to organize work in regard to preventing the neglect of, and violations of law by, minors, to settle the affairs of and protect the rights of minors, to coordinate the efforts of state agencies and social organizations in regard to the said questions, to consider cases concerning violations of law by minors and effectuate control over the conditions for the maintenance and conducting of educational work with minors in institutions of the Ministry of Internal Affairs and special educational institutions.

Article 2. Commissions for cases of minors shall be created attached to executive committees of district, city, national area, regional, and territory soviets of working people's deputies, attached to autonomous republic councils of ministers, and attached to the RSFSR Council of Ministers.

By way of exception, commissions for cases of minors may be created attached to executive committees of settlement soviets of working people's deputies situated a significant distance from district centers. The question of forming such commissions shall be decided by the executive committee of the regional or district soviet of working people's deputies or the Presidium of the autonomous republic supreme soviet.

Commissions for cases of minors attached to executive committees of settlement soviets of working people's deputies shall have the rights and duties of district or city (with district divisions) commissions for cases of minors.

Article 3. District, city, national area, regional, and territory commissions for cases of minors shall be formed by the executive committees of soviets of working people's deputies and their membership shall be confirmed by the respective soviet of working people's deputies for the term of its powers.

Commissions for cases of minors attached to autonomous republic councils of ministers shall be formed by the councils of ministers of these republics, and their membership shall be confirmed by the presidiums of the autonomous republic supreme soviets for the period of their powers.

The commission for cases of minors attached to the RSFSR Council of Ministers shall be formed by the RSFSR Council of Ministers, and its membership shall be confirmed by the Presidium of the RSFSR Supreme Soviet for the period of its powers.

Article 4. In all their activity commissions for cases of minors shall be responsible to the respective soviets of working people's deputies and their executive committees, presidiums of autonomous republic supreme soviets and councils of ministers, and the Presidium of the RSFSR Supreme Soviet and Council of Ministers, and shall be accountable to them. The executive committees of soviets of working people's deputies, autonomous republic council of ministers, and RSFSR Council of Ministers may make changes in the membership of the respective commissions for cases of minors, subsequently submitting them for the confirmation of the soviet of working people's deputies or the Presidium of the autonomous republic supreme soviet or Presidium of the RSFSR Supreme Soviet.

The commissions systematically shall inform social organizations and collectives of working people about their work.

Article 5. Commissions for cases of minors shall function with a membership of a chairman (the deputy chairman or secretary of the executive committee, deputy chairman of the council of ministers), deputy chairman, executive secretary, and 6-12 members of the commission.

The number of commission members shall be established, depending on the amount of work, by the executive committee of the respective soviet of working people's deputies or council of ministers to which the commission formed is attached.

Deputies of soviets, representatives of trade union, komsomol, and other social organizations, and also workers of public education, professional-technical education, public health, social security, agencies of internal affairs, and cultural-enlightenment and other institutions shall be members of a commission.

The post of a full-time executive secretary and, when necessary, also an inspector for work with children shall be introduced for the purpose of carrying on day-to-day work and control over the fulfillment of commission decisions in territory, regional, city, and district commissions for cases of minors.

Article 6. The activity of commissions for cases of minors shall be carried out with the broad participation of the Soviet public.

Representatives of factory, plant, and local trade union committees, komsomol committees, parents' committees attached to schools, guardian councils of children's homes, boarding schools, and special schools, voluntary people's guard detachments, block and house committees, and other representatives of the public shall be enlisted for the commission's work.

From among the aktiv enlisted for work, the commissions shall designate social inspectors and social educators for work among minors.

Commissions for cases of minors shall interact, in regard to all questions relegated to their competence, with the permanent commissions of soviets of working people's deputies.

Article 7. Commissions for cases of minors shall adopt, in regard to questions relegated to their competence, decrees which shall be binding on state institutions, enterprises, social organizations, officials, and citizens.

State institutions, enterprises, social organizations, and officials shall be obliged to notify the commission for cases of minors within a two-week period about measures taken in execution of commission decrees.

II. Prevention of Neglect and of Violations of Law by Minors. Settling the Affairs of Minors

Article 8. District (or city) commissions for cases of minors shall combine and coordinate the efforts of public education, public health, social security, culture, and internal affairs agencies and institutions and other institutions, enterprises, and organizations in the district (or city), and also of pedagogues and organizers, relating to work with children and adolescents at their place of residence, and of social agencies on whom duties relating to the bringing up of children, settling their affairs, strengthening health, preventing neglect and violations of law by minors, and protecting their rights have been entrusted.

District (or city) commissions for cases of minors shall work out and exercise, both directly and through the respective state agencies and social organizations, measures for the prevention of neglect and of violations of law by minors, settling their affairs, and organizing the cultural leisure time of children and adolescents, and also for rendering assistance in the bringing up of minors.

Article 9. District (or city) commissions for cases of minors shall, jointly with public education, professional-technical education, social security, and police agencies and with the broad participation of the public, uncover and register children and adolescents who have been left without parents; minors having parents or persons replacing them who do not provide proper conditions for raising children; adolescents who have left school and who are not working; and also other minors requiring state or social assistance, and shall take measures to settle their affairs.

Commission decrees specifying the form of settling the affairs of minors shall be directed to:

public education sections and other state and social organizations in order to settle children in schools of general education, boarding schools, children's homes, schools for mentally retarded children or for the deaf and blind, and other appropriate educational institutions or in families of working people with a view to subsequently establishing a trusteeship, guardianship, patronization, or adoption;

social security agencies for settlement in children's homes for the mentally retarded and children's homes for physically handicapped children;

professional-technical education agencies in order to settle minors in institutions of professional-technical education;

directors of enterprises, organizations, and institutions, to hire them for work.

Article 10. District (or city) commissions for cases of minors shall exercise control over conditions for the maintenance and upbringing of children and adolescents in therapeutic educational institutions, boarding schools, children's homes, and institutions of professional-technical education; over the organization of cultural leisure time of children and adolescents at their place of residence; and also when necessary over educational work with minors at schools of general education, other educational institutions, cultural-enlightenment institutions, and sport organizations.

The transfer or switchover of a minor who has not finished eight grades of a school of general education to a school for workers or rural youth shall be permitted only by agreement with the district (or city) commission for cases of minors. When deciding the question of transferring or switching a minor to a school for workers or rural youth, the district (or city) commission for cases of minors shall take measures to find him employment.

A minor may be expelled from a school of general education or other educational institution only with the consent of the district (or city) commission for cases of minors.

Article 11. District (or city) commissions for cases of minors shall exercise control over the observance by the administrations of enterprises, institutions, and organizations of the work regime and conditions established for minors, over the state of educational work with them and the creation of the requisite material and domestic conditions and the conditions for raising their general educational, cultural, and professional levels.

The dismissal of persons younger than 18 years of age at the initiative of the administration may occur when the general rules for dismissal are observed and only with the consent of the district (or city) commission for cases of minors. The question of deciding about the dismissal of a minor shall be considered at a commission session.

In all instances when minors submit applications with a request to be released from work at their own wish, the administration of an enterprise, organization, or institution shall be obliged within three days to notify the commission for cases of minors thereof so that the commission can, within the period established by law, look into the real reasons for submitting the application for release and take measures to keep the minor in his previous job or to find him employment in another enterprise, organization, or institution.

Article 12. District (or city) commissions for cases of minors shall exercise constant control over the implementation of educational work, of general or professional-technical training, of conditions for maintenance and the correctness of the organization of labor in the special educational institutions, educational-labor colonies, inspectorates for cases of minors and reception-distribution centers for minors situated on the territory of the particular district (or city), and also render assistance to these institutions in carrying out the said work.

Article 13. District (or city) commissions for cases of minors shall, jointly with agencies of internal affairs, observe the conduct of minors subjected to measures of educational or administrative pressure, sentenced to punishment not connected with deprivation of freedom, or conditionally sentenced or conditionally released early from serving a punishment and the conduct of minors who have returned from special educational or therapeutic educational institutions or who have served a punishment in educational-labor colonies, and shall exercise control over the conduct of persons sentenced with respect to whom execution of a judgment for deprivation of freedom has been deferred, as well as register such minors.

When necessary, commissions shall take measures to find employment for minors or send them to educational institutions.

Article 14. District (or city) commissions for cases of minors shall have the right to:

(a) verify conditions for the maintenance and upbringing of children and adolescents in boarding schools, children's homes, professional-technical schools, special educational and therapeutic-educational institutions, educational-labor colonies, and reception-distribution centers for minors, as well as to verify the state of the work of inspectorates for cases of minors;

(b) verify the organization of educational work with children and adolescents in schools of general education and other educational institutions, cultural-enlightenment institutions, housing-maintenance offices, house administrations, as well as at enterprises, organizations, and institutions where minors work;

(c) demand the submission of information needed for the commission's work from the administrations of enterprises, organizations, and institutions;

(d) hear at commission sessions the reports of administrations of the said enterprises, organizations, and institutions in regard to questions appertaining to conditions for the maintenance and education of children and adolescents;

(e) receive minors in person, consider their complaints and applications, and acquaint themselves with their personal affairs;

(f) enlist the public to participate in the reeducation of minors and appoint social educators;

(g) make recommendations to state institutions, enterprises, and social organizations relating to questions of educational work, production training, finding employment, and sending minors for study;

(h) initiate petitions concerning a pardon for minors; make recommendations to a court concerning the nonapplication of punishment, or the application of a lighter punishment, concerning conditional conviction, early quashing of the conviction of minors; recommending to a court, jointly with an agency executing the punishment, the conditional early relief of minors from punishment or replacing the unserved portion of the punishment with a lighter punishment in the instances provided for by Article 55 of the RSFSR Criminal Code; petition a court jointly with an agency of internal affairs for the relief from punishment of a convicted person who has been granted a deferral of execution of judgment, and also make a recommendation to a court jointly with an agency of internal affairs concerning the vacating of such deferral and sending the convicted person to serve deprivation of freedom assigned by the judgment (Article 46-1 of the RSFSR Criminal Code); give consent to the administration of an educational-labor colony to recommend to a court the modification of conditions for the maintenance of persons sentenced to deprivation of freedom while the punishment is being served (Article 364 of the RSFSR Code of Criminal Procedure);

(i) submit for the consideration of executive committees of district (or city) soviets of working people's deputies questions concerning the state of educational work, production training, arrangement of employment, and sending minors for study, and also questions connected with the activity of enterprises, organizations, and institutions specified in points (a) and (b) of the present Article;

(j) make recommendations to executive committees of the respective soviets of working people's deputies concerning the allocation of a certain number of places in order to fully provide employment for a quota of minors specified in Articles 9 and 13 of the present Statute at the expense of a quota established by prevailing legislation and exercise thereafter control over filling it;

(k) place before the appropriate agencies the question of imposing disciplinary sanctions or, before social organizations, the application of measures of social pressure to officials in the event they fail to fulfill decrees of the commission;

(l) give consent to the administration of an educational-labor colony to grant a convicted person the right to move about outside the colony without being accompanied and to leave a convicted person who has attained eighteen years of age at an educational-labor colony.

Article 15. City (or in cities divided into districts), national area, regional, and territory commissions for cases of minors and commissions for cases of minors attached to autonomous republic councils of ministers shall:

work out and implement through the respective state agencies, enterprises, organizations, and institutions measures for the prevention of the neglect of and violations of law by minors, for eliminating the causes giving rise to such phenomena, to settling the affairs of children and adolescents and protecting their rights about the city, national area, region, territory, or autonomous republic as a whole;

control, direct, and coordinate the activity of district (or city) commissions for cases of minors, render methods assistance to them, and summarize and disseminate their positive work experience;

verify decrees of district (or city) commissions in regard to sending minors to special educational-training institutions and repeal them in those instances when they are deemed illegal or unfounded, if such decrees were not appealed to the executive committee of the district (or city) soviet of working people's deputies.

When fulfilling the said duties, city (in cities divided into districts), national area, regional, and territory commissions for cases of minors and commissions for cases of minors attached to autonomous republic councils of ministers shall enjoy the rights provided in Article 14 of the present Statute.

Article 16. The Commission for Cases of Minors attached to the RSFSR Council of Ministers shall:

combine and direct all work in regard to the prevention of the neglect of, and violations of law by, minors, to eliminating the causes giving rise to such phenomena, to settling the affairs of children and adolescents and protecting their rights;

control and coordinate the activity of commissions for cases of minors attached to autonomous republic councils of ministers, executive committees of territory, regional, national area, city (of cities having district divisions) soviets of working people's deputies, render methods assistance to them, and summarize and disseminate their positive work experience.

III. Cases Considered by Commissions for Cases of Minors. Measures of Pressure and the Procedure for Applying Them

Article 17. District (or city) commissions for cases of minors shall be entrusted with considering cases concerning minors who:

(a) have committed, at an age of up to 14 years, socially dangerous acts;

(b) have committed, at an age of 14 to 16 years, socially dangerous acts not provided for by Article 10 of the RSFSR Criminal Code;

(c) have committed crimes, at an age of from 14 to 18 years, with respect to which the initiation of a criminal case has been refused or a criminal case has been terminated in the procedure provided by Articles 8 and 10 of the RSFSR Code of Criminal Procedure;

(d) have committed, at an age of up to 16 years, petty hooliganism or, at an age of up to 18 years, petty speculation or other administrative violations, responsibility for which is provided directly by acts of supreme agencies of state authority and state administration of the USSR, RSFSR, and autonomous republics, as well as by decisions of local soviets of working people's deputies and their executive committees;

have committed, at an age of from 16 to 18 years, petty hooliganism, if the head of the police agency or a people's judge, taking into account the personality of the offender and the character of the offense committed, finds it advisable to transfer the materials for the consideration of the commission;

(e) have committed other antisocial offenses;

(f) avoid study or work.

Article 18. District (or city) commissions for cases of minors may, in the instances provided for by Article 17 of the present Statute, apply the following measures of pressure to minors:

(a) oblige them to make a public or other form of apology to the victim;

(b) issue a warning;

(c) announce a reprimand or a severe reprimand;

(d) impose on a minor who has attained 15 years of age the duty to compensate for material damage caused if the minor has independent earnings and the amount of damage does not exceed 20 rubles or impose the duty to eliminate by his own labor the material damage caused not exceeding 20 rubles;

(e) impose a fine on a minor who has attained 16 years of age and who has independent earnings in the instances and in the amounts provided for by acts of the highest agencies of state power and state administration of the USSR, RSFSR, and autonomous republics and by decisions of local soviets of working people's deputies and their executive committees;

(f) hand over a minor to the supervision of parents or persons replacing them or to social educators, as well as to the observation of a collective of working people or social organization with their consent;

(g) hand over a minor on probation to a collective of working people or a social organization upon their petitions;

(h) send a minor to a special therapeutic-educational institution;

(i) place a minor in a special educational-training institution if he has committed socially dangerous acts or maliciously and systematically violated rules of public conduct. A minor from 11 to 14 years of age may be sent to a special school, and from 14 to 18 years of age to a special professional-technical school. A commission for cases of minors also may establish the said measure conditionally with an annual probation period.

District (or city) commissions for cases of minors shall have the right to make proposals to a guardianship and curatorship agency concerning the limitation or deprivation of a minor from 15 to 18 years of age of the right to dispose of his earnings or stipend.

Article 19. District (or city) commissions for cases of minors may apply to parents or to persons replacing them, if their attitude to children is improper or they maliciously fail to fulfill duties with regard to raising and bringing up children, or for bringing a minor into a state of intoxication, and also for the consumption by minors of narcotics without the prescription of a doctor or in connection with other violations of law committed by them, the following measures of pressure:

(a) issue a public warning;

(b) impose the duty to compensate damage caused by a minor which does not exceed 20 rubles;

(c) impose a fine in an amount of up to 30 rubles.

A commission for cases of minors may transfer a case concerning parents or persons replacing them to a comrades' court. A commission shall have the right to apply to a district (or city) people's court to limit the dispositive capacity of parents, for depriving parents of parental rights, and also for evicting persons deprived of parental rights or creating impossible conditions for living together with children from apartments on the grounds provided in law.

Minors may be sent to special educational-training and special therapeutic-educational institutions by decision of a commission for cases of minors without the consent of parents or persons replacing them. Cases concerning the sending to special educational-training and special therapeutic-educational institutions shall be considered with the obligatory participation of a procurator.

Minors may be sent to a children's home or boarding school when they have parents or persons replacing them without the consent of the latter only in exceptional instances (their prolonged absence, illness, conviction for crime which they committed, and so forth). At the same time, the commission shall adopt a decision to recover from the parents in the procedure established by law the means to reimburse expenditures connected with the maintenance of the children. In exceptional instances upon the petitions of the commission for cases of minors, the amount of payment may be reduced in the procedure established by law.

Article 20. Commissions for cases of minors shall make recommendations to the respective state agencies or social organizations concerning the application of measures of pressure to parents or to persons replacing them who incorrectly treat the raising of their children or obstruct the fulfillment of a decree of the commission, and also bring persons to responsibility who create conditions for children and adolescents to commit crimes or incite or involve minors in the commission of crimes and other antisocial offenses.

Article 21. When applying the measures of pressure provided for by Article 18 of the present Statute, a district (or city) commission should take into account the character and causes of the violation of law, the age of the minor and conditions of his life, the degree of his participation in the violation of law, as well as his conduct at home, in school, or at work.

The decree of a commission for cases of minors concerning the announcement of a warning, reprimand, or severe reprimand shall be in effect for one year. A measure of pressure shall be considered canceled if the minor to whom it was applied during this period has not committed a new violation of law. The commission for cases of minors which has applied the measure of pressure may, by its own decree, repeal it before the expiry of the year in the event of the exemplary conduct of the minor with respect to whom this measure of pressure was applied.

The effect of a decree of a commission for cases of minors on handing over a minor to the supervision of parents, persons replacing them, social educators, or to the observation of a collective of working people or social organization may be terminated at any time by the commission itself upon the petition of these persons or organizations if the minor has proved his reform by exemplary conduct and a conscientious attitude toward work and study.

When the selected measure of educational pressure with regard to a minor has proved to be unsuccessful, the commission shall have the right to apply a more severe measure to this minor from among those specified in Article 18 of the present Statute.

Article 22. The decree of a district (or city) commission concerning compensation by a minor, as well as by parents or persons replacing them, of damage caused by the minor in the instances provided for by Articles 18 and 19 of the Statute shall be subject to execution by a sheriff.

In the event a minor causes material damage exceeding 20 rubles, the question of compensation of damage shall be decided in a judicial proceeding upon the suits of the interested organizations or citizens.

Article 23. The decree of a district (or city) commission for cases of minors concerning the imposition of a fine shall be subject to execution by the person on whom the fine has been imposed within 15 days from the date that the decree was handed to him.

The fine imposed by a commission for cases of minors shall be paid in to a branch of the USSR State Bank, savings bank, or communications branch and shall enter the budget in the established procedure.

In the event a fine is not paid within 15 days, the commission decree concerning the imposition of a fine shall be sent to the place of work of the person subjected to the fine for withholding of the amount of the fine from his earnings in an uncontested proceeding, and if he has no earnings, to a sheriff at the place of residence of this person in order to levy execution on the property.

Article 24. A minor may be kept in special schools until attaining 15 years of age, and in special professional-technical schools until 18 years of age.

In exceptional instances the stay of pupils in special schools may be extended until they attain 16 years of age.

A minor shall be placed in special educational-training institutions until reformed, but for not more than three years.

The commission for cases of minors at the place were special educational-training institutions are located may authorize a pupil to remain in the special school or special professional-technical school upon the expiry of the three-year period until completing the respective grade of the school of general education or professional training in the current academic year.

Pupils of special schools who have attained 15 years of age but who have not reformed their conduct may be sent by the commission for cases of minors at the place where such schools are located to special professional-technical schools.

In partial compensation of expenses for the maintenance of pupils in special educational-training institutions, payment may be recovered from the parents in the procedure determined by USSR and RSFSR legislation.

The questions of the advisability of the further stay of minors in special educational-training or therapeutic-educational institutions shall be considered periodically, but not less than once per year, by commissions for cases of minors at the place where these institutions are located upon the initiative of the commission, of the recommendation of the administration of the said institutions, or upon the petition of the parents or persons replacing them.

<u>Article 25.</u> Deaf, blind, mentally ill, and mentally retarded minors, and also children and adolescents with physical defects and illnesses provided by lists of medical contra-indications for admission to boarding schools and professional-technical schools, should not be sent to special educational-training institutions for minors.

<u>Article 26.</u> The stay of a minor in a special educational-training or therapeutic-educational institution shall be terminated upon the decree of a district (or city) commission for cases of minors at the place where the said institution is located on the basis of a decision of the pedagogical council, confirmed by the director, the commission for cases of minors at the minor's place of residence being notified thereof at least one month before the minor's release, which shall be obliged to take measures to find employment or send the minor to an educational institution and create for him the requisite material and domestic conditions.

If a minor has been sent for educational purposes by a commission to a children's home or boarding school, the decision to withdraw him from the children's home or boarding school shall be taken by the commission for cases of minors at the place where the children's home or boarding school is located.

<u>Article 27.</u> When after being released from a special educational-training or therapeutic-educational institution, children's home, or boarding school, a pupil may not be sent to parents or to persons replacing them in connection with their being deprived of parental or guardian rights in the procedure established by law, and also when the return of a pupil to the place of former residence is impossible by virtue of other reasons (absence of parents or persons replacing them; lack of proper conditions for domestic life or employment and further education), the district (or city) commission at the place where this institution is located

shall take measures to arrange the domestic life, study, or labor of the minor and, when necessary, may appoint a social educator for him, and also shall have the right to make recommendations to the executive committee of the respective soviet of working people's deputies concerning the appointment of a guardian or curator for the minor.

When deciding the said questions, the district (or city) commission at the place where the institutions enumerated in the present Article are located must have the respective opinion of the district (or city) commission at the place of the minor's former residence or at the place where his parents or the persons replacing them reside.

Article 27-1. A commission for cases of minors at the place of permanent residence of a person released from an educational-labor colony before he has attained 18 years of age shall take measures to settle this person in a job or study and shall exercise control over his conduct.

If the return of the released minor to parents or to persons replacing them is impossible by virtue of the absence of the said persons or of their being deprived of parental or guardian rights, the commission for cases of minors at the place of the released person's former residence shall take measures, upon the recommendation of the administration of the colony, to settle this person in a job in accordance with his specialization or in study, and also to create housing and domestic conditions for him.

In exceptional instances when it is inadvisable to send the released person from a colony to his former place of residence for educational reasons, upon the recommendation of the administration of the colony, his affairs shall be arranged by the commission for cases of minors at the place where the colony is located.

A commission for cases of minors shall be obliged to decide the question of settling the released person within 15 days from the date of his application for assistance.

IV. Preparation and Consideration of Cases by Commissions for Cases of Minors

Article 28. Commissions for cases of minors shall consider cases:

(a) transferred in the procedure provided by Articles 8 and 10 of the RSFSR Code of Criminal Procedure;

(b) upon the recommendation of permanent commissions of soviets of working people's deputies, police agencies, and public education and professional-technical education agencies;

(c) upon the recommendation of voluntary people's guards for the protection of the public order, trade union and komsomol organizations, parent committees attached to schools, house committees attached to housing offices, house administrations, and other social organizations;

(d) upon the applications of citizens;

(e) upon their own initiative.

Commissions for cases of minors shall consider cases within a period of not more than 15 days from when they are received.

Article 29. Materials concerning violations of law by minors subject to consideration by district (or city) commissions shall be studied in advance by the chairman of the commission or by his deputy, who shall make a decision to:

(a) consider the case at a commission session;

(b) conduct a supplementary verification of the materials of the case or an investigation in regard to the applications and recommendations received;

(c) take measures of pressure with regard to the minor before the consideration of the case by a commission session;

(d) transfer materials concerning insignificant violations of law to comrades' courts or social organizations at the minor's place of work or study if educational pressure on the offender can be achieved thereby.

Article 30. Before a commission considers a case concerning a violation of law, the minor may be handed over for the supervision of parents or the persons replacing them, and a minor being brought up in a children's institution, for the supervision of the administration of this institution.

In the event an adolescent from 11 to 14 years of age commits a grave socially dangerous act and it is necessary in this connection to isolate the adolescent immediately, he may be placed in a reception-distribution center for minors upon the written instruction of the commission chairman for a term of not more than 15 days.

If doubt arises about the mental stability of a minor, the case concerning whom must be considered, he shall be subject to being sent for medical examination.

Article 31. When preparing and considering cases, the commission for cases of minors should establish precisely the age, occupation, conditions of life, and education of the minor, the fact of a violation of law and data confirming that it was committed, whether the adolescent had instigators and other accomplices in the violation of law, and whether measures of pressure had been previously taken against the minor.

A commission for cases of minors shall be obliged to uncover the causes and conditions furthering the commissions of violations of law by a minor and shall take measures to eliminate them.

Article 32. A commission for cases of minors may demand needed information and documents, as well as summon officials and citizens, in order to obtain explanations from them in regard to questions being considered by the commission.

If officials and citizens fail to appear upon the summons of a commission without justifiable reasons, the commission may postpone consideration of the case and take measures for their appearance through the administration or social organizations at their place of work or study. In the event a minor whose case is being considered refuses to appear at the commission without justifiable reasons, he may be brought through police agencies.

Article 33. Having deemed a case to be prepared, the chairman, deputy chairman, or member of a commission for cases of minors to whom this has been entrusted shall, before the case is considered, acquaint the minor, his parents, or the persons replacing them and, when necessary, also representatives of educational institutions, with all the materials, establish who should be summoned to the commission session, and designate the time and place for consideration of the case.

The procurator shall be notified about the date of the commission session.

Article 34. A session of a commission for cases of minors shall be empowered to act when not less than half of its membership are present.

The presence of the minor with regard to whom the case is being considered, and also the parents or the persons replacing them and, when necessary, representatives also of educational institutions, shall be obligatory at a session of a commission for cases of minors.

When considering questions concerning the initiation of petitions regarding the conditional early release of sentenced minors from punishment, regarding the replacement of punishment assigned by a lighter one, and regarding other petitions in respect of convicted persons at a commission session, the presence of a representative of the administration of an educational-labor colony and of the convicted person himself shall be obligatory.

The commission shall have the right to remove a minor from the session during the investigation of circumstances whose discussion may negatively influence him.

Article 35. A commission for cases of minors shall consider materials collected in regard to the case, hear explanations of the minor, his parents or the persons replacing them, the victim, witnesses, and after a balanced consideration of all the circumstances of the case, shall make one of the following decisions:

(a) to apply measures of pressure provided by Articles 18 and 19 of the present Statute;

(b) terminate the case;

(c) postpone consideration of the case and conduct a supplementary verification;

(d) transfer the case to agencies of the procuracy.

Article 36. A protocol shall be drawn up at the commission session with a brief record of the explanations of the person with regard to whom the case is being considered and the testimony of the victim and witnesses and also other data relating to the case. The protocol shall be signed by the person presiding and by the secretary.

A commission for cases of minors may hold circuit sessions at the place of work or residence of the persons with regard to whom the cases are being considered.

Article 37. Decrees of the commission shall be adopted by a simple majority vote of commission members taking part in the session.

The decree of a commission must be set out in writing and be justified. In a decree concerning the application of measures of pressure, there shall be specified the essence of a violation, the evidence on the basis of which a decision is made, and the measure of pressure determined by the commission, adducing the reasons for assigning it.

The decree shall be signed by the person presiding, the secretary, and the commission members who considered the particular case, and shall be announced by the person presiding after it is adopted.

The commission shall notify social organizations at the minor offender's place of work, study, or residence, and also the place of work or residence of his parents or the persons replacing them, about the decree adopted.

Article 37-1. If there are sufficient grounds to suppose that a minor who is subject by decree of a commission to being placed in a special educational-training institution, will engage in criminal or other antisocial activity, and also in order to ensure the execution of its decree, the commission shall have the right to take a decision concerning a provisional period of up to 30 days for keeping a minor in a reception-distribution center for minors, which shall complete the formalization of his personal file and deliver the minor to the special educational-training institution.

In exceptional instances the period for the stay of a minor in the reception-distribution center for minors may be extended, but for not more than 15 days, by decree of the commission for cases of minors which rendered the decision for the temporary keeping of the minor in the reception-distribution center.

Article 38. With a view to studying and eliminating the causes and conditions giving rise to violations of law by minors, commissions for cases of minors shall organize a case register concerning violations of law considered at their sessions and shall summarize quarterly the data of this register within the limits of the district, city, national area, region, territory, or republic.

Article 39. A decree of a commission for cases of minors may be appealed to the executive committee of the respective soviet of working people's deputies within ten days from the date it is handed over. The decision of the executive committee regarding the appeal should be taken within seven days and shall be final.

The decree of the commission for cases of minors concerning the imposition of a fine may be appealed within ten days from the date it is handed over to the district (or city) people's court at the place of residence of the person subjected to the fine. Submitting an appeal to the court within the specified period shall suspend recovery of the fine.

Article 40. The material-technical provisioning of a commission for cases of minors shall be entrusted respectively to the executive committees of soviets of working people's deputies, the autonomous republic councils of ministers, and the RSFSR Council of Ministers.

STATUTE CONCERNING SOCIAL EDUCATORS OF MINORS

[Confirmed by Edict of the Presidium of the RSFSR Supreme Soviet, December 13, 1967. Vedomosti RSFSR (1967), no. 51, item 1239]

I. General Provisions

1. The institution of social educators was founded with a view to increasing the role of the public in nurturing minors who have committed a violation of law.

The basic task of social educators is to render assistance to parents or to persons replacing them in the re-education of minor offenders in a spirit of respect for and observance of the laws and rules of socialist community life.

2. Workers, employees, collective farmers, representatives of the intelligentsia, military servicemen, students, pensioners, and other citizens who take an active part in social life and who have the necessary general educational preparation, experience in living, and work experience with children may be social educators, on condition that they agree to assume the duties of a social educator.

Persons recommended as social educators shall be put forward by the general meeting of the collective of working people or social organization of which they are members or by residents of the house of their place of residence. Lists of recommended persons shall be transferred to the commission for cases of minors attached to the executive committee of the district (or city) soviet of working people's deputies. These persons shall become members of the aktiv of the commission.

3. A social educator shall be appointed when this is deemed necessary in order to prevent the neglect and violations of law by a minor:

(a) who has committed a violation of law but has been relieved of criminal responsibility by virtue of age or in connection with the inadvisability of applying measures of criminal punishment to him, if it would be premature to place him in a special educational institution;

(b) who has been conditionally sentenced or sentenced to a measure of punishment not connected with deprivation of freedom;

(c) who has served a punishment or who has been conditionally relieved from punishment;

(d) who has returned from a special school, special professional-technical school, or therapeutic educational institution, children's home, or boarding school.

When a social educator is appointed, the parents or persons replacing them shall not be relieved from the duty to bring up the minor or from responsibility for his conduct.

4. A minor shall be transferred to the supervision of a social educator by the district (or city) commission for cases of minors on the

basis of a ruling, judgment, or decree of a court which deems it necessary to appoint a social educator or at its own personal initiative, or the initiative of state agencies, social organizations, and citizens.

A commission for cases of minors shall, within five days after adopting the decision to appoint a social educator, notify the court, state agencies, social organizations, and citizens at whose initiative the case was considered, as well as the parents of the minor or persons replacing them, of the surname, forename, patronymic, place of work, and residence of the social educator.

5. When appointing a social educator, the nature of the violation of law, the age of the minor, his disposition, other circumstances, as well as the possibility and consent of the social educator himself to fulfill the duties entrusted to him with respect to the said minor, shall be taken into account in each individual instance.

6. The district (or city) commission for cases of minors shall present to the social educator a certificate and booklet in which the duties and rights of a social educator are set forth.

7. Social educators shall carry on their work in close contact with the minor's parents or persons replacing them, with the administrations of enterprises, organizations, and institutions, with the pedagogic collectives of schools and special educational institutions, with police workers, with social organizations at the place of study, work, or residence of the minor as well as with representatives of the public for work among minors.

Officials of enterprises, organizations, institutions, as well as directors of trade union, Komsomol, and other social organizations, should render every possible assistance to the work of social educators.

8. Direction and control over the work of social educators shall be effectuated by the district (or city) commissions for cases of minors, and methods direction, by the district (or city) public education sections, which shall familiarize social educators with the basic principles of pedagogy, psychology, and legal knowledge.

A social educator shall report systematically to commissions for cases of minors and to his collective or the social organization which nominated him about the work he is performing.

9. The replacement of one social educator by another may be done by way of exception when the district (or city) commission for cases of minors deems this necessary.

In the event a minor changes his place of residence, the commission for cases of minors shall notify the respective commission at the minor's new place of residence about the need to designate another social educator.

10. The work of a social educator shall be terminated by the district (or city) commission for cases of minors or by a court, in connection with the correction of the minor or if he attains 18 years of age.

II. Duties of a Social Educator

11. A social educator shall be obliged to:

(a) render assistance to parents or persons replacing them in nurturing the minor; make every effort to correct the minor, eliminating harmful or amoral habits or notions which he has; prepare him for conscious, socially useful activity; nurture the minor in a spirit of revolutionary, labor, and battle traditions of our people, respect for the aged, love for the Motherland; inculcate in him a feeling of responsibility to society and the state;

(b) watch over the punctual attendance of the minor at lessons, his progress, fulfillment of domestic tasks, conduct in school, at work, in the family, on the street, in public places; involve him in the work of extracurricular children's institutions and circles; take measures to create proper conditions for the correct organization of study, labor, and leisure of the minor;

(c) render assistance, when necessary, in enlisting the minor in socially useful labor, in settling him in an educational institution or a sport, technical, or other circle or section.

In the process of his work the social educator should, taking into account the personality of the minor, use the most effective forms and means of educational work, having recourse when necessary to the assistance of the district (or city) commission for cases of minors, social organizations, police workers, teachers, doctors, and other specialists.

III. Rights of a Social Educator

12. A social educator shall have the right to:

(a) visit the minor at the place of residence, study, or work, control his expenditures, give necessary advice in regard to observance of rules of conduct; in the event of the repeated failure to fulfill his demands or of the absence of positive results in reeducating the minor, to bring the question for discussion to the commission for cases of minors in order to apply the necessary measures of pressure to him;

(b) call the attention of parents or persons replacing them to their improper fulfillment of parental duties and to explain the responsibility for bringing up and for the conduct of the minor; to raise before the commission for cases of minors the question of notifying the place of work of the parents about their unsatisfactory fulfillment of duties to bring up children, about the discussion of their conduct at the commission session, and about other measures of pressure taken;

(c) demand from administrations and social organizations at the place of study, work, or residence of the minor the elimination of shortcomings in educational work and the creation of more favorable conditions for his study or work.

IV. Measures of Incentive for Social Educators

13. Social educators who actively and conscientiously execute their duties and who achieve positive results in their work shall be encouraged by the executive committees of district (or city) soviets of working people's deputies, social organizations, and directors of enterprises, institutions, and other organizations by:

an announcement of gratitude;

the awarding of a certificate;

being placed on the Board of Honor;

a monetary bonus or valuable gift.

An additional paid vacation of up to three working days per year may be established by directors of enterprises, organizations, and institutions at the place of work for the most distinguished social educators as an incentive measure.

STATUTE ON COMMISSIONS FOR THE STRUGGLE AGAINST DRUNKENNESS

[Confirmed by Edict of the Presidium of the RSFSR Supreme Soviet, August 21, 1972. Vedomosti RSFSR (1972), no. 34, item 845]

I. Tasks of Commissions for the Struggle Against Drunkenness and the Procedure for Organizing Them

Article 1. The basic tasks of commissions for the struggle against drunkenness shall be to coordinate the activity of state agencies and social organizations directed toward the struggle against drunkenness, as well as to work out and effectuate measures to prevent and suppress drunkenness.

Article 2. Commissions for the struggle against drunkenness shall be formed attached to the executive committees of district, city, national area, region, and territory soviets of working people's deputies, autonomous republic councils of ministers, and attached to the RSFSR Council of Ministers.

Commissions for the struggle against drunkenness may also, when necessary, with the authorization of the executive committee of a region or territory soviet of working people's deputies or the presidium of an autonomous republic supreme soviet, be formed attached to the executive committees of rural or settlement soviets of working people's deputies.

Commissions for the struggle against drunkenness attached to executive committees of rural and settlement soviets of working people's deputies shall have the rights and duties of district or city (not divided into districts) commissions for the struggle against drunkenness.

Article 3. District, city, national area, region, and territory commissions for the struggle against drunkenness shall be formed by executive committees of soviets of working people's deputies, and their membership shall be confirmed by the respective soviets of working people's deputies for their term of office.

Commissions for the struggle against drunkenness attached to autonomous republic councils of ministers shall be formed by the councils of ministers of these republics, and their membership shall be confirmed by the presidiums of autonomous republic supreme soviets for their term of office.

The Commission for the Struggle Against Drunkenness attached to the RSFSR Council of Ministers shall be formed by the RSFSR Council of Ministers, and its membership shall be confirmed by the Presidium of the RSFSR Supreme Soviet for its term of powers.

Article 4. Commissions for the struggle against drunkenness shall be responsible in all their activity to the respective soviets of working people's deputies and their executive committees, presidiums of supreme soviets and councils of ministers of autonomous republics, the Presidium of the RSFSR Supreme Soviet and the Council of Ministers, and shall be accountable to them. The executive committees of soviets of working people's deputies, autonomous republic councils of ministers, and the RSFSR Council of Ministers may make changes in the membership of the respective commissions for the struggle against drunkenness, submitting these thereafter for the confirmation of the soviets of working people's deputies or the presidium of the autonomous republic supreme soviet or of the Presidium of the RSFSR Supreme Soviet.

The commissions systematically shall inform social organizations and collectives of working people about their work.

Article 5. Commissions for the struggle against drunkenness shall function with the membership of a chairman (the deputy chairman or secretary of the executive committee; deputy chairman of the Council of Ministers), deputy chairman, secretary, and 6-10 commission members.

The number of commission members shall be established depending on the amount of work, by the executive committee of the respective soviet of working people's deputies or council of ministers to which the commission is attached.

Deputies of soviets, representatives of trade unions, Komsomol, and other social organizations or collectives of working people, directors of enterprises and construction organizations, as well as workers of public health, education, trade, agencies of internal affairs, cultural-enlightenment, and other institutions shall be commission members.

Article 6. The activity of a commission for the struggle against drunkenness shall be effectuated with the broad participation of the Soviet public.

Representatives of factory, plant, and local trade union committees, Komsomol committees, voluntary people's guard detachments, street and house committees, and other representatives of the public shall be enlisted for work in a commission.

From among the aktiv enlisted for work, the commission shall allocate social inspectors for educational work among persons who abuse alcoholic beverages, who permit violations of labor discipline or rules of conduct in public places, or who negatively influence the upbringing of children in the family.

Commissions for the struggle against drunkenness shall, with regard to all questions relegated to their competence, interact with the permanent commissions of soviets of working people's deputies, as well as with commissions for cases of minors and administrative commissions attached to the executive committees of the respective soviets of working people's deputies.

Article 7. Commissions for the struggle against drunkenness shall, with regard to questions relegated to their competence, adopt decrees which shall be binding on state institutions, enterprises, social organizations, officials, and citizens.

State institutions, enterprises, social organizations, and officials shall be obliged to notify the commission for the struggle against drunkenness within two weeks about measures adopted in execution of the commission decree.

II. Duties and Rights of Commissions for the Struggle Against Drunkenness

Article 8. District and city (cities not divided into districts) commissions for the struggle against drunkenness shall:

(a) ensure the coordination of the activity of state agencies and social organizations for the struggle against drunkenness and alcoholism;

(b) work out and effectuate measures, both directly and through the respective state agencies,and social organizations and collectives of working people, to prevent drunkenness, alcoholism, and violations of law committed under the influence of alcohol, to intensify anti-alcohol propaganda in collectives of working people and among the populace at their place of residence, to actively involve citizens and especially youth in sociopolitical life, scientific-technical activity, and to inspire profound interest for literary activity, art, physical culture, and sport;

(c) ensure the organization of necessary educational work at enterprises, collective farms, and institutions among persons who abuse alcohol, widely enlisting collectives of working people, labor and war veterans, members of voluntary people's guard detachments, and representatives of other social organizations to work with these persons; render assistance to social organizations and collectives of working people in re-educating persons who abuse alcohol; and verify the effectiveness of social and administrative pressure on persons who abuse alcohol;

(d) control the work of agencies of internal affairs and public health in regard to unmasking and registering persons to whom measures of administrative or social pressure for drunkenness have been applied previously; who systematically abuse alcohol; and who repeatedly have been placed in sobering stations -- in order to organize constant social supervision over the conduct of all such persons in daily life and at work, to take necessary measures for the treatment of persons ill with chronic alcoholism in corresponding medical institutions and labor therapy dispensaries, as well as to take other preventive measures and measures to suppress manifestations of drunkenness and alcoholism;

(e) control the activity of medical sobering stations and labor therapy dispensaries for chronic alcoholics, as well as render assistance to the administrations of dispensaries in work for the re-education and correction of persons maintained in them;

(f) organize control of social organizations and collectives of working people over the conduct of persons released from labor therapy dispensaries, and, when necessary, render assistance to them in finding employment;

(g) exercise control over the observance by trade and public dining enterprise workers of the rules established for trade in vodka and other alcoholic beverages;

(h) organize and carry out anti-alcohol propaganda with regard to explaining the harm inflicted by hard drinking on the health of people, the nurturing of children and adolescents, Soviet society, actively using the press, radio, television, and lecture propaganda. Anti-alcohol propaganda by lecture shall be performed in close contact with district (or city) organizations of the "Znanie" Society;

(i) take measures jointly with state agencies and social organizations to unmask persons who engage in home-brewing or in the illegal sale of alcoholic beverages and to bring them to responsibility in the established procedure.

Article 9. District or city (in cities not divided into district) commissions for the struggle against drunkenness shall have the right to:

(a) conduct a verification at enterprises, collective farms, organizations, and institutions of the state of work in regard to the struggle against drunkenness and alcoholism, to anti-alcohol propaganda, and to the organization of the cultural leisure time of workers, employees, and collective farmers;

(b) hear communications at commission sessions of the directors of enterprises, organizations, and institutions and the chairmen of collective farms about measures of struggle against drunkenness and alcoholism, about measures to prevent instances of drunkenness and violations of labor discipline, and about educational work and the organization of the cultural leisure time of workers, employees, and collective farmers;

(c) verify the activity of trade and public dining enterprises in regard to questions of the observance of established rules of trade for alcoholic beverages and, when violations are discovered, to raise the question of bringing the guilty persons to the responsibility established by law;

hear communications of the directors of trade and public dining enterprises about the fulfillment of established rules for trade in alcoholic beverages;

(d) enlist the public to participate in the reeducation of persons who indulge in drunkenness and to appoint social inspectors for educational work among such persons;

(e) make recommendations to the appropriate agencies and departments regarding the intensification of demands on directors of enterprises, institutions, and organizations who do not carry on the necessary struggle against drunkenness and alcoholism and who do not take necessary measures to prevent and suppress drunkenness or to educate workers and employees and organize their rest period. The said agencies and departments shall be obliged to notify the commission within a month about the results of consideration of the recommendation;

(f) bring questions for the consideration of executive committees of district (or city) soviets of working people's deputies concerning:

measures to intensify the struggle against drunkenness and alcoholism;

restriction or prohibition of trade in vodka and other alcoholic beverages in certain localities;

improvement of the state of educational work at enterprises, organizations, institutions, and collective farms.

(g) petition a court about sending chronic alcoholics who avoid voluntary treatment or who continue to drink after treatment, and who violate labor discipline, public order, or the rules of socialist community life notwithstanding measures of social or administrative pressure applied to them, to labor therapy dispensaries for compulsory treatment and labor re-education;

(h) petition a court to acknowledge a citizen to have a limited legal capacity in consequence of abuses of alcoholic beverages.

Article 10. City (in cities divided into districts), national area, region, and territory commissions for the struggle against drunkenness and commissions for the struggle against drunkenness attached to autonomous republic councils of ministers shall:

work out and implement measures through the appropriate state agencies, social organizations, and collectives of working people to prevent drunkenness and alcoholism and violations of law committed under the influence of alcohol, as well as measures to eradicate the causes giving rise to these phenomena;

Control, direct, and coordinate the activity of inferior commissions for the struggle against drunkenness, render methods assistance to them, and summarize and disseminate their positive work experience.

When fulfilling the said duties, city (in cities divided into districts), national area, region, and territory commissions for the struggle against drunkenness and commissions for the struggle against drunkenness attached to autonomous republic councils of ministers shall enjoy the rights provided for in Article 9 of the present statute.

Article 11. The Commission for the Struggle Against Drunkenness attached to the RSFSR Council of Ministers shall:

unify and direct the work to prevent drunkenness, alcoholism, and violations of law committed under the influence of alcohol and to eradicate the causes giving rise to these phenomena;

control and coordinate the activity of commissions for the struggle against drunkenness attached to autonomous republic councils of ministers, executive committees of territory, region, national area, and city (cities divided into districts) soviets of working people's deputies, render methods assistance to them, and summarize and disseminate their positive work experience.

III. Organization of the Work of Commissions for the Struggle Against Drunkenness

Article 12. The chairman of a commission for the struggle against drunkenness shall ensure the regular convening of commission sessions, determine the circle of questions subject to consideration at regular sessions, and prepare the work plan of the commission and reports on its activity for consideration at sessions. In the interval between sessions he shall give commissions to commission members and verify their execution.

A protocol shall be made at commission sessions in which the nature of questions considered shall be indicated. The protocol shall be signed by the presiding officer and the secretary.

Article 13. A session of a commission for the struggle against drunkenness shall be empowered to act when at least half of its membership is present.

A commission decree shall be adopted by a single majority vote of commission members who take part in the session and shall be signed by the chairman and secretary.

Article 14. Depending on the nature of questions being considered, representatives of agencies of internal affairs, public health, enlightenment, culture, transport, trade, public dining, and other state agencies, social organizations, and collectives of working people shall be invited to a session of the commission for the struggle against drunkenness.

Article 15. Sections may be created from the membership of a commission for the struggle against drunkenness for:

educational work and anti-alcohol propaganda;

registration and social observance over persons who abuse alcohol and who suffer from chronic alcoholism;

preventive treatment;

organization of control over the observance by trade and public dining enterprises of established rules for trade in alcoholic beverages.

Commissions also may create other sections.

Article 16. Members of a commission for the struggle against drunkenness shall fulfill their duties, as a rule, in free time from their basic job. During the fulfillment of commissions connected with a digression from their basic activity, earnings shall be retained for commission members at their place of work, and they shall have the right to compensation for expenses incurred.

Article 17. A decree of a commission for the struggle against drunkenness may be appealed to the executive committee of the respective soviet of working people's deputies or to the autonomous republic council of ministers to whom the commission is attached. The decision of these agencies in regard to the appeal shall be final.

Article 18. The material-technical provisions of a commission for the struggle against drunkenness shall be entrusted respectively to executive committees of soviets of working people's deputies, autonomous republic councils of ministers, and the RSFSR Council of Ministers.

ON CONFIRMATION OF THE GENERAL STATUTE ON THE LEGAL SECTION (OR OFFICE), CHIEF (OR SENIOR) JURISCONSULT, AND JURISCONSULT OF A MINISTRY, DEPARTMENT, EXECUTIVE COMMITTEE OF SOVIET OF WORKING PEOPLE'S DEPUTIES, ENTERPRISE, ORGANIZATION, OR INSTITUTION

[Decree of the USSR Council of Ministers, June 22, 1972, No. 467. Biulleten', no. 3 (1972), pp. 3-10]

The USSR Council of Ministers decrees:

1. The appended General Statute on the Legal Section (or Office), Chief (or Senior) Jurisconsult, and Jurisconsult of a Ministry, Department, Executive Committee of Soviet of Working People's Deputies, Enterprises, Organization, or Institution shall be confirmed.

2. Within a two-month period the ministries and departments of the USSR shall work out on the basis of the General Statute and shall confirm a Statute on the Legal Section (or Office), Chief (or Senior) Jurisconsult of the enterprise, organization, or institution of the system of the said ministry (or department), taking into account the peculiarities of work in the respective branch.

The union republic councils of ministers shall:

(a) oblige republic ministries and departments to work out within a two-month period on the basis of the General Statute and confirm a Statute on the Legal Section (or Office), Chief (or Senior) Jurisconsult, and Jurisconsult of the enterprise, organization, or institution of the system of the said ministry (or department), taking into account the peculiarities of work in the respective branch;

(b) within a two-month period work out on the basis of the General Statute and confirm a Statute on the Legal Section (or Office), Chief (or Senior) Jurisconsult, and Jurisconsult of the executive committee of a soviet of working people's deputies.

3. The USSR Ministry of Agriculture and the USSR Ministry of Justice shall be charged to work out within a three-month period and in conformity with the General Statute and shall confirm the procedure for legal services for collective farms, inter-collective farm enterprises and organizations (including services for their interfarm legal groups), taking into account the specific features of these enterprises and organizations.

4. It shall be recommended to the Administration of Tsentrosoiuz and the central agencies of other social organizations that they establish a procedure for carrying out legal work in the respective organizations and in conformity with the General Statute confirmed by the present decree.

General Statute on the Legal Section (or Office), Chief (or Senior) Jurisconsult, and Jurisconsult of a Ministry, Department, Executive Committee of Soviet of Working People's Deputies, Enterprise, Organization, or Institution

1. In order to carry out the legal work in a ministry (or department) of the USSR or of a union or autonomous republic or in an executive committee of a territorial, regional, city, or district soviet of working people's deputies or in an enterprise, organization, or institution, depending on the amount, nature, or complexity of the work, there shall be created a legal section (or office), as a rule an independent structural subdivision, or the post of chief (or senior) jurisconsult or of jurisconsult shall be introduced;[1] in a ministry or department where there is arbitrazh, the legal section (or office) shall be created with the arbitrazh.

The arbitrazh of a ministry or department shall operate on the basis of an individual statute confirmed in the established procedure.

2. The basic tasks of a legal section or jurisconsult of a ministry, department, executive committee of soviet of working people's deputies, enterprise, organization, or institution shall be:

(a) to strengthen socialist legality in the activity of a ministry, department, executive committee of soviet of working people's deputies, enterprise, organization, or institution;

(b) to actively utilize legal means to strengthen economic accountability, to struggle against mismanagement, and to improve the economic indicators of the work of enterprises, organizations, and institutions;

(c) to secure by legal means the preservation of socialist ownership, to increase the quality of products issued, to fulfill planning tasks, delivery obligations, subcontracts for capital construction, and other contracts;

(d) to defend the rights and legal interests of enterprises, organizations, institutions, and citizens;

(e) to propagandize Soviet legislation.

3. The workers of a legal section or a jurisconsult should participate actively in working out and effectuating measures directed toward the observance of state, planning, and contractual discipline, the strengthening of economic accountability, as well as the organization of the struggle against stealing, the issuance of poor-quality products, nonproduction losses, and violations of economic, labor, housing, and other legislation or of the norms of soviet or collective farm democracy.

4. The head of a legal section and the jurisconsult of a ministry or department shall be appointed to the post and relieved therefrom by the director of the ministry or department.

The head of a legal section and the jurisconsult of an enterprise, organization, or institution shall be appointed to and relieved from the post by the superior organization.

---

1) Hereinafter the terms "legal section" and "jurisconsult" shall be used respectively.

The head of a legal section and the jurisconsult of an executive committee of the soviet of working people's deputies shall be appointed to and relieved from the post in the established procedure.

The abolition of a legal section or curtailment of the post of jurisconsult at an enterprise, organization, or institution shall be permitted only with the consent of the superior organization.

5. Persons having a higher legal education shall be appointed to the post of head (or manager) of a legal section or jurisconsult.

In exceptional instances persons may be appointed to the post of jurisconsult who do not have a higher legal education if they have not less than three years work experience in a legal specialization, as well as persons studying in the last years of legal institutions of higher education.

6. The legal section or jurisconsult of a ministry or department shall be subordinated directly to the director of the ministry or department or by his decision to one of the deputy directors. The legal section or jurisconsult of an enterprise, organization, or institution shall be subordinated directly to the director.

With regard to methods questions of conducting legal work, the head of a legal section or jurisconsult shall be guided by the instructions of the legal section or jurisconsult of the superior organization.

7. The legal section or jurisconsult of a ministry or department shall:

(a) jointly with other structural subdivisions work out and effectuate measures directed at ensuring the undeviating observance of socialist legality in the system of the ministry or department and take measures to prevent violations of legislation in force;

(b) jointly with other subdivisions, and in individual instances independently, summarize the practice of the application of legislation in the branch, work out proposals to improve it, and submit them for the consideration of the leadership of the ministry or department;

(c) verify the conformity of requirements of legislation of the draft orders, instructions, decrees, regulations, and other documents of a legal nature submitted for the signature of the leadership of the ministry or department, and also to visa them; prepare independently or jointly with other subdivisions proposals regarding the amendment, or the repeal, of prevailing orders and other ministerial or departmental normative acts which have in reality lost force;

(d) participate in the preparation of draft laws, as well as of decrees and regulations of the government and other normative acts worked out by the ministry or department; prepare independently or jointly with other subdivisions opinions respecting drafts of normative acts received for review by the ministry or department; visa the said draft normative acts and opinions submitted for the signature of the leadership of the ministry or department;

(e) take part in working out proposals to improve the system of administration in the branch and to define the rights and duties of structural subdivisions of the ministry or department and also of enterprises, organizations, institutions, and officials;

(f) carry out work to enhance the role of economic contracts and to intensify responsibility for their fulfillment, to strengthen contractual discipline; take part in working out special conditions of delivery, standard contracts, and other normative acts regulating economic relations;

work out methods instructions regarding the organization of contractual work in the system of the ministry or department; take measures to ensure the timely and correct conclusion of economic contracts, an accounting of the fulfillment of contractual obligations, the application of economic measures of pressure in the event of the nonexecution or improper execution of contractual obligations;

(g) effectuate methods direction over claims work in the system of the ministry or department; analyze the state of work respecting the submission and consideration of claims and arbitrazh practice; work out proposals to eliminate shortcomings in the activity of enterprises, organizations, and institutions unmasked during the consideration of claims and economic disputes and submit these proposals to the leadership of the ministry or department;

(h) take part in working out and effectuating measures aimed at organizing the struggle against the issuance of poor-quality products, the spoilage of material valuables, stealing, and shortages;

(i) effectuate methods direction of legal work in the system of the ministry or department and verify the state of such work; organize the exchange of work experiences of legal sections or jurisconsults; convoke conferences and hold seminars in the established procedure;

(j) represent in the established procedure the interests of the ministry or department in court or arbitrazh, and also in other agencies when legal questions are being considered;

(k) implement jointly with other subdivisions measures to enhance the occupational qualifications of jurisconsults and the legal knowledge of workers of the central apparatus of the ministry (or department) and enterprises, organizations, or institutions within their jurisdiction;

work out measures respecting the propaganda of Soviet legislation in the system of the ministry or department and take part in effectuating them;

(l) give, with regard to the inquiries of enterprises, organizations, or institutions within the jurisdiction of the ministry (or department), explanations concerning legal questions, send them informational materials relating to legislation in force and the practice of its application; advise workers of the central apparatus of the ministry or department on legal questions; prepare informational materials respecting legislation for the leadership of the ministry or department;

(m) organize a systematized record of and keep normative acts received in the ministry (or department) or promulgated thereby; take measures aimed at improving the provision of legal sections or legal consultation offices of enterprises, organizations, or institutions with legislative and reference materials;

(n) analyze the informational and other materials regarding legal work received from enterprises, organizations, or institutions; draw up surveys of them and report on them when necessary to the leadership of the ministry or department;

(o) render legal assistance to the local trade union committee, the voluntary people's guard, and other social organizations of the ministry or department;

8. The legal section and jurisconsult of an executive committee of a territorial, regional, city, or district soviet of working people's deputies shall:

(a) verify the conformity to requirements of legislation of the draft decisions, regulations, and other documents of a legal nature submitted for the consideration of the soviet of working people's deputies and its executive committee, and also visa them;

(b) take part in the preparation and implementation of measures being carried out by a soviet of working people's deputies, its executive committee, or permanent committees to ensure the observance of socialist legality; take part in the preparation of draft documents of a legal nature submitted for the consideration of the soviet and its executive committee;

(c) prepare proposals concerning the amendment, suspension, or repeal of decisions and regulations of lower soviets of working people's deputies and their executive committees that do not conform to the law;

(d) prepare independently or jointly with sections (or administrations) of the executive committee proposals concerning the amendment of decisions or regulations of the soviet of working people's deputies and its executive committee or the repeal of those which have actually lost force;

(e) render legal assistance to permanent commissions of the soviet of working people's deputies, to administrative commissions, observation commissions, commissions for the affairs of minors, and other commissions created and attached to the executive committee of the soviet, as well as to deputies of the soviet and to amateur social agencies of the populace working under the direction of the soviet agencies of the working people's deputies;

(f) advise workers of the sections and administrations of the executive committee and jurisconsults of enterprises, organizations, and institutions subordinate to the soviet of working people's deputies, as well as workers of executive committees of lower soviets of working people's deputies on legal questions; upon the commission of the executive committee, give opinions on legal questions;

(g) organize a systematized record of and keep normative acts received in the executive committee or promulgated by the soviet of working people's deputies and its executive committee; take measures aimed at improving the provision of legal sections or legal consultation offices of executive committees of lower soviets of working people's deputies with legislative and reference materials;

(h) organize jointly with sections and administrations of the executive committee of the soviet of working people's deputies the study of normative acts by workers of the apparatus of the executive committee and its sections and administrations which relate to their activity;

(i) render methods assistance in carrying out legal work to legal sections and jurisconsults of the executive committees of inferior soviets of working people's deputies;

(j) represent in the established procedure the interests of the executive committee of the soviet working people's deputies in court or arbitrazh, and also in other agencies when legal questions are being considered.

9. The legal section and jurisconsult of an enterprise, organization, or institution shall:

(a) verify the conformity to requirements of legislation of the draft orders, instructions, statutes, and other documents of a legal nature, submitted for the signature of the director of the enterprise, organization, or institution, and also visa them;

(b) exercise supervision over the conformity to requirements of legislation of orders and other acts promulgated by the directors of structural subdivisions of the enterprise, organization, or institution and take measures to amend or repeal acts promulgated in violation of legislation in force;

(c) prepare jointly with other subdivisions proposals concerning the amendment of orders and other normative acts promulgated at the enterprise organization, or institution which are in force and the repeal of those which have actually lost force;

(d) take part in the preparation and conclusion of collective contracts, as well as in working out and effectuating measures to strengthen labor discipline at the enterprise, organization, or institution;

(e) organize jointly with other subdivisions work relating to the conclusion of economic contracts at enterprises, organizations, and institutions, take part in preparing the said contracts, and visa them;

(f) organize and conduct claims work; carry out methods direction of such work if it is conducted by other subdivisions of the enterprise, organization, or institution;

(g) participate in the consideration of questions concerning the computation of debtor and creditor indebtedness in the balance sheet of the enterprise, organization, or institution and take, jointly with other subdivisions, measures to liquidate such indebtedness;

(h) exercise supervision over the observance at the enterprise, organization, or institution of the procedure for accepting products and goods in respect of quantity and quality as established by legislation in force;

(i) represent in the established procedure the interests of the enterprise, organization, or institution in court or arbitrazh, and also in other agencies when legal questions are being considered;

(j) summarize and analyze the results of the consideration of court and arbitrazh cases and jointly with other structural subdivisions, the results of the consideration of claims, the practice of concluding and executing economic contracts; submit to the director of the enterprise, organization, or institution proposals concerning the elimination of shortcomings unmasked;

(k) participate in the preparation of draft normative acts worked out by the enterprise, organization, and institution, and in the preparation of opinions respecting draft normative acts sent to the enterprise, organization, or institution for comment;

(l) give advice, opinions, and information on legal questions arising in the activity of the enterprise, organization, or institution;

(m) take part in working out proposals appertaining to the results of the work of the commissions for the consideration of results of financial and economic activity of the enterprise, organization, or institution

(n) render legal assistance to the factory, plant, or local trade union committee, comrades' court, voluntary people's guard, and other social organizations at the enterprise, organization, or institution;

(o) prepare with the participation of other subdivisions materials relating to stealing, waste, shortages, issuance of poor-quality, substandard, or incomplete products, or other violations of law for transmission to investigative or judicial agencies and to comrades' courts, as well as take measures to compensate the damage caused to the enterprise, organization, or institution;

(p) organize a systematized record of and keep normative acts received in the enterprise, (or organization, institution) or promulgated by them;

(q) pass on information concerning legislation in force, organize jointly with other subdivisions the study of normative acts by officials of the enterprise, organization, or institution which relate to their activity;

(r) carry on work relating to the propaganda of Soviet legislation at the enterprise, organization, or institution.

10. The legal section and jurisconsult of a ministry, department, executive committee of soviet of working people's deputies, enterprise, organization, or institution shall have the right to:

(a) verify the observance of legality respectively in the system of the ministry, department, executive committees of lower soviets of working people's deputies, in the activity of the structural subdivisions of the ministry, department, enterprise, organization, or institution, as well as in sections and administrations of the executive committee of soviet of working people's deputies;

(b) receive documents, references, accounts, and other information needed to fulfill duties from officials in the procedure established in the ministry, department, executive committee of soviet of working people's deputies, enterprise, organization, or institution;

(c) enlist with the consent of the director or the structural subdivision of a ministry, department, section (or administration) of an executive committee of soviet of working people's deputies or the director of an enterprise, organization, or institution workers to prepare draft normative acts and other documents, as well as to work out and effectuate measures implemented by the legal section and jurisconsult in conformity with the duties entrusted to them.

11. The head (or manager) of a legal section and the jurisconsult shall participate in sessions of the college of the ministry (or department), in sessions of the executive committee of soviet of working people's deputies, in meetings convoked by the director of the enterprise, organization, or institution, when there is discussion at them of questions relating to the practice of applying legislation in force or other aspects of legal work.

12. The head (or manager) of a legal section and the jurisconsult of a ministry, department, executive committee of soviet of working people's deputies, enterprise, organization, or institution shall bear responsibility for the conformity to legislation in force of draft orders, instructions, statutes, decrees, decisions, regulations, and other documents of a legal nature visaed by him.

13. The head (or manager) of a legal section and jurisconsult who has discovered violations of legality in the work of the ministry, department, organization, institution, section (or administration) of an executive committee of soviet of working people's deputies or their officials shall be obliged to report these violations to the director of the respective ministry, department, enterprise, organization, institution, executive committee of soviet of working people's deputies so that the necessary measures can be taken to eliminate them.

14. In the event draft orders, instructions, and other legal documents submitted for signature to the leadership of the ministry, department, executive committee of soviet of working people's deputies or director of an enterprise, organization, or institution do not conform to legislation in force, the head (or manager) of the legal section and the jurisconsult, without visaing the drafts of these documents, shall give an appropriate opinion with suggestions as to the legal procedure for resolving the questions being considered.

In the event the director of the enterpise, organization, or institution signs the said documents, notwithstanding the opinion of the head of the legal section or the jurisconsult, the latter shall notify the superior organization thereof.

The head of the legal section and the jurisconsult of an enterprise, organization, or institution who has not taken measures in accordance with the present General Statute to eliminate violations of legality shall bear liability together with the director of the enterprise, organization, or institution in the established procedure.

15. Entrusting duties to a legal section or jurisconsult of a ministry, department, executive committee of soviet of working people's deputies, enterprise, organization, or institution which are not provided for by the present General Statute and which do not relate to legal work shall not be permitted.

Ministries, departments, executive committees of soviets of working people's deputies, enterprises, organizations, and institutions shall be obliged to provide the legal section or jurisconsult with legislative and reference materials, collections and other manuals on legal questions, as well as necessary legal literature.

STATUTE ON PEOPLE'S CONTROL AGENCIES IN THE USSR

[Confirmed by Decree of the Central Committee of the CPSU and the Council of Ministers of the USSR, December 19, 1968. SP SSSR (1969), no. 1, item 2]

In the Soviet state, which expresses the interests and the will of the whole people, the right of control belongs to the people, as the sole master of their country.

People's control agencies occupy an important place in Soviet society, being one of the forms of socialist democracy. Through them, the broad masses of working people exercise the right of control in the domain of the economy and of economic and cultural construction, and participate in the administration of the affairs of the state.

In people's control agencies, state control is combined with the social control of working people at enterprises, collective farms, institutions, and organizations. Their chief strength consists of the workers, collective farmers, and employees who work in people's control groups, posts, and committees, who participate in verifying the execution of Party and Government directives, who help transform them into life, and who achieve the unity of decision and deed.

People's control agencies shall work under the direction of the Party and Government and shall support them as active assistants in day-to-day activity by educating cadres in the spirit of high organization and discipline. Party organizations shall direct the activity of people's control agencies and shall render to them all possible support and assistance in work.

I. Fundamental Tasks of People's Control Agencies

1. The primary activity of people's control agencies shall be to render aid to party and state agencies in the systematic verification of the actual execution of Party and Government directives by soviet, economic, and other organizations, in the further improvement of leadership in communist construction, and in the struggle to promote the economy in all ways and to strengthen state discipline and socialist legality.

People's control agencies:

(a) shall exercise systematic control over the course of the fulfillment of state plans and assignments;

(b) shall lead an active struggle to uncover and use reserves of the national economy, to raise the effectiveness of social production and the economic expenditure of labor and material resources and monetary assets, and to introduce everything new and progressive into production;

(c) shall decisively oppose violations of state discipline, manifestations of localist tendencies, a departmental approach to affairs, mismanagement and squandering, any attempts to cheat the state, and infringements of socialist ownership;

(d) shall strictly suppress manifestations of bureaucratism and red tape, and shall strive to improve the work of the state apparatus and its economization, to introduce the scientific organization of labor and administration and the efficient organization of departmental control.

In all their activity, people's control agencies are called upon to develop in Soviet people the feeling of being master of the country, the feeling of the high responsibility of each for the affairs of the whole society.

2. People's control agencies shall systematically exercise control over the observance of Soviet laws by officials in considering proposals, petitions, and complaints of citizens, verify the state of such work, in all ministries and departments, enterprises, institutions, and organizations, as well as collective farms and other cooperative and social organizations, bringing to strict responsibility persons who are guilty of violating laws, red tape, formalism, bureaucratism, and of failing to fulfill decisions taken in accordance with proposals, petitions, and complaints of citizens.

3. A most important task of people's control agencies is, by timely warning, to prevent cadres from making mistakes and blunders in work and achieve the elimination of hidden shortcomings. For such purposes, people's control agencies shall construct their work on the basis of publicity, widely using such means as the press, radio, and television. The results of verifications and measures adopted concerning them shall, as a rule, be brought to the information of the collectives of the corresponding enterprises, collective farms, institutions, and organizations. On persons who are guilty of permitting shortcomings, people's control agencies shall exert pressure by way of comradely criticism, by discussions of their improper actions, and also by means of bringing them to responsibility.

4. People's control agencies shall work on the basis of the principle of collectivity.

People's control agencies shall decide practical questions in close connection with the appropriate party, soviet, economic, cooperative, trade union, komsomol, and other organizations.

5. People's control agencies shall be directed in their activity by legislation in force in the USSR, decisions of the Party and Government, and the present Statute. They shall account periodically to party and soviet agencies about their work, report to them the results of the more important verifications, make suggestions with regard to eliminating hidden shortcomings, and, when necessary, shall transfer for their consideration the cases of workers who have permitted shortcomings and violations.

6. People's control agencies shall educate their workers and activists in the spirit of high responsibility for fulfillment of the honorable duties entrusted to them.

7. Soviet, economic, cooperative, and social organizations, and officials, should render every kind of cooperation to people's control agencies and create the necessary conditions for fulfillment of the duties entrusted to them.

II. Construction and Organization of the Work of People's Control Agencies

8. People's control agencies in the USSR shall be: union republic people's control committees, autonomous republic people's control committees, territory, regional, autonomous region, national area, city, and district people's control committees, people's control groups and posts attached to rural and settlement soviets of working people's deputies, at enterprises, collective farms, institutions, organizations, and military units. The people's control committees, groups, and posts shall comprise a unified system of people's control agencies of the USSR.

People's Control Groups and Posts

9. People's control groups and posts shall comprise the basis of the system of people's control agencies. They shall be called upon to exercise control directly at enterprises, collective farms, and institutions and organizations, to help party organizations and the administration in all sections of production management and servicing, and to achieve the creation of conditions which would exclude the possibility of the manifestation of mismanagement and squandering and the violation of state and production discipline and socialist legality.

10. People's control groups and posts shall, when necessary, conduct verifications, raids, and views at enterprises, collective farms, institutions, and organizations, take part in verifications and inspections of their production and financial-economic activity that are carried out by superior agencies, and have the right to familiarize themselves with documents and materials describing the state of affairs in places being verified, according to the results of verifications to hear explanations of persons who are guilty of frustrating production plans and assignments, who have permitted violations of state discipline, bureaucratism and red tape, mismanagement, and abuses, to pronounce social censure on guilty persons, to oblige them to appear before the collective to report on measures taken to eliminate shortcomings, and to transfer cases for the consideration of comrades' courts.

People's control groups and posts shall raise before administrations, and before party and other social organizations of the collective, questions which arise as a result of verifications, in particular questions of bringing to responsibility workers who are guilty of permitting any kind of shortcomings.

Directors of enterprises, collective farms, institutions, and organizations shall be obliged to render to people's control groups and posts all possible aid in their work, to consider their proposals and recommendations, and to take necessary measures to eliminate hidden shortcomings. Groups and posts shall verify that both their proposals and recommendations are carried out and that the results of the verifications are brought to the information of the collectives of working people.

When necessary, people's control groups and posts shall turn with questions deriving from their activity to party, soviet, and economic agencies and to people's control committees. They shall bring to the consideration of people's control committees proposals to conduct a more thorough verification of the respective enterprise, collective farm, institution, or organization with the participation of representatives of the same or another people's control committee, to suspend clearly illegal orders and actions of officials, to assess monetary deductions, to bring guilty persons to responsibility, and other questions.

11. Members of people's control groups and posts shall be elected at meetings of collectives of working people, and where due to production conditions a general meeting may not be convoked, at conferences of the representatives of collectives and at meetings of authorized persons on collective farms. Groups and posts shall be elected for a term of two years.

People's control groups attached to rural and settlement soviets of working people's deputies shall be formed by election of members of groups at meetings of citizens of population centers located on the territory of the corresponding rural or settlement soviet or at meetings of persons authorized by it. Such groups shall work under the direction of the corresponding party organizations, rural and settlement soviets, and people's control committees. They shall exercise control with respect to questions relating to the competence of rural and settlement soviets, and shall coordinate their work with the activity of people's control groups created at enterprises, collective farms, institutions, and organizations located on the territory of the corresponding soviet.

The outstanding and most active and authoritative workers, collective farmers, employees, students, as well as pensioners and housewives, both communists and non-party members, shall be elected to people's control groups and posts.

The numerical composition of people's control groups or posts shall be determined by a meeting of the collective of working people, taking into account the necessity of a broad involvement of workers, collective farmers, and employees in the cause of control and depending upon the amount of work and the size of the enterprise, collective farm, institution, or organization. Members of groups and posts shall be elected by open ballot. At their meetings, collectives of working people may give instructions to people's control groups and posts. Groups and posts shall report on their activity to the collectives or representatives of a collective.

A meeting or conference of representatives of a collective of working people, on its own initiative or on the proposal of a people's control group or post, may recall a member of a group or post before his term expires if he has not justified the confidence placed in him.

A people's control group of an enterprise (or collective farm, institution, or organization) shall exercise control throughout the entire enterprise (or collective farm, institution, or organization) and shall direct the work of groups and posts in shops, divisions, and brigades.

12. A general meeting of members of a people's control group, by open ballot, shall select a chairman, his deputies, and when necesary, a group bureau, form sectors and permanent or provisional commissions for individual questions of activity, confirm a work plan, discuss the results of the more important verifications, and work out suggestions and recommendations regarding them.

The director of a people's control post shall be elected by open ballot at a meeting of members of the post and shall organize their work.

13. People's control groups and posts at enterprises, on collective farms, and in organizations and institutions shall work under the direction of party organizations and the corresponding committees of people's control. They must display initiative in their work and widely enlist participation in verifications by workers, collective farmers, employees, specialists, and social controllers of trade unions and komsomol organizations.

14. Members of people's control groups and posts shall carry out their activity on social principles. Such work is an honorable social duty.

A people's controller is called upon to constantly display concern for the preservation and augmentation of the national wealth, to set an example of diligence, high organization and discipline, to be exacting toward himself, and to be principled and implacable when the matter concerns the defense of state and social interests.

To reward the most distinguished activists of people's control, people's control committees and party, soviet, economic, cooperative, and other social organizations shall use the prevailing forms of incentive.

Any attempts to persecute people's controllers, reprisals against them for their social activity, or suppression of criticism must be resolutely suppressed, and the persons guilty thereof shall be brought to strict responsibility up to and including removal from posts and bringing to trial.

People's Control Committees

15. District, city, area, regional, and territory people's control committees shall be formed by corresponding soviets of working people's deputies. Such committees shall be composed of chairmen, their deputies, and members of committees -- representatives of party, soviet, trade union, and komsomol organizations, workers, collective farmers, and employees, workers of the press, figures of science and culture and leading workers and activists of people's control. The chairmen of committees shall be appointed by the soviet of working people's deputies.

District, city, area, regional, and territory people's control committees shall work under the direction of the corresponding party and soviet agencies and of the superior people's control agencies. They shall exercise control over the fulfillment of Party and Government directives and state plans and assignments by enterprises, collective farms, institutions, and organizations located on the territory of the district, city, national area, region, or territory irrespective of their departmental affiliation, shall achieve the elimination of hidden shortcomings and the general improvement of matters, and shall bring more important questions to the consideration of corresponding party, soviet, and economic agencies and, in necessary instances, to the consideration of central institutions and organizations.

The important tasks of district, city, national area, regional, and territory people's control committees shall be to exercise direction over people's control groups in order to ensure the active activity of each of them, and to raise the responsibility of groups and posts for the state of affairs at enterprises, collective farms, institutions, and organizations.

16. The personnel of union and autonomous republic people's control committees shall be confirmed by the union and autonomous republic councils of ministers. Such committees shall comprise the chairmen, their deputies, and the members of committees -- representatives of party, soviet, trade union, komsomol, and other organizations, workers, collective farmers, and employees, workers of the press, figures of science and culture, and leading workers of people's control agencies. The chairmen of the committees shall be appointed by the supreme soviets of union or autonomous republics. Union republic people's control committees shall work under the direction of the Central Committee of the Communist Party, the union republic councils of ministers and the People's Control Committee of the USSR. People's control committees of autonomous republics shall work under the direction of regional party committees, the councils of ministers of such republics, and superior people's control committees.

Union and autonomous republic people's control committees shall direct the work of inferior people's control agencies, shall exercise control over the fulfillment of Party and Government directives and of state plans and assignments by ministries and departments of the republic, as well as by enterprises, collective farms, institutions, and organizations irrespective of their affiliation, and shall achieve the elimination of hidden shortcomings and the general improvement of matters. Proceeding from the materials of verifications, committees shall bring to the consideration of the corresponding republic party and soviet agencies, and when necessary to the consideration of corresponding institutions and organizations of the USSR, questions requiring their decisions.

17. The People's Control Committee of the USSR shall be a union-republic agency. The Committee shall work under the immediate direction of the Central Committee of the CPSU and the USSR Council of Ministers.

The personnel of the People's Control Committee of the USSR shall be confirmed by the USSR Council of Ministers. The Committee shall comprise a chairman, deputy chairmen and members of the Committee -- representatives of party, soviet, trade union, komsomol, and other organizations, workers, collective farmers, employees, workers of the press, figures of science and culture, and leading workers of the Committee and people's control agencies in the provinces. The chairman of the People's Control Committee of the USSR shall be appointed by the USSR Supreme Soviet.

The People's Control Committee of the USSR shall direct the activity of all people's control agencies in the country and exercise control over the fulfillment of Party and Government directives and of state plans and assignments by ministries, departments, soviet and economic organizations, enterprises, and collective farms.

The People's Control Committee of the USSR by its activity shall promote the carrying out of tasks placed before ministries and departments, assist the education of their cadres in the spirit of strict observance of state interests and discipline, and raise the responsibility of each worker for the cause entrusted to him.

The People's Control Committee of the USSR, with regard to the results of verifications, shall bring to the Central Committee of the CPSU and the USSR Council of Ministers proposals having general state significance and shall submit reports on the state of affairs in individual branches of the national economy and on the organization of work in ministries and departments.

Control in the Armed Forces of the USSR shall be exercised by the People's Control Committee of the USSR on the basis of the present Statute and in conformity with a special instruction confirmed by the USSR Council of Ministers.

People's control agencies shall exercise control in branches of the defense industry on the basis of the present Statute and in conformity with a special instruction confirmed by the USSR Council of Ministers.

18. People's control committees shall adopt appropriate decrees with regard to the results of verifications and, within the limits of the rights granted to them by the present Statute, they shall determine measures with regard to eliminating hidden shortcomings. Directors of enterprises, collective farms, organizations, ministries, and departments shall without delay eliminate hidden shortcomings and violations and inform the people's control committees of the results.

19. The People's Control Committee of the USSR, union and autonomous republic people's control committees, and territory, regional, national area, city, and district people's control committees, in conformity with the tasks entrusted to them, shall have the right to:

(a) request necessary documents and materials from directors and officials of enterprises, collective farms, organizations, ministries, and departments, hear their reports and explanations with regard to the results of verifications, and give (as appropriate) instructions on the elimination of hidden shortcomings and violations;

(b) prescribe, when necessary, and conduct with the participation of representatives of the appropriate agencies, an inspection of economic-financial activity and production-technical expertise;

(c) suspend clearly illegal orders and actions of officials and to inform the directors of the appropriate enterprises, collective farms, institutions, and organizations, or superior agencies, thereof;

(d) point out shortcomings permitted by officials, give them warnings, transfer materials concerning their offenses for the discussion of collectives of working people and social organizations.

20. In instances when means of social pressure are insufficient and when by their nature the offenses call for bringing the officials who have permitted or committed them to stricter responsibility, peoples's control committees shall:

(a) impose penalties on the guilty (public exposure; reprimand, severe reprimand);

(b) in conformity with Rules confirmed by the Council of Ministers of the USSR, impose monetary deductions on those officials who by their actions caused material damage to the state or cooperative, collective farm, and social enterprises, and organizations;

(c) remove officials from occupied posts for frustrating fulfillment of Party and Government directives and for grave violations of state discipline and other serious omissions in work. The subsequent discharge of the said workers shall be made in the established procedure;

(d) send to agencies of the procuracy materials concerning thefts, abuses, and other criminal actions of officials.

Appeals from decrees of people's control committees on bringing officials to responsibility shall be considered by superior people's control committees or by other agencies to whom the people's control committees imposing a penalty are inferior.

21. Penalties imposed by people's control committees shall be removed by them on the application of persons subjected to punishment or on the petition of appropriate people's control agencies, ministries, departments, enterprises, collective farms, institutions, and organizations, after elimination of the shortcomings for which the penalties were imposed.

22. People's control committees, together with the regular apparatus, shall create sections for branches of the economy, science, and culture, and permanent and provisional commissions, working on social principles. The workers of such sections and commissions shall be chosen from among the most authoritative and experienced workers, collective farmers, employees, as well as pensioners, and shall be confirmed by people's control committees upon the recommendation of party and other social organizations.

Workers of auxiliary sections and commissions of people's control committees shall fulfill commissions, as a rule, in a social procedure, and when necessary, with the consent of the directors of the appropriate enterprises, collective farms, institutions, organizations, with release from basic work for a period of up to two weeks per year, retaining the average monthly wage at the place of work.

For verifications, investigations, and inspections, people's control committees shall enlist workers, collective farmers, specialists, as well as representatives of soviet, economic, trade union, and komsomol organizations, workers of the press, ministries, departments, and members of inspection commissions of cooperative organizations, and with their participation shall work out measures to eliminate shortcomings that have been uncovered and to improve the general state of affairs.

23. People's control committees shall create a bureau for complaints and proposals of working people which shall consider proposals, declarations, and complaints submitted to the committees and shall achieve the proper resolution of questions submitted to them. The bureau of complaints and proposals shall study the reasons for complaints, shall bring the more important questions deriving from letters and petitions for the discussion of committees, and shall exercise control over the execution of committee decisions adopted with regard to complaints and suggestions of working people.

Directors and officials of enterprises, collective farms, institutions, and organizations to whom people's control committees send for consideration the complaints and proposals of working people must give their replies thereto within the established periods.

People's control committees shall receive working people. The reception shall be conducted by chairmen, deputy chairmen, committee members, and workers of the bureau of complaints and proposals and other regular or auxiliary workers of the apparatus.

24. The structure and number of workers of the apparatus of the People's Control Committee of the USSR, as well as the general regular number of workers of people's control committees, shall be confirmed by the USSR Council of Ministers. The People's Control Committee of the USSR shall have the right to make changes in the structure and to confirm the personnel establishment of its apparatus within the limits of the number of workers and wage fund established for the central apparatus, observing the scheme of official rates of pay.

The structure and staffs of people's control committees of union republics and of local people's control committees within the general number of workers of people's control agencies shall be confirmed by the union republic councils of ministers by agreement with the Committee of People's Control of the USSR.

25. The financing of people's control committees shall be at the expense of the assets of the union budget.

26. The People's Control Committee of the USSR shall have a seal depicting the State Arms of the USSR and its own name.

People's control committees of union and autonomous republics and territory, regional, national area, city, and district people's control committees shall have a seal depicting the State Arms of the union republic and its own name.

STATUTE ON COMRADES' COURTS

[Confirmed by Edict of the Presidium of the Supreme Soviet of the RSFSR, March 11, 1977. Vedomosti RSFSR (1977), no. 12, item 254]

I. Tasks of Comrades' Courts and Procedure for their Organization

Article 1. Comrades' courts are elective social agencies called upon actively to promote the nurturing of citizens in the spirit of a communist attitude toward labor, an attitude of care toward socialist ownership, observance of the rules of socialist community life, the development of a feeling of collectivism and comradely mutual assistance in them, and respect for the dignity and honor of Soviet people. The principal task in the work of comrades' courts is the prevention of violations of law, the nurturing of people through persuasion and social pressure, and the creation of a situation of intolerance toward any antisocial offenses. Comrades' courts shall be invested with the trust of the collective, shall express its will, and shall be responsible to it.

Article 2. Comrades' courts at enterprises and in institutions, organizations, and higher and secondary specialized educational institutions shall be created by decision of the general meeting of workers, employees, or students.

Comrades' courts at collective farms and in houses served by housing operations offices, housing administrations, or united in street committees, as well as in rural population centers and settlements, shall be created by decision of a general meeting of collective farm members or a general meeting (or gathering) of the inhabitants of houses or citizens of the rural village or settlement, with the consent of the executive committees of the respective soviets of working people's deputies.

In large collectives, comrades' courts may be created in the shops of enterprises, state farm divisions, collective farm brigades, and certain other subdivisions.

Comrades' courts may be created in collectives numbering not less than 50 persons. In individual instances, with the consent of the superior trade union agency or of the executive committee of the respective soviet of working people's deputies, comrades' courts may be created in collectives numbering less than 50 persons.

Article 3. Citizens who by their professional and moral qualities are capable of successfully fulfilling the tasks placed before comrades' courts may be elected to a comrades' court. Each member of a comrades' court shall be obliged to display high discipline and orderliness, be implacable toward violations of law and antisocial offenses, and be guided in its activity strictly by law.

Article 4. Candidates for members of a comrades' court shall be nominated by party, trade union, komsomol, and other social organizations, as well as by individual citizens.

Lists of candidates for members of a comrades' court shall be posted for general review.

Article 5. Comrades' courts shall be elected by open ballot at general meetings of collectives of working people and at meetings (or gatherings) of citizens at their place of residence for a term of two years.

Meetings for elections of comrades' courts shall be convoked respectively by the factory, plant, and local trade union committees or by the executive committees of local soviets of working people's deputies.

The date for elections of a comrades' court shall be notified in good time.

Citizens who are participating in the election of a comrades' court shall have the right to file a reasoned challenge against any of the candidates, as well as to nominate new candidates. The question of satisfying or rejecting a challenge shall be decided by a majority vote of those participating in the meeting.

Persons who have received a majority of votes with respect to the remaining candidates and more than half of the votes of those cast at the meeting shall be considered to be elected to the membership of the court.

The number of court members shall be established by the meeting; however, their number may not exceed five. Court members shall elect from their membership by open ballot a chairman of the comrades' court, his deputies, and a court secretary.

A special certificate shall be presented to those elected to a comrades' court by the agency entrusted with the guidance of comrades' courts.

Article 6. Comrades' courts shall account not less than once a year for their activity to general meetings of collectives of working people.

The members of a comrades' court who have not justified the trust placed in them may be recalled before time by the general meeting. The question of recall shall, as a rule, be discussed in the presence of the comrades' court member being recalled.

A comrades' court member shall be considered recalled if a majority of participants of a general meeting voted for recall.

Release from the duties of a comrades' court member in the event of his dismissal from work or of the impossibility to fulfill the duties for reasons of health, or for other justifiable reasons shall be by the trade union agency or by the executive committee of the respective local soviet of working people's deputies.

The election of new members of a comrades' court in place of those recalled or who have left for other reasons shall be in the procedure provided for by Articles 2-5 of the present Statute.

II. Cases Considered by Comrades' Courts

Article 7. Comrades' courts shall consider cases concerning:

(1) truancy without valid reasons (including appearing at work in a state of intoxication), late arrival at work or departing prematurely from work, and other violations of labor discipline; unconscientious fulfillment of work or wasted time as a consequence of the unconscientious attitude of a worker toward his duties;

(2) the failure to observe requirements for the protection of labor (safety, production sanitation, labor hygiene) and fire prevention, except for instances entailing criminal responsibility;

(3) loss or damage of equipment, inventory, instruments, materials, and other state or social property as a consequences of an unconscientious attitude of a person toward his duties, unless this entails criminal responsibility;

(4) unauthorized use for personal purposes of means of transport, agricultural equipment, machine tools, instruments, raw materials, and other property belonging to a state enterprise, institution, organization, collective farm, as well as another cooperative or social organization, unless such actions caused material damage to the said enterprises, institutions, and organizations;

(5) drinking alcoholic beverages on the streets and in courtyards and doorways, at stadiums, in public gardens, parks, and other public places, except trade and public dining enterprises in which the retail sale of alcoholic beverages is permitted; appearance in public places in an intoxicated condition, insulting human dignity and public morality; acquisition of home-brew, chacha, arrack, mulberry vodka, home-brewed beer, and other strong home-made alcoholic beverages;

(6) petty stealing of state or social property, petty hooliganism; petty speculation committed for the first time; theft of inexpensive articles on consumption and everyday life in the personal ownership of citizens when the guilty person and the victim are members of a single collective.

Note. Cases enumerated in the present point shall be sent to comrades' courts by agencies of internal affairs, the procuracy, or a court, and cases concerning petty stealing of state or social property also by the administrations of enterprises, institutions, or organizations, or the collective farm boards, notifying the procurator thereof. If there is no comrades' court at the place of work, residence, or study of the offender, the case shall be considered in a district (or city) people's court in the procedure established by law.

(7) insults, slander, beatings and light bodily injuries not entailing impairment of health, if such acts were committed for the first time; foul language;

(8) the failure to fulfill or the improper fulfillment by parents, guardians, or curators of duties relating to the nurturing of children; an unworthy attitude toward parents; unworthy conduct in the family; an unworthy attitude toward women;

(9) damaging of dwelling and non-dwelling premises and communal equipment; the failure to observe fire safety rules;

(10) violations of rules in apartments and dormitories; dispute of inhabitants relating to the use of auxiliary premises, house services, payment for municipal services, and payment for current repair expenses of places of common use;

(11) the procedure for the use of structures comprising the common ownership of two or several citizens; the division of collective farm household property and withdrawal from a collective farm household; the division of property between spouses if the parties in dispute consent to the case being considered in a comrades' court;

(12) the damaging of trees and other greenery; recovery for damage caused by petty forestry violations committed for the first time unless the damage exceeds thirty rubles according to prevailing rates for calculating the extent of recovery for damage;

(13) property disputes between citizens in an amount of up to fifty rubles, if the participants in the dispute consent to the case being considered in a comrades' court;

(14) administrative violations of law, if the agencies or officials granted the right to impose a fine in an administrative proceeding consider it necessary to transfer material for the consideration of a comrades' court.

A comrades' court also may consider cases concerning criminal acts committed for the first time unless they represent a great social danger, and agencies of internal affairs, the procuracy, or a court shall, in accordance with prevailing legislation, transfer such a case for the consideration of a comrades' court.

Article 8. Comrades' courts shall not have the right to consider cases in respect of which judgments or judicial decisions already have been rendered, disciplinary or administrative penalties imposed, or a decision of a comrades' court adopted within the limits of its competence has been taken.

III. Procedure for Consideration of Cases in Comrades' Courts

Article 9. Cases in comrades' courts shall be considered at the place of work, study, or residence of the offender.

Article 10. Comrades' courts shall consider cases relating to:

(1) the representations of factory, plant, or local (or shop) trade union committees, voluntary people's guards for the protection of public order, people's control groups and posts, street, house, sector, and block committees and other social organizations, and meetings of citizens;

(2) representations of executive committees of local soviets of working people's deputies, administrative commissions attached to executive committees of district, city, rural, and settlement soviets of working people's deputies and permanent commissions of soviets;

(3) communications of state agencies, directors of enterprises, institutions and organizations, collective farm boards, as well as of other officials having the right to impose disciplinary sanctions;

(4) materials transferred by a court, procurator, as well as investigator and agency of inquiry with the consent of a procurator;

(5) applications of citizens;

(6) the initiative of the comrades' court itself.

Article 11. A comrades' court shall consider cases within a period of up to 15 days from the moment they are received. Cases concerning petty hooliganism, petty stealing, and petty speculation shall be considered by comrades' courts within 10 days from the moment they are received. The time and place of considering the case shall be determined by the chairman of the comrades' court and shall be publicized widely to citizens.

Article 12. Before consideration of a case in a comrades' court, when necessary, the materials received should be verified.

Directors of enterprises, institutions, and organizations, as well as other officials and citizens, shall be obliged, upon the demand of a comrades' court, to submit information and documents necessary in the case.

The chairman of a court or his deputy shall acquaint the person brought before the court, the victim, and participants of a civil law dispute with the available materials and, when there are grounds for consideration of the case in a comrades' court, establish who should be summoned for the court session as witnesses. The person brought before the court, the victim, as well as participants of the civil law dispute being considered by a court, shall have the right to petition to demand and obtain additional documents and summon witnesses.

When considering the case at the place of residence of the offender, a comrades' court shall, when necessary, take measures ensuring the participation in the comrades' court session of representatives of the collective in which the offender works.

Article 13. Sessions of a comrades' court and the fulfillment by court members of commissions connected with the consideration of a case shall be during non-working time.

Cases shall be considered publicly by not less than three comrades' court members; however, in all instances their number should be uneven.

A person brought before a comrades' court, a victim, and participants in a civil law dispute may challenge the presiding member and members of a comrades' court if there are circumstances giving grounds to believe that the presiding member or member of a comrades' court may be personally interested in the outcome of a case.

The question of satisfying the challenge or rejecting it shall be decided by the entire bench of the comrades' court considering the particular case.

During the examination of cases in a comrades' court, the person brought before the court, the victim, and participants in a civil law dispute shall enjoy equal rights.

The comrades' court shall consider materials available, hear the explanations of the person brought before the court, the victim, the participants in a civil law dispute, and witnesses. Those present at the session may put questions or speak on the substance of the case being considered.

A comrades' court shall keep a protocol, which shall be signed by the presiding member and the secretary of the session.

Article 14. The appearance of citizens upon the summons of a comrades' court shall be obligatory. If the person brought before a comrades' court, the victim, or the participant of a civil law dispute does not appear at the session, the court should elucidate the reasons for the failure to appear and, depending upon the facts established, shall designate the case for hearing a second time. In the event of this person's failure to appear for a second time without valid reasons, the comrades' court may consider the case in his absence.

Article 15. When considering a case and taking a decision, a comrades' court shall be guided by prevailing legislation, by the present Statute, and by an awareness of its social duty. The decision of a comrades' court shall be adopted by a majority vote of court members participating in the consideration of the particular case in conditions excluding extraneous influence of the composition of the court. In the decision shall be specified the time and place of considering the case, the name and composition of the comrades' court, data concerning the person with respect to whom the case is considered, the content of the violation of law or the character of the civil law dispute, the reasons for the decision and the evidence to which the comrades' court refers, the measure of social pressure determined by the court or an indication of the justification or results of the consideration of a civil law dispute, as well as the period and procedure for appealing the decision.

The decision of a comrades' court shall be signed by those participating in rendering it: the presiding member and the members of the court, and shall be announced publicly and brought to the information of the collective.

IV. Measures of Social Pressure Applied by Comrades' Courts

Article 16. A comrades' court may apply one of the following measures of pressure to a guilty person:

(1) oblige him to make a public apology to the victim or collective;

(2) announce a comradely warning;

(3) announce a social censure;

(4) announce a social reprimand, with or without publication in the press;

(5) impose a money fine in an amount not exceeding 10 rubles, unless the offense is connected with a violation of labor discipline, and in cases concerning petty stealing of state or social property, a fine not exceeding 30 rubles, and in the event of repeated petty stealing, not exceeding 50 rubles;

(6) place before the director of an enterprise, institution, or organization the question of the transfer of the guilty person who violated labor discipline, in accordance with prevailing labor legislation, to lower-paid work or demoting him to a lower post;

(7) place before the director of an enterprise, institution, or organization the question of the dismissal, in accordance with prevailing legislation, of a worker who fulfills educational functions or work connected with the direct servicing of money or valuable goods if the comrades' court, taking into account the character of the offenses committed by this person, considers it impossible to trust him with such work thereafter.

Simultaneously with the application to the guilty person of the measures of pressure established by the present article, a comrades' court may, in instances provided for by law, place before the administration of an enterprise, institution, organization, and FZMK the question of depriving the guilty person wholly or in part of compensation for the results of the year's work, a preferential pass for a rest home or sanatorium, as well as being put off in the priority to receive housing premises.

Together with the application of measures of pressure provided for by points 1-7 of the present article, a comrade's court may oblige a guilty person to compensate damage caused by unlawful actions in an amount not exceeding 50 rubles unless another procedure for recovery of damage is established by legislation.

As regards cases concerning petty stealing of state or social property, a comrades' court should in all instances oblige the guilty person to compensate in all instances financial damage caused, establishing a period for the execution of this decision; as regards cases concerning petty speculation, to render a decision concerning the transfer of articles of petty speculation to the revenue of the state.

Article 17. A comrades' court may restrict itself to a public consideration of a case and not apply the measures of social pressure specified in Article 16 if the guilty person, having sincerely repented, publicly makes an apology to the collective or victim and voluntarily compensates the damage caused.

In the absence of grounds for discussion, a comrades' court shall discharge the person brought to responsibility.

When considering property or other civil law disputes, a comrades' court shall satisfy the claim filed in whole or in part or shall reject it.

In the event of attaining conciliation of the participants of a civil law dispute, and in cases concerning insult, slander, beatings, and the infliction of light bodily injuries when the victim is reconciled with the person who inflicted these the comrades' court shall adopt a decision to terminate the proceedings in the case.

If a case was considered at the place of residence of an offender, a comrades' court may bring its decision to the information of social organizations at the place of work or study of this person.

In regard to materials sent by administrative commissions, a court, a procurator, as well as an investigator or agency of inquiry with the consent of a procurator, a comrades' court shall be obliged to notify these agencies concerning the results of the consideration of the case within a ten-day period.

A comrades' court shall bring to the information of social organizations and officials the causes and conditions uncovered by them which furthered the committing of the violation of law. The officials and social organizations shall be obliged to notify a comrades' court within a month about measures taken to eliminate the causes and conditions furthering the committing of petty stealing and other violations of law.

Article 18. If a comrades' court, when considering the case, is convinced of the need to bring the offender to criminal or administrative responsibility, it shall adopt a decision to transfer the materials to the appropriate agencies.

If an offender is an alcoholic or addict, a comrades' court shall, together with applying measures of social pressure to such a person, raise the question of his being treated compulsorily in the procedure established by law.

If when considering a property or other civil law dispute a comrades' court comes to the conclusion that a case, in view of its complexity, can not be decided by it, it shall transfer the case to a district (or city) people's court.

Article 19. The decision of a comrades' court may be appealed by the person with respect to whom the decision was rendered, by the victim, and by the participants in a civil law dispute within 7 days from the date the decision was rendered to the respective factory, plant, or local trade union committee or to the executive committee of the local soviet of working people's deputies. The said agencies, having established that a comrades' court decision is contrary to prevailing legislation, to the present statute, or to the facts of the case, shall vacate the decision and send the material to the same comrades' court for new consideration or shall terminate the proceedings in the case.

The filing of an appeal shall suspend execution of the decision.

Article 20. A decision of a comrades' court concerning compensation of damage caused, the imposition of a fine, or other financial sanction should be executed within the period specified in the decision. A comrades' court shall exercise control over the execution of its own decisions. If a decision is not executed within the established period, as well as for the execution of a comrades' court decision concerning the transfer of articles of petty speculation to the revenue of the state, the chairman of the comrades' court shall send the file of the case to a people's judge, who, after verifying the materials submitted and the legality of the decision, shall issue a writ of execution.

If the decision of the comrades' court is not legal, the people's judge shall refuse by a reasoned decree to issue the writ of execution, and shall notify the comrades' court and respectively the trade union committee or the executive committee of the soviet of working people's deputies thereof in order to consider the question of vacating the comrades' court decision.

Funds recovered from persons subjected to a fine shall enter the state budget in the procedure established by law.

The decision of a comrades' court concerning the imposition of a fine which is not executed within three months from the date rendered shall not be subject to execution.

Article 21. A decision of a comrades' court concerning the announcement of a warning, social censure, or social reprimand shall be valid for a year. If the person with respect to whom the measure of social pressure was applied by a comrades' court does not commit within the year a new violation of law or antisocial offense, he shall be considered as not having been subjected to measures of social pressure.

A comrades' court, upon the petition of a social organization, a director of an enterprise or institution, a collective farm board, or the application of the person brought before the comrades' court, and also at its own initiative, shall have the right to remove measures of pressure before the expiry of the year's period. Decisions adopted regarding this shall be brought to the information of the collective.

V. Direction of Comrades' Courts

Article 22. Direction of the activity of all comrades' courts on the territory of districts, cities, districts in cities, rural villages, and settlements shall be carried out respectively by district, city, district in city, rural village, and settlement soviets of working people's deputies.

The respective factory, plant, and local (or shop) trade union committees shall direct the work of comrades' courts directly at enterprises, institutions, organizations, and higher and secondary specialized educational institutions.

The respective local soviets of working people's deputies and their executive committees shall direct the work of comrades' courts directly at collective farms, in houses served by housing operations offices, house administrations, or combined street committees, as well as in rural population centers and settlements.

With a view to assisting executive committees of local soviets of working people's deputies and factory, plant, or local trade union committees in effectuating direction and control over the activity of comrades' courts, rendering to comrades' courts methods assistance and coordinating their activity, and organizing study and exchange of work experience, there shall be created social councils for the work of comrades' courts attached to executive committees of district, city (in cities not divided into districts) and district in city soviets of working people's deputies.

Agencies of justice, the procuracy, and the courts shall render legal assistance to comrades' courts.

Article 23. The technical servicing of comrades' courts shall be entrusted respectively to the administration of enterprises, institutions, organizations, housing operations offices, and house administrations, collective farm boards, and respective executive committees of soviets of working people's deputies.

Comrades' courts shall present once a year to the respective executive committee of a soviet of working people's deputies data concerning the number and character of cases considered by them and concerning the measures of pressure adopted.

Article 24. The chairman, deputy chairmen, secretary, and members of a comrades' court taking active part in the consideration of cases and carrying on preventive work in collectives of working people shall be stimulated by the executive committee of the local soviet of working people's deputies and factory, plant, or local trade union committee or the representation of administrations of enterprises, institutions, and organizations by:

an announcement of gratitude;

the awarding of a Certificate of Honor;

a valuable gift or cash bonus;

granting of additional paid leave for a period not exceeding three days;

granting a preferential pass to a sanatorium or rest home.

STATUTE ON SOCIAL COUNCILS FOR THE WORK OF COMRADES' COURTS

[Confirmed by Edict of the Presidium of the Supreme Soviet of the RSFSR, March 11, 1977. Vedomosti RSFSR (1977), no. 12, item 254]

1. Social Councils for the Work of Comrades' Courts shall be created attached to the executive committees of district, city (in cities not divided into districts), district in city soviets of working people's deputies.

2. Social councils shall be called upon to assist the executive committees of the respective soviets of working people's deputies and trade union committees in organizing the work of comrades' courts, in effectuating direction and control over the activity of comrades' courts at enterprises, in institutions, in organizations, higher and secondary specialized educational institutions, collective farms, houses served by housing operations offices, house administrations, or combined street committees, as well as in rural population centers and settlements.

3. The basic tasks of social councils for the work of comrades' courts shall be:

furthering improvement of the work organization of comrades' courts and raising the efficiency of their activity;

coordination of the work of comrades' courts, ensuring the observance by them of legality and protection of the rights of citizens;

rendering assistance in holding elections and reports of comrades' courts, as well as their interaction with other social organizations in the cause of preventing violations of law;

organization of legal training of chairmen and members of comrades' courts;

study, summary of practice, and dissemination of positive work experience of comrades' courts.

4. The membership of the social council shall be confirmed by the executive committee of the district, city, or district in city soviet of working people's deputies for a term of two years.

5. Social councils shall function with a chairman, deputy chairman, secretary, and council members. The number of members of the council shall be established depending on the amount of work.

6. The activity of social councils shall be effectuated with the broad participation of the public.

7. Social councils shall be responsible to the executive committees of the respective soviets of working people's deputies and shall account not less than once a year to them concerning the results of work done.

8. In their activity social councils for the work of comrades' courts shall be guided by the present Statute, by the Statute on Comrades' Courts, and by other normative acts.

9. Direction of a social council for the work of comrades' courts shall be effectuated by its chairman and deputy chairman. The council secretary shall keep the correspondence of the social council and store the documents.

10. Social councils shall work according to plans confirmed at their sessions.

11. A social council for the work of comrades' courts shall:

(a) organize the legal study of the chairmen and members of comrades' courts; hold seminars and meetings regarding the application of prevailing legislation, the exchange of work experience of comrades' courts, and their participation in the communist nurturing of citizens;

(b) upon the commission of the executive committee of the soviet of working people's deputies, regularly verify the work of comrades' courts, familiarize themselves with cases and materials in comrades' courts, analyze the data submitted once a year by comrades' courts concerning the number and character of cases considered by them and concerning measures of pressure taken, and submit cumulative data to the executive committee of the soviet of working people's deputies;

(c) render cooperation in holding elections and reports of comrades' courts;

(d) verify, upon the commission of the executive committee of a district, city, or district in city soviet of working people's deputies, appeals against decisions of comrades' courts and make proposals relating to the results of the verification;

(e) hear communications of the chairmen of comrades' courts concerning the work of comrades' courts and give recommendations relating to the elimination of shortcomings and improvement of their activity;

(f) make proposals for the consideration of the executive committee of a local soviet of working people's deputies or a factory, plant, or local trade union committee concerning the elimination of shortcomings uncovered and the future improvement of the activity of comrades' courts, as well as concerning the vacating of decisions of comrades' courts contrary to the facts of the case or to prevailing legislation;

(g) raise before executive committees of local soviets of working people's deputies or factory, plant, or local trade union committees the question of stimulating the chairmen and members of comrades' courts for active work;

(h) take measures to publicize the activity of comrades' courts in the press, on radio, television, and by other means of information.

MODEL STATUTE ON VOLUNTARY PEOPLE'S GUARD DETACHMENTS FOR THE PROTECTION OF PUBLIC ORDER

[Approved by Decree of the Central Committee of the Communist Party of the USSR and the USSR Council of Ministers, May 20, 1974. SP SSSR (1974), no. 12, item 67]

Under the conditions of a developed socialist society and the great economic and social transformations in our country, the tasks of forming the consciousness of and feeling for the high responsibility of every citizen to society, of ensuring discipline and organization, and of strengthening the socialist legal order and legality in every possible way is acquiring ever greater importance.

In solving this task an important role appertains to voluntary people's guard detachments, together with state organizations and social organizations. Created at the initiative of the working people, the voluntary people's guards actively take part in the work to strengthen public order and wage a struggle against violations of the rules of socialist community life and other anti-social manifestations. For their activity they have earned prestige and the gratitude of the broad masses of the populace.

The work of voluntary people's guard detachments, which unite thousands of outstanding and conscientious citizens in their ranks, serves as a brilliant example of the democratism of the Soviet system, based on the broad and ever growing participation of the working people in the state and social life of the country.

I. General Provisions

1. Voluntary people's guards shall be created by collectives of working people at enterprises, institutions, and organizations, as well as at the place of residence of citizens, in order to intensify the protection of public order and the struggle against violations of law.

2. All activity of voluntary people's guard detachments shall be based on the strict observance of socialist legality. People's guard detachments shall be guided in their work by laws of the USSR and of the union and autonomous republics, by decrees and regulations of the USSR Council of Ministers and the union and autonomous republic councils of ministers, by decisions and regulations of the local agencies of state authority and state administration, as well as by the present Statute.

3. People's guard detachments shall be created according to the production-territorial principle at enterprises, construction sites, transport, collective farms, state farms, institutions, organizations, educational institutions, house maintenance offices, house administrations, hostels, and so forth.

4. Citizens of the USSR who have attained 18 years of age shall be accepted in voluntary people's guard detachments from among leading workers, collective farmers, employees, students, pupils, and pensioners who

by virtue of their professional, moral, and political qualities are capable of successfully fulfilling the tasks confronting a guard detachment.

5. People's guard detachments shall be directed by soviets of working people's deputies and by their executive and administrative agencies.

6. State agencies, social organizations, and officials shall render every possible assistance and aid to voluntary people's guard detachments in their activity to strengthen public order and struggle against violations of law.

7. Opposition to the legal activity of people's guard and an infringement against the life, health, and dignity of people's guards in connection with their activity to protect public order shall entail responsibility in accordance with USSR and union republic legislation.

II. Basic Tasks and Functions of Voluntary People's Guards

8. The basic tasks of voluntary people's guards shall be to protect the rights and legal interests of citizens, actively participate in preventing and suppressing violations of law and in protecting public order and socialist ownership, and participate in the work of nurturing the Soviet people in the spirit of respect for the laws and rules of socialist community life.

9. When fulfilling the tasks entrusted to them in point 8 of the present statute and being guided by prevailing legislation, voluntary people's guard detachments shall:

(a) participate in protecting public order on streets and squares, in parks, on transport lines, at stations, on wharfs, at airports and other public places, as well as in maintaining order while various mass arrangements are held;

(b) render assistance to agencies of internal affairs, procuracy, justice, and courts in their activity to strengthen public order and struggle against violation of law;

(c) take part in the struggle against hooliganism, drunkenness, homebrewing, the stealing of state and social property and also the personal property of citizens, against violations of trade rules, and against speculation and other violations of law;

(d) take part in conducting educational work in labor collectives and among the populace in regard to observance of the rules of socialist community life and the prevention of antisocial offenses;

(e) participate in the struggle against child neglect and violation of law by minors;

(f) participate in ensuring the safe movement of transport and pedestrians and in preventing road and transport accidents;

(g) take measures to render first aid to persons suffering from accidents or violations of law, as well as those found in public places in a helpless state; participate in saving people and property and in maintaining public order in the event of natural disasters or other extraordinary circumstances;

(h) render aid to frontier forces in protecting the state frontier of the USSR;

(i) participate in implementing measures to conserve and protect natural wealth and in the struggle against poaching and violations of hunting and fishing rules.

III. Procedure for Creating and Organizing the Work of a Voluntary People's Guard Detachment

10. A voluntary people's guard detachment shall be founded at an organizational meeting of persons wishing to join the guard detachment which is convened at the initiative of a group at an enterprise, institution, or organization consisting of representatives of Party, soviet, trade union, komsomol, and other social organizations.

11. At production associations (or combines), enterprises, institutions, organizations, and educational institutions which have a large number of persons working or studying, guard detachments of factories (or subsidiaries), shops, sections, sectors, brigades, faculties, and so forth, as well as headquarters for directing the said guard detachments, shall be created by decision of the district or city headquarters of voluntary people's guard detachments.

12. Upon the representation of the district, city, rural, or settlement headquarters, voluntary people's guard detachments shall be registered at executive committees of district, city, rural, or settlement soviets of working people's deputies. When a guard detachment is registered, observance of the established procedure for creating it shall be certified.

Individual voluntary people's guard detachments shall be abolished or reorganized by decision of the district, city, rural, or settlement headquarters of guard detachments, with notification of the decision made to the executive committee of the district, city, rural, or settlement soviet of working people's deputies.

13. Admittance to a people's guard detachment shall be on strictly voluntary principles, individually, at a general meeting of the people's guards or at a session of the headquarters of the guard detachment on the basis of a personal application and in the presence of recommendations of the Party, trade union, or Komsomol organization at the place of work, study, or residence of the citizen who wishes to join the guard detachment.

14. Every people's guard shall take a solemn pledge(the text is appended) to conscientiously and faithfully execute his social duty to ensure the protection of public order and struggle against violations of law. The solemn pledge shall be taken at a general meeting of people's guards, representatives of Party and soviet agencies, social organizations, and collectives of working people being invited.

Before citizens admitted to a people's guard detachment take the solemn pledge, the significance of this pledge shall be explained and study of the present statute and the legislative and other normative acts which regulate the protection of public order and the struggle against violations of law, and of the forms and methods of the work of people's guard detachments shall be organized for them.

To a people's guard who has thoroughly mastered his duties and rights and who has taken the solemn pledge, the commander or head of the headquarters of the guard detachment shall present a certificate of the established form, a chest badge, and a people's guard booklet in which the basic duties and rights of a people's guard are set forth, as well as the most important legal provisions regarding the protection of public order. Only then shall a people's guard be permitted to execute his duties.

15. A people's guard who has committed an offense incompatible with this title or who has not fulfilled his duties shall be expelled from the people's guard detachment. The decision to expel shall be made at a general meeting of people's guards or session of the headquarters of the guard detachment; the person expelled from the guard detachment shall hand back the certificate and chest badge of the people's guard.

People's guards who have requested to be relieved of the duties of a people's guard shall leave the membership of the guard detachment. The decision concerning the departure shall be made by the headquarters; the person leaving the detachment shall hand back the certificate and chest badge of a people's guard to the headquarters.

People's guards who leave a people's guard detachment in connection with a change of place of work, study, or residence may be admitted to a guard detachment at the new place of work, study, or residence on the basis of a personal application and references given by the headquarters or commander of the guard detachment in which he was previously enrolled.

16. A commander and his deputies elected by open ballot at a general meeting of people's guards for a two-year term shall head a voluntary people's guard detachment.

In a guard detachment numbering more than 50 people's guards, a headquarters of the guard detachment shall be elected for the same term to direct its work.

17. For the operative direction of the work of voluntary people's guard detachments within the limits of a district or city, a district or city headquarters of voluntary people's guard detachments shall be formed by decision of the district or city party committee and the executive committee of the district or city soviet of working people's deputies from representatives of Party, and other state agencies and social organizations, the heads of headquarters (or commanders) of individual people's guard detachments, and people's guards. Within the limits of a rural or settlement soviet, a rural or settlement headquarters of voluntary people's guard detachments shall be formed by decision of the executive committee of the rural or settlement soviet.

The head of a district, city, rural, or settlement headquarters of voluntary people's guard detachments shall be confirmed by the executive committee of the respective soviet of working people's deputies.

Appropriate headquarters may be formed by decision of the district or city headquarters of voluntary people's guard detachments or city headquarters of voluntary people's guard detachments in order to direct the work of voluntary people's guard detachments in microdistricts of cities, as well as in individual populated points.

18. With a view to better organizing the work of voluntary people's guard detachments in the struggle against individual types of violations of law, specialized guard detachments or specialized groups within a guard detachment shall be created by decision of the district or city headquarters of the guard detachments for the struggle against stealing of socialist ownership and speculation, to prevent violations of law by minors, to ensure the safety of road traffic, and for other orientations of the activity of voluntary people's guard detachments.

Combined operative detachments of people's guard detachments may be created attached to district or city headquarters of guard detachments.

19. By decision of the district or city headquarters of guard detachments and the district or city komsomol committee, operative komsomol detachments may be created from among operative komsomol people's guard detachments in order to struggle against violations of law among youth and minors. The procedure for the organization and activity of operative komsomol detachments shall be defined by the Central Committee of All-Union Leninist Communist Youth League in accordance with the present statute.

20. In order to coordinate the activity of district and city headquarters of voluntary people's guard detachments and to summarize and disseminate their leading work experience and render them necessary methods assistance, national area, region, territory, and republic headquarters of voluntary people's guard detachments may be created by decision of the appropriate Party and soviet agencies in national areas, regions, territories, autonomous republics, and also union republics not divided into regions, from representatives of Party, soviet, and other state agencies and social organizations and the heads of district and city headquarters of voluntary people's guards.

IV. Duties and Rights of a People's Guard

21. A people's guard shall be obliged to:

(a) actively participate in the protection of public order, in the work regarding the prevention of violations of law and the nurturing of citizens in a spirit of observance of Soviet laws and rules of socialist community life; render assistance to agencies of internal affairs, procuracy, justice, and courts in the activity regarding the struggle against violations of law;

(b) everywhere -- at work, in an educational institution, on the street, in public places -- defend the honor, dignity, and also the rights and legal interests of citizens, enterprises, institutions, and organizations; be tactful and courteous in addressing citizens; decisively and fearlessly take measures provided by law to suppress criminal infringements and other antisocial actions;

(c) be an example in labor, study, and daily life, and constantly raise his ideological, cultural, and general educational level;

(d) when fulfilling tasks, fulfill precisely and conscientiously the requirements of the commander of the guard detachment and its headquarters, as well as instructions of police workers when carrying on joint operations for protection of public order;

(e) strictly execute legislative and other legal acts; persistently master the forms and methods of struggle against violations of law; constantly enlarge his knowledge of Soviet legislation;

(f) notify in good time the headquarters of the guard detachment, police, agency, or other appropriate state agencies and social organizations about facts of crimes prepared or committed which have become known to him, about the beginning of natural disasters or other extraordinary circumstances which threaten the safety of citizens, enterprises, institutions, and organizations, as well as take measures to avert their harmful consequences;

(g) during the execution of duties, wear the armband and have with him the people's guard certificate and chest badge;

(h) in the event of an appeal by a deputy of a soviet of working people's deputies, render him assistance in suppressing a violation of law discovered by the deputy;

(i) regularly report about his work to the social organization which recommended him to the people's guard.

22. A people's guard shall have the right to:

(a) demand the observance of the established public order and the cessation of violations of law from citizens;

(b) in the absence of police workers or other authorized persons, draw up a protocol in the event of a malicious violation of public order or the infliction by the violation of law of property or other damage to a citizen, enterprise, institution, or organization, transmitting the protocol subsequently to the head of the headquarters (or commander) of the guard detachment;

(c) demand the presentation of a passport or other documents certifying identity from offenders of public order in instances when the establishment of identity is necessary to elucidate the circumstances of committing the violation of law or involvement therein;

(d) deliver to the police or to the headquarters of the voluntary people's guard detachment persons who have committed a violation of law or with a view to suppressing a violation of law when other measures of pressure have been exhausted, as well as to establish the identity of an offender and draw up a protocol unless it is possible to draw it up at the place of violation; the person delivered to the headquarters of the guard detachment in this connection may not be kept more than one hour;

(e) when suppressing a violation of law, take instruments for committing them from offenders, transferring them to the police immediately thereafter;

(f) enter clubs, stadiums, cinemas, and other public places in order to pursue an offender who has concealed himself, suppress violations of law which have arisen there, and also, with the consent of the administrations of such places, in order to fulfill duties to ensure public order;

(g) when executing duties to protect public order, enjoy the right of free carriage on city passenger transport (except taxis) on special tickets issued for the duty period in the procedure determined by the executive committee of the respective soviet of working people's deputies;

(h) in urgent matters, use means of transport (except special and diplomatic motor vehicles) to deliver persons found in public places in a helpless state from accident or violations of law and who require in this connection urgent medical assistance;

(i) when executing duties to protect public order, use the telephones of enterprises, institutions, and organizations free of charge;

(j) demand from drivers of automotive transport, tractors, and other self-propelled vehicles which violate road traffic rules documents for the right to operate means of transport and deliver drivers who operate these means of transport in a state of intoxication or without drivers' document to the nearest police agency.

23. In the event of the temporary inability to work of a people's guard in connection with the fulfillment of duties to protect public order, the people's guard shall be paid a grant for temporary inability to work irrespective of work experience in an amount of 100 percent of earnings, and in the event of permanent or prolonged loss of ability to work for the same reason, he shall be assigned a disability pension in an amount established for workers and employees who have lost the ability to work as a consequence of occupational injury or illness.

A pension for loss of breadwinner shall be assigned in an amount established for families of workers and employees who have died from occupational injury or disease to family members of a people's guard who has perished when fulfilling duties to protect public order.

In the said instances a people's guard or members of his family shall have the right to demand compensation for damage caused in the established procedure.

V. Forms and Methods of Work of Voluntary People's Guard Detachments

24. Voluntary people's guards shall carry out their activity by means of:

(a) patrolling or manning posts on streets, squares, in parks, and in other public places and conducting raids to unmask violations of law and the persons who have committed them;

(b) conducting individual educational work with persons who have committed violations of law and establishing a patronage of people's guards over such persons; explaining legislation and rules of socialist community life to citizens; holding conversations with parents and other close relatives of minors who have committed a violation of law;

(c) formalizing materials on offenders and sending these materials to the appropriate state agencies and social organizations;

(d) organizing the issuance of satirical posters, wall newspapers, and photo displays; using the press, radio, and television for the purpose of preventing violations of law and of influencing persons who commit antisocial offenses;

(e) discussing the conduct of offenders at sessions of the headquarters of the guard detachment, inviting representatives of social organizations and collectives of working people, of which the offenders are members.

VI. Direction of the Activity of Voluntary People's Guard Detachments

25. District, city, settlement, and rural soviets of working people's deputies and their executive committees shall, when effectuating direction over voluntary people's guard detachments within the limits of their competence, organize and direct their activity, take measures to strengthen guard detachments and enlist in the ranks of people's guards the best representatives of the working people, assure the observance of legality in the activity of guard detachments, organize their interaction with state and social organizations which participate in the protection of public

order, hear communications and reports in regard to questions of the work of guard detachments by directors of enterprises, institutions, and organizations, irrespective of their departmental subordination, and decide questions of material-technical supply for guard detachments.

26. The operative direction of the work of people's guards shall be effectuated by the headquarters (or commander) of the voluntary people's guard detachment, which shall:

(a) carry on work to consolidate and strengthen the guard detachment, nurture people's guards in high discipline, a feeling of social duty, comradeliness, and selflessness and maintain a permanent link with the social organizations which recommended people's guards;

(b) organize the study of people's guards of the fundamental principles of Soviet legislation and exercises for the physical training of people's guards; teach them forms and methods of struggle against violations of law;

(c) plan the work of the guard detachment; instruct people's guards and supervise their activity; keep a record of the work results of the guard detachment; prepare questions of the organization and activity of the guard detachment for discussion at the meeting of people's guards;

(d) consider protocols drawn up by people's guards concerning violations of law and send them to the appropriate state agencies or social organizations;

(e) report not less than once annually on its work to the people's guards and on the work of the guard detachment to the respective collectives of enterprises, institutions, and organizations, as well as to the respective soviet of working people's deputies and its executive committee;

(f) petition directors of enterprises, institutions, and organizations, as well as social organizations, about incentives for the most distinguished people's guards.

27. A district, city, rural, or settlement headquarters of a guard detachment shall:

(a) carry on organizational work in regard to the creation of guard detachments and to the improvement of their activity;

(b) plan the work of voluntary people's guard detachments; work out measures for the interaction of guard detachments; distribute the strength of guard detachments by territory and types of activity; and organize the training for leaders of guard detachments;

(c) verify the activity of guard detachments; take measures to eliminate shortcomings unmasked; summarize and disseminate positive work experience;

(d) take part in working out and implementing measures to prevent violations of law; make recommendations for these purposes to state agencies and social organizations about eliminating the causes of violations of law and the conditions which facilitate their being committed;

(e) petition directors of enterprises, institutions, and organizations, as well as social organizations, about incentives for the most distinguished people's guards;

(f) hold reviews and gatherings of people's guards;

(g) report about the work of the headquarters of the guard detachment to the respective district, city, rural, or settlement soviet of working people's deputies, and its executive committee.

28. A national area, region, territory, or republic headquarters of a voluntary people's guard detachment shall:

(a) summarize and disseminate the positive experience of the activity of district, city, settlement, and rural headquarters and individual guard detachments; render necessary methods assistance in their work;

(b) verify the work of headquarters of guard detachments and take measures to eliminate shortcomings uncovered;

(c) hold national area, region, territory, or republic gatherings of people's guards; organize the training of leaders of district and city headquarters of guard detachments;

(d) make recommendations to respective state agencies and social organizations in regard to questions of the protection of public order and the struggle against violations of law;

(e) report about the work of the headquarters of the guard detachments to the executive committee of the national area, region, or territory soviet of working people's deputies or the union or autonomous republic council of ministers.

VII. Interaction of Agencies of Internal Affairs, Procuracy, Justice, and Courts with Voluntary People's Guard Detachments

29. Agencies of internal affairs, procuracy, justice, and courts shall render every possible assistance and support to voluntary people's guard detachments in the fulfillment of tasks entrusted to them; give information about violations of law necessary for the activity of guard detachments to the commanders or heads of headquarters of people's guard detachments; conduct work in regard to the legal nurturing of people's guards; render aid in supplying them with methods guides and legal reference literature; take part in the work of general meetings, reviews, and gatherings of people's guards and in sessions of headquarters of guard detachments.

30. Agencies of internal affairs shall ensure the organization of day-to-day interaction with voluntary people's guard detachments; instruct people's guards when necessary; teach them the forms and methods of struggle against violations of law; render methods assistance to guard detachments in planning and recording their work; by agreement with the headquarters of guard detachments, hold joint exercises for the protection of public order and the prevention of violations of law. While such exercises are held, operative direction over the work of the people's guards shall be exercised by the appropriate officials of the agencies of internal affairs.

VIII. Incentive Measures and Sanctions

31. People's guards who actively participate in the struggle against violations of law shall be encouraged by the executive committees of local soviets of working people's deputies and appropriate state agencies, institutions, enterprises, and social organizations within the limits of their competence by means of:

an announcement of gratitude;

the presentation of a certificate;

being entered in the Book of Honor;

being placed on the Board of Honor;

the presentation of a gift or monetary bonus;

being awarded the chest badge "Distinguished People's Guard";

being granted additional paid vacation for a period of up to three days;

being granted a preferential right to receive housing accommodation;

being granted accommodation in a sanatorium or rest home.

For special merit in the fulfillment of his social duty and for courage and heroism displayed in this connection, people's guards shall be recommended for the conferment of orders and medals of the USSR in accordance with prevailing legislation.

Additional paid vacation, preferential right to receive housing, and accommodation in a sanatorium or rest home shall be granted to the most distinguished people's guards on the basis of reasoned petitions of headquarters (or commanders) of guard detachments which have been agreed with district or city headquarters of people's guards. There shall be taken into account in this connection the number and the length of the people's guard's tours of duty, the specific results of this work in regard to the struggle against violations of law, and also the labor indicators and personal conduct of the people's guard.

A monetary bonus or gift shall be presented to people's guards at the expense of assets provided for bonuses of collectives of enterprises, institutions, and organizations.

32. An incentive for people's guards shall be announced at a ceremonial situation at meetings or gatherings of people's guards or meetings of the collectives of enterprises, institutions, and organizations.

33. A people's guard detachment which has achieved the best results at work shall be awarded the challenge Red Banner, pennant, or Certificate of Honor by the executive committee of the local soviet of working people's deputies.

34. There may be applied, by decision of the general meeting or the headquarters of a guard detachment, to people's guards who unconscientiously fulfill their duties the following sanctions:

a warning;

a reprimand;

a severe reprimand;

expulsion from the guard detachment.

The social organization which recommended him shall be informed about the expulsion of a people's guard from the guard detachment.

IX. Material-Technical Supply of Voluntary People's Guard Detachments

35. Enterprises, institutions, and organizations shall provide voluntary people's guard detachments of these enterprises, institutions, or organizations with necessary premises, telephone communications, furniture, and supplies.

Republic, territory, region, national area, district, city, rural, and settlement headquarters of voluntary people's guard detachments, the headquarters of guard detachments of microdistricts and populated points, combined operative detachments, as well as komsomol operative detachments of people's guard detachments, shall be provided with official premises, telephone communications, and supplies by the respective executive committees of soviets of working people's deputies.

36. Expenditures for the maintenance of official premises of voluntary people's guard detachments of enterprises, institutions, and organizations, for the acquisition of furniture, supplies, special literature, visual aids, certificate blanks, chest badges, and arm bands for a people's guard, as well as telephone, postal, and other expenditures needed to ensure the activity of the guard detachment, shall be at the expense of assets of the corresponding enterprises, institutions, and organizations.

The said expenditures for republic, territory, region, national area, district, city, rural, and settlement headquarters of voluntary people's guard detachments, headquarters of guard detachments of microdistricts and populated points, combined operative detachments, as well as Komsomol operative detachments of people's guard detachments, shall be at the expense of budget appropriations for the corresponding soviets of working people's deputies.

37. When necessary, the directors of enterprises, institutions, organizations, and executive committees of soviets of working people's deputies shall allocate means of transport for the duty periods to voluntary people's guard detachments or headquarters of guard detachments.

38. When necessary, agencies of internal affairs may grant mobile radio units and other technical means to headquarters of people's guard detachments for the duty period in the procedure determined by the USSR Ministry of Internal Affairs.

X. Supervision over the Observance of Socialist Legality

39. Supervision over the strict execution of laws in the activity of voluntary people's guard detachments shall be exercised by procuratorial agencies in accordance with the Statute on Procuracy Supervision in the USSR.

ANNEX

The Solemn Pledge of a Member of a Voluntary People's Guard Detachment for the Protection of Public Order

I, a citizen of the Union of Soviet Socialist Republics, joining a voluntary people's guard detachment, give before my comrades a solemn pledge to: be a courageous, vigilant, and disciplined people's guard, wage an implacable struggle against violations of public order and violations of law, strictly observe socialist legality, and be an example in labor and daily life.

I pledge myself to honorably and conscientiously fulfill all duties entrusted to me, to selflessly protect the rights and legal interests of citizens, to guard the interests of Soviet society, and in all my activity to be a selfless devotee to my people, socialist Motherland, and the cause of communist construction.

ON THE PROCEDURE FOR CONSIDERING PROPOSALS, APPLICATIONS, AND APPEALS OF CITIZENS

[Edict of the Presidium of the USSR Supreme Soviet, April 12, 1968. Vedomosti SSSR (1968), no. 17, item 144]

In conditions of the construction of communism and of the all-round development and perfection of socialist democracy in our country, the correct and timely consideration of proposals, applications, and appeals of citizens acquires ever greater significance.

Proposals of citizens relating to questions of political, economic, and cultural life and to the improvement of legislation are one form of the participation of working people in state administration, in improving the work of the state apparatus and intensifying control over its activity, in the struggle against bureaucratism and red tape, and in strengthening socialist legality. The ever growing number of proposals relating to various questions of the life of society and the state is one indicator of the uninterrupted growth of the political activeness of the Soviet people.

The consideration of applications of citizens relating to sociocultural, housing, and other questions in connection with effectuating rights granted to citizens occupies a significant place in the work of state and social agencies.

In contemporary conditions of the development of Soviet society, appeals, as a rule, are a form of reaction to facts of a violation of rights and interests of citizens protected by law. The also testify to the still serious shortcomings in the work of many state and social agencies. Consistent improvement in the work of state and social agencies and the growth of material and cultural conditions of life leads to a reduction in the number of appeals by citizens.

There are instances when appeals and complaints are not considered in a timely way and formalistic answers are given to them. Control over the execution of decisions adopted in regard to proposals, applications, and appeals of citizens are inadequately implemented, Frequently, the directors of state agencies, enterprises, institutions, and organizations avoid the resolution of proposals, applications, and appeals and do not hold personal receptions. Officials who are guilty of red tape and bureaucratism often remain unpunished. In certain state and social agencies the proposals, applications, and appeals of citizens are inadequately summarized; the conditions and causes giving rise to appeals are not studied, and timely measures to eliminate such causes are not taken; the explanation of Soviet legislation is inadequately carried on among the populace. In a number of instances citizens who have recourse to superior agencies, bypassing local agencies, observing the law and the interests of citizens and the state, are obliged to direct appropriate inquiries to local agencies and thereby delay consideration of the applications and appeals.

The Presidium of the USSR Supreme Soviet decrees:

1. All state and social agencies must provide the necessary conditions to effectuate the rights granted and guaranteed to USSR citizens to make proposals, applications, and appeals in writing or orally.

State agencies, enterprises, institutions, organizations, collective farms, and other cooperative and social organizations, and their directors and other officials shall be obliged to receive and in accordance with their powers to resolve proposals, applications, and appeals of citizens.

2. Proposals, applications, and appeals of citizens shall be resolved by state agencies in accordance with their competence as established by the USSR Constitution, union, and autonomous republic constitutions, and USSR, union republic, and autonomous republic legislation.

USSR agencies shall resolve proposals, applications, and appeals of citizens which appertain to questions of the jurisdiction of the USSR.

USSR agencies shall resolve proposals, applications, and appeals of citizens in regard to questions of the joint jurisdiction of the USSR and union republics when the particular questions are relegated to the competence of union agencies, and also by way of considering appeals against decisions made in regard to applications and appeals by central union republic agencies if such decisions do not conform to USSR legislation.

Proposals, applications, and appeals of citizens relating to other questions shall be resolved by union republic agencies.

3. With a view to the timely consideration of proposals, applications, and appeals of citizens:

proposals and applications shall be submitted by citizens to those state agencies, enterprises, institutions, and organizations or to those officials within whose direct jurisdiction the resolution of a particular question falls;

appeals shall be submitted to those agencies or to those officials to whom the state agency, enterprise, institution, organization, or official whose actions are being appealed is directly subordinate.

Appeals against decisions of a general meeting of members of collective farms and other cooperative organizations which do not have superior agencies, and also against decisions of social amateur agencies functioning under the direction of local soviets of working people's deputies, shall be submitted to the executive committee of the respective local soviet.

In instances provided for by law, appeals may be submitted to a district (or city) people's court.

4. State agencies, enterprises, institutions, organizations, and their officials whose jurisdiction does not appertain to questions raised in proposals, applications, or appeals shall send them within five days to the appropriate institution, notifying the applicant thereof, and when at a personal reception shall explain where he should apply with the proposal, application, or appeal.

5. It shall be prohibited to send appeals of citizens for resolution to those officials whose actions are being appealed.

6. Directors and other officials of state agencies, enterprises, institutions, organizations, collective farms, and other cooperative and social organizations shall be obliged to hold office hours for citizens.

Citizens shall be received on fixed days and hours which are brought to their information, at a time convenient for the populace, when necessary, in the evening.

The directors shall bear personal responsibility for organizing the reception and consideration of proposals, applications, and appeals of citizens in state agencies, enterprises, institutions, organizations, collective farms, and other cooperative and social organizations.

7. When resolving proposals, applications, and appeals, officials shall be obliged to:

attentively look into their substance and, when necessary, demand necessary documents, send workers to the place for verification, and take other measures to objectively resolve the issue;

render reasoned decisions in regard to proposals, applications, or appeals and ensure the timely and correct execution of such decisions;

inform citizens about decisions made with regard to their proposals, applications, or appeals, and, when rejecting them, indicate the reasons;

uncover and eliminate in a timely manner the causes giving rise to violations of the rights and the interests of citizens protected by law.

8. A citizen who does not agree with a decision made in regard to his application or appeal shall have the right to appeal this decision to the superior agency to whom the state agency, enterprise, institution, or organization making the appealed decisions is directly subordinate.

9. Applications and appeals in all agencies shall be resolved within a period of one month, and those not requiring additional study and verification, without further delay, but in any event not more than 15 days from receiving them in the agency obliged to resolve the substance of the issue.

Shorter periods for resolving applications and appeals in republic and local agencies, and also at enterprises, institutions, and organizations, may be established by union republic legislation.

In those instances when, in order to resolve the application or appeal it is necessary to hold a special verification, to demand additional materials, or to take other measures, the periods for resolving the application or appeal may by way of exception be extended by the director or deputy director of the respective agency, but not by more than one month, notifying the person who submitted the application or appeal thereof.

Proposals of citizens shall be considered within one month, with the exception of those proposals which require additional study.

10. Applications and appeals of military servicemen and members of their families shall be considered:

in USSR agencies and in republic agencies within 15 days from the day they are received in the agency obliged to resolve the substance of the issue;

in local agencies of state authority, and also in enterprises, institutions, and organizations, without delay, but not later than 7 days from the day of application or appeal is received in the agency obliged to resolve the substance of the issue.

In those instances when in order to resolve the application or appeal it is necessary to hold a special verification, to demand additional materials, or to take other measures, the periods for resolving the application or appeal may by way of exception be extended by the director or deputy director of the respective agency, but not more than 15 days, notifying the person who submitted the application or appeal thereof.

Proposals, applications, and appeals of military servicemen connected with service shall be considered and resolved in accordance with the Statute of Internal Service and with the Disciplinary Statute of the USSR Armed Forces.

11. Proposals, applications, and appeals of citizens emanating from the editorial offices of newspapers and journals, as well as speeches and other materials published in the press connected with their resolution, shall be considered in the procedure and within the periods provided for by the present edict.

12. Executive committees of soviets of working people's deputies shall enlist deputies and the aktiv of the respective soviet to consider proposals, applications, and appeals of citizens.

State agencies, enterprises, institutions, and organizations shall enlist representatives of the public, the aktiv of people's control, and leading workers, employees, and collective farmers, for the consideration of proposals, applications, and appeals and for holding supplementary verifications and other measures relating thereto.

When necessary, proposals of citizens, and also the results of considering and resolving applications and appeals having social significance, must be discussed at meetings of the collectives of enterprises, institutions, and organizations, and at the place of residence of citizens.

13. It shall be established that all state agencies shall be obliged systematically to verify the state of affairs relating to the consideration of proposals, applications, and appeals of citizens in enterprises, institutions, and organizations subordinate to them and to take measures to eliminate the causes and conditions giving rise to violations of the rights and to the interests of citizens protected by law which result in the receipt of repeated applications and appeals.

14. Executive committees of soviets of working people's deputies shall be obliged systematically to verify the state of affairs in regard to the consideration of proposals, applications, and appeals of citizens in sections and administrations of the executive committee and at enterprises, institutions, and organizations situated on the territory of the particular soviet, to hear the results of verifications at their sessions, and when necessary, to submit them for discussion at a session of the soviet of working people's deputies.

The directors of executive committees of soviets of working people's deputies, their sections and administrations, and the directors of enterprises, institutions, and organizations must periodically report about the work with proposals, applications, and appeals at sessions of soviets of working people's deputies, sessions of executive committees, and also at meetings of citizens.

15. Violation of the established procedure for the consideration of proposals, applications, and appeals shall entail disciplinary responsibility in accordance with prevailing legislation with regard to the guilty officials.

The same acts of officials which cause material harm to state or social interests or to the rights or to the interests of citizens protected by law, as well as the persecution of citizens by officials in connection with appeals or applications which they submit, shall entail criminal responsibility under the respective articles of union republic criminal codes concerning official crimes.

The submission of an appeal or application by a citizen for slanderous purposes shall entail responsibility in accordance with prevailing legislation.

16. Agencies of the procuracy and people's control systematically shall exercise supervision and control over the observance of Soviet laws when considering proposals, applications, and appeals of citizens and shall hold verifications of the state of such work in all ministries and departments and in enterprises, institutions, and organizations subordinate to them, as well as in collective farms and other cooperative and social organizations, bringing those guilty of violating the laws, of red tape, formalism, bureaucratism, and of the failure to fulfill decisions adopted in regard to proposals, applications, and appeals to strict responsibility.

17. The effect of the present edict shall not extend to appeals, applications, and proposals of citizens considered in the procedure established by criminal procedure or civil procedure legislation of the USSR and union republics, by the Statute on the Procedure for Considering Labor Disputes, by the Statute on Discoveries, Inventions, and Rationalization Proposals, and by other legislation.

18. The presidiums of union republic supreme soviets shall be charged with bringing union republic legislation into conformity with the present edict.

19. The decree of the Presidium of the USSR Central Executive Committee of April 13, 1933, "On Considering the Appeals of Working People and Taking Necessary Measures in Regard to Them" (SZ SSSR [1933], no. 26, item 153), the decree of the USSR Central Executive Committee of December 14, 1935, "On the State of Affairs in Analyzing Appeals of Working People" (SZ SSSR [1936], no. 31, item 274), with the addition made by the explanation of the Presidium of the USSR Central Executive Committee of May 7, 1937, shall be deemed to have lost force.

CHAPTER IV

THE ROLE OF SOCIAL ORGANIZATIONS

RULES OF THE COMMUNIST PARTY OF THE SOVIET UNION

[Confirmed by the XXII Congress, with partial changes made by the XXIII and XXIV Congresses of the Communist Party of the Soviet Union]

The Communist Party of the Soviet Union is the battle-tested vanguard of the Soviet people, uniting on a voluntary basis the progressive, most conscious part of the working class, collective farm peasantry, and intelligentsia of the USSR.

Founded by V.I. Lenin as the advance detachment of the working class, the Communist Party has passed along the glorius path of struggle and has led the working class and the toiling peasantry to the triumph of the Great October Socialist Revolution and the establishment of the dictatorship of the proletariat in the USSR. Under the direction of the Communist Party, exploiting classes in the USSR have been liquidated and the moral and political unity of Soviet society has been formed and strengthened. Socialism has triumphed fully and completely. The Communist Party, the party of the working class, now has become the party of the entire Soviet people.

The Party exists for the people and serves the people. It is the highest form of socio-political organization and the guiding and directing force of Soviet society. The Party guides the great creative activity of the Soviet people and imparts an organized, planned, scientifically well-founded character to its struggle for the achievement of the ultimate aim: the triumph of communism.

The CPSU builds its work on the basis of the rigorous observance of Leninist norms of Party life, the principle of the collectivity of leadership, the all-round development of intra-party democracy, the activeness, and the initiative of communists, and of criticism and self-criticism.

The inviolable law of life of the CPSU is ideological and organizational unity, the monolithicity of its ranks, and the high conscious discipline of all communists. Any manifestation of factionalism and groupism is incompatible with Marxist-Leninist party loyalty and with staying in the party. The party relieves itself of persons who violate the Program, the Rules of the CPSU, and who compromise by their conduct the high title of communist.

In all its activity the CPSU is guided by Marxist-Leninist teachings and the Program worked out on its basis, in which the basic tasks of the party during the period of building a communist society have been determined.

In creatively developing Marxism-Leninism, the CPSU struggles resolutely against any manifestations of revisionism and dogmatism, which are profoundly alien to revolutionary theory.

The Communist Party of the Soviet Union is an inseparable integral part of the international communist and workers' movement. It stands firmly on tested Marxist-Leninist principles of proletarian internationalism, actively furthers the strengthening of the unity of the entire international communist and workers' movement, and fraternal links with the great army of communists of all countries.

I

Party Members, Their Duties and Rights

1. Any citizen of the Soviet Union who acknowledges the Program and Rules of the party, actively participates in the construction of communism, works in one of the party organizations, fulfills party decisions, and pays membership dues may be a member of the CPSU.

2. A party member shall be obliged to:

(a) struggle for the creation of the material-technical base of communism, serve as a model of the communist attitude toward labor, raise labor productivity, act as a skirmisher of everything new and progressive, support and disseminate progressive experience, master technology, improve his qualifications, care for and increase social, socialist ownership: the basis of the might and the prosperity of the Soviet Motherland;

(b) firmly and steadfastly implement party decisions, explain the policy of the party to the masses, promote the strengthening and expansion of the links of the party with the people, display tact and attentiveness toward people, and respond in a timely manner to the inquiries and needs of the working people;

(c) actively participate in the political life of the country, in the administration of state affairs, and in economic and cultural construction, set an example in the fulfillment of social duty, and aid in developing and consolidating communist social relations;

(d) have a command of Marxist-Leninist theory, raise their ideological level, further the formation and upbringing of the man of communist society. Wage a resolute struggle against any manifestations of bourgeois ideology, the remnants of a private ownership psychology, religious prejudices and other survivals of the last, observe the principles of communist morality, and place social interests above personal;

(e) be an active conductor of the ideas of socialist internationalism and Soviet patriotism in the mass of working people, wage a struggle against survivals of nationalism and chauvinism, promote by word and deed the strengthening of friendship of the peoples of the USSR and fraternal links of the Soviet people with the peoples of the countries of the socialist camp and with the proletarians and working people of all countries;

(f) strengthen in every possible way the ideological and organizational unity of the party, protect the party from the penetration into its ranks of people unworthy of the high title of communist, be truthful and honest before the party and people, display vigilance, and keep party and state secrecy;

(g) develop criticism and self-criticism, boldly expose shortcomings and strive to eliminate them, struggle against ostentation, conceit, complacency, localism, and give a resolute rebuff to any attempts to suppress criticism, speak out against any actions causing harm to the party and state and notify party agencies, up to and including the Central Committee of the CPSU, thereof;

(h) steadfastly carry out the party line in the selection of cadres for their political and professional qualities. Be implacable in all instances when Leninist principles for the selection and education of cadres are violated;

(i) observe party and state discipline binding on all party members alike. The party has one discipline, one law for all communists, irrespective of their services or posts occupied;

(j) further in every possible way the strengthening of the defense might of the USSR and wage an unceasing struggle for peace and friendship between peoples.

3. A party member shall have the right to:

(a) elect and be elected to party agencies;

(b) freely to discuss at party meetings, conferences, congresses, at sessions of party committees, and in the party press questions of the policy and practical activity of the party, make proposals, and openly express and defend their opinion until the organization adopts a decision;

(c) criticize at party meetings, conferences, congresses, and plenums of committees any communist, irrespective of post occupied. Persons guilty of suppressing criticism and persecuting for criticism should be brought to strict party responsibility up to and including expulsion from the ranks of the CPSU;

(d) personally take part in party meetings, and sessions of the bureau and committees when the question of its activity is discussed;

(e) address questions, applications, and proposals to any party instance up to and including the Central Committee of the CPSU and demand a reply on the substance of the address.

4. Party members shall be admitted exclusively on an individual basis. Conscious, active workers, peasants, and representatives of the intelligentsia who are dedicated to the cause of communism shall be admitted as party members. New members shall be admitted from among candidates who have undergone the established candidate probation period.

Persons who have attained 18 years of age shall be admitted to the party. Youths up to 23 years of age inclusive shall enter the party solely through the All-Union Leninist Communist Youth League.

The procedure for admitting candidates to party membership shall be:

(a) applicants for party membership shall submit recommendations of three members of the CPSU having party experience of not less than five years and who know the recommended person from joint production and social work for at least one year.

Note one. Applicants for party membership from the All-Union Leninist Communist Youth League shall submit a recommendation of the district or city committee of the All-Union Leninist Communist Youth League, which shall be equivalent to a recommendation of one party member.

Note two. Members and candidate members of the Central Committee of the CPSU shall refrain from supporting recommendations;

(b) the question of admission to party membership shall be discussed and decided by a general meeting of the primary party organization; its decision shall be considered adopted if at least two-thirds of the party members present at the meeting vote for it and shall enter into force after confirmation by the district committee, and in cities not divided into districts, by the city party committee.

When discussing the question of admission to the party, the presence of the recommending persons shall not be obligatory;

(c) citizens of the USSR who previously were members of communist and workers' parties of other countries shall be admitted to the Communist Party of the Soviet Union on the basis of rules established by the Central Committee of the CPSU.

Persons who previously were in other parties shall be admitted to the CPSU on the general grounds, but with obligatory confirmation by the regional party committee, territory party committee, or central committee of the union republic communist party.

5. The recommending person shall bear responsibility to party organizations for the objectivity of the description of the political, professional, and moral qualities of the persons recommended.

6. The party experience of persons entering the party shall be computed from the date of the decision of the general meeting of the primary party organization admitting the said candidate to party membership.

7. The procedure for registering members and candidate members of the party and their transfer from one organization to another shall be determined by the respective instructions of the Central Committee of the CPSU.

8. The question of a member or candidate member of the party who has not paid membership dues without justifiable reasons during three months shall be subject to discussion at the primary party organization. If it is revealed that the particular member or candidate member of the party has actually lost contact with the party organization, he shall be considered as having withdrawn from the party, and the primary party organization shall adopt a decision thereof and submit it for confirmation of the district or city party committee.

9. For the failure to fulfill duties in the Rules and other offenses, a member or candidate member of the party shall be brought to responsibility and sanctions may be imposed on him: admonition, reprimand (or strict reprimand), and reprimand (or strict reprimand) with entry on his registration card. The highest measure of party punishment shall be expulsion from the party.

Measures of party education and influence in the form of comradely criticism or rendering a party censure, warning, or instruction should be applied for insignificant offenses.

When deciding the question of expulsion from the party, maximum attention and a careful analysis of the well-foundedness of the accusations brought against a communist should be ensured.

10. The question of expulsion of a communist from the party shall be decided by the general meeting of the primary party organization. The decision of a primary party organization to expel from the party shall be considered adopted if at least two thirds of the party members present at the meeting voted for it and shall acquire force after confirmation by the district or city party committee.

Until confirmation of the district or city party committee of a decision to expel from the CPSU, the party card or candidates card shall remain in the hands of the communist, and he shall have the right to attend closed party meetings.

The right shall be retained to file an appeal within two months to superior party agencies, including up to the Central Committee of the CPSU, against expulsion from the party.

11. The question of bringing to party responsibility members and candidate members of the central committees of communist parties of a union republic, territory, regional, national area, city, or district communist party, and also members of auditing commissions, shall be discussed at primary party organizations.

Decisions of party organizations on imposing sanctions on members and candidate members of these party committees and members of auditing commissions shall be adopted in the usual procedure.

Proposals of party organizations to expel from the CPSU shall be communicated to the appropriate party committee of which the particular communist is a member. Decisions concerning expulsion from the party of members and candidate members of the central committee of a union republic communist party or a territory, regional, national area, city, and district communist party and members of auditing commissions shall be taken at a plenum of the respective committee by a two-thirds majority vote of its members.

The question of expelling from the party a member or candidate member of the Central Committee of the CPSU and a member of the Central Auditing Commission shall be decided by a party congress, and in the intervals between congresses, by the Plenum of the Central Committee by a two-thirds majority of Central Committee members.

12. If a party member has committed offenses punishable in a criminal proceeding, he shall be expelled from the party and brought to responsibility in accordance with the law.

13. Appeals of persons expelled from the party or who have received sanctions, and also decisions of party organizations to expel from the party, shall be considered by the respective party agencies within a period of not more than a month from the date of their receipt.

II

Candidates for Party Membership

14. Persons joining the party shall pass through a candidate probation period, necessary so as to become more familiar with the Program and Rules of the CPSU and to prepare for becoming a party member. The party organization should assist a candidate to prepare himself for becoming a member of the CPSU and verify his personal qualities.

The candidate probation period shall be established as a term of one year.

15. The procedure for admission as a candidate (individual admission, submission of recommendations, decision of primary organization on admission and its confirmation) shall be the same as the admission of party members.

16. Upon the expiry of the candidate probation period, the primary party organization shall consider and decide the question of admitting the candidate to party membership. If during the candidate probation period a candidate has not proved himself and by his personal qualities may not be admitted as a member of the CPSU, the party organization shall

render a decision refusing his admission to party membership, and after confirmation of the said decision by the district or city party committee, he shall be considered as having withdrawn from candidate membership in the CPSU.

17. Candidates for party membership shall participate in all activity of the party organization and shall enjoy at party meetings the right of a consultative vote. Candidates for party membership may not be elected to executive party agencies nor as delegates to party conferences and congresses.

18. Candidates for membership in the CPSU shall pay party dues in the same amounts as party members.

III

Organizational Structure of the Party. Intraparty Democracy

19. The guiding principle of the organizational structure of the party shall be democratic centralism, which signifies:

(a) the electivity of all executive agencies of the party from bottom to top;

(b) periodic accountability of party agencies to their own party organizations and to superior agencies;

(c) strict party discipline and subordination of the minority to the majority;

(d) unconditional binding nature of decisions of highest agencies upon the lowest.

20. The party is built on a territorial and production basis: primary organizations shall be created at the place of work of communists and shall be united in district, city, etc. organizations by territory. The organization serving a particular territory shall be the highest with respect to all party organizations serving its parts.

21. All party organizations shall be autonomous in deciding local questions unless such decisions are contrary to party policy.

22. The highest directing agency of a party organization shall be: the general meeting (for primary organizations), conference (for district, city, national area, region, and territory organizations), and congress (for communist parties of union republics, for the Communist Party of the Soviet Union).

23. The general meeting, conference, or congress shall elect the bureau or committee, which shall be the executive agencies and direct all current work of the party organization.

24. Elections of party agencies shall be held by closed (or secret) ballot. All party members during elections shall have an unlimited right to challenge candidates and criticize the latter. Voting should be for each candidate individually. Candidates shall be considered elected for whom more than half of the participants of the meeting, conference, or congress have voted.

The principle of systematic renewal of their membership and continuity of leadership shall be observed during elections of all party agencies, from primary organizations to the Central Committee of the CPSU.

25. A member of the Central Committee of the CPSU and a candidate member of the Central Committee of the CPSU should justify by all his activity the high trust placed in him by the party. If a member or candidate member of the Central Committee of the CPSU has ruined his honor and dignity, he may not remain as a member of the Central Committee. The question of the removal of a member or candidate member of the Central Committee from the membership of the Central Committee of the CPSU shall be decided at a Plenum of the Central Committee by a closed (or secret) ballot. The decision shall be considered adopted if not less than two thirds of all members of the Central Committee of the CPSU voted for it.

The question of the removal of a member or candidate member of the Central Committee of a union republic communist party or a territory, regional, national area, city, or district party committee from membership of a party agency shall be decided at a plenum of the respective committee. The decision shall be considered adopted if as a result of a closed (or secret) ballot not less than two-thirds of the votes of members of the particular committee have voted for it.

If a member of the Central Auditing Commission does not justify the high trust rendered him by the party, he should be removed from membership on the Commission. This question shall be decided at a session of the Central Auditing Commission. The decision shall be considered adopted if as a result of a closed (or secret) ballot not less than two-thirds of the votes of members of the Central Auditing Commission have been cast for the removal of a particular member of the Central Auditing Commission from its membership.

The question of the removal of members of auditing commissions of republic, territory, regional, national area, city, and district party organizations from the membership of such commissions shall be decided at sessions of the respective commissions in the procedure provided for members and candidates for membership of party committees.

26. The free and business-like discussion of questions of party policy and individual party organizations or in the party as a whole shall be the inalienable right of a party member and an important principle of intraparty democracy. Only on the basis of intraparty democracy may criticism and self-criticism be developed and party discipline strengthened, which should be conscious, and not mechanical.

Within the framework of individual organizations or the party as a whole, discussions of controversial or insufficiently clear issues are possible.

A general party discussion is necessary if:

(a) this need is acknowledged by party organizations on a regional or republic scale;

(b) within the Central Committee there is not a sufficiently firm majority on the most important questions of party policy;

(c) the Central Committee of the CPSU deemed it necessary to consult the entire party on particular questions of policy.

A broad discussion, especially a discussion of all-union scale on questions of party policy, should be so implemented that the free manifestation of the views of party members is ensured and the possibility of attempts to form factional groupings damaging to party unity or attempts to split the party are precluded.

27. The highest principle of party leadership shall be the collectivity of leadership: an absolute condition for the normal activity of party organizations, the proper education of cadres, the development of activeness and initiative of communists. The cult of personality and violations of intraparty democracy connected therewith may not be tolerated in the party; they are incompatible with Leninist principles of party life.

The collectivity of leadership shall not remove the personal responsibility of workers for a task entrusted to them.

28. The central committees of communist parties of union republics and territory, regional, national area, city, and district party committees shall, in the period between congresses and conferences, systematically inform party organizations about their work.

29. Meetings of the _aktiv_ of district, city, national area, regional, and territory party organizations and of union republic communist parties shall be convoked in order to discuss the most important decisions of the party and working out measures for their effectuation, and also to consider questions of local life.

IV

Highest Party Agencies

30. The party congress shall be the supreme agency of the Communist Party of the Soviet Union. Regular congresses shall be convoked by the Central Committee at least once every five years. The convocation of a party congress and the agenda shall be announced not later than one and a half months before the congress. Extraordinary congresses shall be convoked by the Central Committee of the party upon its own initiative or upon the demand of at least one-third of the total number of party members represented at the last party congress. Extraordinary congresses shall be convoked within two months. A congress shall be considered valid if at least half of all party members are represented there.

Norms of representation at a party congress shall be established by the Central Committee.

31. In the event the Central Committee of the party fails to convoke an extraordinary congress within the period specified in point 30, the organizations which demanded the convocation of an extraordinary congress shall have the right to form an organizing committee enjoying the rights of the Central Committee of the party to convoke an extraordinary congress.

32. A congress shall:

(a) hear and confirm reports of the Central Committee, Central Auditing Commission, and other central organizations;

(b) review, change, and confirm the Program and Rules of the party;

(c) determine the party line on questions of internal and foreign policy and consider and decide the most important questions of communist construction;

(d) elect the Central Committee and Central Auditing Commission.

33. The Central Committee and the Central Auditing Commission shall be elected in a membership established by the congress. In the event of the departure of members of the Central Committee, its membership shall

be augmented from among candidate members of the Central Committee of the CPSU elected by the congress.

34. The Central Committee of the Communist Party of the Soviet Union shall, in the invervals between congresses, direct the entire activity of the party, local party agencies, select and distribute leading cadres, direct the work of central state and social organizations of working people through party groups therein, create various agencies, institutions, and enterprises of the party and direct their activity, appoint the editorial boards of central newspapers and journals working under their control, distribute the assets of the party budget, and control its execution.

The Central Committee shall represent the CPSU in relations with other parties.

35. The Central Committee of the CPSU regularly shall inform party organizations about its work.

36. The Central Auditing Commission of the CPSU shall audit the expeditious and correct handling of affairs in central agencies of the party, and the bank and enterprises of the Central Committee of the CPSU.

37. The Central Committee of the CPSU shall hold at least one plenary session every six months. Candidate members of the Central Committee shall be present at sessions of plenums of the Central Committee with a right of consultative vote.

38. The Central Committee of the Communist Party of the Soviet Union shall elect: for directing the work of the party between plenums of the Central Committee: a Politburo; for directing current work, principally to select cadres and organization verifications of execution: a Secretariat. The Central Committee shall elect a General Secretary of the Central Committee of the CPSU.

39. The Central Committee of the Communist Party of the Soviet Union shall organize a Party Control Committee attached to the Central Committee.

The Party Control Committee attached to the Central Committee of the CPSU shall:

(a) verify the observance by members and candidate members of the CPSU of party discipline and bring to responsibility communists guilty of violating the Program and Rules of the party and state discipline, and also offenders of party morality;

(b) consider appeals against decisions of the Central Committees of union republic communist parties and territory and regional party committees concerning expulsion from the party and party sanctions.

40. In the period between party congresses, the Central Committee of the CPSU may, when necessary, convoke an All-Union Party Conference to discuss questions of party policy which have arisen. The procedure for holding an All-Union Party Conference shall be determined by the Central Committee of the CPSU.

V

Republic, Territory, Regional, National Area, City, and District Party Organizations

41. Republic, territory, regional, national area, city, and district party organizations and their committees shall be guided in their activity by the Program and Rules of the CPSU, shall carry out all work to implement party policy within the limits of the republic, territory, region, national area, city, and district, and shall organize the execution of directives of the Central Committee of the CPSU.

42. The basic duties of republic, territory, regional, national area, city, and district organizations of the party and their directing agencies shall be:

(a) political and organizational work in the masses, mobilizing them to carry out tasks of communist construction, all possible development of industrial and agricultural production, and the fulfillment and overfulfillment of state plans; concern for the steady increase of material well-being and the cultural level of the working people;

(b) organization of ideological work, propaganda of Marxism-Leninism, raising the communist consciousness of the working people, direction of the local press, radio, and television, and control over the activity of cultural-enlightenment institutions;

(c) direction of soviets, trade unions, komsomol, cooperative, and other social organizations through party groups therein, more extensive involvement of the working people in the work of these organizations, development of the initiative and activeness of the masses as a necessary condition of the gradual transition from socialist statehood to communist social self-administration;

Party organizations shall not supplant soviet, trade union, cooperative and other social organizations of working people nor allow the mixing of functions of party and other agencies of unnecessary parallelism in work;

(d) selection and distribution of leading cadres, educating them in the spirit of communist ideology, honor, and truthfulness and high responsibility to the party and people for the task entrusted to them;

(e) extensive involvement of communists in the implementation of party work as non-establishment workers by way of social activity;

(f) organization of various institutions and enterprises of the party within the limits of its own republic, territory, region, national area, city, or district and direction of their activity; distribution of party assets within their own organization; systematic information for the superior party agency and accountability to them for their work.

Directing Agencies of Republic, Territory, and Regional Party Organizations

43. The regional or territory party conference or the congress of a union republic communist party shall be the highest agency of a regional, territory, or republic party organization, and in the interval between such, the regional committee, territory committee, or central committee of the union republic communist party.

44. The regular regional or territory conference shall be convoked by the regional or territory committee once every two or three years. A regular congress of a union republic communist party shall be convoked by the central committee of the communist party at least once every five years. Extraordinary conferences or congresses shall be convoked by decision of the regional or territory committee or the central committee of the union republic communist party, or at the demand of one-third of the total number of members of the organizations within the regional, territory, or republic party organization.

Norms of representation for a regional or territory conference or a congress of a union republic communist party shall be established by the respective party committee.

A regional or territory conference or congress of a union republic communist party shall hear reports of the regional or territory committee or the central committee of the union republic communist party and the auditing commission, shall discuss at its discretion other questions of party, economic, and cultural construction, shall elect the regional and territory committee, the central committee of the union republic communist party, the auditing commission, and the delegates to the congress of the CPSU.

In the period between congresses of the union republic communist parties, in order to discuss important questions of the activity of party organizations, the central committees of the communist parties may, when necessary, convoke republic party conferences. The procedure for holding republic party conferences shall be determined by the central committees of the union republic communist parties.

45. Regional and territory committees, and the central committee of the union republic communist parties, shall elect the bureau, including the secretary of the committee. For a secretary, party experience of not less than five years is obligatory. The chairmen of party commissions, the heads of sections of such committees, and the editors of party newspapers and journals also shall be confirmed at plenums of committees.

Secretariats may be created in order to consider current questions and verify execution in regional and territory party committees and the central committee of union republic communist parties.

46. The plenum of a regional or territory committee and the central committee of a union republic communist party shall be convoked at least once every four months.

47. The regional or territory committee or central committee of a union republic communist party shall direct national area, city, and district party organizations, verify their activity, and systematically hear reports of national area, city, and district party committees.

Party organizations of autonomous republics, and also of autonomous and other regions within territories and union republics, shall work under the direction of territory committees and the central committee of union republic communist parties.

Directing Agencies of National Area, City, and District (or Rural and City) Party Organizations

48. A national area, city, or district party conference or a general meeting of communists convoked by a national area, city, or district committee once every two or three years shall be the highest agency of a

national area, city, or district party organization, and extraordinary conferences and meetings convoked by decision of the committee or upon the demand of one-third of the total number of party members within the respective party organization.

The national area, city, or district conference (or meeting) shall hear reports to the committee and the auditing commission and shall discuss at their discretion other questions of party, economic, and cultural construction, elect a national area, city, or district committee and auditing commission and delegates to the regional or territory conference or to the congress of the union republic communist party.

Norms of representation at a national area, city, or district conference shall be established by the respective party committee.

49. The national area, city, or district committee shall elect a bureau, including the secretary of the committee, and also shall confirm the heads of the committee sections and the editors of newspapers. Party experience of not less than three years shall be obligatory in order to be the secretary of a national area, city, or district committee. Committee secretaries shall be confirmed by the regional or territory committee or the central committee of the union republic communist party.

50. A national area, city, or district committee shall organize and confirm primary party organizations, direct their activity, and systematically hear reports concerning the work of the party organization and register communists.

51. The plenum of the national area, city, or district committee shall be convoked at least once every three months.

52. A national area, city, or district committee shall have non-staff instructors, create permanent or temporary commissions for various questions of party work, and use other forms for involving communists in the activity of the party committee on social principles.

VI

Primary Party Organizations

53. Primary organizations shall be the base of the party.

Primary party organizations shall be created at the place of work of party members: plants, factories, state farms, and other enterprises, collective farms, units of the Soviet Army, institutions, educational institutions, and the like where there are at least three party members. Territorial primary party organizations also may be created at the place of residence of communists in villages and attached to house administrations.

In individual instances with the authorization of the regional or territorial committee or central committee of a union republic communist party, primary party organizations may be created within the framework of several enterprises comprising a production association and situated, as a rule, on the territory of a single district or several districts of one city.

54. Party organizations for shops, sectors, farms, brigades, sections and the like may be created with the authorization of the district, city, or national area committee at enterprises, collective farms, institutions where there are more than 50 party members and candidates within a general primary party organization.

Party groups for brigades and other production links may be created within shop, sector, and other organizations, and also within primary party organizations numbering less than 50 members and candidates.

55. The highest agency of a primary party organization shall be the party meeting, which shall be held at least once a month. In party organizations having shop organizations, the general party meeting shall be held at least once every two months.

In large party organizations numbering more than 300 communists, the general party meeting shall be convoked as necessary within periods established by the party committee or at the demand of several shop party organizations.

56. In order to carry on current work, a primary or shop party organization shall elect a bureau for one year in a quantity established by the party meeting. In primary and shop party organizations numbering at least 15 party members, not a bureau, but a secretary, of the party organization and his deputy shall be elected.

Party experience of at least one year shall be obligatory to be a secretary of primary and shop party organizations.

Posts for released party workers shall not, as a rule, be established in primary party organizations combining less than 150 party members.

57. At large enterprises and institutions numbering more than 300 party members and candidates and, when necessary, taking into account the production peculiarities and territorial dispersion, and in organizations numbering more than 100 communists, party committees may be created with the authorization of the regional or territory committee or the central committee of the union republic communist party, the shop party organizations of these enterprises and institutions being granted the rights of a primary party organization.

Party committees may be created in party organizations of collective farms and state farms if there are 50 communists.

In party organizations numbering more than 500 communists, party committees may be created in individual instances with the authorization of the regional and territory committee and the central committee of the union republic communist party in large shops, and the party organizations of production sectors shall be granted the rights of a primary party organization.

Party committees shall be elected for a term of two or three years, their numerical composition being determined by the general party meeting or conference.

58. Party committees of primary organizations numbering more than 1000 communists may, with the authorization of the central committee of the union republic communist party, be granted the rights of a district party committee on questions of admission to the CPSU, registration of party members and candidates, and considering the personnel files of communists.

59. A primary party organization shall be guided in its activity by the Program and the Rules of the CPSU. It shall carry on work directly among the populace, rally them around the Communist Party of the Soviet Union, and organize the masses to implement party policy and struggle for the building of communism.

A primary party organization shall:

(a) admit new members into the CPSU;

(b) nurture communists in a spirit of devotion to the cause of the party, ideological convictions, and communist morality;

(c) organize the study by communists of Marxist-Leninist theory in close connection with the practice of communist construction, oppose any attempts of revisionist distortions of Marxism-Leninism and its dogmatic interpretation;

(d) concern itself with raising the vanguard role of communists in labor and the socio-political and economic life of the enterprise, collective farm, institution, educational institution, and the like;

(e) act as an organizer of the working people in deciding the regular tasks of communist construction, head the socialist competition for the fulfillment of state plans and obligations of working people, mobilize the masses for uncovering and better use of the internal reserves of enterprises and collective farms, for the extensive introduction into production of the achievements of science, technology, and the experience of peredoviki, strive to strengthen labor discipline, steadfastly increase labor productivity, improve product quality, be concerned for preserving and multiplying social wealth at enterprises, state farms, and collective farms;

(f) carry on mass agitation and propaganda work, educate the masses in the spirit of communism, and help the working people develop skills in the administration of state and social affairs;

(g) wage, on the basis of the extensive development of criticism and self-criticism, a struggle against manifestations of bureaucratism, localism, violations of state discipline, thwart efforts to defraud the state, take measures against laxity, mismanagement, and waste at enterprises, collective farms, and institutions;

(h) render assistance to the national area, city, and district committee in all its activity and report to them about their work.

The party organization should strive so that every communist in his own life has himself observed and imparted to the working people moral principles set forth in the Program of the CPSU, the moral code of a builder of communism:

-- devotion to the cause of communism and love for the socialist Motherland and the countries of socialism;

-- conscientious labor for the good of society: he who does not work, neither shall he eat;

-- concern of everyone for the preservation and multiplying of social wealth;

-- high consciousness of social duty and intolerance of violations of social interests;

-- collectivism and comradely mutual assistance: one for all, and all for one;

-- humane relations with and mutual respect between people: man is to man a friend, comrade, and brother;

-- honesty and truthfulness, moral purity, simplicity, and modesty in public and personal life;

-- mutual respect for the family and concern for the upbringing of children;

-- implacability toward injustice, parasitism, dishonesty, careerism, and greed;

-- friendship and fraternity of all peoples of the USSR and intolerance of national and racial enmity;

-- implacability toward the enemies of communism and the cause of peace and freedom of peoples;

-- fraternal solidarity with the working people of all countries and with all peoples.

60. Primary party organizations of enterprises of industry, transport, communications, construction, material-technical supply, trade, public dining, and municipal-domestic services, collective farms, state farms, and other agricultural enterprises, design organizations, construction design offices, scientific research institutes, educational institutions, cultural-enlightenment and treatment institutions shall enjoy the right of control over the activity of the administration.

Party organizations of ministries, state committees, and other central and local soviet and economic institutions and departments shall exercise control over the work of the apparatus relating to the fulfillment of party and government directives and the observance of Soviet laws. They should actively influence the improvement of the work of the apparatus, educate associates in the spirit of high responsibility for the task entrusted to them, take measures to strengthen state discipline and improve services for the populace, wage a resolute struggle against bureaucratism and red tape, and notify in a timely manner the appropriate party agencies about the shortcomings in the work of institutions, and also individual workers, irrespective of the posts they occupy.

VII

The Party and the Komsomol

61. The All-Union Leninist Communist Youth League is an independent social organization of youth, the active helper and reserve of the party. The komsomol shall help the party educate youth in the spirit of communism, involve it in the practical construction of the new society, prepare a generation of all-round developed people who will live, work, and administer public affairs under communism.

62. Komsomol organizations shall enjoy the right of extensive initiative in discussing and raising before the appropriate party organizations questions of the work of an enterprise, collective farm, or institution. They should be in practice the active conductors of party directives in all branches of communist construction, especially where there are no primary party organizations.

63. The VLKSM shall work under the direction of the Communist Party of the Soviet Union. The work of local organizations of the VLKSM shall be directed and controlled by the respective republic, territory, regional, national area, city, and district party organizations.

Local party agencies and primary party organizations shall rely on komsomol organizations in the work of the communist nurturing of youth and shall support and disseminate their useful beginnings.

64. Members of the VLKSM admitted to the CPSU shall withdraw from the komsomol from the moment they join the party unless they occupy executive posts in komsomol organizations.

VIII

Party Organizations in the Soviet Army

65. Party organizations of the Soviet Army shall be guided in their activity by the Program and Rules of the CPSU and shall work on the basis of instructions confirmed by the Central Committee.

Party organizations of the Soviet Army shall ensure the implementation of party policy in the Armed Forces, shall rally their personnel around the Communist Party, shall educate soldiers in the spirit of the ideas of Marxism-Leninism and selfless devotion to the socialist Motherland, actively further the strengthening of the unity of the army and the people, be concerned to strengthen military discipline, mobilize personnel to fulfill the tasks of battle and political training, have a command of new technology and weapons, and irreproachably execute their military duty, orders, and regulations of the command.

66. The direction of party work in the Armed Forces shall be carried out by the Central Committee of the CPSU through the Chief Political Administration of the Soviet Army and the Navy, working with the rights of a section of the Central Committee of the Communist Party of the Soviet Union.

Five years of party experience shall be obligatory to be heads of political administrations of districts and fleets or heads of political sections of the army, and three years to be heads of political sections of formations.

67. Party organizations and political agencies of the Soviet Army shall maintain a close connection with local party committees and systematically inform them about political work in military units. Secretaries of military party organizations and directors of political agencies shall take part in the work of local party committees.

IX

Party Groups in Non-Party Organizations

68. Party groups shall be organized at congresses, conferences, and meetings convoked by soviet, trade union, cooperative, and other mass organizations of working people, and also at elected agencies of such organizations, where there are at least three party members. The task of these groups shall be the all-round intensification of the influence of the party and the implementation of its policy among non-party members, the strengthening of party and state discipline, the struggle against bureaucratism, and verification of the execution of party and soviet directives.

69. Party groups shall be subordinate to the respective party agencies: the Central Committee of the Communist Party of the Soviet Union, the central committees of the union republic communist parties, and the territory, regional, national area, city, and district party committee.

In all questions party groups shall be obliged to strictly and steadfastly be guided by decisions of the leading party agencies.

X

Party Funds

70. The funds of the party and its organizations shall be composed of membership dues, revenues from party enterprises, and other receipts.

71. Monthly membership dues for party members and candidates shall be established in the following amount:

Those having monthly earnings:

up to 50 rubles	shall pay	10 kopecks
from 51 to 100 rubles	" "	0.5 percent
from 101 to 150 rubles	" "	1.0 percent
from 151 to 200 rubles	" "	1.5 percent
from 201 to 250 rubles	" "	2.0 percent
from 251 to 300 rubles	" "	2.5 percent
over 300 rubles	" "	3.0 percent of monthly earnings

72. An entrance fee shall be recovered upon joining as a candidate member of the party in an amount of two percent of monthly earnings.

CHAPTER V

THE CHURCH

ON RELIGIOUS ASSOCIATIONS

[Decree of the All-Russian Central Executive Committee and the Council of People's Commissars, April 8, 1929, as amended January 1, 1932, and June 23, 1975. SU RSFSR (1929), no. 35, item 353; (1932), no. 8, item 41; Vedomosti RSFSR (1975), no. 27, item 572]

The All-Russian Central Executive Committee and the Council of People's Commissars of the RSFSR decree:

I.

1. Churches, religious groups, groupings, religious movements, and other cult associations of all denominations shall come within the effect of the Decret of the RSFSR Council of People's Commissars of January 23, 1918, on the separation of church from state and of the school from church (SU RSFSR (1918), no. 18, item 263).

2. Religious associations of believing citizens of all cults shall be registered as religious societies or groups of believers.

Each citizen may be a member of only one religious cult association (or society or group).

3. A religious society is a local association of believing citizens who have attained 18 years of age and who are of one and the same cult, faith, orientation, or grouping, numbering at least 20 persons who have united for the joint satisfaction of their religious requirements.

Believing citizens who by virtue of their small numbers can not form a religious society shall be granted the right to form a group of believers.

Religious societies shall have the right to acquire church utensils, articles of the religious cult, means of transport, and to lease, construct, and purchase structures for their own needs in the procedure established by law.

4. A religious society or group of believers may commence its activity only after the adoption of a decision concerning registration of the society or group of believers by the Council for Religious Affairs attached to the USSR Council of Ministers.

A decision concerning the registration of a religious society or group of believers and the opening of a prayer building shall be adopted by the Council for Religious Affairs attached to the USSR Council of Ministers upon the recommendation of autonomous republic councils of ministers or executive committees of territory, regional, and city (or cities of Moscow and Leningrad) soviets of working people's deputies.

5. In order to register a religious society, its founders, numbering at least 20 persons, shall send a petition for registration of the religious society and the opening of a prayer building (or church, kostel, kirkh, mecheta, synagogue, and others) to the executive committee of a district or city soviet of working people's deputies.

The executive committee of the district or city soviet of working people's deputies shall send the petition of the believers which it has received with its opinion to the autonomous republic council of ministers or the executive committee of the territory, regional, or city (or cities of Moscow and Leningrad) soviet of working people's deputies.

6. In order to register a group of believers, a petition signed by all the believers of this group shall be submitted to the executive committee of the district or city soviet of working people's deputies, which shall send this petition with its opinion to the autonomous republic council of ministers or executive committee of the territory, regional, or city (or cities of Moscow and Leningrad) soviet of working people's deputies.

7. An autonomous republic council of ministers or executive committee of a territory, regional, or city (or cities of Moscow and Leningrad) soviet of working people's deputies, having received the materials concerning registration of the society or group of believers, shall consider them within a month and send their recommendations with them for decision to the Council for Religious Affairs attached to the USSR Council of Ministers.

After considering the materials concerning the registration of the society or group of believers, the Council for Religious Affairs attached to the USSR Council of Ministers shall adopt a decision concerning the registration or refusal of registration of the religious society or group of believers and notify them thereof.

8. A register of religious associations, prayer houses, and buildings shall be kept by the Council for Religious Affairs attached to the USSR Council of Ministers which shall establish the procedure for the submission of the respective data concerning the religious society or group of believers and their executive and auditing agencies and priests.

9. Only those believers who have expressed their consent thereto may be entered in the lists of members of religious societies or groups.

10. In order to satisfy religious requirements, believers who comprise a religious society may, by decision of the Council for Religious Affairs attached to the USSR Council of Ministers, receive a special prayer building for use free of charge on the conditions and in the procedure provided by a contract concluded between the religious society and an authorized representative of the executive committee of the district or city soviet of working people's deputies.

In addition, believers who comprise a religious society or a group of believers may use other premises for prayer meetings granted to them by individual persons or the executive committees of district or city soviets of working people's deputies by lease. All the rules established by the present decree for prayer buildings shall extend to these premises; contracts for the right to use such premises shall be concluded by individual believers upon their personal liability. Moreover, these premises should satisfy construction, technical, and sanitary rules.

Each religious society or group of believers may use only one prayer premise.

11. Legal transactions connected with the management and use of cult property, such as: contracts to hire watchmen, for the delivery of fuel, for the repair of prayer buildings and property of the cult, for the acquisition of products and property for the performance of religious rites

and ceremonies and similar activities, and closely and directly connected with the teachings and ritual of the particular religious cult, and also for the hire of premises for prayer meetings, may be concluded by individual citizens who are members of the executive agencies of religious societies or authorized groups of believers.

Such legal transactions may not have contractual relations as their content which even though connected with the cult nonetheless pursue trade or industrial purposes, such as: leasing a candle plant or a printing establishment for the printing of religious books, and the like.

12. The general meetings of religious societies and groups of believers (except prayer meetings) shall take place with the permission of the executive committee of the district or city soviet of working people's deputies.

13. In order to directly fulfill the functions connected with the management and use of cult property (Article 11), and also with a view to external representation, religious associations shall elect, by open ballot, executive agencies from among their members at the general meeting of believers: three persons in religious associations, and one representative in a group of believers.

14. The right to remove individual persons from membership of the executive agency of a religious society or group of believers shall be granted to the registering agencies.

15. An auditing commission comprising not more than three members may be elected at a general meeting of believers from the members of the religious associations in order to verify cult property and money received from donations and voluntary offerings.

16. Meetings (or sessions) of the executive and auditing agencies of religious societies and groups of believers shall take place without informing or without the permission of agencies of authority.

17. A religious association shall be prohibited from:

(a) creating mutual aid societies, cooperatives, production associations, and in general using the property at their disposal for any other purposes except the satisfaction of religious requirements;

(b) rendering material support to their members;

(c) organizing either special childrens', youth, women's, prayer, and other meetings or general bible, literary, handicraft, labor, religious study, or other meetings, groups, circles, sections, and also arranging excursions and children's playgrounds, opening libraries and reading rooms, or organizing sanatoriums and medical assistance.

Only the books necessary for the exercise of the particular cult may be kept in prayer buildings and premises.

18. The teaching of any religious teachings in educational institutions whatever shall not be permitted. The teaching of religious teachings may be permitted exceptionally in ecclesiastical educational institutions opened in the established procedure.

19. The area of activity of the priests of a cult, religious preachers, teachers, and so forth shall be restricted to the place of residence of the members of the religious association which they serve and the place where the prayer premises are situated.

The activity of the priests of a cult, religious teachers, and teachers who permanently serve two or several religious associations shall be restricted to the territory on which the believers in the said religious associations permanently reside.

20. Religious societies and groups of believers may convoke religious congresses and meetings only upon the authorization in each individual instance of the Council for Religious Affairs attached to the USSR Council of Ministers.

Religious centers, ecclesiastical boards, and other religious organizations elected at meetings, congresses, and meetings shall direct only the religious (or canonical) activity of the associations of believers. They shall be supported from assets deducted by religious associations exclusively on a voluntary basis.

Religious centers and diocesan boards shall have the right to produce church utensils, articles of the religious cult, and to sell them to societies of believers, and also to acquire means of transport and to lease, construct, and purchase buildings for their own needs in the procedure established by law.

21. Repealed

22. Repealed

23. The executive agencies of religious societies and groups, and also of religious congresses, may use stamps, seals, and blank forms which designate their name, but exclusively for matters of a religious character only. These stamps, seals, and blank forms may not incorporate emblems and slogans established for institutions and agencies of Soviet authority.

24. Repealed

25. Property necessary for the exercise of the cult, both transferred by contract to the believers who comprise a religious society or newly acquired by them or donated to them for the needs of the cult, shall be nationalized and recorded at the respective executive committee of the district or city soviet of working people's deputies and shall be for the use of the believers.

26. Premises serving especially as a dwelling for the watchman and located on the grounds of a prayer building or near a prayer building shall, together with other cult property, be transferred under contract for the use of the believers free of charge.

27. Prayer buildings and cult property shall be transferred for the use of the believers who comprise a religious society on the conditions and in the procedure provided for by the contract concluded by the religious society with the authorized representative of the executive committee of the district or city soviet of working people's deputies.

28. The building of a cult and property situated therein shall be received under contract from the representation of the executive committee of the district or city soviet of working people's deputies by not less than 20 members of the religious society in order to grant the said property for the use of all the believers.

29. It shall be provided in the contract that the persons who have received the cult building and property for use (Article 28) shall be obliged to:

(a) keep and care for it, as state property entrusted to them;

(b) repair the cult building and also bear expenses connected with the possession and use of this property, such as: heating, insurance, protection, payment of taxes, charges, and so forth;

(c) use this property exclusively to satisfy religious requirements;

(d) compensate damage caused to the state by the deterioration of defects of the property;

(e) have an inventory of all cult property in which all newly received (by purchase, donation, or transfer from other prayer buildings, and so forth) articles of the religious cult which do not belong to individual citizens by right of personal ownership, and in which articles which have become unfit for use are excluded with the knowledge and consent of the executive committee of the district or city soviet of working people's deputies with whom the contract was concluded;

(f) admit, without hindrance, at any time except when religious rites are being performed, authorized representatives of executive committees of district, city, or rural soviets of working people's deputies.

30. Prayer buildings having historical, artistic, or archeological significance and which are on the special register of the RSFSR Ministry of Culture shall be transferred in the same procedure and on the same grounds, but with obligatory observance of the rules established for the registration and protection of monuments of art and antiquity.

31. All local inhabitants of the respective faith, orientation, or grouping shall have the right to sign a contract concerning the receipt and use of cult buildings and property, and after the cult property is transferred, acquire thereby the right to participate in the management of such property on the same basis as the persons who initially signed the contract.

32. Each signatory of the contract may cancel his signature on the said contract, filing an appropriate application therefor at the executive committee of the district or city soviet of working people's deputies, which, however, shall not relieve him of liability for the integrity and preservation of the property during the period before he filed the said application.

33. Buildings of a religious cult shall be subject to compulsory insurance at the expense of the persons who signed the contract for the benefit of the executive committee of the district or city soviet of working people's deputies on whose territory the building is situated.

The insurance amounts for burned prayer buildings shall be used by decision of the autonomous republic council of ministers or the executive committee of the territory, regional, or city (or cities of Moscow and Leningrad) soviet of working people's deputies, agreed with the Council for Religious Affairs attached to the USSR Council of Ministers, for the restoration of burned prayer buildings or for cultural needs of the district or city in which the burned prayer building was situated.

34. If petitions are not received from believers concerning the granting of a cult building and property for use to satisfy religious requirements on the conditions provided for by Articles 27-33 of the present Decree, the autonomous republic council of ministers or executive committee of the territory, regional, or city (or cities of Moscow and Leningrad) soviet of working people's deputies shall decide the future purpose of the prayer building and all property therein in accordance with Articles 40 and 41 of the present Decree.

35. Repealed.

36. The transfer of a cult building in the use of believers for other needs (or the closing of a prayer building) shall be permitted exclusively by decision of the Council for Religious Affairs attached to the USSR Council of Ministers upon the recommendation of the autonomous republic council of ministers or the executive committee of the territory, regional, or city (or cities of Moscow and Leningrad) soviet of working people's deputies if this building is needed for state or social needs. The believers who comprise the religious society shall be notified of such a decision.

37. Repealed.

38. Contracts for the lease of premises of nationalized, municipalized, or private houses for the needs of religious associations (Article 10, para. 2) may be dissolved before the expiry of the period of the contract in an ordinary judicial proceeding.

39. The closing of prayer buildings in the respective instances shall be only by decision of the Council for Religious Affairs attached to the USSR Council of Ministers upon the recommendation of the autonomous republic council of ministers or executive committee of the territory, regional, or city (or cities of Moscow or Leningrad) soviet of working people's deputies.

40. When a prayer building is closed, the cult property shall be distributed as follows:

(a) all articles of platinum, gold, silver, and brocade, and also precious stones, shall be subject to being entered in the state fund and transferred to the disposal of local financial agencies or the disposal of the RSFSR Ministry of Culture, if these articles are on their register;

(b) all articles of historical, artistic, or museum value shall be transferred to agencies of the RSFSR Ministry of Culture;

(c) remaining articles (icons, clerical vestments, gonfalons, palls, and so forth) having special significance for the exercise of the cult shall be transferred to the believers for being carried over to other prayer buildings of the same cult; these articles shall be entered in the inventory of cult property on the general grounds;

(d) everyday articles (bells, furniture, carpets, chandeliers, and so forth) shall be subject to being entered in the state fund and transferred to the disposal of local financial agencies or to the disposal of agencies of the RSFSR Ministry of Culture if they were registered with the latter;

(e) so-called transient property, money, and also frankincense, candles, oil, wine, wax, wood, and coal having particular special significance for fulfilling the conditions of a contract or for the performance of religious rites of the cult, shall not be subject to withdrawal if the religious society retains its existence after the prayer building is closed.

41. Prayer buildings subject to closure which are not under state protection as monuments of culture may be used and re-equipped for other purposes or demolished only by decision of the Council for Religious Affairs attached to the USSR Council of Ministers upon the recommendation of the autonomous republic council of ministers or executive committee

of the territory, regional, or city (or cities of Moscow or Leningrad) soviet of working people's deputies.

42. Repealed.

43. Religious associations may be removed from registration if they violated legislation on cults.

Religious associations shall be removed from registration by decision of the Council for Religious Affairs attached to the USSR Council of Ministers upon the recommendation of the autonomous republic council of ministers or executive committee of the territory, regional, or city (or cities of Moscow or Leningrad) soviet of working people's deputies.

44. If a religious association fails to observe a contract for the use of the prayer building or cult property, this contract may be dissolved by decision of the Council for Religious Affairs attached to the USSR Council of Ministers upon the recommendation of the autonomous republic council of ministers or the executive committee of the territory, regional, or city (or cities of Moscow or Leningrad) soviet of working people's deputies.

45. The construction of new prayer buildings with the efforts and assets of the believers shall be permitted in individual instances at the request of religious societies with the authorization of the Council for Religious Affairs attached to the USSR Council of Ministers upon the recommendation of the autonomous republic council of ministers or the executive committee of the territory, regional, or city (or cities of Moscow or Leningrad) soviet of working people's deputies.

46. If a prayer building, by virtue of dilapidation, threatens to collapse completely or partially, the executive committee of the district, city, or rural soviet of working people's deputies shall be granted the right to propose to the executive agency of the religious association or to a representation of a group of believers that the holding of services and meetings of believers cease temporarily until the building is inspected by a special technical commission.

47. Simultaneously with the proposal to close a prayer building, the officials who have made the proposal shall notify the executive committee of the district or city soviet of working people's deputies.

If a cult building having historical, artistic, or archeological significance is subject to protection as a monument of culture, the proposal to close the prayer building shall be sent to the respective agency of the RSFSR Ministry of Culture.

48. A representative of the religious association shall be involved in the technical commission (Article 46) formed by the executive committee of the district or city soviet of working people's deputies.

49. The opinion of the technical commission set forth in its examination report shall be binding and subject to execution.

50. If the technical commission recognizes that the building is threatened with collapse, then it should be specified in the act drawn up whether the building is subject to being demolished or whether only appropriate repairs will be sufficient. In the latter instances the act shall establish precisely the necessary repair for the prayer building and the period sufficient for the repair. Until the repair is completed, religious associations shall not have the right to be admitted to the building for either prayer or any other meetings.

51. If the believers refuse to carry out the repairs specified in the examination report, the contract concluded with them for the use of the building and property of the cult shall be subject to dissolution by decision of the Council for Religious Affairs attached to the USSR Council of Ministers upon the recommendation of local agencies of authority.

52. If the technical commission deems the building to be subject to being demolished, the contract concluded with the believers for the granting and use of this building shall be dissolved by decision of the Council for Religious Affairs attached to the USSR Council of Ministers upon the recommendation of local agencies of authority.

53. Repealed.

54. Religious societies and members of groups of believers shall have the right to make donations and gather voluntary offerings in the prayer building among members of the particular religious association and only for purposes connected with the maintenance of the prayer building, cult property, hiring of cult priests, and support of executive agencies.

55. All cult property, both donated and acquired by voluntary donation, shall be subject to compulsory entry in the inventory of cult property.

Voluntary contributions (or donations) made with a view to beautifying the prayer building with a donated article or with a view to beautifying articles of the cult shall be entered in the inventory of all cult property in the use of the religious society free of charge.

All remaining types of voluntary donations in kind made without mentioning the above purposes, and also cash donations either for the needs of the religious society for maintenance (repairs, heating, etc.) of the prayer building or premises and for the benefit of priests of the cult shall not be subject to entry in the inventory of cult property.

Voluntary cash donations of believers shall be accounted for by the treasurer of the religious association in the daily account book.

56. The expenditure of donated amounts in accordance with the purposes relating to the management of the prayer building and cult property may be made by members of the executive agencies of the religious societies and authorized representatives of groups of believers.

57. Prayer meetings of believers united in groups or a society shall take place without informing or without the authorization of agencies of authority in buildings of the religious cult or in specially adapted premises which satisfy the construction, technical, and sanitary rules.

Prayer meetings of believers shall take place in premises not specially adapted with notification in rural localities of the executive committee of the rural soviet of working people's deputies and in urban settlements, of the executive committee of the district or city soviet of working people's deputies.

58. The performance of any religious rites and ceremonies of a cult, as well as any articles of a cult, shall not be permitted in all state, social, and cooperative institutions and enterprises.

The present prohibition shall not extend to the exercise of religious cult rites in especially isolated premises, nor to the exercise of religious rites at cemeteries or crematoriums, at the request of dying or gravely ill persons who are in hospitals or places of confinement.

59. Religious festivals, the performance of religious rites and ceremonies under an open sky, and also in apartments and houses of believers, shall be permitted with the special permission in each case of the executive committee of the district or city soviet of working people's deputies.

Petitions for the issuance of permits for religious festivals and the performance of religious rites under an open sky shall be submitted not less than two weeks before the period of the said ceremony.

The exercise of religious cult rites in apartments and houses of believers at the request of dying or gravely ill persons may take place without the authorization or notification of the executive committee of the district or city soviet of working people's deputies.

60. Special permits or notification of agencies of authority shall not be required for religious festivals which are an integral part of services performed around the cult building or in cities or rural localities on condition that such festivals do not disturb normal street traffic.

61. Religious festivals, and also the performance of religious rites and ceremonies beyond the place where the religious association is situated, may be permitted with the special authorization in each instance of the agency which concluded the contract for the use of the cultural property. Such authorization may be issued after agreement in advance with the executive committee of that local soviet of working people's deputies in whose district the performance of the festival, rite, or ceremony is proposed.

62. Religious societies, and also groups of believers, shall be registered by the executive committee of the district or city soviet of working people's deputies.

63. The autonomous republic council of ministers or executive committee of the territory, regional, or city (or cities of Moscow or Leningrad) soviet of working people's deputies shall communicate information concerning religious associations according to the established form to the Council for Religious Affairs attached to the USSR Council of Ministers.

64. Supervision over the activity of religious associations, as well as over the preservation of the building and property of the cult transferred for their use on the basis of the contract, shall be entrusted to the registering agencies, in rural localities such supervision also being entrusted to the rural soviets.

II.

65. All religious associations actually existing on the territory of the RSFSR on the date of issuance of the present Decree shall be obliged to be registered within a year at the place where they are situated in the procedure and at the agencies specified in the present Decree.

66. Religious cult associations which have not fulfilled the requirements of the preceding Article shall be considered closed with the consequences provided for by the present Decree.

CHAPTER VI

CIVIL LAW AND PROCEDURE

FUNDAMENTAL PRINCIPLES OF CIVIL LEGISLATION OF THE USSR AND UNION REPUBLICS

[Adopted by Law of the USSR Supreme Soviet, December 8, 1961, as amended November 9, 1966, May 13, 1969, June 12, 1970, August 7, 1972, February 21, March 13, and October 31, 1973, October 13, 1976, and May 16, 1977. Vedomosti SSSR (1961), no. 50, item 525; (1962), no. 2, item 148; (1966), no. 45, item 955; (1969), no. 21, item 185; (1970), no. 24, item 207; (1972), no. 33, item 289; (1973), no. 9, item 138; no. 12, item 173; no. 45, item 637; (1976), no. 42, item 585; (1977), no. 21, item 313]

The Soviet Union, having achieved the full and complete victory of socialism, has embarked upon a period of the expanded construction of a communist society.

The tasks of this period are: the creation of the material-technical base of communism, ensuring an abundance of material and cultural blessings and fuller satisfaction of the requirements of society and all of its citizens; the gradual transformation of socialist into communist social relations; the nurturing of citizens in a spirit of high communist ideology and a communist attitude toward labor and the social economy.

The economy of the period of the expanded construction of communism is based on socialist ownership of the means of production in the form of state (or the whole people) and collective farm and cooperative ownership. Collective farm and cooperative ownership gradually will be merged in character with that of the whole people until the formation of a single communist ownership of the whole people of the means of production.

Personal ownership shall be produced from socialist ownership and serve as one of the means of satisfying the requirements of citizens. With the movement toward communism, the personal requirements of citizens will be satisfied to a greater degree from social funds.

Commodity-money relations shall be used wholly in communist construction in accordance with the new content which they have in planned socialist economy, and such important instruments for the development of the economy as economic accountability, money, price, cost of production, profit, trade, credit, and finance shall be employed. The construction of communism rests on the principle of material interest of citizens, enterprises, collective farms, and other economic organizations.

The Soviet state shall carry out the planned direction of the development of the USSR national economy in accordance with the Leninist principle of democratic centralism. The future strengthening and development of the operative and property independence and initiative of enterprises and other economic organizations and the expansion of their rights within the framework of a uniform national economic plan is linked therewith.

Soviet civil legislation shall regulate property relations conditioned by the use of the commodity-money form in communist construction and personal nonproperty relations connected therewith.

Soviet civil legislation is an important means for the future strengthening of legality in the domain of property relations and the protection of the rights of socialist organizations and citizens.

Soviet civil legislation has been called upon to actively promote the resolution of the tasks of the construction of communism. It furthers the strengthening of the socialist system of economy and socialist ownership and the development of its forms into a single communist ownership, the strengthening of planning and contractual discipline, economic accountability, the timely and proper fulfillment of deliveries, a steady increase in product quality, the fulfillment of capital construction plans and increasing the efficiency of capital investments, carrying out state procurements of agricultural products, development of Soviet trade, protection of material and cultural interests of citizens and the proper combining of these interests with the interests of all of society and the development of creative initiative in the domain of science and technology, literature, and art.

Section I. General Provisions

Article 1. Tasks of Soviet Civil Legislation

Soviet civil legislation shall regulate property and personal nonproperty relations connected therewith with a view to creating the material-technical base of communism and satisfying more fully the material and spiritual requirements of citizens. In instances provided for by law, civil legislation also shall regulate other personal nonproperty relations.

The socialist system of economy and socialist ownership of the instruments and means of production shall be the basis of property relations in Soviet society. The economic life of the USSR shall be determined and directed by the state national economic plan.

Article 2. Relations Regulated by Soviet Civil Legislation

The relations specified in Article 1 of the present Fundamental Principles shall be regulated by Soviet civil legislation:

state, cooperative, and social organizations between themselves;

citizens with state, cooperative, and social organizations;

citizens between themselves.

Other organizations also may be participants of relations regulated by Soviet civil legislation in the instances provided for by USSR legislation.

USSR and union republic civil legislation shall not apply to property relations based on the administrative subordination of one party to another, nor to tax and budget relations.

Family, labor, and land relations, and also relations in collective farms arising from their charter, shall be regulated respectively by family, labor, land, and collective farm legislation.

Article 3. USSR and Union Republic Civil Legislation

In accordance with the present Fundamental Principles, the civil codes and other union republic acts of civil legislation shall regulate property and personal nonproperty relations both provided for by the Fundamental Principles and also not provided for by them.

Relations between socialist organizations for deliveries of produce and for capital construction, relations relating to state procurements of agricultural produce from collective and state farms, relations of railway, maritime, river, air, pipeline transport, and communications organizations and credit institutions with clients and between themselves, state insurance relations, relations arising in connection with discoveries, inventions, and rationalization proposals, and also other relations whose regulation is relegated by the USSR Constitution and by the present Fundamental Principles to the jurisdiction of the USSR, shall be regulated by USSR civil legislation in accordance with the present Fundamental Principles. Questions relegated by USSR legislation to the jurisdiction of the union republics may be settled by their legislation in regard to such relations.

Foreign trade relations shall be determined by special USSR legislation regulating foreign trade and by general USSR and union republic civil legislation.

Article 4. Bases for Origin of Civil Rights and Duties

Civil rights and duties shall arise from the bases provided for by USSR and union republic legislation, and also from the activities of citizens and organizations which, even though not provided for by law, give rise to civil rights and duties by virtue of the general principles and sense of civil legislation.

In accordance therewith, civil rights and duties shall arise from:

legal transactions provided for by law, and also from legal transactions which, although not provided for by law, are not contrary thereto;

administrative acts, including -- for state, cooperative, and social organizations -- planning acts;

as a result of discoveries, inventions, rationalization proposals and the creation of works of science, literature, and art;

as a consequence of causing harm to another person, and equally as a consequence of acquiring or saving property at the expense of the assets of another pěrson without sufficient grounds;

as a consequence of other actions of citizens and organizations;

as a consequence of events with which the law links civil law consequences.

Article 5. Exercise of Civil Rights and Execution of Duties

Civil rights shall be protected by law, except for instances when they are exercised contrary to the purpose of such rights in a socialist society in the period of the construction of communism.

When exercising rights and executing duties, citizens and organizations should observe the laws and respect the rules of socialist community life and the moral principles of a society building communism.

Article 6. Protection of Civil Rights

The protection of civil rights shall be exercised in the established procedure by a court, arbitrazh, or arbitration tribunal by means of: recognition of such rights; restoration of the situation which existed before the violation of the right and the prevention of actions which violate the right; awarding the specific performance of duties; termination or modification of legal relations; sanctions from the person who has violated the right, caused losses, and if provided by law or contract, a penalty (or fine, forfeit), and also by other means provided for by law.

The protection of civil rights in the instances and in the procedure established by USSR and union republic legislation also shall be exercised by comrades' courts, trade unions, and other social organizations.

In instances specially provided for by law, the protection of civil rights shall be carried out in an administrative procedure.

Before filing a suit arising from relations between organizations, it shall be obligatory to file a claim. Exceptions from this rule shall be established by USSR legislation.

Article 7. Protection of Honor and Dignity

A citizen or organization shall have the right to demand the retraction of information defaming their honor and dignity through a court, unless the person who disseminated such information proves that it corresponds to reality.

If the said information is disseminated in the press and if it does not conform to reality, it should be retracted also in the press. The procedure for retraction in other instances shall be established by the court.

If the court decision is not fulfilled, the court shall have the right to impose a fine on the offender recovered for the revenues of the state. The payment of the fine shall release the offender from the duty to fulfill the action provided for by the court decision.

Article 8. Legal Capacity and Dispositive Capacity of Citizens

The capacity to have civil rights and duties (civil legal capacity) shall be recognized in equal measure for all citizens of the USSR. The legal capacity of a citizen shall arise at the time of his birth and cease at death.

The capacity of a citizen by his actions to acquire civil rights and to create civil duties for himself (civil dispositive capacity) shall arise in full measure with the coming of majority, that is, upon the attainment of eighteen years of age. The limited dispositive capacity of minors, and also the instances and procedure for limiting the dispositive capacity for persons who have attained majority, shall be determined by USSR and union republic legislation.

No one may be limited in legal capacity or dispositive capacity other than in the instances and in the procedure provided for by law. Legal transactions directed toward the limitation of legal capacity or dispositive capacity shall be void.

Article 9. Content of Legal Capacity of Citizens

Citizens may, in accordance with law, have property in personal ownership, the right to use dwelling premises and other property, inherit and bequeath property, select the nature of occupation and place of residence, the right of an author of a work of science, literature, and art, discovery, invention, or rationalization proposal, and also other property and personal nonproperty rights.

Article 10. Recognition of A Citizen as Missing or Declaration that He is Dead

A citizen may, in a judicial proceeding, be deemed to be missing if during the course of a year there is no information at his permanent place of residence as to his whereabouts.

A citizen may, in a judicial proceeding, be declared to be dead if during the course of three years there is no information at his permanent place of residence as to his whereabouts, and if he is missing in circumstances of impending death or giving grounds to suppose he has perished in a particular accident, in the course of six months.

A military serviceman or other citizen missing in connection with military activities may not be declared dead in a judicial proceeding until two years have expired from the date the military activities ended.

If a citizen deemed to be missing or declared to be dead appears or his whereabouts are discovered, the respective decision shall be vacated by a court. The property rights of the citizen shall be restored in accordance with union republic legislation.

Article 11. Juridical Persons

Organizations which possess separate property, may acquire property and personal nonproperty rights and bear duties in their own name, and be plaintiffs or defendants in court, arbitrazh, or arbitration tribunal shall be juridical persons.

Juridical persons shall be:

state enterprises and other state organizations which are on economic accountability and have basic and circulating assets allocated to them and an independent balance; institutions and other state organizations which are on the state budget and have an independent estimate and whose directors enjoy the rights of disposing of credits (with exceptions established by law); state organizations financed at the expense of other sources and having an independent estimate and an independent balance;

collective farms, inter-collective farm, and other cooperative and social organizations and their associations, and also in instances provided for by USSR and union republic legislation the enterprises and institutions of such organizations and their associations which have separate property and an independent balance;

state-collective farm and other state-cooperative organizations.

A juridical person shall operate on the basis of a charter (or statute). Institutions and other state organizations on the state budget, and in instances provided for by USSR and union republic legislation also other organizations, may operate on the basis of a general statute concerning organizations of the particular type.

The institutions and other state organizations specified in the present Article which are on the state budget shall operate, in instances provided for by USSR and union republic legislation, in the name respectively of the USSR or union republic.

Article 12. Legal Capacity of a Juridical Person

A juridical person shall possess civil legal capacity in accordance with the established purposes of its activity.

The rights and duties of economic organizations connected with the use of a firm name, production marks, and trademarks shall be determined by USSR legislation.

Article 13. Liability of a Juridical Person for Its Obligations

A juridical person shall be liable for its obligations with property belonging to it (and a state organization which is a juridical person, allocated to it) on which execution may be levied according to USSR and union republic legislation.

The state shall not be liable for the obligations of state organizations which are juridical persons, and these organizations shall not be liable for obligations of the state.

The conditions and procedure for the release of assets to cover the indebtedness of institutions and other state organizations which are on the state budget, if such indebtedness can not be covered from their estimates, shall be established by USSR and union republic legislation.

Article 14. Legal Transactions

Actions of citizens and organizations directed toward the establishment, modification, or termination of civil rights and duties shall be deemed legal transactions.

Legal transactions may be unilateral and bilateral or multilateral (contracts).

A legal transaction which does not conform to the requirements of the law shall be void.

The failure to observe the form required by law shall entail the invalidity of a legal transaction only when such a consequence is expressly specified in a law. The failure to observe the form of foreign trade transactions and the procedure for signing them (Article 125 of the present Fundamental Principles) shall entail the invalidity of the legal transaction.

If a legal transaction is void, each party shall be obliged to restore to the other party everything received under the legal transaction, and if it is impossible to restore that received in kind, to reimburse its cost in money unless other consequences of invalidity of the legal transaction are provided for in a law.

If a legal transaction is performed for a purpose knowingly contrary to the interests of the socialist state and society and if there is intent on the part of both parties, then, if both parties have executed the legal transaction, everything received by them under the legal transaction shall be recovered for the income of the state, and if the legal transaction has been executed by one party, everything received shall be recovered from the other party for the income of the state and everything due to the first party as compensation for that received; if only one party has intent, everything received by it under the legal transaction should be restored to the other party, and that received by the latter or due to it as compensation for that executed shall be recovered for the income of the state.

Article 15. Representation

A legal transaction performed by one person (representative) in the name of another person (person represented) by virtue of authority based on a power of attorney, law, or administrative act shall directly create, modify, or terminate civil rights and duties of the person represented.

Article 16. Limitation of Actions

The general period for protecting the right of a person to sue whose right has been violated (limitation of actions) shall be established as three years, and for suits of state organizations, collective farms, and other cooperative or social organizations against one another, one year.

A reduced period of limitation of actions may be established by USSR legislation for individual types of actions arising out of relations whose regulation is relegated to the jurisdiction of the USSR, and for other actions, by union republic legislation.

The running of the period of limitation of actions shall commence from the date the right to sue arises; the right to sue shall arise from the date when the person knew or should have known about the violation of his right. Exceptions from this rule, and also the grounds for suspending and interrupting the running of the period of limitation of actions, shall be established by USSR and union republic legislation.

An action to protect a violated right shall be accepted for consideration by a court, arbitrazh, or arbitration tribunal irrespective of the expiry of the period of limitation of actions. The limitation of actions shall be applied by a court, arbitrazh, or arbitration tribunal irrespective of the application of the parties. If a court, arbitrazh, or arbitration tribunal deems the reason for the passage of the period of limitation of actions to be justifiable, the violated right shall be subject to protection.

Article 17. Actions to Which the Limitation of Actions shall not Extend

The limitation of actions shall not extend to:

actions arising from the violation of personal nonproperty rights, except for instances provided for by law;

actions of state organizations concerning the return of state property from illegal possession of collective farms and other cooperative and social organizations or citizens;

actions of depositers concerning the payment of deposits made in state labor savings banks and the USSR State Bank;

in instances established by USSR legislation, also to other actions.

Article 18. Application of Civil Legislation of One Union Republic in Another Union Republic

The civil legislation of one union republic shall be applied in another union republic according to the following rules:

(1) to relations arising from the right of ownership the law of the place where the property is located shall be applied;

(2) in the performance of legal transactions, legal capacity and dispositive capacity shall be determined according to the law of the place where the legal transaction is performed;

(3) the law of the place where a legal transaction is performed shall be applied to the form of legal transactions; the law of the place where a legal transaction is performed also shall be applied to obligations arising from the legal transaction unless otherwise provided by law or agreement of the parties;

(4) the law of the place where a dispute is considered shall be applied to obligations arising from the causing of harm, and at the petition of the victim, the law of the place where the harm is caused;

(5) the law of the place where an inheritance is opened shall be applied to relations regarding inheritances;

(6) questions of the limitation of actions shall be settled according to the law of that union republic whose legislation regulated the particular relation.

Section II. Law of Ownership

Article 19. Powers of an Owner

An owner shall have the right to possess, use, and dispose of property within the limits established by law.

Article 20. Socialist Ownership

Socialist ownership shall be: state (or of the whole people) ownership; ownership of collective farms, other cooperative organizations, their associations; ownership of social organizations.

Article 21. State Ownership

The state shall be the sole owner of all state property.

State property allocated to state organizations shall be in the operative management of such organizations exercised within the limits established by law in accordance with the purposes of their activity, planning tasks, purpose of the property, and the right to possess, use, and dispose of the property.

Land, its minerals, water, forests, plants, factories, mines, quarries, electric power stations, railway, water, air, and automotive transport, banks, means of communications, agricultural, trade, municipal, and other enterprises organized by the state, and also the basic housing fund in cities and city-type settlements shall be in state ownership. Any other property also may be in the ownership of the state.

Land, its minerals, water, and forests, being in the exclusive ownership of the state, may be granted only for use.

Article 22. Procedure for the Disposition of State Property and Levying Execution on It

The procedure for transferring state enterprises, buildings, installations, equipment, and other property relegated to the basic assets of state organizations, to other state organizations, and also collective farms and other cooperative and social organizations shall be determined by USSR and union republic legislation.

State enterprises, buildings, and installations shall be transferred from one state organization to another free of charge.

State property specified in the present Article shall not be subject to alienation to citizens, except for individual types of property whose sale to citizens is permitted by USSR and union republic legislation.

Enterprises, buildings, installations, equipment, and other property relegated to the basic assets of state organizations may not be the subject of a pledge or execution levied thereon in respect of the claims of creditors. Execution may be levied on other property with the exceptions established by union republic legislation, and with respect to monetary assets, by USSR legislation. The procedure for levying execution in respect of claims of credit institutions concerning the return of loans issued by them shall be determined by USSR legislation.

Article 23. Ownership of Collective Farms, Other Cooperative Organizations, and Their Associations

Enterprises, cultural and domestic institutions, buildings, installations, tractors, combines, other machines, means of transport, working and productive livestock, produce produced by such organizations, and other property corresponding to the purposes of the activity of such organizations shall be the ownership of collective farms, other cooperative organizations, and their associations.

Execution may not be levied in respect of claims of creditors on enterprises, cultural and domestic institutions, buildings, installations, tractors, combines, other machines, means of transport, and other property relegated to their basic assets, as well as seed and forage funds, belonging to collective farms, other cooperative organizations, and their associations. Execution may be levied on other property with the exceptions established by union republic legislation, and with respect to monetary assets, by USSR legislation. The procedure for levying execution in respect of claims of credit institutions for the return of loans issued by them shall be determined by USSR legislation.

Article 24. Ownership of Trade Union and Other Social Organizations

The ownership of trade union and other social organizations shall be their enterprises, buildings, installations, sanatoriums, rest homes, palaces of culture, clubs, stadiums, and pioneer camps with their equipment, cultural-enlightenment funds, and other property corresponding to the purposes of the activity of these organizations.

Execution may not be levied in respect of creditors on enterprises, buildings, installations, equipment, and other property relegated to the basic assets of the enterprise, sanatoriums, rest homes, palaces of culture, clubs, stadiums, and pioneer camps, and also cultural-enlightenment funds, belonging to trade union and other social organizations. Execution may be levied on other property with the exceptions established by union republic legislation, and with respect to monetary assets, by USSR legislation. The procedure for levying execution in respect of claims of credit institutions concerning the return of loans issued by them shall be determined by USSR legislation.

Article 25. Personal Ownership

Citizens may have in personal ownership property intended for the satisfaction of their material and cultural requirements. Each citizen may have in personal ownership labor income and savings, a dwelling house (or part thereof) and subsidiary household economy, household articles, and articles of personal use and convenience. Property in the personal ownership of citizens may not be used to derive nonlabor income.

A citizen may have one dwelling house in personal ownership. Spouses living together and their minor children may have only one dwelling house belonging by right of personal ownership to one of them or in their common ownership. The maximum size of a dwelling house which may be in the personal ownership of a citizen and the procedure and conditions for leasing premises in such a house shall be established by union republic legislation.

The maximum number of livestock which may be in the personal ownership of a citizen shall be established by union republic legislation.

A citizen who is a member of a collective farm household may not have property in personal ownership which in accordance with the collective farm charter may belong only to the collective farm household.

Article 26. Common Ownership

Property may belong by right of common ownership to two or several collective farms or other cooperative and social organizations or to the state and one or several collective farms or other cooperative and social organizations, or to two or several citizens.

Common ownership with a specific share (share ownership) or without shares (joint ownership) shall be distinguished.

Article 27. Collective Farm Household Ownership

The property of a collective farm household shall belong to its members by right of joint ownership (Article 26 of the present Fundamental Principles).

A collective farm household may have in ownership the subsidiary husbandry on its household land plot, a dwelling house, productive livestock, poultry, and minor agricultural implements, in accordance with the collective farm charter.

In addition, there shall belong to a collective farm household the labor income transferred to its ownership by household members from participation in the general economy of the collective farm or other property transferred by them to the ownership of the household, as well as household articles and articles of personal consumption acquired with common assets.

The procedure for the possession, use, and disposition of collective farm household property, and also the allocation of the share of a household member and partition of a household shall be established by union republic legislation.

Article 28. Protection of the Right of Ownership

An owner shall have the right to demand and obtain his property from the illegal possession of another.

If property is acquired for value from a person who did not have the right to alienate it, of which the acquirer did not know and should not have known (good-faith acquirer), then the owner shall have the right to recover this property from the acquirer only when the property has been lost by the owner or person to whom the property was transferred in possession by the owner, or has been stolen from one or the other, or otherwise left their possession against their will.

If the property was acquired gratuitously from a person who did not have the right to alienate it, the owner shall have the right to recover the property in all instances.

State property, and also the property of collective farms and other cooperative and social organizations, unlawfully alienated by whatever means may be demanded and obtained by the respective organizations from any acquirer.

Money, and also demand securities, may not be demanded and obtained from a good-faith acquirer.

An owner may require the elimination of any violations of his right, even though such violations were not linked with deprivation of possession.

Article 29. Protection of the Rights of a Possessor Who is Not an Owner

The rights provided by Article 28 of the present Fundamental Principles also shall belong to a person even though not an owner who possesses property by virtue of law or contract.

Article 30. Time at Which the Right of Ownership Arises in an Acquirer of Property by Contract

The right of ownership of an acquirer of property by contract (and of state organizations, the right of operative management of property) arises from the time the article is transferred unless otherwise provided by law or contract.

Transfer shall be deemed the handing over of the article to the acquirer, and equally the surrender to a transport organization or post office for dispatch of the article to the acquirer alienated without an obligation to deliver. The transfer of a bill of lading or other document for disposing of the article shall be equivalent to the transfer of the article.

Article 31. Requisition and Confiscation

The appropriation by the state of property from an owner in the interests of the state or of social interests with the payment of the value of the property (requisition), and also the appropriation by the state of property without compensation as a sanction for a breach of law (confiscation) shall be permitted only in the instances and in the procedure established by USSR and union republic legislation.

Article 32. Ownerless Property

Property which has no owner or whose owner is unknown (ownerless property) shall enter state ownership. Ownerless property which belonged to a collective farm household shall enter into collective farm ownership. The procedure for the transfer of ownerless property into ownership of the state or collective farm shall be established by union republic legislation.

Section III. Law of Obligations

Chapter 1. General Provisions on Obligations

Article 33. An Obligation and its Execution

By virtue of an obligation, one person (the obligor) shall be obliged to perform for the benefit of another person(the obligee) a certain action such as to transfer property, fulfill work, pay money, and so forth, or to refrain from a certain action, and the obligee shall have the right to demand the execution of the duty from the obligor.

Obligations shall arise from a contract or other bases specified in Article 4 of the present Fundamental Principles.

Obligations should be executed properly and within the established period in accordance with the ukazaniia of the law, planning act, contract, and in the absence of such ukazaniia, in accordance with the requirements customarily presented.

Unilateral refusal to execute an obligation and a unilateral modification of the conditions of a contract shall not be permitted except for instances provided for by law.

Article 34. Conclusion of a Contract

A contract shall be considered concluded when an agreement regarding all its essential points is achieved in the appropriate form required. Those points of the contract are essential which are so deemed by law or are necessary for contracts of the particular type, as well as all those points relative to which agreement must be achieved at the request of one of the parties.

The content of a contract concluded on the basis of a planning task should correspond to this task.

Disagreements which arose when concluding the contract which is based on a planning task binding upon both parties shall be settled by a court, even if one of the parties is a collective farm or an inter-collective farm organization, or by the appropriate arbitrazh (or arbitration tribunal) if the parties are state, cooperative (except collective farms and inter-collective farm organizations), and other social organizations insofar as is not established otherwise by law.

Disagreements between the said organizations which arose when concluding the contract not based on a planning task binding upon both parties may be settled respectively by a court or arbitrazh if this is specially provided for by law or by agreement of the parties.

Article 35. Ensuring the Execution of Obligations

The execution of obligations may be secured according to law by a penalty (or fine, forfeit), pledge, or surety. In addition, obligations between citizens or with their participation may be secured by a deposit and obligations between socialist organizations, by a guarantee.

Article 36. Liability for Breach of Obligations

In the event of the failure to execute or of the improper execution of an obligation by a debtor, he shall be obliged to compensate the creditor for losses caused thereby. "Losses" includes expenses made by a creditor, the loss of or damage to his property, as well as revenues not received by a creditor which he would have received if the obligation had been executed by a debtor.

If a forfeiture (fine, penalty) has been established for the failure to execute or for the improper execution of an obligation, the losses shall be compensated in that part not covered by the forfeiture (or fine, penalty).

Instances may be provided for by law or contract when only the recovery of a forfeiture (or fine, penalty) is permitted, but not for losses when losses may be recovered in full amount above the forfeiture (or fine, penalty); when at the choice of the creditor either a forfeiture (or fine, penalty), or losses may be recovered.

Limited liability for the failure to execute or for the improper execution of obligations may be established for individual types of obligations by USSR and union republic legislation.

An agreement between socialist organizations to limit their liability shall not be permitted if the amount of liability for a particular type of obligation is determined precisely by law.

The payment of a penalty (or fine, forfeit) established in the event of delay or other improper execution of an obligation and compensation of losses caused by improper performance shall not release the debtor from specific execution of the obligation except for instances when a planning task on which the obligation between socialist organizations is based has lost force.

Article 37. Fault as a Condition of Liability for Breach of Obligations

A person who has not executed an obligation or has executed it improperly shall be financially liable (Article 36 of the present Fundamental Principles) only if there is fault (intent or negligence) except for instances provided for by law or contract. The absence of fault shall be proved by the person who has breached the obligation.

If the failure to execute or the improper execution of an obligation occurred through the fault of both parties, the court, arbitrazh, or arbitration tribunal respectively shall reduce the amount of liability of the debtor.

Article 38. Entrusting the Execution of an Obligation to a Third Person

The execution of an obligation which arose from a contract may be entrusted to a third person in whole or in part if this is provided for by the established rules, and equally if the third person is linked with one of the parties by administrative subordination or respective contract.

In this event liability for the failure to execute or the improper execution of the obligation shall be borne by the party to the contract from which it arose, unless USSR or union republic legislation provides that the direct executor bears liability.

Chapter 2. Purchase-Sale

Article 39. Purchase-Sale Contract

Under a purchase-sale contract, the seller shall be obliged to transfer property to the ownership of the buyer, and the buyer shall be obliged to accept the property and pay a specific sum of money for it.

If a state organization is the buyer, the right of operative management of the property shall arise therefrom (Article 21 of the present Fundamental Principles).

Article 40. Price

Goods shall be sold by state, cooperative, and social organizations at the established state prices, except for instances provided for by USSR legislation and within the limits established thereby, by union republic legislation.

The sale by collective farms of surplus agricultural produce not bought by the state, and also the sale by citizens of their property, shall be at prices established by agreement of the parties.

Article 41. Liability of Seller for Poor Quality of Articles Sold

The quality of an article sold should correspond to the conditions of the contract, and if there are no specifications in the contract, to the requirements customarily presented. An article being sold by a trade organization should correspond to the state standard, technical conditions, or models established for this type of article unless it follows otherwise from the nature of the particular type of purchase sale.

The buyer to whom a poor-quality article has been sold, unless its defects were stipulated by the seller, shall have the right at his election either to demand the replacement of the article as defined in the contract by generic characteristics by an article of proper quality, or a corresponding reduction in the sale price, or the elimination of the defects in the article without charge by the seller or reimbursement of the buyer's expenditures to correct them, or dissolution of the contract with compensation of losses to the buyer.

The procedure for the effectuation of these rights by a person who has bought the article from a retail trade enterprise shall be determined by union republic legislation.

Article 42. Periods for Filing Claims and Periods for Limitation of Actions in Connection with Defective Articles Sold

The periods during which a claim may be filed because of defects in the article sold, and also periods for limitation of actions connected with such defects, shall be established by USSR and union republic legislation.

In instances when guarantee periods have been established in accordance with Article 48 of the present Fundamental Principles for articles sold through retail trade organizations, these periods shall be calculated from the date of sale. During the guarantee period, the buyer may file a claim against the seller because of defects in the article sold which prevent its normal use. The seller shall be obliged to ensure elimination of the defects in the article without charge, replace it with an article of proper quality, or take it back, returning to the buyer the amount that he paid, unless it is proved that the defects arose as a consequence of a violation by the buyer of rules for the use of the article or for storing it.

Article 43. Sale of Goods on Credit

Durable goods may be sold to citizens by retail trade enterprises on credit (with deferred payment) in the instances and procedure established by union republic legislation.

The right of ownership in goods sold on credit shall arise in the buyer in accordance with the rules of Article 30 of the present Fundamental Principles.

Chapter 3. Delivery

Article 44. Contract of Delivery

Under a contract of delivery, a supplier organization shall be oblige to transfer a specific product within specific periods or period to the ownership or, in accordance with Articles 21 and 30 of the present Fundamental Principles, to the operative management of a buyer organization (or customer) according to a planning act for the distribution of the product which is binding upon both organizations; the supplier organization shall be obliged to accept the product and pay the established prices for it. A contract concluded between organizations at their discretion by which the supplier is obliged to transfer a product to the buyer which is not distributed by way of planning within a period not coinciding with the time of concluding the contract also shall be a contract of delivery.

The delivery of a product without concluding a contract shall take place only in the instances established by the USSR Council of Ministers or union republic council of ministers.

Article 45. Partial Delivery or Selection of a Product

The quantity of a product not delivered by a supplier or not selected by a buyer within the stipulated period should be delivered (or selected) in the procedure and within the periods provided for by statutes on deliveries, special conditions for the delivery of individual types of products (Article 50 of the present Fundamental Principles), or by contract.

A buyer shall have the right, having informed the supplier, to refuse to accept a product whose delivery has been delayed, unless provided otherwise in the contract. The latter shall be obliged to accept and pay for a product loaded by the supplier before receiving the notification of the buyer.

Article 46. Assortment of the Product Delivered

A product should be delivered in the assortment provided by the contract.

The delivery of a product of certain types included in a particular assortment in a larger quantity than provided by the contract shall not be counted as covering the partial delivery of other types of product except for instances when such a delivery is made with the consent of the buyer.

The supplier shall pay the established penalty for the partial delivery of particular types of a product included in the assortment even though the delivery of the total value of the product has been fulfilled within the period provided for by the contract.

Article 47. Quality of Delivered Product

The quality of a delivered product should correspond to the state standards, technical conditions, or models. The delivery of a higher quality product in comparison with state standards and of confirmed technical conditions or models may be provided for in the contract.

If a lower quality product than that required by a state standard or confirmed technical conditions or model is delivered, the buyer shall be obliged to refuse to accept and pay for the product, and if the product already has been paid for by the buyer, the amount paid shall be subject to return.

However, if the defects of a delivered product can be eliminated without returning it to the supplier, the buyer shall have the right to demand from the supplier the elimination of the defects at the place where the product is located or eliminate them by their own means but at the expense of the supplier.

If a product delivered corresponds to the state standards or technical conditions but is of a lower grade than stipulated, the buyer shall have the right to accept the product, paying the price established for a product of the respective grade, or refuse to accept and pay for the product.

A six month period of limitations from the date the buyer ascertains in the proper procedure that the product delivered to him is defective shall be established for suits arising from the delivery of a product of poor quality.

Article 48. Periods for Filing Claims in Connection with Defects in a Delivered Product

The periods and procedure for a buyer to establish defects in a product delivered to him which could not be discovered during the ordinary reception and the filing of a claim against the supplier arising out of the delivery of a poor quality product shall be determined by USSR legislation.

With respect to a product intended for long-term use or storage, state standards or technical conditions may provide for a longer period for the buyer to establish the said defects in the proper procedure (guarantee periods) with the subsequent filing of claim actions against the supplier concerning the elimination of the said defects or the replacement of the product. A supplier shall be obliged to correct defects in a product free of charge for which a guarantee period has been established or to replace it unless it is proved that the defects arose as a consequence of a violation by the buyer of rules for the use of the product or its storage.

Guarantee periods may be established by contracts unless they are provided for by standards or technical conditions, as well as guarantee periods longer than those provided for by standards or technical conditions. With respect to consumer goods sold through retail trade organizations, the guarantee period shall be computed from the date of the retail sale of the article (Article 42 of the present Fundamental Principles).

Article 49. Delivery of a Product in Complete Sets

A product should be delivered in a complete set in accordance with the requirements of state standards, technical conditions, or price lists. The delivery of a product with additional items (or parts) to the complete set or without individual items (or parts) included in the complete set which are unnecessary to the buyer may be provided for in the contract. If the completeness of a set is not determined by a state standard, confirmed technical conditions, or price list, it may be determined by the contract when necessary.

If an incomplete set of a product is delivered, the buyer shall be obliged to demand that the set be completed or that the incomplete set of the product be replaced by a complete set, and until it is complete or replaced shall refuse payment, and if the product already has been paid for, to demand the return of the amounts paid for it.

If a supplier fails to complete the set of a product within the period established by agreement of the parties, the buyer shall have the right to refuse the product.

Article 50. Statutes on Deliveries and Special Conditions of Deliveries. Liability for Violation of the Contract of Delivery

Contracts of delivery shall be concluded and executed in accordance with the statutes on deliveries confirmed by the USSR Council of Ministers and the special conditions of delivery for individual product types confirmed in the procedure established by the USSR Council of Ministers, and in the instances provided thereby, by the union republic councils of ministers.

A penalty (or fine, forfeit) and losses for breach of duties under a contract of delivery shall be recovered in accordance with these statutes and special conditions.

If a poor quality or incomplete set of a product is delivered, the buyer shall recover the established penalty (or fine) from the supplier and, in addition, the losses caused by such delivery without deducting the penalty (or fine).

Chapter 4. State Purchase of Agricultural Produce from Collective and State Farms

Article 51. Procurement Contract for Agricultural Produce

The state procurement of agricultural produce from collective and state farms shall be carried out by procurement contracts, which shall be concluded on the basis of state plans for procurements of agricultural produce and plans for the development of agricultural production in collective and state farms.

Article 52. Content of a Procurement Contract

Procurement contracts should provide for:

the quantity (by product types), quality, periods, procedure, and conditions for delivery and the place for surrendering the agricultural product;

the duty of procurement organizations and enterprises to accept the produce in a timely manner and to pay for it at the established prices, and also the periods and amounts for issuing cash advances to collective farms;

the duty to render assistance to collective and state farms in organizing the production of agricultural produce and its transport to receiving centers and enterprises;

the mutual property liability of the parties in the event they fail to fulfill their duties.

Model procurement contracts shall be confirmed in the procedure established by the USSR Council of Ministers.

Chapter 5. Lease of Property

Article 53. Contract for Lease of Property

By a contract for the lease of property, the lessor shall be obliged to grant property for temporary use to the lessee for payment.

The lessor shall be obliged to grant the property to the lessee in a state corresponding to the conditions of the contract and purpose of the property and to make capital repairs of this property at his own expense unless provided otherwise by law or contract.

The lessee shall be obliged to make timely payment for the use of the property, to use the property in accordance with the contract and the purpose of the property, to maintain it in a proper state, to make current repairs at his own expense, unless otherwise provided by law or contract, and when the loan contract is terminated, to return the property in the state in which he received it, taking into account normal wear, or in the state stipulated by the contract.

Article 54. Preservation of Force of a Lease Contract if the Property is Transferred to Another Owner

If the right of ownership to leased property is transferred from the lessor to another person, the lease contract shall retain force for the new owner. A lease contract also shall preserve its force if property is transferred from one state organization (lessor) to another.

Article 55. Domestic Rental

The conditions and procedure for state, cooperative, and social organizations to grant citizens the temporary use of domestic household articles, musical instruments, sporting equipment, passenger motor vehicles, and other property (domestic rental) for payment shall be established by union republic legislation.

Model contracts shall be confirmed by the union republic councils of ministers for individual types of domestic rental. Deviations from the conditions of the model contracts which restrict the rights of users shall be void.

Chapter 6. Lease of Dwelling Premises

Article 56. Procedure for Granting Dwelling Premises and Lease Contract for Dwelling Premises

Dwelling premises in houses of local soviets of working people's deputies shall be granted by the executive committee of the local soviet with the participation of representatives of social organizations. Dwelling premises shall be granted in houses of state, cooperative, and social organizations by joint decision of the administration and of the factory, plant, and local trade union committee confirmed by the executive committee of the soviet of working people's deputies, and in instances provided for by the USSR Council of Ministers, by joint decision of the administration and the factory, plant, and local trade union committee with subsequent notification of the executive committee of the soviet of working people's deputies about the dwelling premises granted for occupancy. The use of dwelling premises in houses of local soviets of working people's deputies and in houses of state, cooperative, and social organizations shall be formalized by a contract for lease of dwelling premises with the respective house administration.

The contract for lease of dwelling premises in houses belonging to citizens by right of personal ownership shall be concluded by the lessee with the owner of the house.

The rights and duties of the parties shall be determined in the contract. Articles 53 and 54 of the present Fundamental Principles shall be applied to a contract for the lease of dwelling premises.

Article 57. Apartment Rent

Until the establishment of free use of dwelling premises, a lessee shall be obliged to make timely apartment rental payments.

The amounts of apartment rent shall be established by USSR legislation.

Payment for the use of dwelling premises in houses belonging to citizens by right of personal ownership shall be determined by agreement of the parties, but may not exceed the maximum rates established for such houses by union republic legislation.

Article 58. Right of Lessee to Renew the Contract

If a contract for the lease of dwelling premises in a house of the local soviet of working people's deputies or in a house of a state, cooperative, or social organization has been concluded for a specific period, the lessee shall, upon the expiry of the contract period, have the right to renew the contract. This right may be contested by the lessor in court only in the event of the systematic failure of the lessee to fulfill his duties under the contract.

The same right shall appertain to the lessee of dwelling premises in a house belonging to a citizen by right of personal ownership, except for instances:

when the lessee resides in premises under a contract concluded for a period not exceeding one year with the obligation to vacate the premises upon the expiry of this period;

when it is established by a court that the premises are needed for the personal use of the owner of the house and members of his family.

Article 59. Modification of a Contract for the Lease of Dwelling Premises

The possibility of the withdrawal in a court of surplus dwelling space (exceeding the established norm) in the form of a separate isolated apartment may be provided for by union republic legislation. In such instances the norm for dwelling space established by union republic legislation may not be less than 9 square meters per person. A norm of supplemental dwelling space also shall be established for individual categories of lessees.

A surplus isolated room in houses of local soviets of working people's deputies may be withdrawn only if the lessee himself does not occupy the released premise within three months after a warning in writing from the housing agency.

If a surplus isolated room is formed in an apartment granted for use to one family, the lessee shall have the right either to occupy it in accordance with the rules of the present Article or to demand resettlement in a separate smaller apartment.

Other instances when the withdrawal of a surplus isolated room is not permitted also may be established by union republic legislation.

If in an apartment in which the lessee resides a room has been vacated which is not isolated from the dwelling premise which he occupies and is adjacent to him, this room shall be subject to transfer to his use.

Article 60. Dissolution of a Contract by a Lessee. Exchange and Sublease of Dwelling Premises

A lessee of dwelling premises shall have the right to dissolve the contract at any time.

A lessee of dwelling premises shall have the right to exchange the premises which he occupies.

The exchange of dwelling premises in houses of state, cooperative, and social organizations, and also in houses belonging to citizens by right of personal ownership, shall be permitted only with the consent of the lessor. The procedure for the exchange of dwelling premises shall be established by union republic legislation.

A lessee may sublease dwelling premises in the instances and procedure established by union republic legislation.

Article 61. Dissolution of a Contract by the Lessor

A contract for the lease of dwelling premises may not be dissolved and a lessee may not be evicted from the dwelling premises he occupies other than in a judicial proceeding (with the exceptions specified in Article 63) and on the grounds established by law.

A lessor should grant other comfortable dwelling premises, except for the instances specified below, to a lessee evicted on the grounds provided by law from a house of the local soviet of working people's deputies or from a house of a state, cooperative, or social organization.

If a lessee or members of his family systematically destroy or damage dwelling premises or systematically violate the rules of socialist community life, making it impossible for others residing with them in one apartment or in a single house, and warnings and measures of social pressure have been without result, the guilty persons shall be evicted without granting other dwelling premises.

The conditions for dissolution of a lease contract without granting other dwelling premises also shall be provided by union republic legislation in instances of the prolonged absence of the lessee and members of his family; in instances when a lessee possesses by right of personal ownership a dwelling house in the same population center which is suitable for permanent residence and it is possible for him to occupy it; and equally in instances of the systematic failure to pay apartment rent by lessees of dwelling premises in houses which belong to citizens by right of personal ownership.

Article 62. Special Instances of Eviction from Houses of Enterprises and Institutions

Lists of enterprises and institutions of the most important branches of the national economy and individual departments from whose houses eviction shall be permitted in a judicial proceeding without granting dwelling space for workers and employees who have ceased labor relations in connection with dismissal at their own wish or for violation of labor discipline or for committing a crime may be established by the USSR Council of Ministers and union republic councils of ministers.

However, disabled war veterans, I and II group labor invalids, old age pensioners, personal pensioners, family of persons in the service of the USSR Armed Forces, and also families of military servicemen and partisans who perished or are missing while defending the USSR or executing other duties of military service, may not be evicted without granting dwelling space in such instances.

Article 63. Administrative Eviction

The eviction of citizens in an administrative proceeding shall not be permitted except for the eviction of persons who have arbitrarily occupied dwelling premises, and also the eviction of lessees from houses threatened with collapse. Other comfortable dwelling premises shall be granted to lessees evicted from houses threatened with collapse.

An administrative procedure for eviction from official premises, dormitories, and hotels may be established by union republic legislation.

Chapter 7. Independent Work Contract

Article 64. Independent Work Contract

By an independent work contract, an independent contractor shall be obliged to fulfill specific work at his own risk under an order of a customer from his or his own materials, and the customer shall be obliged to accept and pay for the work fulfilled.

An independent contractor shall be obliged to take all measures to ensure the preservation of property entrusted to him by the customer and bear responsibility for any omission entailing the loss or damage of such property.

Article 65. Rights of a Customer in the Event of a Breach of the Contract by an Independent Contractor

If an independent contractor allowed deviations from the conditions of the contract which have lowered the quality of the work or permitted other defects in the work, the customer shall have the right at his election to demand: correction of the said defects free of charge within a commensurate period or compensation of necessary expenses borne by the customer for the correction of the defects in the work by his own means if such a right for the customer is provided by the contract or a corresponding reduction in the compensation for the work.

A customer shall have the right to demand dissolution of the contract and compensation for losses if there are material deviations from the contract in the work or other material defects.

Article 66. Rules Concerning Independent Work Contracts for Servicing the Domestic Requirements of Citizens

Rules concerning independent work contracts for servicing the domestic requirements of citizens (domestic order) shall be established by union republic legislation.

Model contracts shall be confirmed by union republic councils of ministers for individual types of services for citizens. Deviations from the conditions of model contracts which limit the rights of customers shall be void.

Chapter 8. Independent Work Contract for Capital Construction

Article 67. Independent Work Contract for Capital Construction

By an independent work contract for capital construction, an independent contractor organization shall be obliged to build with its own efforts and means and to surrender to the customer organization an object provided for by the plan in accordance with confirmed design estimate documentation and within the established period, and the customer shall be obliged to grant to the independent contractor a building site, to transfer the confirmed design estimate documentation to him, to ensure the timely financing of the construction, to accept the objects whose construction is completed, and to pay for them.

The provision of the construction with technological, power, electrotechnical, and general plant equipment and apparatus shall be entrusted to the customer, except for instances provided for by special decrees. The provision of construction materials may be entrusted by special decrees to the customer.

Article 68. General Independent Contractor and Sub-Independent Contractor

An independent work contract for capital construction shall be concluded by a customer with one construction organization and, in the instances and procedure determined by the USSR Council of Ministers, with two or more construction organizations, which shall have the right as the general independent work contractor to entrust the fulfillment of individual units of work to specialized organizations on the basis of a sub-independent work contract (Article 38 of the present Fundamental Principles).

A contract for the fulfillment of work for the assembly of equipment shall be concluded by the customer or with a general independent work contractor or with the supplier of the equipment.

Contracts for the fulfillment of assembly and other special work may, with the consent of the general independent work contractor, be concluded by a customer with assembly or other specialized organizations.

Article 69. Rights of a Customer

A customer shall exercise control and technical supervision over the conformity of the amount, cost, and quality of work fulfilled to the designs and estimates. He shall have the right at any time to verify the course and the quality of construction and assembly work, and also the quality of materials used, without interfering in the operational and economic activity of the independent work contractor.

Defects in the fulfillment of work or materials used for the work which are permitted through the fault of the independent work contractor (or sub-independent work contractor) should be eliminated by the independent work contractor at his own expense.

Article 70. Liability of Parties for Breach of an Independent Work Contract for Capital Construction

For the failure to execute or for the improper execution of duties under an independent work contract for capital construction the liable party shall pay the established penalty (or forfeit), and also compensate losses not covered by the penalty which are reflected in expenditures made by the other party or the loss or damage to its property.

The amount of the penalty (or forfeit) paid by an independent work contractor for breach of the periods for the fulfillment of specific work shall be repaid to the independent work contractor if all the work on the object is completed by the final period established by the contract.

Article 71. Rules on Independent Work Contracts for Capital Construction

Independent work contracts for capital construction shall be concluded and executed in accordance with the rules confirmed by the USSR Council of Ministers or in the procedure established thereby. Special rules on independent work contracts for capital construction on collective farms may be established by union republic legislation.

Chapter 9. Carriage

Article 72. Contract of Carriage

By a contract for the carriage of freight, a transport organization (carrier) shall be obliged to deliver freight entrusted to it by the sender to a destination and issue it to a person authorized to receive the freight (recipient), and the sender shall be obliged to pay the established charge for carriage of the freight.

By a contract for the carriage of a passenger, the carrier shall be obliged to carry a passenger to a destination, and if the passenger brings baggage, also to deliver the baggage to the destination and issue the baggage to a person authorized to receive it; the passenger shall be obliged to pay the established charge for the passage, and if baggage is brought, also for the carriage of the baggage.

Conditions for the carriage of freight, passengers, and baggage and the liability of the parties for such carriage in accordance with the present Fundamental Principles shall be determined by the charters (or codes) for particular types of transport and the rules issued in the established procedure.

Article 73. Plan for Freight Carriage and Liability for the Failure to Fulfill It

A contract for the carriage of freight of state, cooperative, and social organizations shall be concluded on the basis of a carriage plan binding upon both parties.

The conclusion of contracts for the carriage of freight not provided for by plan shall be permitted in the procedure established by transport charters (or codes).

The carrier and sender shall bear financial liability for the failure to supply means of carriage, the failure to submit freight for carriage, and for other breaches of the duties arising from a carriage plan, and equally for such breaches in the instances provided for by paragraph two of the present Article.

Article 74. Liability of a Carrier for Loss, Shortage, or Damage to Freight or Baggage

A carrier shall be liable for loss, shortage, and damage to freight and baggage accepted for carriage unless it is proved that the loss, shortage, or damage occurred not by his fault (Article 37 of the present Fundamental Principles).

Instances may be provided in transport charters (or codes) when proof of the fault of a carrier in the loss, shortage, or damage of freight is imposed on the recipient or sender.

Article 75. Period for Delivery of Freight and Baggage and Liability for Delay

A carrier shall be obliged to deliver freight or baggage to the destination within the period established by transport charters (or codes) or by rules issued in the established procedure. If the period for delivery in the said procedure has not been established, the parties shall have the right to establish the period in the contract.

A carrier shall be released from liability for delay in the delivery of freight or baggage if the delay occurred not by its fault.

Article 76. Claims and Suits Relating to Carriage

Before filing suit against a carrier arising out of carriage, it shall be obligatory to file a claim.

Claims may be filed within six months, and claims concerning the payment of fines and bonuses, within 45 days. A carrier shall be obliged to consider a claim filed and to inform the claimant about its satisfaction or rejection within three months, and with respect to claims for carriage effectuated by carriers of different types under a single document, within six months, and claims concerning the payment of a fine or bonus, within 45 days.

If a claim is rejected or a reply is not received within the period established by the present Article, the claimant shall be allowed to file suit two months from the date of receiving the reply or from the expiry of the period established for reply.

A six-month period shall be established for a carrier to file suit arising from carriages against senders, recipients, or passengers.

Periods of limitation of actions and the procedure for filing suits regarding disputes connected with carriages on foreign transport shall be established by transport charters (or codes) or international agreements.

Article 77. Liability of a Carrier for Causing Death or Injury to the Health of a Passenger

The liability of a carrier for causing death or damage to the health of a passenger shall be determined according to the rules of Chapter 12 of the present section, unless higher liability is provided for by law.

Chapter 10. State Insurance

Article 78. Types of Insurance

State insurance shall be effectuated in the form of compulsory or voluntary insurance.

Article 79. Compulsory Insurance

Property shall be subject to compulsory insurance which is specified in a law on the conditions established therein.

Under compulsory insurance, an insurance organization shall, if the event provided for by law happens (insured event), pay the insured or other person to whom the property belongs the damage which he has incurred; if the property is a complete loss, the full amount of the insurance protection, and if the damage is partial, in the amount of the respective portion of the insurance protection. The insured shall be obliged to make the established insurance payments.

The types of compulsory personal insurance shall be established by USSR legislation.

Article 80. Voluntary Insurance Contract

By a voluntary insurance contract, an insurance organization shall, if the event specified in the contract happens (insured event), be obliged:

under property insurance: to compensate the insured or other person to whose benefit the contract has been concluded for the damage incurred (or to pay insurance compensation) within the limits of the amount stipulated under the contract (insured amount), and when property has not been insured for the full value, the corresponding portion of the damage unless otherwise provided for by insurance rules;

under personal insurance: to pay the insured or other person to whose benefit the contract has been concluded the insured amount stipulated under the contract irrespective of amounts due him under state social insurance, social security, or amounts due by way of compensation for damage.

The insured shall be obliged to make the insurance payments established by the contract.

Article 81. Transfer to an Insurance Organization of Rights of an Insured with Respect to a Person Liable for the Damage Caused

The right of action which an insured (or other person who has received insurance compensation) has against the person liable for the damage caused shall pass within the limits of this amount to the insurance organization which paid insurance compensation under property insurance.

Article 82. Insurance Rules

Insurance Rules shall be confirmed in the procedure established by the USSR Council of Ministers.

Chapter 11. Accounts and Credit Relations

Article 83. Accounts Between Organizations

Payments under obligations between state organizations, collective farms, and other cooperative and social organizations shall be made in the procedure of non-cash accounts through credit institutions in which the said organizations in accordance with law keep their cash assets. The procedure and forms for accounts shall be determined by USSR legislation.

Cash accounts between state organizations, collective farms, and other cooperative and social organizations shall be permitted in the instances and within the limits established by USSR legislation.

Article 84. Disposal of Cash Assets Kept in Accounts of Organizations at Credit Institutions

Organizations shall dispose of cash assets kept in their accounts at credit institutions in accordance with the special purpose of these assets.

Assets needed for payment of wages and payments equivalent thereto shall be issued from the account of the organization irrespective of the existence of any claim against the possessor of the account. Exceptions from this rule may be established by the USSR Council of Ministers.

The writing off of assets in its account in a credit institution without the consent of the organization shall be permitted only in the instances provided for by USSR legislation.

The priority established by USSR legislation shall be observed when satisfying claims.

Article 85. Credit for Organizations

Credit for state organizations, collective farms, and other cooperative and social organizations shall be according to confirmed plans through the issuance of special time loans by the USSR State Bank and other USSR banks in the procedure established by USSR legislation.

Credit by one organization to another in kind or in cash, including the issuance of advance payments, shall be permitted only in the instances established by USSR legislation.

The conditions and procedure for credit by one collective farm to another when rendering production assistance shall be established by union republic legislation.

Article 86. Bank Loans to Citizens

Loans to citizens shall be issued by USSR banks in the instances and procedure established by USSR legislation.

Article 87. Deposits of Citizens in Credit Institutions

Citizens may keep cash assets in state labor savings banks and in other credit institutions, dispose of deposits, receive income for deposits in the form of interest or prizes, and make non-cash accounts in accordance with the charters of credit institutions and rules issued in the established procedure.

The state shall guarantee the secrecy of deposits, their safekeeping, and their issuance at the first demand of the depositer.

The procedure for the disposal of deposits made in state labor savings banks and in other credit institutions shall be determined by their charters and specified in the rules of paragraph one of the present Article.

Execution may be levied on deposits of citizens in state labor savings banks and in the USSR State Bank on the basis of a judgment or decision of a court by which a civil suit has been satisfied which arose out of a criminal case, or a court decision in a suit for recovery of alimony (in the absence of earnings or other property on which execution may be levied) or for a division of a deposit which is the joint property of spouses. Deposits of citizens in the said credit institutions may be deposited on the basis of a judgment which has entered into legal force or a decree concerning the confiscation of property rendered in accordance with the law.

Chapter 12. Obligations Arising as a Consequence of Causing Harm

Article 88. General Bases of Liability for Causing Harm

Harm caused to the person or property of a citizen, as well as harm caused to organizations, shall be subject to compensation in full by the person who has caused the harm.

One who has caused harm shall be relieved from compensating it if he proves that the harm was caused not by his fault.

Harm caused by lawful actions shall be subject to compensation only in the instances provided for by law.

Article 89. Liability of State Institutions for Harm Caused by Actions of Their Officials

State institutions shall be liable for harm caused to citizens by the improper official actions of their officials in the domain of administrative management on the general bases (Article 88 of the present Fundamental Principles) unless otherwise provided by a special law. State institutions shall be liable in the procedure established by law for harm caused by such actions of officials to organizations.

The respective state agencies shall bear financial liability in the instances and within the limits specially provided for by law for harm caused by the improper official actions of officials of agencies of inquiry, preliminary investigation, the procuracy, and court.

Article 90. Liability for Harm Caused by a Source of Increased Danger

Organizations and citizens whose activity is connected with an increased danger for surrounding persons (transport organizations, industrial enterprises, construction sites, owners of automobiles, etc.) shall be obliged to compensate harm caused by a source of increased danger unless it is proved that the harm arose as a consequence of insuperable force or the intention of the victim.

Article 91. Liability for Injury to Health and for Death of a Citizen for Whom the Person Who Has Caused the Harm is Obliged to Pay Insurance Premiums

If a worker in connection with the performance by him of his labor (or official) duties is caused mutilation or other injury to health by the fault of the organization or citizen obliged to pay premiums for state social insurance for him, this organization or citizen should compensate the victim for the harm in that part exceeding the amount of benefit received by him or assigned to him after the injury to his health and the pension actually received by him. Exceptions from this rule may be established by USSR legislation.

In the event of the death of the victim, the right to compensation for harm shall appertain to persons unable to work who were dependent on the deceased or had on the date of his death the right to receive support from him, as well as a child of the deceased born after his death.

Article 92. Liability for Injury to Health and Death of a Citizen for Whom the Person Who Has Caused the Harm is Not Obliged to Pay Insurance Premiums

If mutilation or other injury to health is caused to a citizen who is subject to state social insurance by an organization or citizen not obliged to pay for the victim's premiums under state social insurance, this organization or citizen should compensate the victim for the harm according to the rules of Articles 88 and 90 of the present Fundamental Principles in that part exceeding the amount of benefits received by him or the pension assigned to him after the injury to his health and in fact received by him.

In the event of the death of the victim, the right of compensation for harm shall appertain to the persons specified in the second paragraph of Article 91 of the present Fundamental Principles.

Article 93. Taking Account of the Fault of the Victim and Financial Status of the Person Who Caused the Harm

If the gross negligence of the victim himself facilitated the origin or the aggravation of the harm, then depending on the extent of the victim's fault (and if the person who caused the harm is at fault, also depending upon the extent of his fault), the amount of compensation unless otherwise provided for by a law of the USSR should be reduced or compensation of the harm should be refused.

A court may reduce the amount of compensation for harm caused by a citizen, depending on his financial status.

Article 94. Indemnification Actions

An organization or citizen liable for causing harm shall be obliged under an indemnification action of an agency of state social insurance or social security to compensate the amount of a grant or pension which has been paid to persons specified in Articles 91 and 92 of the present Fundamental Principles.

In instances of reducing the amount of compensation for harm (Article 93 of the present Fundamental Principles), the amount of compensation under an indemnification action also shall be reduced correspondingly.

Chapter 13. Obligations Arising as a Consequence of Saving Socialist Property

Article 95. Compensation of Harm Sustained When Saving Socialist Property

Harm sustained by a citizen when saving socialist property from a danger threatening it should be compensated by that organization whose property was saved by the victim.

The procedure for compensation of harm shall be established by union republic legislation.

Section IV. Copyright

Article 96. Works to Which Copyright Extends

Copyright shall extend to works of science, literature, or art irrespective of the form, purpose, or value of the work, and also of the means of reproducing it.

Copyright shall extend to works, published or unpublished, but expressed in some objective form which permits reproduction of the result of the creative activity of the author (manuscript, drawing, picture, public recital or performance, film; mechanical or magnetic recording, etc.).

Article 97. Copyright on Works Published on the Territory of the USSR and Abroad

Copyright on a work published for the first time on the territory of the USSR or not published but situate on the territory of the USSR in some objective form shall be recognized for the author and his heirs irrespective of their citizenship, and also for other legal successors of the author.

Copyright shall be recognized also for citizens of the USSR whose works are published for the first time or are situate in some objective form on the territory of a foreign state, and equally for their legal successors.

Copyright in a work first published or situate in some objective form on the territory of a foreign state shall be recognized for other persons in accordance with international treaties or international agreements in which the USSR participates.

Copyright shall be recognized on the territory of the USSR for foreign legal successors of authors who are citizens of the USSR if this right is transferred to them in the procedure established by USSR legislation.

Article 98. Rights of an Author

The right belongs to an author:

to publish, reproduce, and disseminate his work by all means permitted by law under his own name, under an assumed name (or pseudonym), or without an indication of name (anonymously);

to the integrity of the work;

to receive remuneration for use of the work by other persons except for instances specified in law. Rates of an author's remuneration shall be established by USSR and union republic legislation.

The procedure for an author who is a citizen of the USSR to transfer the right to use his work on the territory of a foreign state shall be established by USSR legislation.

Article 99. Co-authorship

Copyright on a work created by the joint labor of two or more persons (collective work) shall belong to the co-authors jointly irrespective of whether this work forms an integral whole or consists of parts, each of which also has independent significance. Each co-author shall retain his copyright in the part of a collective work having independent significance which he created.

Article 100. Copyright of Juridical Persons. Copyright in a Work Created by Way of Fulfilling an Official Task

Copyright shall be recognized for juridical persons in the instances and within the limits established by USSR and union republic legislation.

Copyright shall belong to an author of a work created by way of fulfilling an official task in a scientific or other organization. The procedure for the use of such a work by the organization and instances for the payment of remuneration to the author shall be established by USSR and union republic legislation.

Article 101. Use of an Author's Work by Other Persons

The use of an author's work (including translation into another language) by other persons shall be permitted not otherwise than on the basis of a contract with the author or his legal successors, except for instances specified in law.

Model contracts concerning the use of a work (publisher's, public performance, scenario, and other authors' contracts) shall be confirmed in the procedure established by USSR and union republic legislation.

Conditions of a contract concluded with an author which worsen his position in comparison with the position established in a law or a model contract shall be void and replaced by the conditions established by law or the model contract.

Article 102. Translation of a Work into Another Language

The translation of a work into another language with a view to publication shall be permitted not otherwise than with the consent of the author or his legal successors.

Competent agencies of the USSR may authorize, in the procedure established by USSR legislation, the translation of a work into another language and the publication of this translation, observing as appropriate the conditions of international treaties or international agreements in which the USSR participates.

Copyright shall belong to the translator in the translation which he has fulfilled.

Article 103. Use of a Work Without the Consent of an Author and Without Payment of Royalties

There shall be permitted without the consent of the author and without payment of royalties, but with the obligatory specification of the surname of the author whose work is used and the source from which it was borrowed:

(1) the use of another's published work for the creation of a new, creatively independent work, except for reworking a narrative work in dramatic or scenario form, and vice versa, and also reworking a dramatic work into a scenario and vice versa;

(2) the reproduction in scientific and critical works, textbooks, and political-enlightenment publications of individual published works of science, literature, and art of selections therefrom within the limits established by union republic legislation;

(3) information in the periodical press, film, radio, and television concerning published works of literature, science, and art;

(4) the reproduction in film, radio, and television of publicly delivered speeches, reports, and also published works of literature, science, and art;

(5) the reproduction in newspapers of publicly delivered speeches, reports, and also published works of literature, science, and art in the original or translation;

(6) the reproduction by any method, except mechanical contract copying, of works of decorative art situate in places open to the public, except for exhibitions and museums;

(7) the reproducing of printed works for scientific, textbook, and enlightenment purposes without deriving profits;

(8) the publication of published works in braille for the blind.

Article 104. Use of a Work Without the Consent of the Author and With Payment of Royalties

There shall be permitted without the consent of the author, but specifying his surname and payment of a royalty:

(1) the public performance of published works; however, if a payment from visitors is not recovered, an author shall have a right to remuneration only in the instances established by union republic legislation;

(2) the recording of works with a view to public reproduction or circulation of published works on film, record, magnetic tape, or other equipment except for the use of the work on film, radio, or television (Article 103, point 4, of the present Fundamental Principles);

(3) the use by a composer of published literary works to create musical works with a text;

(4) the use of works of decorative art, and also photographic works, on industrial articles; in such instances specifiying the author's surname is not obligatory.

Article 105. Period of Validity of Copyright

A copyright shall be valid throughout the entire life of the author and for twenty-five years after his death, commencing from January 1st of the year following the year of the author's death.

Shorter periods for the validity of copyright on photographic works and decorative art works may be established by union republic legislation. These periods may not be less than 10 years from the time such a work is published by way of reproduction.

A copyright shall pass by inheritance. If there is a shorter period for the validity of copyright, it shall pass to the heirs for the unexpired portion of the period before the author's death.

A group of author's rights which do not pass by inheritance shall be established by union republic legislation.

Article 106. Purchase of Copyright by the State

Copyright in a publication, public performance, or other use of a work may be compulsorily purchased by the state from an author or his heirs in the procedure established by union republic legislation.

Section V. Law of Discovery

Article 107. Rights of a Discoverer

A discoverer shall have the right to demand recognition of his authorship and priority in a discovery certified by a diploma which shall be issued in the instances and in the procedure provided for by the Statute on Discoveries, Inventions, and Rationalization Proposals confirmed by the USSR Council of Ministers.

A discoverer shall have the right to remuneration paid him when receiving the diploma, and also to the benefits provided by the Statute on Discoveries, Inventions, and Rationalization Proposals.

Article 108. Transfer of Rights of Discoverer by Inheritance

The right of a deceased discoverer to receive a diploma, and also remuneration for a discovery, shall pass by inheritance in the procedure established by law.

Article 109. Disputes Concerning Authorship of a Discovery

Disputes concerning the authorship (or co-authorship) of a discovery shall be decided by a court.

Section VI. Law of Invention

Article 110. Author's Certificate and Patent

An author of an invention may at his election demand either recognition solely of his authorship or recognition of authorship and the granting to him of the exclusive right to the invention. In the first case an author's certificate shall be issued for the invention; in the second case, a patent. Authors' certificates and patents shall be issued on the conditions and in the procedure provided for by the Statute on Discoveries, Inventions, and Rationalization Proposals.

The patenting abroad of inventions made within the limits of the USSR and of inventions made abroad by Soviet citizens, as well as any transfer of Soviet inventions abroad, shall be permitted only in the procedure established by the USSR Council of Ministers.

Article 111. Use of an Invention for Which an Author's Certificate Has Been Issued

In those instances when an author's certificate has been issued for an invention, the right to use the invention shall belong to the state, which shall assume the concern for realizing the invention, taking into account the advisability of introducing it.

Cooperative and social organizations may on an equal basis with state organizations use inventions relating to the area of their activity.

An inventor to whom an author's certificate has been issued shall, if his invention is used, have the right to remuneration depending on the economies or other positive effect derived as a result of introducing the invention, and also the right to the benefits in accordance with the Statute on Discoveries, Inventions, and Rationalization Proposals.

Article 112. Rights of a Patentee

A patent shall be issued for a period of fifteen years, calculated from the date the application was filed. The rights of the applicant shall be protected from the same date. No one may use the invention without the consent of the person to whom the patent (patentee) belongs. The patentee may issue a permit (or license) to use his invention or completely assign the patent.

An organization which before an application for an invention has been filed independently of the inventor has used the particular invention within the limits of the USSR or made all preparations necessary to do so shall retain the right to future use of the particular invention free of charge. Disputes regarding this question shall be settled in a judicial proceeding.

In those instances when an invention has specially important significance for a state but agreement is not reached with the patentee for an assignment of the patent or the issuance of a license, by decision of the USSR Council of Ministers the patent may be compulsorily purchased by the state or permission to use the invention may be given to the respective organization, establishing remuneration for the patentee.

Article 113. Rights of the Author of a Rationalization Proposal

A certificate establishing authorship shall be issued to the author of a rationalization proposal accepted for introduction. He shall have the right to remuneration, depending on the economies or other positive effect obtained as a result of introducing the proposal, and also the right to the benefits in accordance with the Statute on Discoveries, Inventions, and Rationalization Proposals.

Article 114. Participation of an Inventor and Rationalizer in Introducing a Proposal

Inventors and rationalizers should actively promote the introduction and further development of their proposals and shall have the right to participate in effectuating work relating to the introduction of these proposals in the procedure provided for by the Statute on Discoveries, Inventions, and Rationalization Proposals.

Article 115. Transfer of the Rights of the Author of an Invention or Rationalization Proposal by Inheritance

The right to receive an author's certificate or patent for an invention, a certificate for a rationalization proposal, and remuneration for an invention or rationalization proposal, and also the exclusive right to an invention based on a patent shall pass by inheritance in the procedure established by law.

Article 116. Disputes Concerning Authorship and Payment of Remuneration

Disputes concerning authorship (or co-authorship) of an invention shall be settled by a court. Disputes concerning the priority of a rationalization proposal also shall be settled by a court, unless they have been settled at the organization at the place where the proposal is introduced.

Disputes relating to questions of the amount, procedure for computing, and periods for payment of remuneration for an invention or rationalization proposal shall be settled in the procedure provided for by the Statute on Discoveries, Inventions, and Rationalization Proposals; the inventor or rationalizer may have recourse to a court if the decision adopted is considered to be incorrect.

Section VII. Law of Inheritance

Article 117. The Bases of Inheritance

Inheritance shall be effectuated by operation of law and by will.

Inheritance by operation of law shall take place when and insofar as it has not been altered by will.

If there are no heirs either by operation of law or by will, or if none of the heirs has accepted the inheritance, or if all heirs have been disinherited by the testator, the property of the deceased shall pass to the state by right of succession.

Article 118. Inheritance by Operation of Law

In the event of inheritance by operation of law, the heirs of the first class, in equal shares, shall be the children (including adopted children), the spouse, and parents (or adoptive parents) of the deceased. A child of the deceased born after his death also shall be an heir of the first class.

The grandchildren and great-grandchildren of the testator shall be heirs by operation of law if at the time of the opening of the inheritance none of their parents are living who would be an heir; they shall inherit in equal share that which their deceased parent would have received in the event of an inheritance by operation of law.

The legislation of the union republics may designate additional groups of heirs by operation of law. Heirs of this additional class shall inherit by operation of law only if there are no heirs belonging to the preceding class or in the event of their failure to accept the inheritance.

Among the heirs by operation of law shall be disabled persons who were dependent on the deceased for not less than one year before his death. If there were other heirs, they shall inherit equally with heirs of the class entitled to inherit.

Articles of ordinary household furnishings or use shall pass to heirs by operation of law who live together with the decedent irrespective of their class or their share of the inheritance. The terms of the inheritance of such property shall be determined by union republic legislation.

Article 119. Inheritance by Will

Every citizen may leave all of his property or part thereof by will (including articles of ordinary household furnishing or use) to one or several persons, either within or not within the group of heirs by operation of law, as well as to the state or to individual state, cooperative, or social organizations.

Minors or disabled children of the decedent (including adopted children), as well as the spouse, the parents (or adoptive parents), and dependents of the deceased who are unable to work, shall inherit, irrespective of the content of the will, not less than two-thirds of the share which would have been due each of them in the event of inheritance by operation of law (statutory share). In determining the amount of the statutory share, the value of the estate property consisting of articles of ordinary household furnishings or use also shall be taken into account.

The procedure for the disposition, in the event of death, of deposits in state savings banks or in the USSR State Bank according to the special instructions of the depositers shall be determined by the statutes of the said financial institutions issued in accordance with the established procedure.

Article 120. Liability of Heir for Debts of Decedent

An heir who has accepted an inheritance shall be liable for debts of the decedent within the limits of the actual value of the estate property which has passed to him. The state shall be liable on the same bases for property which has passed in the procedure of Articles 117 and 119 of the present Fundamental Principles.

Article 121. Place of Opening an Inheritance

The place of opening an inheritance shall be deemed the last permanent place of residence of the decedent, and if it is unknown, the place where the property or the principal part thereof is located.

Section VIII. Legal Capacity of Foreigners and Stateless Persons. Application of Civil Laws of Foreign States, International Treaties and Agreements

Article 122. Civil Legal Capacity of Foreign Citizens

Foreign citizens shall enjoy civil law capacity in the USSR equally with Soviet citizens. Individual exceptions may be established by USSR law.

Reciprocal limitations may be established by the USSR Council of Ministers in respect of citizens of those states in which there are special limitations on the civil law capacity of Soviet citizens.

Article 123. Civil Law Capacity of Stateless Persons

Stateless persons shall enjoy civil law capacity in the USSR on an equal basis with Soviet citizens. Individual exceptions may be established by the law of the USSR.

Article 123-1. Law Applicable to Civil Dispositive Capacity of Foreign Citizens and Stateless Persons

The civil dispositive capacity of a foreign citizen shall be determined by the law of the country of which he is a citizen.

The civil law capacity of a stateless person shall be determined by the law of the country in which he has a permanent place of residence.

The civil dispositive capacity of foreign citizens and stateless persons with respect to legal transactions performed in the USSR and obligations arising as a consequence of the causing of harm in the USSR shall be determined according to Soviet law.

Foreign citizens and stateless persons permanently residing in the USSR may be deemed not to have dispositive capacity or to have a limited dispositive capacity in the procedure established by legislation of the USSR and respective union republic.

Article 124. Civil Legal Capacity of Foreign Enterprises and Organizations

Foreign enterprises and organizations may, without special authorization, perform legal transactions in the USSR relating to foreign trade and to accounts connected therewith, insurance, and other operations with Soviet foreign trade combines and other Soviet organizations which have been granted the right to perform such legal transactions.

The civil law capacity of foreign enterprises and organizations when performing legal transactions relating to foreign trade and to accounts connected therewith, insurance, and other operations shall be determined by the law of the country where the enterprise or organization was founded.

Article 125. Law Applicable to the Form of a Legal Transaction

The form of a legal transaction performed abroad shall be subordinate to the law of the place where it is performed. However, a legal transaction may not be deemed void as a consequence of the failure to observe the form if the requirements of legislation of the USSR and respective union republic have been observed.

The form of foreign trade transactions performed by Soviet organizations and the procedure for signing them, irrespective of the place where these legal transactions are performed, shall be determined by USSR legislation.

The form of legal transactions relating to structures situated in the USSR shall be subordinate to legislation of the USSR and respective union republic.

Article 126. Law Applicable to Obligations Relating to Foreign Trade Transactions

The rights and duties of the parties under a foreign trade transaction shall be determined by the laws of the place where it is performed unless otherwise established by agreement of the parties.

The origin and termination of the right of ownership in an article under a foreign trade transaction shall be determined by the law of the place where it is performed unless otherwise established by agreement of the parties.

The right of ownership in an article en route under a foreign trade transaction shall be determined by the law of the country from which this article was sent unless otherwise established by agreement of the parties.

The place where a legal transaction is performed shall be determined according to Soviet law.

Article 126-1. Law Applicable to the Form and Period of Validity of a Power of Attorney

The form and period of validity of a power of attorney shall be determined according to the law of the country where the power of attorney was issued. However, a power of attorney may not be deemed void as a consequence of the failure to observe the form if the latter satisfies the requirements of Soviet law.

Article 126-2. Law Applicable to Limitation of Actions

Limitation of actions shall be determined according to the law of the country whose legislation is applied to determine the rights and duties of the participants of the respective legal relation.

Actions to which a limitation of actions does not extend shall be determined according to Soviet legislation.

Article 126-3. Law Applicable to the Right of Ownership

The right of ownership in an article shall be determined according to the law of the country where this article is situated.

The origin and termination of the right of ownership in an article shall be determined according to the law of the country where this article was situated at the time when the action or other circumstance serving as the basis for the origin or termination of the right of ownership took place unless otherwise provided by USSR and union republic legislation.

Article 126-4. Law Applicable to Obligations Arising as a Consequence of Causing Harm

The rights and duties of parties in regard to obligations arising as a consequence of causing harm shall be determined according to the law of the country where the action or other circumstance serving as the basis for an action concerning compensation of harm took place.

The rights and duties of the parties in regard to obligations arising as a consequence of causing harm abroad, if the parties are Soviet citizens or Soviet organizations, shall be determined according to Soviet law.

Foreign law shall not be applied if the action or other circumstance serving as the basis for an action concerning compensation of harm is not unlawful according to Soviet legislation.

Article 127. Law Applicable to Inheritance

Relations relating to inheritance shall be determined by the law of the country where the decedent had his last permanent place of residence.

The capacity of a person to draw up and revoke a will, as well as the form of the will and act of revocation, shall be determined by the law of the country where the testator had a permanent place of residence at the time the act was drawn up. However, the will or its revocation may not be deemed void as a consequence of the failure to observe the form if the latter satisfies the requirements of the law of the place where the act was drawn up or the requirements of Soviet law.

The inheritance of structures situated in the USSR shall be determined in all instances by Soviet law. The capacity of a person to draw up or revoke a will, as well as the form of the latter if a structure situated in the USSR is bequeathed, shall be determined by the same law.

Article 128. Limitation of the Application of Foreign Law

Foreign law shall not be applied if its application would be contrary to the bases of the Soviet system.

Article 129. International Treaties and Agreements

If other rules have been established by an international treaty or international agreement in which the USSR participates than those which are contained in Soviet civil legislation, the rules of the international treaty or international agreement shall be applied.

The same situation shall apply on the territory of a union republic if other rules have been established in an international treaty or international agreement in which the union republic participates than those provided for by the union republic civil legislation.

FUNDAMENTAL PRINCIPLES OF CIVIL PROCEDURE OF THE USSR AND UNION REPUBLICS

[Confirmed by Law of the USSR Supreme Soviet, December 8, 1961, as amended August 7, 1972, and May 16, 1977. Vedomosti SSSR (1961), no. 50, item 526; (1972), no. 33, item 289; (1977), no. 21, item 313]

Section I. General Provisions

Article 1. Legislation on Civil Procedure

The procedure for proceeding in civil cases shall be determined by the present Fundamental Principles and other USSR laws issued in accordance therewith and the union republic codes of civil procedure.

Legislation on civil procedure shall establish the procedure for considering cases in disputes arising from civil, family, labor, and collective farm legal relations, cases arising from administrative legal relations, and cases of special procedure. Cases arising from administrative legal relations and cases of special procedure shall be considered in accordance with the general rules of procedure, with individual exceptions established by USSR and union republic legislation.

Article 2. Tasks of Civil Procedure

The tasks of Soviet civil procedure shall be the proper and speedy consideration and settlement of civil cases with a view to protecting the social and state system of the USSR, the socialist system of economy and socialist ownership, the protection of political, labor, housing, and other personal and property rights and interests of citizens protected by law, and also the rights and interests protected by law of state institutions, enterprises, collective farms, and other cooperative and social organizations.

Civil procedure should further the strengthening of socialist legality, the prevention of violations of law, and the nurturing of citizens in a spirit of undeviating execution of Soviet laws and respect for the rules of socialist community life.

Article 3. Procedure for Proceedings in Civil Cases

Proceedings in civil cases shall be conducted in union republic courts according to the civil procedure laws of the USSR and that union republic whose courts are considering the case, or performing individual procedural actions, or are executing a court decision.

Proceedings in civil cases in the USSR Supreme Court shall be conducted according to the civil procedure laws of the USSR and that union republic whose court has considered or should have considered the case in accordance with the rules of territorial jurisdiction.

Proceedings in civil cases shall be conducted according to civil procedural laws prevailing at the time the case is considered, the individual procedural actions are performed, or a court decision is executed.

Article 4. Civil Cases Within the Jurisdiction of Judicial Agencies

Cases concerning disputes arising from civil, family, labor, and collective farm legal relations shall be within the jurisdiction of courts if one of the parties to the dispute is a citizen, collective farm, or intercollective farm organization, except for instances when the settlement of such disputes is relegated by law to the jurisdiction of administrative or other agencies.

In the instances provided for by law, civil cases may be considered by comrades' courts. The procedure for the activity of comrades' courts shall be established by union republic legislation.

Cases concerning appeals against the irregularity of voter lists, against the actions of administrative agencies in connection with the imposition of a fine, and other cases arising from administrative legal relations relegated to the competence of judicial agencies by law shall be within the jurisdiction of courts.

Cases of special procedure shall be within the jurisdiction of courts: concerning the establishment of facts having legal significance unless another procedure is provided for by law for establishing them, concerning the deeming of a citizen to be missing or declaring him deceased, or deeming a citizen to lack dispositive legal capacity as a consequence of mental illness or feeble-mindedness.

Other cases relegated by law to the competence of judicial agencies also shall be within the jurisdiction of courts.

Courts also shall consider cases in which foreign citizens, stateless persons, foreign enterprises, and organizations participate.

Article 5. The Right to Apply to a Court for Judicial Protection

Any interested person shall have the right, in the procedure established by law, to apply to a court for the protection of a right violated or contested or of an interest protected by law.

Renunciation of the right to apply to a court shall be void.

Article 6. Initiation of a Civil Case in Court

A court shall commence to consider a civil case upon:

(1) the application of a person applying for the protection of his right or of an interest protected by law;

(2) the application of a procurator;

(3) the application of agencies of state administration, trade unions, state institutions, enterprises, collective farms and other cooperative and social organizations, or individual citizens in the instances when by law they may apply to a court for protection of the rights and interests of other persons.

Article 7. Effectuation of Justice Only by a Court and on the Basis of Equality of Citizens Before the Law and Court

Justice in civil cases shall be effectuated only by a court and on the basis of equality before the law and court of all citizens, irrespective of their social, property, and official status, national or racial affiliation, or confession of faith.

Article 8. Participation of People's Assessors and Collegiality in the Consideration of Cases

Civil cases in all courts shall be considered by judges and people's assessors elected in the procedure established by law.

Civil cases in all courts of first instance shall be considered by a judge and two people's assessors.

People's assessors shall enjoy equal rights with the person presiding at the judicial session in deciding all questions arising during the consideration of the case and decreeing of the decision.

Consideration of cases by way of cassation shall be carried out by courts composed of three members of the court, and by way of judicial supervision, composed of at least three members of the court.

Article 9. Independence of Judges and Their Subordination Only to Law

When effectuating justice in civil cases, judges and people's assessors shall be independent and subordinate only to law. Judges and people's assessors shall decide civil cases on the basis of law and in accordance with socialist legal consciousness in conditions excluding outside influence on the judges.

Article 10. Language in Which a Proceeding is Conducted

A proceeding shall be conducted in the language of a union or autonomous republic, or autonomous region, and in the instances provided by union or autonomous republic constitutions, in the language of the national area or in the language of the majority of the local populace.

Persons who do not have command of the language in which a proceeding is conducted shall be ensured the right to make applications, give explanations, and testimony, speak in court, and file petitions in their native language, and also to use the services of an interpreter in the procedure established by law.

Judicial documents shall, in accordance with the procedure established by law, be handed over to persons participating in a case in a translation into their native language or in another language of which they have command.

Article 11. Publicity of Judicial Examination

Examination of cases in all courts shall be open, except for instances when this is contrary to the interests of protecting state secrecy.

A closed judicial session shall, in addition, be allowed by a reasoned court ruling for the purpose of preventing the disclosure of information about the intimate aspects of the life of those persons participating in the case.

Decisions of courts in all instances shall be announced publicly.

Article 12. Settlement of Cases on the Basis of Prevailing Legislation

A court shall be obliged to settle cases on the basis of laws of the USSR and the union and autonomous republics, edicts of the Presidium of the USSR Supreme Soviet and the presidiums of the union and autonomous republic supreme soviets, and decrees of the highest agencies of state administration of the USSR and the union and autonomous republics. The court also shall apply acts issued by other agencies of state power and administration within the limits of the competence granted to them.

The court shall apply norms of foreign law in accordance with the law.

In the absence of a law regulating a relation in dispute, the court shall apply the law regulating similar relations, and in the absence of such a law, the court shall proceed from the general principles and meaning of Soviet legislation.

Article 13. Supervision of the USSR Supreme Court and the Union and Autonomous Republic Supreme Courts Over Judicial Activity

The USSR Supreme Court shall exercise supervision over the judicial activity of judicial agencies of the USSR and also of union republic judicial agencies, within the limits established by law.

Union republic supreme courts and autonomous republic supreme courts shall exercise supervision over the activity of judicial agencies of the respective republics.

Article 14. Procuracy Supervision in Civil Proceeding

Supervision over the exact execution of the laws of the USSR and the union and autonomous republics in a civil proceeding shall be exercised by the USSR Procurator General both directly and through the procurators subordinate to him.

A procurator shall be obliged at all stages of a civil proceeding to take, in a timely way, the measures provided by law to eliminate any violations of the law from wherever such violations emanate.

A procurator shall exercise his powers in a civil proceeding independently of any agencies or officials, being subordinate only to law and being guided by instructions of the USSR Procurator General.

Article 15. Binding Nature of Decisions, Rulings, and Decrees of a Court

A decision, ruling, or decree of a court which has entered into legal force shall be binding upon all state institutions, enterprises, collective farms, and other cooperative and social organizations, officials, and citizens and shall be subject to execution on the entire territory of the USSR.

The binding nature of a decision, ruling, or decree shall not deprive interested persons of the possibility of applying to a court for protection of the rights and the interests protected by law, the dispute concerning which has not been considered and settled by a court.

Article 16. Elucidation by a Court of the Actual Facts of a Case and the Rights and Duties of the Parties

The court shall be obliged, without limiting itself to the materials and explanations submitted, to take all measures provided by law for an all-round, complete, and objective elucidation of the actual facts of a case and the rights and duties of the parties.

The court should explain to the persons participating in the case their rights and duties and warn them about the consequences of the performance or the failure to perform procedural actions and render assistance to persons participating in the case in carrying out their rights.

Article 17. Evidence

Any factual data on the basis of which a court shall, in the procedure determined by law, establish the existence or the absence of facts supporting the claims or objections of the parties and other facts having significance for the proper settlement of the case shall be evidence in a civil case.

Such data shall be established by the following means: explanations of the parties or third persons, witness testimony, documentary evidence, real evidence, and opinions of experts.

The facts of the case which by law should be confirmed by specified means of proof may not be confirmed by any other means of proof.

Article 18. Duty of Proof and Submission of Evidence

Each party should prove those facts to which they refer both on the basis of their claims and their objections.

Evidence shall be submitted by the parties and other persons participating in the case. If the evidence submitted is inadequate, the court shall propose to the parties and other persons participating in the case to submit additional evidence or collect it at their initiative.

Article 19. Evaluation of Evidence

The court shall evaluate evidence according to its own inner conviction based on an all-round, complete, and objective consideration in a judicial session of all the facts of the case in their aggregate, being guided by law and socialist legal consciousness.

No evidence shall have any previously established weight for a court.

Article 20. Judicial Commissions

A court considering a case shall, if it is necessary to collect evidence in another city or district, commission the appropriate court to carry out the particular procedural actions.

Protocols and all materials collected when fulfilling a commission shall be sent immediately to the court considering the case.

Article 21. The Binding Nature of a Judgment for a Court Considering a Civil Case

The judgment of a court which has entered into legal force in a criminal case shall be binding for a court considering a case concerning the civil law consequences of the actions of a person with respect to which there is the court judgment or relating to questions of whether the actions took place or whether the particular person committed them.

Article 22. Challenge of Judge, Procurator, and Other Participants in a Trial

A judge, people's assessor, procurator, secretary of a judicial session, expert, or interpreter may not participate in the consideration of a case and shall be subject to challenge if they personally, directly or indirectly, are interested in the outcome of the case or there are other circumstances giving rise to doubt as to their impartiality.

Article 23. Judicial Expenses

The judicial expenses shall consist of a state duty and costs connected with the consideration of the case.

There shall be exempted from the payment of judicial expenses for state revenue:

(1) plaintiffs: workers and employees in suits concerning the recovery of earnings and other claims arising out of labor relations, and collective farmers in suits against collective farms for payment of labor;

(2) plaintiffs in cases arising from copyright, and also from the right to a discovery, invention, or rationalization proposal;

(3) plaintiffs in suits concerning the recovery of alimony;

(4) plaintiffs in suits concerning compensation for harm caused by mutilation or other injury to health, and also by death of a breadwinner.

Other instances of relieving parties from the payment of judicial expenses for state revenue may be provided by USSR and union republic legislation.

A court or judge shall, proceeding from the property status of a citizen, have the right to relieve him from payment of judicial expenses for the revenue of the state.

Section II. Persons Participating in a Case; Their Rights and Duties

Article 24. Parties, Their Rights and Duties

Citizens, and also state institutions, enterprises, collective farms, and other cooperative and social organizations enjoying the rights of a juridical person, may be parties, either plaintiff or defendant, in a civi trial.

The parties shall enjoy equal procedural rights. The parties may familiarize themselves with the materials of the case, make challenges, submit evidence, participate in the analysis of evidence, file petitions, give oral or written explanations to the court, submit their arguments and reflections, object to the petitions, arguments, and reflections of the other party, appeal against the decision or ruling of the court, demand compulsory execution of a court decision, be present during the actions of a sheriff when executing the decision, and also perform other procedural actions provided by law.

The parties shall be obliged to use the procedural rights belonging to them in good faith.

Persons participating in cases arising out of administrative legal relations and in cases of special procedure shall enjoy the rights and bear the duties of the parties with the exceptions established by law.

A plaintiff shall have the right to change the grounds or subject of a suit, to increase or reduce the amount of the claim, or to withdraw the suit. A defendent shall have the right to recognize the suit. The parties may terminate a case by a friendly agreement.

A court shall not accept the withdrawal of a plaintiff from a suit, nor the recognition of a suit by a defendant, nor confirm a friendly agreement of the parties if these actions are contrary to law or violate the rights and the interests protected by law of any person.

Article 25. Participation of Several Plaintiffs or Defendants in a Case

A suit may be filed jointly by several plaintiffs or several defendants. Each of the plaintiffs or defendants shall appear in the trial independently with respect to the other party.

Article 26. Replacement of Inappropriate Party

The court, having established while examining a case that the suit has not been brought by the person to whom the right of claim appertains nor against the person who should defend the suit, may with the consent of the plaintiff and without terminating the case allow the replacement of the initial plaintiff or defendant by the proper plaintiff or defendant.

If the plaintiff does not agree to replacement of the defendant by another person, the court may join this person as a second defendant.

Article 27. Third Persons

Third persons filing independent claims to the subject of a dispute may appear in a case before the court decrees a decision. They shall enjoy all the rights and bear all the duties of a plaintiff.

Third persons who have not filed independent claims to the subject of a dispute may appear in a case on the side of the plaintiff or defendant before the decision is decreed by a court, if the decision in the case may affect their rights or duties in respect of one of the parties. They may be joined to participate in a case also upon the petition of the parties, the procurator, or upon the initiative of the court. Third persons not filing independent claims shall enjoy the procedural rights and bear the procedural duties of a party except for the right to change the grounds or subject of a suit, to increase or reduce the amount of the claim, and also to withdraw the suit, recognize the suit, or conclude a friendly agreement.

Article 28. Representation in Court

Citizens may conduct their own cases in court personally or through representatives. Cases of persons not having dispositive legal capacity shall be conducted by their legal representatives.

Cases of juridical persons shall be conducted in court by their agencies or their representatives.

Article 29. Participation of a Procurator in a Trial

The procurator shall have the right to file a suit or appear in a case at any stage of the trial if the protection of state or social interests or of the rights and interests of citizens protected by law require this.

The participation of the procurator in the examination of a civil case shall be obligatory in instances when this is provided by law or when the participation of the procurator in a particular case is deemed necessary by the court.

The procurator participating in a case shall familiarize himself with the materials of the case, make challenges, submit evidence, participate in the analysis of evidence, file petitions, give opinions on questions arising during the examination of the case and on the substance of the case as a whole, and also perform other procedural actions provided for by law.

Article 30. Participation of Agencies of State Administration, Trade Unions, Institutions, Enterprises, Organizations, and Individual Citizens Defending the Rights of Other Persons in a Trial

In instances provided by law, agencies of state administration, trade unions, state institutions, enterprises, collective farms, and other cooperative and social organizations or individual citizens may file suit to protect the rights and the interests protected by law of other persons.

Agencies of state administration may, in the instances provided by law, be joined by a court to participate in a trial or appear in a trial upon their own initiative to give an opinion in the case with a view to carrying out duties entrusted to them and to protect the rights of citizens and the interests of the state.

The agencies of state administration specified in the present Article, institutions, enterprises, or organizations in the person of their representatives, and individual citizens may familiarize themselves with the materials of the case, make challenges, give explanations, submit evidence, participate in the analysis of evidence, file petitions, and also perform other procedural actions provided for by law.

Section III. Procedure of Cases in the Court of First Instance

Article 31. Acceptance of Applications in Civil Cases

A judge shall decide alone the question of accepting an application in a civil case.

The judge shall refuse to accept an application if:

(1) the application is not subject to consideration in judicial agencies;

(2) the procedure for preliminary extra-judicial settlement of the dispute for the particular category of cases has not been observed by the plaintiff;

(3) there is a court decision which has entered into legal force rendered in the dispute between the same parties, on the same subject, and on the same grounds or a court ruling accepting the plaintiff's withdrawal of the suit or confirming a friendly agreement of the parties;

(4) there is a case regarding the dispute between the same parties, on the same subject, and on the same grounds in a judicial proceeding;

(5) a decision of a comrades' court adopted within the limits of its competence has been given in a dispute between the same parties, on the same subject, and on the same grounds;

(6) a contract has been concluded between the parties to transfer the particular dispute for settlement by an arbitration tribunal;

(7) the case is not within the jurisdiction of the particular court;

(8) the application is filed by a person lacking dispositive capacity

(9) the application in the name of a plaintiff has been filed by a person not having the power to conduct the case.

The judge, in refusing to accept an application, shall render a reasoned ruling thereof.

The refusal of a judge to accept an application on the grounds provided by points 2, 7, 8, and 9 of the present Article shall not prevent a second application to the court in the same case if the violation permitted has been eliminated.

Article 32. Security for a Suit

The court or judge, at the request of persons participating in the case or upon their own initiative, may take measures to secure a suit. Security for a suit shall be permitted at any position in the case if the failure to take measures of security may make it difficult or impossible to execute the court decision.

Article 33. Preparation of Civil Cases for Judicial Examination

After accepting an application, the judge shall prepare the case for judicial examination, the purpose of which shall be to ensure the timely and correct settlement of the case.

Article 34. Judicial Examination

A civil case shall be examined in a judicial session with the obligatory notification of the persons participating in the case.

The court shall hear the explanations of the parties and other persons participating in the case, analyze other evidence, and also perform other procedural actions.

After the judicial pleadings and the opinion of the procurator, the court shall recess to the conference room to decree the decision.

Article 35. Judicial Examination to be Direct, Oral, and Uninterrupted

A court of first instance shall, when considering a case, be obliged to directly analyze the evidence in the case: hear the explanations of the persons participating in the case, witness testimony, opinions of experts, familiarize itself with documentary evidence, view real evidence. Exceptions from the present rules shall be permitted only in the instances established by union republic legislation.

Cases shall be examined orally and with an unchanged composition of the court. If one of the judges is replaced during the consideration of the case, the examination of the case should commence from the very beginning.

A judicial session in every case shall proceed without interruption except for the time designated for recess. The court shall not have the right to consider other cases before completing consideration of the case begun or adjourning it.

Article 36. Participation of the Public in a Judicial Examination

Representatives of social organizations and collectives of working people who are not a party in a case may by court ruling be permitted to participate in a judicial examination to set forth for the court the opinions of the organizations or collectives which authorized them with regard to the case being considered by the court.

The rights and duties of representatives of social organizations and collectives of working people shall be determined by union republic legislation.

Article 37. Decision of a Court

A court decision should be lawful and well-founded.

The court shall base the decision only on that evidence which was analyzed in the judicial session. In every instance the decision should specify: the facts of the case established by the court; the evidence on which the conclusions of the court are based and the arguments for which the court rejects particular evidence; the laws by which the court was guided; the conclusion of the court to satisfy the suit or to reject the suit wholly or in part; the period and procedure for appealing against the decision.

Depending upon the facts of the case elucidated, the court may go beyond the limits of the claim filed by the plaintiff if this is necessary to protect the rights and the interests protected by law of state institutions, enterprises, collective farms, and other cooperative and social organizations or citizens.

A court decision shall be decreed by a majority vote, shall be set forth in writing, and shall be signed by all the judges. A judge who remains in a minority shall have the right to set forth a special opinion in writing, which shall be attached to the file of the case.

The USSR Supreme Court shall render a decision in the name of the Union of Soviet Socialist Republics, and union republic courts, in the name of the union republic.

A court which has decreed a decision in a case may determine the procedure for its execution, grant deferment of execution or execution by installment, explain its decision without changing its content, and also render a supplementary decision regarding a claim considered at a judicial session but not settled by the court.

Article 38. Special Rulings of a Court

A court, having discovered a violation of legality or of the rules of socialist community life by officials or citizens when considering a case or material shortcomings in the work of state institutions, enterprises, collective farms, and other cooperative and social organizations, shall render a special ruling and send it to the appropriate institutions, enterprises, organizations, officials, or collectives of working people, which shall be obliged to notify the court about measures which it has taken.

If when considering a civil case the court discovers the indicia of a crime in the actions of a party or other person, it shall notify the procurator thereof or initiate a criminal case.

Article 39. Entry of Court Decision into Legal Force

A court decision shall enter into legal force upon the expiry of the period for cassational appeal or protest unless it has been appealed or protested. In the event a cassational appeal or a cassational protest is brought, unless it is vacated, the decision shall enter into legal force upon the consideration of the case by a superior court.

Upon the entry of a decision into legal force, the parties and other persons who participated in the case, and also their legal successors, may not again file the same suit in court, on the same grounds, nor contest in another trial the facts and legal relations established by the court.

Article 40. Suspension of Proceedings in a Case

The court shall be obliged to suspend the proceeding in a case in the instances of:

(1) the death of a citizen, if the legal relation in dispute allows legal succession, or the termination of the existence of a juridical person who was a party in the case;

(2) loss by a party of dispositive legal capacity;

(3) the defendant being in an active unit of the USSR Armed Forces or the request of the plaintiff who is in an active unit of the USSR Armed Forces;

(4) the impossibility of considering a particular case before settlement of another case being considered in a civil, criminal, or administrative proceeding.

Other grounds may be established by union republic legislation for which a court may suspend the proceedings in a case at the request of the persons participating in the case or upon its own initiative.

Article 41. Termination of Proceedings in a Case

The court shall terminate the proceedings in a case if:

(1) the case is not subject to consideration in judicial agencies;

(2) the procedure for preliminary extra-judicial settlement of a dispute for the particular category of cases was not observed by the plaintiff and the possibility for using this procedure has been lost;

(3) there is a court decision which has entered into legal force and was rendered in a dispute between the same parties, on the same subject, and on the same grounds or a court ruling accepting the withdrawal of the plaintiff from the suit or confirming a friendly agreement of the parties;

(4) the plaintiff withdrew the suit and the court accepted the withdrawal;

(5) the parties concluded a friendly agreement and it was confirmed by the court;

(6) a decision of a comrades' court adopted within the limits of its competence has been given in a dispute between the same parties, on the same subject, and on the same grounds;

(7) a contract has been concluded between the parties to transfer the particular dispute for settlement by an arbitration tribunal;

(8) after the death of the citizen who was one of the parties in the case the legal relation in dispute does not allow legal succession.

If the proceeding in a case is terminated, a second application to the court in a dispute between the same parties, on the same subject, and on the same grounds shall not be permitted.

Article 42. Leaving a Suit Without Consideration

The court shall leave a suit without consideration if:

(1) the procedure for preliminary extra-judicial settlement of the dispute established for the particular category of cases has not been observed by the plaintiff and the possibility of applying this procedure has not been lost;

(2) the suit was brought by a person lacking dispositive legal capacity;

(3) the application in the name of the plaintiff was filed by a person not having the power to conduct the case.

Other grounds for which a court shall leave a suit without consideration also may be established by union republic legislation.

After eliminating the conditions which served as a basis for leaving a suit without consideration, the plaintiff shall have the right again to file the same suit in the usual procedure.

Article 43. Transfer of Cases from the Court of One Union Republic to the Court of Another Union Republic

Cases shall be transferred from the court of one union republic to the court of another union republic on the basis of a court ruling upon the expiry of the period for appeal or protest of this ruling, and if an appeal is filed or a protest is brought, after the ruling is rendered to leave the appeal or protest without satisfaction.

If a dispute arises between courts of different union republics concerning the place for considering the case, the question shall be decided by the USSR Supreme Court.

Section IV. Proceedings in Cases in Cassational and Supervisory Instances

Article 44. Right of Cassational Appeal and to Protest a Decision

Decisions of all courts, except for decisions of the USSR Supreme Court and the union republic supreme courts, may be appealed by way of cassation within the periods established by union republic legislation by the parties and other persons participating in the case.

The procurator shall bring a protest against an illegal or unfounded court decision irrespective of whether or not he participated in the particular case.

Copies of appeals or protests brought in their cases should be handed over to the parties and other persons participating in the case. The parties and other persons participating in the case shall be notified about the time and place for consideration of the case by way of cassation.

The procedure for handing over copies of appeals and protests and the procedure for notification of the time and place for consideration of the case by way of cassation shall be established by union republic legislation.

Article 45. Consideration of Case by Way of Cassation

When considering a case by way of cassation, the court shall, from the materials available in the case and additionally submitted by the parties and other persons participating in the case, verify the legality and well-foundedness of the decision of the court of first instance, both in the appealed and non-appealed parts, and also with respect to persons who have not filed an appeal.

The court shall not be bound by the arguments of the cassational appeal or protest and shall be obliged to verify the case as a whole.

When a case is considered by way of cassation, the procurator shall give an opinion concerning the legality and well-foundedness of the decision.

Article 46. Powers of Cassational Instance

The court, having considered the case by way of cassation, shall have the right by its ruling to:

(1) leave the decision without change, and the appeal or protest without satisfaction;

(2) vacate the decision wholly or in part and send the case for new consideration to the court of first instance;

(3) vacate the decision wholly or in part and terminate the proceeding in the case or leave the suit without consideration;

(4) change the decision or render a new decision, without transferring the case for new consideration, unless the collection or additional verification of evidence is required in the case, or the facts of the case have been established by the court of first instance fully and correctly but an error in the application of norms of material law has been allowed.

Article 47. Grounds for Vacating a Court Decision by Way of Cassation

The grounds for vacating the decision of a court of first instance and transferring a case for new consideration to a court of first instance shall be: incomplete elucidation of facts having significance for the case; unproved facts having significance for the case which the court considered established; the failure of the conclusions of the court set forth in the decision to conform to the facts of the case; the violation or incorrect application of norms of material law or norms of procedural law.

A court decision shall be subject to being vacated by way of cassation with termination of the proceedings in the case or the suit being left without consideration on the grounds specified in Articles 41 and 42 of the present Fundamental Principles.

A court decision correct in substance may not be vacated for only formal considerations.

Article 48. Appeal and Protest of Rulings of a Court of First Instance

The ruling of a court of first instance may, except for rulings of the USSR Supreme Court and the union republic supreme courts, be appealed separately from the court decision by the parties or other persons participating in the case or protested by the procurator to a court of second instance in the instances provided by law, and also in those instances when a court ruling bars the possibility of further movement of the case.

Article 49. Review by Way of Judicial Supervision of Decisions, Rulings, and Decrees Which Have Entered into Legal Force

Decisions, rulings, and decrees which have entered into legal force may be reviewed by way of judicial supervision upon the protests of procurators, the chairmen of courts, and their deputies who have been granted this right by law.

Officials who have been granted the right to bring protests by way of supervision may suspend execution of the respective decisions, rulings, and decrees until the proceeding by way of supervision is completed.

When considering a case by way of supervision, the court shall, from the materials available in the case and additionally submitted, verify the legality and well-foundedness of a decision, ruling, or decree, both in the protested and non-protested parts, and also with respect to persons not specified in the protest.

The court shall not be bound by the arguments of the protest and shall be obliged to verify the case as a whole.

The procurator shall take part in the consideration of a case by way of judicial supervision, supporting the protest brought by him or a superior procurator or giving an opinion in the case being considered upon the protest of the chairman of the court or his deputy.

Copies of the protest brought in the case shall be sent to the parties and other persons participating in the case. If necessary, the parties and other persons participating in the case shall be notified of the time and place where the case is being considered.

The procedure for sending copies of protests and the procedure of notification concerning the time and place for considering the case shall be established by union republic legislation.

Article 50. Powers of a Court Considering a Case by Way of Supervision

A court, having considered a case by way of supervision, shall have the right by its ruling or decree to:

(1) leave the decision, ruling, or decree without change, and the protest, without satisfaction;

(2) vacate a decision, ruling, or decree wholly or in part and send the case for new consideration to a court of first or cassational instance

(3) vacate a decision, ruling, or decree wholly or in part and terminate the proceeding in the case or leave the suit without satisfaction;

(4) leave in force one of the previously rendered decisions, rulings, or decrees in the case;

(5) change the decision, ruling, or decree or render a new decision, without transferring the case for new consideration, unless the collection or additional verification of evidence is required in the case, or the facts of the case have been established by the court of first instance fully and correctly but an error in the application of norms of material law has been allowed.

Article 51. Grounds for Vacating Decisions, Rulings, or Decrees of a Court by Way of Supervision

The grounds for vacating decisions, rulings, or decrees of a court by way of supervision shall be their unfoundedness or material violations of the norms of material or procedural law.

A decision, ruling, or decree of a court shall be subject to being vacated by way of supervision with termination of the proceedings in the case or the suit being left without consideration on the grounds specified in Articles 41 and 42 of the present Fundamental Principles.

Article 52. Binding Nature of Instructions of Superior Courts

The instructions of a court considering a case by way of cassation or by way of judicial supervision set forth in a ruling or decree shall be binding upon the court which considers the particular case anew.

A court considering a case by way of cassation or by way of judicial supervision shall not have the right to establish or consider as proved facts which have not been established in the decision or refuted by it, predetermine questions of the reliability or unreliability of particular evidence or the priority of some evidence over other, and also which norm of material law should be applied or which decision should be rendered in a new consideration of the case.

Moreover, a court, when considering a case by way of judicial supervision, in repealing a cassational ruling, shall not have the right to predetermine conclusions which may be made by the cassational instance during a second consideration of the case.

Article 53. Review of Decisions, Rulings, and Decrees Which Have Entered into Legal Force for Newly Discovered Facts

Decisions, rulings, and decrees which have entered into legal force may be reviewed for newly discovered facts.

The grounds for review of decisions, rulings, and decrees for newly discovered facts shall be:

(1) facts material for the case which were not or could not be known to the applicant;

(2) knowingly false witness testimony, knowingly false expert opinion, knowingly incorrect translation, false documents or real evidence which itself involves the decreeing of an unlawful or unfounded decision established by a court judgment which has entered into legal force;

(3) establishment by judgment of a court which has entered into legal force of criminal actions of the parties, other persons who participated in the case, or their representatives or criminal acts of judges committed when considering the particular case;

(4) vacating of a decision, judgment, ruling, or decree of a court or the decree of another agency which served as a basis for rendering the particular decision or ruling.

The periods and procedure of review for newly discovered facts of decisions, rulings, and decrees which have entered into legal force shall be established by union republic legislation.

Section V. Execution of Judicial Decisions

Article 54. Execution of Judicial Decisions Which Have Entered into Legal Force

Judicial decisions shall be executed upon their entry into legal force, except for instances of immediate execution, which shall be established by union republic legislation.

Compulsory execution of judicial decisions shall take place upon the expiry of the period for voluntary execution of a judicial decision granted to the debtor in accordance with union republic legislation.

The decision of a court in a case in which one of the parties is a citizen may be filed for compulsory execution within three years from the moment of its entry into legal force, and in all other cases, within one year.

Other periods for execution of judicial decisions may be established for individual categories of cases by USSR and union republic legislation.

Article 55. Binding Nature of Claims for Execution of Judicial Decisions

The claims of a sheriff for execution of judicial decisions shall be binding upon all state institutions, enterprises, collective farms, and other cooperative and social organizations, officials, and citizens on the entire territory of the USSR.

Article 56. Control Over the Correct and Timely Execution of Judicial Decisions

Control over the correct and timely execution of judicial decisions shall be carried out by judges.

The parties and other persons participating in a case may appeal the actions of a sheriff. The procedure for considering such appeals shall be determined by union republic legislation.

Article 57. Levying Execution on Property of Citizens, State Institutions, Enterprises, Collective Farms, and Other Cooperative and Social Organizations

Execution shall be levied against citizens on personal property of a debtor, and also on his share in common ownership or in joint ownership of spouses, and also in the property of a collective farm household or one-man peasant farm.

Recovery of compensation for damage caused by a crime also may be levied against property which is the joint ownership of spouses and against property of a collective farm household or one-man peasant farm if it is established by the judgment of a court in a criminal case that such property was acquired from assets obtained by criminal means.

Execution against deposits of citizens in state labor savings banks and in the USSR State Bank may be levied on the basis of a judgment or decision of a court which satisfied a civil suit that arose from a criminal case or the decision of a court in a suit for the recovery of alimony (in the absence of earnings or other property which may be levied against) or for the division of a deposit which is the joint property of spouses.

Execution may be levied against the wages or other earnings, pension, or stipend of a debtor if the debtor lacks property or such property is insufficient for full recovery.

Execution shall not be levied against the property of a debtor if the amount of recovery does not exceed that portion of monthly wages or other earnings, pension, or stipend for which execution may be levied under the law.

Execution may be levied only by a court decision for the recovery of alimony or for compensation of harm caused by mutilation or other injury to health, and also for death of a breadwinner, against social insurance allowances paid during temporary incapacity to work, and also against grants paid by collective farm mutual assistance banks.

Execution shall be levied against state institutions, enterprises, collective farms, and other cooperative and social organizations first of all on cash assets of the debtor in credit institutions according to the rules established by USSR legislation.

The list of types of property of citizens, state institutions, enterprises, collective farms, and other cooperative and social organizations and the portion of wages or other earnings, pensions, and stipends of pupils on which execution may not be levied, and also the priority for satisfying claims concerning recovery if the amounts recovered are insufficient shall be established by USSR and union republic legislation.

Article 58. Execution of Judgments in Respect of Recovery of Property and Friendly Agreements Confirmed by a Court, and Other Decisions and Decrees

The execution of judgments in respect of recovery of property, judicial rulings and decrees, friendly agreements confirmed by a court, decisions of arbitration tribunals, awards of the maritime and foreign trade arbitration commissions, decisions of commissions for labor disputes, decrees regarding labor disputes rendered by factory, plant, and local trade union committees, executory endorsements of notarial offices, and also, in the instances provided by law, decisions of arbitrazh agencies and other decisions and decrees, shall be carried out in the procedure established for the execution of judicial decisions.

Section VI. Civil Procedure Rights of Foreign Citizens and Stateless Persons. Suits Against Foreign States, Judicial Commissions, and Decisions of Foreign Courts. International Treaties and Agreements

Article 59. Civil Procedure Rights of Foreign Citizens, Foreign Enterprises, and Organizations

Foreign citizens shall have the right to apply to courts of the USSR and shall enjoy civil procedural rights on the same basis as Soviet citizens.

Foreign enterprises and organizations shall have the right to apply to courts of the USSR and shall enjoy the civil procedural rights in order to protect their interests.

Reciprocal restrictions with respect to citizens, enterprises, and organizations of those states in which special restrictions on civil procedure rights for Soviet citizens, enterprises, or organizations are permitted may be established by the USSR Council of Ministers.

Article 60. Civil Procedure Rights of Stateless Persons

Stateless persons shall have the right to apply to courts of the USSR and shall enjoy civil procedure rights on the same basis as Soviet citizens.

Article 60-1. Jurisdiction of USSR Courts in Civil Cases Regarding Disputes in Which Foreign Citizens, Stateless Persons, and Foreign Enterprises and Organizations Participate, and also Disputes in Which One of the Parties Resides Abroad

The jurisdiction of USSR courts in civil cases regarding disputes in which foreign citizens, stateless persons, and foreign enterprises and organizations participate, and also disputes in which one of the parties resides abroad, shall be determined by USSR legislation, and in instances not provided by USSR legislation, proceeding from the rules for jurisdiction provided by union republic legislation.

Article 61. Suits Against Foreign States. Diplomatic Immunity

Bringing a suit against a foreign state, securing the suit, and levying execution on the property of a foreign state which is in the USSR may be permitted only with the consent of competent agencies of the respective state.

Diplomatic representatives of foreign states accredited in the USSR and other persons specified in respective laws and international agreements shall be subject to the jurisdiction of a Soviet court in civil cases only within the limits determined by norms of international law or agreements with the respective states.

In those instances when the same judicial inviolability in a foreign state is not secured for the Soviet state, its property, or representatives of the Soviet state which, according to the present Article, is secured for foreign states, their property, or representatives of foreign states in the USSR, the application of reciprocal measures may be ordered with respect to this state, its property, or representative of such state by the USSR Council of Ministers or other authorized agency.

Article 62. Execution of Judicial Commissions of Foreign Courts and Application by USSR Courts with Commissions for Foreign Courts

Courts of the USSR shall execute commissions of foreign courts transmitted to them in the established procedure concerning the performance of individual procedural actions (serving writs and other documents, interrogation of parties and witnesses, performance of expert examination and views on the spot, and others), except for instances when:

(1) execution of the commission would be contrary to the sovereignty of the USSR or would threaten the security of the USSR;

(2) execution of the commission is not within the competence of the court.

Commissions of foreign courts concerning the performance of individual procedural actions shall be executed on the basis of Soviet legislation.

Courts of the USSR may apply to foreign courts with commissions concerning the execution of individual procedural actions. The procedure for relations of Soviet courts with foreign courts shall be determined by USSR and union republic legislation and by international agreements of the USSR and union republics.

Article 63. Execution in the USSR of Decisions of Foreign Courts and Arbitration Tribunals

The procedure for the execution in the USSR of decisions of foreign courts and arbitration tribunals shall be determined by respective agreements of the USSR with foreign states or by international conventions in which the USSR participates. A decision of a foreign court or arbitration tribunal may be submitted for compulsory execution in the USSR within three years from the moment the decision entered into legal force.

Article 64. International Treaties and Agreements

In those instances when other rules are established by an international treaty or international agreement in which the USSR participates than those which are contained in the present Fundamental Principles, the rules of the international treaty or international agreement shall be applied.

The same provision shall apply on the territory of a union republic if other rules are established in an international treaty or international agreement in which the union republic participates than are provided by the civil procedure legislation of the union republic.

CHAPTER VII

FAMILY LAW

FUNDAMENTAL PRINCIPLES OF LEGISLATION OF THE USSR AND UNION REPUBLICS ON MARRIAGE AND THE FAMILY

[Confirmed by Law of the USSR Supreme Soviet, June 27, 1968. Vedomosti SSSR (1968), no. 27, item 241]

Concern for the Soviet family, in which the social and personal interests of citizens are harmoniously combined, is one of the most important tasks of the Soviet state.

The most favorable conditions for the strengthening and flourishing of the family have been created in the Soviet Union. The material well-being of citizens is growing steadily, and the housing and cultural conditions of life for the family are improving. Socialist society devotes great attention to the protection and encouragement of motherhood and to ensuring a happy childhood.

A communist upbringing for the growing generation and the development of its physical and spiritual forces are the most important duty of the family. The state and society help the family in every possible way in the upbringing of children and is expanding the network of kindergartens, day nurseries, boarding schools, and other children's institutions.

The necessary social and domestic conditions are provided to Soviet woman in order to combine a happy motherhood with an ever more active and creative participation in production and in socio-political life.

Soviet legislation on marriage and the family is called upon to actively promote the final cleansing of family relations from material calculations, to eliminate the remnants of the unequal status of women in daily life, and to create a communist family in which the deepest personal feelings of people find their complete satisfaction.

Section I. General Provisions

Article 1. Tasks of Soviet Legislation on Marriage and the Family

The tasks of Soviet legislation on marriage and the family shall be:

the further strengthening of the Soviet family based on principles of communist morality;

the structuring of family relations on a voluntary marital union of a woman and a man of feelings of mutual love free from material calculations and of friendship and respect for all family members.

the bringing up of children of the family in an organic combination with social nurturing in a spirit of devotion to the Motherland, of a Communist attitude toward labor, and of training children to actively participate in the construction of a communist society;

all possible protection of the interests of the mother and children and ensuring a happy childhood to each child;

the final elimination of harmful survivals and customs of the past in family relations;

nurturing a feeling of responsibility toward the family.

Article 2. Relations Regulated by Legislation on Marriage and the Family

Legislation on marriage and the family shall establish the procedure and conditions of entry into marriage, regulate personal and property relations arising in a family between spouses, between partners and children, and between other family members, relations arising in connection with adoption, guardianship, and curatorship, the adoption of children for upbringing, the procedure and conditions for the termination of marriage, and the procedure for the registration of acts of civil status.

Article 3. Equality of Women and Men in Family Relations

The woman and man shall have equal personal and property rights in family relations.

Equality of rights in the family shall be based on the equal rights of a woman with a man consolidated by the USSR Constitution in all domains of state, socio-political, economic, and cultural life of the country.

Article 4. Equality of Citizens in Family Relations Irrespective of Their Nationality, Race, or Attitude Toward Religion

All citizens, irrespective of nationality, race, and attitude toward religion, shall have equal rights in family relations.

Any direct or indirect limitation of rights or the establishment of express or indirect privileges when entering into a marriage or family relations dependent on national or racial affiliation or attitude toward religion shall not be permitted.

Article 5. Protection and Encouragement of Motherhood

Motherhood in the USSR shall be honored and respected by all the people and shall be protected and encouraged by the state.

The protection of the interests of mother and child shall be ensured by the organization of a broad network of maternity homes, children's day nurseries, and kindergartens, boarding schools, and other children's institutions, by granting to a woman leave for pregnancy and birth while retaining maintenance, by establishing privileges and benefits for pregnant women and mothers, protection of labor in production, the payment of state benefits to mothers of one child or many children, as well as other state and social assistance to the family.

Article 6. Legal Regulation of Marriage and Family Relations by the State

Legal regulation of marriage and family relations in the USSR shall be exercised only by the state.

A marriage concluded only in state agencies for the registry of acts of civil status shall be recognized. A religious marriage rite, just as other religious rites, shall have no legal significance.

This rule shall not appertain to religious rites performed before the formation or restoration of Soviet agencies for acts of civil status or to documents concerning birth, the conclusion of a marriage, dissolution of a marriage, and death obtained therein.

Article 7. USSR and Union Republic Legislation on Marriage and the Family

Legislation concerning marriage and the family shall consist of the present Fundamental Principles and other legislative acts of the USSR issued in accordance therewith, and union republic codes on marriage and the family and other legislative acts.

Union republic legislation shall decide questions relegated to their jurisdiction by the present Fundamental Principles, and questions of marriage and family relations not expressly provided for by the Fundamental Principles.

Article 8. Application of Union Republic Legislation on Marriage and the Family

The conclusion of a marriage, relations between spouses, between parents and children, adoption, the establishment of paternity, the recovery of alimony, guardianship and curatorship, dissolution of marriage, and registration of acts of civil status shall be regulated by legislation of the union republic whose agency performs or registers the respective act of civil status or settles the dispute which has arisen.

The validity of a marriage, adoption, establishment of guardianship and curatorship, and the validity of acts of civil status shall be determined by union republic legislation on whose territory the marriage was concluded, the adoption performed, the guardianship or curatorship established, or the act of civil status registered.

Section II. Marriage

Article 9. Conclusion of a Marriage

A marriage shall be concluded in state agencies for the registry of acts of civil status.

The registration of a marriage shall be established both in the interests of the state and society and also with a view to protection of the personal and property rights and interests of spouses and children.

Only a marriage concluded in state agencies for the registry of acts of civil status shall give rise to rights and duties of spouses.

The conclusion of a marriage shall take place upon the expiry of a month after those wishing to marry file an application at the state agency for the registry of acts of civil status. A reduction or increase in this period may be provided for in individual instances by union republic legislation.

A marriage shall be concluded in solemnity. Agencies for the registry of acts of civil status shall ensure a situation of solemnity for the registration of a marriage with the consent of the persons being married.

Article 10. Conditions for Conclusion of a Marriage

The mutual consent of the persons entering into a marriage and the attainment by them of marriageable age are necessary for the conclusion of a marriage.

Marriage age shall be established as eighteen years. A lower marriageable age may be provided for by union republic legislation, but not less than two years.

The conclusion of a marriage shall not be allowed;

between persons one of whom is already married;

between relatives in direct line of ascendance or descendance, between full or half brothers or sisters, and also between adoptive and adopted persons;

between persons one of whom is deemed by a court to lack capacity as a consequence of mental illness or feeble-mindedness.

Article 11. Personal Rights of Spouses

When concluding a marriage, the spouses at their own wish shall select the surname of one of the spouses as their common surname or each spouse shall retain his premarital surname.

The right of spouses to have a compound surname may be provided for by union republic legislation.

Questions of the upbringing of children and other questions of family life shall be decided by the spouses jointly.

Each spouse shall be free to select an occupation, profession, and place of residence.

Article 12. Property of Spouses

The property acquired by spouses during marriage shall be their common joint ownership. Spouses shall have equal rights to possession, use, and disposition of such property.

Spouses shall enjoy equal rights to property also in the event that one of them was occupied with keeping the household, caring for children, or for other justifiable reasons had no independent earnings.

In the event of a division of property in the common joint ownership of spouses, their shares shall be deemed equal. In individual instances a court may depart from the principle of equality of shares of spouses, taking into account the interests of minor children or the interests of one of the spouses which deserves attention.

Property belonging to spouses before marriage, and also received by them during marriage as a gift or by way of inheritance, shall be the ownership of each of them.

The rules of the present Article shall extend only to that property of spouses who are collective farm members which constitutes their personal ownership.

The rights of spouses to the possession, use, and disposition of the ownership of a collective farm household shall be established by union republic legislation.

Article 13. Duties of Spouses Regarding Mutual Support

Spouses shall be obliged to support each other materially. In the event of a refusal of such support, a spouse who is not capable of working and who needs material assistance, and also a wife during pregnancy and one year after the birth of the child, shall have the right to obtain support (or alimony) from the other spouse through a court if the latter is in a state to grant it. This right shall be retained also after the dissolution of a marriage.

A divorced needy spouse also shall have a right to support if he became incapable of working within one year after the dissolution of the marriage. If the spouses had been married for a lengthy time, a court shall have the right to recover alimony to the benefit of a divorced spouse also in the event this spouse has reached pension age nor more than five years from the date the marriage was dissolved.

In individual instances a spouse may be relieved of the duty to support the other spouse or his duty may be limited to a period. The conditions under which a court may relieve a spouse of the duty to support the other spouse or limit this duty to a period shall be established by union republic legislation.

Article 14. Termination of Marriage

A marriage shall be terminated as a consequence of the death or the declaration of one of the spouses as deceased in a judicial proceeding.

During the life of the spouses, a marriage may be dissolved by a divorce upon the application of one or both spouses.

A marriage shall be dissolved in a judicial proceeding. The court shall take measures to reconcile the spouses.

A marriage shall be dissolved if it is established by a court that the further joint life of the spouses and preservation of the family has become impossible.

A husband shall not have the right to initiate a case concerning dissolution of a marriage without the consent of the wife during the pregnancy of the wife nor within one year after the birth of a child.

When rendering a decision concerning dissolution of a marriage, the court shall take measures when necessary to protect the interests of minor children and a spouse incapable of working.

With the mutual consent for dissolution of a marriage of spouses not having minor children, a marriage shall be dissolved in agencies for the registry of acts of civil status. In such instances the divorce shall be formalized and a certificate concerning dissolution of the marriage shall be issued to the spouses upon the expiry of three months from the date the spouses filed the application for divorce.

A marriage shall be dissolved at agencies for the registry of acts of civil status also with persons who are:

deemed missing in the procedure established by law;

deemed to lack dispositive capacity as a consequence of mental illness or feeble-mindedness in the procedure established by law;

sentenced to deprivation of freedom for a term of not less than three years for the commission of a crime.

If there is a dispute between the spouses, the marriage shall be dissolved through a court.

A spouse who has changed his surname to another when being married also shall have the right after dissolution of marriage to have this surname or at his request to take his premarital surname.

Article 15. Invalidity of a Marriage

A marriage may be deemed void if the conditions established in Article 10 of the present Fundamental Principles are violated, as well as in instances of registration of a marriage without an intention to create a family (fictitious marriage). A marriage shall be deemed void in a judicial proceeding.

Deeming a marriage void shall not affect the rights of children who were born of this marriage. Other consequences of deeming a marriage void shall be established by union republic legislation.

Section III. Family

Article 16. Bases of Origin of Rights and Duties of Parents and Children

The mutual rights and duties of parents and children shall be based on the parentage of the children certified in the procedure established by law.

The parentage of a child from parents who are married shall be certified by an entry concerning the marriage of the parents. The parentage of a child from parents who are not married shall be established by means of the father and mother filing a joint application at state agencies for the registry of acts of civil status.

If a child is born of parents who are not married, in the absence of a joint application of the parents, paternity may be established in a judicial proceeding.

When establishing paternity, the court shall take into account the cohabitation and keeping of a common household of the child's mother and the defendant before the birth of the child or the joint upbringing or maintenance by them of the child, or evidence reliably confirming the acknowledgement of paternity by the defendant.

Article 17. Entry of Parents in Birth Registry Books

The father and mother who are married shall be entered as the parents of a child in the birth registry book upon the application of either of them.

If the parents are not married, the mother of the child shall be entered upon the application of the mother, and the entry concerning the father, upon the joint application of the father and mother of the child, or the father shall be entered according to a decision of a court. In the event of the mother's death, and also if it is impossible to establish her place of residence, the father of the child shall be entered upon the application of the father.

If a child is born of a mother who is not married, unless there is a joint application of the parents or a decision of a court concerning the establishment of paternity, the father of the child shall be entered in the birth registry book according to the surname of the mother; the name and patronymic of the father of the child shall be entered at her instruction.

Article 18. Rights and Duties of Parents

The father and mother shall have equal rights and duties with respect to their children.

Parents should bring up their children in the spirit of the moral code of a builder of communism, concern for their physical development, and training and preparation for socially useful activity.

Parents shall be obliged to support their minor children and children who have attained majority, are not capable of working, and require assistance.

The protection of the rights and interests of minor children lies on their parents.

Parents shall have the right to demand the return of children from any person keeping children with them not on the basis of law or a judicial decision.

Parental rights may not be exercised contrary to the interests of children.

Parents shall enjoy equal rights and bear equal duties with respect to their children also in instances when the marriage is dissolved. The procedure for the settlement of disputes between parents relating to questions of the residence and upbringing of children shall be established by union republic legislation.

Article 19. Deprivation of Parental Rights

The parents, or one of them, may be deprived of parental rights if it is established that they are avoiding the fulfillment of their duties to bring up the children or abuse their parental rights, treat children cruelly, exert a harmful influence on children by their amoral, antisocial conduct, and also if the parents are chronic alcoholics or drug addicts.

Cases concerning deprivation of parental rights shall be considered upon the application of state or social organizations, one of the parents or the guardian (or curator) of a child, and also upon the suit of a procurator.

If both parents are deprived of parental rights, the child shall be transferred to the care of agencies of guardianship and curatorship.

A court may take a decision to remove a child and transfer him to the care of agencies of guardianship and curatorship irrespective of the deprivation of parental rights if leaving a child with the persons with whom he is would be dangerous for him.

Restoration of parental rights shall be permitted if the interests of the children require this and if the children have not been adopted.

Parental rights shall be deprived and restored only in a judicial proceeding.

Deprivation of parental rights shall not relieve parents of the duty to support the children.

Article 20. Duty of Children to Support Parents

Children who have attained majority shall be obliged to support parents who are not capable of working and require assistance and to care for them.

Children may be relieved of the duty to support their parents if it is established by a court that the parents have avoided the fulfillment of parental duties.

Article 21. Alimony Duties of Other Family Members

The duty to support minor children, if they have no parents, may be entrusted to other relatives: grandfather, grandmother, brother, sister, and also to the step-father and step-mother of the child.

The duty to support family members who have attained majority and are not capable of working and require assistance, if they have no spouses, parents, or children who have attained majority, may be entrusted to grandchildren or stepchildren.

Other grounds for the origin of rights and duties relating to the mutual support of parents and other persons also may be established by union republic legislation.

Article 22. Amount of Alimony

Alimony for minor children shall be recovered from their parents in an amount: for one child, one quarter; for two children, one third; for three or more children, one-half of the earnings (or income) of the parents.

The amount of these shares may be reduced by a court if the parents obliged to pay alimony have other minor children who, if the amount of alimony established by the present Article were recovered, would be less provided for materially than the children receiving the alimony, as well as in those instances if the parent from whom alimony is recovered is a first or second group invalid or if the children work and have adequate earnings.

The court shall have the right to reduce the amount of alimony or to exempt it from being paid if the children are fully supported by the state or a social organization. Expenses for the support of children placed in a children's institution may be recovered to the benefit of these institutions from the parents of the children in amounts established in the present Article.

For individual instances when the recovery of alimony as a share of a parent's earnings is impossible or difficult, a specific lump sum amount of alimony for minor children may be provided for by union republic legislation. The amount of this sum shall be determined by proceeding from the proposed earnings (or income) of the parent pursuant to the aforementioned provisions.

Parents who are paying alimony for minor children may be involved in additional expenses resulting from exceptional circumstances (grave illness, injury of the child, etc.).

The types of earnings (or income) subject to reckoning in the withholding of alimony shall be determined in a procedure established by the USSR Council of Ministers.

When recovering alimony from parents for children who have attained majority and require assistance, and also in all remaining instances of recovering assets for support, the amount of alimony shall be determined in a lump sum, proceeding from the material and family position of the person from whom the alimony is recovered and of the person receiving it.

Article 23. Procedure for Payment and Recovery of Alimony

Alimony shall be paid in a voluntary procedure personally by the person obliged to pay the alimony or through the administration at the place of his work or the receipt by him of a pension or stipend.

The voluntary procedure for the payment of alimony shall not preclude the right of the person recovering the alimony to bring suit in court at any time regarding recovery of alimony.

The administration of an enterprise, institution, and organization shall, on the basis of a written application of the person paying the alimony, withhold the alimony monthly from earnings (or pension, benefit, stipend, and others) and shall pay or transfer it to the person specified in the application.

Article 24. Adoption

Adoption shall be permitted only with respect to minor children and in their interests.

Adoption shall be by decision of the executive committee of the district or city soviet of working people's deputies at the request of the person wishing to adopt a child.

The consent of the parents of a child not deprived of parental rights, and also the consent of the adopted person if he has attained ten years of age, shall be required for adoption. The procedure for expressing consent of a child shall be established by union republic legislation.

If parents avoid participation in bringing up a child, adoption by way of exception may be without their consent. The procedure for adoption and the conditions under which it shall be permitted without the consent of the parents shall be established by union republic legislation.

When a person who is married adopts a child, if both spouses do not adopt the child, the consent of the other spouse to the adoption shall be required. The conditions under which adoption by way of exception may be without the consent of the other spouse shall be established by union republic legislation.

An adoption shall be deemed void or shall be vacated only in a judicial proceeding.

The rules of adoption, the conditions for deeming an adoption void, and the conditions for vacating the adoption, and also the consequences of the repeal, shall be established by union republic legislation.

The conditions ensuring the secrecy of adoption shall be established by union republic legislation.

Article 25. Rights and Duties of Adoptive Persons, Adopted Persons, and Their Relatives

Adopted persons and their descendants with respect to their adoptive persons and their relatives, and the adoptive persons and their relatives with respect to the adopted persons and their descendants, shall be equal in personal and property rights and duties to the relatives by descent.

Adopted persons shall lose personal and property rights and be relieved of duties with respect to their parents and their relatives. In the event of the adoption of a child by one person, these rights and duties may be preserved at the wish of the mother, if the adoptive person is a man, or of the father, if the adoptive person is a woman. Minors who at the time of adoption have a right to a pension or benefit from state or social organizations due to them for loss of a breadwinner shall retain this right also if they are adopted.

At the request of the adoptive persons, they may be registered in the birth entry books as the parents of the adopted persons.

Article 26. Guardianship and Curatorship

Guardianship and curatorship shall be established to bring up minor children who as a consequence of the death of parents, the deprivation of parents of parental rights, illness of parents, or for other reasons were left without parental care, as well as for the protection of the personal and property rights and interests of such children.

Guardianship and curatorship shall be established also for the protection of the personal and property rights and interests of persons who have attained majority and who by the state of their health can not independently exercise their rights and fulfill their duties.

Guardianship and curatorship shall be established by the executive committee of a district (or city), settlement, or rural soviet of working people's deputies.

The rights and duties of guardians and curators, and also the rules of guardianship and curatorship, shall be established by union republic legislation.

Section IV. Acts of Civil Status

Article 27. Registration of Acts of Civil Status

Birth, death, conclusion of a marriage, dissolution of marriage, adoption, establishment of paternity, change of name, patronymic, and surname, shall be subject to registration in state agencies for the registry of acts of civil status.

Article 28. Procedure for Contesting Entries for Acts of Civil Status

If there are sufficient grounds and in the absence of a dispute between the interested persons, errors shall be corrected and changes made in entries of acts of civil status by agencies for the registry of acts of civil status. The refusal of agencies for the registry of acts of civil status to correct or change an entry may be appealed to a court.

If there is a dispute between the interested persons, an entry shall be corrected on the basis of a court decision.

Article 29. Document Books. Rules for the Registration of Acts of Civil Status

The basic provisions determining the procedure for changing and restoring entries of acts of civil status, and also the forms of registration books for acts of civil status and forms of certificates issued on the basis of entries in such books, and the procedure and periods for keeping document books shall be established by the USSR Council of Ministers.

The rules for registration of acts of civil status, including the procedure for the solemn registration of marriages and births, as well as the procedure for mutually informing those being married about the state of health and family status and explaining their rights and duties as future spouses and parents, shall be established by union republic legislation.

Section V. Application of Soviet Legislation on Marriage and the Family to Foreigners and Stateless Persons. Application of Laws on Marriage and the Family of Foreign States, International Treaties, and Agreements

Article 30. Citizenship of Children

A child both of whose parents at the time of his birth were USSR citizens shall be deemed a citizen of the USSR wherever he was born.

In the event of the different citizenship of the parents, one of whom at the time of the child's birth was a citizen of the USSR, the child shall be deemed a citizen of the USSR even if one of the parents at this time resided on the territory of the USSR. If at this time both parents resided beyond the limits of the USSR, the citizenship of the child shall be determined by their agreement.

Article 31. Conclusion of Marriages of Soviet Citizens with Foreigners and of Foreigners between Themselves in the USSR

Marriages of Soviet citizens with foreigners, as well as marriages of foreigners between themselves, shall be concluded in the USSR on the general principles.

The entry into marriage of Soviet citizens with foreigners shall not in itself entail a change of citizenship.

Marriages between foreigners concluded in the USSR at embassies or consulates of foreign states shall be deemed valid in the USSR on the basis of reciprocity if such persons at the time of entering into marriage were citizens of the state which appointed the ambassador or consul.

Article 32. Conclusion of Marriages of Soviet Citizens and Performance of Other Acts of Civil Status in Embassies and Consulates of the USSR. Recognition of Marriages Concluded Beyond the Limits of the USSR

Marriages of Soviet citizens who are residing beyond the limits of the USSR shall be concluded at embassies or consulates of the USSR.

The laws of that union republic of which the persons concerned are citizens shall be applied when concluding a marriage or performing other acts of civil status in embassies and consultates of the USSR abroad. If the persons concerned are citizens of different union republics or it has not been established as to which union republic they are citizens of, by their agreement the laws of one of the union republics shall be applied, and if there is disagreement, by decision of the official registering the act of civil status.

In those instances when marriages between Soviet citizens and marriages of Soviet citizens with foreigners are concluded beyond the limits of the USSR, observing the form of marriage established by the laws of the place where it was performed, such marriages shall be deemed valid in the USSR unless there are obstacles arising from Articles 10 and 15 of the present Fundamental Principles.

Marriages of foreigners concluded beyond the limits of the USSR according to the laws of the respective states shall be deemed valid in the USSR.

Article 33. Dissolution of Marriages of Soviet Citizens with Foreigners and Marriages of Foreigners between Themselves in the USSR. Recognition of Divorces Performed Beyond the Limits of the USSR

Marriages of Soviet citizens with foreigners, as well as marriages of foreigners between themselves, shall be dissolved in the USSR on the general bases.

The dissolution of marriages between Soviet citizens and foreigners performed beyond the limits of the USSR according to the laws of the respective states shall be deemed valid in the USSR even if at the time the marriage was dissolved one of the spouses resided beyond the limits of the USSR.

The dissolution of marriages between Soviet citizens performed beyond the limits of the USSR according to the laws of the respective states shall be deemed valid in the USSR if both spouses at the time the marriage is dissolved resided beyond the limits of the USSR.

The dissolution of marriages between foreigners performed beyond the limits of the USSR according to the laws of the respective states shall be deemed valid in the USSR.

Soviet citizens permanently residing abroad shall have the right to dissolve a marriage in judicial agencies of the USSR.

Article 34. Adoption of Children Holding Soviet Citizenship and Residing Beyond the Limits of the USSR. Rules for Adoption of Children by Foreigners in the USSR

The adoption of a child holding Soviet citizenship and residing beyond the limits of the USSR shall be at an embassy or consulate of the USSR. If the adoptive person does not hold Soviet citizenship, it shall be necessary to obtain the authorization of the authorized union republic agency.

The adoption of a child holding Soviet citizenship performed in agencies of the state on whose territory the child resides also shall be deemed valid on condition of obtaining in advance the authorization for such adoption from the authorized union republic agency.

The rules for the adoption of children holding Soviet citizenship by foreigners on the territory of the USSR shall be established by union republic legislation.

Article 35. Application of USSR Legislation and Union Republic Legislation on Marriage and the Family in Regard to Stateless Persons

Stateless persons residing in the USSR shall enter into marriage and dissolve marriage, shall enjoy the rights arising from legislation on marriage and the family, and shall bear the duties provided for by such legislation on the general bases with Soviet citizens.

Article 36. Application of Foreign Laws and International Treaties and Agreements

The application of foreign laws on marriage and the family or the recognition of acts of civil status based on such laws may not occur if such application or recognition would be contrary to the bases of the Soviet system.

If other rules than those contained in Soviet legislation on marriage and the family have been established by an international treaty or an international agreement in which the USSR participates, the rules of the international treaty or international agreement shall be applied.

The same situation shall apply on the territory of a union republic, if other rules than those provided for by legislation on marriage and the family of this union republic have been established in an international treaty or international agreement in which the particular union republic participates.

CHAPTER VIII

NATURAL RESOURCES AND ENVIRONMENT LAW

FUNDAMENTAL PRINCIPLES OF LAND LEGISLATION OF THE USSR AND UNION REPUBLICS

[Confirmed by Law of the USSR Supreme Soviet, December 13, 1968, as amended September 14, 1977 and December 16, 1977. Vedomosti SSSR (1968), no. 51, item 485; (1977), no. 51, item 771]

The Great October Socialist Revolution destroyed the quasi-serfdom land system of Tsarist Russia, which condemned the peasantry to poverty while inhibiting the development of the productive forces of the country. Private ownership in land was abolished forever by the Decret of the Second All-Russian Congress of Soviets of October 26 (November 8) 1917, "On the Land," and all the land became national property and was transferred without payment to the use of the working people.

The state ownership of land which arose as a result of nationalization constitutes the basis of land relationships in the USSR. The land, which served as an instrument in the exploitation of man by man under conditions of private ownership, is used in the USSR to develop the productive forces of the country in the interests of the people as a whole.

The state ownership of land has played an enormous role in ensuring the victory of socialism in the USSR. It has permitted the optimum distribution of all branches of the economy and has been one of the most important factors in the transition to socialist forms of land use.

As the conditions for mass collectivisation of scattered individual holdings were created in the course of the construction of socialism, the peasantry, under the leadership of the Communist Party and with every kind of assistance and support from the working class, set out on the path of socialism. The implementation of Lenin's cooperative plan and the victory of the collective farm system provided the true solution to the peasant question.

The state ownership of land furthers the creation of the managerial and technical base of communism in our country for the gradual transition to communist social relationships and the elimination of differences between town and country.

The land -- that most important resource of Soviet society -- is the principal means of production in agriculture and provides space for the distribution and development of all branches of the economy. The scientifically well-founded and rational utilization of all lands, their conservation, and the improvement of soil fertility in every way are tasks common to all.

Section I. General Provisions

Article 1. The Tasks of Soviet Land Legislation

The tasks of Soviet land legislation shall be to regulate land relationships in order to ensure rational land use and to create conditions for increasing its efficiency, to safeguard the rights of socialist organizations and citizens, and to strengthen legality in the domain of land relationships.

Article 2. Land Legislation of the USSR and Union Republics

Land relationships in the USSR shall be regulated by the present Fundamental Principles and by other acts of USSR land legislation issued in accordance therewith, by land codes, and by other union republic acts of land legislation.

Mining, forest, and water relationships shall be regulated by special USSR and union republic legislation.

Article 3. State Ownership of Land in the USSR

In accordance with the Constitution of the USSR, land in the Union of Soviet Socialist Republics shall be in state ownership, that is to say, the property of the whole people.

Land in the USSR shall be in the exclusive ownership of the state and only shall be granted for use. Activities which infringe on the right of state ownership to land, whether direct or covert, shall be prohibited.

Article 4. Unified State Land Fund

All land in the USSR shall form the unified state land fund, which shall consist of the following, according to its basic special designation:

(1) designated agricultural land, granted for use to collective farms, state farms, and other land users for agricultural purposes;

(2) land in population centers (cities, workers' settlements, resorts, and dacha and rural population centers);

(3) designated land for industry, transport, resorts, preserves, and other nonagricultural users;

(4) land of the state forest fund;

(5) land of the state water fund;

(6) land of the state reserve.

The procedure for relegating land to the said categories and the transfer of land from one category to another shall be determined by USSR and union republic legislation.

Article 5. Competence of the USSR in Regulation of Land Relationships

There shall be subject to USSR jurisdiction in the regulation of land relationships:

(1) disposal of the unified state land fund within the limits necessary to implement the powers of the USSR in accordance with the Constitution of the USSR;

(2) establishment of the basic statutes for land use and land tenure;

(3) establishment of long-term plans for the rational use of the country's land resources, providing the requirements for agricultural production and for other branches of the national economy;

(4) establishment of plans for all-union measures relating to land conservation and also the establishment of basic statutes for the protection of soil from erosion, salinization, and other processes which cause soil deterioration;

(5) establishment of state control over land use;

(6) establishment of a system of state land registration uniform for the USSR, state registration of land use, and a procedure for keeping the land register;

(7) establishment of the procedure for drawing up the annual land balance of the USSR.

Article 6. Competence of the Union Republics in Regulation of Land Relationships

There shall be subject to the jurisdiction of a union republic in the regulation of land relationships: disposal of the unified state land fund within the limits of the republic and the establishment of long-term plans for its use; establishment of land use procedures and of land tenure organization; establishment of plans to conserve the land; the struggle against erosion and to increase soil fertility; and also the regulation of land relationships in other matters, unless they have been relegated to the competence of the USSR.

Article 7. Land Users

Land in the USSR shall be granted for the use of:

collective farms, state farms, and other agricultural state, cooperative, and social enterprises, organizations, and institutions;

industrial, transport, and other nonagricultural state, cooperative, and social enterprises, organizations, and institutions;

citizens of the USSR.

In instances provided for by USSR legislation, land may be granted for use also to other organizations and persons.

Article 8. Use of Land Without Payment

Land shall be granted to collective farms, state farms, and to other state, cooperative, and social enterprises, organizations, and institutions, and to citizens of the USSR and their use without payment.

Article 9. Periods of Land Use

Land shall be granted in perpetuity or for temporary use.

Where no period is established in advance, land use shall be deemed to be in perpetuity (permanent).

Land occupied by collective farms shall be allotted to them for use in perpetuity, that is to say, eternally.

Temporary land use may be short-term -- up to three years -- or long-term -- from three to ten years. In case of industrial necessity, these periods may be extended for a period not exceeding the periods of short- or long-term temporary use respectively.

Individual types of land use may be established by union republic legislation for a longer period of long-term use, but not exceeding 25 years.

Article 10. Procedure for the Granting of Land for Use

Land plots shall be granted for use by a special allocation procedure.

Land plots shall be allocated on the basis of a decree of a union republic council of ministers or a decision of the executive committee of the respective soviet of people's deputies in the procedure established by USSR and union republic legislation. The decrees or decisions on granting land plots shall indicate the purpose for which they are allocated and the basic conditions for use of the land.

A land plot already in use shall be granted to another land user only after withdrawal of the plot in the procedure provided for by Article 16 of the present Fundamental Principles.

Land which has been deemed in the established procedure suitable for the needs of agriculture must first of all be granted to agricultural enterprises, organizations, and institutions.

Designated nonagricultural land, unsuitable for agriculture, or agricultural areas of the lowest quality shall be granted for the construction of industrial enterprises, dwellings, railways, highways, electric power lines, pipelines, and for other nonagricultural needs. Land plots for these purposes from the state forest fund shall be granted primarily from areas not covered by forest or from areas occupied by scrub or plantings of low value. Land plots to be built over shall be granted in areas where mineral beds occur by agreement with state mining supervision agencies. Electric power and telephone lines and other communications shall be laid mainly along roads, existing routes, and the like.

The right of land use of collective farms, state farms, and other land users shall be certified by state documents for the right of land use, issued by the executive committees of district and city soviets of people's deputies.

The procedure for formalizing the temporary use of land shall be established by union republic legislation.

Article 11. Rights and Duties of Land Users

Land users shall have the right and shall be obliged to use land plots for those purposes for which they have been granted to them.

Depending upon the special purpose of each land plot granted for use the land users shall have the right in the established procedure to:

erect dwelling, production, cultural, domestic, and other structures and installations;

sow agricultural crops and plant forest, fruit, decorative, and other plantings;

use hay-growing, pasture, and other areas;

use, for the needs of the husbandry, minerals in general use, peat, and waters which are on the land, as well as exploit other useful properties of the land.

Losses caused to land users shall be subject to compensation.

The rights of land users which are violated shall be subject to being restored in the procedure provided for by USSR and union republic legislation.

The rights of land users may be restricted by law in the interests of the state, as well as in the interests of other land users.

The use of land to derive nonlabor income shall be prohibited.

Land users shall be obliged to use rationally the land plots granted to them and not to perform on their plot actions which violate the interests of neighboring land users.

Enterprises, organizations, and institutions working deposits of minerals by stripping or underground means or carrying out geological prospecting, construction, or other works on agricultural lands or forest areas granted to them for temporary use shall be obliged at their own expense to bring these land plots into a state suitable for use in agriculture, forestry, or fisheries, and when performing the said works on other lands, into a state suitable for their designated use. Land plots shall be brought into a suitable state during the course of the work, and if this is impossible, within a year after the work is completed.

Enterprises, organizations, and institutions carrying out industrial or other construction, working mineral deposits by strip methods, as well as carrying on other works connected with a disturbance of the soil cover, shall be obliged to remove and preserve the top layer of soil with a view to using it for recultivation of the land and increasing the fertility of low-productive areas.

Article 12. Secondary Land Use

Collective farms, state farms, and other enterprises, organizations, and institutions may in the instances established by law grant the land plots allotted to them for a secondary use.

The procedure and conditions for secondary use shall be determined by Articles 25, 27, 28, 41, 42, and 43 of the present Fundamental Principles, as well as by other USSR and union republic legislation.

Article 13. Conservation of Land and Increasing Soil Fertility

Land users shall be obliged to take effective measures to increase soil fertility, shall implement a system of organizational, economic, cropping, forest improvement, and hydraulic engineering measures to prevent soil erosion by wind or water, and shall not permit salinization, waterlogging, or pollution of the land, overgrowth of weeds, or other processes causing deterioration of the soil.

Measures relating to land irrigation, drainage, and conservation, shelter-belt cultivation, the struggle against soil erosion, and other measures directed toward the basic improvement of the land shall be provided for in state plans for the development of the national economy and shall be carried out by the appropriate ministries, departments, and land users.

Agricultural areas and specially irrigated or drained lands shall be subject to special conservation. Collective farms, state farms, and other enterprises, organizations, and institutions using designated agricultural land shall be obliged to conserve, restore, and increase the fertility of the soil.

Industrial and construction enterprises, organizations, and institutions shall not permit the pollution of agricultural or other land by production or other wastes or by sewage waters.

Material incentive measures for land users stimulating the implementation of measures to protect land, increase soil fertility, and bring unused lands into agricultural circulation may be established by USSR and union republic legislation.

Article 14. Grounds for Terminating the Right of Enterprises, Organizations, and Institutions to Use Land

The right of enterprises, organizations, and institutions to use the land granted to them shall be subject to termination either wholly or in part, respectively, in instances of:

(1) the need for the land plot no longer exists;

(2) expiry of the period for which the plot was granted;

(3) liquidation of the enterprise, organization, or institution;

(4) the necessity arises to withdraw the land plot for other state or social needs;

(5) failure to exploit the plot granted for two years in succession.

The right of land use also may be terminated when the land plot is not used in accordance with the purpose for which it was granted.

Other grounds for the termination of the rights of an enterprise, organization, and institution to use land also may be provided by the union republic land codes.

Article 15. Grounds for Terminating the Right of Citizens to Use Land

The right of citizens to use land plots granted to them shall be subject to termination either wholly or in part, respectively, in instances of:

(1) voluntary renunciation of use of the land plot;

(2) expiry of the period for which the land plot was granted;

(3) resettlement by all of the members of the household or family to another permanent place of residence;

(4) termination of the labor relationships in connection with which the employment allotment was made, unless provided otherwise by USSR and union republic legislation;

(5) death of all the members of the household or family;

(6) the necessity arises to withdraw the land plot for state or social needs.

The right to use a land plot may be terminated if the citizen commits any of the acts provided for by Article 50 of the present Fundamental Principles, as well as if the land plot is not used for two years in succession or is not used in accordance with the purpose for which it was granted.

Other grounds for the termination of the right of a citizen to use land also may be provided by the union republic land codes.

Article 16. Procedure for Withdrawal of Land for State or Social Needs

A land plot or part thereof shall be withdrawn for state or social needs on the basis of a decree of a union republic council of ministers or an autonomous republic council of ministers or a decision by the executive committee of the appropriate soviet of people's deputies in the procedure established by USSR and union republic legislation.

The withdrawal of land plots in the use of collective farms, state farms, and other agricultural enterprises, organizations, and institutions and of lands having cultural or scientific significance shall be permitted only in instances of special need.

The withdrawal of irrigated or drained land, fields, land plots with established orchards and vineyards and for nonagricultural needs, as well as land with water conservancy, shelter-belt, or other first group forests for use for purposes not connected with forestry shall occur in exceptional instances and only by decree of the union republic council of ministers.

Enterprises, organizations, and institutions interested in the withdrawal of land plots for nonagricultural needs shall be obliged before beginning design work to agree in advance with the land users and agencies exercising state control over the use of land, the place for siting the objects, and the appropriate dimensions of the area marked for withdrawal.

Land plots in the use of collective farms may be withdrawn only with the consent of general meetings of collective farm members of meetings of authorized representatives, and land in the use of state farms and other state, cooperative, social enterprises, organizations, and institutions of union or republic subordination, by agreement with the land users and with the respective USSR and union republic ministries and departments.

Article 17. Procedure for Use of Land Plots for Prospecting Work

Enterprises, organizations, and institutions carrying out geological survey, searches, geodesic, and other prospecting work may carry on such work on all lands in the procedure established by USSR and union republic legislation without the land plots being withdrawn from land users. The periods for beginning and the site of the said work shall be agreed with the land users, and in the event of the failure to reach agreement, shall be determined by the executive committees of district or city soviets of people's deputies.

Enterprises, organizations, and institutions carrying on the work specified in the first paragraph of the present Article shall be obliged at their own expense to bring the land plots which they occupied into a state suitable for their intended use. Land plots shall be brought into a suitable state in the course of the work, and if this is impossible, within a month after completion of the work, excluding the period when the soil is frozen.

Article 18. Compensation of Land Users for Losses Caused by the Withdrawal or Temporary Occupation of Land Plots

Losses caused to land users by the withdrawal of land plots for state or social needs or land plots temporarily occupied shall be subject to compensation.

Losses shall be compensated by the enterprises, organizations, and institutions to which the land plots are allocated in accordance with a statute confirmed by the USSR Council of Ministers.

Article 19. Compensation for Loss of Agricultural Production Connected With the Withdrawal of Land for Nonagricultural Needs

Enterprises, organizations, and institutions to which land plots occupied by agriculture are allocated for construction work or other nonagricultural needs shall pay compensation for the loss of agricultural production connected with the withdrawal of these plots (in addition to the compensation for loss to land users in conformity with Article 18 of the present Fundamental Principles).

The amounts of and procedure for determining the loss of agricultural production subject to compensation, as well as the procedure for using the appropriate assets, shall be established by the USSR Council of Ministers.

Article 20. State Control of Land Use

State control of the use of all lands shall have as its task to ensure the observance of land legislation by ministries, departments, state, cooperative, and social enterprises, organizations, and institutions, as well as by citizens, and the procedure for land use and that the land register and land tenure are properly kept for the rational use and conservation of the land.

State control of the use of all land shall be exercised by the soviets of people's deputies and by their executive and administrative agencies and also by specially authorized state agencies in the procedure established by USSR legislation.

Section II. Designated Agricultural Lands

Article 21. Designated Agricultural Lands

All lands granted for agricultural needs or designated for such purposes shall be deemed designated agricultural lands.

Designated agricultural lands shall be used by socialist agricultural enterprises, organizations, and institutions in accordance with plans for the development of agriculture with a view to satisfying the growing requirements of the national economy for agricultural products.

Reducing the area of irrigated or drained land, fields, valuable established orchards and vineyards as well as other highly productive lands including their transfer to less productive areas, shall not be permitted except for instances of special need provided for by union republic legislation.

Article 22. Granting Designated Agricultural Lands for Use

Agricultural lands shall be granted for use in perpetuity to:

collective farms, state farms, and other agricultural state, cooperative, and social enterprises and organizations: for carrying on agriculture;

scientific research, training, and other agricultural institutions: for carrying on field research and the practical application and dissemination of the achievements of science and progressive experience in agriculture, as well as for productive purposes;

nonagricultural enterprises, organizations, and institutions: for conducting subsidiary husbandry;

citizens: for conducting subsidiary husbandry without using hired labor.

Land plots may be granted to enterprises, organizations, and institutions for collective horticulture and truck gardening in the procedure and on the conditions established by legislation of the USSR and union republics.

In addition to land granted for use in perpetuity which are specified in the present Article, land users also may be granted lands for temporary use.

Changing the boundaries and dimensions of land use of collective farms, state farms, and other state agricultural enterprises and organizations, as well as scientific research, experimental and training, and other agricultural institutions when amalgamating and dividing farms, and a redistribution of lands among land users may occur on the basis of scientifically well-founded land tenure schemes confirmed in the established procedure.

Article 23. Duties of Land Users for the Use of Designated Agricultural Lands

Collective farms, state farms, and other enterprises, organizations, and institutions using designated agricultural lands shall be obliged, on the basis of the achievements of science and of progressive experience and taking into account local conditions, to:

(1) provide for concrete measures to raise soil fertility and for rational land use in organizational and economic tenure plans and in production and financial plans;

(2) introduce, in accordance with zonal conditions and farm specialization, the most efficient system of agriculture and most economically advantageous combination of the branches of the farm, introduce and use crop-rotation, and bring unused lands into agricultural production;

(3) develop irrigation, drainage, and water supply of land, improve the meadow and pasture, and to chalk and put gypsum in the soil;

(4) take measures against soil erosion, the waterlogging and salinization of land, to plant shelter-belt greenery and to afforest and consolidate sands, ravines, and steep slopes, and not allow soil pollution;

(5) clear agricultural fields of stones, scrubs, and bushes and wage a struggle against weeds and harmful or diseased agricultural plants.

Article 24. Lands for Common Use and Personal Plots of Collective Farms

Lands granted to a collective farm by a state act for use in perpetuity shall consist of lands for common use and personal plots. The personal plots shall be delimited with actual boundaries from common use land.

If the personal plot lands are insufficient to grant land plots to collective farm households according to the norms provided by the collective farm charter, it shall be allowed to increase the area of personal plot lands at the expense of common use lands by a decision of the general meeting of collective farm members or a meeting of authorized persons which is confirmed by the executive committee of the regional or territory soviet of people's deputies or autonomous republic council of ministers, and in republics not divided into regions, by the union republic council of ministers.

Intra-farm use of lands allotted to collective farms shall be on the basis of the collective farm charter in accordance with the present Fundamental Principles, as well as with other USSR and union republic legislation.

Article 25. Right of a Collective Farm Household to a Personal Plot

Each collective farm household shall have the right to a personal plot granted in the procedure and within the limits of norms provided by the collective farm charter.

The right to a granted personal plot shall be preserved for collective farm households in which a single able-bodied household member is called to active military service in the ranks of the Armed Forces of the USSR or holds an elective post, undertakes study, is temporarily transferred to other work with the consent of the collective farm or by way of an organized selection, as well as when only minors remain in the collective farm household.

The right to use a personal plot also shall be preserved for collective farm households, all members of which have lost the capacity to work as a result of age or disability.

Collective farm households shall be allotted pastures for their livestock in accordance with the collective farm charter.

Article 26. Personal Plots of State Farms and Other State Agricultural Enterprises, Organizations, and Institutions

Personal plots designated to be granted to workers and employees as personal plots within the limits of norms established by union republic legislation shall be allotted and demarcated with actual boundaries in accordance with the confirmed intra-farm land tenure scheme from lands granted for use to the state farm or other state agricultural enterprise, organization, and institution for agricultural needs.

If the personal plot lands are insufficient to provide land plots to workers and employees, the area of these lands may be increased upon the petition of the farm directors with the authorization of the executive committee of the regional or territory soviet of people's deputies or the autonomous republic council of ministers, and in republics not divided into regions, by the union republic council of ministers.

Article 27. Granting Personal Land Plots to Workers and Employees of State Farms and Other Citizens Residing in a Rural Locality

State farms and other state agricultural enterprises, organizations, and institutions shall grant personal land plots or kitchen gardens from lands designated for these purposes to permanent workers and employees, as well as to teachers, doctors, and other specialists working and residing in a rural locality.

A collective farm shall, by decision of the general meeting of collective farm members or meeting of authorized representatives, grant personal land plots to teachers, doctors, and other specialists working and residing in a rural locality.

Where there exist free personal land plots on collective farms, state farms, and other state agricultural enterprises, organizations, and institutions the personal plots may be granted to workers, employees, pensioners, and invalids residing in a rural locality respectively by decision of the general meeting of collective farm members or a meeting of authorized representatives or the administration of a state farm, enterprise, organization, and institution, to be confirmed by the executive committee of a rural soviet of people's deputies.

Personal land plots shall be preserved in their former dimensions for workers and employees specified in the present Article in the event of their transfer to old age pension or invalid status, as well as for families of workers and employees called to active military service in the ranks of the USSR Armed Forces or enrolling for study during the entire period of military service or at an educational institution.

The categories of citizens enumerated in the present Article who have livestock in personal ownership shall be allotted land plots to pasture the livestock from the state reserve lands, state forestry fund, or from cities, workers', resort, and dacha settlements, as well as nonagricultural land. In the absence of such land, plots to pasture livestock may be allotted from lands of collective farm, state farm, and other agricultural enterprises, organizations, and institutions, with compensation by the livestock owners to the land users for expenditures for the maintenance and improvement of such plots.

Land plots for haying shall be granted to the categories of citizens of the said categories from lands of the state reserve, the state forestry fund, the belt allotted to railways and highways, and lands of other nonagricultural designation.

Land plots shall be granted in the procedure and within the norms established by union republic legislation.

Article 28. Procedure and Conditions for Granting Agricultural Lands to Land Users for Temporary Use by Other Land Users

Collective farms, state farms, and other state agricultural enterprises and organizations which are not using temporarily a part of the agricultural area allocated to them may transfer these areas for temporary use to collective farms, state farms, and other farms needing them by a decision of the executive committee of the district soviet of people's deputies. A farm receiving a land plot for a fixed period shall compensate the land user for the unused expenditure of the respective period of the land use.

A part of land area shall be transferred from one farm to the permanent use of another farm in the procedure provided by Article 10 of the present Fundamental Principles.

Article 29. Land Use by Family Peasant Farms

Family peasant farms which exist in some areas shall use the personal plots and the fields granted to them for agriculture in the procedure and within the limits of norms established by union republic legislation.

Section III. Lands of Population Centers (Cities, Workers', Resort, and Dacha Settlements) and Rural Population Centers

Article 30. Composition of City Lands

All lands within the limits of the city boundary shall be relegated to city lands.

Such lands shall comprise:

(1) lands for city building;

(2) lands for common use;

(3) lands for agricultural use and other areas;

(4) lands occupied by urban forests;

(5) lands for rail, water, air, and pipeline transport, mining industry, and others.

Article 31. Procedure for the Use of City Lands

All lands within the limits of the city boundary shall be in the jurisdiction of city soviets of people's deputies.

The procedure for establishing and modifying the city boundary, for the economic and land tenure of the territory of cities, for granting and withdrawing land plots, and the conditions for using them shall be determined by union republic legislation, and the procedure for the use of lands specified in Article 30, points 3-5 of the present Fundamental Principles, by USSR and union republic legislation.

Article 32. Land Use of Collective Farms and State Farms Within the Limits of the City Boundary

Common use lands of collective farms and lands of state farms and other state agricultural enterprises, organizations, and institutions located within the limits of the city boundary and not subject to being built on or to amenities pursuant to the city planning and building design shall be allotted to them in perpetuity.

Dwelling, cultural, domestic, and production structures and installations shall be placed on them by agreement with the executive committees of city soviets of people's deputies.

Article 33. Transfer of Right of Land Plot Use when Transferring the Right of Ownership in a Building in Cities

When transferring the right of ownership in a structure on the lands of cities, the right to use the land plot or part thereof also shall pass in the procedure established by union republic legislation.

Article 34. Suburban Zones and Green Belts

Lands outside the city boundary serving as a reserve for urban expansion and a site for the location and construction of essential installations connected with public amenities and the normal functioning of the city economy, as well as occupied by forests, parkland, and other green plantings fulfilling shelter-belt, sanitary, and hygienic functions and being a place of leisure for the populace, shall be allocated respectively as the suburban zone and the green belt of the city.

The procedure for allocating suburban zones and green belts, and also for land use in them, shall be established by USSR and union republic legislation.

Article 35. Lands of Urban-Type Settlements

The provisions of Articles 30, 31, 32, 33, and 37 of the present Fundamental Principles shall extend to the lands of population centers relegated in accordance with union republic legislation to the category of urban-type settlements.

All lands within the limits of the settlement boundary shall be in the jurisdiction of settlement soviets of people's deputies.

Article 36. Lands of Rural Population Centers

All lands within the limits of boundaries established for such centers shall be relegated to lands of rural population centers. Lands of rural population centers relegated in long-term development plans shall be demarcated from other lands by establishing the boundary of population centers in accordance with their planning and building designs. Lands of rural population centers not relegated in long-term plans shall be demarcated from other lands by way of intra-farm land tenure.

Within the limits of rural population centers, a rural soviet of people's deputies shall exercise control over the granting of all land plots and shall take decisions concerning the granting of land plots from lands not within the land use of collective farms, state farms, and other agricultural enterprises.

Land plots within the limits of a rural population center allotted to collective farms, state farms, and other agricultural enterprises shall be used by them for the building of dwelling, cultural, domestic, and production structures and installations, as well as for personal land use in accordance with Articles 24, 25, 26, and 27 of the present Fundamental Principles, and other USSR and union republic legislation. Dwelling, cultural, domestic, and production structures and installations shall be sited by agreement with the executive committees of rural soviets of people's deputies.

The procedure for establishing and modifying the boundaries of rural population centers, for relegating them to long-term development, and also the procedure for use of lands of rural population centers shall be determined by union republic legislation.

Article 37. Granting Land Plots for Use of Housing Construction and Dacha Construction Cooperatives, as well as to Citizens for Individual Housing Construction

Land plots shall be granted to housing construction and dacha construction cooperatives, as well as to citizens, for individual housing construction from lands of population centers, the state reserve, and lands of the state forestry fund located beyond the limits of the green zone of urban lands, in the procedure and on the conditions established by USSR and union republic legislation.

Section IV. Lands for Industry, Transport, Resorts, Preserves, and Other Nonagricultural Designation

Article 38. Lands for Industry, Transport, Resorts, Preserves, and Other Nonagricultural Designation

Lands granted for use to enterprises, organizations, and institutions in order for them to carry out the special tasks entrusted to them (industrial production, transport, the organization of resorts, preserves, and so forth) shall be deemed lands for industry, transport, resorts, preserves, and other nonagricultural designation.

The dimensions of land plots granted for the said purposes shall be determined in accordance with the norms and the design and technical documentation confirmed in the established procedure.

The procedure for the use of lands for industry, transport, resorts, preserves, and other nonagricultural designation and the establishment of zones with special conditions of land use (sanitary protection area, etc.) shall be determined by statutes concerning such lands confirmed by the USSR Council of Ministers and the union republic councils of ministers.

Article 39. Resort Land

Land plots having medicinal significance and favorable conditions for the organization of therapeutic measures and granted in the established procedure for use to medicinal and resort institutions shall be relegated to resort lands. Resort lands shall be subject to special protection.

A sanitary protection area shall be established at all resorts in the interests of ensuring the necessary conditions for treatment and leisure of the populace and in order to conserve natural medicinal factors. Within these areas it shall be prohibited to grant land plots for the use of those enterprises, organizations, and institutions whose activities are incompatible with the conservation of the natural medicinal properties and with favorable conditions for leisure of the populace.

Article 40. Lands of Preserves

Land plots allotted in the established procedure within whose limits there are natural objects of special scientific or cultural value (typical or rare landscapes, communities of plant and animal organisms, rare geological formations, plant and animal species, and the like) shall be deemed to be preserve lands.

Any activity which disturbs the natural structures of the preserves or threatens the preservation of natural objects or special scientific or cultural value shall be prohibited both on the territory of preserves and within the limits of the protective zones established around the preserves.

Article 41. Granting by Industrial, Transport, and Other Nonagricultural Enterprises, Organizations, and Institutions of Lands for Agricultural Purposes

Industrial, transport, and other nonagricultural enterprises, organizations, and institutions shall, by decision of executive committees of district or city soviets of working people's deputies, grant lands not being used by them for temporary use to collective farms, state farms, and other enterprises, organizations, institutions, and citizens for agricultural purposes in the procedure and on the conditions established by USSR and union republic legislation.

Article 42. Auxiliary Land Strips

Auxiliary land strips shall be granted to individual categories of transport, forest industry, communications, water, fishery, and hunting workers, as well as certain other branches of the national economy.

Auxiliary land strips shall be allotted from lands in the use of enterprises, organizations, and institutions of the respective ministries and departments, and if such lands are insufficient, from lands of the state reserve and lands of the state forestry fund.

A list of categories of workers having the right to an auxiliary land strip, the dimensions of auxiliary strips, and the conditions for granting and procedure for using them shall be determined by union republic legislation.

Section V. Lands of the State Forest Fund

Article 43. Lands of the State Forest Fund

Lands covered by forest, and also not covered by forest but which have been designated for the needs of forestry, shall be deemed to be lands of the state forest fund.

By decision of the executive committees of district or city soviets of people's deputies, state forestry enterprises, organizations, and institutions shall grant to collective farms, state farms, and other enterprises, organizations, institutions, and citizens agricultural areas from the lands of the state forest fund available for use but not being used for the needs of forestry and the timber procurement industry, for temporary use for agricultural purposes if such use is compatible with the forestry interests.

The procedure for the use of lands of the state forest fund shall be determined by USSR and union republic legislation.

Section VI. Lands of the State Water Fund

Article 44. Lands of the State Water Fund

Lands occupied by bodies of water (rivers, lakes, reservoirs, canals, internal seas, territorial waters, and the like), glaciers, and hydraulic engineering and other water installations, as well as lands allocated for drainage belts on banks and shores, conservation zones, and the like, shall be deemed to be lands of the state water fund.

The procedure for the use of lands of the state water fund shall be determined by USSR and union republic legislation.

Section VII. State Reserve Lands

Article 45. State Reserve Lands

All lands not granted to land users for long-term use or use in perpetuity shall be state reserve lands.

State reserve lands shall be granted for the permanent or temporary use of collective farms, state farms, and other state, cooperative, and social enterprises, organizations, and institutions, and of citizens in the procedure provided by Article 10 of the present Fundamental Principles.

Section VIII. State Land Register

Article 46. The State Land Register, Its Constituent Parts and Purpose

In order to ensure the rational use of land resources, a state land register shall be kept containing the aggregate of authentic and necessary information concerning the natural, economic, and legal status of land.

The state land register shall include data of land use registration, a record of the quantity and quality of land, botanization of soils, and an economic evaluation of the land.

Data from the state land register shall serve the purposes of organizing the efficient use of lands and their protection, of planning the national economy, of the siting and specialization of agricultural production, of soil conservation and chemicalization of agriculture, as well as the effectuation of other national economic measures connected with land use.

The land register shall be kept at state expense according to a system uniform for the USSR. The procedure for keeping the state land register, the forms of register documentation, and the periodicity of clarifying and updating register data shall be established by the USSR Council of Ministers.

Section IX. State Land Tenure

Article 47. Land Tenure and Land Tenure Activities

Land tenure shall include the system of state measures aimed at effectuating decisions of state agencies in the domain of land use.

The tasks of state land tenure shall be the organization of the fullest, most rational and efficient use of lands and of increasing agricultural crops and protection of the land.

Land tenure shall include the following land tenure activities:

(1) the formation of new, as well as the regulation of existing, land use, eliminating the open-field system and other inconvenience in the arrangement of land; clarification and modification of boundaries of land users on the basis of a district planning scheme;

(2) intra-farm organization of the territory of collective farms, state farms, and other agricultural enterprises, organizations, and institutions, introducing economically well-founded crop rotation and the layout of all other agricultural lands (hay fields, pastures, gardens, etc.), as well as working out measures regarding the struggle against soil erosion;

(3) bringing to light new lands for agricultural and other national economic exploitation;

(4) allotment and withdrawal of land plots;

(5) establishment and modificaticn of city boundary, settlement boundary, and boundaries of rural population centers;

(6) carrying on topographical, geodesic, soil, geobotanical, and other investigations and prospecting.

Land tenure, including planned prospecting, survey, and inspection work, shall be at state expense.

Article 48. Land Tenure Documentation

Land tenure designs, as well as documents for the right to use land provided for by Article 10 of the present Fundamental Principles, shall be drawn up in the process of land tenure.

Land tenure designs shall be drawn up with the participation of interested land users and after confirmation shall be transferred in actuality (on the ground), marking the boundaries of land use with survey marks of the established form.

The intra-farm organization of territory established by way of land tenure shall be binding on collective farms, state farms, and other agricultural enterprises.

Section X. Settlement of Land Disputes

Article 49. Procedure for the Settlement of Land Disputes

Land disputes between collective farms, state farms, other state, cooperative, and social enterprises, organizations, and institutions, and citizens shall be settled by union republic councils of ministers, autonomous republic councils of ministers, and executive committees of territory, regional, national area, district, city, rural, and settlement soviets of people's deputies in the procedure established by union republic legislation.

Disputes of collective farms, state farms, and other state, cooperative, and social enterprises, organizations, and institutions from one union republic and relating to the use of land on the territory of another union republic shall be considered by a commission formed from representatives of the interested union republics on an equal footing. Where the commission has not arrived at an agreed decision, disputes relating to these questions shall be subject to consideration by the USSR Council of Ministers.

Disputes between joint owners of individual buildings on the land of cities, settlements of the urban type, and land plots in rural population centers allocated by executive committees of rural soviets of people's deputies concerning the procedure for the use of a common land plot shall be considered by the courts.

Property disputes connected with land relationships shall be considered in the procedure established by USSR and union republic legislation.

Section XI. Responsibility for Violations of Land Legislation

Article 50. Responsibility for Violation of Land Legislation

The purchase, sale, mortgage, testamentary disposition, gift, leasing, and unauthorized exchange of land plots or other legal transactions, which directly or covertly violate the right of state ownership in land, shall be void.

Persons guilty of performing the said legal transactions, as well as:

unauthorized occupation of land plots;

uneconomic land use and its use for the purpose of deriving nonlabor income;

despoiling agricultural or other land, or pollution of land with industrial or other waste or sewage waters;

failure to fulfill obligatory measures to improve the land and protect the soil from wind or water erosion or other processes causing soil deterioration;

failure to return temporarily occupied land at the appointed time or failure to fulfill obligations to bring the land to a state suitable for use for the specified purpose;

destruction of survey marks showing land use boundaries;

shall bear criminal or administrative responsibility in the procedure established by USSR and union republic legislation.

Responsibility for other forms of violations of land legislation may be established by USSR and union republic legislation.

Land plots occupied without authority shall be returned to those to whom they belong without compensation for expenditures incurred during the time of illegal use.

In instances established by USSR and union republic legislation, land users permitting systematic violations of the rules for land use may be deprived of the land plots not being correctly used by them.

Enterprises, organizations, institutions, and citizens shall be obliged to compensate harm caused by them as a result of violations of land legislation.

FUNDAMENTAL PRINCIPLES OF WATER LEGISLATION OF THE USSR AND UNION REPUBLICS

[Confirmed by Law of the USSR Supreme Soviet, December 10, 1970. Vedomosti SSSR (1970), no. 50, item 566]

Water, just as other natural wealth in our country, was nationalized and became the property of the people as a result of the victory of the Great October Socialist Revolution.

State ownership of water constitutes the basis of water relationships in the USSR, creates favorable conditions for the effectuation of planned and integrated use of water to the best advantage of the national economy, and allows the provision of optimum conditions for the labor, life, leisure, and health protection of the Soviet people.

The development of social production and urban development and the growth of the material well-being and cultural level of the populace increase the all-round demand for water and the significance of the rational use and conservation of water.

Soviet water legislation has been called on to promote actively the most efficient and scientifically well-founded use of water and to protect them from pollution, obstruction, and depletion.

Section I. General Provisions

Article 1. Tasks of Soviet Water Legislation

The tasks of Soviet water legislation shall be the regulation of water relationships with a view to ensuring the rational use of water for the needs of the population and the national economy, the protection of water from pollution, obstruction, and depletion, the prevention and elimination of the harmful effects of water, the improvement of the state of water installations, and also the protection of the rights of enterprises, organizations, institutions, and citizens and the strengthening of legality in the domain of water relationships.

Article 2. Water Legislation of the USSR and Union Republics

Water relationships in the USSR shall be regulated by the present Fundamental Principles and other acts of USSR water legislation issued in accordance therewith, and by the water codes and other acts of water legislation of the union republics.

Land, forestry, and mining relations shall be regulated by the respective legislation of the USSR and union republics.

Article 3. State Ownership of Water in the USSR

In accordance with the USSR Constitution, waters in the Union of Soviet Socialist Republics shall be in state ownership, that is, the property of the whole people.

Water in the USSR shall be in the exclusive ownership of the state and shall be granted only for use. Actions which directly or covertly violate the right of state ownership of water shall be prohibited.

Article 4. Unified State Water Fund

All waters (or water objects) in the USSR shall constitute the unified state water fund.

The unified state water fund shall include:

(1) rivers, lakes, water reservoirs, other surface waters and water sources, and also the waters of canals and ponds;

(2) underground waters and glaciers;

(3) internal seas and other internal sea waters of the USSR;

(4) territorial waters (or territorial sea) of the USSR.

Article 5. Competence of the USSR in the Domain of Regulating Water Relationships

There shall be subject to the jurisdiction of the USSR in the domain of regulating water relationships:

(1) disposal of the unified state water fund within the limits necessary for the exercise of powers of the USSR in accordance with the USSR Constitution;

(2) establishment of basic provisions in the domain of water use, protection from pollution, obstruction, and depletion, and prevention and liquidation of the harmful effect of water;

(3) establishment of all-union standards for water use, water quality, and methods for assessing it;

(4) establishment of a state system uniform for the USSR for recording water, and its use, registration of water use, and a state water register;

(5) confirmation of an integrated water use and conservation scheme, as well as water resource balances of all-union significance;

(6) planning of all-union measures for the use and conservation of water and for the prevention and elimination of its harmful effects;

(7) state control over the use and conservation of water and the establishment of the procedure for its implementation;

(8) determination of water objects whose use is to be regulated by agencies of the USSR.

Article 6. Competence of Union Republics in the Domain of Regulating Water Relationships

There shall be subject to the jurisdiction of a union republic in the domain of regulating water relationships, outside the limits of the competence of the USSR: disposal of the unified state water fund on the territory of the republic; establishment of the procedure for the use of water, for protecting it from pollution, obstruction, and depletion, and for the prevention and elimination of the harmful effects of water; planning of measures for the use and conservation of water and for the prevention and elimination of its harmful effects; confirmation of integrated water use and conservation schemes and water resource balances; exercise of state control over the use and conservation of water; as well as the regulation of water relationships on other questions unless they have been relegated to the jurisdiction of the USSR.

Article 7. State Administration in the Domain of Water Use and Conservation

State administration in the domain of water use and conservation shall be exercised by the USSR Council of Ministers, union republic councils of ministers, autonomous republic councils of ministers, and executive committees of local soviets of working people's deputies, as well as by specially authorized state agencies for regulating water use and conservation, either directly or through basic (or territorial) administrations and by other state agencies in accordance with USSR and union republic legislation.

Article 8. State Control Over Water Use and Conservation

State control over water use and conservation shall have as its task to ensure the observance by all ministries, departments, state, cooperative, and social enterprises, organizations, institutions, and citizens of the established procedure for water use, the fulfillment of duties in respect of water conservation, the prevention and liquidation of its harmful effects, rules for recording water, and also other rules established by water legislation.

State control over water use and conservation shall be exercised by soviets of working people's deputies and their executive and administrative agencies, and also by specially authorized state agencies in the procedure established by legislation of the USSR.

Article 9. Participation of Social Organizations and Citizens in the Implementation of Measures for the Rational Use and Conservation of Water

Trade unions, youth organizations, nature conservation societies, scientific societies, and other social organizations, as well as citizens, shall render assistance to state agencies in implementing measures for rational use and conservation of water.

Social organizations shall participate in activities directed toward ensuring the rational use and conservation of water in accordance with their charters (or statutes) and with USSR and union republic legislation.

Article 10. Siting, Design, Construction, and Putting into Operation of Enterprises, Installations, and Other Objects Affecting the State of Water

When siting, designing, constructing, or putting into operation new and converted enterprises, installations, and other objects, as well as when introducing new technological processes which affect the state of water, the rational use of water should be ensured, with priority being given to satisfying the needs of the populace for drinking and domestic water. In these circumstances, measures shall be provided ensuring the recording of water drawn from water objects and water returned to them, protection of water from pollution, obstruction, and depletion, prevention of the harmful effects of water, restricting the flooding of land to the minimum necessary amounts; protection of land from salinization, saturation, and drying out, as well as the preservation of favorable natural conditions and landscapes.

When siting, designing, constructing, or putting into operation new and converted enterprises, installations, and other objects on waters for fishing, measures ensuring the conservation of fish and other aquatic animals and plants and the conditions for their reproduction should be carried out in addition in good time.

The determination of construction sites for enterprises, installations, and other objects affecting the state of water shall be agreed with agencies for regulating the use and conservation of water, executive committees of local soviets of working people's deputies, agencies carrying out state sanitary supervision and protection of fishery stocks, and with other agencies in accordance with USSR and union republic legislation. Designs for the construction of the said enterprises, installations, and other objects shall be subject to agreement with agencies for regulating the use and conservation of water and other agencies in the instances and in the procedure established by USSR legislation.

It shall be prohibited to put into operation:

new and converted enterprises, workshops, production units, municipal and other objects not provided with devices to prevent the pollution and obstruction of water or its harmful effects;

irrigation and water supply systems, reservoirs, and canals, before carrying out measures provided for by the designs to prevent flooding, saturation, waterlogging, and salinization of land and soil erosion;

drainage systems before water receptacles and other installations are ready in accordance with the confirmed designs;

water-intake installations without fish-protection devices in accordance with confirmed designs;

hydraulic engineering installations, until devices for the passage of flood water and fish are ready in accordance with the confirmed designs;

boreholes for water, without equipping them with water-regulating devices and establishing sanitary protection zones in appropriate instances.

The filling of water reservoirs shall be prohibited until the bed preparations provided for in the designs have been carried out.

Article 11. Procedure for Performing Work on Water Objects and in Coastal Belts (or Zones)

Construction, dredging, and blasting, extracting minerals and aquatic plants, laying cables, pipelines, and other communications, cutting timber drilling, agricultural, and other work on water objects or in coastal belt (or zones) of waters which affects the state of the water shall be by agreement with agencies for regulating the use and conservation of water, executive committees of local soviets of working people's deputies, and other agencies, in accordance with USSR and union republic legislation.

Section II. Water Use

Article 12. Water Users

State, cooperative, and social enterprises, organizations, institutions, and citizens of the USSR may be water users in the USSR.

Other organizations and persons also may be water users in the instances provided for by USSR legislation.

Article 13. Objects of Water Use

The water objects enumerated in Article 4 of the present Fundamental Principles shall be granted for use.

The use of water objects of special state significance or of special scientific or cultural value may be prohibited in part or wholly in the procedure established by the USSR Council of Ministers and the union republic councils of ministers.

Article 14. Types of Water Use

Water objects shall be granted for use if the requirements and conditions provided for by law for the satisfaction of drinking, domestic, medicinal, resort, therapeutic, and other needs of the populace, and agricultural, industrial, power, transport, fishery, and other state and social needs are observed. The use of water objects for the discharge of sewage water may be permitted only in the instances and with observance of the special requirements and conditions provided for by USSR and union republic legislation.

A distinction shall be drawn between general water use, exercised without the use of installations or technical devices which affect the state of water, and special water use, exercised with the use of such installations or devices. The use of water without the use of installations or technical devices but exerting influence on the state of water also may be relegated in individual instances to special water use.

A list of the types of special water use shall be established by agencies regulating the use and conservation of water.

Water objects may be in joint or solitary use.

Enterprises, organizations, and institutions to which water objects have been granted for solitary use shall be primary water users; in instances established by USSR and union republic legislation they shall have the right to authorize secondary water use for other enterprises, organizations, institutions, and citizens by agreement with agencies regulating use and conservation of water.

Article 15. Procedure and Conditions for Granting Water Objects for Use

Water objects shall be granted for use first of all to satisfy drinking and domestic needs of the populace.

Water objects shall be granted for solitary use wholly or in part on the basis of a decree of the union republic council of ministers or the autonomous republic council of ministers, a decision of the executive committee of the respective soviet of working people's deputies or other authorized state agency in the procedure established by USSR and union republic legislation.

Special water use shall be exercised on the basis of permits issued by agencies regulating the use and conservation of water, and in instances provided for by USSR and union republic legislation, by the executive committees of local soviets of working people's deputies. Such permits shall be issued after agreement with agencies of the state sanitary inspectorate, for the protection of fish stocks, as well as other interested agencies. The procedure for agreement and the issuance of permits for special water use shall be established by the USSR Council of Ministers.

General water use shall be exercised without a permit in the procedure established by union republic legislation. At general water objects granted for solitary use, general water use shall be permitted on the conditions established by a primary water user by agreement with agencies regulating the use and conservation of water, but if necessary may be prohibited.

Water use shall be free of charge. Special water use may be subject to payment in the instances and in the procedure established by the USSR Council of Ministers.

Article 16. Periods of Water Use

Water objects shall be granted in perpetuity or for temporary use.

Water use without a period established in advance shall be deemed in perpetuity (permanent).

Temporary use may be short-term, up to three years, or long-term, from three to twenty-five years. If necessary, periods for water use may be extended for a period not exceeding respectively the periods for short-term or long-term temporary use.

General water use shall be unrestricted as to period.

Article 17. Rights and Duties of Water Users

Water users shall have the right to use water objects only for those purposes for which they have been granted.

In instances provided for by USSR and union republic legislation, the rights of water users may be restricted in the interests of the state, as well as in the interests of other water users. In such circumstances there should be no deterioration in the conditions for the use of water objects for drinking and domestic needs of the populace.

Water users shall be obliged to:

use water objects rationally and concern themselves with the economic expenditure of water and the restoration and improvement of water quality;

take measures for the complete cessation of the discharge of sewage waters containing pollutants into water objects;

not permit the violation of rights granted to other water users, as well as the infliction of damage on economic and natural objects (land, forests, wildlife, minerals, and others);

maintain purification and other water installations and technical devices affecting the state of water in good repair, improve their operational qualities, and record water use in established instances.

Article 18. Grounds for Termination of Water Use Rights

The right of water use by enterprises, organizations, institutions, and citizens shall be subject to termination respectively in instances of:

(1) no further need of water use or renunciation thereof;

(2) expiry of the period of water use;

(3) liquidation of an enterprise, organization, or institution;

(4) transfer of water installations to other water users;

(5) necessity arising to withdraw water objects from solitary use.

The right of water use by enterprises, organizations, institutions, and citizens (except the right of water use for drinking and domestic needs) also may be terminated in the event of the violation of rules for water use and their conservation and for the failure to use a water object in accordance with the purpose for which it was granted.

Other grounds for terminating the right of water use by enterprises, organizations, institutions, and citizens may be provided for by union republic legislation.

Article 19. Procedure for Termination of Water Use Rights

The right of water use shall be terminated by:

cancellation of a permit for special, as well as secondary, water use;

withdrawal of water objects granted for solitary use.

Special water use shall be terminated by decision of the agency which issued the permit therefor.

Secondary water use may be terminated by decision of the primary water user, agreed with an agency regulating water use and conservation.

Withdrawal of water objects from solitary use shall be in the procedure established by USSR and union republic legislation.

Water objects shall be withdrawn from solitary use of enterprises, organizations, and institutions of union subordination by agreement with the water users and the ministries and departments to which they are directly subordinate.

Article 20. Compensation for Losses Caused by the Conducting of Water Measures or the Termination or Alteration of Water Use Conditions

Losses caused to enterprises, organizations, institutions, and citizens as a result of the conducting of water measures (hydraulic engineering works and the like) or as a result of the termination or alteration of water use conditions shall be subject to compensation in the instances and in the procedure established by the USSR Council of Ministers.

Article 21. Use of Water Objects for Drinking, Domestic, and Other Needs of the Populace

Water objects whose water quality corresponds to the established sanitary requirements shall be granted for the drinking and domestic water supply, as well as for other needs of the populace.

The use of underground water of drinking quality for needs not connected with drinking and domestic water supply shall not, as a rule, be permitted. In districts which lack the necessary surface water sources and which have sufficient reserves of underground water of drinking quality, agencies regulating use and conservation of water may permit the use of such waters for purposes not connected with drinking and water supply.

Article 22. Use of Water Objects for Medicinal, Resort, and Therapeutic Purposes

Water objects relegated in the established procedure to the category of medicinal shall be used first of all for medicinal and resort purposes. In exceptional instances agencies regulating the use and conservation of water may authorize the use of water objects relegated to the category of medicinal for other purposes by agreement with the respective public health agencies and resort administrations.

The discharge of sewage waters into water objects relegated to the category of medicinal shall be prohibited.

The procedure for the use of waters for leisure and sport shall be established by USSR and union republic legislation.

Article 23. Use of Water Objects for Needs of Agriculture

The use of water objects for the needs of agriculture shall be by way of both general and special water use.

In special water use, irrigation, water-supply, drainage, and other water installations and devices belonging to state organizations, collective farms, state farms, and other water users shall be employed.

Collective farms, state farms, and other enterprises, organizations, institutions, and citizens using water objects for the needs of agriculture shall be obliged to observe the established plans, rules, norms, and regime of water use, take measures to reduce the loss of water in filtration and by evaporation in drainage and irrigation systems, prevent inefficient discharges of water from them, not allow fish from fishery waters into the drainage and irrigation systems, and also create the more favorable regime of soil moisture.

Irrigation of agricultural land with sewage waters shall be authorized by agencies regulating the use and conservation of water by agreement with state sanitary and veterinary supervision agencies.

The provisions of the present Article also shall extend to the irrigation and drainage of land occupied by forests, forest belts, and tree nurseries.

Article 24. Use of Water Objects for Industrial Purposes

Water users using water objects for industrial purposes shall be obliged to observe established plans, technological forms, and rules for water use, as well as take measures to reduce the expenditure of water and to stop the discharge of sewage waters by improving production technology and water supply schemes (employment of waterless technological processes, air cooling, recirculating water supply, and other technical methods).

In the event of natural disaster, emergency, or other exceptional circumstances, and also when an enterprise exceeds the established limit of water consumption from the main, the executive committees of local soviets of working people's deputies shall have the right to reduce or prohibit the consumption of drinking water for industrial purposes from municipal water mains and restrict temporarily from departmental economic and drinking mains in the interests of priority satisfaction of the drinking and domestic needs of the populace.

Underground waters (fresh, mineral, or thermal) not relegated to the category of drinking or medicinal waters may be used in the established procedure for technical water supply, extraction of chemical elements contained therein, obtaining thermal energy, and for other production needs, observing the requirements of rational use and conservation of water.

Article 25. Use of Water Objects for Hydroelectric Engineering Needs

The use of water objects for the needs of hydroelectric engineering shall be carried out by taking into account the interests of other branches of the national economy, as well as by observing the requirements for integrated use of water, unless expressly provided otherwise by decree of the USSR Council of Ministers or by decrees of the union republic councils of ministers, and in appropriate instances by decision of an agency regulating the use and conservation of water.

Article 26. Use of Water Objects for Needs of Water Transport and Logging

Rivers, lakes, reservoirs, canals, internal seas, and other internal sea waters of the USSR, as well as territorial waters (or territorial sea) of the USSR, shall be waterways of general use, except for instances when their use for such purposes is wholly or partially prohibited or they have been granted for solitary use.

The procedure for relegating waterways to the category of navigable and logging waterways and also for establishing rules for the use of waterways, shall be determined by USSR and union republic legislation.

The floating of unrafted logs, as well as the floating of timber in bundles and chained rafts without tugs, shall be prohibited on:

(1) navigable waterways;

(2) water objects, a list of which shall be confirmed by the USSR Council of Ministers or union republic councils of ministers, taking into account the special significance of these objects for fishing, water supply, or other national economic purposes.

The said types of logging shall be permitted on other water objects on the basis of permits issued by agencies regulating the use and conservation of water after agreement with fishery protection agencies.

Logging organizations shall be obliged regularly to clear sunken timber from logging routes.

Article 27. Use of Water Objects for Air Transport Needs

The procedure for the use of water objects for berthing, take-off, and landing of aircraft, as well as for other air transport needs, shall be established by USSR legislation.

Article 28. Use of Water Objects for Fishery Needs

The rights of water users may be restricted in the interests of fishing on fishery waters or individual areas thereof having particular importance for the preservation and reproduction of valuable fish species and other useful stocks. A list of such waters or areas thereof and the types of restriction of water use shall be determined by agencies regulating the use and conservation of water upon the representation of fishery protection agencies.

When hydraulic engineering and other installations are in operation on fishery waters, timely measures should be carried out ensuring the conservation of fish stocks and the conditions for their reproduction.

The procedure for the use of water objects for fishing needs shall be established by USSR and union republic legislation.

Article 29. Use of Water Objects for Hunting and Trapping Needs

Preferential rights of water use may be granted to hunting and trapping enterprises and organizations, taking into account integrated water use requirements, by agencies regulating the use and conservation of water on rivers, lakes, and other water objects which are the habitat of wild waterfowl and valuable furbearing animals (beaver, muskrat, coypu, and others).

The procedure for the use of water objects for hunting and trapping needs shall be established by USSR and union republic legislation.

Article 30. Use of Waters for the Needs of Preserves

Water objects of special scientific or cultural value shall be declared to be preserves in the procedure established by USSR and union republic legislation and shall be granted for solitary use in perpetuity as preserves for purposes of nature conservation and conducting scientific research.

The procedure for the use of preserve waters shall be determined by statutes on preserves.

The withdrawal of water objects from use as preserves shall be permitted only in instances of special need on the basis of a decree of a union republic council of ministers.

Article 31. Use of Water Objects for the Discharge of Sewage Waters

Water objects may be used for the discharge of industrial, municipal, domestic, drainage, and other sewage waters only with the authorization of agencies regulating the use and conservation of water after agreement with agencies carrying out state sanitary supervision, fishery protection, and other interested agencies.

The discharge of sewage waters shall be permitted only in instances if it will not lead to an increase in the pollutant content exceeding the established norms and on condition that the sewage water is purified by the water user up to the limits established by agencies regulating the use and conservation of water.

If the said requirements are violated, the discharge of sewage water should be restricted, suspended, or prohibited by agencies regulating the use and conservation of water until the individual industrial establishments, workshops, enterprises, organizations, and institutions cease the activity. In instances threatening the health of the populace, agencies exercising state sanitary supervision shall have the right to suspend the discharge of sewage waters until the operation of the production or other objects ceases, notifying the agencies regulating the use and conservation of water thereof.

The procedure and conditions for the use of water objects for the discharge of sewage waters shall be established by USSR and union republic legislation.

Article 32. Use of Water Objects for Fire-Fighting Needs and Other State and Social Necessities

It shall be permitted to take water from any water objects for fire-fighting needs.

The procedure for the use of water objects for fire-fighting needs, as well as other state and social needs, shall be established by USSR and union republic legislation.

Article 33. Use of Reservoirs

Enterprises, organizations, and institutions which use installations creating a head of water, allowing the passage of water, or the taking of water at reservoirs shall be obliged to observe the regime for filling and operating the reservoirs established by taking into account the interests of water users and land users in the zones of influence of the reservoirs.

The procedure for the use of reservoirs shall be determined by rules confirmed by agencies regulating the use and conservation of water for each reservoir, cascade, or reservoir system by agreement with agencies exercising state sanitary supervision, fishery protection, and other interested agencies.

The organization and coordination of measures ensuring the proper technical state and amenities of reservoirs, as well as control over the observance of rules for their use, shall be carried out by agencies regulating the use and conservation of water in the procedure established by the USSR Council of Ministers or union republic councils of ministers.

The provisions of the present Article also shall extend to the use of lakes and other waters used as reservoirs.

Article 34. Regulation of the Use of Water Objects Situated on the Territory of Several Union Republics

The regulation of the use of water objects situated on the territory of two or several union republics in a part affecting the interests of these republics shall be carried out by agreement between the agencies of the interested republics, except for water objects whose regulation of use is relegated to the competence of the USSR.

Article 35. Procedure for Settlement of Water Use Disputes

Disputes concerning water use shall be settled by union republic councils of ministers, autonomous republic councils of ministers, executive committees of local soviets of working people's deputies, as well as agencies regulating the use and conservation of water and other authorized state agencies, in the procedure established by USSR and union republic legislation.

Disputes between water users of one union republic and water users of another union republic concerning water use shall be considered by a commission formed on an equal footing from representatives of the interested union republics. If a commission fails to reach an agreed decision, disputes on the said matters shall be subject to consideration in the procedure determined by the USSR Council of Ministers.

Property disputes connected with water relationships shall be settled in the procedure established by USSR and union republic legislation.

Article 36. Water Use on Frontier Waters of the USSR

Water use on frontier waters of the USSR shall be on the basis of international agreements.

To the extent that water use in the Soviet part of frontier waters has not been regulated by international agreements with the participation of the USSR, it shall be exercised in accordance with USSR and union republic legislation.

The procedure for water use on frontier waters of the USSR shall be established by competent agencies by agreement with the border guard command.

Section III. Water Conservation and the Prevention of its Harmful Effects

Article 37. Conservation of Water

All waters (or water objects) shall be subject to protection from pollution, obstruction, and depletion which may harm the health of the populace, as well as entail diminution of fish stocks, deterioration of water supply conditions, and other unfavorable phenomena as a consequence of a change of physical, chemical, biological properties of water, reduction of its capacity for natural purification, and disturbance of the hydrological and hydrogeological regime.

Enterprises, organizations, and institutions whose activity affects the state of water shall be obliged to carry out technological, forest improvement, cropping, hydraulic engineering, sanitary, and other measures ensuring the protection of waters from pollution, obstruction, and depletion, as well as improving the state and regime of waters agreed with agencies regulating the use and conservation of water, executive committees of local soviets of working people's deputies, agencies exercising state sanitary supervision, fishery protection, and other interested state agencies or by instruction of authorized state agencies.

Water conservation measures shall be provided for in state plans for the development of the national economy.

Article 38. Protection of Water from Pollution and Obstruction

The discharge of production, domestic, and other types of waste and refuse into water objects shall be prohibited. The discharge of sewage waters shall be permitted only with the observance of requirements provided for by Article 31 of the present Fundamental Principles.

The owners of means of water transport, pipelines, and floating and other installations on water objects, logging organizations, as well as other enterprises, organizations, and institutions shall be obliged not to permit pollution and obstruction of water as a consequence of the loss of oil, timber, and chemical, petroleum, and other products.

Enterprises, organizations, and institutions shall be obliged not to permit the pollution and obstruction of surfaces of catchments, the ice cover of waters, and the surface of glaciers by production, domestic, and other waste, refuse, or scrap material, as well as oil and chemical products which, if washed down, entail a deterioration of the quality of surface and underground waters.

The administrations of state water systems, collective farms, state farms, and other enterprises, organizations, and institutions shall be obliged to prevent the pollution of water by fertilizers and toxic chemicals.

With a view to the protection of water used for drinking and domestic water supply, medicinal, resort, and therapeutic needs of the populace, sanitary protection areas and zones shall be established in accordance with USSR and union republic legislation.

Article 39. Protection of Waters from Depletion

With a view to maintaining a favorable water regime for rivers, lakes, reservoirs, underground waters, and other water objects, to preventing water erosion of soil, silting-up of waters, deterioration of habitat conditions for aquatic animals, and to reducing fluctuations in drainage, and so forth, forest water conservation zones shall be established, and also forest improvement, antierosion, hydraulic engineering, and other measures in the procedure provided for by USSR and union republic legislation.

In agreeing the question of the siting and construction of enterprises, installations, and other objects affecting the state of water, as well as in issuing permits for special water use, agencies regulating the use and conservation of water shall be obliged to be guided by schemes for the integrated use and conservation of water and by water balances, taking into account the interests of water users and land users.

If underground water levels are discovered when carrying on drilling and other mining work connected with the search or prospecting for and exploitation of deposits of gas, petroleum, coal, and other minerals, the organizations carrying on mining work shall be obliged immediately to notify the agencies regulating the use and conservation of water thereof and to take measures to protect the underground waters in the established procedure.

Selfpumping boreholes shall be subject to being equipped with regulatory devices, temporarily shut, or liquidated in the procedure established by USSR and union republic legislation.

Article 40. Prevention and Elimination of Harmful Effect of Water

Enterprises, organizations, and institutions shall be obliged to carry out measures for the prevention and elimination of the harmful effects of water which are agreed with agencies regulating the use and conservation of water, executive committees of local soviets of working people's deputies, and other interested state agencies or by instructions of authorized state agencies:

inundation, flooding, and saturation;

breaking of banks, dikes, and other installations;

saturation and salinization of land;

soil erosion, formation of ravines, landslides, flood streams, and other harmful phenomena.

The effectuation of urgent measures for the prevention and liquidation of natural disasters caused by the harmful effect of water shall be regulated by USSR and union republic legislation.

Measures for the prevention and liquidation of the harmful effects of water shall be provided for in state plans for the development of the national economy.

Section IV. State Recording and Planning of Water Use

Article 41. Tasks of State Recording and Planning of Water Use

The state recording of water and its use shall have as its task the establishment of the quantity and quality of water and data concerning water use for the needs of the populace and the national economy.

The planning of water use should ensure the scientifically well-founded distribution of water among water users, taking into account the priority satisfaction of drinking and domestic needs of the populace, water conservation, and prevention of its harmful effects. When planning water use, data from the state water register, water balances, and integrated water use and conservation schemes shall be taken into account.

Article 42. State Water Register

The state water register shall include data recording water by quantitative and qualitative indicators, registration of water use, as well as data recording water use.

Article 43. Water Balances

Water balances evaluating the existence and extent of water use shall be drawn up by basins, economic areas, union republics, and the USSR.

Article 44. Integrated Water Use and Conservation Schemes

General and basin (or territorial) schemes for the integrated use and conservation of water shall define the principal water and other measures subject to implementation in order to satisfy the long-term water requirements of the populace and the national economy, as well as for the conservation of water and prevention of its harmful effects.

Article 45. Procedure for State Recording of Water and Its Use, for Keeping the State Water Register, for Compiling Water Balances, and for Working Out Schemes for the Integrated Use and Conservation of Water

The state recording of water and its use, keeping the state water register, compiling water balances, and working out schemes for the integrated use and conservation of water shall be carried out at state expense and according to systems uniform for the USSR.

The procedure for state recording of water and its use, for keeping the state water register, for compiling water balances, and for working out and confirming schemes for the integrated use and conservation of water shall be established by the USSR Council of Ministers.

Section V. Responsibility for Violation of Water Legislation

Article 46. Responsibility for Violation of Water Legislation

Reassignment of the right of water use and other legal transactions directly or covertly violating the right of state ownership of water shall be void.

Persons guilty of performing the said legal transactions, as well as:

unauthorized seizure of water objects or unauthorized water use;

taking of water in violation of water use plans;

pollution and obstruction of water;

putting enterprises, municipal, or other objects into operation without installations and devices to prevent pollution and obstruction of water or its harmful effects;

wasteful use of water (extracted or drained from water objects);

violations of the water conservation regime in catchments, causing pollution, water erosion of soil, and other harmful phenomena;

unauthorized hydraulic engineering works;

damaging of water installations and devices;

violation of rules for the operation of water installations and devices;

bear criminal or administrative responsibility in accordance with USSR and union republic legislation.

Responsibility for other types of violations of water legislation also may be established by union republic legislation.

Water objects seized without authorization shall be returned according to their affiliation without compensation for expenditure incurred during the time of illegal use.

Enterprises, organizations, institutions, and citizens shall be obliged to compensate losses caused by a violation of water legislation in the amounts and in the procedure established by USSR and union republic legislation. Officials and other workers by whose fault the enterprises, organizations, and institutions have borne expenditures connected with the compensation of losses shall bear material liability in the established procedure.

FUNDAMENTAL PRINCIPLES OF FORESTRY LEGISLATION OF THE USSR AND UNION REPUBLICS

[Confirmed by Law of the USSR Supreme Soviet, June 17, 1977. Vedomosti SSSR (1977), no. 25, item 388]

As a result of the triumph of the Great October Socialist Revolution, the forests, just as other natural wealth in our country, were nationalized and became the property of the people. The Decret of the All-Russian Central Executive Committee "On the Forests" of 27(14) May 1918 determined the basic principles of the socialist organization of forestry with a view to the use of forests in the interests of the entire people.

State ownership of forests in the USSR shall constitute the basis of forestry relations, that is, of social relations in the domain of the use, regeneration, and protection of forests, and shall serve as a principal prerequisite for the rational conduct of forestry.

Forests in the USSR shall play a large role in the development of the economy, improvement of the environment, and raising the well-being of the people. They shall be a source for satisfying the requirements of the country for timber and other forestry products, shall render a favorable influence on the climate, air, and the hydrological regime of rivers and other water objects, shall protect soil from wind and water erosion, and shall have other useful natural properties. Forests shall be used more and more for therapeutic purposes and for satisfying the cultural and aesthetic needs of the populace.

The multifaceted significance of forests and the length of time to cultivate them imparts to the cause of rational use, care, and multiplication of forestry riches the character of an all-state task.

Soviet forestry legislation is called upon to actively further the scientifically well-founded, integrated use of forests, their planned regeneration and effective protection in the interests of the present and future generations, and the education of the Soviet people in the spirit of high responsibility for a zealous and solicitous attitude toward the forest as an important integral part of the natural wealth of our Motherland.

Section I. General Provisions

Article 1. Tasks of Soviet Forestry Legislation

The tasks of Soviet forestry legislation shall be the regulation of forestry relations with a view to ensuring the rational use of forests and their protection and defense, regeneration, and increased productiveness in order to satisfy the requirements of the national economy and the populace for timber, other forestry products, and to intensify the water protection, protective, climate regulating, sanitary-hygienic, therapeutic, and other useful natural properties of forests, and also the protection of the rights of enterprises, organizations, institutions, and citizens and the strengthening of legality in the domain of forestry relations.

Article 2. Forestry Legislation of the USSR and Union Republics

Forest relations in the USSR shall be regulated by the present Fundamental Principles and other acts of forestry legislation of the USSR issued in accordance therewith, forestry codes, and other union republic acts of forestry legislation.

Land, water, and mining relations shall be regulated by the respective USSR and union republic legislation.

Article 3. State Ownership of Forests in the USSR

In accordance with the USSR Constitution, forests in the Union of Soviet Socialist Republics shall be state ownership, that is, the property of the entire people.

Forests in the USSR shall be in the exclusive ownership of the state and shall be granted only for use. Actions, direct or indirect, violating the right of state ownership of forests shall be prohibited.

Article 4. Unified State Forestry Fund. State Forestry Fund Lands

All the forests in the USSR shall constitute the unified state forestry fund.

The unified state forestry fund shall consist of:

(1) forests of state significance, that is, forests in the jurisdiction of state forestry agencies, city forests, allocated forests, and preserve forests;

(2) collective farm forests, that is, forests on lands granted to collective farms for use in perpetuity.

Lands covered by forest and also not covered by forest but earmarked for forestry needs shall be deemed state forestry fund lands in accordance with the Fundamental Principles of Land Legislation of the USSR and Union Republics. Boundaries of state forestry fund lands separating them from lands of other categories shall be determined in the established procedure.

Article 5. Shrubbery Plantings Not Within the State Forestry Fund

There shall not be in the state forest fund:

trees and groups of trees, and also shrubbery on designated agricultural lands;

protective plantings on belts of railway, highway, and canal plots;

trees and groups of trees, and also greenery in cities and other population centers growing on lands not occupied by urban forests;

trees and groups of trees on personal, dacha, and garden plots.

The creation of the said plantings and the caring for and use thereof shall be carried out in the procedure determined by USSR and union republic legislation.

Article 6. Competence of the USSR in Regulating Forestry Relations

There shall be subject to the jurisdiction of the USSR in the domain of regulating forestry relations:

(1) disposal of the unified state forest fund within the limits necessary to carry out the powers of the USSR in accordance with the USSR Constitution;

(2) establishment of basic provisions for the use of forests, regeneration, raising productiveness, and protecting and defending forests;

(3) establishment of the size of the forest-cutting fund of the USSR, the procedure for distributing it, and the distribution of standing timber;

(4) establishment of the basic orientations and long-term plans for the development of forestry of the country and the use of forest resources and useful natural properties of the forest;

(5) planning of all-union measures for the rational use, regeneration, raising the productiveness, protection, and defense of forests;

(6) establishment of the procedure for relegating forests to the respective groups and transferring them from one group to another;

(7) establishment of systems of forest tenure uniform for the USSR, registration of forests, and the procedure for keeping the state forest register;

(8) state control over the state, use, regeneration, protection, and defense of forests and establishment of the procedure for carrying them out.

Article 7. Competence of Union Republics in Regulating Forestry Relations

There shall be subject to union republic jurisdiction in the domain of regulating forestry relations beyond the limits of USSR competence: disposal of the unified state forest fund on the territory of the republic; establishment of the procedure for the use of forests, the regeneration, raising the productiveness, protecting and defending forests; establishment of long-term plans for the development of forestry, use of forest resources and useful natural properties of the forest; planning of republic measures for the rational use, regeneration, raising the productiveness, protecting, and defending forests; exercising state control over the state, use, regeneration, protection, and defense of forests, and also the regulation of forestry relations on other questions unless they have been relegated to the competence of the USSR.

Article 8. State Administration in the Domain of the Use, Regeneration, Protection, and Defense of Forests

State administration in the domain of the use, regeneration, protection, and defense of forests shall be carried out by the USSR Council of Ministers, union republic councils of ministers, autonomous republic councils of ministers, and executive committees of local soviets of working people's deputies, and also by state forestry agencies and other state agencies in accordance with USSR and union republic legislation.

Article 9. State Control Over the State, Use, Regeneration, Protection, and Defense of Forests

State control over the state, use, regeneration, protection, and defense of forests shall have as its task to ensure the observance by all ministries, departments, state, cooperative, and social enterprises, organizations, institutions, and citizens of the established procedure for the use of forests, rules for conducting forestry, for forest regeneration, for their registration and protection, and also other rules and norms provided for by forestry legislation.

State control over the state, use, regeneration, protection, and defense of all forests shall be carried out by soviets of working people's deputies, their executive and administrative agencies, and also by state forestry agencies and other specially authorized state agencies in the procedure established by USSR legislation.

Article 10. Participation of Social Organizations and Citizens in Carrying Out Measures for the Rational Use, Regeneration, Protection, and Defense of Forests

Trade unions, youth organizations, nature conservation societies, scientific societies, and other social organizations, and also citizens, shall render assistance to state agencies and collective farms in carrying out measures for the rational use, regeneration, protection, and defense of forests.

Social organizations shall take part in activity directed toward ensuring the rational use, regeneration, protection, and defense of forests in accordance with their charters (or statutes) and USSR and union republic legislation.

State agencies shall be obliged to take into account in every possible way the proposals of social organizations and citizens when carrying out measures for the rational use, regeneration, protection, and defense of forests.

Article 11. Basic Requirements for Conducting Forestry

State agencies, enterprises, organizations, and institutions carrying out planning and organizing and conducting forestry and the use of forest resources, taking into account the national economic significance of forests and natural conditions, shall be obliged to ensure:

the intensification of water protection, protective, climate regulating, therapeutic, and other use of natural properties of forests in the interests of protecting the health of people, improving the environment, and developing the national economy;

the uninterrupted, inexhaustible, and rational use of the forest for the planned satisfaction of the requirements of the national economy and the populace for timber and other forest products;

the expanded regeneration and improved pedigree and quality of forests, and their increased productiveness;

care for forests, protecting them from fires, and defending them from pests and diseases;

rational use of state forestry fund lands and other lands occupied by forests;

increasing the efficiency of forestry production on the basis of a uniform technological policy and the achievements of science and technology.

Caring for the forest, and also defending it from pests and diseases, should be carried out by means and methods not harmful to man and the environment.

Measures for conducting forestry shall be provided in state plans for the development of the national economy, taking the long-term perspective, and shall be carried out by the appropriate ministries, departments, and forestry enterprises.

Article 12. Rights and Duties of State Forestry Agencies in the Use and Protection of Lands

State forestry agencies and forestry enterprises within their jurisdiction shall organiza the specially designated use and ensure the protection of lands in the use of such enterprises, determine the area in which various types of forest uses should be carried out and measures for the regeneration of forests and care for forests should be implemented, shall grant land plots in accordance with Article 22, paragraph two, of the present Fundamental Principles in order to effectuate forest uses and needs connected therewith, allot plots for organizing forest nurseries, plantations, and the like, and also may have other rights and duties in the domain of the use and protection of the said lands in accordance with USSR and union republic legislation.

The rights and duties provided for by paragraph one of the present Article also shall extend to other enterprises, organizations, and institutions conducting forestry and their superior agencies.

State forestry agencies of the USSR and union republics shall exercise control over the use of state forestry fund lands in accordance with their special designation and over the protection of such lands in the procedure established by USSR legislation.

Article 13. Conducting Forestry in Forests of State Significance

Conducting forestry in forests of state significance shall be entrusted to:

forestry enterprises of state forestry agencies (except urban forests, allocated forests, and preserve forests);

forestry and other enterprises, organizations, and institutions of executive committees of city, district (in city) soviets of working people's deputies: in urban forests. Forestry in urban forests may be conducted jointly with forestry enterprises of state forestry agencies;

forestry and other enterprises, organizations, and institutions of ministries and departments to which these forests have been allocated: in allocated forests;

preserves: in preserve forests.

The regeneration, protection, defense, and improvement of the sanitary state of forests, caring for them, raising the productiveness of forests and the fertility of forest soils, organizing forest use, registration of forests, and other duties relating to conducting forestry established by USSR and union republic legislation shall be entrusted to the enterprises, organizations, and institutions conducting forestry in forests of state significance.

The rules, instructions, and *ukazaniia* of state forestry agencies of the USSR and union republics shall, within the limits of rights established by USSR and union republic legislation, be binding upon ministries, departments, enterprises, organizations, and institutions to whom the conducting of forestry has been entrusted, upon forest users, and also upon enterprises, organizations, institutions, and citizens who are carrying out work in forests and on state forest fund lands not covered by forests which is not connected with conducting forestry or carrying out forest uses.

Ukazaniia of enterprises, organizations, and institutions conducting forestry in forests of state significance shall, within the limits of rights established by USSR and union republic legislation, be binding upon all forest users, and also upon enterprises, organizations, institutions, and citizens carrying out work in these forests and on corresponding state forest fund lands not covered by forest which is not connected with conducting forestry or carrying out forest uses.

Enterprises, organizations, and institutions conducting forestry in forests of state significance may carry out the forest uses in the established procedure provided for by Article 21 of the present Fundamental Principles.

Article 14. Conducting Forestry in Collective Farm Forests

Forests on lands granted to collective farms for use in perpetuity and registered in the established procedure on land registration documents shall be deemed collective farm forests.

Collective farm forests shall be in the use of collective farms in perpetuity.

Conducting forestry in collective farm forests shall be carried out by collective farms in accordance with the Statute on Collective Farm Forests confirmed by the USSR Council of Ministers. Collective farms may conduct forestry jointly with other collective farms, state farms, and other enterprises, organizations, and institutions in the procedure determined by USSR and union republic legislation.

The direction of organizations and the conducting of forestry on collective farms shall be carried out by state agricultural agencies.

State forestry agencies shall render assistance to collective farms in planning and organizing the conducting of forestry, and, if necessary, shall organize the fulfillment by enterprises within their jurisdiction under contracts with collective farms (or organizations conducting forestry on collective farm forests) of forestry, forest cultivation, and forest-protective work.

Article 15. Division of Forests into Groups

A division of forests into groups shall be established in accordance with the national economic significance of forests, their location, and the functions they fulfill. Forests of state significance shall be divided into a first, second, and third group, and collective farm forests, into a first and second group.

Forests fulfilling primarily the following functions shall be relegated to the first group:

water protection (restricted belts of forests along the coasts of rivers, lakes, water reservoirs, and other water objects, including restricted forest belts protecting the spawning of commercially valuable fish);

protective (antierosion forests, including forest plots for steep mountain slopes, state protective forest belts, coniferous forests, steppe growth and forests, protective belts of forest along railways and highways of all-state, republic, and regional significance, and especially valuable forest blocks);

sanitary-hygienic and therapeutic (urban forests, green zone forests around cities, other population centers, and industrial enterprises, fores zones for sanitary protection of sources of water supply and areas for the sanitary protection of resorts).

Forests of preserves and national and natural parks, preserve forest parcels, forests having scientific or historical significance, natural monuments, forest parks, brazil-nut forestry zones, fruit tree plantings, tundra, and sub-alpine forests also shall be relegated to the first group.

Forests in areas with a high population density and a developed network of transport routes having a protective and limited exploitation significance, and also forests with inadequate forestry raw material resources shall be relegated to the second group in order to preserve the protective functions for which uninterrupted and inexhaustible use requires a stricter regime of forest use.

All collective farm forests not within the first group also shall be relegated to the second group.

Forests of heavily-forested areas having primarily significance for exploitation and earmarked for the uninterrupted satisfaction of the requirements of the national economy for timber without damaging the protective properties of these forests shall be relegated to the third group.

Third group forests shall be subdivided into exploited and reserve groups.

Forests which have not been involved in exploitation as a consequence of their remoteness from transport routes and for other reasons shall be deemed reserve forests.

When relegating forests to respective groups, the boundaries of the lands occupied by forests of each group shall be determined at the same time. Depending upon the group of forests, the procedure for conducting forestry in them, the use of forests and the corresponding lands, and also the procedure for withdrawal of these lands for state or social needs shall be established.

Especially protective parcels with a restricted forest use regime may be allocated within first and second group forests and in mountain forests of all groups.

The relegation of forests to groups, the transfer from one group to another, the determination of the breadth of restricted and protective belts, the relegation of forest parcels for steep mountain slopes to protective forests, and also the allocation of especially protective forest parcels, shall be carried out by proceeding from the national economic significance of the forests, their location, the functions they fulfill, and the economic grounds in the procedure established by USSR legislation. The transfer of forests from one group to another in connection with the construction of large-scale national economic objects shall be carried out until construction of the object begins.

Article 16. Transfer of Forest Areas to Nonforest Areas

The lands comprising the state forestry fund shall be allotted into:

forest areas (covered by forest, and also not covered by forest: nonafforested wood-cutting, burning, thinning, glades, wasteland, and so forth);

nonforest areas (agricultural land, roads, cuttings, and so forth).

The transfer of forest areas into nonforest areas in order to use them for purposes not connected with conducting forestry and to exercise forest uses shall be:

in first group forests: in exceptional instances by decree of the union republic council of ministers;

in second and third group forests: in the procedure established by USSR and union republic legislation.

When withdrawing land plots occupied by forests for state or social needs, the state agencies adopting the decision to withdraw shall simultaneously decide the question of preserving or cutting the timber and of the procedure for using the timber obtained.

Article 17. Use of Lands for Erecting Production Objects Connected with the Conducting of Forestry

Enterprises, organizations, and institutions conducting forestry in forests of state significance may erect, in the established procedure, in forests and on state forestry fund lands not covered by forest production objects connected with conducting forestry, transferring when necessary (with the authorization of agencies to which these enterprises, organizations, and institutions are subordinate) of the forest areas to nonforest areas.

Collective farms in whose use there are forests may erect on state forestry fund lands granted them for use in perpetuity production objects connected with the conducting of forestry, with the authorization of executive committees of district or city soviets of working people's deputies.

Article 18. Siting, Designing, Construction, and Introduction into Use of Enterprises, Installations, and Other Objects Affecting the State and Regeneration of Forests

When siting, designing, constructing, and introducing into use new and converted enterprises, installations, and other objects, and also when introducing new technological processes affecting the state and regeneration of forests, measures should be provided and carried out ensuring the protection of forests from the negative influence on them of sewage waters, chemical substances, and industrial and municipal-domestic effluents, wastes, and refuse.

The determination of places for the construction of enterprises, installations, and other objects affecting the state and regeneration of forests shall be agreed with executive committees of local soviets of working people's deputies, state forestry agencies, and other agencies in accordance with USSR and union republic legislation. Construction designs of the said enterprises, installations, and other objects shall be subject to agreement with state forestry agencies and other agencies in the instances and procedure established by USSR legislation.

The introduction into use of new and converted enterprises, shops, assemblies, transport routes, municipal, and other objects not provided with devices preventing the harmful influence on the state and regeneration of forests shall be prohibited.

Article 19. Procedure for Performance in Forests of Work Not Connected with Conducting Forestry and Carrying Out Forest Uses

Construction and blasting work, extraction of minerals, laying of cables, pipelines, and other communications, boring, and other work in forests, and also on state forestry fund lands not covered by forest and not connected with conducting forestry, and the carrying out of forest uses shall be performed by agreement with the executive committees of local soviets of working people's deputies, state forestry agencies, and other agencies in connection with USSR and union republic legislation.

The said works should be carried out by means not causing the deterioration of the fire-prevention and sanitary state of forests and conditions for their regeneration.

Section II. Forest Use

Article 20. Forest Users

State, cooperative, and social enterprises, organizations, and institutions, and also citizens of the USSR, may be forest users.

In the instances provided by USSR legislation, other organizations and persons also may be forest users.

Article 21. Types and Periods of Forest Uses

The following types of forest uses may be carried out in forests, and also on state forestry fund lands not covered by forest, with observance of the requirements and conditions provided for by legislation:

(1) procurement of timber;

(2) procurement of soft resin;

(3) procurement of secondary forestry materials (stumps, basts, bark, etc.);

(4) collateral forest uses: haying, pasturage of livestock, siting of beehives and apiaries, procurement of tree saps, procurement and gathering of wild fruit, nuts, mushrooms, berries, medicinal plants, and technical raw materials. Haying and livestock pasturage on agricultural lands within state forestry fund lands shall be carried out in accordance with the requirements of USSR and union republic land legislation, taking into account the interests of forestry. Other collateral forest uses also may be provided by union republic legislation;

(5) use of the forest for scientific research purposes;

(6) use of the forest for cultural and therapeutic purposes;

(7) use of the forest for needs of hunting.

Periods for carrying out forest uses shall be established:

for the procurement of timber and soft resins: by USSR legislation;

for carrying out other forest uses: by USSR and union republic legislation.

Article 22. Procedure for Granting Right to Carry Out Forest Uses

Enterprises, organizations, and institutions conducting forestry shall grant, in the established procedure, plots in kind to forest users for the procurement of timber, soft resins, and secondary forestry materials, for haying, livestock pasturage and other forest uses.

Carrying out forest uses (with the exception provided for by Article 35 of the present Fundamental Principles) shall be permitted only by special permit: a timber-cutting card (or order) or forestry card, the forms of which shall be confirmed in the procedure established by the USSR Council of Ministers. A timber-cutting card (or order) or forestry card shall give the right to use the land plot needed to carry out the forest use. Forest users shall have the right to use the respective areas only for those forest uses for which the timber-cutting card (or order) or forestry card was issued to them.

A timber-cutting card (or order) and forestry card shall be issued by enterprises, organizations, and institutions conducting forestry.

Enterprises, organizations, and institutions conducting forestry shall, when carrying out forest uses, be obliged to formalize the right of forest use on the general grounds.

The procedure for issuing permits for the siting of tourist camps, leisure bases, and other similar objects with the erection of non-capital type structures shall be regulated by union republic legislation.

The procedure for granting the right to use the forest for scientific research purposes and for hunting needs shall be established by USSR and union republic legislation.

Article 23. Procedure for the Procurement of Timber

The procurement of timber in forests shall be carried out by way of principal use felling (including forest-restoration fellings) of mature tree stands.

Timber also shall be procured when conducting intermediate use fellings (fellings to care for the forest, sanitary fellings, and fellings connected with the reconstruction of forestry plantings of little value) and when conducting other fellings (cleaning forest areas in connection with the construction of hydrojunctions, pipelines, roads, and also when laying cuttings, creating fire safety breaks, and so forth). The procurement of timber when conducting intermediate use fellings and other felling shall be carried out in forests of all groups.

Principal use fellings in third group forests shall be carried out by means directed toward the efficient exploitation of forests and furthering the restoration of economically valuable species of timber.

In second group forests principal use fellings shall be carried out by means directed toward the restoration of forests with economically valuable timber species, the preservation of the protective and water conservation properties of forests, allowing their efficient exploitation in this connection.

In first group forests, forest restoration fellings shall be carried out in the procedure determined by the USSR Council of Ministers by means directed toward the improvement of the forest environment, the state of tree stands, water conservation, protective, and other properties of forests and their timely and rational use of mature trees.

In forests of preserves, national and natural parks, preserve forest sectors, forests having scientific or historical significance, natural monuments, forest parks, forest nut zones, fruit tree plantings, urban forests, forest park areas of green zones, sanitary protection zone forests for water supply sources and areas for the sanitary protection of resorts, state forest belts, antierosion forests and especially valuable forest blocks, fellings shall be permitted only for the care of the forest and for sanitary fellings.

Fellings to care for the forest and sanitary fellings shall be carried on in restricted forest belts protecting the spawning of valuable commercial fish and selective forest restoration fellings shall be permitted in the procedure determined by the USSR Council of Ministers.

Means of felling shall be applied in mountain forests which take into account the special protective, antierosion, and water regulating significance of these forests.

The application of dense timber felling methods may be completely or partially prohibited in especially protective sectors of forest, and, when necessary, also the application of other means of principal use felling.

The procedure for the procurement of timber shall be established by Rules for Standing Timber in Forests of the USSR, confirmed by the USSR Council of Ministers.

Rules for timber felling shall be confirmed in the procedure established by the USSR Council of Ministers.

Article 24. Determining the Amount of Timber Procurement

The planning and procurement of timber by way of principal use felling shall be carried out by proceeding from the necessity of satisfying the requirements of the national economy for timber with the limits of rated wood-cutting areas.

Principal use fellings in amounts exceeding the rated wood-cutting area may be permitted when necessary in third or second group forests in the procedure determined by the USSR Council of Ministers.

The amount of timber procurement when conducting intermediate use fellings shall be determined by proceeding from the need to improve the species composition and quality of forests, and the amount of timber procurement when conducting other fellings, by the amount of work for thinning forest areas, laying cuttings, and so forth.

Article 25. Timber-cutting Fund

The timber-cutting fund shall be formed from reserves of mature tree stands earmarked for timber procurement.

The amount of annually allotted timber-cutting fund shall be determined in state plans for the development of the national economy separately by forest groups.

The timber-cutting fund in kind (or allocation of timber-cutting area) to forest users (or timber procurers) shall be transferred by enterprises, organizations, and institutions conducting forestry.

The procedure for the transfer of the timber-cutting fund to forest users shall be established by the Rules for Standing Timber in Forests of the USSR.

Article 26. Allocation of Standing Timber Reserves to Timber Procurement Enterprises

In order to ensure the planned and prolonged industrial exploitation of forests, standing timber reserves on a specified area (or forest raw material base), and also the long-term use timber-cutting fund, shall be allocated for an economically justified period in third and second group forests to timber procurement enterprises.

In instances determined by the USSR Council of Ministers, standing timber reserves in the form of a long-term use timber cutting fund shall be allocated to timber-cutting enterprises also in first group forests (except for forests of preserves, national and natural parks, preserve forest sectors, forests having scientific or historical significance, natural monuments, forest parks, forest nut zones, fruit tree plantings, urban forests, forest park areas of green zones, sanitary protection zone forests for water supply sources and areas for the sanitary protection of resorts, state forest belts, antierosion forests and especially valuable forest blocks, and restricted forest belts protecting the spawning of valuable commercial fish).

Forestry raw material bases and the long-term use timber-cutting fund shall be allocated in priority to timber procurement enterprises of the forestry industry.

The procedure for the allocation and exploitation of standing timber reserves shall be established depending on the forest groups.

The satisfaction of local timber requirements shall be provided for when allocating standing timber reserves to timber procurement enterprises

In the forest raw material bases and long-term use timber-cutting fund allocated to them, timber procurement enterprises shall carry out the procurement of timber in accordance with Articles 22, 23, 24, and 25 of the present Fundamental Principles.

The allocation, redistribution, and withdrawal of forest raw material bases and the long-term use timber-cutting fund shall be in the procedure established by the USSR Council of Ministers.

Article 27. Distribution of Standing Timber

Standing timber in forests shall be distributed for payment at the established rates. Standing timber in collective farm forests shall be distributed free of charge for the needs of the social economy of the collective farms.

Enterprises, organizations, and institutions conducting forestry shal be relieved from payment for timber obtained when caring for the forest an carrying out other forestry measures.

The procedure for payment of standing timber, for the establishment of the rate, for the partial or complete exemption in individual instances of state, cooperative, and social enterprises, organizations, institutions and citizens from paying for standing timber shall be determined by USSR legislation.

Article 28. Procedure for Procurement of Soft Resins

Soft resins in forests may be procured only by state and cooperative enterprises, organizations, and institutions. The procedure for payment for the procurement of soft resins shall be established by USSR legislation.

Conducting principal use fellings shall be prohibited until the periods of sap flow have ended in those coniferous plantings which have been earmarked in the established procedure for the procurement of soft resins. Felling of the said plantings before sap-flow, and also the withdrawal before time of plantings from sap-flow, may, as an exception, be permitted in the procedure determined by the USSR Council of Ministers.

Article 29. Procedure for Procurement of Secondary Forest Materials

The procurement of secondary forest materials for industrial processing, the development of forest trades, and the satisfaction of the needs of the populace should be carried out without causing harm to the forest.

The procedure for the procurement of secondary forest materials, confirmation of the rate for such materials, or exemption from payment therefor shall be established by USSR and union republic legislation.

Article 30. Procedure for Carrying Out Collateral Forestry Uses

Collateral forest uses shall be carried out free of charge, except for the trade procurement of timber saps, wild fruits, nuts, mushrooms, berries, and technical raw materials. Rates for the said products shall be established by union republic legislation.

Enterprises, organizations, and institutions conducting forestry shall carry out all types of collateral forest uses free of charge.

All collateral forest uses should be carried out without harm to the forest.

Haying and livestock pasturage in forests and on state forestry fund lands not covered by forest shall be prohibited in sectors where this may harm the forest.

In forests of state significance haying and pasturage not used for the needs of forestry and the timber-procurement industry shall be granted to collective farms, state farms, other enterprises, organizations, institutions, and citizens for temporary use if such use is compatible with the interests of forestry. Haying and pasturage shall be granted with observance of the requirements of land legislation.

The procedure and conditions for carrying out collateral forest uses shall be established by USSR and union republic legislation.

Article 31. Procedure for Using the Forest for Scientific Research Purposes

Special sectors may be allocated to the appropriate enterprises, organizations, and institutions in order to carry out scientific research work in forests.

Forest uses for other enterprises, organizations, and institutions, and also citizens, may be restricted or wholly prohibited on the allotted sectors if this is incompatible with the aims of conducting scientific research work.

The procedure for using a forest for scientific research purposes shall be established by USSR and union republic legislation.

Article 32. Procedure for Using the Forest for Cultural-Therapeutic Purposes

With a view to organizing the leisure of the populace, executive committees of soviets of working people's deputies, forestry enterprises of state forestry agencies, and also other enterprises, organizations, and institutions, by agreement with them, in forests of green zones and other forests used for the leisure of the populace shall carry out measures for the public amenities of forest parcels and for the cultural-domestic servicing of the populace, taking into account the need to preserve the forest environment and natural landscapes, observing the architectural planning of suburban zones and sanitary requirements.

The procedure for using the forest for cultural-therapeutic purposes shall be established by USSR and union republic legislation.

Article 33. Procedure for Using the Forest for Hunting

Forest uses and forestry measures in forests should be carried out, taking into account the need to preserve favorable conditions for wildlife to feed.

The numbers of wildlife in forests shall be regulated within the limits of density permissible for forest lands so that wildlife do not harm forestry and agriculture.

The procedure for forest use for hunting needs shall be established by USSR and union republic legislation.

Article 34. Rights and Duties of Forest Users

Forest users shall have the right and shall be obliged to carry out only those forest uses which they have been authorized.

Forest users procuring timber shall have the right, within the established periods, to receive the timber-cutting fund in amounts necessary to fulfill the planning tasks of state plans for the development of the national economy.

Depending on the type of forest use, forest users shall have the right in the established procedure to lay roads, equip areas for storing forest products, erect production and domestic structures, fix equipment and appliances for exploring for and processing timber, build transport stops, and so forth.

In the instances provided for by USSR and union republic legislation, the rights of forest users may be restricted in the interests of the state and also in the interests of other forest users.

Carrying out forest uses to derive nonlabor income shall be prohibited.

The violated rights of forest users shall be subject to restoration, and losses caused to them, to compensation in the procedure established by the present Fundamental Principles and other USSR and union republic legislation.

Depending on the type of forest use, forest users shall be obliged to:

use as fully as possible and rationally the timber-cutting areas transferred to them and forest plantings allotted for tapping, forest haying, and other forest lands;

not leave small cuttings (or parts of felled timber), nor also cut timber on felling sites or in the forest after the expiry of the periods for its cutting and transport established by Rules for Standing Timber in Forests of the USSR;

carry on work with means not allowing soil erosion to commence and precluding or limiting the negative influence of forest uses on the state and regeneration of forests, and also on the state of waters and other natural objects;

observe fire safety, carry out fire prevention measures at the sites when conducting work, and if forest fires start, to extinguish them;

not allow the loss of timber, nor the conversion of timber into firewood, nor the use of timber for other than its purpose;

clean woodcutting areas of cutting remnants and bring the land plots disturbed as a result of forest uses into a state, at their own expense, suitable for its designated use;

fulfill other requirements established by the Rules for Standing Timber in Forests of the USSR and rules for cutting forests.

The state agency of the forestry industry of the USSR shall determine the technical policy binding upon all forest procurers, while observing the requirements of the present Fundamental Principles, based on the application of progressive technological processes, machines, and mechanisms.

Article 35. Sojourn of Citizens in Forests

Citizens shall have the right to freely stay in forests, gather wild fruits, nuts, mushrooms, berries, and so forth.

Citizens shall be obliged to observe the fire safety rules in forests, not to permit the breakage and cutting of trees and bushes, harm forest growth, litter forests, destroy anthills, nesting birds, and so forth.

The sojourn of citizens in forests, collecting of wild fruits, nuts, mushrooms, berries, and so forth may be restricted in the procedure determined by USSR and union republic legislation in the interests of fire safety or carrying on nut gathering, fruit picking, or seeding, and in preserve forests and other forests, in connection with the special use procedure established therein.

Article 36. Bases for Terminating the Right of Forest Use of Enterprises, Organizations, and Institutions

The right of forest use for enterprises, organizations, and institutions shall be subject to termination wholly or partially, respectively, in instances of:

(1) the need for forest use having passed;

(2) expiry of the period of forest use;

(3) liquidation of the enterprise, organization, or institution.

The right of forest use of enterprises, organizations, and institutions also may be terminated in the event of the withdrawal of state forestry fund lands or other lands occupied by forests for other state or social needs or if forest uses are not exercised in accordance with their purposes or the requirements provided in the timber-cutting card (or order) or forestry card.

Other grounds for terminating the right of forest use of enterprises, organizations, and institutions also may be provided by USSR and union republic legislation.

Article 37. Grounds for Terminating Right of Forest Use of Citizens

The right of forest use of citizens shall be subject to termination wholly or partially, respectively, in instances of:

(1) voluntary renunciation of forest use;

(2) expiry of period of forest use;

(3) not exercising forest uses in accordance with the purposes or requirements provided in the timber-cutting card (or order) or forestry card.

The right of forest use of citizens also may be terminated in the event of the withdrawal of state forestry fund lands or other lands occupied by forests, for state or social needs.

Other grounds for terminating the right of forest use of citizens also may be provided by USSR and union republic legislation.

Article 38. Peculiarities of Forest Use in Urban Forests

Urban forests shall be used primarily for cultural-therapeutic purposes and for leisure of the populace.

Timber procurement by way of principal use cutting and the procurement of soft resins and wood sap shall be prohibited in urban forests.

Other types of forest uses also may be prohibited by union republic legislation in urban forests, if they are incompatible with carrying on cultural-therapeutic measures and with organizing the leisure of the populace.

The provisions of the present Article shall extend also to forests of population centers relegated in accordance with union republic legislation to categories of urban-type settlements.

Article 39. Peculiarities of Forest Use in Allocated Forests

Enterprises, organizations, and institutions of ministries and departments for whom forests have been allocated in order to fulfill scientific, training, and other tasks entrusted to them shall have a preferential right to carry out, in the established procedure in such forests, the appropriate types of forest uses.

Forest uses of other enterprises, organizations, and institutions, and also citizens, may be restricted or completely prohibited in allocated forests if they are incompatible with the purposes of allocating the forests.

The procedure for allocating the forests, and also the procedure for forest use in allocated forests, shall be established by USSR and union republic legislation.

Article 40. Restriction of Forest Use in Preserve Forests

In preserve forests the principal use felling, procurement of soft resins, and also other forest uses not compatible with the purposes of a preserve, shall be prohibited.

The procedure for forest use in preserve forests shall be determined by USSR and union republic legislation.

Article 41. Peculiarities of Forest Use in Collective Farm Forests

Forest uses in collective farm forests shall be carried out first of all by collective farms and collective farmers.

Collective farms (or inter-collective farm forestry organizations) shall carry out all types of forest uses in collective farm forests for the needs of the social economy free of charge. Collective farm members shall carry out forest uses in such forests on the basis of exemptions or free of charge.

After satisfying the requirements of the social economy of the collective farm and the needs of the collective farmers for timber and other forest products, a collective farm may allow other forest users to carry out forest uses. Payment for products procured by such forest users in collective farm forests shall be recovered by the collective farm according to rates established for forests of state significance. Funds derived from forest uses in collective farm forests shall be expended to conduct forestry.

Collective farm forests may, with the consent of general meetings of collective farm members or meetings of authorized representatives and by decree of the union republic council of ministers, be transferred wholly or in part to forests of state significance.

Article 42. Peculiarities of Forest Use in a Border Zone

The use of forests in a border zone shall be carried out in the procedure established by the present Fundamental Principles and other USSR and union republic legislation.

The peculiarities of forest use in a border zone shall be established by competent agencies by agreement with the command of the border forces.

Article 43. Procedure for Settling Disputes on Forest Use

Disputes between enterprises, organizations, institutions, and citizens concerning forest use shall be settled by union republic councils of ministers, autonomous republic councils of ministers, executive committees of local soviets of working people's deputies, and also by state forestry agencies and other specially authorized state agencies, in the procedure established by USSR and union republic legislation.

Property disputes connected with forestry relations shall be considered in the procedure established by USSR and union republic legislation.

Section III. Regeneration and Raising the Productivity of Forests

Article 44. Restoration of Forests and Forest Cultivation

Restoration of forests shall be carried out in clearings, burned areas, and other areas formerly afforested, and on other lands earmarked for the creation of new forests, forest cultivation shall be carried out.

The amount of work relating to forest restoration and forest cultivation shall be provided in state plans for the development of the national economy.

The restoration and cultivation of forests, the procurement of forestry seeds, and the growing of planting material shall be carried out by forestry enterprises of state forestry agencies, and also by other enterprises, organizations, and institutions conducting forestry. The fulfillment of the said work also may be entrusted to other organizations by USSR and union republic legislation.

When procuring and dragging timber, forestry procurers shall be obliged to observe the requirements aimed at preserving favorable conditions for the restoration of forests in clearings. These requirements should be taken into account also when working out new technology for the procurement and dragging of timber.

Forest restoration work shall be carried out by means ensuring the creation in the briefest possible periods of highly productive forests from economically valuable timber species in the procedure established by state forestry agencies.

In order to ensure optimal woodiness, the afforestation of river banks, waters, and in other necessary instances, lands of other categories may be transferred to state forestry fund lands, above all land plots not suitable for use in agriculture (ravines, gullies, gravel, and the like), and also state reserve lands overgrown with shrubbery. Lands of other categories shall be transferred to state forestry fund lands in the procedure established by land legislation of the USSR and union republics.

Article 45. Raising the Productiveness of Forests and Caring for Forests

Felling to care for the forest, sanitary fellings, and fellings connected with the reconstruction of forest plantings of little value should be carried out with a view to improving the quality of forests, and measures to improve the growth of forests shall be carried out, including to prevent the accumulation of plantings which have stood too long, and also to increase soil fertility and other work furthering the increased productiveness of forests.

Forestry enterprises of state forestry agencies and other enterprises, organizations, and institutions conducting forestry shall be obliged to:

care for the forest, carry on work relating to the selection, forest seeding, and quality experimentation of the most valuable timber species economically, measures to increase soil fertility, drainage of plentiful wet lands, prevention of water and wind erosion of soil, swamping, salinization, and other processes worsening the state of soil, and also carry out other measures aimed at improving the species composition, and quality of forests, and raising their productiveness and protective qualities;

take measures for the fullest and most efficient use of state forestry fund lands for the restoration and creation of new forests in areas earmarked for this.

Section IV. Protection and Defense of Forests

Article 46. Protection and Defense of Forests

All forests shall be subject to protection from fires, illegal felling, violations of the established procedure for forest use, and other actions causing harm to the forest, and also defense against pests and diseases.

Carrying out measures for the protection and defense of forests shall be entrusted:

in forests of state significance: to forestry enterprises of state forestry agencies, other enterprises, organizations, and institutions to whom the conduct of forestry in such forests has been conducted, and also to the corresponding ministries and departments and executive committees of city soviets of working people's deputies;

in collective farm forests: to collective farms, other organizations to whom the conduct of forestry in such forests has been entrusted, and also to the corresponding agricultural agencies.

Union republic councils of ministers, autonomous republic councils of ministers, and executive committees of local soviets of working people's deputies shall, in accordance with USSR and union republic legislation, ensure the effectuation of measures for the protection and defense of forests, the struggle against forest fires, enlist the populace to extinguish them, and also fire-fighting technology and means of transport, and prohibit the populace from visiting the forest in a period of high fire danger, when necessary, and the entry of means of transport therein.

Enterprises, organizations, and institutions whose activity affects the state and regeneration of forests shall be obliged to carry out technological, sanitary, and other measures aimed at protecting forests and agreed with state forestry agencies, executive committees of local soviets of working people's deputies, and other state agencies in accordance with USSR and union republic legislation.

The protection and defense of semi-protective forest belts on collective farm and state farm lands and other protective or planted shrubbery which are not within the state forestry fund shall be ensured by land users, the respective ministries and departments, and the executive committees of local soviets of working people's deputies.

Measures of material and moral incentive for enterprises, organizations, institutions conducting forestry, and forest users may be established by USSR and union republic legislation, stimulating the effectuation of measures for the rational conducting of forestry, improvement of forest use, and intensifying their protection and defense.

Article 47. Forest Protection in the USSR

There shall carry out the protection and defense of forests: state forestry protection service of the USSR; forestry protection service of ministries and departments in whose system there are enterprises, organizations, and institutions conducting forestry; forest production service of executive committees of city soviets of working people's deputies; forest protection service of collective farms.

The state forestry protection service of the USSR, the forestry protection service of ministries and departments and of executive committees of city soviets of working people's deputies, and also the forestry protection service of collective farms, shall be given the rights to cease and prevent violations of rules for the protection and defense of forests, of the established procedure for carrying out forest uses, of the use of state forestry fund lands in accordance with their special purpose, and also to cut off and prevent other actions causing harm to the forest.

The exercise of control over the cause of protecting and defending all forests of the USSR shall be entrusted to state forestry agencies.

Section V. State Registration of Forests and State Forestry Register. Forestry Tenure

Article 48. State Registration of Forests and the State Forestry Register

The state registration of forests shall be carried out and a state forestry register shall be kept according to a system uniform for the USSR in order to organize the rational use of forests, their regeneration, protection, and defense, planning the development of forestry, and distributing the timber-cutting fund, at state expense.

The state registration of forests and the state forestry register shall be kept in the procedure established by the USSR Council of Ministers.

The branch registration of the state and use of state forestry fund lands shall be carried out in the procedure established by the USSR Council of Ministers.

Article 49. Forest Tenure

Forest tenure shall include the system of state measures aimed at ensuring the rational use, increased productiveness, regeneration, protection, and defense of forests, and also increasing the conducting of forestry.

Forest tenure shall include the following forest tenure actions:

determination of the boundaries of territories of forestry enterprises, intra-entity organization of the territory of forestry enterprises of state forestry agencies, and also the territories occupied by forests in which the conducting of forestry is entrusted to other enterprises, organizations, and institutions;

determination of forestry resources, species, and growth composition of forests in order to establish the rated wood-cutting area for principal use fellings and the amounts of other types of forest use, and also means of felling;

uncovering plots on which it is necessary to carry out fellings to care for the forest, sanitary fellings, and fellings connected with the reconstruction of forestry plantings of little value, and drainage and other forestry measures;

clarification of areas earmarked for the restoration of forests and forest cultivation, and determination of the means for forest regeneration;

determination of categories of protectiveness of forests and well-foundedness of transfer of forests, if necessary, from one group to another;

effectuation of topographic, geodesic, forestry biological, and other research and inquiries, and also other forest tenure activities.

Appropriate drafts, which shall be the basis for conducting forestry and carrying out forestry uses shall be drawn up and confirmed by state forestry agencies or by other state agencies, by agreement with them, according to forest tenure materials for enterprises, organizations, and institutions conducting forestry, and shall serve as base data for long-term and current planning.

The rated wood cutting area shall be computed for principal use fellings for an extended period with forest tenure for each enterprise, organization, and institution conducting forestry, separately by forest groups and farms (coniferous, hardwood, and softwood) and shall be determined by region, territory, and republic. The procedure for confirmation of the rated wood-cutting area shall be established by the USSR Council of Ministers.

Forest tenure shall be carried out in all forests by state forest tenure enterprises according to a system uniform for the USSR established by state forestry agencies of the USSR.

Section VI. Responsibility for Violation of Forestry Legislation

Article 50. Responsibility for Violation of Forestry Legislation

The unauthorized cession of the right of forest use, and also other legal transactions, direct or indirect, violating the right of state ownership in forests shall be void.

Persons guilty of performing the said legal transactions, and also of:

illegal felling and harm to trees and bushes;

destruction or damage to forests as a result of arson or negligence with fire;

violation of the requirements of fire safety in forests;

damage to forests by sewage waters, chemical substances, industrial or municipal-domestic effluents, wastes, and refuse entailing its drying out or swamping;

destruction or damage to forest crops, seedlings, or saplings in forest nurseries and plantations, and also undergrowth of natural origin and self-sown on areas earmarked for forest restoration;

use of land plots of the state forestry fund for feeding, erecting structures, processing timber, building warehouses, and the like, without proper authorization for the use of such plots;

unauthorized haying and pasturage of livestock in forests and on state forestry fund lands not covered by forest;

unauthorized collecting of wild fruits, nuts, mushrooms, berries, and the like on plots where this is prohibited or permitted only by forestry cards;

violation of the established procedure for the use of the wood-cutting fund, the procurement and transport of timber, or the procurement of soft resins;

destruction and harm of boundary markers in forests;

destruction of fauna useful for forests;

bear criminal, administrative, or other responsibility in accordance with USSR and union republic legislation.

Responsibility for other violations of forestry legislation also may be established by USSR and union republic legislation.

Enterprises, organizations, institutions, and citizens shall be obliged to compensate harm caused by a violation of forestry legislation within the amounts and in the procedure established by USSR and union republic legislation.

Illegally extracted timber and other forest products shall be subject to seizure and transfer to the respective enterprise, organization, or institution conducting forestry or to the forest user, if his rights have been violated. If it is impossible to seize the illegally extracted products, its value shall be recovered.

If the established procedure for forest use is violated by forest users, the exercise of forest use may be suspended in instances and in the procedure determined by the USSR Council of Ministers.

Work carried out by enterprises, organizations, and institutions may be suspended in the instances and procedure established by USSR legislation if it represents a danger for the state and regeneration of forests in connection with the failure to fulfill technological, sanitary, and other measures when carrying out such work to ensure the protection of forests from fires and the elimination of a harmful influence on the state and regeneration of forests.

Persons guilty of the illegal destruction or harm to semi-protective forest belts on lands of collective farms and state farms or other protective or shrubbery plantings not within the state forestry fund shall bear responsibility established by legislation for the destruction or damage to specially protected first group forests, unless a stricter responsibility for the said actions has been established by USSR and union republic legislation.

Persons guilty thereof shall bear responsibility in accordance with USSR and union republic legislation for the failure to fulfill obligatory measures for the restoration, improvement of the state of and species composition of forests, raising their productivity, and also for using the mature timber resources.

Section VII. International Treaties and Agreements

Article 51. International Treaties and Agreements

In instances when by international treaty or international agreement in which the USSR participates other rules have been established than those which are contained in Soviet forestry legislation, the rules of the international treaty or international agreement shall be applied.

The same provision shall apply on the territory of the respective union republic if in an international treaty or an international agreement in which a union republic participates other rules than those provided for by union republic forestry legislation have been established.

FUNDAMENTAL PRINCIPLES OF LEGISLATION OF THE USSR AND UNION REPUBLICS ON MINERALS

[Confirmed by Law of the USSR Supreme Soviet, July 9, 1975. Vedomosti SSSR (1975), no. 29, item 435]

As a result of the victory of the Great October Socialist Revolution, the mineral wealth of the land in our country was nationalized and became the heritage of the people.

State ownership of minerals in the USSR constitutes the basis of mining relations, that is, of social relations in the domain of using and protecting minerals, creates conditions for the planned, rational, integrated use of minerals, allows one to ensure the correct allocation of productive forces of the country and the high rates of the development of the national economy, and is one of the major factors in the creation of the material-technical base of communism.

The USSR possesses large reserves of minerals. At the same time, the uninterrupted growth of the consumption of mineral raw materials in the national economy increases the significance of scientifically justified, efficient use of minerals, and requires from all enterprises, organizations, institutions, and citizens a careful attitude toward mineral wealth.

The Soviet state is concerned to provide not only the ever-growing requirements of the country for mineral raw materials and to satisfy other needs of the national economy connected with the use of minerals, but also to preserve the natural wealth for future generations.

Soviet legislation on minerals is called upon to actively promote the most rational use of minerals and their protection.

Section I. General Provisions

Article 1. Tasks of Soviet Legislation on Minerals

The tasks of Soviet legislation on minerals are to regulate mining relations with a view to ensuring the rational, integrated use of minerals in order to satisfy requirements for mineral raw materials and other needs of the national economy, to protect minerals, to ensure work safety when using minerals, and also to protect the rights of enterprises, organizations, institutions, and citizens, and to strengthen legality in this domain.

Article 2. Legislation of the USSR and Union Republics on Minerals

Mining relations in the USSR shall be regulated by the present Fundamental Principles and other acts of USSR legislation on minerals issued in conformity therewith, and by laws (or codes) and other acts of union republic legislation on minerals.

Land, water, and forestry relations shall be regulated by respective USSR and union republic legislation.

Article 3. State Ownership of Minerals in the USSR

In accordance with the USSR Constitution minerals in the Union of Soviet Socialist Republics are state ownership, that is, the property of the whole people.

Minerals in the USSR shall be in the exclusive ownership of the state and shall be granted only for use. Actions, direct or indirect, which violate the right of state ownership of minerals shall be prohibited.

Article 4. Unified State Mineral Fund

All minerals in the USSR shall constitute the unified state mineral fund, in which are both exploited and unexploited portions of minerals.

Article 5. Competence of the USSR in the Regulation of Mining Relations

There shall be subject to the jurisdiction of the USSR in the regulation of mining relations:

(1) disposal of the unified state mineral fund within the limits necessary for effectuating the powers of the USSR in accordance with the USSR Constitution;

(2) establishment of the basic provisions and determination of a uniform technological policy in using and protecting minerals;

(3) establishment of all-union plans for the protection of minerals and the rational use of mineral resources;

(4) state supervision and control over the use and protection of minerals and over the conduct of work relating to the geological study of minerals; establishment of the procedure for exercising supervision and control;

(5) regulation of other questions in the use and protection of minerals in accordance with the USSR Constitution and the present Fundamental Principles.

Article 6. Competence of Union Republics in Regulation of Mining Relations

There shall be subject to the jurisdiction of a union republic in the regulation of mining relations outside the limits of the competence of the USSR: disposition of the unified state mineral fund within the limits of the territory of the republic; establishment of the procedure for the use and protection of minerals; establishment of republic plans for the protection of minerals and the rational use of mineral resources; effectuation of state supervision and control over the use and protection of minerals and conducting work relating to the geological study of minerals, as well as the regulation of other questions in the use and protection of minerals unless they are relegated to the competence of the USSR.

Article 7. State Administration in the Use and Protection of Minerals

State administration in the use and protection of minerals shall be exercised by the USSR Council of Ministers, the union republic councils of ministers, the autonomous republic councils of ministers, the executive committees of local soviets of working people's deputies, as well as state agencies specially authorized therefor in a procedure established by USSR and union republic legislation.

Article 8. Users of Minerals

State, cooperative, and social enterprises, organizations, and institutions, as well as citizens of the USSR, may be users of minerals.

In instances provided for by USSR legislation, minerals may be granted for use also to other organizations and persons.

Article 9. Types of Mineral Use

Minerals shall be granted for use for:

geological study;

extraction of minerals;

construction and exploitation of underground installations not connected with the extraction of minerals, including installations for the underground storage of oil, gas, and other substances and materials, the burial of harmful substances and production wastes or sewage waters;

satisfaction of other state and social needs.

Minerals shall be granted for use free of charge except for instances established by the USSR Council of Ministers.

Article 10. Granting Minerals for Geological Study

Minerals shall be granted for use on the basis of permits issued by state agencies specially authorized therefor in a procedure established by USSR legislation for geological study, that is, for obtaining data on the geological structure of minerals and the processes flowing within them, uncovering and analyzing mineral deposits, study of the laws of their formation and allocation, explaining mining technology and other conditions for working mineral deposits and using minerals for purposes not connected with the extraction of minerals.

Article 11. Granting Minerals for Extraction of Minerals

Minerals shall be granted for use on the basis of an act certifying a mining allotment for the extraction of minerals.

Mining allotments for working mineral deposits (except mining allotments for working deposits of generally distributed minerals) shall be granted by state mining supervision agencies in a procedure established by USSR legislation.

Mining allotments for working deposits of generally distributed minerals shall be granted by executive committees of district (or city) soviets of working people's deputies and shall be subject to registration in state mining supervision agencies. Minerals shall be relegated to generally distributed by state mining supervision agencies in a procedure established by USSR legislation.

Working mineral deposits outside mining allotments shall be prohibited.

Experimental industrial working of mineral deposits or part thereof, as well as working peat deposits and fresh underground waters shall be carried out without the grant of a mining allotment in the procedure established by USSR and union republic legislation.

Enterprises, organizations, institutions, and citizens shall have the right to use minerals within the limits of land plots granted to them for the purpose of extraction for their own economic and daily needs of generally distributed minerals, peat, and fresh underground waters without the grant of a mining allotment in the procedure established by union republic legislation.

Article 12. Granting Minerals for Purposes Not Connected With the Extraction of Minerals

Minerals shall be granted for use in the procedure established by USSR and union republic legislation for construction and exploitation of underground installations and other purposes not connected with the extraction of minerals. Granting minerals for the burial of harmful substances and production wastes or sewage waters shall be permitted only in exceptional instances and with observance of special requirements and conditions.

Enterprises, organizations, institutions, and citizens shall have the right within the limits of the land plots granted to them to use minerals for their economic and domestic needs not connected with the extraction of minerals in the procedure established by union republic legislation.

Article 13. Periods of Mineral Use

Mineral use may be in perpetuity or temporary.

Mineral use without a previously established period shall be deemed in perpetuity (permanent).

In instances of temporary use minerals shall be granted for a period not exceeding ten years. When necessary, the period of temporary use may be extended.

Article 14. Basic Rights and Duties of Mineral Users

Mineral users shall have the right and shall be obliged to use minerals in accordance with the purposes for which they have been granted.

In instances provided for by USSR and union republic legislation, the rights of a mineral user may be restricted in the interests of the state, as well as in the interests of other mineral users.

Mineral users shall be obliged to ensure:

(1) the completeness of geological study; rational, integrated use and protection of minerals;

(2) safe conducting of work connected with mineral use for workers and the populace;

(3) protection of the air, land, forests, waters, and other objects of the environment, as well as buildings and installations, from the harmful influence of work connected with mineral use;

(4) preservation of reserves, monuments of nature and culture from the harmful influence of work connected with mineral use;

(5) bringing land plots disturbed during mineral use into safe condition, as well as into a state suitable for their being used in the national economy in accordance with USSR and union republic legislation.

Article 15. Bases and Procedure for Terminating Right of Mineral Use

The right to use minerals shall be terminated wholly or in part in instances:

(1) of the need to use minerals having passed;

(2) expiry of the period established for mineral use;

(3) arising of the need to withdraw a mineral plot for other state or social needs;

(4) liquidation of the enterprise, organization, or institution to which the minerals were granted for use;

(5) arising of a clear threat to the health of the populace.

The right of mineral use may be terminated if the user:

has not begun to use the minerals within two years;

does not use the minerals in accordance with the purpose for which they were granted;

violated other rules for mineral use and protection.

The right to use minerals in instances provided for by points 1, 3, 4, and 5 of paragraph one and of paragraph two of the present Article shall be terminated by annulment of the mining allotment act or permit by the respective agencies which issued them.

Enterprises, organizations, institutions, and citizens may be deprived of the right to extract generally distributed minerals, peat, and fresh underground waters within the limits of the land plots granted to them in the event of a violation of the procedure or conditions for extraction.

Other bases for terminating the right of mineral use may be provided for by USSR and union republic legislation.

Section II. Geological Study of Minerals

Article 16. Basic Requirements for Geological Study of Minerals

Enterprises, organizations, and institutions carrying on geological study of minerals shall be obliged to ensure:

(1) the rational, scientifically well-founded direction and efficiency of work relating to the geological study of minerals;

(2) completeness of the study of the geological structure of minerals, mining technology, hydrogeological, and other conditions for working out exploratory deposits, construction and exploitation of underground installations not connected with the extraction of minerals;

(3) authenticity of determining the quantity and quality of reserves of basic minerals and those lying with them or containing components in them; geological and economic analysis of mineral deposits;

(4) conducting work relating to the geological study of minerals by methods and means excluding the unjustified loss of minerals or reduction of quality;

(5) distribution of rock and minerals extracted from minerals excluding their harmful influence on the environment;

(6) preservation of exploratory mining works and drilling which may be used when working the deposits or for other national economic purposes, and the liquidation in the established procedure of workings and holes not subject to use;

(7) preservation of geological and administrative and technical documentation, samples of rock and ores, cores, duplicates of assays of minerals which may be used in the further study of the minerals, exploration, or working of the mineral deposits, as well as when using the minerals for purposes not connected with the extraction of minerals.

Article 17. State Registration and State Registry of Work Relating to Geological Study of Minerals

Work relating to the geological study of minerals shall be subject to state registration and state registry for the purposes of summarizing and using maximally the results of the study of minerals, as well as to prevent duplication of the said work.

State registration and state registry of work relating to the geological study of minerals shall be carried out in the procedure established by USSR legislation.

The performance of work relating to the geological study of minerals shall be prohibited without state registration.

Article 18. Standards for Mineral Raw Material

In order to determine the industrial value of deposits and calculate the reserves of minerals in them, standards shall be established for mineral raw material for each deposit, which shall constitute the aggregate economically justified requirements for quality and quantity of minerals, mining technology, and other conditions for working the deposit.

Standards for mineral raw material shall be worked out taking into account the use of basic minerals and those lying with them, as well as valuable components contained in them, and shall be confirmed in the procedure established by USSR legislation.

Article 19. Transfer of Prospected Mineral Deposits for Industrial Exploitation

Prospected deposits or parts thereof for which mineral reserves have been confirmed shall be subject to transfer for industrial exploitation to ministries and departments exercising direction of the working of mineral deposits.

The procedure for the transfer of prospected mineral deposits (except deposits of generally distributed minerals) for industrial exploitation shall be established by USSR legislation, and deposits of generally distributed minerals, by union republic legislation.

Article 20. Discoverers of Mineral Deposits

Persons who have discovered a previously unknown deposit having industrial value, as well as uncovered additional reserves of minerals or a new mineral raw material in a previously known deposit materially increasing its industrial value, shall be deemed the discoverers.

Discoverers shall have a right to compensation.

The rights of the discoverer and the procedure for payment of compensation to them shall be determined by USSR legislation.

Section III. Designing, Construction, and Introduction into Use of Extractive Mining Enterprises, As Well As Underground Installations Not Connected with the Extraction of Minerals

Article 21. Peculiarities of Designing Extractive Mining Enterprises, as Well as Underground Installations Not Connected with Extraction of Minerals

Extractive mining enterprises and underground installations not connected with the extraction of minerals shall be designed on the basis of a geological or other study of the minerals on the plot of the proposed construction, taking into account the integrated development of the economic area.

Extractive mining enterprises shall be designed only after the confirmation of mineral reserves and the transfer of the deposits for industrial exploitation. In exceptional instances, with the authorization of the USSR Council of Ministers, extractive mining enterprises may be designed before confirmation of the mineral reserves.

Places for locating extractive mining enterprises or underground installations not connected with the extraction of minerals shall, before beginning design work, be agreed with the executive and administrative agencies of the respective soviets of working people's deputies, state mining supervision agencies, and other interested agencies.

Article 22. Basic Requirements for the Designing, Construction, and Introduction into Use of Extractive Mining Enterprises, as well as of Underground Installations Not Connected with Extraction of Minerals

Designs of extractive mining enterprises should provide for:

(1) placing of surface and underground installations of extractive mining enterprises at mineral deposits, ensuring the most rational and efficient use of mineral reserves;

(2) means for opening and the systems for working the mineral deposits and technological schemes for processing (or preparing) mineral raw materials, ensuring the fullest and most integrated and economically advisable extraction from mineral reserves of basic minerals and those lying with them, as well as the use of components contained in them which have industrial significance;

(3) rational use of strata uncovered when working mineral deposits;

(4) storage and preservation of incidentally extracted and temporarily unused minerals, as well as of production wastes containing useful components;

(5) geological study of minerals uncovered in the process of construction and exploitation of mining enterprises and the drawing up of geological and mine survey documentation;

(6) measures ensuring the safety of the populace and protection of minerals and other objects of the natural environment, buildings, and installations.

When designing, constructing, and introducing into use mining enterprises, the fulfillment of the requirements specified in Article 14 of the present Fundamental Principles also should be guaranteed.

When designing, constructing, and introducing into use underground installations not connected with the extraction of minerals, the fulfillment of the requirements specified in points 3-6 of the present Article and respectively in Article 14, paragraph three, points 1-5 of the present Fundamental Principles should be guaranteed.

The construction, reconstruction, and introduction into use of mining enterprises, as well as of underground installations not connected with the extraction of minerals, shall be prohibited unless the requirements provided for by the present Article are observed when designing them.

Section IV. Use of Minerals to Work Mineral Deposits and for Purposes Not Connected with the Extraction of Minerals

Article 23. Procedure for Working Mineral Deposits

Mineral deposits shall be worked in accordance with confirmed project of mining enterprises, plans for the development of mining work, projects and schemes for working deposits of oil, gas, and underground waters, and technical exploitation rules.

Technical exploitation rules of mining enterprises, rules for working oil and gas deposits, and plans for the development of mining work shall be confirmed by the appropriate agencies by agreement with state mining supervision agencies.

Article 24. Basic Requirements for Working Mineral Deposits

When working mineral deposits there should be ensured:

(1) application of the most rational and efficient methods for extracting basic minerals and those lying with them and deriving components in them which have industrial significance, and not permitting the loss or depletion of minerals in excess of standards, nor the selective processing of rich deposits leading to unjustified losses of mineral reserve balances;

(2) carrying out of prospecting of mineral deposits and other geological work, mine surveys, as well as technical documentation provided for;

(3) inventory of the state and movement of reserves and the loss or depletion of minerals;

(4) inadmissibility of spoiling mineral deposits and those neighboring them as a result of carrying on mining work, as well as the preservation of mineral reserves conserved in the earth;

(5) preservation and inventory of incidentally extracted and temporarily unused minerals, as well as production wastes which contain useful components;

(6) rational use of uncovered strata and production wastes, as well as their proper allocation;

(7) safety of workers and the populace, protection of minerals and other objects of the natural environment, buildings, and installations; working out and confirmation of plans for the elimination of accidents.

Article 25. Liquidation and Temporary Closure of Mining Enterprises

Upon completion of the working of mineral reserves, as well as in instances when according to technical and economic accounts and other reasons the further working of a deposit or part thereof is inadvisable or impossible, the mining enterprise working the deposit or respective sector of this enterprise shall be subject to liquidation or to temporary closure.

In the event of the complete or partial liquidation or temporary closure of a mining enterprise, the mine workings and boreholes should be placed in a state ensuring the safety of the populace, the protection of the natural environment, buildings and installations, and in the event of temporary closure also the preservation of a deposit, mine workings and boreholes for the entire period of temporary closure. In the event of the liquidation of a mining enterprise, the question also should be resolved of the possible use of the mine workings and boreholes for other national economic purposes.

When liquidating or temporarily closing a mining enterprise or part thereof, the geological and mine survey documentation shall be supplemented to the time the mining work is completed and handed over in the established procedure for safekeeping.

Measures ensuring the safety of mining works should be carried out at mining enterprises adjoining the enterprise being liquidated or temporarily closed.

The liquidation or conservation of a mining enterprise or part thereof shall be carried out by agreement with the state mining supervision agencies and other interested agencies.

Article 26. Prospecting for Minerals

At deposits of minerals or sectors thereof, the working of which by mining enterprises is inadvisable, the extraction of minerals by the personal labor of prospectors shall be permitted.

The extraction of minerals by artels of prospectors shall be by contract with mining enterprises within the limits of their mining allotments, and by individual citizens, by an authorization permit issued by mining enterprises. Control over the extraction of minerals by prospectors shall be entrusted to mining enterprises.

A list of minerals whose extraction by prospectors is permitted, and a Model Charter for a Prospectors' Artel shall be confirmed in the procedure established by the USSR Council of Ministers.

Article 27. Procedure for Using Minerals for Purposes Not Connected With the Extraction of Minerals

The use of minerals for construction and exploitation of underground installations and other purposes not connected with the extraction of minerals shall be by special projects confirmed in the procedure established by USSR and union republic legislation.

Measures should be provided in the projects which ensure respectively the neutralization of sewage waters, harmful substances, production wastes, and other substances and materials or their localization within strictly defined boundaries and the prevention of penetration into mine workings, the land surface, or water objects.

In instances of the violation of the requirements of the present Article, the flow of sewage waters into the minerals, the burial of harmful substances and production wastes, and the underground storage of substances and minerals should be limited, suspended, or prohibited by state mining supervision agencies or by other specially authorized state agencies.

Section V. Safety of Work Connected with Mineral Use

Article 28. Ensuring the Safe Conduct of Work Connected with Mineral Use

In the event of the construction, reconstruction, and exploitation of mining enterprises, as well as underground installations not connected with the extraction of minerals, and when fulfilling geological survey and other work connected with mineral use, the safety of the workers and the populace should be ensured.

Responsibility for ensuring the observance of safety rules and norms at enterprises, organizations, and institutions using minerals shall be entrusted to their managers, who shall determine the group of persons exercising control over the observance of the said safety rules and norms in structural subdivisions of the enterprises, organizations, and institutions.

Article 29. Basic Requirements for Ensuring the Safe Conduct of Work Connected with Mineral Use

When conducting work connected with mineral use, there should be ensured:

(1) the study and fulfillment by workers of rules and norms relating to the safe conduct of work, as well as the planning and implementation of measures to prevent and eliminate accidents;

(2) the suspension of work in the event a danger arises to the life of workers, the bringing out of people to a safe place, and the implementation of measures necessary to eliminate the danger;

(3) the application of machines, equipment, and materials corresponding to the requirements of safety rules and norms and sanitary norms;

(4) the registration, appropriate storage, and expenditure of explosive substances and means for explosions, as well as their proper and safe use;

(5) the timely supplementation of technical documentation provided for by safety rules, including plans for mining work, with data clarifying the boundaries of safety zones for conducting work and plans for eliminating accidents.

The charter on discipline for persons working in especially dangerous underground conditions shall be confirmed by the USSR Council of Ministers.

Article 30. Special Requirements for the Safe Conduct of Mining Work

Ministries, departments, and enterprises, organizations, and institutions subordinate to them which carry on mining work shall be obliged to work out, taking into account modern achievements of science and technology, and to carry out special integrated organizational and technical measures which provide improvement of the composition of mine air and improve the technology of carrying on mining work and means of collective and individual protection and are aimed at preventing professional illnesses and production injuries.

With a view to ensuring the most favorable conditions for the normal life and safety of workers and employees engaged in mining work, ministrie and departments, as well as other interested agencies, shall be obliged systematically to improve the safety rules and norms and sanitary rules and norms.

Persons having the appropriate special education shall be allowed to direct mining and explosive work. Persons having the right to conduct such work shall be allowed to perform explosive work.

Article 31. Duties of Persons Engaged in Mining Work Relating to the Observance of Safety Rules and Norms

Persons engaged in mining work shall be obliged to:

(1) fulfill the requirements of rules and norms relating to the safe conduct of work;

(2) systematically conduct inspections of working places and equipment and take measures to eliminate immediately violations of safety rules and norms uncovered;

(3) be at work in special clothing and use means for individual protection;

(4) not employ means when fulfilling work which might create the danger of damage or an accident;

(5) cease work in the event the danger of an accident arises, immediately notify the director of the work thereof, and act in strict accordance with the plan to eliminate accidents.

Article 32. Mining Rescue Service

Enterprises, organizations, and institutions carrying on mining work shall be serviced in the established procedure by mining rescue units, and those carrying on drilling work when exploring and working oil and gas deposits, by services for the prevention and elimination of open gas and oil gushers. The deployment of such units and services shall be determined by the respective ministries and departments by agreement with state mining supervision agencies.

Statutes on mining rescue units and services for the prevention and elimination of open gas and oil gushers shall be confirmed in the procedure established by the USSR Council of Ministers.

The executive committees of local soviets of working people's deputies as well as enterprises, organizations, and institutions, irrespective of their departmental subordination, shall be obliged in the event of accident at mining enterprises to supply means of transport, materials, and equipment, means of communication, medical supplies, and render other forms of assistance in eliminating the damage.

Section VI. Protection of Minerals

Article 33. Basic Requirements in Domain of Protection of Minerals

All minerals in the USSR shall be subject to protection.

The basic requirements in the protection of minerals shall be:

ensuring the complete and integrated geological study of minerals;

observance of the established procedure for granting minerals for use and not allowing the arbitrary use of minerals;

fullest extraction of minerals and the rational use of reserves of basic minerals and those lying with them and containing components in them;

not allowing the harmful influence of work connected with mineral use on the preservation of mineral reserves;

protection of mineral deposits from caving in, flooding, fires, and other factors reducing the quality of minerals and the industrial value of deposits or complicating their working;

prevention of unjustified and unauthorized building on beds of minerals and observance of the established procedure for the use of such areas for other purposes;

prevention of the harmful influence of work connected with mineral use, protection of mine workings and boreholes, and also underground installations, being exploited or temporarily closed;

prevention of pollution of minerals in the event of underground storage of oil, gas, and other substances and materials, the burial of harmful substances and production wastes, and the flow of sewage waters.

In the event of a violation of the requirements of the present Article, the use of minerals may be restricted, suspended, or prohibited by state mining supervision agencies or other specially authorized state agencies in the procedure established by USSR legislation.

Measures of material and moral incentive may be established by USSR and union republic legislation for users of minerals which stimulate the implementation of measures to improve mineral use and intensify their protection.

Article 34. Conditions for Building on Bed Areas for Minerals

The designing and construction of population centers, industrial complexes, and other national economic objects before obtaining data from the appropriate territorial geological organization concerning the absence of minerals in the ground under the plot of the forthcoming building shall be prohibited.

In exceptional instances the building on bed areas for minerals (except widely distributed minerals), as well as placing underground installations in beds which are not connected with the extraction of minerals, shall be permitted only by agreement with state mining supervision agencies. In this connection construction and other measures ensuring the possibility of extracting minerals from the ground should be provided for an carried out.

The building on bed areas of widely distributed minerals, as well as placing underground installations in beds which are not connected with the extraction of minerals, shall be permitted in the procedure establish by union republic legislation.

Article 35. Protection of Mineral Plots Representing Special Scientific or Cultural Value

Rare geological outcrops, mineralogical formations, paleontologica objects, and other mineral plots representing special scientific or cultural value may be declared in the established procedure to be reserves or monuments of nature or culture. Any activity violating the preservatic of the said reserves and monuments shall be prohibited.

In the event rare geological outcrops and mineralogical formations meteorites, paleontological, archeological, and other objects representir interest for science and culture are discovered when using minerals, the mineral user shall be obliged to suspend work on the respective plot and notify the interested state agencies thereof.

Article 36. Participation of Social Organizations and Citizens in Implementing Measures for the Protection of Minerals and their Rational Use

Trade unions, youth organizations, nature protection organizations, scientific societies, and other social organizations, as well as citizens, shall render assistance to state agencies in carrying out measures relating to the protection of minerals and their rational use.

Social organizations shall take part in activity aimed at ensuring the protection of minerals and their rational use in accordance with their charters (or statutes) and USSR and union republic legislation.

State agencies shall be obliged to take into account in every possible way proposals of social organizations and citizens when carrying out measures relating to the protection of minerals and their rational use.

Section VII. State Registry of Reserves and Deposits of Minerals, as well as Mineral Plots Granted for Use which are Not Connected with the Extraction of Minerals

Article 37. State Registry of Mineral Reserves and Deposits

Mineral reserves and deposits, as well as the revealing of minerals, shall be subject to state registration according to systems uniform for the USSR.

With a view to facilitating the planning of work relating to the geological study of minerals and siting mining industry enterprises and the rational, integrated use of mineral deposits, as well as to resolve other national economic tasks, a state register of mineral deposits shall be kept and state mineral reserve balances shall be drawn up.

Article 38. State Register of Mineral Deposits

The state register of mineral deposits should contain information for each deposit describing the quantity and quality of reserves of basic minerals and layers with them and components contained therein, mining technological, hydrogeological, and other conditions for working deposits and its geological and economic evaluation, as well as information for each revealing of minerals.

Article 39. State Mineral Reserve Balances

State mineral reserve balances should contain information concerning the quantity, quality, and degree of study of mineral reserves for deposits having industrial significance, their siting, degree of industrial exploitation, extraction, losses, and being provided industry with explored mineral reserves.

Article 40. Confirmation of Mineral Reserves

Mineral resources of explored deposits, as well as mineral reserves explored additionally in the process of working deposits, shall be subject to confirmation by state agencies specially empowered for this in the procedure established by USSR legislation.

When confirming reserves, the authenticity of explored mineral reserves, their quantity and quality, condition of the beds, extent of study, national economic significance, and readiness of the deposit for industrial exploitation shall be established.

Article 41. Writing off of Balance Mineral Reserves

Extracted minerals, as well as mineral reserves which have lost industrial significance, wasted while being extracted, or were not confirmed during subsequent geological survey work or in working the deposit shall be subject to being written off from the state mineral balance in the procedure established by USSR legislation.

The writing off from the record of a mining enterprise of balance mineral reserves which have lost industrial significance, been wasted while being extracted, or were not confirmed by subsequent geological survey work or in working the deposit shall be by agreement with state mining supervision agencies.

Article 42. State Record of Mineral Plots Granted for Use Which Are Not Connected With the Extraction of Minerals

Mineral plots granted for construction and exploitation of underground installations and for other purposes not connected with the extraction of minerals shall be subject to state registration according to systems uniform for the USSR.

Section VIII. Supervision and Control Over the Use and Protection of Minerals and Conduct of Work Relating to the Geological Study of Minerals

Article 43. Tasks of State Supervision and Control Over the Use and Protection of Minerals and Conduct of Work Relating to Geological Study of Minerals

State supervision and control over the use and protection of minerals shall have as its task to ensure the observance by all ministries, departments, enterprises, organizations, institutions, and citizens of the established procedure for the use of minerals, the fulfillment of duties relating to the protection of minerals, the safe conduct of work connected with mineral use, the prevention and elimination of their harmful influence on the populace, the natural environment, buildings, and installations, and the observance of rules for keeping the state registry of mineral reserves and deposits, as well as other rules and norms established in legislation on minerals.

State control over the conduct of work relating to the geological study of minerals shall have as its task to ensure the observance of the established procedure and the efficiency of the performance of geological survey, search, exploration, hydrogeological, geological engineering, geophysical, geochemical, and other work relating to the geological study of minerals fulfilled by enterprises, organizations, and institutions irrespective of the departmental subordination.

Article 44. Agencies Exercising State Supervision and Control Over the Use and Protection of Minerals and the Conduct of Work Relating to the Geological Study of Minerals

State supervision over the use and protection of minerals (state mining supervision) and state control over the conduct of work relating to the geological study of minerals (state geological control) shall be carried out by specially empowered state agencies.

Soviets of working people's deputies and their executive and administrative agencies shall exercise state control in the domain of the use and protection of minerals in accordance with USSR and union republic legislation.

Article 45. Exercise of State Supervision Over the Use and Protection of Minerals

Agencies of state mining supervision shall verify:

(1) the correctness of working mineral deposits and the fulfillment of requirements relating to protection of minerals;

(2) observance of the established procedure for the recording of mineral reserves by mining enterprises and the correctness and timeliness of writing them off;

(3) observance of the rules and norms relating to the safe conduct of work when using minerals;

(4) the correctness and timeliness of carrying on measures ensuring the safety of the populace, protection of the environment, buildings, and installations, mining works and boreholes being exploited or temporarily closed from the harmful influence of work connected with mineral use;

(5) observance of the requirements relating to the prevention of the penetration of oil, gas, and other substances and materials stored underground, of sewage waters following into the minerals, and of harmful substances and production wastes buried in minerals into mine workings, the land surface, and waters;

(6) observance of rules for carrying on geological and mine survey work when working mineral deposits.

State mining supervision agencies shall have the right to:

suspend work connected with mineral use in instances of the violation of rules and norms for the safe conduct of work and protection of minerals;

terminate the arbitrary use of minerals and arbitrary building on bed areas of minerals;

give *ukazaniia* binding for execution concerning the elimination of violations of rules and norms for the safe conduct of work and protection of minerals at enterprises, organizations, and institutions using minerals;

investigate the circumstances and causes of accidents and instances of production injuries in the established procedure when using minerals and take decisions according to the results of the investigation binding for execution on managers of the respective enterprises, organizations, and institutions.

Other functions also may be entrusted to state mining supervision agencies regarding supervision over the use and protection of minerals, and other rights may be granted them regarding the prevention and stopping of violations of rules and norms for the safe conduct of work and protection of minerals.

Article 46. Exercise of State Control Over the Conduct of Work Relating to Geological Study of Minerals

State geological control agencies shall verify the direction, method, complexity, and quality of work relating to the geological study of minerals.

State geological control agencies shall have the right to:

give *ukazaniia* binding for execution concerning the elimination of shortcomings and violations when conducting work relating to the geological study of minerals;

suspend work relating to the geological study of minerals unless they correspond to confirmed projects or are carried out without state registration, as well as in instances of violations of rules and norms determining the procedure for carrying on such work.

State geological control agencies also may be granted other rights regarding the prevention and stopping of violations of rules and norms for the conduct of work relating to the geological study of minerals.

Article 47. Departmental Control Over the Use and Protection of Minerals

Departmental control over the observance of the established procedure for mineral use, the conduct of work relating to the geological study of minerals, the fulfillment of requirements regarding the protection of minerals, obtaining complete extraction of basic minerals and those lying with them and conponents contained therein, including during the concentration and reprocessing of mineral raw materials, requirements for the safe conduct of work connected with mineral use, the implementation of measures ensuring the safety of the populace, protection of the environment, buildings, and installations, observance of rules for recording mineral reserves and deposits, as well as other rules and norms established by legislation on minerals and carried out by agencies in whose jurisdiction are the enterprises, organizations, and institutions using the minerals.

Control over the correctness of working mineral deposits shall be carried out by mine survey, geological, and other services.

Model statutes on mine survey and geological surveys shall be confirmed by the USSR Council of Ministers.

Section IX. Settlement of Disputes on Questions of Mineral Use

Article 48. Procedure for the Settlement of Disputes

Disputes between enterprises, organizations, institutions, and citizens on questions of mineral use shall be settled respectively by the executive committees of district (or city) soviets of working people's deputies, state mining supervision agencies, state geological control agencies, and other state agencies empowered for this in the procedure established by USSR and union republic legislation.

Section X. Responsibility for Violation of Legislation on Minerals

Article 49. Responsibility for Violation of Legislation on Minerals

Legal transactions in express or concealed form which violate the right of state ownership in minerals shall be void.

Persons who are guilty of performing the said legal transactions, and also:

of unauthorized use of minerals;

of violating rules and requirements for conducting work relating to the geological study of minerals which have led to an inaccurate evaluation of explored mineral reserves or of conditions for the construction and exploitation of mining enterprises, as well as of underground installations not connected with the extraction of minerals;

of selective processing of such sectors of deposits which leads to unjustified losses of balance mineral reserves; losses and depletions of minerals in excess of norms during extraction; spoilage of mineral deposits and other violations of requirements for the rational use of mineral reserves;

unauthorized building on bed areas of minerals;

violation of rules and norms for the safe conduct of work connected with mineral use;

the failure to fulfill rules for the protection of minerals, as well as requirements for the protection of the environment, buildings, and installations from the harmful influence of work connected with mineral use;

the destruction or damaging of classified observatory slits for underground waters, as well as mine survey and geological marks;

loss of mine survey or geological documentation, as well as duplicate assays of minerals and cores which are needed for the future geological study of minerals and the working of deposits;

the failure to fulfill the requirements relating to bringing liquidated or temporarily closed mine workings and boreholes into a state ensuring the safety of the populace, as well as requirements for the preservation of deposits, mine workings, and boreholes at the time of temporary closure;

bear criminal, administrative, or other responsibility in accordance with USSR and union republic legislation.

Responsibility for other violations of legislation on minerals also may be established by USSR and union republic legislation.

The unauthorized use of minerals and unauthorized building on bed areas of minerals shall be terminated without compensation of losses made.

Article 50. Compensation of Losses

Enterprises, organizations, institutions, and citizens shall be obliged to compensate losses caused by violation of legislation on minerals in amounts and in the procedure established by USSR and union republic legislation. Officials and other workers at whose fault enterprises, organizations, and institutions have borne expenses connected with the compensation of losses shall bear material liability in the established procedure.

Section XI. International Treaties and Agreements

Article 51. International Treaties and Agreements

If other rules are established by an international treaty or an international agreement in which the USSR or a union republic participates than those which are contained in USSR or union republic legislation on minerals, the rules of the international treaty or international agreement shall be applied.

ON THE PROTECTION AND USE OF MONUMENTS OF HISTORY AND CULTURE

[Law of the USSR, adopted by the USSR Supreme Soviet, October 29, 1976. Vedomosti SSSR (1976), no. 44, item 628]

In the USSR monuments of history and culture are the property of the people. The Soviet state, following Leninist principles of relations toward the cultural heritage, creates all the conditions for the preservation and efficient use of the monuments in the interests of communist construction.

The monuments of history and culture of the peoples of the USSR reflect the material and spiritual life of past generations, the history of our Motherland for many centuries, the struggle of the popular masses for its freedom and independence, the revolutionary movement, and the origin and development of the Soviet socialist state.

In monuments of history and culture are embodied the outstanding events of the Great October Socialist Revolution, the Civil and Great Fatherland Wars, the labor exploits of the working class, collective farm peasantry, and intelligentsia, the fraternal friendship of the peoples of our country, and the heroic struggle of the Soviet people to build socialism and communism.

The monuments of history and culture of the peoples of the USSR constitute an integral part of a world cultural heritage and testify to the enormous contribution of the peoples of our country to the development of world civilization.

In the USSR monuments serve the purposes of the development of science, public education, and culture, the formation of a high feeling of Soviet patriotism, and the ideological, moral, international, and aesthetic nurturing of the working people.

The protection of monuments is an important task of state agencies and social organizations. A careful attitude toward monuments of history and culture is the patriotic duty of every citizen of the USSR.

Soviet legislation is called upon actively to further the improvement of the cause of the protection and use of monuments of history and culture and the further strengthening of legality in this domain.

I. General Provisions

Article 1. Monuments of History and Culture

Monuments of history and culture shall be buildings, memorial places, and articles connected with historical events in the life of the people or the development of society and the state, and works of material and spiritual creativity which are of historical, scientific, artistic, or other cultural value.

All monuments of history and culture situated on the territory of the USSR shall be protected by the state.

Article 2. Tasks of Soviet Legislation on the Protection and Use of Monuments of History and Culture

Soviet legislation on the protection and use of monuments of history and culture shall regulate social relations in the domain of the protection and use of monuments with a view to ensuring their preservation for the present and future generations and efficient use for the scientific study and propaganda of monuments in the interests of the communist nurturing of the working people.

Article 3. Legislation of the USSR and Union Republics on the Protection and Use of Monuments of History and Culture

Legislation of the USSR and union republics on the protection and use of monuments of history and culture shall consist of the present Law and other acts of USSR legislation issued in accordance therewith and laws and other acts of union republic legislation on the protection and use of monuments of history and culture.

Article 4. Ownership of Monuments of History and Culture

Monuments of history and culture shall be in the ownership of the state, as well as of collective farms, other cooperative organizations, their associations, and social organizations, and in the personal ownership of citizens.

The sale, gift, or other alienation of monuments of history and culture shall be permitted with the obligatory notification in advance of state agencies for the protection of monuments. In the event of the sale of monuments, the state shall have a priority right of purchase.

Article 5. Types of Monuments of History and Culture

There shall be relegated to monuments of history and culture in accordance with Article 1 of the present Law:

monuments of history: buildings, structures, memorial places, and articles connected with the most important historical events in the life of the people, the development of society and the state, the revolutionary movement, the Great October Socialist Revolution, the Civil and Great Fatherland Wars, socialist and communist construction, the strengthening of international solidarity, as well as the development of history and technology, culture, and life of peoples, the life of outstanding political, state, and military public figures, people's heroes, and public figures of science, literature, and art;

monuments of architecture: ancient towns, burial mounds, remains of ancient settlements, fortifications, production sites, canals, roads, ancient burial sites, stone sculptures, stone paintings, ancient articles, and parcels of the historical and cultural layer of ancient population centers;

monuments of urban construction and architecture: architectural ensembles, and complexes, historical centers, quarters, squares, streets, remains of the ancient planning and building of cities and other population centers; buildings of civil, industrial, military, and cult architecture, folk architecture, and monumental works connected therewith, decorative, applied, garden and parks art, and natural landscapes;

monuments of art: works of monumental, decorative, applied, and other types of art;

documentary monuments: acts of agencies of state power and state administration, other written and graphic documents, cinema film documents and recordings, and also ancient and other manuscripts and archives, music and folklore records, and rare printed publications.

Other objects of historical, scientific, artistic, and other cultural value also may be relegated to monuments of history and culture.

Article 6. State Administration in the Domain of the Protection and Use of Monuments of History and Culture

State administration in the domain of the protection and use of monuments of history and culture shall be effectuated by the USSR Council of Ministers, union republic councils of ministers, autonomous republic councils of ministers, executive committees of territory, regional, national area, district, city, rural, and settlement soviets of working people's deputies, and also specially authorized state agencies for the protection of monuments in accordance with USSR and union republic legislation.

Article 7. State Control Over the Protection and Use of Monuments of History and Culture

State control over the protection and use of monuments of history and culture shall have as its task to ensure the fulfillment by all ministries, departments, state, cooperative, and social enterprises, organizations, institutions, and by citizens of duties relating to the observance of the established procedure for the protection, use, recording, and restoration of monuments, as well as other rules provided for by USSR and union republic legislation.

State control over the protection and use of monuments of history and culture shall be effectuated by soviets of working people's deputies, their executive and administrative agencies, and specially authorized state agencies in accordance with USSR and union republic legislation.

Article 8. Participation of Social Organizations and Citizens in Effectuating Measures for the Protection and Use of Monuments of History and Culture

Trade unions, youth organizations, societies for the protection of monuments of history and culture, scientific societies, creative unions, and other social organizations, and also citizens, shall render assistance to state agencies in effectuating measures for the protection, use, uncovering, recording, and restoration of monuments of history and culture and the dissemination of knowledge concerning them. Societies for the protection of monuments of history and culture shall promote the involvement of the broad masses of the populace in the active and direct participation in protecting monuments, carry out propaganda of the monuments and legislation concerning them, their protection and use, and actively further the work of state agencies for the protection of monuments.

Social organizations shall take part in work directed toward ensuring the preservation of monuments of history and culture in accordance with the charters (or statutes) of these organizations and USSR and union republic legislation.

II. State Record of Monuments of History and Culture

Article 9. Organization of a State Record of Monuments of History and Culture

Monuments of history and culture, irrespective of in whose ownership they are, shall be subject to state recording.

The state recording of monuments of history and culture shall be carried out in the procedure determined by the USSR Council of Ministers.

Article 10. Relegation of Monuments of History and Culture to Monuments of All-Union, Republic, and Local Significance

With a view to organizing the recording and protection of monuments of history and culture, immovable monuments shall be subdivided into monuments of all-union, republic, and local significance.

Monuments of history and culture shall be relegated to the categories of monuments of all-union, republic, or local significance in accordance with USSR and union republic legislation.

Article 11. State Recording of Monuments of History and Culture in Museums, Libraries, and Archives

Monuments of history and culture in museums, libraries, archives, and other organizations and institutions shall be recorded by the state in the procedure determined by USSR legislation on the museum and archive funds of the USSR.

Article 12. State Registration of Monuments of History and Culture in the Personal Ownership of Citizens

Articles of antiquity, works of decorative and applied art, structures, manuscripts, collections, rare printed publications, and other articles and documents in the personal ownership of citizens and of significant historical, scientific, artistic, or other cultural value shall be deemed monuments of history and culture and shall be subject to state registration for the purpose of fully making known the monuments and rendering assistance in ensuring their preservation.

Citizens in whose personal ownership there are monuments of history and culture shall be obliged to observe the rules for the protection, use, registration, and restoration of monuments.

III. Ensuring the Preservation of Monuments of History and Culture. The Procedure and Conditions for the Use of Monuments

Article 13. Use of Monuments of History and Culture

Monuments of history and culture shall be used with a view to the development of science, public education and culture, and patriotic, ideological, moral, internationalist, and aesthetic upbringing.

The use of monuments of history and culture for economic and other purposes shall be permitted unless this inflicts damage to the preservation of the monuments and disturbs their historical and artistic value.

The granting of monuments of history and culture for use to state, cooperative, and social enterprises, organizations, and institutions, and also to other organizations and persons for scientific, cultural, enlightenment, tourist, and other purposes, shall be carried out in the procedure and with observance of the conditions determined by USSR and union republic legislation.

Article 14. Procedure for Expenditure of Assets Received from the Use of Monuments of History and Culture

Monies received from the use of monuments of history and culture, and also assets received in accordance with Article 32 of the present Law, shall be deducted in the established procedure for the special accounts of state agencies for the protection of monuments in whose jurisdiction the monuments are, and shall be expended by them only on measures for the protection, restoration, conservation, and repair of monuments.

Article 15. Duties of Enterprises, Organizations, Institutions in Whose Ownership or Use There Are Monuments of History and Culture

Enterprises, organizations, and institutions in whose ownership or use there are monuments of history and culture shall bear responsibility for their preservation and shall be obliged to observe the rules for the protection, use, registration, and restoration of the monuments.

Rules for the protection, use, and restoration of monuments of history and culture shall be established in the procedure determined by the USSR Council of Ministers.

Article 16. Withdrawal of Monuments of History and Culture

Monuments of history and culture not used in accordance with their character and purpose or subjected to threat of destruction or deterioration may be withdrawn from enterprises, organizations, and institutions in the procedure determined by USSR legislation.

If a citizen does not ensure the preservation of a monument of history and culture belonging to him, this monument may, in accordance with union republic legislation, be withdrawn in a judicial proceeding with appropriate compensation.

Article 17. Ensuring the Preservation of Monuments of History and Culture on Lands Granted for Use

Enterprises, organizations, institutions, and citizens shall be obliged to ensure the preservation of monuments of history and culture on lands granted for use to them.

Article 18. Restoration, Conservation, and Repair of Monuments of History and Culture

Restoration, conservation, and repair of monuments of history and culture shall be carried out only with the knowledge of state agencies for the protection of monuments and under their control.

Restoration, conservation, and repair of monuments shall be exercised at the expense of assets of the users or owners of the monuments, and also at the expense of state agencies for the protection of monuments.

Article 19. Zones for the Protection of Monuments of History and Culture

Protection zones, building regulation zones, and protected natural landscape zones shall be established in a procedure determined by USSR and union republic legislation with a view to ensuring the protection of monuments of history, archeology, urban construction and architecture, and monumental art.

Land, construction, and other work, and also economic activity, shall be prohibited within the limits of the said zones without the authorization of the respective agencies for the protection of monuments of the USSR or union republic.

Article 20. Protection of Historical or Cultural Preserves

Ensembles and complexes of monuments of history and culture of special historical, scientific, artistic, or other cultural value may be declared to be historical or cultural preserves, whose protection is carried out on the basis of a special statute for each of them, by decisions of the USSR Council of Ministers or a union republic council of ministers.

Article 21. Protection of Newly Discovered Monuments of History and Culture

Newly discovered objects of historical, scientific, artistic, or other cultural value shall, until the question of accepting them for state registration as monuments of history and culture is decided, be subject to protection in accordance with the requirements of the present Law.

Article 22. Agreement of Drafts for the Planning, Building, and Reconstruction of Cities and Other Population Centers Having Monuments of History and Culture with Agencies for the Protection of Monuments

Drafts for the planning, building, and reconstruction of cities and other population centers having monuments of history, archeology, urban construction, and architecture and monumental art shall be subject to agreement with the respective agencies for the protection of monuments.

Article 23. Prohibition of the Demolition, Re-Siting, or Modification of Monuments of History and Culture

The demolition, re-siting, or modification of immovable monuments of history and culture shall be prohibited. An exception from this rule may be permitted only with the special authorization in each individual instance of the USSR Council of Ministers, with regard to monuments of all-union significance, and of a union republic council of ministers, with regard to monuments of republic and local significance.

An enterprise, organization or institution, having received such authorization, shall, when carrying out the demolition, re-siting, or modification of a monument, be obliged to ensure the observance of the condition provided for by USSR and union republic legislation, and the respective state agency for the protection of monuments shall be obliged to carry on work relating to the scientific study and fixing of monuments.

Expenditures connected with the effectuation of the said work shall be at the expense of the enterprise, organization or institution which has received the authorization for demolition, re-siting, or modification of a monument.

Article 24. Ensuring the Preservation of Monuments of History and Culture When Performing Construction and Other Work

Construction, irrigation, road, and other work which may create a threat to the existence of monuments of history and culture shall be carried out only by agreement with the state agencies for the protection of monuments and after the effectuation of measures ensuring the preservation of monuments.

The financing of the said measures shall be at the expense of the organizations carrying out construction, irrigation, road, or other works.

Enterprises, organizations, and institutions shall, if archeological and other objects having historical, scientific, artistic, or other cultural value are discovered in the process of carrying on work, be obliged to notify the state agency for the protection of monuments thereof and suspend further work.

Article 25. The Suspension of Construction and Other Work Representing a Danger for Monuments of History and Culture

State agencies for the protection of monuments shall have the right to suspend construction, irrigation, road, and other works if a danger arises in the process of conducting these works for monuments of history and culture or a violation of the rules for their protection.

Article 26. Carrying on Diggings and Explorations for Monuments of Archeology

The carrying on of diggings and explorations for monuments of archeology shall be permitted only if there exists a permit (or open lists) issued and registered in the established procedure.

Organizations and citizens carrying on archeological work shall be obliged to ensure the preservation of the monuments.

Article 27. Collecting of Monuments of History and Culture

The collecting of antique documentary monuments, ancient paintings, and ancient applied art by organizations or citizens shall be permitted if there exist special permits issued and registered in the established procedure.

Article 28. Prohibition of Exporting of Monuments of History and Culture Beyond the Limits of the USSR

The export of monuments of history and culture beyond the limits of the USSR shall be prohibited.

An exception to this rule shall be permitted only with a special permit issued in each individual instance in the procedure determined by USSR legislation.

Article 29. Procedure for Temporary Export of Monuments of History and Culture Beyond the Limits of the USSR

With a view to the development of international cultural exchange, the temporary export of monuments of history and culture beyond the limits of the USSR shall be authorized with observance of the rules and conditions specially established for each instance by the respective USSR state agency.

Article 30. Protection of Monuments of History and Culture Imported into the USSR

Monuments of history and culture which are in the ownership of foreign states, organizations, and persons and are temporarily imported into the USSR for the purposes of cultural exchange on the basis of the respective agreements shall be protected by the state.

IV. Responsibility for Violations of Legislation on the Protection and Use of Monuments of History and Culture

Article 31. Responsibility for Violation of Legislation on the Protection and Use of Monuments of History and Culture

Persons guilty of the failure to fulfill rules for the protection, use, registration, and restoration of monuments of history and culture, of violating the regime of the zone for their protection, and also of other violations of legislation on the protection and use of monuments, shall bear criminal, administrative, or other responsibility in accordance with USSR and union republic legislation.

Article 32. Restoration of a Monument of History and Culture and Compensation of Losses in the Event of Inflicting Harm on the Monument

Enterprises, organizations, institutions, and citizens who have harmed a monument of history and culture or its protection zone shall be obliged to restore the monument or protection zone to its former state, and if this is impossible, to compensate the losses inflicted in accordance with USSR and union republic legislation. Restoration of the monument or its protection zone shall be carried out with observance of the established procedure for the restoration of monuments of history and culture.

Officials and other workers through whose fault an enterprise, organization, or institution incurred expenses connected with the compensation of losses specified in the first paragraph of the present Article shall bear material liability in the established procedure.

V. International Treaties and Agreements

Article 33. International Treaties and Agreements on Monuments of History and Culture

If rules other than those which are contained in USSR or union republic legislation on the protection and use of monuments of history and culture have been established by an international treaty or international agreement in which the USSR or union republic participates, the rules of the international treaty or international agreement shall be applied.

CHAPTER IX

ADMINISTRATIVE LAW

ON THE PROCEDURE FOR THE PUBLICATION AND ENTRY INTO FORCE OF LAWS OF THE USSR, DECREES OF THE USSR SUPREME SOVIET, AND EDICTS AND DECREES OF THE PRESIDIUM OF THE USSR SUPREME SOVIET

[Edict of the Presidium of the USSR Supreme Soviet, June 19, 1958, as amended March 11, 1960. *Vedomosti SSSR* (1958), no. 14, item 275]

With a view to putting in order the matter of publishing the laws of the USSR and the edicts of the Presidium of the USSR Supreme Soviet and of clarifying the periods for their entry into force, the Presidium of the USSR Supreme Soviet decrees:

1. To establish that the laws of the USSR and decrees and other acts of the USSR Supreme Soviet shall be subject to publication in the *Vedomosti Verkhovnogo Soveta SSSR* not later than seven days after their adoption.

2. The most important of the acts specified in Article 1, which are subject to wide and immediate promulgation, shall be published in the newspaper *Izvestiia Sovetov deputatov trudiashchikhsia SSSR*.

When necessary, these acts may be promulgated also by radio or transmitted by telegraph.

3. Edicts and decrees of the Presidium of the USSR Supreme Soviet not having general significance or bearing a normative character shall be sent to the appropriate departments and institutions and brought by them to the information of the persons to whom the effect of such acts extends. They may not be published by decision of the Presidium of the USSR Supreme Soviet.

4. Treaties, agreements, and conventions concluded by the USSR with foreign states and ratified in the established procedure, and the respective edicts concerning ratification, shall be published in *Vedomosti* upon the representation of the USSR Ministry of Foreign Affairs to the Presidium of the USSR Supreme Soviet.

5. Laws of the USSR, decrees and other acts of the USSR Supreme Soviet, and edicts and decrees of the Presidium of the USSR Supreme Soviet of a general normative character shall enter into force simultaneously on the entire territory of the USSR upon the expiry of ten days after their publication in *Izvestiia* or in *Vedomosti*, unless another period is specified in the acts themselves for their introduction into effect; such acts published in accordance with Article 2 of the present Edict in *Izvestiia* before publication in *Vedomosti* shall enter into force on the expiry of ten days after publication in *Izvestiia*.

All other acts not having a general normative character shall enter into force from the moment of their adoption, unless another period is specified in the acts themselves for their introduction into effect.

6. Edicts and decrees of the Presidium of the USSR Supreme Soviet which are not published in accordance with Article 3 of the present Edict

shall enter into force from the moment of their receipt of the appropriate departments and institutions, unless in the acts themselves another period is specified for their introduction into effect.

7. In connection with the issuance of the present Edict:

b) The USSR Council of Ministers shall be commissioned to establish the procedure for the publication and entry into force of decrees and regulations of the USSR Council of Ministers.

8. The present Edict shall be submitted for confirmation by the USSR Supreme Soviet.

ON THE PROCEDURE FOR THE PUBLICATION AND ENTRY INTO FORCE OF DECREES AND REGULATIONS OF THE GOVERNMENT OF THE USSR

[Decree of the Council of Ministers of the USSR, March 30, 1959. SP SSSR (1959), no. 6, item 37]

The Council of Ministers of the USSR decrees:

1. To establish that decrees of the Government of the USSR having general significance or bearing a normative character shall be published in the Sobranie postanovlenii Pravitel'stva SSSR, issued by the Administrative Department of the USSR Council of Ministers.

Decrees of the Government of the USSR which in view of their importance or the urgency of the measures provided therein are subject to wide and immediate promulgation shall be published in the newspapers and in necessary instances shall be broadcast also on the radio or transmitted by telegraph.

2. To establish that in decrees of the Government of the USSR of a normative character there should be specified the period for their entry into effect.

In those instances when the period for entry into effect is not specified in decrees of the Government of the USSR, they shall enter into force from the moment of their adoption.

3. Regulations of the USSR Council of Ministers shall enter into force from the moment of their adoption and are not subject to publication in the Sobranie postanovlenii Pravitel'stva SSSR.

4. Treaties, agreements, and conventions concluded by the USSR with foreign states and not subject to ratification, and also the respective decrees of the Government concerning their confirmation, shall be published in the Sobranie postanovlenii Pravitel'stva SSSR upon the representation of the USSR Ministry of Foreign Affairs.

5. Decrees of the Government of the USSR not published in the Sobranie postanovlenii Pravitel'stva SSSR or in newspapers, and also regulations of the USSR Council of Ministers, may be published in other printed publications upon the proposal of the appropriate organizations only with the authorization of the Administrative Department of the USSR Council of Ministers.

6. On the original copies of decrees of the Government of the USSR which are subject to publication in accordance with Paragraph 1 of the present Decree, the following inscriptions shall be made:

"Subject to publication in the Sobranie postanovlenii";

"Subject to publication in the Sobranie postanovlenii and in the newspapers;

"Subject to publication in the Sobranie postanovlenii and in newspapers and to broadcast on the radio."

7. Decrees of the Government of the USSR, irrespective of their publication in accordance with the present decree, shall be distributed by the Administrative Department of the USSR Council of Ministers immediately after their adoption, to the councils of ministers of the union republics, to the state committees of the USSR Council of Ministers, to the ministries of the USSR, to the Commission of Soviet Control of the USSR Council of Ministers, to the Procuracy of the USSR, to the USSR Supreme Court, to the State Bank of the USSR, to the USSR Central Statistical Administration, to the Committee of State Security attached to the USSR Council of Ministers, and also to other organizations on a list determined by the Administrative Department of the USSR Council of Ministers.

STATUTE ON ENTRY INTO THE USSR AND ON EXIT FROM THE USSR

[Confirmed by Decree of the USSR Council of Ministers, September 22, 1970. SP SSSR (1970), no. 18, item 139]

Entry into the USSR

1. The entry of Soviet citizens into the USSR shall be permitted on Soviet diplomatic, service, and general citizen's foreign passports, sailor's passports, or certificates for return.

Soviet citizens residing abroad permanently and having valid Soviet general citizen's foreign passports shall be permitted to enter the USSR if notations of registration exist in the passports in connection with exit from the Soviet Union which were made by Soviet embassies, missions, or consulates.

2. The entry of foreign citizens or stateless persons to the USSR shall be permitted on valid foreign passports or documents replacing them with Soviet entry visas, unless another entry procedure has been established by an agreement of the USSR with the respective country.

3. Entry visas of the USSR for foreign citizens, as well as for stateless persons, shall be issued abroad by Soviet embassies, missions, and consulates or, in individual instances, by Soviet representatives especially empowered therefor.

Entry visas to the USSR may be issued in appropriate instances also on the territory of the USSR (or exit-entry visas) in the event of the departure of citizens abroad for a specific period. Such visas shall be issued by the USSR Ministry of Foreign Affairs, by union republic ministries of foreign affairs, by diplomatic agencies of the USSR Ministry of Foreign Affairs, by the USSR Ministry of Internal Affairs, by union and autonomous republic ministries of internal affairs, and by the administrations of internal affairs of the executive committees of regional and city soviets of working people's deputies in the established procedure.

4. The passage of the crew of means of transport who are traveling abroad across the state frontier of the USSR shall be regulated by special rules.

Exit from the USSR

5. The exit of Soviet citizens from the USSR shall be permitted on valid documents enumerated in Article 8(a)-(d) of the present Statute.

6. The exit of foreign citizens from the USSR, as well as stateless persons, shall be permitted on valid foreign passports or documents replacing them, with exit visas, unless another procedure has been established by an agreement of the USSR with the respective country.

7. Exit visas from the USSR shall be issued by the USSR Ministry of Foreign Affairs, union republic ministries of foreign affairs, diplomatic agencies of the USSR Ministry of Foreign Affairs, the USSR Ministry of

Internal Affairs, union and autonomous republic ministries of internal affairs, administrations of the ministries of internal affairs of executive committees of territory, region, and city soviets of working people's deputies in the established procedure.

Exit visas from the USSR also may be issued abroad to foreign citizens and stateless persons (or entry-exit visas) for entry to the USSR for a specific period. Such visas shall be issued by Soviet embassies, missions, and consulates or, in individual instances, by Soviet representatives specially empowered therefor.

Documents on the Right to Cross the USSR State Frontier

8. There may be issued to a citizen of the USSR for exit from the USSR, residence abroad, and return to the USSR: (a) a diplomatic passport; (b) service passport; (c) seaman's passport; (d) general citizen's foreign passport.

In the absence of the enumerated documents for return to the USSR, a certificate for return may be issued.

9. Diplomatic, service, and general citizen's foreign passports shall be issued to citizens of the USSR going abroad by the USSR Ministry of Foreign Affairs or the union republic ministries of foreign affairs in accordance with Articles 13, 14, and 16-18 of the present Statute.

Diplomatic, service, and general citizen's passports and certificates for return to the USSR shall be issued to citizens of the USSR who are abroad by Soviet embassies, missions, or consulates or, in individual instances, by Soviet representatives especially empowered therefor.

10. Service passports shall be issued in the established procedure in place of those certificates previously issued also by the USSR Ministry of Internal Affairs and the union republic ministries of internal affairs to persons going abroad on official business to socialist countries, and general citizen's foreign passports, by the USSR Ministry of Internal Affairs, union and autonomous republic ministries of internal affairs, and by the administrations of internal affairs of executive committees of territory, regional, and city soviets of working people's deputies.

11. Seaman's passports shall be issued to citizens of the USSR by the port masters of the Ministry of the Maritime Fleet and by the masters of fishing seaports of the USSR Ministry of Fisheries.

12. Stateless persons residing on the territory of the USSR shall be issued the necessary documents for exit from the Soviet Union with exit visas. The issuance of such documents shall be in the established procedure by the USSR Ministry of Internal Affairs, union and autonomous republic ministries of internal affairs, and administrations of internal affairs of executive committees of territory, regional, and city soviets of working people's deputies.

13. Diplomatic passports shall be issued to:

(a) members and candidate members of the Central Committee of the Communist Party of the Soviet Union; members and candidate members of the central committees of the union republic communist parties; members of the Central Auditing Committee of the Communist Party of the Soviet Union and members of the auditing committees of the union republic communist parties; secretaries of territory and regional committees of the Communist Party of the Soviet Union and union republic communist parties; executive workers of the apparatus of the Central Committee of the Communist Party of the Soviet Union;

(b) the Chairman of the Presidium of the USSR Supreme Soviet and his deputies; chairmen of the presidiums of the union and autonomous republic supreme soviets and their deputies; the Secretary of the Presidium of the USSR Supreme Soviet and secretaries of the presidiums of the union and autonomous republic supreme soviets; deputies of the USSR Supreme Soviet and deputies of the union and autonomous republic supreme soviets; the head of the Secretariat and section heads of the Presidium of the USSR Supreme Soviet; assistants of the Chairman of the Presidium of the USSR Supreme Soviet;

(c) the Chairman of the USSR Council of Ministers and his deputies; chairmen of the union and autonomous republic councils of ministers and their deputies; ministers, chairmen of state committees of the USSR, managers of central state institutions of the USSR and union and autonomous republics and their deputies, chairmen of executive committees of territory and regional soviets of working people's deputies; members of collegia of ministries, USSR state committees, and central state institutions of the USSR; the Administrative Officer of the USSR Council of Ministers; the Deputy Administrative Officer of the USSR Council of Ministers; heads of secretariats and assistants to the Chairman and deputy chairmen of the USSR Council of Ministers; heads of administrative sections of the USSR Council of Ministers;

(d) ambassadors and envoys of the USSR, counsellors, first, second, and third secretaries, and attaches of the USSR Ministry of Foreign Affairs and union republic ministries of foreign affairs, embassies and missions of the USSR, as well as Soviet consuls-general, consuls, vice consuls, consular agents, and secretaries of consulates-general and consulates; diplomatic couriers;

(e) military, naval, and air attaches and their aides;

(f) trade representatives of the USSR and their deputies, trade counsellors, counsellors on economic questions and their deputies; commercial attaches;

(g) heads and members of governmental delegations of the USSR and union republics at international conferences, meetings, and negotiations; heads, representatives, and members of delegations of the USSR and union republics at a session of the United Nations and its organs, United Nations specialized agencies, and conferences of inter-governmental international organizations;

(h) Soviet personnel of international organizations holding a post equivalent to a diplomatic post.

14. Service passports shall be issued to:

(a) personnel of ministries, departments, and other state institutions and enterprises of the USSR and union and autonomous republics going abroad on official business;

(b) correspondents of TASS attached to the USSR Council of Ministers or of _Izvestia_ and _Pravda_.

15. Seaman's passports shall be issued to citizens of the USSR who are members of a crew of a vessel of foreign navigation of the Ministry of the Maritime Fleet or of the USSR Ministry of Fisheries.

16. General citizen's foreign passports shall be issued to Soviet citizens, in addition to those enumerated in Articles 13-15 of the present

Statute, who are going abroad on official, social, or private business, as well as to Soviet citizens residing abroad permanently.

17. Diplomatic, service, or general citizen's foreign passports shall be issued respectively for wives, children under 18 years of age, and unmarried daughters over 18 years of age who are traveling with the persons enumerated in Articles 13, 14, and 16, or to them. Children under 16 years of age also may be entered in the passport of one of the parents or the persons with whom they are traveling.

18. The issuance of documents for exit from the USSR, residence abroad, and return to the USSR shall be in the established procedure upon the written applications of the ministries, departments, or organizations of the USSR concerned, as well as upon the applications of citizens who are going abroad for private business.

19. Foreign visas for those going abroad on official business shall be obtained by the USSR Ministry of Foreign Affairs, by representatives of the Soviet Union abroad, by union republic ministries of foreign affairs, by embassies and missions of the USSR abroad, and for private business, by direct recourse of citizens to the foreign representations.

STATUTE ON THE PASSPORT SYSTEM IN THE USSR

[Confirmed by Decree of the USSR Council of Ministers, August 28, 1974. SP SSSR (1974), no. 19, item 109]

I. General Provisions

1. The passport of a citizen of the Union of Soviet Socialist Republics shall be the basic document certifying the identity of a Soviet citizen.

All Soviet citizens who have attained 16 years of age shall be obliged to have the passport of a citizen of the USSR.

Military servicemen and Soviet citizens who reside permanently abroad and who have returned to the USSR for temporary residence shall reside without the said passports.

Identity certificates and military passes issued by the command of military units and military institutions shall be the documents which certify the identity of military servicemen.

The documents certifying the identity of Soviet citizens who reside permanently abroad and who have returned to the USSR for temporary residence shall be their ordinary foreign passports.

Foreign citizens and stateless persons shall reside on the territory of the USSR in accordance with documents established by USSR legislation.

2. Passports shall be manufactured to a specimen uniform for the entire USSR, in the Russian language and the language of the respective union republic, and for autonomous republics, also in the language of the respective autonomous republic.

3. The following information concerning the identity of the citizen shall be entered in the passport:

- surname, forename, patronymic;
- day, month, and year of birth;
- nationality.

The entry concerning nationality in the passport shall be respectively the nationality of the parents. If the parents are of different nationalities, when issuing a passport for the first time the nationality shall be entered according to the nationality of the father or mother, depending on the wish of the passport holder. Thereafter, the entry concerning nationality shall not be subject to change. The following information concerning children who have been born thereof also shall be entered in the passport of a citizen: surname, forename, patronymic, day, month, and year of birth. Such information shall be entered by agencies for the registry of acts of civil status.

4. Notations shall be made in the passports of citizens concerning:

- the registration and dissolution of a marriage, by agencies for the registry of acts of civil status;

- the relationship to military service, by military commissariats;

- the residence permit and departure from residence by agencies of internal affairs or persons empowered therefor by the executive committees of rural or settlement soviets of working people's deputies.

In instances provided for by legislation, agencies of internal affairs shall make notations concerning the duty to pay alimony in the passports of citizens who avoid the payment of alimony.

With the consent of citizens, public health institutions shall make notations in passports concerning the blood group and type of the passport holder.

Notations in passports shall be made by stamps, the form and dimensions of which shall be established by the USSR Ministry of Internal Affairs.

It shall be prohibited to make any other notations in the passports of citizens.

5. The validity of a passport shall not be limited as to time.

When citizens attain 25 and 45 years of age, new photographs corresponding to this age shall be inserted in the passport by agencies of internal affairs. Passports not having such photographs shall be invalid.

6. Citizens shall be subject to residence registration in the established procedure at the place of residence, as well as to residence registration or to registration at a place of temporary residence and to departure registration when departing from a place of residence.

Residence registration, registration, and departure registration of citizens shall be performed in accordance with USSR legislation.

7. There shall be responsible for observance of the passport system rules:

heads of housing administration offices and of municipal housing offices (or sections),

house administrators, commandants of houses and hostels, chairmen of housing construction or dacha construction cooperatives;

directors (or managers) of hotels, sanatoriums, rest homes, pensions, tourist parks, hospitals, boarding houses for the aged and handicapped, boarding homes for children, and other similar institutions in which are situate citizens who are subject to residence registration or registration;

house owners and other persons in whose jurisdiction there are dwelling buildings or premises.

8. Control over the fulfillment of the passport system rules shall be exercised by the executive committees of local soviets of working people's deputies and agencies of internal affairs.

II. Issuance of Passports and Use Thereof

9. The issuance and exchange of passports and the insertion in the passport of new photographs upon the attainment by citizens of 25 or 45 years of age shall be performed by agencies of internal affairs at the citizen's place of residence.

10. In order to receive a passport, citizens shall submit:

(a) an application of the form established by the USSR Ministry of Internal Affairs;

(b) a birth certificate. If it is impossible to submit a birth certificate, the passport shall be issued upon the submission of other documents which confirm the time and place of birth, in a procedure determined by the USSR Ministry of Internal Affairs;

(c) two photographs, 50 x 60 mm.

Passports may be issued on the basis of military passes to servicemen discharged from the ranks of the USSR Armed Forces.

Passports shall be issued on the basis of established documents to persons admitted to Soviet citizenship, as well as to persons who have arrived in the USSR by way of repatriation.

11. In order to insert new photographs in the passport upon the attainment by citizens of 25 or 45 years of age, they shall submit to agencies of internal affairs the passports and two photographs, 50 x 60 mm., corresponding to the age attained.

12. Passports shall be exchanged in instances of:

(a) change of surname, forename, or patronymic;

(b) establishment of an inaccuracy in the entries;

(c) unsuitability for use.

13. In order to exchange a passport, citizens shall submit:

(a) an application of the established form;

(b) the passport subject to exchange;

(c) two photographs, 50 x 60 mm.

To exchange a passport in connection with a change of surname, forename, patronymic, or the establishment of an inaccuracy in the entries, documents confirming these circumstances also shall be submitted.

14. To obtain or exchange passports, citizens shall give the documents and photographs to the persons responsible for the observance of passport system rules or to persons empowered to perform passport work, who shall be obliged to submit these documents and photographs within three days to the agencies of internal affairs.

15. To obtain and exchange passports or insert new photographs in a passport, documents and photographs should be surrendered by citizens not later than a month after attaining the respective age or the change of surname, forename, or patronymic.

16. In passports issued to citizens by way of exchange or to replace those lost, entries about children who have not attained 16 years of age and notations concerning the registration of marriage, relationship to military service, residence registration, and also about the duty to pay alimony if this duty remains, should be made by agencies of internal affairs.

17. Payment in the amount of two rubles shall be exacted for the passport issued.

18. Citizens shall be obliged to preserve the passport carefully.

A citizen should immediately notify agencies of internal affairs about the loss of a passport, which at his request shall issue him a certificate thereof. The certificate form shall be established by the USSR Ministry of Internal Affairs.

19. Passports should be surrendered by citizens when:

(a) being called for military service, to the military commissariats at the place of call, and when enrolling in a military training institution, to these institutions for subsequent forwarding to agencies of internal affairs;

(b) when exiting abroad for temporary residence, to the respective institutions at the place of obtaining documents to exit abroad. Upon the return of citizens from abroad, the passports shall be returned to them.

The passports of persons who have exited abroad for permanent residence, as well as persons who have given up Soviet citizenship, shall be subject to surrender to agencies of internal affairs.

Passports of deceased persons shall be surrendered to agencies for the registry of acts of civil status, which shall forward them to agencies of internal affairs after registering the death.

Passports which have been found shall be subject to surrender to agencies of internal affairs.

20. Passports shall be confiscated by agencies of inquiry, preliminary investigation, or by a court from persons confined under guard, as well as those sentenced to deprivation of freedom or exile, and from persons conditionally sentenced to deprivation of freedom with compulsory labor. Upon release from being under guard or from serving a punishment, the passports shall be returned to their holders. Passports shall be returned to persons conditionally released from places of deprivation of freedom for work on the construction of enterprises of the national economy after removing therefrom restrictions on the place of work.

21. It shall be prohibited to confiscate passports from citizens except for instances provided for by legislation of the USSR, as well as to receive or transfer passports as a pledge.

III. Residence Registration, Registration, Departure Registration

22. Citizens shall be registered for residence at their place of residence:

citizens who have passports, according to the passports;

children who have not attained 16 years of age residing separately from their parents (or trustees, guardians), according to the birth certificate;

military servicemen residing outside barracks, ships, or vessels, according to certificates issued in the established procedure by military units or by military institutions;

Soviet citizens residing permanently abroad who have arrived for a temporary residence in the USSR, according to ordinary foreign passports.

The residence registration of children who have not attained 16 years of age and who reside together with their parents (or trustees, guardians) shall be performed by entering the information concerning them in the respective residence registration documents of one of the parents (or trustee, guardian).

Citizens who have arrived for temporary residence from one locality to another for a period exceeding one and a half months shall be provisionally registered for residence, and those who have arrived for a period of up to one and a half months shall be registered in the established procedure.

23. Citizens who change their place of residence, as well as those who depart to another locality for temporary residence for a term exceeding one and a half months, except those departing on a business trip, on holidays, for a dacha, for rest or recuperation, shall be obliged to register their departure before leaving.

Citizens not having notations concerning departure registration in the passports or other documents provided by point 22 of the present Statute shall not be subject to residence registration.

24. Residence registration and departure registration of citizens in cities, as well as in settlements of an urban type and in rural population centers in which there are agencies of internal affairs, as well as in population centers located in a frontier zone, shall be performed by agencies of internal affairs; in other settlements of an urban type and rural population centers, by persons empowered therefor by the executive committees of rural or settlement soviets of working people's deputies.

25. Citizens shall submit:

for residence registration: an application of the established form containing the consent to the residence registration also of the person who is giving the dwelling space; passport or one of the documents provided for by point 22 of the present Statute; military registration documents.

for departure registration: applications; passport or one of the documents provided for by point 22 of the present Statute; military registration documents.

for registration: passport or one of the documents provided for by point 22 of the present Statute.

For residence registration or registration in population centers located in a frontier zone, a permit for entry into this zone obtained in the established procedure shall also be submitted to an agency of internal affairs at the place of residence before exit to the frontier zone.

26. Citizens subject to residence registration shall be obliged within three days from the date of arrival to surrender residence registration documents to the persons responsible for the observance of passport system rules or to the persons empowered to perform passport work. Departure registration documents shall be surrendered to those same persons at the place of departure registration. Documents received from citizens should be submitted to the organ effectuating residence and departure registration within three days.

Citizens who have come from one locality to another for a period of up to a month and a half shall be registered not later than three days from the date of arrival, and in hotels, sanatoriums, rest homes, pensions, hospitals, and other similar institutions in which are situate citizens subject to registration, upon arrival.

27. Persons who have been refused residence registration at a population center where they arrived shall be obliged to leave this population center within seven days.

28. A state fee for residence registration shall be exacted in accordance with prevailing legislation.

29. The procedure for the residence and departure registration of persons who by virtue of the nature of their occupation constantly move about (members of the crews of vessels, workers of geological survey parties, etc.) shall be established by the USSR Ministry of Internal Affairs by agreement with the interested ministries and departments.

30. Persons called to military service shall be subject to departure registration upon their receipt of the notice to appear at the assembly point.

31. The departure registration of persons sentenced to deprivation of freedom, exile, as well as persons conditionally sentenced to deprivation of freedom with compulsory labor, shall be performed after the entry into legal force of the judgments in respect of these persons. The procedure for the departure registration of such persons shall be established by the USSR Ministry of Internal Affairs.

32. Deceased persons shall be subject to departure registration after the registration of death.

33. The forms for residence registration applications, residence registration cards, address blanks, house books, and other documents relating to residence registration, registration, and departure registration shall be established by the USSR Ministry of Internal Affairs.

Blanks for applications and other documents relating to residence registration, registration, and departure registration, shall be issued to citizens free of charge. Payment shall be exacted for house books within the amounts of their actual cost.

IV. Responsibility for Violation of Passport System Rules

34. Citizens obliged to have passports shall, for residence without a passport or with an invalid passport, as well as citizens residing without a residence registration or registration, be subjected to a fine in an amount of up to 10 rubles in an administrative procedure. Citizens shall bear the same responsibility for intentional damage to a passport, as well as for the careless keeping of a passport which entails its loss.

For malicious violation of passport system rules, citizens shall be brought to criminal responsibility in accordance with legislation.

35. Persons responsible for the observance of passport system rules who allow the residence of citizens without passports or with invalid passports or without residence registration or registration, and also citizens who allow the residence of persons in dwelling premises which they occupy without passports, residence registration, or registration, shall be subjected to a fine in an amount of up to 10 rubles in an administrative procedure.

36. The same violation allowed by a person after the application to him in the course of a year of a measure of administrative exaction for such acts shall itself entail the imposition of a fine in an amount of up to 50 rubles in an administrative procedure.

37. Persons who have violated the rules for entry into a frontier zone, as well as rules for residence or residence registration therein, shall be subjected to a fine in an amount of up to 10 rubles in an administrative procedure.

38. Officials who illegally confiscate a passport from a citizen or who take a passport as a pledge shall be subject to a fine in an amount of up to 10 rubles in an adminstrative procedure.

ON THE FURTHER LIMITATION OF THE APPLICATION OF FINES IMPOSED BY ADMINISTRATIVE PROCEDURE

[Edict of the Presidium of the USSR Supreme Soviet, June 21, 1961, as amended November 11, 1963, December 14, 1966, November 19, 1969, and October 13, 1976. Vedomosti SSSR (1961), no. 35, item 368; (1963), no. 47, item 490; (1966), no. 50, item 1020; (1969), no. 48, item 431; (1976), no. 42, item 584]

The successive development of Soviet democracy, the extensive involvement of the public in the protection of the Soviet legal order, and the strengthening of legality in the period of the expanded construction of a communist society create the conditions for the further limitation of the application of a fine as a measure of administrative sanction.

At the present time, when the sphere of administrative coercion is narrower, such a measure as a fine should be applied to citizens, as well as to officials, in instances when measures of social or disciplinary pressure will be recognized as inadequate.

In connection with the strengthening of state discipline in the activity of institutions, enterprises, and organizations, and the further increase of the personal responsibility of officials, the application of fines imposed by administrative procedure to institutions, enterprises, and organizations at the present time is unnecessary, the more so since the complex practice of imposing fines on institutions, enterprises, and organizations in many instances actually leads to officials who are the true perpetrators of the violation going unpunished.

For the purposes of the further limitation of the application of fines imposed by administrative procedure, it is necessary to reduce the group of state agencies empowered to establish fines, the group of agencies and officials who have the right to impose fines, to limit the list of violations for which fines may be imposed, to decrease the amount of fines for individual types of violations, and to strengthen legality and the principles of collegiality in the activity of agencies imposing fines.

In conditions of the enlargement of the rights of union republics in state construction, legislation on fines imposed by administrative procedure should be brought within the jurisdiction of the union republics, reserving to the USSR only the determination of the fundamental provisions of this legislation and the establishment of fines for violation of rules whose confirmation is within the jurisdiction of the USSR.

The Presidium of the USSR Supreme Soviet decrees:

1. Fines as a measure of administrative sanction shall be established by the highest agencies of state power and state administration of the USSR and the highest agencies of state power and state administration of the union and autonomous republics within the limits of their competence and may be imposed only in the instances expressly provided for by acts of the highest agencies of state power and state administration.

2. Fines as a measure of administrative sanction may be established by laws of the USSR, by edicts of the Presidium of the USSR Supreme Soviet,

and by decrees of the USSR Council of Ministers for the violation of rules whose confirmation is relegated to the exclusive jurisdiction of the USSR; rules ensuring the safe movement of railway, maritime, and air transport, and rules for the use of these types of transport; rules for military registration, border regime, customs rules and smuggling, as well as for a violation of the rules enumerated in Article 3 of the present Edict whose establishment is relegated to the joint jurisdiction of the USSR and union republics.

Fines as a measure of administrative sanction may be established by laws of the USSR and edicts of the Presidium of the USSR Supreme Soviet for a violation of other rules whose confirmation is relegated to the jurisdiction of the USSR.

3. Fines as a measure of administrative sanction may be established in accordance with USSR legislation by laws of the union republics, edicts of the presidiums of the union republic supreme soviets, and decrees of the union republic councils of ministers for: violation of rules for technical safety and labor protection in industry, construction, transport, and agriculture; violation of registration rules for non-cooperative handicraftsmen and artisans, and for engaging in prohibited trades; violation of sanitary-antiepidemic and sanitary-hygienic rules, and of rules for the quarantine of livestock, other veterinary-sanitary rules and rules for the quarantine of plants; for violation of the public order and rules of the passport system; violation of rules for the protection of the air, soil, minerals, forests, water resources and fisheries; violation of fire safety rules; violation of rules ensuring the safe movement of automotive and river transport and rules for the use of these types of transport; violation of rules of communications.

Fines as a measure of administrative sanction may be established in accordance with USSR legislation, laws of the union republics, and edicts of the presidiums of the union republic supreme soviets for the violation of other rules whose establishment is relegated to the joint jurisdiction of the USSR and the union republics.

4. A list of violations concerning questions within the exclusive jurisdiction of the union republics for which fines as a measure of administrative sanction may be provided shall be established by union republic legislation.

5. It is considered advisable that the group of questions with regard to which local agencies of state power may adopt decisions providing for the imposition of fines by administrative procedure for their violation be limited by union republic legislation and that only the territory, regional, autonomous region, national area, district, and city soviets of workings people's deputies and the executive committees of the said soviets possess the right to adopt such decisions, and only with regard to questions of the struggle against natural disasters, epidemics, and epizootics.

6. The imposition of fines by administrative procedure on institutions, enterprises, and organizations is repealed.

Fines shall be imposed in conformity with prevailing legislation on those officials who in the course of carrying out their official duties must take measures to simultaneously fulfill the established rules. The assumption of fines imposed on officials at the expense of institutions, enterprises, and organizations shall be prohibited.

7. A fine may be imposed on a person who is guilty of committing an administrative offense.

The amount of the fine shall be established depending on the gravity of the offense committed, taking into account the personality and the financial position of the guilty person.

8. A fine may be imposed only on a person who prior to committing the administrative offense had attained 16 years of age.

9. Military servicemen, and also enlisted men and officers of agencies of the MVD, shall bear responsibility in conformity with disciplinary statutes for offenses involving the imposition of a fine by administrative procedure.

10. The amount of fines imposed on citizens by administrative procedure may not exceed 10 rubles, and on officials, 50 rubles.

A higher amount of fines may be established by laws of the USSR and union republic laws, edicts of the Presidium of the USSR Supreme Soviet, and edicts of the presidiums of the union republic supreme soviets in instances of special need to strengthen responsibility for individual types of violations: on citizens up to 50 rubles, and on officials up to 100 rubles.

11. Fines by administrative procedure shall be imposed by administrative commissions attached to executive committees of district and city soviets of working people's deputies, and in instances provided for by Article 13 of the present Edict, by the respective state agencies and officials.

The right to impose fines by administrative procedure for individual types of violation may, by way of exception, be granted to executive committees of rural and settlement soviets of working people's deputies by union republic laws and edicts of the presidiums of union republic supreme soviets.

The right to impose fines on citizens, in instances provided for by USSR and union republic legislation when considering cases relegated to the jurisdiction of commissions for cases of minors may be granted by union republic legislation to district and city commissions for cases of minors.

12. Administrative commissions shall be formed from the deputies of soviets and representatives of social organizations by district, city, and, when necessary, with the authorization of the executive committee of the superior soviet, by rural and settlement soviets of working people's deputies and shall be attached to the executive committees of the respective soviets. Administrative commissions shall rely in their activity on the broad aktiv of the public.

The membership and procedure for activity of administrative commissions shall be determined by union republic legislation.

13. The right to impose fines in an administrative procedure without recourse to administrative commissions shall be retained for:

police agencies: for violation of the public order, consumption of narcotics without a doctor's prescription, violation of rules of the border regime, rules of sojourn, registration, and movement of foreigners and stateless persons on the territory of the USSR, rules ensuring safe movement of transport, and also rules for the use of transport;

railway, maritime, river, and air transport agencies: for violation of rules for the use of means of transport, rules for protecting order and safe movement, and also rules for fire safety and sanitary rules on transport;

city and intercity automotive passenger transport and electrotransport (trolleybus and streetcars): for violation of rules for the use of automotive transport and electrotransport;

legal labor inspectors: for violation of labor legislation; technical labor inspectors: for violation of rules for the protection of labor;

state mining technical supervision agencies: for repeated violation of rules, norms, and instructions for the safe conduct of work in branches of industry and at objects under the control of state mining technical supervision agencies;

agencies of the inspectorates of the Ministry for Machine-Building and the Ministry for Medium Machine-Building: for repeated violation of rules, norms, and instructions for the safe conduct of work at objects under their control;

customs agencies: for violation of customs rules and smuggling;

agencies of the Ministry of Defense: for violation of rules for military registration and for the failure of reservists and men called to military service to appear at a military commissariat without justifiable reasons;

agencies and institutions carrying out state sanitary supervision and medical services of the USSR Ministry of Defense, the USSR Ministry of Internal Affairs, and the Committee of State Security attached to the USSR Council of Ministers exercising sanitary supervision: for violation of sanitary-hygienic and sanitary-antiepidemic rules;

state fire supervision agencies: for violation of fire safety rules;

agencies for the conservation of water resources, fisheries, and forests and agencies exercising state supervision over the observance of hunting rules: respectively for a violation of rules for the protection and use of water resources, fishing rules, fire safety rules in forests, and hunting rules;

agencies of the State Inspectorate of the electrical communications system of the USSR Ministry of Communications: for violation of rules for the acquisition, installation, construction, and use of radio electronic means, rules for the use of radio frequencies, radio waves, and permitted industrial interference with radio reception.

The consideration of individual categories of cases concerning violations provided for by the present Article may be transferred to administrative commissions attached to the executive committees of district and city soviets of working people's deputies, and also to rural and settlement soviets of working people's deputies and their executive committees or administrative commissions attached to the executive committees of rural and settlement soviets of working people's deputies, by USSR legislation and union republic legislation.

The agencies and officials specified in the present Article also may transfer materials with respect to offenders to administrative commissions for the imposition of a fine.

14. A protocol (or act) should be drawn up specifying the identity of the offender, the nature, place, and time of violation, as well as witnesses, concerning each administrative offense, except for instances when in conformity with prevailing legislation the fine is to be recovered on the spot.

The procedure in cases of administrative violations shall be established by union republic legislation.

15. A fine by administrative procedure may not be imposed later than one month from the date the offense was committed.

A decree of an administrative commission and of another agency or official imposing a fine which is not executed within three months from the date it was rendered shall not be subject to execution.

16. Agencies and officials to whom the right of imposing fines on citizens by administrative procedure is granted shall have the right, instead of imposing a fine, to give the offender a warning or to transfer the materials with respect to him to a comrades' court or to social organizations at his place of work or residence for the application of measures of social pressure.

The agency or official imposing an administrative sanction should, as a rule, bring this to the information of the collective at the place of work or the residence of the offender.

17. A fine imposed on a citizen, as well as on an official, which has not been paid within the 15-day period from the date the decree imposing the fine was handed down, shall be recovered in an uncontested proceeding from the wages of the person fined in conformity with the decree of the administrative commission or other agency or official imposing the fine.

If a person subjected to a fine does not work, the fine shall be recovered by the sheriff by resorting to levying against the property on the basis of the decree of the administrative commission or corresponding state agency or official imposing the fine.

18. Citizens, as well as officials, subjected to a fine by administrative procedure shall have the right to appeal against the decree imposing the fine to a district (or city) people's court at the place of their residence within a 10-day period from the date the decree was handed down.

Filing an appeal in a court within the specified period shall suspend recovery of the fine. In this event the three-month time period established by Article 15 of the present Edict shall be suspended.

19. The procedure for the consideration of appeals in courts against the improper imposition of a fine, as well as the list of property not subject to seizure when recovering the fine, shall be established by union republic legislation.

20. Substitution of the fine by correctional tasks in the event of failure to pay shall be prohibited.

21. The presidiums of the union republic supreme soviets shall make the necessary changes in union republic legislation providing for the imposition of fines by administrative procedure.

22. [List of enactments no longer in force in consequence of adopting the present Edict].

23. The present Edict shall enter into force on January 1, 1962, and shall have retroactive force with respect to unrecovered fines imposed on citizens and officials, as well as on institutions, enterprises, and organizations.

CHAPTER X

FINANCE LAW

ON BUDGET RIGHTS OF THE USSR AND UNION REPUBLICS

[Law of the USSR Supreme Soviet, adopted October 30, 1959, as amended June 27, 1969. Vedomosti SSSR (1959), no. 44, item 221; (1969), no. 27, item 234]

Section I. General Provisions

Article 1. The state budget of the USSR shall be the basic financial plan for forming and using the general state fund of monetary assets of the Soviet state. The portion of the national income of the Soviet Union being directed to the planned development of industry, agriculture, transport, trade, and other branches of the national economy, to raise the material well-being and cultural level of the working people, for the defense of the country, and for the maintenance of agencies of state power and agencies of state administration shall be concentrated in the state budget of the USSR.

Assets of the state budget of the USSR shall be formed primarily at the expense of revenues from the socialist economy, constantly growing on the basis of the uninterrupted expansion and improvement of socialist production. Citizens of the USSR shall take part in forming the revenues of the state budget of the USSR with their personal incomes by paying taxes established by laws of the USSR and the voluntary contribution of funds.

Control over the financial and economic activity of enterprises and organizations and over the fulfillment by them of planning tasks of the national economic plan shall be effectuated in the process of drawing up and executing the state budget of the USSR.

Article 2. The budgetary structure of the USSR shall be determined by the state structure of the Union of Soviet Socialist Republics as a union state formed on the basis of a voluntary combining of equal Soviet Socialist Republics. In accordance therewith the state budget of the USSR shall combine the union budget and the state budgets of the union republics.

The financing of measures provided for by the plan for the development of the national economy of the USSR, the participation of the union republics in effectuating measures of all-union significance, and the all-round development of the economy and culture of the union republics and their mutual assistance shall be ensured on the basis of combining the union budget and the state budgets of the union republics in the state budget of the USSR.

Article 3. The drawing up, confirmation, and execution of the state budget of the USSR and the delimitation of its revenues and expenditures between the union budget and the state budgets of the union republics shall be effectuated on the basis of the principle of democratic centralism, ensuring the observance of the sovereign rights of the union republics, the rights of the autonomous republics and local soviets of working people's deputies, and the unity of the budget system and financial policy of the Soviet socialist state.

Article 4. The state budget of the USSR shall be confirmed by the USSR Supreme Soviet for a period of one year, from January 1st to December 31st inclusive. The confirmed state budget of the USSR shall be a law.

Ministries and departments, enterprises, organizations, and institutions shall be obliged to fulfill precisely and without deviation the USSR state budget, to make established payments in full and in good time to the budget, and to observe strict economizing in the expenditure of state funds.

Article 5. Each Soviet Socialist Republic shall have a union republic state budget confirmed by the union republic supreme soviet.

The state budgets of the union republics shall combine the republic budgets of the union republics, the state budgets of the autonomous republics, and local budgets.

Article 6. Each autonomous soviet socialist republic shall have an autonomous republic state budget confirmed by the autonomous republic supreme soviet.

Autonomous republic state budgets shall combine the republic budgets of autonomous republics and local budgets.

Article 7. Each territory, region, autonomous region, national area, district, city, settlement soviet, and rural soviet shall have a local budget confirmed by the respective soviet of working people's deputies.

Article 8. The budget for state social insurance shall be included in the state budget of the USSR.

The budget for state social insurance shall be drawn up by the All-Union Central Trade Union Council and shall be executed by trade union agencies.

Article 9. Social insurance of workers and employees shall be effectuated in the USSR at the expense of the state.

State social insurance funds shall be directed for the payment of pensions, allowances, temporary incapacity to work, pregnancy and birth, the acquisition of passes for sanatoriums and rest homes, and for other expenses relating to the material security and cultural and everyday servicing of the working people.

Section II. State Budget of the USSR

Article 10. The state budget of the USSR shall be drawn up by revenues and expenditures in accordance with the plan for the development of the national economy as a whole for the USSR and for the union republics.

Article 11. The revenues of the state budget of the USSR shall include:

(a) a portion of the revenues of enterprises and economic organizations in the form of a tax on turnover and profits;

(b) an income tax from collective farms, enterprises, and organizations of the cooperative systems and enterprises of social organizations;

(c) taxes from the populace;

(d) other revenues provided for by USSR legislation.

Article 12. Payments of state enterprises and economic organizations, as well as of collective farms, enterprises, and organizations of cooperative systems and enterprises of social organizations received in the state budget of the USSR shall be established by laws of the USSR and by decrees of the USSR Council of Ministers issued in accordance therewith.

Tax payments of the populace shall be established by the USSR Supreme Soviet.

Article 13. The expenditures in the state budget of the USSR shall include:

(a) the national economy;

(b) socio-cultural measures and science;

(c) defense of the country;

(d) maintenance of agencies of state power and agencies of state administration, courts, and procuracy;

(e) formation of state material and financial reserves;

(f) other measures provided for by USSR legislation.

Article 14. The state budget of the USSR shall provide for reserve funds for the USSR Council of Ministers and union republic councils of ministers to cover urgent expenditures for the national economy and socio-cultural and other measures which could not be foreseen when confirming the state budget of the USSR and union republic state budgets.

Article 15. In accordance with the procedure and periods established by the USSR Council of Ministers, the draft state budget of the USSR shall be drawn up:

(a) union republic councils of ministers on the basis of the plan for the development of the USSR national economy and plans for the development of the union republic national economies shall draw up draft union republic state budgets and submit them to the USSR Council of Ministers for consideration and inclusion in the draft state budget of the USSR;

(b) ministries and departments of the USSR on the basis of planning tasks provided for by the plan for the development of the USSR national economy shall draw up draft financial plans and estimates and submit them to the USSR Council of Ministers for drawing up the draft union budget;

(c) All-Union Central Trade Union Council shall draw up the draft state social insurance budget and submit it to the USSR Council of Ministers for consideration and inclusion in the draft USSR state budget;

(d) the USSR Ministry of Finances shall consider in advance:

draft union republic state budgets with the participation of union republic representatives and draw up opinions on these drafts;

the draft state social insurance budget with the participation of representatives of the All-Union Central Trade Union Council and draw up an opinion on this draft;

draft financial plans and estimates of USSR ministries and departments with the participation of their representatives.

Upon considering the said drafts, the USSR Ministry of Finances shall:

draw up a draft union budget;

draw up, on the basis of drafts of the union budget, union republic state budgets, and state social insurance budget, a draft state budget of the USSR and submit it to the USSR Council of Ministers together with opinions regarding the drafts of union republic state budgets and the draft state social insurance budget.

Article 16. The USSR Council of Ministers shall consider the draft state budget of the USSR and submit to the USSR Supreme Soviet:

(a) the USSR state budget: a total amount of revenues with an apportionment of basic revenue sources, and a total amount of expenditures with an apportionment of appropriations for financing the national economy, socio-cultural measures, defense of the country, and maintenance of agencies of state power, agencies of state authority, the courts, and the procuracy;

(b) the union budget: a total amount of revenues with an apportionment of basic revenue sources, and a total amount of expenditures with an apportionment of basic types of expenditures, as well as with a distribution of payments into the budget and appropriations by individual USSR ministries and departments;

(c) union republic state budgets and the state social insurance budget included in the state budget of the USSR;

(d) proposals concerning amounts from all-union state taxes and revenues for the union republic state budgets.

Article 17. The state budget of the USSR submitted by the USSR Council of Ministers to the USSR Supreme Soviet shall be considered beforehand in the standing commissions of the Soviet of the Union and the Soviet of Nationalities of the USSR Supreme Soviet.

Article 18. The standing commissions of the Soviet of the Union and the Soviet of Nationalities of the USSR Supreme Soviet shall:

(a) when considering the state budget of the USSR, hear reports of USSR ministries and departments regarding their financial plans and estimates, reports of union republic councils of ministers regarding revenues and expenditures of union republic state budgets, the report of the All-Union Central Trade Union Council regarding revenues and expenditures of the state social insurance budget, as well as consider proposals regarding changes in revenues and expenditures of the state budget of the USSR submitted by USSR ministries and departments, union republic councils of ministers, and the All-Union Central Trade Union Council;

(b) draw up and submit to the USSR Supreme Soviet opinions relating to the state budget of the USSR.

Article 19. The USSR Supreme Soviet shall consider the state budget of the USSR upon the report of the USSR Council of Ministers and opinions of the standing commissions of the Soviet of the Union and the Soviet of Nationalities, as well as consider the proposals of deputies of the USSR Supreme Soviet made during the discussion of the state budget of the USSR.

Article 20. The USSR Supreme Soviet shall confirm:

(a) the state budget of the USSR: a total amount of revenues with an apportionment of basic revenue sources, and a total amount of expenditures with an apportionment of appropriations:

for financing the national economy;

for socio-cultural measures, including the state social insurance budget;

for defense of the country;

for maintenance of agencies of state power, agencies of state administration, the courts, and the procuracy;

(b) the union budget;

(c) amounts from all-union state taxes and revenues for the union republic state budgets.

Union republic state budgets shall be established in the state budget of the USSR in a total amount of revenues and a total amount of expenditures for each union republic.

Article 21. The Law on the State Budget of the USSR shall be published for general information.

Article 22. The USSR Council of Ministers shall organize the execution of the state budget of the USSR through the USSR Ministry of Finances, USSR ministries and departments, and union republic councils of ministers.

The USSR Ministry of Finances, USSR ministries and departments, and union republic councils of ministers shall ensure the fulfillment of all revenues provided for by the budget, the economical expenditure of budget funds strictly for the designated purpose and within the fulfillment of production and financial plans.

The cash execution of the state budget of the USSR shall be effectuated by the USSR State Bank.

Article 23. A report concerning the execution of the state budget of the USSR shall be drawn up by the USSR Ministry of Finances and submitted to the USSR Council of Ministers in the procedure and within the periods established by the USSR Council of Ministers.

Article 24. The USSR Council of Ministers shall submit a report to the USSR Supreme Soviet concerning the execution of the state budget of the USSR.

Article 25. The standing commissions of the Soviet of the Union and the Soviet of Nationalities of the USSR Supreme Soviet shall consider the report concerning the execution of the state budget of the USSR, draw up opinions regarding the report, and submit them to the USSR Supreme Soviet.

Article 26. The USSR Supreme Soviet shall, in regard to the report of the USSR Council of Ministers and the opinions of the standing commissions of the Soviet of the Union and the Soviet of Nationalities, consider and confirm the report concerning the execution of the state budget of the USSR, including the reports concerning the execution of the union budget, the union republic state budgets, and the state social insurance budget.

A decree of the USSR Supreme Soviet regarding the report concerning the execution of the state budget of the USSR shall be published for general information.

Article 26-1. The preliminary consideration of the state budget of the USSR and the report concerning the execution of the state budget of the USSR submitted by the USSR Council of Ministers to the USSR Supreme

Soviet and the drawing up and submission to the USSR Supreme Soviet of opinions regarding the state budget of the USSR and the report concerning the execution of the state budget of the USSR shall be by the standing commissions of the Soviet of the Union and the Soviet of Nationalities in the procedure provided for by the present Law, as well as by the Statute on the Standing Commissions of the Soviet of the Union and the Soviet of Nationalities of the USSR Supreme Soviet.

Article 27. Control over the execution of the state budget of the USSR shall be exercised by the USSR Ministry of Finances in the procedure established by the USSR Council of Ministers.

Section III. The Union Budget

Article 28. The union budget shall provide with the requisite monetary funds the financing of measures having all-union significance in the domain of economic and cultural construction and the defense of the country. The redistribution of the portion of financial resources among union republics with a view to the all-round development of their economies and ensuring the growth of the material well-being and cultural level of the life of the peoples of the union republics shall be effectuated through the union budget.

Article 29. The union budget shall include revenues:

(a) a turnover tax from enterprises and organizations, except for the portion transferred to the union republic state budgets;

(b) deductions from the profits of state enterprises and economic organizations of union subordination;

(c) repealed;

(d) an income tax from the populace, except for the portion transferred to the union republic state budgets;

(e) customs and other revenues provided for by USSR legislation.

Article 30. The union budget shall include expenditures:

(a) for financing enterprises and economic organizations of union subordination;

(b) for financing measures carried out by institutions and organizations of union subordination relating to enlightenment, science, culture, public health, physical culture, as well as for the payment of pensions and other social security measures;

(c) for the formation of state material and financial reserves;

(d) for the defense of the country;

(e) for the maintenance of agencies of state power and agencies of state administration of the USSR, the USSR Supreme Court, and the procuracy;

(f) for other measures being financed in accordance with USSR legislation from the union budget.

In accordance with Article 14 of the present Law, a reserve fund of the USSR Council of Ministers shall be formed as part of the union budget.

Article 31. The union budget shall be executed according to the list of revenues and expenditures drawn up by the USSR Ministry of Finances in accordance with the budget confirmed by the USSR Supreme Soviet.

Section IV. Union Republic State Budgets

Article 32. The union republic state budgets shall provide with the requisite monetary funds the financing of economic and cultural construction being carried out by agencies of state power and agencies of state administration of the union republics.

Article 33. The budget structure of union republics shall be determined by their state structure and shall be established by the union republic supreme soviets in accordance with the present Law.

Each union republic shall possess equal rights in regard to the drawing up, consideration, confirmation, and execution of the republic state budget.

Article 34. In the event of the issuance of laws of the USSR or decrees of the USSR Council of Ministers after the confirmation of the state budget of the USSR, in accordance with which expenditures are increased or the revenues of union republic state budgets are reduced, these budgets shall in the process of executing the state budget of the USSR be compensated with funds from the union budget: in the event the expenditures of union republic state budgets are reduced or revenues increased, the respective amounts shall be transferred to the union budget.

Article 35. The following revenues shall enter into the union republic state budgets:

(a) deductions from profits and other receipts from enterprises and economic organizations within the jurisdiction of union and autonomous republic ministries and departments and executive committees of soviets of working people's deputies;

(b) forestry revenues, income tax from collective farms, income tax from enterprises and organizations of cooperative systems and enterprises of social organizations;

(c) agricultural tax;

(d) deductions from the income tax from the populace in the amount of fifty percent;

(e) state duty, local taxes, and fees, and other revenues established in the procedure provided for by USSR legislation.

Article 36. There shall be transferred to the union republic state budgets above the revenues provided for in Article 35 of the present Law:

(a) state social insurance funds for the payment of pensions;

(b) deductions from the turnover tax and other all-union state revenues in the amounts provided for in the state budget of the USSR.

Article 37. Expenditures shall be included in the union republic state budgets for:

(a) financing enterprises and economic organizations within the jurisdiction of union and autonomous republic ministries and departments and the executive committees of soviets of working people's deputies;

(b) financing measures being carried out by union republic institutions and organizations relating to enlightenment, science, culture, public health, physical culture, the payment of pensions, allowances for mothers with many children and unmarried mothers, and other social security measures;

(c) maintaining agencies of state power and agencies of state administration of the union republics, people's courts, and other judicial institutions of the union republics, as well as notarial offices;

(d) other measures being financed in accordance with legislation of the USSR and union republics from the union republic state budgets.

In accordance with Article 14 of the present Law, reserve funds of the union republic councils of ministers shall be formed as part of the union republic state budgets.

Article 38. The delimitation of revenues and expenditures of union republic state budgets among republic budgets of union republics, autonomous republic state budgets, and local budgets shall be determined by union republic legislation.

Article 39. The union republic supreme soviets may, when confirming the union republic state budgets, increase the total amount of revenues and the total amount of expenditures established in accordance with Article 20 of the present Law for the union republic in the state budget of the USSR without modifying the amounts from all-union state taxes and revenues provided for in the state budget of the USSR for the union republic state budget.

Article 40. A circulating cash fund shall be formed in the union republic state budgets above the expenditures provided for, at the expense of remaining funds for the said budgets at the beginning of the planning year. The amount of the circulating cash fund shall be determined when confirming the union republic state budgets.

The circulating cash fund may be used during the year to cover temporary cash gaps and should be restored in the same year to the amounts established when confirming the budget.

Article 41. Revenues additionally received when executing the union republic state budgets shall be directed in a procedure determined by USSR and union republic legislation for the financing of the national economy and socio-cultural measures, including capital investments.

Article 42. The amounts of excess of revenues over expenditures for the union republic state budgets at the end of the year as a result of the overfulfillment of revenues or of economies in expenditures, except for unused funds relating to appropriations for capital investments of enterprises and organizations, shall remain at the disposal of the union republic councils of ministers and shall be spent at their discretion.

The procedure for spending the funds formed in connection with the unused appropriations for capital investments for enterprises and organizations shall be determined when confirming the state budget of the USSR.

Article 43. Reports concerning the execution of union republic state budgets shall be confirmed by the union republic supreme soviets.

Article 44. Control over the execution of the union republic state budgets shall be effectuated in the procedure determined by union republic legislation in accordance with the present Law.

Article 45. The union republic supreme soviets shall, in accordance with the present Law, determine the budget rights of autonomous republics and local soviets of working people's deputies.

Article 46. The USSR Council of Ministers shall establish the procedure for confirming the Rules for Drawing Up and Execution of the State Budget of the USSR.

CHAPTER XI

LABOR LAW

FUNDAMENTAL PRINCIPLES OF LEGISLATION OF THE USSR AND UNION REPUBLICS ON LABOR

[Confirmed by Law of the USSR Supreme Soviet, July 15, 1970, as amended August 10, 1973 and October 7, 1977. Vedomosti SSSR (1970), no. 29, item 265; (1973), no. 33, item 440; (1977), no. 41, item 619]

The Great October Socialist Revolution destroyed the system of exploitation and oppression. For the first time, after centuries of forced labor for the exploiters, the working people received the opportunity to work for themselves, for their own society.

With the triumph of socialism in the Soviet Union, the exploitation of man by man has been liquidated completely and forever. Socialist ownership constitutes the basis of the social organization of labor in the USSR, having opened an epoch of free labor in the name of the best life for the working man. The freedom of labor from exploitation guaranteed by the socialist system shall be the basic condition for the genuine freedom of the individual.

In a socialist society, where there are no exploiters and exploited, the universality of labor for all able-bodied members of society shall be realized and the opportunity to work ensured for all citizens. The principle of socialism shall be operative in the USSR: "From each according to his ability, to each according to his labor"; labor shall be a duty and moral obligation of every able-bodied citizens according to the principle: "He who does not work, neither shall he eat".

The socialist social system shall create the material and moral interest of people in the best labor results and in the constant development and improvement of social production. The growth of socialist production shall provide a stable base for the steady increase of material well-being and the cultural level of the Soviet people. The Soviet state shall improve the forms of material and moral stimuli for labor and further in every possible way the development of mass socialist competitions of working people and the movement for communist labor.

The most important condition for building communism is the attainment of high labor productivity and increasing the efficiency of social production. Resolving this task required the acceleration of scientific-technical progress in the entire national economy, the steady growth of the cultural and technical training of the working people, and raising the level of their labor organization and discipline.

In the USSR scientific-technical progress is combined with full employment of the populace and used to fundamentally ease labor, reduce the work week, and liquidate heavy manual and any unskilled labor. With the development of scientific-technical progress, the process of the organic combining of mental and physical labor in the production activity of people gradually occurs. The implementation on an extensive scale of free specialized and professional-technical education guarantees the free choice of kind of work and profession, taking account of the interests of society.

The health protection of the working people, provision of safe labor conditions, and liquidation of professional diseases and industrial injuries constitutes one of the principal concerns of the Soviet state.

In Soviet society the working people shall manage enterprises, which constitute all-people's (or state) ownership, through soviets of working people's deputies and agencies of state administration created by them. Trade unions play an enormous role in the cause of involving workers and employees in production management.

In accordance with the USSR Constitution, equal rights shall be secured for citizens in the domain of labor, irrespective of nationality and race. Women in the USSR shall be granted the right to labor, payment for labor, leisure, and social security on the same basis as men.

Labor rights of citizens shall be protected by law. The protection of labor rights shall be protected by state agencies, and also by trade unions and other social organizations.

Chapter I. General Provisions

Article 1. Tasks of Soviet Legislation on Labor

Soviet legislation on labor shall regulate labor relations of all workers and employees, furthering the growth of labor productivity, raising the efficiency of social production and the material and cultural level of the life of the working people on this basis, strengthen labor discipline, and gradually transform labor into the wealth of society as a prime vital requirement for each able-bodied person.

Legislation on labor shall establish a high level of labor conditions and every possible protection for the labor rights of workers and employees

Article 2. Basic Labor Rights and Duties of Workers and Employees

The right of citizens of the USSR to labor shall be secured by the socialist organization of the national economy, the steady growth of the productive forces of Soviet society, elimination of the possibility of economic crises, and the liquidation of unemployment.

Workers and employees shall realize the right to labor by concluding a labor contract concerning work at an enterprise, institution, or organization. Workers and employees shall have the right to wages guaranteed by the state in proportion to the quantity and quality of labor expended, the right to leisure in accordance with laws limiting the work day and work week and on annual paid leaves, and the right to health and safe labor conditions, free professional training and free raising of qualifications, joint trade unions, participate in production management, in material security at the expense of state funds by way of state social insurance for old-age, and also in the event of illness and loss of capacity to work.

The observance of labor discipline, an attitude of care toward the public weal, the fulfillment of labor norms established by the state with the participation of trade unions shall comprise the duty of all workers and employees.

Article 3. Regulation of Labor of Collective Farm Members

The labor of collective farm members shall be regulated by collective farm charters adopted on the basis of and in accordance with the Mode

Collective Farm Charter, and also USSR and union republic legislation relating to collective farms.

Article 4. Legislation of the USSR and Union Republics on Labor

Legislation of the USSR and union republics on labor shall consist of the present Fundamental Principles and other acts of USSR labor legislation issued in accordance therewith, codes of labor laws, and other union republic acts of labor legislation.

The regulation of the labor of workers and employees on questions provided for by the present Fundamental Principles shall be effectuated by:

legislation of the USSR;

legislation of the USSR and union republics;

legislation of the union republics.

The competence of the USSR and the union republics in the domain of regulating the labor of workers and employees shall be demarcated according to the rules of Article 107 and other articles of the present Fundamental Principles.

Questions of the labor of workers and employees not provided for by the present Fundamental Principles shall be regulated by USSR and union republic legislation.

Article 5. Invalidity of Terms of Labor Contracts Which are Contrary to Labor Legislation

The terms of labor contracts which worsen the position of workers and employees in comparison with USSR and union republic labor legislation or are otherwise contrary to such legislation shall be void.

Chapter II. The Collective Contract

Article 6. Conclusion of the Collective Contract and its Effect

The collective contract shall be concluded by the factory, plant, and local trade union committee in the name of the collective of workers and employees with the administration of an enterprise or organization.

The conclusion of the collective contract should be preceded by a discussion and approval of a draft at meetings (or conferences) of workers and employees.

The collective contract shall extend to all workers and employees of the enterprise or organization irrespective of whether they are trade union members.

Article 7. Content of Collective Contract

The collective contract should contain basic provisions on questions of labor and wages established for the particular enterprise or organization in accordance with prevailing legislation, and also provisions in the domain of work time, rest time, payment of labor, and material incentives, labor protection worked out by the administration and the factory, plant, and local trade union committee within the limits of the rights granted them and bearing a normative character.

The mutual obligations of the administration and the collective of workers and employees for the fulfillment of production plans, improvement in organizing production and labor, introducing new technology and raising labor productivity, improving the quality and reducing the production cost of products, development of the socialist competition, strengthening production and labor discipline, and raising the qualifications and training cadres directly in production shall be established by the collective contract.

Obligations of the administration and factory, plant, and local trade union committee for involving workers and employees in production management, improvement of labor standards, forms for payment of labor and material incentive, labor production, granting exemptions and privileges to peredoviki of production, improvement of housing conditions and the cultural-domestic servicing of the working people, and the development of educational and cultural-mass work should be contained in the collective contract.

Chapter III. The Labor Contract

Article 8. Parties to and Content of Labor Contract

The labor contract is an agreement between the working people and the enterprise, institution, or organization, according to which the working people shall be obliged to fulfill work of a particular specialization, skill, or post while being subordinate to internal labor discipline, and the enterprise, institution, or organization shall be obliged to pay the working people a wage and ensure labor conditions provided for by labor legislation, the collective contract, and the agreement of the parties.

Article 9. Guarantees of Being Hired for Work

An unfounded refusal to hire for work shall be prohibited.

In accordance with the USSR Constitution, any direct or indirect limitation of the rights or the establishment of direct or indirect priorities when hiring for work depending on sex, race, national affiliation, or attitude toward religion shall not be permitted.

Article 10. Term of Labor Contract

Labor contracts shall be concluded for:

(1) an indeterminate term;

(2) a specified term of not more than three years;

(3) for the time of fulfilling specified work.

Article 11. Probationary Hiring

When concluding a labor contract, probation may be stipulated by agreement of the parties with a view to verifying whether a worker or employee conforms to the work entrusted to him.

Maximum probation periods shall be established by USSR and union republic legislation.

Article 12. Prohibition Against Requiring Fulfillment of Work Not Stipulated by Labor Contract

The administration shall not have the right to require from a worker or employee the fulfillment of work not stipulated by a labor contract.

Article 13. Transfer to Other Work

Transfer to other work in the same enterprise, institution, organization, and also transfer to work in another enterprise, institution, or organization or to another locality, even though with the enterprise, institution, or organization, shall be permitted only with the consent of the worker or employee except for instances provided for in Articles 14 and 56 of the present Fundamental Principles.

Article 14. Temporary Transfer to Other Work in Event of Production Necessity or Stoppage

In the event of production necessity for an enterprise, institution, or organization, the administration shall have the right to transfer workers and employees for a period of up to one month to work not stipulated by the labor contract in the same enterprise, institution, or organization, or to another enterprise, institution, or organization, but in the same locality with payment of labor for work fulfilled, but not lower than average earnings for the previous work. Such transfer shall be permitted to prevent or liquidate natural disasters, industrial accidents, or the prompt elimination of their consequences; to avert accidents, stoppage, the perishing or damaging of state or social property, and in other exceptional instances, and also to replace an absent worker or employee. The duration of transfer to other work in order to replace an absent worker may not exceed one month during the calendar year.

In the event of stoppage, workers and employees shall be transferred, taking into account their specialization and skills, to other work in the same enterprise, institution, or organization for the entire time of stoppage or to another enterprise, institution, or organization but in the same locality for a period of up to one month. In the event of a transfer to lower-paid work as a consequence of stoppage, average earnings for previous work shall be retained for workers and employees fulfilling output norms, and the tariff scale (or salary) shall be retained for workers and employees not fulfilling norms or transferred to being paid for work by time.

In the event of stoppage and in the event of the temporary replacement of an absent worker, the transfer of skilled workers and employees to unskilled work shall not be permitted.

Article 15. Grounds for Terminating a Labor Contract

The grounds for terminating a labor contract shall be:

(1) agreement of the parties;

(2) expiry of the term (Article 10, points 2 and 3), except for instances when labor relations are continued de facto and neither party has requested their termination;

(3) being called up or enlistment of a worker or employee for military service;

(4) dissolution of a labor contract upon the initiative of a worker or employee (Article 16), upon the initiative of the administration (Article 17), or upon the demand of a trade union agency (Article 20);

(5) transfer of a worker, with his consent, to other work or transfer to an elective office;

(6) refusal of a worker or employee to transfer to work in another locality together with the enterprise, institution, or organization;

(7) entry into legal force of a court judgment by which a worker or employee (except for instances of conditional conviction) is sentenced to

deprivation of freedom, correctional tasks not at the place of work, or to another punishment precluding the possibility of continuing the particular work.

Article 16. Dissolution of Labor Contract upon the Initiative of the Worker or Employee

Workers and employees shall have the right to dissolve a labor contract concluded for an indefinite term, warning the administration thereof in writing two weeks in advance.

A periodic labor contract (Article 10, points 2 and 3) shall be subject to dissolution before time upon the demand of a worker in the event of his illness or disability preventing the fulfillment of work under the contract, a violation by the administration of labor legislation or of the collective or labor contract, or for other justifiable reasons.

Article 17. Dissolution of Labor Contract Upon the Initiative of the Administration

A labor contract concluded for an indeterminate term, and also a periodic labor contract, may, upon the expiry of the term of its validity, be dissolved by the administration of an enterprise, institution, or organization only in instances of:

(1) liquidation of the enterprise, institution, or organization or a reduction of the numbers or personnel establishment of workers;

(2) having discovered the failure of a worker or employee to conform to the post occupied or the work fulfilled as a result of inadequate qualifications or a state of health precluding continuation of the said work;

(3) systematic failure of a worker or employee to execute duties without justifiable reasons which were imposed on him by a labor contract or rules for internal labor discipline, if measures of disciplinary or social sanctions have previously been applied to the worker or employee;

(4) shirking without justifiable reasons (including appearing at work in a state of intoxication);

(5) the failure to appear at work for more than four months in a row as a consequence of temporary incapacity to work, not counting pregnancy or birth leave, unless a longer period for retention of place of work (or post) in the event of a specified illness has been established by USSR legislation. A place of work (or post) shall be retained for workers and employees who have lost capacity to work in connection with a labor injury or professional disease until restoration of the capacity to work or establishment of disability;

(6) restoration at work of a worker or employee who previously fulfilled such work.

Dismissal on the grounds specified in points 1, 2, and 6 of the present Article shall be permitted if it is impossible to carry over the worker, with his consent, to other work.

Article 18. Prohibition of Dissolution of Labor Contract upon the Initiative of the Administration without the Consent of the Factory, Plant and Local Trade Union Committee

Dissolution of a labor contract upon the initiative of the administration of the enterprise, institution, organization shall not be permitted without the prior consent of the factory, plant, and local trade union committee, except for instances provided for by USSR legislation.

Dissolution of a labor contract in violation of the requirements of paragraph one of the present Article shall be illegal, and the dismissed worker shall be subject to be being restored to his former work (Article 91).

Article 19. Severance Allowance

When terminating a labor contract on the grounds specified in Article 15, points 3 and 6, and Article 17, points 1, 2, and 6 of the present Fundamental Principles, or as a consequence of a violation by the administration of labor legislation or the collective or labor contract (Article 16, paragraph two), a severance allowance in an amount of two weeks average earnings shall be paid to workers and employees.

Article 20. Dissolution of a Labor Contract upon the Demand of a Trade Union

Upon the demand of a trade union agency (not lower than district), the administration shall be obliged to dissolve a labor contract with an executive worker or to remove him from the post occupied, if he violates labor legislation, does not fulfill obligations under the collective contract, displays bureaucratism, or allows red tape.

The demand of a trade union agency may be appealed by the worker or the administration to the superior trade union agency, whose decision shall be final.

Chapter IV. Work Time and Leisure Time

Article 21. Normal Duration of Work Time

The normal duration of work time for workers and employees at enterprises, institutions, and organizations may not exceed 41 hours per week. Transfer to a shorter work week shall be carried out as the economic and other necessary conditions are created.

Article 22. Reduced Duration of Work Time

A reduced duration of work time shall be established for:

(1) workers and employees from 16 to 18 years of age: 36 hours per week; persons from 15 to 16 years of age (Article 74): 24 hours per week;

(2) workers and employees engaged in work with harmful labor conditions: not more than 36 hours per week.

In addition, a reduced duration of work time for individual categories of workers (teachers, doctors, and others) shall be established by USSR legislation.

Article 23. Five-day and Six-day Work Week and Duration of Day Work

A five-day work week with two days off shall be established for workers and employees. Under a five-day work week, the duration of the work day (or shift) shall be determined by rules for internal labor discipline or shift profiles confirmed by the administration by agreement with the factory, plant, and local trade union committee with observance of the established duration of the work week (Articles 21 and 22).

At those enterprises, institutions, and organizations where by virtue of the character of production and work conditions the introduction of a five-day work week is inadvisable, a six-day work week with one day off shall be established. Under a six-day work week, the duration of the work day may not exceed 7 hours with a weekly norm of 41 hours, 6 hours with a weekly norm of 36 hours, and 4 hours with a weekly norm of 24 hours.

Article 24. Duration of Work on Eve of Holidays and Days Off

On the eve of holidays (Article 31), the duration of work for workers and employees, except the workers and employees specified in Article 22 of the present Fundamental Principles, shall be reduced by one hour for both the five-day and the six-day work week.

On the eve of days off, the duration of work under the six-day work week may not exceed 6 hours.

Article 25. Duration of Work at Night

The established duration for work (or shift) shall be reduced by one hour for night work. This rule shall not extend to workers and employees for whom a reduction of work time already has been provided (Article 22, paragraph one, point 2, and paragraph two).

The duration of night work shall be equated with day work in those instances when this is necessary for production conditions, in particular, in continuous production units, and also in shift work during a six-day work week with one day off.

The time from 10:00 p.m. to 6:00 a.m. shall be considered night.

Article 26. Incomplete Work Time

An incomplete work day or incomplete work week may be established by agreement between a worker, employee, and the administration both when hiring for work and subsequently. Labor in such instances shall be paid proportionally for the time worked or depending upon output.

Article 27. Limitation of Overtime Work

Overtime work, as a rule, shall not be permitted.

The administration may apply overtime work only in exceptional instances provided for by union republic legislation. Overtime work may be carried out only with the authorization of the factory, plant, and local trade union committee.

Overtime work should not exceed four hours for each worker or employee on two days in succession or 120 hours per year.

Article 28. Summary Record of Work Time

At continuously operating enterprises, institutions, and organizations and also in individual production units, shops, sectors, divisions, and at certain types of work, where by virtue of production (or work) conditions the daily or weekly duration of work time established for a particular category of workers and employees can not be observed, the introduction of a summary record of work time shall be permitted by agreement with the factory, plant, and local trade union committee so that the duration of work time for the record period does not exceed the normal number of work hours (Articles 21 and 22).

Article 29. Rest and Food Breaks

Rest and food breaks shall be granted to workers and employees of not less than two hours in duration. The break shall not be included in work time.

At that work where by virtue of production conditions a break can not be established, the opportunity to receive food during work time should be granted to the worker or employee. A list of such work and the procedure and place for receiving food shall be established by the administration by agreement with the factory, plant, and local trade union committee.

Article 30. Days Off

During a five-day work week, workers and employees shall be granted two days off per week, and during a six-day work week, one day off.

The duration of weekly continuous leisure should be at least forty-two hours.

Work shall be prohibited on days off. Involving individual workers and employees in work on such days shall be permitted only with the authorization of the factory, plant, and local trade union committee and solely in exceptional instances determined by union republic legislation. Another day of leisure during the nearest fortnight shall be granted for work on a day off.

If granting another day of leisure is impossible (in connection with the dismissal of a worker or employee and in other instances provided for by legislation), work on a day off shall be paid at a double rate.

Article 31. Holidays

Work at enterprises, institutions, and organizations shall not be carried on at the following holidays:

1 January	New Year
8 March	International Women's Day
1-2 May	Day of International Solidarity Working People
9 May	Victory Day
7 October	USSR Constitution Day
7-8 November	Anniversary of Great October Socialist Revolution
5 December	USSR Constitution Day

Work whose suspension is impossible for technical production reasons (continuously operating enterprises, institutions, organizations), work caused by the need to service the populace, and also urgent repair and loading or unloading work, shall be permitted on holidays.

Article 32. Annual Leaves

All workers and employees shall be granted annual leaves while retaining place of work (or post) and average earnings (Articles 33 and 34).

The priority for granting leaves shall be established by the administration, by agreement with the factory, plant, and local trade union committee.

Replacement of leave with monetary compensation shall not be permitted except for instances of the dismissal of a worker or employee who has not used the leave.

Article 33. Duration of Leave

Annual leave shall be granted to workers and employees for a duration of not less than 15 work days, with gradual transition to being granted leave for a longer duration. The procedure for computing the duration of annual leave shall be determined by USSR legislation.

Annual leave shall be granted to workers and employees younger than 18 years of age for one calendar month.

Article 34. Supplementary Leaves

Annual supplementary leaves shall be granted to:

(1) workers and employees engaged in work with harmful labor conditions;

(2) workers and employees engaged in individual branches of the national economy and having extended work experience at one enterprise or organization;

(3) workers with a non-standard work day;

(4) workers and employees working in areas of the Far North and localities equated thereto;

(5) in other instances provided by legislation.

Article 35. Leave Without Retention of Wages

Short-term leave without retention of wages may be granted for family obligations and other justifiable reasons to a worker or employee, upon his application.

Chapter V. Wages, Guarantees, and Compensation

Article 36. Payment for Labor. Minimum Wage

In accordance with the USSR Constitution, the labor of workers and employees shall be paid by quantity and quality. Any lowering of amounts of payment for labor whatever depending upon sex, age, race, and national affiliation shall be prohibited.

The monthly wage of a worker or employee may not be lower than the minimum amount established by the state.

Article 37. Wage Norms. Establishment of Tariff Rates and Salaries

Wage norms shall be effectuated by the state with the participation of trade unions.

Labor of workers shall be paid on the basis of tariff rates (or salaries) confirmed in a centralized procedure. The relegation of work fulfilled to particular tariff classes and the conferment of qualification classes upon workers shall be carried out by the administration of the enterprise or organization by agreement with the factory, plant, and local trade union committee in accordance with the tariff-qualifications manual.

Labor of employees shall be paid on the basis of a scheme of post salaries confirmed in a centralized procedure. Post salaries for employees shall be established by the administration of the enterprise, institution, or organization in accordance with the post and qualifications of the worker.

Higher payment for labor shall be established for heavy work, work with harmful labor conditions, and work in localities with grave climate conditions.

Article 38. Systems for Payment of Labor

Labor of workers and employees shall be paid for by time or by piece work.

Time-bonus and piece work-bonus systems for payment of labor may be introduced in order to intensify the material interest of workers and employees in the fulfillment and overfulfillment of production plans, raising the efficiency and profitability of production, the growth of labor productivity, and improvement of product quality and resource economies.

The time or piece work system for payment of labor shall be established, and statutes on bonuses for workers and employees also shall be confirmed, by the administration of the enterprise or organization by agreement with the factory, plant, and local trade union committee.

Compensation for workers and employees of an enterprise or organization for the annual work results may be established as a supplement to the systems for payment of labor, from the fund formed at the expense of profit obtained by the enterprise or organization. The amount of compensation shall be determined by taking into account the results of the labor of the worker or employee and the length of his continuous work experience at the enterprise or organization.

Article 39. Output Norms (or Time Norms), Service Norms, Numerical and Piece Work Rate Standards

Output norms (or time norms), service norms, and numerical and piece work rate standards for workers and employees shall be established by taking into account the level of technology achieved, scientific organization of labor and production, and progressive work experience. These norms and standards shall be subject to being replaced by new ones through the introduction into production of technological, economic, and organizational measures ensuring the growth of labor productivity. Norms and standards shall be introduced and reviewed by the administration of the enterprise, institution, or organization by agreement with the factory, plant, and local trade union committee.

Uniform or model (inter-branch, branch, departmental) norms and standards may be established for work of the same kind.

In the case of piece work payment of labor, the rates shall be determined by proceeding from the established classes of work, tariff rates (or salaries) and output norms (or time norms).

In the case of time payment of labor, service norms for machine tools, assemblies, or rated production tasks for a particular time period assigned to them shall be established for workers and employees. Numerical standards for workers and employees may be established for the fulfillment of individual functions or amounts of work.

Article 40. Payment for Overtime Work

In the case of time payment of labor, overtime work shall be paid at one and a half times the rate for the first two hours and at double the rate for subsequent hours.

In the case of piece work payment of labor, and also in those branches of the national economy where uniform tariff rates for piece-work workers and time-workers have been established for overtime work, the additional payment shall be in the amount established by USSR legislation.

Article 41. Payment for Holiday Work

Holiday work (Article 31, paragraph two) shall be paid at double the rate.

Another day of leisure may be granted a worker or employee, at his wish, who works on a holiday.

Article 42. Payment for Night Work

Night work (Article 25) shall be paid at a higher rate established by USSR legislation.

Article 43. Payment of Labor in the Event of the Failure to Fulfill Output Norms, Defective Products, and Payment of Stoppage Time

In the event of the failure to fulfill output norms, of the manufacture of defective products, and stoppage which occurred not through the fault of the worker or employee, payment shall be in the amounts determined by USSR legislation.

Monthly wages in the said instances may not be lower than the established minimum amount (Article 36).

Defective products wholly through the fault of the worker or employee and stoppage time through his fault shall not be subject to being paid. Partial defective products through the fault of the worker or employee shall be paid at a lower rate, depending upon the degree of fitness of the manufactured product.

Article 44. Retention of Wages During Transfer to Other Permanent Lower Paid Work

In the event of the transfer of a worker or employee to other permanent lower paid work, the worker shall retain his previous average wages for two weeks from the date of the transfer.

Article 45. Periods for Wage Payment

Wages shall be paid not less than once every half-month.

Other periods for payment of wages may be established for individual categories of workers and employees by union republic legislation.

Article 46. Guarantees for Workers and Employees Elected to Elective Posts

Workers and employees released from work as a consequence of their being elected to elective posts in state agencies, and also in party, trad union, komsomol, cooperative, and other social organizations, shall, after completing their powers in the elective post, be granted their previous work (or post), and in the absence thereof, other equivalent work (or post in the same or, with the consent of the worker, another enterprise, institution, or organization.

Article 47. Guarantees for Workers and Employees During the Fulfillment of State or Social Duties

During the fulfillment of state or social duties, if according to prevailing legislation of the Soviet Union and union republics, these duties may be carried out at night, workers and employees shall be guaranteed their place of work (or post) and average wage.

For workers and employees enlisted to fulfill duties provided for by the Law of the USSR on University Military Obligation, the guarantees and exemptions in accordance with this Law shall be granted.

Article 48. Guarantees and Compensation during Business Trips and Travel to Work in Another Locality

Workers and employees shall have the right to compensation for expenditures and to receive other compensation in connection with official business trips or being transferred, hired, or sent to work in another locality.

Place of work (or post) and average earnings shall be retained during the entire time of a business trip for workers sent on a business trip.

Article 49. Guarantees When Material Responsibility is Imposed on Workers and Employees for Damage Caused to the Enterprise, Institution, or Organization

For damage caused to an enterprise, institution, or organization when executing labor duties, workers and employees through whose fault the damage was caused shall bear material responsibility in the amount of the direct actual damage, but not less than one-third of their monthly tariff rate (or salary).

Material responsibility exceeding one-third of the monthly tariff rate (or salary) but not the full amount of the damage caused shall be permitted only in the instances specified in USSR legislation.

Damage in the amount provided for by paragraph one of the present Article shall be compensated, with the written consent of the worker, through withholding from wages by order of the administration of the enterprise, institution, or organization. The order of the administration to withhold may be made not later than two weeks from the date of discovery of the damage caused by the worker. Withholding shall not be made in the absence of the consent of the worker in writing, and the question of compensation of damage shall be considered, upon the application of the administration, by a district (or city) people's court.

In other instances compensation of damage shall be made by the administration filing suit in a district (or city) people's court.

Article 50. Limitation of Withholdings from Wages

Withholdings from wages may be made only in the instances provided for by USSR and union republic legislation.

During each payment of wages the total amount of all withholdings may not exceed twenty percent, and in instances specially provided for by USSR and union republic legislation, fifty percent of the wages due to be paid to a worker or employee.

In any event, fifty percent of earnings should be retained for a worker or employee in the event of wages being withheld under several executory documents.

Limitations established by paragraphs two and three of the present Article shall not extend to withholdings from wages while serving correctional tasks.

Withholdings shall not be permitted from a severance allowance, compensation, and other payments against which execution may not be levied according to legislation.

Chapter VI. Labor Discipline

Article 51. Duties of Workers and Employees

Workers and employees shall be obliged to work honorably and conscientiously, to observe labor discipline, to execute precisely and in a timely manner the orders of the administration, to raise labor productivity, to improve product quality, to observe technological discipline, requirements for labor protection, technical safety, and production sanitation, and to care for and strengthen socialist ownership.

Article 52. Ensuring Labor Discipline

Labor discipline at enterprises, institutions, and organizations shall be ensured by a conscious attitude toward labor, methods of persuasion, and also incentive for conscientious labor. Measures of disciplinary and social pressure shall be applied, if necessary, to individual unconscientious workers.

Article 53. Duties of the Administration

The administration of an enterprise, institution, or organization shall be obliged to properly organize the labor of workers and employees, create conditions for the growth of labor productivity, ensure labor and production discipline, steadfastly observe labor legislation and rules for labor protection, and attentively attend to the needs and inquiries of workers, and improve their labor and domestic conditions.

Article 54. Rules for Internal Labor Discipline. Discipline Charters

Labor discipline at enterprises, institutions, and organizations shall be determined by rules for internal labor discipline established by the administration by agreement with the factory, plant, and local trade union committee on the basis of model rules confirmed in the established procedure.

Discipline charters shall operate in certain branches of the national economy for individual categories of workers and employees.

Article 55. Incentives for Success in Work

For the model fulfillment of labor duties, successes in the socialist competition, raising labor productivity, improving product quality, continuous and irreproachable work, innovation in labor, and other work achievements, the following incentives shall be applied:

(1) announcement of gratitude;

(2) issuance of bonus;

(3) awarding of valuable gift;

(4) awarding of honorary certificate;

(5) entry into the Book of Honor or on the Board of Honor.

Other incentives also may be provided by rules of internal labor discipline and discipline charters.

Incentives shall be applied by the administration jointly or by agreement with the factory, plant, and local trade union committee.

Privileges and exemptions in the domain of socio-cultural and housing and domestic services (passes to sanatoriums and rest homes, improvement of housing conditions, etc.) shall be granted in priority to workers and employees who have successfully and conscientiously fulfilled their labor duties. Priority in promotions at work also shall be granted to such workers.

For special labor services, workers and employees shall be recommended to superior agencies for an incentive, the awarding of orders, medals, honorary certificates, lapel pins, and for the conferment of honorary titles and titles of best worker for the particular profession.

Article 56. Penalties for Violation of Labor Discipline

The administration of an enterprise, institution, or organization shall apply the following disciplinary penalties for violation of labor discipline:

(1) reproof;

(2) reprimand;

(3) strict reprimand;

(4) transfer to lower-paid work for a term of up to three months or demotion to a lower post for the same term;

(5) dismissal (Article 17, points 3 and 4).

Other disciplinary penalties also may be provided for individual categories of workers and employees by legislation on disciplinary responsibility and by discipline charters.

The administration shall have the right, instead of applying a disciplinary penalty, to transfer the question of a violation of labor discipline for the consideration of a comrades' court or a social organization.

Chapter VII. Labor Protection

Article 57. Securing Health and Safe Labor Conditions

Healthy and safe labor conditions shall be created at all enterprises, institutions, and organizations.

Securing healthy and safe labor conditions shall be entrusted to the administration of enterprises, institutions, and organizations.

The administration shall be obliged to introduce modern means of technical safety which prevent industrial injuries and ensure the sanitary-hygienic conditions, preventing the breaking out of professional diseases of workers and employees.

Article 58. Observance of Requirements for Labor Protection During the Construction and Exploitation of Production Buildings, Installations, and Equipment

Production buildings, installations, equipment, and technological processes should meet the requirements ensuring healthy and safe labor conditions.

These requirements shall include the rational use of territory and production premises, proper exploitation of equipment and organization of technological processes, protection of persons working from the effects of harmful labor conditions, maintenance of production premises and workers' places in accordance with sanitary-hygienic norms and rules, and the arrangement of sanitary-domestic premises.

Rules and norms for labor protection should be observed when designing, constructing, and using production buildings and installations.

Article 59. Prohibition of Introduction into Use of Enterprises Not Meeting Labor Protection Requirements

No enterprise, shop, sector, or production unit may be accepted and introduced into use unless healthy and safe labor conditions have been secured therein.

The introduction into use of new and converted production designated objects shall not be permitted without the authorization of agencies exercising state sanitary and technical supervision, technical inspectorates of trade unions (Article 104), and the factory, plant, and local trade union committee of the enterprise, institution, or organization introducing the object into use.

Article 60. Rules for Labor Protection Binding Upon the Administration

The administration of an enterprise, institution, or organization shall be obliged to provide the proper technical equipment for all workers' places and create work conditions in them which correspond to the rules for labor protection (rules for technical safety, sanitary norms and rules, and others). Such rules (uniform for all branches of the national economy or inter-branch) shall be confirmed by the USSR Council of Ministers or, upon its commission, by other state agencies jointly or by agreement with the All-Union Central Trade Union Council.

Branch rules and norms for labor protection shall be confirmed in the established procedure by ministries, departments, and state supervision agencies (Article 104) jointly or by agreement with the central committees of the respective trade union.

In the absence in the rules of requirements whose observance during production work is essential in order to secure safe labor conditions, the administration of the enterprise, institution, or organization shall, by agreement with the factory, plant, or local trade union committee, take measures ensuring safe labor conditions.

To the administration shall be entrusted the instruction of workers and employees in safety technique, production sanitation, fire protection, and other labor protection rules, and also permanent control over the observance by workers of all instruction requirements for labor protection.

Article 61. Instructions Concerning Labor Protection Binding Upon Workers and Employees

Workers and employees shall be obliged to observe instructions for labor protection which establish rules for the fulfillment of work and conduct in production premises and at construction areas. Such instructions shall be worked out and confirmed by the administration of an enterprise, institution, and organization jointly with the factory, plant, and local trade union committee. Model instructions for labor protection for workers of basic professions may be confirmed by ministries and department by agreement with the central committees of trade unions and, when necessary, also with corresponding state supervision agencies (Article 104).

Workers and employees shall also be obliged to observe established requirements for the use of machines and mechanisms and to use individual protective means issued to them.

Article 62. Funds for Labor Protection Measures

Funds shall be allocated in the established procedure for the implementation of labor protection measures and necessary materials. The expenditure of these funds and materials for other purposes shall be prohibited.

The procedure for using the said funds and materials shall be determined in collective contracts or in labor protection agreements concluded between the administration and the factory, plant, and local trade union committee.

Article 63. Issuance of Special Clothing and Other Individual Protective Means. Issuance of Soap and Neutralizing Means

Special clothing, special footwear, and other individual protective means shall be issued free of charge according to the established norms to workers and employees for work with harmful labor conditions, and also for work carried on in special temperature conditions or connection with pollution.

Soap shall be issued free of charge according to the established norms for work connected with pollution. At work where harmfully active substances possibly affect leather, cleaning and neutralizing means shall be issued free of charge according to the established norms.

Article 64. Issuance of Milk and Therapeutic-Prophylactic Food

Milk and other equivalent food products shall be issued free of charge according to the established norms to workers and employees for work with harmful labor conditions.

Therapeutic-prophylactic food shall be granted free of charge according to the established norms for work with especially harmful labor conditions.

Article 65. Medical Examinations of Workers and Employees of Certain Categories

Workers and employees engaged in heavy work and work with harmful or dangerous labor conditions, and also work connected with the movement of transport, shall undergo compulsory preliminary, upon commencing work, and periodic medical examinations in order to determine their fitness for the work entrusted and to prevent professional diseases.

Workers of enterprises of the food industry, public dining, and trade, waterpipe installations, therapeutic-prophylactic and children's institutions, and also certain other enterprises, institutions, and organizations, shall undergo the said medical examinations with a view to protecting the health of the populace.

Article 66. Transfer to Lighter Work

Workers and employees who by their state of health need to be granted lighter work the administration shall be obliged to transfer, with their consent, to such work in accordance with a medical opinion temporarily or without limit of time.

In the event of transfer by reason of state of health to lighter lower-paid work, the previous average earnings shall be retained for workers and employees for two weeks from the date of transfer, and in instances provided for by USSR and union republic legislation, the previous average earnings shall be retained for the entire time of lower-paid work or a state social insurance benefit shall be paid.

Article 67. Material Responsibility of Enterprises, Institutions, and Organizations for Damage Caused to Workers and Employees by Impairing Their Health

Enterprises, institutions, and organizations shall bear material responsibility in accordance with USSR and union republic legislation for damage caused to workers and employees by mutilation or other impairment to health connected with their executing their labor duties.

Chapter VIII. Labor of Women

Article 68. Work for Which the Use of Women's Labor is Prohibited

The use of women's labor for heavy work and work with harmful labor conditions, and also underground work, except for certain underground work (nonphysical work or work for sanitary and domestic services) shall be prohibited.

Article 69. Limitation of Women's Labor for Night, Overtime Work and Sending Them on Business Trips

Involving women in night work shall not be permitted except for those branches of the national economy where there is a special need and is authorized as a temporary measure.

Involving women in night work, overtime work, and work on days off, or sending pregnant women and nursing mothers, and also women having children less than one year of age, shall be prohibited.

Women having children in age of from one year to eight years may not be involved in overtime work or sent on a business trip without their consent.

Article 70. Transfer of Pregnant Women, Nursing Mothers, and Women Having Children of up to One Year in Age to Lighter Work

Pregnant women shall, in accordance with a doctor's opinion, be transferred during pregnancy for other lighter work while retaining average earnings for the previous work.

Nursing mothers and women having children of up to one year of age shall, if it is impossible to fulfill their former work, be transferred to other work while retaining the average earnings for their former work during the time of nursing the child or until the child attains one year of age.

Article 71. Pregnancy and Birth Leaves

Women shall be granted pregnancy and birth leaves of fifty-six calendar days in length before birth and fifty-six calendar days after birth with payment of a state social security benefit during this period. In the event of abnormal births or the birth of twins or triplets, the leave after birth shall be extended to seventy calendar days.

In addition to pregnancy or birth leave, a supplemental leave shall be granted to women upon their application without retention of earnings until the child attains one year of age.

Article 72. Breaks for Nursing a Child

Nursing mothers and women having children of up to one year of age shall, besides the ordinary rest and dining break, also be granted an additional break for nursing the child.

Such breaks shall be granted not less than once every three hours, each being not less than thirty minutes in duration.

Breaks for nursing a child shall be included in work time and shall be paid according to the average earnings.

Article 73. Guarantees When Hiring and Prohibition Against Dismissal of Pregnant Women, Nursing Mothers, and Women Having Children of up to One Year in Age

To refuse to hire women or to reduce their wages for reasons connected with pregnancy or nursing a child shall be prohibited.

The dismissal of pregnant women, nursing mothers, and women having children of up to one year in age upon the initiative of the administration shall not be permitted except for instances of the complete liquidation of the enterprise, institution, or organization, when dismissal is permitted with obligatory arrangement of employment.

Chapter IX. Labor of Youth

Article 74. Age From Which Hiring is Permitted

The hiring of persons younger than sixteen years of age shall not be permitted.

In exceptional instances, by agreement with the factory, plant, and local trade union committee, persons who have attained fifteen years of age may be hired.

Article 75. Work for Which Use of Labor of Persons Younger than Eighteen Years of Age is Prohibited

The use of the labor of persons younger than eighteen years of age shall be prohibited for heavy work and work with harmful or dangerous labor conditions, and also for underground work.

Article 76. Medical Examinations for Persons Younger Than Eighteen Years of Age

All persons younger than eighteen years of age shall be hired only after a preliminary medical examination and thereafter, until attaining eighteen years of age, annually shall be subject to a compulsory medical examination.

Article 77. Payment of Labor for Workers and Employees Younger than Eighteen Years of Age with a Reduced Work Day

Earnings for workers and employees younger than eighteen years of age shall, in the event of a reduced work day, be paid in the same amount as a worker or employee of the respective category in the case of a full work day.

The labor of workers and employees younger than eighteen years of age who have been admitted to piece work shall be paid at the piece work rates established for adult workers, with supplementary payment according to the tariff rate for the time for which their work day is reduced in comparison with the work day for adult workers.

Article 78. Prohibition Against Involving Workers and Employees Younger Than Eighteen Years of Age in Night or Overtime Work

Involving workers and employees younger than eighteen years of age in night or overtime work and in work on days off shall be prohibited.

Article 79. Leaves for Workers and Employees Younger than Eighteen Years of Age

Annual leaves for workers and employees younger than eighteen years of age (Article 33) shall be granted in the summer time or, at their wish, at any other time.

Article 80. Quotas for Hiring Youth and for Production Training

A quota for the hiring and production training of youth who have completed general education schools, professional-technical, and technical schools, and also other persons younger than eighteen years of age, shall be established for all enterprises and organizations.

Article 81. Providing Young Workers and Specialists Who Have Completed Education Institutions with Work According to Specialization and Qualifications

Young workers who have completed professional-technical and technical schools, and young specialists who have completed higher and secondary specialized educational institutions, shall be provided with work in accordance with the specialization and qualifications obtained.

Article 82. Limitation of Dismissal of Workers and Employees Younger Than Eighteen Years of Age

The dismissal of workers and employees younger than eighteen years of age at the initiative of the administration shall be permitted only, in addition to observing the general procedure for dismissal, with the consent of the district (or city) commission for cases of minors. Dismissal on the grounds specified in Article 17, points 1, 2, and 6, of the present Fundamental Principles shall be only in exceptional instances and shall not be permitted without the arrangement of employment.

Chapter X. Exemptions for Workers and Employees Combining Work With Study

Article 83. Organization of Production Training and Creation of Necessary Conditions for Combining Work with Study

The administration of an enterprise, organization, and institution shall organize individual, brigade, course, and other production training at the expense of the enterprise, organization, and institution for the professional training and raising the qualifications of workers and employees, especially youth.

The administration shall be obliged to create the necessary conditions for combining work with study for workers and employees undergoing production training or studying in educational institutions while continuing work.

The successful passing by a worker or employee of production training, general education, and professional training, and also the obtaining of higher or secondary specialized education, should be taken into account when raising qualification classes or in promotion for work.

Article 84. Exemptions for Workers and Employees Studying in General Education and Professional-Technical Educational Institutions

A reduced work week or a reduced work day with retention of earnings in the established procedure shall be established for workers and employees studying while continuing to work in general education and professional-technical educational institutions; other exemptions also shall be granted to them.

Article 85. Exemptions for Workers and Employees in Connection with Study in Higher and Secondary Specialized Educational Institutions

Leave without retention of earnings shall be granted to workers and employees admitted to entry examinations for higher and secondary specialized educational institutions.

Workers and employees studying in night and correspondence higher and secondary specialized educational institutions shall be granted leave paid in the established procedure in connection with study, and also other exemptions.

Chapter XI. Labor Disputes

Article 86. Agencies Considering Labor Disputes

Labor disputes shall be considered by:

(1) commissions for labor disputes organized at enterprises, institutions, and organizations from an equal number of trade union committee and administration representatives;

(2) factory, plant, and local trade union committees;

(3) district (or city) people's courts.

Labor disputes of certain categories of workers shall be considered by superior agencies by way of subordination (Article 94).

Article 87. Commissions for Labor Disputes

Commissions for labor disputes shall be the compulsory primary agency for the consideration of labor disputes arising at enterprises, institutions, and organizations between workers and employees, on one side, and the administration, on the other, except for disputes subject to consideration according to law directly in district (or city) people's courts and other agencies.

Decisions of a commission shall be adopted by agreement of the parties.

Article 88. Consideration of Labor Disputes by Factory, Plant, and Local Trade Union Committees

Factory, plant, and local trade union committees shall consider labor disputes upon the applications of workers and employees when agreement of the parties in a commission for labor disputes was not attained and upon the appeals of workers and employees against the decisions of this commission. The factory, plant, and local committee may leave the commission decision in force or vacate it and render a decree on the substance of the dispute.

A factory, plant, and local trade union committee shall, upon its own initiative or the protest of a procurator, vacate a commission decision contrary to prevailing legislation and render a decree on the substance of the dispute.

Article 89. Consideration of Labor Disputes in District (or City) People's Courts

Labor disputes shall be considered in district (or city) people's courts upon:

(1) applications of workers and employees, when they do not agree with a decree of a factory, plant, or local trade union committee, or the

applications of the administration, when it considers that the decree of the factory, plant, and local trade union committee is contrary to prevailing legislation;

(2) applications of workers and employees, when they do not agree with a decision of a commission for labor disputes composed of the trade union organizer and director of the enterprise, institution, or organization or when agreement of the parties was not attained in this commission, and also when there is no factory, plant, and local trade union committee or trade union organizer at the enterprise, institution, or organization.

In addition, labor disputes shall be considered directly in district (or city) people's courts, without recourse to a commission for labor disputes of the factory, plant, and local committee:

(1) upon the applications for the restoration to work of workers and employees dismissed at the initiative of the administration of an enterprise, institution, or organization, except for disputes of workers occupying a post provided in a special list (Article 94);

(2) upon the applications of the administration for compensation by workers and employees of damage caused to the enterprise, institution, or organization.

Article 90. On Periods to Apply for Settlement of Labor Disputes

Workers and employees may apply to a commission for labor disputes at any time, without any period of limitation, and in cases concerning dismissal, to a district (or city) people's court within a month from the date of being handed the order concerning dismissal.

The following periods shall be established for the administration to apply to a court regarding questions of recovering material damage from workers caused to the enterprise, institution, or organization:

(1) in instances provided by Article 49, paragraph one: one month from the date of discovering the damage caused by a worker;

(2) in instances provided by Article 49, paragraph two: one year from the date of discovering the damage caused by a worker.

A court may restore these periods established in the present Article if they pass for justifiable reasons.

Article 91. Restoration to Work

A worker or employee should be restored to his previous work by the agency considering a labor dispute in the event of dismissal without legal grounds or in violation of the established procedure for dismissal.

Article 92. Payments for Time of Enforced Idleness or for Fulfillment of Lower Paid Work

A worker or employee illegally dismissed from work and restored to his former work shall be paid, by court decision, the average earnings for the time of enforced idleness from the date of dismissal, but for not more than three months.

A worker or employee illegally transferred to other work and restored to his former work shall be paid, by decision or decree of the agency considering labor disputes, average earnings for the time of enforced idleness or the difference in earnings for the time fulfilling lower-paid work, but for not more than three months.

A decision or decree adopted by an agency for the consideration of labor disputes concerning restoration to work of an illegally dismissed or transferred worker shall be subject to immediate execution. If the administration delayed the execution of this decision or decree, then the worker shall be paid the average earnings or the difference in earnings for the time of delay from the date the decision or decree was rendered until the date of execution.

Article 93. Imposing Material Responsibility on Person Guilty of Illegal Dismissal or Transfer

The court shall impose on an official guilty of illegal dismissal or transfer of a worker to other work the duty to compensate the damage caused to the enterprise, institution, and organization in connection with payment for the time of enforced idleness or for the time of fulfillment of lower-paid work. Such a duty shall be imposed if the dismissal or transfer was made in clear violation of the law or if the administration delayed execution of the court decision for restoration to work. The amount of compensation of damage may not exceed three months salary of the official.

Article 94. Procedure for Consideration of Disputes on Questions of Dismissal and Transfer to Other Work of Certain Categories of Workers and Imposing Disciplinary Penalties on Them

Disputes concerning questions of dismissal and transfer to other work of workers occupying posts provided for in a special list, and also questions of imposing disciplinary sanctions, shall be considered by superior agencies by way of subordination. Disputes regarding questions of imposing disciplinary penalties on workers bearing disciplinary responsibility under discipline charters shall be considered in the same procedure.

In the event a worker is restored to his former work by decision of a superior agency by way of subordination, payment for the time of enforced idleness from the date of dismissal or for the time of fulfillment of lower paid work, but for not more than three months, shall be made. Articles 92 and 93 of the present Fundamental Principles shall be applied respectively in this connection.

Chapter XII. Trade Unions. Participation of Workers and Employees in Production Management

Article 95. Right of Workers and Employees to Join Trade Unions

In accordance with the USSR Constitution, workers and employees shall be ensured the right to join trade unions.

Trade unions shall operate in accordance with charters adopted by them and shall not be subject to registration in state agencies.

State agencies, enterprises, institutions, and organizations shall be obliged in every possible way to assist trade unions in their activity.

Article 96. Rights of Trade Unions

Trade unions shall represent the interests of workers and employees in the domain of production, labor, daily life, and culture.

Trade unions shall take part in working out and realizing state plans for the development of the national economy, deciding questions of the distribution and use of material and financial resources, involve workers and employees in production management, organize socialist competition, mass technical creativity, and promote the strengthening of production and labor discipline.

Establishment of labor conditions and wages, application of labor legislation, and the use of social consumption funds in the instances provided by USSR and union republic laws and decrees of the USSR Council of Ministers and union republic councils of ministers shall be carried out by enterprises, institutions, and organizations and their superior agencies jointly or by agreement with trade unions.

Trade unions shall exercise supervision and control over the observance of labor legislation and rules for labor protection and control housing and domestic services of workers and employees.

Trade unions shall administer state social insurance, and also sanatoriums, dispensaries, rest homes, and cultural-enlightenment, tourist, and sport institutions within their jurisdiction.

Trade unions in the person of the All-Union Central Trade Union Council shall possess the right of legislative initiative.

Article 97. Right of Workers and Employees to Take Part in Production Management

Workers and employees shall have the right to take part in the discussion and decision of questions of production development, make proposals to improve the work of enterprises, institutions, and organizations, and also on questions of socio-cultural and domestic services.

Workers and employees shall take part in production management through trade unions and other social organizations, people's control agencies, general meetings, production meetings, conferences, and various forms of social initiative of workers and employees.

The administration of enterprises, institutions, and organizations shall be obliged to create conditions ensuring the participation of workers and employees in production management. Officials of enterprises, institutions, and organizations shall be obliged to consider in a timely manner the critical remarks and the proposals of workers and employees and to notify them of measures taken.

Article 98. Mutual Relations of Factory, Plant, and Local Trade Union Committee with the Administration

The mutual relations of the factory, plant, and local trade union committee with the administration of the enterprise, institution, or organization shall be determined by the Law of the USSR on the Rights of the Factory, Plant, and Local Trade Union Committee.

Enterprises and organizations shall be obliged to assign cash assets to trade union agencies for mass cultural and physical-cultural work.

Article 99. Additional Guarantees for Elected Trade Union Workers

Workers and employees elected to a factory, plant, and local or shop trade union committee and not released from their production work may not be transferred to other work or subjected to a disciplinary penalty without the prior consent of the factory, plant, and local trade union committee, and the chairmen of such committees and trade union organizers, without the prior consent of the superior trade union agency.

Dismissal of the chairmen and members of factory, plant, and local trade union committees not released from production work may take place, upon the initiative of the administration, in addition to observing the general procedure for dismissal, only with the consent of the superior trade union agency. The dismissal of trade union organizers upon the initiative of the administration shall be permitted only with the consent of the superior trade union agency.

Chapter XIII. State Social Insurance

Article 100. Extension of Social Insurance to All Workers and Employees. Social Insurance Funds

All workers and employees shall be subject to compulsory state social insurance.

State social insurance of workers and employees shall be carried out at the expense of the state. Social insurance contributions shall be paid by enterprises, institutions, and organizations without any deductions from earnings of workers and employees. The failure of an enterprise, institution, or organization to pay insurance contributions shall not deprive workers and employees of the right to security under state social insurance.

Article 101. Types of Security Under Social Insurance

Workers and employees, and in appropriate instances also members of their families, shall be provided by way of state social insurance with:

(1) benefits for temporary incapacity to work, and women, in addition, benefits for pregnancy and birth;

(2) benefits for the birth of a child; burial benefits;

(3) pensions for old-age, disability, death of a breadwinner, and also for service of years established for certain categories of workers.

State social insurance funds shall be used also for sanitary-resort treatment of workers and employees, servicing their dispensaries and rest homes, therapeutic (or dietary) food, maintenance of pioneer camps, and other measures for state social insurance.

Article 102. Benefits for Temporary Incapacity to Work, Pregnancy, and Birth

Benefits for temporary incapacity to work shall be paid in the event of illness, mutilation, temporary transfer to other work in connection with disease, caring for an ill family member, quarantine, sanitorium-resort care and prosthetics: in an amount of up to full earnings. In the event of illness or mutilation, benefits shall be paid until restoration of capacity to work or establishment of disability.

Pregnancy and birth benefits shall be paid during the entire pregnancy or birth leave in an amount of full earnings.

Article 103. Pensions for Old-Age, Disability, and Loss of Breadwinner

Pensions for old-age, disability of workers and employees, and for loss of breadwinner to members of their families shall be assigned in accordance with the Law of the USSR on State Pensions.

Chapter XIV. Supervision and Control Over the Observance of Labor Legislation

Article 104. Agencies of Supervision and Control Over the Observance of Labor Legislation

Supervision and control over the observance of labor legislation and rules for labor protection shall be exercised:

(1) by specially authorized state agencies and inspectorates not dependent in their activity on the administration of the enterprise, institution, or organization or their superior agencies;

(2) trade unions, and also technical and legal labor inspectorates within their jurisdiction, according to statutes concerning such inspectorates confirmed by the All-Union Central Trade Union Council.

Soviets of working people's deputies and their executive and administrative agencies shall exercise control over the observance of labor legislation in the procedure provided for by USSR and union republic legislation.

Ministries and departments shall exercise departmental control over the observance of labor legislation with respect to enterprises, institutions, and organizations subordinate to them.

Supreme supervision over the precise execution of labor laws by all ministries and departments, enterprises, institutions, and organizations and their officials shall be entrusted to the USSR Procurator General.

Article 105. Responsibility for Violation of Labor Legislation

Officials guilty of violating labor legislation and labor protection rules or of the failure to fulfill obligations under collective contracts or agreements for labor protection or of hindering the activity of trade unions shall bear responsibility in the procedure established by USSR and union republic legislation.

Chapter XV. Concluding Provisions

Article 106. Peculiarities of Regulating the Labor of Certain Categories of Workers and Employees

There shall be established by USSR legislation and, within the limits determined for such, by union republic legislation:

(1) exemptions in the domain of labor for workers and employees working in areas of the Far North and localities equated thereto, and also for certain other categories of workers and employees;

(2) peculiarities of regulating work time and leisure time on transport and at communications and agricultural enterprises and organizations, within the limits of norms established by the present Fundamental Principles;

(3) special labor conditions for workers and employees engaged in seasonal work or in work in the forestry industry or forestry, for temporary workers and employees, and also for persons working for citizens under contracts (household workers and others), with individual exceptions from the present Fundamental Principles with respect to the regime for work time and leisure time, involvement in overtime work and on non-working

days, compensation for such work, temporary transfer to other work, and dismissal;

(4) additional grounds for termination of the labor contract of certain categories of workers and employees under specified conditions (single flagrant violation of labor duties by a worker bearing disciplinary responsibility by way of subordination; guilty actions of a worker directly servicing cash or goods if such actions give grounds for loss of trust in him on the part of the administration; commission of an amoral offense incompatible with continuing work by a worker fulfilling educational functions; sending of a worker to a treatment-labor dispensary by court decree; violation of established rules for hiring, and others).

The limits of material responsibility of workers and employees for damage caused to an enterprise, institution, or organization in those instances when the actual amount of damage exceeds a nominal amount shall be established by USSR legislation and by decrees of the USSR Council of Ministers.

Other peculiarities of labor regulation for certain categories of workers and employees on individual questions may be established only by laws of the USSR and decrees of the USSR Council of Ministers.

Article 107. Delimitation of Competence of USSR and Union Republics on Questions Provided for by the Fundamental Principles

To the jurisdiction of the USSR, in addition to the matters provided for by individual articles of the present Fundamental Principles, shall be relegated the establishment of rules determining: unskilled work to which workers may not be transferred in connection with idleness (Article 14, paragraph three); duration of night work (Article 25, paragraph two); minimum monthly earnings (Article 36, paragraph two); amount of payment for partially defective products (Article 43, paragraph three); compensation in connection with official business trips and travel to work in another locality (Article 48, paragraph one); restriction of women's labor at night (Article 69, paragraph one); categories of workers whose labor disputes shall be considered by way of subordination (Article 94, paragraph one); the procedure and amount of deductions for trade union agencies for mass-cultural and physical-cultural work (Article 98, paragraph two); the procedure and amounts of security for state social insurance (Articles 100, 101, 102, 103).

To the jurisdiction of the USSR and, within the limits determined for them, to the jurisdiction of union republics shall be relegated the establishment of rules determining: the reduction of work time for individual categories of workers (Article 22, paragraph one, point 2); application of the six-day work week (Article 23, paragraph two); instances of impossibility to grant time off for work on days off (Article 30, paragraph four); work done on holidays (Article 31, paragraph two); the granting and the duration of annual supplementary leaves (Article 34); wage norms (Article 37); bonus system for payment of labor (Article 38, paragraphs two and three); payment of remuneration for annual work results (Article 38, paragraph four); uniform or model output norms (Article 39, paragraph two); granting time off for work on holidays (Article 41, paragraph two); limiting withholdings from wages (Article 50, paragraph five); model rules for internal labor discipline and discipline charters (Article 54, Article 55, paragraph two, Article 56, paragraph two); rules for labor protection (Article 60, paragraphs one and two); allocation and expenditure of assets for labor protection measures (Article 62, paragraph one); the procedure for issuing special clothing, milk, and treatment-prophylactic food (Articles 63, 64); carrying out medical examinations (Article 65); work for which labor of women and minors is not permitted (Articles 68, 75); hiring quota for youth (Article 80); ensuring the work of young workers and specialists (Article 81); exemptions for studying while continuing to work (Articles 84, 85); rights of trade unions (Article 96); agencies of state supervision and control over the observance of labor legislation (Article 104, point 1); peculiarities of regulation of labor of certain categories of workers and employees (Article 106, paragraph one).

To the jurisdiction of union republics shall be relegated the establishment of rules determining: instances of the application of overtime work (Article 27, paragraph two); instances of work on days off (Article 30, paragraph three); periods for payment of wages (Article 45, paragraph two).

STATUTE ON THE RIGHTS OF A FACTORY, PLANT AND LOCAL TRADE UNION COMMITTEE

[Confirmed by Edict of the Presidium of the USSR Supreme Soviet, September 27, 1971. Vedomosti SSSR (1971), no. 39, item 382]

1. A factory, plant, and local trade union committee elected on the basis of the charter of the respective trade union shall represent the interests of workers and employees of an enterprise, institution, or organization in the domain of production, labor, daily life, and culture and shall enjoy the rights of a juridical person.

2. A factory, plant, and local trade union committee shall ensure the participation of workers and employees in the management of production through general meetings, production meetings, conferences, and various forms of social initiative of workers and employees.

The administration of an enterprise, institution, and organization shall be obliged to create the conditions ensuring the participation of workers and employees in the management of production. Officials of the enterprise, institution, and organization shall be obliged to consider critical remarks and proposals of workers and employees in a timely way and notify them of measures taken.

3. A factory, plant, and local trade union committee shall participate in working out the drafts of production plans and plans for introducing new technology and capital construction of the enterprise, institution, or organization, draft plans for the construction and repair of dwelling houses and cultural-domestic objects, as well as plans for the social development of the collective.

4. A factory, plant, and local trade union committee shall conclude a collective contract in the name of the collective of workers and employees with the administration of the enterprise or organization and exercise systematic control over the timely fulfillment of measures provided by the collective contract and jointly organize with the administration the fulfillment of obligations under the collective contract.

5. The material incentive fund and fund for socio-cultural measures and housing construction shall be distributed according to the established directions, and also the estimate for expenditures from these funds shall be confirmed, by the administration of the enterprise or organization jointly with the factory, plant, and local trade union committee.

The assets shall be redistributed between the material incentive fund and the fund for socio-cultural measures and housing construction within the established limits by the administration, by agreement with the factory, plant, and local trade union committee.

The amounts of bonuses and other types of incentive, material assistance, and remuneration for annual work results of the enterprise or organization from the material incentive fund shall be determined by the administration of the enterprise or organization jointly with the factory, plant, and local trade union committee.

The factory, plant, and local trade union committee shall, jointly with the administration, confirm the estimate for the use of assets from the enterprise fund to improve cultural-domestic conditions for workers and improve production, and also issue individual bonuses and render one-time assistance.

6. Title lists for construction of objects at the expense of assets of the enterprise or organization fund and the consumption fund, and also title lists for work to ensure the protection of labor, safety techniques, and production sanitation shall be confirmed by the director of the enterprise or head of the organization by agreement with the factory, plant, and local trade union committee.

7. The factory, plant, and local trade union committee shall have the right to hear reports of the directors of the enterprise, institution, and organization concerning the fulfillment of the production plan, obligations under the collective contract, and measures for the organization and improvement of labor conditions, material-domestic and cultural services for workers and employees and to demand the elimination of shortcomings uncovered.

When necessary, the factory, plant, and local trade union committee shall raise the question before the respective organizations of removing or punishing executive workers who do not fulfill obligations under the collective contract, display bureaucratism, allow red-tape, and violate labor legislation.

Workers shall be appointed to executive economic posts of an enterprise, organization, or institution by the administration, taking into account the opinion of the factory, plant, and local trade union committee

8. A factory, plant, and local trade union committee shall direct production meetings, hold general meetings, and exercise systematic control over the fulfillment of decisions adopted and proposals of workers and employees;

convoke, jointly with the administration of the enterprise or organization, regularly the production-technical and economic conferences, meetings of outstanding production workers, at which questions of technical progress and economic development of the enterprise shall be discussed and measures to eliminate shortcomings in the activity of the enterprise or organization and of individual shops, sections, and other internal links shall be worked out.

The factory, plant, and local trade union committee shall, jointly with the administration, organize the socialist competition and the movement for a communist attitude toward labor and total the results, determine the victors in the competition, award challenge Red Banners and certificates of honor to collectives of the outstanding shops, sections, brigades, and other internal links of the enterprise or organization, decide the question of awarding of certificates and cash bonuses, and also entering outstanding production workers on the Board of Honor and the Book of Honor, extensively popularize the results of the socialist competition, and disseminate progressive experience.

All assets for bonuses in a socialist competition shall be disbursed by the director of the enterprise or organization by agreement with the factory, plant, and local trade union committee.

9. The factory, plant, and local trade union committee shall promote in every possible way the development of inventions and rationalization

proposals and exercise control over the timely introduction of inventions accepted and rationalization proposals. They shall consider, jointly with the administration of the enterprise or organization, appeals of workers and employees against the rejection of their rationalization proposals, and also appeals on questions concerning the procedure for calculating and the periods for payment of remuneration for rationalization proposals and inventions accepted.

10. The factory, plant, and local trade union committee shall make proposals to superior economic and soviet agencies on questions of improving the activity of the enterprise, institution, or organization, and also on questions of labor conditions and material-domestic and cultural services for the working people. The said agencies shall be obliged to consider these proposals and notify the factory, plant, and local trade union committee about the results of the consideration.

11. The rules of internal labor discipline at an enterprise, institution, and organization shall be established by the administration by agreement with the factory, plant, and local trade union committee on the basis of model rules confirmed in the established procedure.

12. By agreement with the factory, plant, and local trade union committee and within the limits of the rights granted to the enterprise or organization, the administration shall:

(a) establish the piece and time system for payment of labor;

(b) determine lists of professions of workers for whom tariff piece rates shall be applied in time payment of labor and monthly payments in place of tariff rates for time-rate workers;

(c) determine lists of professions of workers and of work paid by tariff rates established for workers engaged in hot and heavy work, work with harmful labor conditions, work with specially heavy and harmful labor conditions, in accordance with prevailing model lists of such professions and work by branches of production;

(d) establish categories of work and confer categories on workers in accordance with prevailing tariff-qualifications manuals and rate workers of new professions in conformity with the characteristics of analogous work contained in the manuals, notifying the superior agency;

(e) confirm statutes on bonuses for workers and employees of the enterprise or organization and payment for remuneration for the results of annual work from the fund formed from profits received from the enterprise or organization;

(f) decide questions concerning the relegation of shops, sectors, divisions, farms, and other internal links of an enterprise or organization to the respective group for the payment of labor of executive, engineering, and technical workers and employees, and also their transfer from one group to another in connection with a modification of the volume of production in accordance with indicators confirmed in the established procedure;

(g) introduce and review output norms (or time norms), servicing norms, and standards for the numbers of workers and employees;

(h) confirm lower output norms for young workers, in the instances provided by legislation, who come to the enterprise and organization upon completing schools of general education, professional-technical educational institutions, courses, and also training directly in production;

(i) allow, when advisable, the combining of the professions of workers, and also establish additional payment for the combining of professions in accordance with prevailing legislation.

13. The factory, plant, and local trade union committee shall exercise control over the fulfillment by the administration of an enterprise, institution, or organization of labor legislation, safety technique and production sanitation rules and norms, and the proper application of the established conditions for the payment of labor and recovery of taxes from earnings of workers and employees.

The introduction into use of new and converted production objects shall not be permitted without the authorization of the agencies which effectuate state sanitary and technical supervision and the technical inspectorate of the trade unions and factory, plant, and local trade union committee of the enterprise, institution, or organization introducing the object into use.

14. By agreement with the factory, plant, and local trade union committee and within the limits of the rights granted to an enterprise, institution, or organization, the administration shall:

(a) establish, on the basis of branch norms, lists of work and professions giving workers and employees the right to receive special clothing, special footwear, and other means of individual protection free of charge and shall grant workers and employees special soap according to the established norms and, in the established instances, washing and neutralizing means;

(b) establish a list, in accordance with medical indicators, of work and professions giving the right to receive milk or other equivalent food products;

(c) establish a list of work where production conditions preclude an interruption for rest and food, and also the procedure and place for eating;

(d) permit the introduction of a summary record of work time for work ers and employees at constantly operating enterprises, institutions, and organizations, as well as at individual production units, shops, sectors, divisions, and at certain types of work where because of the production (or work) conditions, the daily or weekly length of the work period established for the particular category of workers and employees can not be observed, so that the duration of the work time during the record period does not exceed the normal number of work hours;

(e) establish the priority for granting leave;

(f) confirm the shift profile during a five-day work week;

(g) establish the length of additional leave for workers with a non-standard work day in accordance with labor legislation and a list of posts of workers with a non-standard work day, confirmed by the ministry (or with regard to workers of enterprises, institutions, and organizations of republic ministries, departments, and of local subordination, by the union republic council of ministers) by agreement with the respective trade union agency;

(h) hire adolescents from 15 to 16 years of age for work;

(i) authorize the combining of jobs in instances established by legislation.

15. In the absence of requirements in rules for labor protection whose observance during production work is necessary to ensure safe labor conditions, the administration of an enterprise, institution, or organization shall, by agreement with the factory, plant, and local trade union committee, take measures ensuring safe labor conditions.

16. Instructions for labor protection which establish rules for the fulfillment of work and conduct in production premises and at construction areas shall be worked out and confirmed by the administration of the enterprise, institution, and organization jointly with the factory, plant, and local trade union committee.

17. Overtime work and enlisting individual workers and employees to work on days off may, in the exceptional instances provided by prevailing legislation, occur only with the authorization of the factory, plant, and local trade union committee.

18. Workers and employees may not be dismissed from an enterprise, institution, or organization at the initiative of the administration without the consent in advance of the factory, plant, and local trade union committee, except for instances provided for by USSR legislation.

19. The factory, plant, and local trade union committee shall consider labor disputes upon the applications of workers and employees when agreement of the parties is not achieved within the commissions for labor disputes and upon appeals of workers and employees against the decision of this commission. It shall have the right to leave the commission decision in force or to vacate it and render a decree on the substance of the dispute.

The factory, plant, and local trade union committee shall, at its own initiative or upon the protest of a procurator, repeal a commission decision which is contrary to prevailing legislation and render a decree on the substance of the dispute.

20. The factory, plant, and local trade union committee shall consider appeals against a decision of the administration concerning compensation by the enterprise, institution, and organization for damage caused to workers and employees or mutilation or other impairment of health connected with work.

21. The factory, plant, and local trade union committee shall effectuate state social insurance of workers and employees of the enterprise, institution, or organization, assign benefits under social insurance, grant passes to workers and employees for sanitarium and resort care, for a rest home, for a tourist-therapeutic institution, and for dietary food, send children of working people to pioneer camps, verify the organization of medical services for workers, employees, and members of their families.

By agreement with the factory, plant, and local trade union committee, the administration shall grant passes to workers and employees for a rest home, sanatorium, boarding house, tourist base and excursions paid for from the fund for socio-cultural measures and housing construction.

The factory, plant, and local trade union committee shall, jointly with the administration, prepare documents needed when assigning pensions to workers, employees, and their families and submit them for the assignment of a pension, decide questions of arranging employment for disabled persons, and take part through their representatives in the assignment of pensions to workers and employees by social security agencies.

The factory, plant, and local trade union committee shall watch over the timely payment by the enterprise, institution, and organization of contributions for social insurance and, when necessary, seek the uncontested recovery of insurance contributions in the established procedure.

When a factory, plant, and local trade union committee established that a labor mutilation or professional illness of a worker or employee is the result of a violation by the administration of labor protection or safety technique rules, the factory, plant, and local trade union committee shall render a decree binding on the administration concerning the compensation by the enterprise, institution, or organization to the state social insurance budget in an uncontested procedure of expenditures for the payment of benefits for the temporary disability in connection with this mutilation or illness.

22. The factory, plant, and local trade union committee shall verify the fulfillment of plans for housing and cultural-domestic construction, watch over the use of the housing fund and municipal-domestic enterprises. A representative of the trade union committee shall participate with the rights of a member in the commission for accepting dwelling houses earmarked for occupancy by workers and employees of the enterprise, institution, and organization, and also buildings and installations built for servicing their cultural-domestic requirements.

23. Dwelling premises in houses of state, cooperative, and social organizations shall be granted by joint decision of the administration and the factory, plant, and local trade union committee confirmed by the executive committee of the soviet of working people's deputies. All dwelling premises built at the expense of the fund for socio-cultural measures and housing construction, the enterprise fund, and consumption fund, and other assets of the enterprise which may, in accordance with legislation, be directed for housing construction shall be occupied by persons according to a list confirmed by joint decision of the administration of the enterprise and the factory, plant, and local trade union committee, with subsequent notification of the executive committee of the soviet of working people's deputies.

24. The factory, plant, and local trade union committee shall, joint with the administration of the enterprise, institution, and organization, take measures directed toward the observance of the exemptions and privileges established by legislation for women, protection of their health, and the improvement and cleanliness of labor conditions and services for women.

25. The factory, plant, and local trade union committee and the administration of the enterprise, institution, and organization shall consider questions of bonuses for young workers and employees, the distribution of housing and places in dormitories for them, protection of the labor of adolescents, dismissal of youths, and the use of assets for the development of mass cultural and sport work with the participation of a representative of the komsomol committee of the respective enterprise, institution, and organization.

26. Assets allocated to an enterprise in a centralized procedure for the construction of preschool children's institutions shall be used for housing construction by the administration by a joint decision with the factory, plant, and local trade union committee.

27. The factory, plant, and local trade union committee shall exercise social control over the work of state and cooperative trade and publ

dining enterprises servicing the workers and employees of the enterprise, institution, and organization. Prices for meals and food products, and also the work hours of lunch rooms, buffets, stores, and booths situated on the territory of the enterprise, institution, and organization shall be established with the participation of the factory, plant, and local trade union committee.

28. An enterprise, institution, or organization shall be obliged to grant the necessary premises free of charge to the factory, plant, and local trade union committee with all equipment, heating, lighting, cleaning, and protection for the work of the committee itself and for holding meetings of workers and employees. The administration shall grant the factory, plant, and local trade union committee means of transport and means of communications free of charge.

The buildings, premises, installations, gardens, and parks designated for carrying on cultural-enlightenment, therapeutic, physical culture, and sport work among workers and employees of the enterprise, institution, or organization and members of their families, as well as pioneer camps on the balance sheet of the enterprise, institution, and organization, shall be transferred to the use, free of charge, of the factory, plant, and local trade union committee. Buildings, premises, and installations leased by an enterprise, institution, and organization and designated for the said purposes also shall be transferred for use free of charge to the trade union committee.

The economic maintenance, repair, heating, lighting, cleaning, protection, and also the equipment of the buildings, premises, and installations specified in the present Article, and pioneer camps shall be at the expense of the enterprise, institution, and organization.

A list of equipment and economic inventory acquired for the premises granted by enterprises, institutions and organizations to factory, plant, and local trade union committees, and also for carrying on cultural-enlightenment, therapeutic, physical culture, and sport work among workers and employees and members of their families, and of equipment and inventory for pioneer camps, shall be determined by the director of the enterprise, institution, or organization jointly with the trade union committee within the limits of the assets provided in the estimate for such purposes.

An enterprise or organization shall transfer without charge, from balance sheet to balance sheet, to the trade union committee and other social organizations the cultural-domestic and sport inventory acquired by the enterprise at the expense of the enterprise fund, the consumption fund, and the fund for socio-cultural measures and housing construction and the amounts of bonuses for the socialist competition.

The factory, plant, and local trade union committee shall ensure the proper use of buildings, premises, installations, gardens, and parks placed at its disposal, and also of pioneer camps, shall establish an appropriate procedure therein, shall organize cultural-enlightenment, therapeutic, physical culture, and sport work among workers, employees, and members of their families.

29. Workers and employees released from work at an enterprise, institution, and organization as a consequence of being elected a member of the factory, plant, and local trade union committee shall, after their powers have terminated, be granted their former work (or post), and in the absence thereof, other equivalent work (or post) at the same or, with the consent of the worker, at another enterprise, institution, or organization.

30. Workers and employees elected to a factory, plant, local, and shop trade union committee and who are not released from production work may not be transferred to other work or subjected to disciplinary sanction without the consent in advance of the factory, plant, and local trade union committee, and the chairman of such committees and trade union organizers, without the consent in advance of the superior trade union agency.

The dismissal of the chairman and members of factory, plant, and local trade union committees who are not released from production work at the initiative of the administration may take place, besides observing the usual dismissal procedure, only with the consent of the superior trade union agency. The dismissal of trade union organizers at the initiative of the administration shall be permitted only with the consent of the superior trade union agency.

31. The present Statute also shall extend to shop trade union committees of an enterprise within the limits of the competence of the shop trade union committee.

The factory, plant, and local trade union committee to which the rights of a district trade union committee have been granted may transfer certain rights to shop trade union committees which are relegated to the competence of the factory, plant, and local trade union committee.

CHAPTER XII

PUBLIC HEALTH

FUNDAMENTAL PRINCIPLES OF LEGISLATION OF THE USSR AND UNION REPUBLICS ON PUBLIC HEALTH

[Confirmed by Law of the USSR Supreme Soviet, December 19, 1969. Vedomosti SSSR (1969), no. 52, item 466]

Protection of the health of the people is one of the most important tasks of the Soviet state.

The socialist social system ensures the constant growth of material well-being and culture of the people and improvement of conditions for labor, life, and leisure. An extensive system of socio-economic and medical measures is being carried out in the USSR which promote a higher level of health protection for the populace, and also generally accessible, free, and qualified medical assistance, therapeutic and sanitary measures are expanding, and physical culture and sport are receiving all-round development. The special attention of socialist society is being devoted to protecting the health of mother and child.

Constantly developing medical science constitutes an important basis for Soviet public health. Scientific research in medicine is subordinated to concern for the health and a long active life for the individual.

The system for protecting the health of the people in the USSR, being one of the greatest conquests of socialism, has allowed a significant improvement in the state of health of the populace, a reduction of the incidence of disease, the liquidation of a number of previously widespread contagious diseases, a sharp reduction in general and infant mortality, and a significant increase in the life expectancy of people.

Soviet legislation on public health has been called upon to actively serve the further improvement of protection for the health of the populace and to strengthen legality in this domain of social relations.

Section I. General Provisions

Article 1. Tasks of Soviet Legislation on Public Health

USSR and union republic legislation on public health shall regulate social relations in the domain of protecting the health of the populace with a view to ensuring the harmonious development of physical and spiritual forces, health, high level of capacity to work, and a long active life for citizens; prevention and reduction of the incidence of disease and a further reduction of disability and mortality; elimination of the factors and conditions which harmfully affect the health of citizens.

Article 2. Legislation of the USSR and Union Republics on Public Health

Legislation of the USSR and Union Republics on public health shall consist of the present Fundamental Principles and other acts of USSR and union republic legislation on public health corresponding thereto.

Article 3. Protection of the Health of the Populace: Duty of All State Agencies and Social Organizations

The health protection of the populace shall be the duty of all state agencies, enterprises, institutions, and organizations. The powers of the said agencies, enterprises, institutions, and organizations for health protection of the populace shall be determined by USSR and union republic legislation.

Trade unions, cooperative organizations, the Red Cross and Red Crescent Societies, and other social organizations shall, in accordance with their charters (or statutes), take part in ensuring health protection of the populace in the procedure provided by USSR and union republic legislation.

Citizens of the USSR should treat their own health and the health of other members of society with care.

Article 4. Provision of Medical Assistance to Citizens

Generally accessible, free, and qualified medical assistance rendered by state public health institutions shall be provided to citizens of the USSR.

Article 5. Fundamental Principles for Organizing Public Health in the USSR

Health protection for the populace in the USSR shall be ensured by a system of socio-economic and medico-sanitary measures and shall be carried by means of:

(1) carrying on extensive therapeutic and prophylactic measures and being especially concerned for the health protection of the rising generation;

(2) creation at production and in daily life of the proper sanitary-hygienic conditions, elimination of the causes of industrial injuries, professional diseases, and also other factors negatively affecting health;

(3) carrying out measures to sanitize the external environment and ensuring the sanitary protection of waters, soil, and air;

(4) planned development of a network of public health enterprises and medical industry enterprises;

(5) satisfying free of charge the requirements of the populace for all types of medical assistance; raising the quality and culture of medical assistance; gradual expansion of clinic observation; development of specialized medical assistance;

(6) granting treatment and diagnostic means free of charge during out-patient treatment, with a gradual expansion of granting means of treatment and other types of medical assistance free of charge or on preferential terms;

(7) expanding the network of sanatoriums, dispensaries, rest homes, boarding houses, tourist bases, and other institutions for the treatment and leisure of the working people;

(8) physical and hygienic upbringing of citizens; development of mass physical culture and sport;

(9) development of science, planned implementation of scientific research, training of scientific cadres and highly qualified specialists in public health;

(10) using the achievements of science, technology, and medical practice in the activity of public health institutions, and equipping these institutions with the most modern apparatus;

(11) development of scientifically hygienic principles for feeding the populace;

(12) extensive participation of social organizations and collectives of working people in protecting the health of the populace.

Article 6. Competence of the USSR in the Domain of Public Health

There shall be subject to the jurisdiction of the USSR in the person of its highest agencies of state power and agencies of state administration in the domain of public health:

(1) establishment of all-union plans for the development of public health and carrying on therapeutic measures;

(2) establishment of all-union plans for the development of scientific research, working out new medical preparations and equipment, the coordination of such research and work, introducing the achievements of science and new methods of diagnosis, treatment, and prophylaxis in medical practice;

(3) establishment of all-union plans for the development of medical and pharmaceutical education, distribution of specialists who have completed higher medical and pharmaceutical educational institutions, training of scientific cadres and improvement of the knowledge of medical and pharmaceutical workers; establishment of medical and pharmaceutical titles and training periods for medical and pharmaceutical workers;

(4) establishment of all-union plans for the production and distribution of medical industry products among the union republics and USSR ministries and departments, the export and import of medicines, articles of medical technology, and other medical manufactures;

(5) ensuring a uniform technological policy in the medical industry, establishment of uniform medical technological requirements in designing public health institutions; confirmation of state and branch standards and technical conditions for medical products, and prices for this product; organization of control over the quality of medical products produced in the USSR or imported from abroad; determination of the volume of production of narcotics and the organization of control over their turnover and consumption;

(6) direction of USSR public health agencies and institutions; administration of medical industry enterprises, organizations, and scientific research institutions for public health, higher medical and pharmaceutical educational institutions, and institutes for improvement of doctors of union subordination;

(7) confirmation of all-union sanitary-hygienic and sanitary-antiepidemic rules and norms; establishment of the procedure for exercising state sanitary supervision; carrying out measures for sanitary protection of the USSR state territory from the importation of quarantine diseases, and also of all-union measures to ensure the sanitary-epidemic well-being and radiation safety;

(8) confirmation of standards for servicing the populace with medical assistance, equipping public health institutions with equipment, inventory, and transport and norms for the expenditure of medicines, confirmation of norms for feeding persons in treatment-prophylactic and other public health institutions;

(9) confirmation of a uniform nomenclature for public health institutions and of model statutes concerning them; establishment of the procedure for determining personnel establishment standards for medical, pharmaceutical, engineering-technical, pedagogical, and other personnel of public health institutions;

(10) establishment of basic statutes defining the procedure for the organization and conducting of examinations of the capacity to work and forensic medical and forensic psychiatric examinations;

(11) establishment of a system for uniform statistical records and reports in public health agencies and institutions;

(12) settlement of other questions of public health relegated to the jurisdiction of the USSR in accordance with the USSR Constitution and the present Fundamental Principles.

Article 7. Competence of Union Republics in the Domain of Public Heal

The establishment of republic plans for the development of public health and carrying out of therapeutic measures, the direction of union republic public health agencies and institutions, the adoption of acts of legislation in public health, and also the settlement of other questions of directing public health relegated to union republic jurisdiction in accordance with the USSR Constitution and union republic constitution and the present Fundamental Principles, shall be subject to union republic jurisdiction in the person of its highest agencies of state power and agencies of state administration in the domain of public health.

Article 8. Direction of Public Health in the USSR

The highest agencies of state power and agencies of state administration of the USSR and union and autonomous republics, and also local soviet of working people's deputies and their executive committees, shall exercise direction over public health in accordance with the USSR Constitutio and the union and autonomous republic constitutions.

The USSR Ministry of Public Health shall direct public health, as a rule, through union republic public health agencies and administer institutions, enterprises, and organizations directly subordinate to it.

Union republic ministries of public health shall direct public healt through the autonomous republic ministries of public health and public health agencies of executive committees of the respective local soviets of working people's deputies and shall administer institutions, enterpris and organizations directly subordinate to them.

The USSR Ministry of Public Health, the union and autonomous republi ministries of public health, and their agencies shall bear responsibility for the state and further development of public health, medical science, and the quality of medical assistance rendered to the populace.

Local soviets of working people's deputies and their executive committees shall direct public health agencies and institutions subordinate to them, take measures to develop the network of public health institutions and properly site them and strengthen the material-technical base, organize medical assistance for the populace, coordinate and control the activity of all enterprises, institutions, and organizations to work out and implement measures for protecting public health, ensure the sanitary well-being of the populace, organize the leisure of the working people, develop physical culture, protect and sanitize the external environment, and also exercise control over observance of legislation on the protectio of the health of the populace.

Article 9. Jurisdiction of Public Health Institutions

Public health institutions shall be in the jurisdiction of the USSR Ministry of Public Health, union and autonomous republic ministries of public health, and public health agencies of executive committees of the respective local soviets of working people's deputies.

Other ministries, departments, and organizations may have public health institutions in their jurisdiction only with the authorization of the USSR Council of Ministers and shall be obliged to administer them in accordance with USSR and union republic public health legislation.

The USSR Ministry of Public Health shall coordinate the activity of public health institutions which are not within its system on questions of treatment-prophylactic assistance, sanitary-epidemiological servicing of the populace, protecting the territory of the USSR from the importation and dissemination of quarantine and other contagious diseases, and also exercise control over their activity.

Article 10. Development of Network of Public Health Institutions, Children's Institutions, and Sport Installations

The development of the network of public health institutions and their siting should be carried out, proceeding from the established standards of medical assistance for the populace and taking into account the economic, geographic, and other peculiarities of the areas of the country.

When designing and constructing population centers, dwelling blocks, enterprises, and other objects, the necessary public health institutions, children's preschool and extracurricular institutions, schools, and sport buildings and installations should be provided.

Article 11. Procedure for Organizing the Activity of Public Health Institutions

The basic provisions concerning the procedure for organizing the activity of treatment-prophylactic, sanitary-prophylactic, and pharmaceutical institutions shall be established by the USSR Ministry of Public Health.

Section II. Engaging in Medical and Pharmaceutical Activity

Article 12. Engaging in Medical and Pharmaceutical Activity

Persons who have received special training and title in the appropriate higher and secondary specialized education institutions of the USSR shall be admitted to medical and pharmaceutical activity.

Foreign citizens and stateless persons having a permanent place of residence in the USSR who have received special training and title in appropriate higher and secondary specialized educational institutions of the USSR may engage in medical and pharmaceutical activity on the territory of the USSR in accordance with the specialization and title received.

Persons who have received medical and pharmaceutical training and title in appropriate educational institutions of foreign states shall be admitted to medical or pharmaceutical activity in the USSR in the procedure established by USSR legislation.

Persons who have not been admitted to such activity in the established procedure shall be prohibited from engaging in medical and pharmaceutical activity.

Responsibility for the illegal practice of medicine shall be established by union republic legislation.

Article 13. Oath of a Doctor

Citizens of the USSR who have completed higher medical educational institutions of the USSR and have received the title of doctor shall take the oath of a doctor of the Soviet Union.

The text of the oath and the procedure for administering it shall be determined by the Presidium of the USSR Supreme Soviet.

Article 14. Professional Duties, Rights, and Privileges of Medical and Pharmaceutical Workers

The basic professional duties and rights of medical and pharmaceutical workers, and also exemptions granted to the said workers, shall be established by USSR legislation and by union republic legislation.

The professional duties and rights of medical, pharmaceutical, and other workers of public health institutions for individual specializations shall be determined by the USSR Ministry of Public Health.

The professional rights, honor, and dignity of doctors and other medical workers shall be protected by law.

Article 15. Improvement of Professional Knowledge of Medical and Pharmaceutical Workers

The working out and carrying out of measures for the specialization and improvement of professional knowledge of medical and pharmaceutical workers carried out by means of periodically passing through training in institutes for improvement and other appropriate public health institutions shall be entrusted to public health agencies.

The directors of public health agencies and institutions shall be obliged to create the necessary conditions for medical and pharmaceutical workers so that they may work systematically to raise their qualifications

The procedure for certifying medical and pharmaceutical workers shall be established by the USSR Ministry of Public Health jointly with the Central Committee of the Trade Union for Medical Workers.

Article 16. Duty to Preserve Medical Secrecy

Doctors and other medical workers shall not have the right to disclose information concerning the illness or intimate and family aspects of the life of a sick person which has become known to them by virtue of performing their professional duties.

Directors of public health institutions shall be obliged to communicate information concerning the illness of citizens to public health agencies in instances when the interests of protecting the health of the populace require this, and to investigative and judical agencies, at their request.

Article 17. Responsibility of Medical and Pharmaceutical Workers for Violation of Professional Duties

Medical and pharmaceutical workers who have violated professional duties shall bear disciplinary responsibility established by legislation unless such violations entail criminal responsibility under the law.

Section III. Ensuring the Sanitary-Epidemic Well-Being of the Populace

Article 18. Sanitary-Epidemic Well-Being of the Populace

The sanitary-epidemic well-being of the populace of the USSR shall be ensured by carrying out integrated sanitary-hygienic and sanitary-antiepidemic measures and a system of state sanitary supervision.

Carrying out sanitary-hygienic and sanitary-antiepidemic measures aimed at the liquidation and prevention of pollution of the environment, making labor conditions, daily life, and leisure of the populace more healthy, and preventing illness shall be the duty of all state agencies, enterprises, institutions, and organizations, collective farms, trade unions, and other social organizations.

Violation of sanitary-hygienic and sanitary-antiepidemic rules and norms shall entail disciplinary, administrative, or criminal responsibility in accordance with USSR and union republic legislation.

Article 19. Agencies Exercising State Sanitary Supervision

State sanitary supervision over the implementation of sanitary-antiepidemic measures and the observance of sanitary-hygienic and sanitary-antiepidemic rules and norms by state agencies, and also by all enterprises, institutions, and organizations, officials, and citizens shall be entrusted to agencies and institutions of the sanitary-epidemiological service of the USSR Ministry of Public Health and the union republic ministries of public health.

The powers of agencies and institutions of the sanitary-epidemiological service carrying out state sanitary supervision shall be determined by USSR legislation.

Article 20. Sanitary Requirements in Planning and Building Population Centers

The planning and building of population centers should provide for the creation of the most favorable conditions for the life and health of the populace.

Dwelling blocks, industrial enterprises, and other objects should be so sited that the unfavorable influence of harmful factors on the health and sanitary and domestic conditions of the life of the populace is precluded.

There should be provided when designing and constructing cities and city-type settlements: water supply, sewage system, street cover system, greenery, lighting, and provision of sanitary purification and other types of amenities.

The obligatory opinion of sanitary-epidemiological service agencies shall be required when granting land plots for construction, confirming design norms, designs for the planning and building of population centers, introducing dwelling houses into use or cultural-domestic buildings, industrial, and other enterprises and installations.

The procedure for agreeing drafts for the construction and conversion of enterprises, buildings, and installations with sanitary-epidemiological service agencies shall be determined by USSR legislation.

Article 21. Ensuring Measures for the Purification and Neutralizing of Industrial and Municipal-Domestic Effluents, Waste, and Refuse

The directors of enterprises and institutions, design, construction, and other organizations, and collective farm boards shall be obliged, when designing, constructing, converting, and using enterprises and municipal-domestic objects, to provide for and carry out measures to prevent the pollution of air, waters, underground waters, and soil and shall bear responsibility established by USSR and union republic legislation for the failure to fulfill these duties.

The introduction of new or converted enterprises, shops, sectors, installations, and other objects not supplied with an efficient purification, neutralization, and detector of harmful effluents, waste, and refuse shall be prohibited.

Sanitary-epidemiological service agencies shall have the right to prohibit or temporarily suspend the use of operating objects which might cause harm to the health of people through effluents, waste, or refuse.

Article 22. Sanitary Requirements for Occupation of Dwelling Premises

The sanitary requirements for the occupation of dwelling premises shall be established by union republic councils of ministers.

The occupation of premises not meeting sanitary requirements shall not be permitted.

Additional dwelling space shall be granted to persons suffering grave forms of certain chronic illnesses in the instances and procedure established by USSR and union republic legislation.

Article 23. Observance of Sanitary Rules for Maintaining Production Premises, Dwelling and Other Buildings, and Territories

The directors of enterprises, institutions, and organizations shall be obliged to ensure the maintenance of production premises and work places in accordance with sanitary-hygienic norms and rules.

Enterprises, institutions, and organizations should ensure the necessary conditions for satisfying the sanitary-domestic needs of workers.

Ensuring the observance of sanitary rules for the maintenance of dwelling and public buildings and territories on which they are situated shall be carried out by the respective enterprises, institutions, organizations, and citizens, in the jurisdiction, use, or ownership of which these buildings are located.

The implementation of general measures to ensure the observance of sanitary rules for the maintenance of dwelling and social buildings and the proper sanitary state of population centers shall be entrusted to the executive committees of local soviets of working people's deputies. Supervision over the observance of sanitary rules for the maintenance of street courtyards, and other territories of population centers shall be carried out by the police and sanitary supervision agencies.

Article 24. Noise Prevention and Elimination

Executive committees of local soviets of working people's deputies and other state agencies, enterprises, institutions, and organizations shall be obliged to carry out measures for the prevention, reduction of intensity, and elimination of noise in production, dwelling, and public buildings, courtyards, streets, and squares of cities and other population centers.

Observance of the rules for the prevention and elimination of noise in domestic conditions shall be the duty of all citizens.

Article 25. Sanitary Requirements for Drinking and Household Use

The quality of water used for drinking and household consumption should correspond to the requirements of the state standard confirmed in the established procedure upon the recommendation of the USSR Ministry of Public Health.

Sanitary protection zones shall be established for household and drinking waterpipes and their sources, with a special regime ensuring proper water quality.

The procedure for determining the sanitary protection zones for waterpipes and their sources shall be established by USSR legislation, and the sanitary regime of such zones, by USSR and union republic legislation.

Article 26. Obligatoriness of Agreeing Standards and Technical Conditions with Public Health Agencies

Draft standards and technical conditions for new types of raw materials, products, food, industrial manufactures, new construction materials, packaging, and packing materials, polymer, and synthetic materials and articles therefrom shall be confirmed by agreement with the USSR Ministry of Public Health, and in instances determined by the USSR Ministry of Public Health, by agreement with the union republic public health agencies. The introduction of new technological processes, types of equipment, instruments, and working tools which might exert a harmful influence on health also shall be authorized in the said procedure.

Article 27. Sanitary Requirements During the Production, Processing, Storage, Transport, and Realization of Food Products

The production, storage, and transport of food products, technological equipment for manufacturing and subsequent culinary processing of products, production of packaging and packing materials, and crockery for food products, as well as the realization of food products, shall be authorized with observance of the sanitary-hygienic norms and rules.

The application of new chemical substances, means, and methods for the production and processing of food products, and also the application of growth stimulators for feeding agricultural plants and livestock and of chemical means for protecting plants, and polymer and plastic mass and other chemical products shall be permitted with the authorization of the USSR Ministry of Public Health.

Article 28. Sanitary Supervision Over the Production, Application, Storage, and Transport of Radioactive, Poisonous, and Virulent Substances

The production, application, storage, transport, and burial of radioactive substances, sources of ionized rays, poisonous, and virulent substances shall be carried out under the supervision of sanitary-epidemiological service agencies and institutions.

Article 29. Compulsory Medical Examinations

With a view to protecting the health of the populace and preventing contagious and professional diseases, workers of food industry, public dining, and trade enterprises, waterpipe installations, treatment-prophylactic and children's institutions, livestock farms, and certain other enterprises, institutions, and organizations, and also enterprises, institutions, and organizations with harmful labor conditions, shall undergo compulsory preliminary medical examinations when commencing work and periodic medical examinations.

A list of professions and production units for work in which medical examinations are compulsory and the procedure for conducting such examinations, shall be established by the USSR Ministry of Public Health by agreement with the All-Union Central Trade Union Council.

Article 30. Prevention and Liquidation of Contagious Diseases

Executive committees of local soviets of working people's deputies, directors of enterprises, institutions, organizations, and other officials shall be obliged to ensure the timely implementation of measures to prevent the dissemination of contagious diseases, and also to liquidate them in the event they arise.

If there is a threat of the arising or spreading of epidemic contagious diseases, the union and autonomous republic councils of ministers and executive committees of local soviets of working people's deputies may introduce in the established procedure on the respective territories special conditions and regimes for labor, study, movement, and transport directed toward preventing the spreading and the liquidation of these diseases.

Persons ill with contagious diseases who represent a danger for surrounding persons shall be subject to compulsory in-patient treatment, and persons having contact with contagiously ill persons, to quarantine.

Persons who are bacteria carriers of contagious diseases shall be subject to being made healthy. These persons, if they may be a source of spreading contagious diseases in connection with the peculiarities of production in which they are engaged or with work they fulfill, shall be transferred temporarily to other work, and if it is impossible to transfer them temporarily, to release them from work with payment of a social insurance benefit in accordance with USSR legislation.

Lists of contagious diseases and illnesses for which persons shall be deemed bacteria carriers shall be determined by the USSR Ministry of Public Health.

Prophylactic inoculations shall be performed on citizens with a view to preventing contagious diseases.

The procedure and periods for carrying out inoculations shall be determined by the USSR Ministry of Public Health.

Article 31. Sanitary Enlightenment of the Populace

Public health agencies and institutions shall, jointly with agencies and institutions of science, culture, and public education with the active participation of Red Cross and Red Crescent Societies and other social organizations, be called upon to provide propaganda for scientific medical and hygienic knowledge among the populace.

Section IV. Treatment-Prophylactic Assistance to the Populace

Article 32. Provision of Citizens with Treatment-Prophylactic Assistance

Specialized medical care shall be rendered to citizens of the USSR in polyclinics, hospitals, dispensaries, and other treatment-prophylactic institutions, as well as urgent medical assistance and medical care at home.

Medical care for invalids of the Great Fatherland War also shall be rendered in special treatment-prophylactic institutions, and in the event of treatment in out-patient clinics, they shall enjoy additional privileges established by USSR legislation.

For a period of illness with temporary loss of capacity to work, citizens shall be granted relief from work with payment of a social insurance benefit in the established procedure.

Enterprises, institutions, and organizations shall, jointly with public health institutions and trade union organizations, be obliged to take necessary measures for the prophylaxis of industrial injuries, professional diseases, and restoration of the capacity to work.

Foreign citizens and stateless persons having a permanent place of residence in the USSR shall enjoy medical assistance on the same basis as citizens of the USSR.

Medical assistance for foreign citizens and stateless persons temporarily staying in the USSR shall be rendered in the procedure established by the USSR Ministry of Public Health.

Article 33. Procedure for Rendering Treatment-Prophylaxis Assistance to Citizens

Treatment-prophylaxis assistance shall be rendered to citizens by public health institutions at their place of residence or work.

For persons suffering from an accident or as a consequence of sudden illness being in a state requiring urgent medical assistance, such assistance shall be rendered without delay by the nearest treatment-prophylaxis institution irrespective of departmental subordination.

Medical and pharmaceutical workers shall be obliged to render immediate first aid to citizens on the road, in the street, or in other public places and at home.

If necessary, ill persons may be sent to appropriate treatment-prophylaxis institutions of other union republics in the procedure established by the USSR Ministry of Public Health, and to treatment-prophylaxis institutions within the limits of a union republic, in the procedure established by the union republic ministry of public health.

When necessary, doctors shall be enlisted by the appropriate public health agencies to participate in commissions for medical examination of citizens.

Article 34. Application of Diagnosis Methods, Treatment, and Medicines

Doctors in medical practice shall apply methods of diagnosis, prophylaxis, and treatment, and medicines authorized by the USSR Ministry of Public Health.

In the interests of the recovery of an ill person and with his consent, and with respect to ill persons who have not attained sixteen years of age, and of mentally ill persons, with the consent of their parents, guardians, or curators, a doctor may apply new scientifically well-founded, but not yet universally applied methods of diagnosis, prophylaxis, treatment, and medicines. The procedure for applying the said methods of diagnosis, prophylaxis, treatment, and medicines shall be established by the USSR Ministry of Public Health.

Article 35. Procedure for Surgical Intervention and Application of Complex Diagnosis Methods

Surgical operations shall be performed and complex methods of diagnosis shall be applied with the consent of ill persons, and to an ill person who has not attained sixteen years of age, and mentally ill persons, with the consent of their parents, guardians, or curators.

Urgent surgical operations shall be performed and complex diagnosis methods applied by doctors without the consent of the ill persons themselves or their parents, guardians, or curators only in exceptional instances when time spent in establishing the diagnosis or performing the operation threatens the life of the ill person and it is not possible to obtain the consent of the said persons.

Article 36. Special Measures for Prophylaxis and Treatment

With a view to protecting the health of the populace, public health agencies shall be obliged to carry out special measures for the prophylaxis and treatment of diseases representing a danger for surrounding persons (tuberculosis, psychiatric and venereal diseases, leprosy, chronic alcoholism, drug addiction), and also quarantine diseases.

Persons ill with tuberculosis shall be provided anti-tuberculosis medicines free of charge; their treatment in sanatoriums and dispensaries also shall be carried out free of charge.

The instances and procedure for compulsory treatment and compulsory hospitalization of persons suffering from the said diseases may be established by USSR and union republic legislation.

Article 37. Assistance to Medical Workers in Rendering Treatment-Prophylactic Assistance to Citizens

In order to organize public health institutions at enterprises, institutions, and organizations, the administration shall be obliged to allocate the necessary premises and transport, and also to assist doctors and other medical workers in the fulfillment of their professional duties.

Executive committees of local soviets of working people's deputies, directors of enterprises, institutions, and organizations, and other officials shall be obliged to assist medical workers in rendering urgent medical care to citizens, providing transport, means of communication, and other necessary assistance.

In instances threatening the life of an ill person, a doctor or other medical worker may use free of charge any forms of transport available in the particular situation in order to travel to the place where the ill person is or for transporting him to the nearest treatment-prophylactic institution.

Section V. Protection of Motherhood and Childhood

Article 38. Incentive for Motherhood. Guarantees for Protecting the Health of Mother and Child

Motherhood in the USSR shall be encouraged and protected by the state.

Protection of the health of mother and child shall be ensured by organizing an extensive network of women's consultation offices, maternity homes, sanatoriums and rest homes for pregnant women and mothers with children, nurseries, kindergartens, and other children's institutions; granting women pregnancy and birth leave with payment of a social insurance benefit; establishing intervals at work to feed a child; payment of allowances in the established procedure for the birth of a child and allowances while nursing an ill child; prohibition against using female labor in production heavy or harmful for women, and transferring pregnant women to lighter work with retention of average earnings; improvement and more sanitary labor and domestic conditions; state and social assistance for the family and other measures in the procedure established by USSR and union republic legislation.

With a view to the health protection of women, they shall be granted the right to decide for themselves the question of motherhood.

Article 39. Provision of Pregnant Women and Newly Born Children with Medical Assistance

Public health institutions shall provide each woman with qualified medical supervision during pregnancy, in-patient medical care during birth, and treatment-prophylactic care for the mother and new born child.

Article 40. Provision of Children and Adolescents with Medical Assistance

Medical assistance for children and adolescents shall be provided by treatment-prophylactic and therapeutic institutions: children's polyclinics, clinics, hospitals, sanatoriums, and other public health institutions. Passes shall be granted to children free of charge for children's sanatoriums.

Children and adolescents shall be under clinic observation.

Article 41. Concern for Strengthening and Protecting the Health of Children and Adolescents

With a view to bringing up a healthy young generation with the harmonius development of physical and spiritual forces, state agencies, enterprises, institutions, and organizations, collective farms, trade unions, and other social organizations shall ensure the development of an extensive network of children's nurseries and kindergartens, schools, boarding schools, forestry schools, pioneer camps, and other children's institutions.

Necessary conditions shall be provided for children being brought up in children's institutions and studying in schools to preserve and strengthen their health and hygienic upbringing. The study and work load, and also a model regime of exercises for children, shall be determined by agreement with the USSR Ministry of Public Health.

Control over the health protection of children and implementation of therapeutic measures in children's institutions and schools shall be carried out by public health agencies and institutions jointly with public education agencies and institutions with the participation of social organizations.

Article 42. State Assistance to Citizens in Caring for Children. Privileges Granted to Mothers in the Event of Illness of Children

Basic expenses for the maintenance of children in nurseries, kindergartens, and other children's institutions shall be at the expense of the state budget, and also of the assets of enterprises, institutions, organizations, collective farms, trade unions, and other social organizations.

Children with physical or mental defects shall be maintained in child homes, children's homes, and other specialized children's institutions at state expense.

If hospitalization is impossible or in the absence of the indicators for in-patient treatment of a sick child, the mother or other family member caring for the child may be relieved of work with payment of a social insurance benefit in the established procedure.

In the event of in-patient treatment of children of up to one year of age, and also of gravely ill older children requiring, in the opinion of a doctor, maternal care, the mother shall be granted the possibility of being with the child in a treatment institution, a benefit being paid to her under social insurance in the established procedure.

Article 43. Control Over Labor and Production Training and Labor Conditions of Adolescents

The production training of adolescents shall be authorized for those professions which correspond to their age, physical and mental development and state of health. Labor and production training shall be carried out under systematic medical control.

Control over the observance of labor conditions of adolescents established by USSR and union republic legislation, and also over the implementation of special measures aimed at preventing the illness of adolescents, shall be carried out by public health agencies and institutions jointly with professional-technical education agencies, public education agencies, trade unions, komsomol, and other social organizations.

Section VI. Sanatorium-Resort Treatment, Organization of Leisure, Tourism, and Physical Culture

Article 44. Sanatorium-Resort Treatment of Citizens

Indicators and contraindicators for in-patient and out-patient treatment in all resorts and sanatoriums of the USSR shall be established by the USSR Ministry of Public Health.

The procedure for medical selection and the sending of ill persons for sanatorium-resort treatment shall be established by the USSR Ministry of Public Health by agreement with the All-Union Central Trade Union Council. Ill persons shall be sent in the established procedure to sanatorium-resort institutions free of charge, on the basis of exemptions, or for ful payment.

Article 45. Resorts and Sanitary Protection Area

Localities possessing natural medicinal means, mineral sources, layers of medicinal muds, climatic, and other conditions favorable for treatment and prophylaxis may be deemed resorts.

Deeming a locality to be a resort, the establishment of the boundarie of sanitary protection areas of resorts, and determining their regime shal be carried out by the USSR Council of Ministers or the union republic coun cil of ministers upon the joint recommendation of the USSR Ministry of Pub lic Health and the All-Union Central Trade Union Council or union republic ministry of public health or republic trade union council agreed with the executive committee of the respective local soviet of working people's deputies on whose territory the particular resort is situated.

Article 46. Organization and Opening of Sanatorium-Resort Institutions

The organization and opening of sanatorium-resort institutions shall be permitted with the authorization of the USSR Ministry of Public Health and the All-Union Central Trade Union Council by agreement with the union republic council of ministers.

The specialization (or medical profile) of sanatorium-resort institutions shall be determined by the USSR Ministry of Public Health and the All-Union Central Trade Union Council.

Article 47. Coordination of Activity of Sanatorium-Resort Institutions

The coordination of the activity of sanatorium-resort institutions, irrespective of their departmental subordination, in using means of treatment and resort factors and organizing the sanatorium-resort regime shall be effectuated by the respective agencies for the administration of resorts.

The USSR Ministry of Public Health and the union and autonomous republic ministries of public health shall exercise control over the organization of therapeutic-prophylactic work in sanatorium-resort institutions, and also render them scientific-methods and consultation assistance.

Article 48. Use of Rest Homes, Boarding Houses, Tourist Bases, and Other Leisure Institutions

Citizens shall use, in the established procedure, rest homes, boarding houses, tourist bases, and other leisure institutions free of charge, on the basis of exemptions, or for full payment.

Article 49. Organization of Physical Culture, Sport, and Tourism

State agencies, trade unions, komsomol and cooperative organizations, sport societies, enterprises, institutions, and organizations should further therapeutic physical culture, sport, tourist, and excursion work among the populace, the creation and strengthening of collectives for physical culture, tourist clubs, and organizations, and the introduction of practical gymnastics.

Physical education shall be provided in work plans of children's preschool and extracurricular institutions and in syllabi of general education schools, professional-technical schools, secondary specialized and higher education institutions.

Sport installations, sport inventory, and tourist equipment shall be granted in the established procedure to citizens for physical culture and sport exercises.

Medical control over the state of health of citizens engaging in physical culture and sport shall be carried out by public health institutions.

Section VII. Medical Examination

Article 50. Performing Medical Examination for Capacity to Work

Examination of the temporary incapacity to work of citizens shall be carried out in public health institutions by a doctor or commission of doctors, which shall grant leave for illness or injury, pregnancy and birth, caring for ill family members, and quarantine, prosthetics, sanatorium-resort treatment, and shall determine the necessity of and periods for temporary transfer of a worker because of illness to other work in the established procedure, and also take the decision to send him to a medical-labor examination commission.

The prolonged or permanent loss of capacity to work shall be examined by medical-labor examination commissions which shall establish the extent of loss of capacity to work, and the group and reason for disability, determine the conditions and types of labor for disabled persons and the work and professions open to them by their state of health; verify the correctness of using disabled persons for work in accordance with the particular opinions; promote the restoration of the capacity to work of disabled persons.

Opinions of medical-labor examination commissions concerning the conditions and character of labor of disabled persons shall be binding upon the administration of enterprises, institutions, and organizations.

The procedure for the organization and performance of examinations for capacity to work shall be established by USSR and union republic legislation.

Article 51. Forensic Medical and Forensic Psychiatric Examination

Forensic medical and forensic psychiatric examinations shall be performed in accordance with USSR and union republic legislation by decree of the person performing the inquiry, the investigator, the procurator, and also by a court ruling.

The procedure for organizing and the performance of forensic medical and forensic psychiatric examination shall be established by the USSR Ministry of Public Health by agreement with the USSR Supreme Court, the Procuracy of the USSR, the USSR Ministry of Internal Affairs, and other departments.

Section VIII. Medicines and Prosthetic Assistance

Article 52. Procedure for Rendering Medicine Assistance to Citizens

Medicine assistance to citizens shall be rendered by state pharmacy institutions, and also by treatment-prophylactic institutions.

The procedure for providing citizens, free of charge or on the basis of exemptions, with medicine assistance during out-patient or polyclinic treatment shall be determined by USSR legislation.

Pharmacy institutions may issue only those medicines which are authorized for use by the USSR Ministry of Public Health.

Article 53. Ensuring Control Over the Production of Medicines

The production of new medicines for medical purposes shall be permitted with the authorization of the USSR Ministry of Public Health after establishing their treatment or prophylactic effectiveness.

The quality of medicines should correspond to the requirements of the State Pharmacopoeia of the USSR or technical conditions confirmed in the established procedure.

Control over the quality of medicines shall be carried out by the USSR Ministry of Public Health.

Article 54. Provision of Prosthetic Assistance to Citizens

When necessary, citizens shall be provided with prosthetic, orthopedic and correctional manufactures, hearing aids, physical culture treatment means, and special means for movement.

The categories of persons subject to provision free of charge or on the basis of exemptions with the said manufactures and articles, and also the conditions and procedure for providing them, shall be established by USSR and union republic legislation.

Section IX. International Treaties and Agreements

Article 55. International Treaties and Agreements

If by an international treaty or international agreement in which the USSR participates other rules have been established than those which are contained in USSR and union republic legislation on public health, then the rules of the international treaty or international agreement shall be applied.

CHAPTER XIII

PUBLIC EDUCATION

FUNDAMENTAL PRINCIPLES OF LEGISLATION OF THE USSR AND UNION REPUBLICS ON PUBLIC EDUCATION

[Confirmed by Law of the USSR Supreme Soviet, July 19, 1973. Vedomosti SSSR (1973), no. 30, item 392]

The Great October Socialist Revolution has created the political, economic, and social conditions for the development of public education, science, and culture in our country.

Socialist ideology has been confirmed within a brief historical period in all spheres of spiritual life of Soviet society. Under the leadership of the Communist Party of the Soviet Union, the task of forming the new man, the builder of communism, is being successfully resolved.

For the first time in the history of mankind, a genuinely democratic system of public education has been created in our country. Citizens of the USSR have the real opportunity to receive secondary and higher education, and also work in accordance with their specialization and qualification.

The triumph of socialism in the USSR has ensured the steady growth of material well-being, of the cultural and educational level of the Soviet people, allowed the creation of favorable conditions for preschool education of children and effectuating successively compulsory eight-year study and the transition to universal secondary education for youth, and the extensive development of professional-technical, secondary specialized, and higher education.

The construction of communism in our country and the uninterrupted growth of productive forces and scientific-technical progress urgently require the all-round development of the rising generation, providing the national economy with highly qualified workers and specialists, and a further increase in the level of general and professional education of the populace of the USSR.

The realization of secondary education everywhere and the improvement of general, professional-technical, secondary specialized, and higher education will promote the future growth of the culture of the Soviet people, the formation of a communist world outlook, and the attainment of higher labor productivity are an important factor in gradually overcoming the essential differences between mental and physical labor, between city and village.

The purpose of public education in the USSR is the training of highly educated, well-developed active builders of a communist society nurtured in the ideas of Marxism-Leninism, in the spirit of respect for Soviet laws and the socialist legal order, a communist attitude toward labor, physically healthy and capable of working successfully in various branches of economic and socio-cultural construction, to actively participate in social and state activity, ready wholeheartedly to defend the socialist Motherland, preserve and multiply its material and spiritual wealth, care for and protect nature. Public education in the USSR is called upon to ensure the development and satisfaction of the spiritual and intellectual requirements of Soviet Man.

Education in the USSR shall be a genuinely all-people's cause. The state, the family, and social organizations shall, by their joint efforts, ensure the nurturing and education of the rising generation. A special role in the development of public education belongs to pedagogical workers, whose activity is based on a high consciousness of the professional and social responsibility for the proper quality of study and a communist upbringing of the young generation.

Soviet legislation on public education is called upon actively to serve the improvement of public education in the country and the further strengthening of socialist legality in this domain of social relations.

Section I. General Provisions

Article 1. Tasks of Soviet Legislation on Public Education

USSR and union republic legislation on public education shall regulate social relations in the domain of public education with a view to the fullest satisfaction of the spiritual needs of Soviet citizens and the requirements of a developed socialist society for the education and communist upbringing of the rising generation and providing the national economy with workers and specialists with appropriate qualifications.

Article 2. Legislation of the USSR and Union Republics on Public Education

Legislation of the USSR and union republics on public education shall consist of the present Fundamental Principles and other acts of USSR and union republic legislation on public education issued in accordance therewith.

Article 3. Right of Citizens of the USSR to Education

In accordance with the USSR Constitution, citizens of the USSR shall have the right to education.

This right shall be secured by compulsory general eight-year education, by universal secondary education for youth, by the extensive development of professional-technical, secondary specialized, and higher education on the basis of linking study with life and with the practice of communist construction, by study in schools in the native language, by enlarging the network of preschool and extracurricular institutions, by all types of education being free of charge, by the system of state stipends and other types of material assistance for pupils and students, by organizing various forms of production training, and by raising the qualifications of working people.

With a view to creating the most favorable conditions for study and for bringing up the rising generation, appropriate exemptions shall be established for pupils and students by USSR and union republic legislation.

Article 4. Basic Principles of Public Education in the USSR

The basic principles of public education in the USSR shall be:

(1) equality of all citizens of the USSR to receive education irrespective of racial and national affiliation, sex, attitude toward religion, or property and social status;

(2) compulsory education for all children and adolescents;

(3) the state and social character of all training and educational institutions;

(4) freedom to select the language of study; study in the native language or the language of another people of the USSR;

(5) all types of education being free of charge, maintaining a portion of the pupils on complete state security, stipend provision for pupils and students and rendering other material assistance to them;

(6) unity of systems of public education and continuity of all types of educational institutions ensuring the possibility of transition from the lowest levels of study to the highest;

(7) unity of study and communist upbringing; cooperation of school, family, and the public in bringing up children and youths;

(8) linking the study and upbringing of the rising generation with life and with the practice of communist construction;

(9) scientific character of education and its constant improvement on the basis of the most recent achievements of science, technology, and culture;

(10) humanistic and high moral character of education and upbringing;

(11) co-education;

(12) secular character of education, excluding the influence of religion.

Article 5. System of Public Education in the USSR

The system of public education in the USSR shall include:

preschool education;

general secondary education;

extracurricular education;

professional-technical education;

secondary specialized education;

higher education.

Article 6. Competence of the USSR in the Domain of Public Education

There shall be subject to the jurisdiction of the USSR in the person of its highest agencies of state power and agencies of state administration in the domain of public education:

(1) establishment of general principles of direction and the system of administration for public education in the USSR;

(2) establishment of all-union plans for the development of public education and plans for training qualified workers and specialists for the national economy of the country;

(3) direction by public education agencies of the USSR; administration by training and educational and scientific research institutions and enterprises of the public education system of union subordination;

(4) establishment of types of educational institutions and other public education institutions, confirmation of statutes (or charters) concerning them, establishment of the age for admission to educational institutions and periods of study therein;

(5) organization, reorganization, and liquidation of institutions of higher education, and also secondary specialized and professional-technical educational institutions and general education schools of union subordination;

(6) establishment of the procedure for determining personnel establishments, standards, and payment for labor of workers of educational institutions and other public education institutions;

(7) establishment of general principles of study and methods guidance for all training and educational institutions, confirmation of study plans, and determining the procedure for the confirmation of study syllabi;

(8) establishment of all-union plans for the development of the study and material base of educational institutions and other public education institutions;

(9) establishment of types and norms of material assistance for persons being trained or educated in training and educational institutions;

(10) state control in the domain of public education and the establishment of the procedure for exercising it;

(11) establishment of a uniform system for statistical records and reports in the domain of public education;

(12) deciding other questions of public education relegated to the jurisdiction of the USSR in accordance with the USSR Constitution and the present Fundamental Principles.

Article 7. Competence of Union Republics in the Domain of Public Education

There shall be subject to the jurisdiction of a union republic in the person of its highest agencies of state power and agencies of state administration in the domain of public education:

(1) establishment of republic plans for the development of public education and plans for training qualified workers and specialists;

(2) direction of union republic public education agencies; administration of training and educational and scientific research institutions and enterprises of the public education system of republic subordination;

(3) organization, reorganization, and liquidation of general education schools, professional-technical educational institutions, and also secondary specialized educational institutions of republic subordination in the procedure established by legislation;

(4) carrying out study and methods guidance in the established procedure by training and educational institutions of republic and local subordination;

(5) establishment of republic plans for the development of the study and material base for public education institutions of republic and local subordination;

(6) exercise of state control over the activity of educational institutions and other institutions of public education on the territory of the union republic;

(7) deciding other questions of public education relegated to union republic jurisdiction in accordance with the USSR Constitution, the union republic constitution, and the present Fundamental Principles.

Article 8. Direction of Public Education in the USSR

The highest agencies of state power and agencies of state administration of the USSR and the union and autonomous republics, and also local soviets of working people's deputies and their executive committees, shall direct public education in accordance with the USSR Constitution and the union and autonomous republic constitutions.

Agencies of state administration for public education of the USSR shall, in accordance with statutes concerning them confirmed by the USSR Council of Ministers, direct general secondary, professional-technical, secondary specialized, and higher education, as a rule, through the system of union republic ministries and union republic departments therein and manage training and educational institutions directly subordinate to them, and also shall work out general statutes relating to study, educational, methods, and scientific work binding upon training and educational institutions irrespective of their departmental subordination and shall exercise control over their activity.

The executive committees of local soviets of working people's deputies shall direct training and educational institutions subordinate to them, take measures for developing the network of these institutions, their proper siting, and strengthening their study and material base, ensure universal compulsory education and direction of preschool and adult education, and render assistance to the work of professional-technical, secondary specialized, and higher education institutions situated on the territory of the soviets.

Article 9. Jurisdictional Subordination of Training and Educational Institutions

Training and educational institutions shall be in the jurisdiction of state agencies. Individual types of training and educational institutions may also be in the jurisdiction of collective farms, cooperative, and other social organizations.

Article 10. Direction of Training and Educational Institutions

A training and educational institution shall be directed by the head, director, or rector of the respective training and educational institution, who shall rely in his work on the pedagogical collective and social organizations.

In order to ensure the collegial consideration of basic questions of study, educational, methods, and scientific work in a training and educational institution, a pedagogical council (or council of an institution of higher education) shall be formed from among the pedagogical workers and representatives of the public.

Social organizations of a training and educational institution shall take part in working out and effectuate measures directed toward the improvement of study, education, and the cultural-domestic services for pupils and students.

Article 11. Participation of Enterprises, Institutions, and Organizations in the Development of Public Education

State enterprises, institutions, and organizations, collective farms, cooperative, trade union, komsomol, and other social organizations shall take part actively in the development of public education, production training, and raising the qualifications of the working people and assist workers, collective farmers, and employees in receiving an education.

Article 12. Self-Education of Citizens

With a view to promoting self-education and raising the cultural level of citizens, people's universities, lectures, courses, schools of communist labor, and other social forms of disseminating political and scientific knowledge shall be organized.

Public education agencies and institutions shall render assistance in organizing the self-education of citizens.

Section II. Preschool Education

Article 13. Children's Preschool Institutions

With a view to the creation of the most favorable conditions for bringing up children of preschool age and rendering necessary assistance to the family, children's nurseries, kindergartens, general and special children's nurseries and kindergartens, and other children's preschool institutions shall be created.

Children shall be enrolled in children's preschool institutions at the wish of their parents or persons replacing them.

Article 14. Tasks of Preschool Education

Children's preschool institutions shall, in close cooperation with the family, effectuate the all-round harmonious development and upbringing of children, protect and strengthen their health, inculcate elementary practical skills and love for labor, be concerned for their esthetic upbringing, prepare children for study in school, and nurture them in a spirit of respect for the elderly and love for the socialist Motherland and native territory.

Article 15. Organization of Children's Preschool Institutions

Children's preschool institutions shall be organized by the executive committees of district, city, rural, and settlement soviets of working people's deputies, and also with their authorization by state enterprises, institutions, and organizations, collective farms, cooperatives, and other social organizations.

Article 16. Pedagogical Direction of Children's Preschool Institutions and Their Medical Service

Pedagogical direction and providing pedagogical workers to children's preschool institutions shall, irrespective of their departmental subordination, be carried out by the USSR Ministry of the Enlightenment and the ministries of enlightenment (or public education) of the union and autonomous republics and their local agencies.

Public health agencies shall carry out therapeutic-prophylactic work with children and provide children's preschool institutions with medical personnel.

Section III. Secondary Education

Article 17. Universal Secondary Education

With a view to the further raising of the educational level of the populace of the USSR, universal secondary education of the rising generation, being one of the most important conditions of socio-political and economic development of our society on the path to communism and the growth of socialist consciousness and culture of the working people, shall be effectuated everywhere.

Universal secondary education shall be carried out in secondary general education schools, in secondary professional-technical schools, and secondary specialized educational institutions.

Section IV. General Secondary Education

Article 18. General Secondary Education Schools

The secondary general education school (the basic form of receiving a general secondary education) shall be a unified, labor, polytechnic school for the training and upbringing of children and youths.

The unity of secondary general education school shall be ensured by the common principles for organizing the training and educational process, unifying on this basis the content and level of general education throughout the entire territory of the USSR, while taking account comprehensively of the national peculiarities of the populace of the union republics.

The polytechnic training, labor education, and professional orientation of pupils shall be carried out in the process of studying the basic principles of the sciences, labor training, organizing various extracurricular activity, and the socially useful labor of pupils, taking into account their ages and individual characteristics, state of health, and in accordance with the requirements of scientific technical progress.

With a view to developing the various interests and capacities of pupils and their professional orientation in secondary general education schools, elective exercises selected by the pupils shall be organized. To these ends may be organized schools and classes for deeper theoretical and practical study of individual subjects, various types of labor, art, and sport. Production training also may be carried on in secondary general education schools where conditions exist. The compulsory amount of general education knowledge should be uniform in all secondary general education schools.

The training and education of pupils of secondary general education school shall be carried out in the process of teaching, homework, and extra curricular activities and socially useful labor. The lesson shall be the basic form for organizing training and educational work in school.

Secondary general education schools shall carry out their activity on the basis of a Charter of a Secondary General Education School confirmed by the USSR Council of Ministers.

Article 19. Principal Tasks of a Secondary General Education School

The principal tasks of a secondary general education school shall be:

carrying out general secondary education for children and youths responding to modern requirements of social and scientific-technical progress, arming pupils with profound and firm knowledge of the basic principles of the sciences, nurturing in them the aspiration to a constant improvement of their knowledge and the ability to augment it independently and apply it in practice;

forming a Marxist-Leninist world outlook in the young generation, nurturing socialist internationalism, Soviet patriotism, and a readiness to defend the socialist Motherland;

nurturing in pupils high moral qualities in the spirit of the requirements of the moral code of a builder of communism;

ensuring the all-round harmonious development of pupils and their culture; strengthening health and the esthetic and physical upbringing of pupils;

preparation of pupils for active labor and social activity and the conscious choice of profession.

Article 20. Language of Studying in a General Education School

Pupils of a general education school shall be granted the opportunity to study in their native language or the language of another people of the USSR. Parents or persons replacing them shall have the right to select for their children at their wish a school with the appropriate language of study. Besides the language in which teaching is carried on, pupils may at their wish study the language of another people of the USSR.

Article 21. Ensuring Accessibility of General Education Schools for Pupils

The territorial accessibility of schools for pupils shall be ensured through optimal school districting and the transport free of charge of pupils from a rural locality to school and from school, and by well-equipped boarding schools attached to schools.

Depending on local conditions, primary schools comprising I-III (or IV) grades, eight-year schools comprising I-VIII grades, and secondary schools comprising I-X (or XI) grades shall be created separately while retaining the unity and continuity of all grades of general secondary education.

Article 22. Preparatory Classes

Preparatory classes shall be organized when necessary for the purpose of preparing children for school who will be studying in a non-native language and children who have not been brought up in children's preschool institutions.

Preparatory classes shall be organized in the procedure established by the USSR Council of Ministers.

Article 23. Extended Day General Education Schools and Extended Day Groups. Boarding Schools

With a view to expanding social education and creating more favorable conditions for the all-round development of pupils and rendering assistance to the family in bringing them up, where the study and material base exists there shall be created extended day general education schools or extended day groups.

Boarding schools shall be created to the same ends for children and adolescents who do not have the requisite conditions for being brought up in the family.

Article 24. Children's Homes

Children's homes in which the maintenance of children and adolescents and their training and upbringing is ensured shall be organized for children deprived of parental care.

Article 25. Special General Education Schools and Boarding Schools

For children and adolescents requiring prolonged care, general education therapeutic sanitary and forestry schools shall be organized, and teaching exercises in hospitals, sanatoriums, and at home shall be carried on with them.

For children and adolescents who have physical or mental defects which prevent their being trained in an ordinary general education school, and also for those requiring special conditions for education, special general education schools and boarding schools shall be organized which provide them training, education, care, and preparation for socially useful labor.

Article 26. Secondary General Education Schools for Working Youth

Secondary general education evening (or shift) and correspondence schools shall be organized for persons working in various branches of the national economy and not having a secondary education.

Enterprises, institutions, and organizations shall be obliged to promote the involvement of working youth in evening schools and to create the necessary conditions for combining work with training and for the normal activity of such schools and the exercises for pupils.

Article 27. Certificate of Eight-Year Education and Certificate of Secondary Education

Persons who have completed eight grades shall be issued a certificate of eight-year education which gives the right to enter the ninth grade of a general education school, professional-technical, or secondary specialized educational institution.

Persons who have completed secondary general education school shall be issued a certificate of secondary education.

Persons who have completed a secondary general education school with production training shall be issued a certificate of secondary education and a certificate for the specialization obtained, specifying the rank conferred by the qualification commission.

Article 28. Awarding of Gold Medal and Honorary Certificate to Persons Who Have Completed Secondary General Education Schools

Persons who have especially distinguished themselves and who have completed a secondary general education school shall be awarded the gold medal "For Outstanding Success in Study, Labor, and Model Conduct", and those who have attained special success in individual subjects shall be awarded an honorary certificate "For Special Success in the Study of Individual Subjects".

Section V. Extracurricular Education

Article 29. Extracurricular Institutions

With a view to the all-round development of the capacities and inclinations of pupils, nurturing social activeness, an interest in labor, science, technology, art, sport, military affairs, and also organizing the culture leisure time and strengthening their health, state enterprises, institutions, and organizations, collective farms, cooperative, trade union, komsomol, and other social organizations shall create Palaces or Houses of Pioneers, stations for young technicians, young naturalists, young tourists, children's libraries, sport, art, and music schools, pioneer camps, and other extracurricular institutions.

Section VI. Professional-Technical Education

Article 30. Professional-Technical Educational Institutions

Professional-technical educational institutions shall be the basic school for the professional-technical education of youth and forming the worthy replenishment of the working class.

Citizens of the USSR who have completed an eight-year or secondary general education school shall be admitted to professional-technical educational institutions (or professional schools).

Admission to professional-technical educational institutions shall be in accordance with the rules confirmed by the State Committee of the USSR Council of Ministers for Professional-Technical Education.

Professional-technical educational institutions shall carry out their activity on the basis of Statutes confirmed by the USSR Council of Ministers.

Article 31. Principal Tasks of Professional-Technical Educational Institutions

The principal tasks of professional-technical educational institutions shall be:

the training for the national economy of all-round developed, technically educated, and cultured young qualified workers possessing a professional skill responding to the requirements of modern production, scientific-technical progress, and the prospects for their development;

carrying out the professional and general secondary education of youth in secondary professional-technical schools;

the formation in pupils of a Marxist-Leninist world outlook, nurturing in them high moral qualities, socialist internationalism, Soviet patriotism, a communist attitude toward labor, and social ownership, and a readiness to care for and augment the revolutionary and labor traditions of the working class;

the esthetic and physical upbringing of pupils, strengthening their health, and training them to protect the socialist Motherland.

Article 32. Interrelationships of Professional-Technical Educational Institutions with Base Enterprises, Institutions, and Organizations

Professional-technical educational institutions shall specialize in training worker cadres by branches of the national economy and shall carry on their work on the base of appropriate enterprises, institutions, and organizations.

The mutual relations of professional-technical educational institutions with base enterprises, institutions, and organizations, and also the duties of ministries, departments, enterprises, institutions, and organizations for the creation and further strengthening of the study and material base and ensuring the necessary conditions for successful work with such educational institutions shall be determined in the procedure established by the USSR Council of Ministers.

Article 33. Training and Raising Qualifications of Workers Directly in Production

Evening (or shift) professional-technical schools, and also courses, study-course combinations, and other forms of training and raising the qualifications directly in production shall be organized for youth beginning in production after completing a general education school and for persons working in the national economy and wishing to receive a new profession or raise their qualifications.

Enterprises, institutions, and organizations shall create the necessary conditions and production training base for carrying on theoretical and practical study when training and raising the qualifications of workers directly in production.

Article 34. Conferment of Qualification, Issuance of Certificate and Diploma

The appropriate qualification (or rank, class, category) by profession shall be conferred on persons who have completed professional-technical educational institutions, and a certificate of the established form issued, and a certificate with distinction issued to those who have achieved special successes in study with exemplary conduct.

A diploma concerning the conferment of a qualification by profession and of receiving a secondary education shall be issued to persons who have completed secondary professional-technical schools, and a diploma with distinction to those who have especially distinguished themselves.

Production ranks, classes, categories conferred on persons who have completed professional-technical educational institutions shall be binding upon all enterprises, institutions, and organizations of the USSR.

A certificate of uniform form concerning the specialization received and the rank, class, or category conferred shall be issued to persons who have been trained in a new profession or whose qualification has been raised directly in production and who have successfully taken a qualification examination.

Section VII. Secondary Specialized Education

Article 35. Secondary Specialized Educational Institutions

Secondary specialized education shall be carried out in technical schools, schools, and other educational institutions relegated in the established procedure to secondary specialized educational institutions.

Day, evening, and correspondence study may be carried on in secondary specialized educational institutions.

Study in secondary specialized educational institutions without interrupting production shall be the form for receiving a specialization and raising qualifications by persons who work in various branches of the national economy.

Secondary specialized educational institutions shall carry out their activity on the basis of the Statute on Secondary Specialized Educational Institutions of the USSR confirmed by the USSR Council of Ministers and charters which are worked out in accordance with the said Statute by each secondary specialized educational institution and confirmed by the ministry or department to which the secondary specialized educational institution is subordinate.

Article 36. Principal Tasks of Secondary Specialized Educational Institutions

The principal tasks of secondary specialized educational institutions shall be:

the training of qualified specialists with a secondary specialized or general secondary education who have the necessary theoretical knowledge and practical skills in a specialization, who are brought up in the ideas of Marxism-Leninism, and who possess the skills of organizing mass political and educational work;

the constant improvement of the quality of training specialists, taking into account the requirements of modern production, science, technology, culture, and prospects for their development;

nurturing in pupils high moral qualities, a communist attitude toward labor, and social ownership, culture, socialist internationalism, Soviet patriotism, readiness to defend the socialist Motherland; physical training of pupils.

Article 37. Right to Admission to Secondary Specialized Educational Institutions

Citizens of the USSR having an eight-year or secondary education shall enjoy the right to admission to secondary specialized educational institutions. Admission to secondary specialized institutions shall be in accordance with rules confirmed by the USSR Ministry of Higher and Secondary Specialized Education.

Article 38. Practice of Pupils of Secondary Specialized Educational Institutions

Practice of pupils of secondary specialized educational institutions shall be an integral part of the training and educational process, as a result of which the pupils obtain work skills as specialists, and for technical and agricultural specializations, also a qualification for one of the workers' professions.

Practice for pupils shall be carried out in accordance with a Statute on Practice for Pupils of Secondary Specialized Educational Institutions confirmed by the USSR Ministry of Higher and Secondary Specialized Education.

Article 39. Conferment of Qualifications and Issuance of Diploma

A qualification shall be conferred on persons who have completed secondary specialized educational institutions in accordance with the specialization obtained, and a diploma or lapel pin of the established form shall be issued.

A diploma with distinction shall be issued to persons who have completed secondary specialized educational institutions and who have achieve great success in study and proved themselves in social work.

Section VIII. Higher Education

Article 40. Higher Educational Institutions

Higher education shall be carried out in universities, institutes, academies, and other educational institutions relegated in the established procedure to higher educational institutions.

Day, evening, and correspondence study may be carried out in higher educational institutions.

Study in higher educational institutions while continuing to work shall be the form of obtaining a specialization and raising qualifications for persons working in various branches of the national economy.

Higher educational institutions shall carry out their activity on the basis of the Statute on Higher Educational Institutions of the USSR, confirmed by the USSR Council of Ministers, and charters which shall be worked out in accordance with the said Statute for each higher educational institution and shall be confirmed by the ministry or department to which the higher educational institution is subordinate.

Article 41. Principal Tasks of Higher Educational Institutions

The principal tasks of higher educational institutions shall be:

the training of highly qualified specialists having a command of Marxist-Leninist theory, profound theoretical knowledge and practical skills in their specialization and in organizing mass-political and educational work;

nurturing in students high moral qualities, communist consciousness, culture, socialist internationalism, Soviet patriotism, readiness to defend the socialist Motherland; physical training of students;

the constant improvement of the quality of training specialists, taking into account the requirements of modern production, science, technology, and culture, and the prospects for their development;

the fulfillment of scientific research work which promotes the increased quality of training specialists and social and scientific-technical progress;

the creation of textbooks and study aids;

training of scientific-pedagogical cadres;

raising the qualifications of the pedagogical staff of higher and secondary educational institutions, and also of specialists with a higher education employed in the respective branches of the national economy.

Article 42. Right to Admission to Higher Educational Institutions

Citizens of the USSR having a secondary education shall enjoy the right to admission to a higher educational institution. Admission to higher educational institutions shall be in accordance with the rules confirmed by the USSR Ministry of Higher and Secondary Specialized Education.

Article 43. Practice for Students and Probation for Graduates of Higher Educational Institutions

Practice for students of higher educational institutions shall be an integral part of the training and educational process. Practice for students of higher educational institutions shall be carried out in accordance with the Statute on Practice, confirmed by the USSR Ministry of Higher and Secondary Specialized Education.

In order to improve practical skills, graduates of higher educational institutions shall pass through probation in their specialization under the direction of the administration of the respective enterprises, institutions, and organizations and under the control of higher educational institutions.

Article 44. Conferment of Qualification and Issuance of Diploma

A qualification shall be conferred on persons who have completed higher educational institutions in accordance with the specialization obtained, and a diploma or lapel pin of the established form shall be issued.

A diploma with distinction shall be issued to persons who have completed higher educational institutions and who have achieved great success in study and proved themselves in scientific and social work.

Article 45. Raising Qualifications of Specialists of the National Economy

Raising the qualifications of specialists of the national economy shall be carried out in the institutes for raising qualifications, at faculties and divisions of higher educational institutions, at scientific research institutes, at courses for raising qualifications, and at outstanding enterprises in the procedure determined by the USSR Council of Ministers.

Section IX. Rights and Duties of Pupils and Students

Article 46. Rights of Pupils and Students

Pupils and students shall have the right to use, free of charge, laboratories, study rooms, auditoriums, reading rooms, libraries, and other teaching and auxiliary study institutions, and also sport bases, installations, sport inventory, and other equipment of educational institutions.

Pupils and students shall, in the procedure established by legislation, be provided with stipends, grants, dormitories, boarding schools, medical assistance in educational institutions, and shall have the right to passage, concessionary or free of charge, on transport and other types of material assistance.

Pupils and students studying while continuing to work shall, in accordance with legislation, have the right to additional leave from their place of work, a reduced work week, and other exemptions.

Persons who have completed professional-technical, secondary specialized, and higher education institutions shall be provided with work in accordance with the specialization and qualification obtained.

Pupils and students shall have the right to take part through their social organizations in discussing questions for improving the learning process, ideological and educational work, and also questions of study progress, labor and study discipline, and other questions connected with the teaching and life of pupils and students.

Article 47. Duties of Pupils and Students

Pupils and students shall be obliged to systematically and profoundly gain a command of knowledge and practical skills, attend study exercises, fulfill assignments within the established periods provided in the teaching plan and syllabus, raise their ideological and cultural level, take part in socially useful labor and self-service, and observe the rules for internal order of the training and educational institution.

Pupils and students should be disciplined and organized, observe the rules of socialist community life, care for and strengthen socialist ownership, be intolerant of any antisocial manifestations, and take part in the social life of the collective.

Section X. Training of Pedagogical Cadres. Pedagogical Activity. Professional Rights and Duties of Public Education Workers

Article 48. Training of Pedagogical Cadres for Training and Educational Institutions

The training of pedagogical cadres for training and educational institutions shall be carried out in universities, institutes, and other higher education institutions, and, for individual specializations, also in secondary specialized educational institutions.

Article 49. Training of Scientific-Pedagogical and Scientific Cadres

Graduate study, organized in higher educational institutions and scientific research institutions, shall be the basic form for training scientific-pedagogical and scientific cadres.

Citizens of the USSR having a higher education shall be admitted to graduate study. A Statute on Graduate Study shall be confirmed in the procedure established by the USSR Council of Ministers.

Article 50. Engaging in Pedagogical Activity

Persons having the appropriate education and professional training shall be admitted to work in children's preschool and extracurricular institutions, general education schools, professional technical, secondary specialized, and higher educational institutions as teachers, educators, instructors, production training master craftsmen, and other pedagogical workers.

With a view to raising pedagogical skills and developing the creative initiative of teaching cadres, the certification of general education school teachers and production training master craftsmen and instructors of professional-technical educational institutions shall be carried out.

Vacant professorial and instructor posts of higher educational institutions shall be filled by competition in the established procedure for a specified term, the persons occupying such posts subsequently being reelected.

Persons who engage in pedagogical activity shall, in the event they are discovered not to conform to the post occupied as a consequence of the inadequate qualifications or state of health preventing the fulfillment of pedagogical and educational functions, and also in the event of committing an amoral offense not compatible with the continuation of pedagogical activity, be relieved from pedagogical work in the procedure established by USSR and union republic labor legislation.

Article 51. Professional Rights and Duties of Pedagogical Workers

The professional rights and duties of pedagogical workers of children's preschool institutions, secondary general education schools, extracurricular institutions, professional-technical, secondary specialized, and higher education institutions shall be determined by the present Fundamental Principles and acts of USSR and union republic legislation adopted in accordance therewith, and statutes and charters of the respective educational and training institutions.

Professional rights, honor, and dignity of teachers and other pedagogical workers shall be protected by law.

Article 52. Raising the Qualifications of Pedagogical Workers

Raising the qualifications of pedagogical workers shall be carried out in higher education institutions, institutes for the improvement of teachers, institutes for raising qualifications, scientific research institutions, progressive enterprises, and also courses for raising qualifications.

The training of executive workers of secondary general education schools, professional-technical, secondary specialized, and other educational institutions shall be carried out by persons with a higher education and pedagogical work experience.

The implementation of measures to improve professional knowledge of pedagogical workers shall be carried by the respective public education agencies.

Article 53. Ensuring Conditions for Pedagogical and Other Public Education Workers to Fulfill Professional Duties

Executive committees of local soviets of working people's deputies, public education agencies and institutions, and ministries and departments shall ensure the creation of the necessary conditions for pedagogical and other public education workers for successful work and the systematic raising of qualifications, grant them the exemptions and privileges established by law, and also display constant concern for maintaining the authority of pedagogical workers, the proper use of their labor and work time, without allowing these persons to be drawn away from executing their real duties.

Article 54. Exemptions and Privileges

In accordance with legislation, public education workers shall enjoy extended leaves paid at state expense, dwelling space with heating and lighting free of charge in a rural locality, pension security privileges, and other exemptions and privileges.

Article 55. Incentives for Public Education Workers for Special Services

For special services in training and educating the rising generation and in training specialists, public education workers shall be recommended in the established procedure:

for the awarding of orders and medals of the USSR;

for the awarding of inscribed medals, and medals and decorations of distinction established for public education workers by USSR and union republic legislation;

for the conferment of honorary titles of the USSR and union republic honorary titles.

Section XI. Rights and Duties of Parents and Persons Replacing Them in Bringing Up and Training Children

Article 56. Rights of Parents and Persons Replacing Them

Parents and persons replacing them shall have the right to:

enroll children for upbringing and training in children's preschool institutions and general education schools at their place of residence, and also in professional-technical or secondary specialized educational institutions;

take part in discussing questions of the training and upbringing of children, and in carrying on homework, extracurricular, and therapeutic work in training and educational institutions where their children are being trained and brought up;

elect and be elected to parents' social committees (or councils) attached to schools and other educational and training institutions.

Article 57. Duties of Parents and Persons Replacing Them

Parents and persons replacing them shall be obliged to:

bring up children in the spirit of high communist morality and an attitude of care toward socialist ownership, inculcate labor skills, and train them for socially useful activity, and be concerned for their physical development and for strengthening the health of children;

enroll children in school when they attain school age and ensure the attendance of pupils of educational institutions without allowing lapses in exercises without justifiable reasons;

create the necessary conditions for the timely receiving of secondary education and professional training for children.

The upbringing in the family shall be organically combined with the educational work of educational institutions, preschool and extracurricular institutions, and social organizations.

Article 58. Dissemination of Pedagogical Knowledge Among the Populace

Public education agencies and institutions shall, jointly with agencies and institutions of science and culture, pedagogical societies, and other social organizations, ensure the dissemination of pedagogical knowledge among the populace and render pedagogical assistance to parents and persons replacing them in bringing up children and adolescents.

Section XII. Study and Material Base for Public Education Institutions

Article 59. Conditions for Opening Training and Educational Institutions

Training and educational institutions may be opened only if there exist the appropriate buildings, study equipment, and pedagogical cadres.

Article 60. Use of Buildings of Training and Educational Institutions

Buildings of training and educational institutions shall be used only for their express designation.

Article 61. Development of the Study and Material Base of Public Education Institutions

The study and material base of public education institutions shall be developed from assets of the state budget, and also capital investments provided in the national economic plan. Assets of enterprises, collective farms, cooperative, and other organizations may, with their consent, also be used for such purposes.

Buildings of educational and training institutions should be built according to designs confirmed in the established procedure.

Article 62. Participation of Enterprises, Institutions, and Organizations in Strengthening the Study and Material Base of Educational and Training Institutions

State enterprises, institutions, and organizations, collective farms, cooperative, trade union, komsomol, and other social organizations shall take part in the established procedure in strengthening the study and material base of training and educational institutions.

Section XIII. Responsibility for Violation of Legislation on Public Education

Article 63. Responsibility for Violation of Legislation on Public Education

Officials and citizens who have allowed a violation of legislation on universal compulsory eight-year education, on the separation of school from the church, or other violations of legislation in the domain of public education, shall bear the responsibility established by USSR and union republic legislation.

Section XIV. Right of Foreign Citizens and Stateless Persons to Receive Education in the USSR. International Treaties and Agreements

Article 64. Right of Foreign Citizens and Stateless Persons to Receive Education in the USSR

Foreign citizens and stateless persons residing on the territory of the USSR shall have the right to receive education in the USSR on the same basis as Soviet citizens in accordance with the procedure established by USSR legislation.

Article 65. International Treaties and Agreements

If an international treaty or international agreement in which the USSR participates has established other rules than those which are contained in USSR and union republic legislation on public education, then the rules of the international treaty or international agreement shall be applied.

CHAPTER XIV

CRIMINAL LAW, CRIMINAL PROCEDURE, AND PENOLOGY

FUNDAMENTAL PRINCIPLES OF CRIMINAL LEGISLATION OF THE USSR AND UNION REPUBLICS

[Confirmed by Law of the USSR, December 25, 1958, as amended May 18, 1961, April 4, 1962, July 11, 1969, May 18, 1972, March 9, 1973, April 11, 1974, April 25, 1974, February 8, 1977, and February 15, 1977. Vedomosti SSSR (1959), no. 1, item 6; (1961), no. 21, item 222; (1962), no. 14, item 147; (1969), no. 29, item 249; (1972), no. 22, item 176; (1973), no. 11, item 157; (1974), no. 16, item 245; no. 18, item 275; (1977), no. 7, item 116; no. 8, item 137]

Section I. General Provisions

Article 1. Tasks of Soviet Criminal Legislation

Criminal legislation of the USSR and union republics shall have as its tasks the protection of the Soviet social and state system, socialist ownership, the person and rights of citizens, and the entire socialist legal order from criminal infringements.

In order to carry out these tasks the criminal legislation of the USSR and union republics shall determine which socially dangerous acts are criminal and shall establish the punishments which are applicable to persons who have committed crimes.

Article 2. Criminal Legislation of the USSR and Union Republics

Criminal legislation of the USSR and union republics shall consist of the present Fundamental Principles, which determine the principles and establish the general provisions of USSR and union republic criminal legislation, all-union laws, which provide responsibility for individual crimes, and the union republic criminal codes.

All-union criminal laws shall determine responsibility for crimes against the state and military crimes and, when necessary, also for other crimes directed against the interests of the USSR.

Article 3. Bases of Criminal Responsibility

Only a person who is guilty of committing a crime, that is, who intentionally or negligently committed a socially dangerous act provided for by a criminal law, shall be subject to criminal responsibility and punishment.

Criminal punishment shall be applied only by judgment of a court.

Article 4. Operation of Criminal Laws of the USSR and Union Republics with Respect to Acts Committed on the Territory of the USSR

All persons who have committed crimes on the territory of the USSR shall be subject to responsibility according to the criminal laws operating at the place where the crime was committed.

The question of the criminal responsibility of diplomatic representatives of foreign states and other citizens who according to prevailing laws and international agreements are not within the jurisdiction, for criminal cases, of Soviet judicial institutions, in the event such persons commit a crime on the territory of the USSR, shall be settled by diplomatic means.

Article 5. Operation of Criminal Laws of the USSR and Union Republics with Respect to Acts Committed Beyond the Limits of the USSR

Citizens of the USSR who have committed a crime abroad shall be subject to criminal responsibility according to the criminal laws operating in the union republic on whose territory they are brought to criminal responsibility or are brought to trial.

Stateless persons who have committed crimes beyond the limits of the USSR and who are situated in the USSR shall bear responsibility on the same grounds.

If the said persons have undergone punishment abroad for the crimes committed, the court may accordingly mitigate the punishment assigned by them or completely relieve the guilty person from serving the punishment.

Foreigners shall be subject to responsibility according to Soviet criminal laws for crimes committed beyond the limits of the USSR in instances provided for by international agreements.

Article 6. Operation of a Criminal Law in Time

The criminality and punishability of an act shall be determined by a law which prevailed at the time this act was committed.

A law eliminating the punishability of an act or mitigating punishment shall have retroactive force, that is, also shall extend to those acts committed before its issuance.

A law establishing the punishability of an act or increasing a punishment shall not have retroactive force.

Section II. On Crime

Article 7. Concept of Crime

A socially dangerous act (an action or omission to act) infringing the Soviet social or state system, socialist system of the economy, socialist ownership, the person, political, labor, property, and other rights of citizens, and also any other socially dangerous act infringing the socialist legal order which is provided for by a criminal law, shall be deemed a crime.

An action or an omission to act shall not be a crime, even though it formally contains the indicia of an act provided for by a criminal law, if by virtue of its insignificance it does not represent a social danger.

Article 7-1. Concept of a Grave Crime

The intentional acts enumerated in the second paragraph of the present Article and representing a higher social danger shall be deemed grave crimes.

There shall be relegated to grave crimes: especially dangerous crimes against the state; banditism; actions disrupting the work of correctional labor institutions; smuggling; mass disorders; damaging routes of communication and means of transport; making or passing counterfeit money or securities; violation of rules for currency transactions and speculation in currencies or securities under aggravating circumstances; stealing of state or social property on an especially large scale; stealing of state or social property committed by open stealing under aggravating circumstances; assault with intent to rob; intentional destruction or damaging of state or social property or the personal property of citizens committed under aggravating circumstances; intentional homicide (except homicide when exceeding the limits of necessary defense or in a state of strong mental agitation); intentional grave bodily injury (except grave bodily injury when exceeding the limits of necessary defense or in a state of strong mental agitation); rape; speculation under aggravating circumstances; abuse of authority or official position under aggravating circumstances; giving a bribe or acting as an intermediary in bribery under aggravating circumstances; taking a bribe; instituting criminal proceedings against a person known to be innocent under aggravating circumstances; rendering a judgment, decision, ruling, or decree known to be unjust which entails grave consequences; compelling to give testimony under aggravating circumstances; infringement against the life of a policeman or people's guard; malicious or especially malicious hooliganism; hijacking an aircraft; stealing of firearms, ammunition, or explosives; stealing of narcotics under aggravating circumstances, and also the sale or stealing committed for the purpose of sale, manufacture, acquisition, keeping, carriage, or sending of such substances; insubordination under aggravating circumstances; resisting of superior or compelling him to violate official duties; forcible actions against superior; desertion; intentional destruction or damaging of military property under aggravating circumstances; violation of rules for performing combat lookout under aggravating circumstances.

Article 8. Commission of a Crime Intentionally

A crime shall be deemed to be committed intentionally if the person who committed it was conscious of the socially dangerous character of his action or omission to act, foresaw its socially dangerous consequences, and desired them or consciously allowed these consequences to occur.

Article 9. Commission of a Crime Through Negligence

A crime shall be deemed to be committed through negligence if the person who committed it foresaw the possibility of the occurrence of the socially dangerous consequences of his action or omission to act but frivolously counted on their being averted or did not foresee the possibility of the occurrence of such consequences although he should and could have foreseen them.

Article 10. Responsibility of Minors

Persons who have attained 16 years of age before the commission of a crime shall be subject to criminal responsibility.

Persons who have committed a crime at an age of 14 to 16 years shall be subject to criminal responsibility only for homicide, intentional infliction of grave bodily injuries causing impairment of health, rape, assault with intent to rob, theft, malicious hooliganism, intentional destruction or damaging of state or social property or personal property of citizens entailing grave consequences, and also for the intentional commission of actions which might cause a train wreck.

If a court finds that the reform of a person who has committed a crime at an age of under 18 years which does not represent great social danger is possible without applying criminal punishment, it may apply compulsory measures of an educational character which are not a criminal punishment to this person.

Types of compulsory measures of an educational character and the procedure for applying them shall be established by union republic legislation.

Article 11. Nonimputability

A person shall not be subject to criminal responsibility who at the time of committing a socially dangerous act was in a state of nonimputability, that is, could not account for his actions or direct them as a consequence of a chronic mental illness, temporary mental derangement, feeble-mindedness, or other state of illness. Compulsory measures of a medical character established by union republic legislation may be applied to such a person by designation of a court.

A person also shall not be subject to punishment who has committed a crime in a state of imputability but before a court renders judgment has become mentally ill, depriving him of the possibility to account for his actions or direct them. Compulsory measures of a medical character may be applied to such a person by designation of a court, but upon recovery he may be subject to punishment.

Article 12. Responsibility for a Crime Committed in a State of Intoxication

A person who committed a crime in a state of intoxication shall not be relieved of criminal responsibility.

Article 13. Necessary Defense

An action shall not be a crime, even though it falls within the indicia of an act provided for by a criminal law but was committed in a state of necessary defense, that is, when protecting the interests of the Soviet state, social interests, the person or the rights of the defender or other person from a socially dangerous infringement by causing harm to the infringer, provided that the limits of necessary defense were not exceeded.

The limits of necessary defense shall be deemed to be exceeded if the defense is clearly not in conformity with the character and danger of the infringement.

Article 14. Extreme Necessity

An action shall not be a crime, even though it falls within the indicia of an act provided for by a criminal law but was committed in a state of extreme necessity, that is, in order to eliminate a danger threatening the interests of the Soviet state, social interests, the person or rights of the particular person or other citizens, unless in the particular circumstances this danger could be eliminated by other means and if the harm caused is less significant than the harm prevented.

Article 15. Responsibility for the Preparation of a Crime and for Attempted Crime

Finding or adapting the means or instruments or other intentional creation of the conditions to commit a crime shall be deemed to be the preparation of a crime.

An intentional action expressly directed toward the commission of a crime shall be deemed to be an attempted crime unless the crime was not brought to completion for reasons independent of the will of the guilty person.

Punishment for the preparation of a crime and for an attempted crime shall be assigned according to the law providing responsibility for the particular crime. When assigning punishment, the court shall take into account the character and degree of social danger of the action committed by the guilty person, the degree to which the criminal intention is realized, and the reasons by virtue of which the crime was not brought to completion.

Article 16. Voluntary Refusal to Commit a Crime

A person who voluntarily refused to bring a crime to completion shall be subject to responsibility only in the event that the act which he actually committed contains the constituent elements of another crime.

Article 17. Complicity

The intentional joint participation of two or more persons in the commission of a crime shall be deemed complicity.

The organizers, instigators, and accessories, together with the perpetrators, shall be deemed to be accomplices.

The person who directly committed a crime shall be deemed the perpetrator.

The person who organized the commission of a crime or directed its commission shall be deemed to be an organizer.

The person who incited the commission of the crime shall be deemed to be an instigator.

The person who furthered the commission of a crime by advice, instructions, providing the means or eliminating obstacles, and also a person who beforehand promised to conceal the criminal, the instruments and means of committing the crime, traces of the crime, or articles obtained by criminal means, shall be deemed to be an accessory.

The degree and character of participation of each of the accomplices in the commission of a crime should be taken into account by a court when assigning punishment.

Article 18. Concealment

The concealment of a criminal not promised beforehand, and also of the instruments and means for committing a crime, traces of the crime, or articles obtained by criminal means, shall entail responsibility only in the instances specially provided for by a criminal law.

Article 19. Failure to Report

The failure to report a crime reliably known to have been prepared or committed shall entail criminal responsibility only in the instances specially provided for by a criminal law.

Section III. On Punishment

Article 20. Purposes of Punishment

Punishment shall not only be a chastisement for a crime committed but also shall have the purpose of the reform and re-education of convicted persons in the spirit of an honorable attitude toward labor, strict execution of the laws, respect for the rules of socialist community life, and also prevention of the commission of new crimes both by the convicted persons and by other persons.

Punishment shall not have the purpose of causing physical suffering or lowering human dignity.

Article 21. Types of Punishment

The following basic punishments may be applied to persons who have committed a crime:

(1) deprivation of freedom;

(2) exile;

(3) banishment;

(4) correctional tasks without deprivation of freedom;

(5) deprivation of the right to occupy particular posts or engage in a particular activity;

(6) fine;

(7) social censure.

Punishment in the form of being sent to a disciplinary battalion also may be applied to military servicemen on active service.

In addition to the basic punishments, the following supplementary punishments may be applied to convicted persons:

confiscation of property;

deprivation of military or special rank.

Banishment, exile, deprivation of the right to occupy particular posts or engage in a particular activity, and a fine may be applied not only as basic, but also as supplementary, punishments.

Other types of punishment, besides those specified in the present Article, may be established in accordance with the principles and general provisions of the present Fundamental Principles by union republic legislation.

Article 22. Death Penalty: Exceptional Measure of Punishment

As an exceptional measure of punishment, until its complete abolition the application of the death penalty -- by shooting -- shall be permitted for crimes against the state in the instances provided for by the Law of the USSR "On Criminal Responsibility for Crimes Against the State", for intentional homicide under aggravating circumstances specified in articles of USSR and union republic criminal laws which establish responsibility for intentional homicide, and in individual instances specially provided for by USSR legislation, also for certain other especially grave crimes.

Persons may not be condemned to the death penalty who have not attained eighteen years of age before the crime was committed, nor women who were pregnant at the time the crime was committed or at the moment judgment is rendered. The death penalty may not be applied to a woman who is pregnant at the moment the judgment is executed.

Article 23. Deprivation of Freedom

Deprivation of freedom shall be established for a term not exceeding ten years, and for especially grave crimes, for crimes entailing especially grave consequences, and for especially dangerous recidivists in the instances provided for by USSR and union republic legislation, not exceeding fifteen years.

When assigning punishment to a person who had not attained 18 years of age before the commission of a crime, the term of deprivation of freedom may not exceed ten years.

The serving of a punishment in the form of deprivation of freedom shall, by judgment of a court, be designated in correctional labor colonies or settlements for persons who have committed a crime through negligence and colonies of general, reinforced, strict, and special regimes or in a prison, and also in educational labor colonies of general and reinforced regimes.

Serving a punishment in correctional labor colonies shall be designated for men:

sentenced for the first time to deprivation of freedom for a term not exceeding five years for crimes committed through negligence: in colonies and settlements for persons who have committed crimes through negligence;

sentenced for the first time to deprivation of freedom for intentional crimes which are not grave or sentenced for the first time to deprivation of freedom for a term not exceeding three years for grave crimes, and also sentenced for the first time to deprivation of freedom for a term exceeding five years for crimes committed through negligence: in colonies of general regime;

sentenced for the first time to deprivation of freedom for a term exceeding three years for grave crimes: in colonies of reinforced regime;

sentenced for especially dangerous crimes against the state or who has previously served a punishment in the form of deprivation of freedom: in colonies of strict regime;

deemed especially dangerous recidivists: in colonies of special regime.

Serving a punishment in correctional labor colonies shall be designated for women sentenced to deprivation of freedom: deemed especially dangerous recidivists, and also sentenced for especially dangerous crimes against the state: in colonies of strict regime; sentenced for the first time for a term not exceeding five years for crimes committed through negligence: in colonies or settlements for persons who committed crimes through negligence; other women sentenced to deprivation of freedom: in colonies of general regime.

Serving a punishment in educational labor colonies shall be designated for:

minors of the male sex sentenced for the first time to deprivation of freedom for crimes which are not grave or sentenced for the first time to deprivation of freedom for a term not exceeding three years for grave crimes, and also minors of the female sex: in colonies of general regime;

minors of the male sex who have previously served punishment in the form of deprivation of freedom, and also sentenced to deprivation of freedom for a term exceeding three years for grave crimes: in colonies of reinforced regime.

Depending on the character and degree of social danger of the crime committed, the personality of the guilty person, and other circumstances of the case, a court may, specifying the reasons for the decision taken, designate the serving of deprivation of freedom for a person sentenced for the first time to deprivation of freedom for a term not exceeding ten years for crimes committed through negligence: in colonies or settlements for persons who committed crimes through negligence; sentenced but not deemed especially dangerous recidivists: in correctional labor colonies of any type except colonies of special regime; and sentenced minors of the male sex: in educational labor colonies of general regime instead of colonies of reinforced regime.

Deprivation of freedom in the form of confinement in a prison for the entire term of punishment or part thereof may be assigned to:

especially dangerous recidivists;

persons who upon attaining eighteen years of age have committed especially dangerous crimes against the state;

persons who upon attaining eighteen years of age have committed other grave crimes for which they are sentenced to deprivation of freedom for a term exceeding five years.

The type of correctional labor institution designated for a convicted person shall be changed by a court on the grounds and in the procedure established by USSR and union republic legislation.

Article 23-1. Especially Dangerous Recidivist

There may be deemed an especially dangerous recidivist by a judgment of a court:

(1) a person previously sentenced to deprivation of freedom for an especially dangerous crime against the state; banditism; making or passing counterfeit money or securities under aggravating circumstances; violation of rules for currency transactions under aggravating circumstances; stealing of state or social property in especially large amounts; assault with intent to rob with a view to taking possession of state or social property or personal property of citizens under aggravating circumstances; intentional homicide (except homicide when exceeding the limits of necessary defense or in a state of strong mental agitation, and also homicide by a mother of a newly born child); rape committed by a group of persons or entailing especially grave consequences, and also rape of a minor; infringement on the life of a police worker or people's guard in connection with their official or social activity to protect public order; hijacking an aircraft or committing anew any of the enumerated crimes for which he is sentenced to deprivation of freedom for a term of not less than five years;

(2) a person twice previously, in any sequence, sentenced to deprivation of freedom for an especially dangerous crime against the state; banditism; mass disorders; making or passing counterfeit money or securities, violation of rules for currency transactions; stealing of state or social property under aggravating circumstances (except petty stealing); assault with intent to rob with a view to taking possession of state or social property or the personal property of citizens; intentional homicide (except homicide when exceeding the limits of necessary defense or in a state

of strong mental agitation, and also homicide by a mother of her newly born child); intentional grave bodily injury (except grave bodily injury when exceeding the limits of necessary defense or in a state of strong mental agitation); rape; theft; open stealing or swindling committed under aggravating circumstances; speculation under aggravating circumstances; taking bribes; infringement on the life of a police worker or people's guard in connection with their official or social activity to protect public order; especially malicious hooliganism; hijacking an aircraft; stealing a firearm, ammunition, or explosives under aggravating circumstances; stealing, making, acquiring, keeping, carriage, or sending of narcotics with a view to marketing, marketing such substances, and also stealing them under aggravating circumstances or committing anew any of the enumerated crimes for which he is sentenced to deprivation of freedom for a term exceeding three years;

(3) a person three times or more, in any sequence, sentenced to deprivation of freedom for malicious hooliganism or for crimes enumerated in point 2 of the first paragraph of the present Article for which he is sentenced to deprivation of freedom.

(4) a person serving punishment in the form of deprivation of freedom for any of the crimes enumerated in point 2 and 3 of the present Article who commits again an intentional crime for which he is sentenced to deprivation of freedom for a term of not less than five years.

In considering the question of whether to deem a person to be an especially dangerous recidivist, a court shall take into account the personality of the guilty person, the degree of social danger of the crimes committed, their motives, the degree of realizing criminal intentions, the degree and character of participation in the commission of the crimes and other circumstances of the case. The decision of the court should be reasoned in the judgment.

When deciding the question of whether to deem a person to be an especially dangerous recidivist, account shall not be taken of a conviction for a crime committed by this person before he was eighteen years of age, and also a conviction which was canceled or removed in the procedure established by law.

The deeming of a person to be an especially dangerous recidivist shall be rescinded when canceling his conviction.

The articles of the USSR and union republic criminal laws providing responsibility for the commission of a crime by an especially dangerous recidivist shall be applied in instances when the person was deemed an especially dangerous recidivist in the procedure established by law before the commission of the particular crime.

Article 23-2. Conditional Sentence to Deprivation of Freedom with Compulsory Enlistment of the Convicted Person for Labor

When assigning punishment to an able-bodied person who has attained majority sentenced for the first time to deprivation of freedom for an intentional crime for a term of up to three years, and for a crime committed through negligence, for a term of up to five years, a court may, taking into account the character and degree of social danger of the crime committed, the personality of the guilty person and other circumstances of the case, and also the possibility of his reform and re-education without isolation from society but under conditions of exercising supervision over him, decree a conditional sentence of this person to deprivation of freedom with compulsory enlistment of him for labor for the period of the assigned punishment in places determined by agencies which execute the judgment, specifying the reasons for this decision in the judgment.

In the event of a conditional sentence to deprivation of freedom with compulsory enlistment of the convicted person for labor, he also may be assigned supplementary measures of punishment by a court in the instances and in the procedure provided for by USSR and union republic legislation. The rules of Article 38, paragraph three, of the present Fundamental Principles shall not apply with regard to such convicted persons.

A conditional sentence to deprivation of freedom with compulsory enlistment of the convicted person for labor shall not be applied to:

(1) persons sentenced for an especially dangerous crime against the state; banditism; intentional homicide (except homicide when exceeding the limits of necessary defense or in a state of strong mental agitation); intentional grave bodily injury (except grave bodily injury when exceeding the limits of necessary defense or in a state of strong mental agitation); rape committed by a group of persons or entailing especially grave consequences, and also rape of a minor; especially malicious hooliganism;

(2) persons to whom, together with punishment for a crime committed, there are assigned measures of compulsory treatment for alcoholism or narcotics addiction, and also who have not undergone the full course of treatment for a venereal disease;

(3) convicted foreigners and stateless persons.

If a conditionally sentenced person avoids work in the place determined by agencies executing the judgment or systematically or maliciously violates labor discipline, public order, or rules of residence established therefor, he shall be sent by ruling of a court to serve deprivation of freedom assigned by the judgment. The time for which work was avoided shall not be counted, but the time during which the convicted person worked may be counted by the court partially or wholly, day by day, toward the term for serving punishment.

If a conditionally sentenced person committed an intentional crime during the term of deprivation of freedom determined by a court for which he is sentenced to deprivation of freedom, the court shall assign punishment to him according to the rules provided for by Article 36 of the present Fundamental Principles.

Article 24. Exile and Banishment

Exile shall consist of the removal of a convicted person from his place of residence with obligatory settlement in a specific locality.

Banishment shall consist of the removal of a convicted person from his place of residence with a prohibition against living in specific localities.

Exile and banishment both as a basic and as a supplementary punishment may be assigned for a term not exceeding five years.

Exile and banishment as a supplementary punishment may be applied only in the instances specially specified in a law.

Exile and banishment shall not be applied to persons who have not attained 18 years of age before the commission of a crime. Exile shall also not be applied to pregnant women and to women having dependent children under eight years of age.

The procedure, places, and conditions for serving exile, and also the procedure and conditions for banishment, shall be established by USSR and union republic legislation.

Article 25. Correctional Tasks Without Deprivation of Freedom

Correctional tasks without deprivation of freedom shall be assigned for a term of up to one year and shall be served either at the convicted person's place of work or other places in the convicted person's district of residence. A deduction from the wages of a person sentenced to correctional tasks without deprivation of freedom shall be made for the revenue of the state in an amount established by judgment of the court, but not exceeding 20%.

In the event of the malicious evasion of serving punishment by a person sentenced to correctional tasks without deprivation of freedom, the court may replace the unserved term of correctional tasks by punishment in the form of deprivation of freedom for the same term.

The procedure for serving correctional tasks without deprivation of freedom shall be established by USSR and union republic legislation.

Article 26. Deprivation of the Right to Occupy Specified Posts or to Engage in a Specified Activity

Deprivation of the right to occupy a specified post or to engage in a specified activity may be assigned by a court for a term of up to five years as a basic or supplementary punishment.

This punishment may be assigned in instances when, by virtue of the character of the crimes committed by the guilty person in his post or when engaging in a specified activity, a court deems it impossible to preserve his right to hold a specified post or engage in a specified activity.

Article 27. Fine

A fine is a monetary sanction imposed by a court in the instances and within the limits established by a law.

The amount of a fine shall be established depending on the gravity of the crime committed, taking into account the financial position of the guilty person.

Replacement of a fine by deprivation of freedom and of deprivation of freedom by a fine shall not be permitted.

Article 28. Social Censure

Social censure shall consist of a public expression by a court of censure of a guilty person, bringing this, when necessary, to the information of the public through the press or other means.

Article 29. Sending Military Servicemen Who Have Committed a Crime to a Disciplinary Battalion and Replacement of Correctional Tasks by Detention in a Guardhouse

Military servicemen on active duty who have committed a crime may be sent to a disciplinary battalion for a term of from three months to two years in the instances provided for by law, and also in those instances when a court, taking into account the circumstances of the case and the personality of the convicted person, finds it advisable to send him to a disciplinary battalion for a term of up to two years in place of deprivation of freedom for the same term.

Correctional tasks without deprivation of freedom shall be replaced for military servicemen by confinement in a guardhouse for a term of up to two months.

Article 30. Confiscation of Property

Confiscation of property shall consist of the compulsory seizure for state ownership, without compensation, of all or part of the property which is the personal ownership of the convicted person.

Confiscation of property may be assigned only in the instances provided for by USSR legislation, and for mercenary crimes, also in the instances provided for by union republic legislation.

The procedure for applying confiscation of property, a list of articles not subject to confiscation which are necessary for the convicted person himself and persons dependent on him, and also the conditions and procedure for satisfying claims from the confiscated property relating to obligations of the convicted person shall be established by union republic legislation.

Article 31. Deprivation of Military and Other Ranks, and Also Orders, Medals, and Honorary Titles

When convicted for a grave crime, a person having a military or special rank may be deprived of this rank by judgment of a court.

When convicting for a grave crime a person awarded an order or medal or having an honorary title conferred by the Presidium of the USSR Supreme Soviet, the Presidium of a union or autonomous republic supreme soviet, or a military or other rank conferred by the Presidium of the USSR Supreme Soviet or USSR Council of Ministers, the court in rendering judgment shall decide the question of the advisability of recommending to the agency which awarded the order or medal to the convicted person or conferred a title on him that the convicted person be deprived of the order or medal or honorary military or other title.

Section IV. On Assignment of Punishment and On Relief from Punishment

Article 32. General Principles for Assignment of Punishment

A court shall assign punishment within the limits established by articles of a law providing responsibility for a crime committed in exact conformity with the provisions of the present Fundamental Principles and union republic criminal code. When assigning punishment, a court, being guided by a socialist legal consciousness, shall take into account the character and degree of social danger of the crime committed, the personality of the guilty person, and the circumstances of the case mitigating or aggravating responsibility.

Article 33. Circumstances Mitigating Responsibility

When assigning punishment, the circumstances mitigating responsibility shall be deemed to be:

(1) prevention by the guilty person of the harmful consequences of the crime committed or voluntary compensation for damage inflicted or the elimination of the harm caused;

(2) commission of a crime as a consequence of the concurrence of grave personal or family circumstances;

(3) commission of a crime under the influence of a threat or compulsion or by virtue of material or other dependence;

(4) commission of a crime under the influence of strong mental agitation caused by the unlawful actions of the victim;

(5) commission of a crime when defending against a socially dangerous infringement, even though when exceeding the limits of necessary defense;

(6) commission of a crime by a minor;

(7) commission of a crime by a woman in a state of pregnancy;

(8) sincere repentance or giving oneself up.

Other circumstances mitigating responsibility also may be provided in the union republic criminal codes.

When assigning punishment, a court may also take into account mitigating circumstances not specified in a law.

Article 34. Circumstances Aggravating Responsibility

When assigning punishment, the circumstances aggravating responsibility shall be deemed to be:

(1) commission of a crime by a person who has previously committed any crime whatever.

A court shall have the right, depending on the character of the first crime, not to acknowledge for it the significance of an aggravating circumstance;

(2) commission of a crime by an organized group;

(3) commission of a crime from mercenary or other base motives;

(4) causing of grave consequences by the crime;

(5) commission of a crime with respect to a young or aged person or a person in a helpless state;

(6) incitement of minors to commit a crime or involving minors to participate in a crime;

(7) commission of a crime with special cruelty or humiliation for the victim;

(8) commission of a crime while exploiting conditions of a public disaster;

(9) commission of a crime by generally dangerous means;

(10) commission of a crime by a person in a state of intoxication. The court shall have the right, depending on the character of the crime, not to acknowledge this circumstance as aggravating responsibility.

Other circumstances aggravating the responsibility of the guilty person besides those specified in the present Article also may be provided in the union republic criminal codes.

Article 35. Assignment of Punishment When Several Crimes Have Been Committed

If a person is deemed guilty of committing two or more crimes provided for by various articles of a criminal law and he has not been convicted for any of them, the court, having assigned punishment separately for each crime, shall determine a final aggregate punishment by absorbing the less severe punishment in the more severe or by wholly or partially cumulating the assigned punishments within the limits established by the articles of the law providing for the more severe punishment.

Any of the supplementary punishments provided for by articles of a law establishing responsibility for those crimes of which the person was deemed guilty of committing may be joined to the basic punishment.

Punishment shall be assigned according to the same rules if it is established after the judgment is rendered in the case that the convicted person is guilty of yet another crime committed by him before judgment is rendered in the first case. In this event, a punishment wholly or partially served under the first judgment shall be counted in the term of punishment.

Article 36. Assignment of Punishment Under Several Judgments

If a convicted person, after judgment is rendered but before a punishment is wholly served, committed a new crime, the court shall join to the punishment assigned under the new judgment the unserved part of the punishment under the preceding judgment.

When cumulating punishments in the procedure provided for by the present Article, the total term of punishment should not exceed the maximum term established for the particular type of punishment. When cumulating punishments in the form of deprivation of freedom, the total term of punishment should not exceed ten years, and for crimes for which assignment of deprivation of freedom for a term of more than ten years is permitted by law, it should not exceed fifteen years.

Article 37. Assignment of Milder Punishment Than Provided by Law

A court, taking into account exceptional circumstances of a case and the personality of a guilty person and deeming it necessary to assign him a punishment lower than the minimum limit provided for by law for the particular crime or to move to another milder form of punishment, may allow such mitigation, with an obligatory indication of its reasons.

Article 38. Conditional Sentence

If when assigning punishment in the form of deprivation of freedom or correctional tasks a court, taking into account the circumstances of the case and the personality of the guilty person, becomes convinced of the inadvisability of the guilty person serving the assigned punishment, it may decree the conditional nonapplication of punishment to the guilty person, with an obligatory indication in the judgment of the reasons for the conditional sentence. In such event the court shall decree not to bring the judgment into execution if during a probation period determined by the court the convicted person does not commit a new intentional crime.

In the event that a conditionally sentenced person commits a new intentional crime during the probation term for which he is sentenced to deprivation of freedom, the court shall assign him a punishment according to the rules provided for by Article 36 of the present Fundamental Principles.

If there is a conditional sentence, supplementary punishments, except for a fine, may not be assigned.

The limits of the probation term, the procedure for observing a conditionally sentenced person and for carrying on educational work with him shall be established by union republic legislation.

Taking into account the circumstances of the case, the personality of the guilty person, and also the petitions of social organizations or a collective of workers, employees, and collective farmers at the guilty person's place of work concerning his conditional sentence, a court may transfer the conditionally sentenced person to these organizations or collective for re-education and reform.

Article 39. Stay of Execution of Judgment for a Military Serviceman or Person Liable to Military Service in Wartime

In wartime the execution of a judgment for deprivation of freedom rendered with respect to a military serviceman or person liable to call-up or mobilization may be deferred by a court until the ending of military operations, sending the convicted person to active duty. The court may in such instances defer also the execution of supplementary punishments.

If a convicted person sent to active duty shows himself to be a stalwart defender of the socialist Motherland, then upon the petition of the respective military command the court may relieve him from punishment or replace the punishment with another milder one.

In the event a person with respect to whom the execution of a judgment has been deferred commits a new crime, the court shall join to the new punishment that previously assigned according to the rules provided in Article 36 of the present Fundamental Principles.

Article 39-1. Stay of Execution of Judgment for a Minor

When assigning punishment to a minor sentenced for the first time to deprivation of freedom for a term of up to three years, the court, taking into account the character and degree of social danger of the crime committed, the personality of the guilty person and other circumstances of the case, and also the possibility of his reform and re-education without isolation from society, may defer the execution of judgment for deprivation of freedom with respect to this person for a term of from six months to two years. In such instances the court may defer execution also of supplementary punishments.

When deferring execution of judgment for a minor, the court may oblige him to commence work or study for a specified term, eliminate harm caused, and impose other duties on him provided for by union republic legislation whose fulfillment may further the reform and re-education of the convicted person. The court also may entrust to a specified collective of working people or a person, with their consent, the duty to observe the convicted person and carry on educational work with him.

Control over the conduct of the convicted person with respect to whom execution of judgment for deprivation of freedom has been deferred shall be effectuated by commissions for cases of minors attached to the executive committees of district (or city) soviets of working people's deputies and by agencies of internal affairs in accordance with USSR and union republic legislation.

If the convicted person during the term established by a court for deferral of execution of judgment proves his reform by exemplary conduct and an honorable attitude toward labor and study, then upon the petition of a commission for cases of minors attached to the executive committee of a district (or city) soviet of working people's deputies or agency of internal affairs the court may relieve him from punishment.

If a convicted person with respect to whom the execution of judgment to deprivation of freedom has been deferred does not fulfill the duties entrusted to him by a court or allows violations of public order entailing the application of measures of administrative pressure, then upon the recommendation of the commission for cases of minors attached to the executive committee of the district (or city) soviet of working people's deputies or agency of internal affairs, the court may render a ruling repealing the deferral of execution of judgment to deprivation of freedom and sending the convicted person to serve the deprivation of freedom assigned by the judgment.

In the event the convicted person with respect to whom execution of judgment has been deferred commits a new crime, the court shall join to the new punishment that previously assigned according to the rules provided for in Article 36 of the present Fundamental Principles.

Article 40. Deducting Preliminary Confinement

Preliminary confinement shall be deducted by a court from the term of punishment when sentencing to deprivation of freedom and sending to a disciplinary battalion, a day for a day, and when sentencing to correctional tasks, exile, or banishment, a day for three days.

Article 41. Period of Limitation for Bringing to Criminal Responsibility

A person may not be brought to criminal responsibility if the following periods have elapsed from the date he committed the crime:

(1) three years from the date the crime was committed for which, under the law, deprivation of freedom may be assigned for a term not exceeding two years or a punishment not connected with deprivation of freedom;

(2) five years from the date the crime was committed for which, under the law, deprivation of freedom may be assigned for a term not exceeding five years;

(3) ten years from the date the crime was committed for which, under the law, a more severe punishment may be assigned than deprivation of freedom for a term of five years.

Lower periods of limitation for individual types of crimes may be established by union republic legislation.

The running of a period of limitation shall be interrupted if the person commits a new crime before the terms specified in law elapse, for which, under the law, deprivation of freedom may be assigned for a term exceeding two years. Calculation of the period of limitation in this event shall commence from the moment the new crime is committed.

The running of a period of limitation shall be suspended if the person who has committed a crime hides from investigation or the court. In such instances the running of the period of limitation shall resume from the moment the person is detained or gives himself up. A person may not be brought to criminal responsibility if fifteen years have passed since the time the crime was committed and the period of limitation was not interrupted by the commission of a new crime.

The question of applying the period of limitation to a person who has committed a crime for which under the law the death penalty may be assigned shall be settled by a court. If the court does not find it possible to apply the period of limitation, the death penalty may not be assigned and shall be replaced by deprivation of freedom.

Article 42. Period of Limitation for Execution of Judgment of Conviction

A judgment of conviction shall not be brought into execution if it was not brought into execution within the following periods, calculated from the date of the entry of the judgment into legal force:

(1) three years: when sentenced to deprivation of freedom for a term not exceeding two years or to a punishment not connected with deprivation of freedom;

(2) five years: when sentenced to deprivation of freedom for a term not exceeding five years;

(3) ten years: when sentenced to a more severe punishment than deprivation of freedom for a term of five years.

Lower periods of limitation for individual types of crimes may be established by union republic legislation.

The running of the period of limitation shall be interrupted if the convicted person evades serving the punishment or commits a new crime before the periods elapse for which punishment was assigned by a court in the form of deprivation of freedom for a term of not less than one year or exile or banishment for a term of not less than three years. Calculation of the period of limitation shall commence, in the event a new crime is committed, from the moment of its commission, and in the event of evasion of serving a punishment, from the moment the convicted person gives himself up to serve the punishment or from the moment a convicted person in hiding is detained. A judgment of conviction may not be brought into execution if fifteen years have passed from the time it was rendered and the period of limitation was not interrupted by the commission of a new crime.

The question of the application of a period of limitation to a person condemned to the death penalty shall be settled by a court. If the court does not find it possible to apply the period of limitation, the death penalty shall be replaced by deprivation of freedom.

Article 43. Relief from Criminal Responsibility and Punishment

A person who has committed a crime may be relieved from criminal responsibility if it is deemed that by the time of the investigation or consideration of the case in court, as a consequence of a change in the situation, the act committed by the guilty person has lost the character of being socially dangerous or this person has ceased to be socially dangerous.

A person who has committed a crime may be relieved from punishment if it is deemed that by virtue of subsequent irreproachable conduct and an honorable attitude toward labor this person may not, by the time the case is considered in court, be considered socially dangerous.

A person who has committed a crime not representing a great social danger may be relieved from criminal responsibility if it is deemed that his reform and re-education are possible without the application of criminal punishment. In this event one of the following decisions shall be taken in accordance with USSR and union republic legislation:

(1) to bring the person to administrative responsibility;

(2) to transfer the materials of the case for consideration of a comrades' court;

(3) to transfer the materials of the case for consideration of a commission for cases of minors;

(4) to transfer the person on surety to a social organization or collective of working people.

Relief from criminal responsibility while bringing to administrative responsibility shall be permitted only in cases concerning crimes for which punishment is provided by law in the form of deprivation of freedom for a term not exceeding one year or other milder punishment.

Article 44. Conditional Early Relief from Punishment and Replacement of Punishment by Milder Punishment

Conditional early relief from punishment or replacement of the unserved part of the punishment by a milder punishment may be applied to persons sentenced to deprivation of freedom, conditionally sentenced to deprivation of freedom with compulsory enlistment for labor, exile, banishment, correctional tasks, or being sent to a disciplinary battalion, and also to persons conditionally released from places of deprivation of freedom with compulsory enlistment for labor in accordance with Article 44-2 of the present Fundamental Principles, except the persons enumerated in Article 44-1 of the present Fundamental Principles.

Conditional early relief from punishment or replacement of the unserved part of the punishment by a milder punishment shall be applied by a court at the place of serving the punishment upon the joint recommendation of the agency executing the punishment and the supervisory commission attached to the executive committee of the local soviet of working people's deputies and with respect to persons conditionally sentenced to deprivation of freedom with compulsory enlistment for labor and conditionally released from places of deprivation of freedom with compulsory enlistment for labor, also upon the joint recommendation of the administration and social organizations at the place of work of the convicted person.

Conditional early relief from punishment or replacement of the unserved part of the punishment by a milder punishment may be applied after the convicted person actually has served at least half of the assigned term of punishment.

Conditional early relief from punishment or replacement of the unserved part of the punishment by a milder punishment may be applied after not less than two thirds of the assigned term of punishment has been actually served to persons:

(1) sentenced to deprivation of freedom for a term exceeding three years for an intentional crime;

(2) who have previously served a punishment in places of deprivation of freedom for an intentional crime and before cancelling or removing the conviction have again committed an intentional crime for which they have been sentenced to deprivation of freedom;

(3) have committed an intentional crime while serving a punishment in places of deprivation of freedom for which they have been sentenced to deprivation of freedom.

Conditional early relief from punishment or replacement of the unserved part of punishment by a milder punishment may be applied after at least three-fourths of the assigned term of punishment has actually been served to persons:

(1) sentenced for banditism; actions disrupting work of correctional labor institutions; making or passing counterfeit money or securities under aggravating circumstances; violation of the rules for currency transactions under aggravating circumstances; stealing state or social property on an especially large scale; assault with intent to rob with a view to taking possession of state or social property or the personal property of citizens under aggravating circumstances; rape committed by a group of persons or entailing especially grave consequences, and also rape of a minor; taking or giving bribes or acting as intermediary in bribery under aggravating circumstances; infringement on the life of a policeman or people's guard in connection with their official or social activity to protect public order under aggravating circumstances; especially malicious hooliganism; hijacking of an aircraft; stealing of a firearm, ammunition, or explosives by assault with intent to rob; making, acquiring, keeping, carriage, or sending with a view to marketing or the marketing of narcotics under aggravating circumstances; stealing of narcotics under aggravating circumstances;

(2) previously sentenced to deprivation of freedom for an intentional crime for which conditional early relief from punishment or replacement of the unserved part of the punishment by a milder punishment was applied if they have committed an intentional crime again before the unserved term of punishment has elapsed for which they have been sentenced to deprivation of freedom.

In the event of the conditional early relief from punishment or the replacement of punishment by a milder punishment, the convicted person may be relieved also from supplementary punishments in the form of exile, banishment, deprivation of the right to occupy specified posts or to engage in a specified activity.

When replacing the unserved part of deprivation of freedom by exile, banishment, or correctional tasks, they shall be assigned within the limits of the terms established by law for these types of punishment and should not exceed the unserved term of deprivation of freedom.

In applying the conditional early relief from punishment or replacement of the unserved part of punishment by a milder punishment, the court may entrust to a specified collective of working people, with its consent, the duty to supervise the person granted conditional early relief during the unserved part of the term of punishment assigned by the court or the person for whom the unserved part of the punishment was replaced by a milder punishment and to carry on educational work with him.

In the event the person to whom conditional early relief was applied commits an intentional crime during the unserved part of the punishment for which he is sentenced to deprivation of freedom, the court shall assign a punishment to him according to the rules provided for by Article 36 of the present Fundamental Principles.

Article 44-1. Nonapplication of Conditional Early Relief from Punishment and Replacement of a Punishment by a Milder Punishment

Conditional early relief from punishment and replacement of the unserved part of a punishment by a milder punishment shall not be applied to:

(1) an especially dangerous recidivist;

(2) a person sentenced for an especially dangerous crime against the state;

(3) a person sentenced for intentional homicide under aggravating circumstances;

(4) a person for whom punishment in the form of a death penalty has been replaced by deprivation of freedom by way of pardon or amnesty.

Article 44-2. Conditional Release from Places of Deprivation of Freedom with Compulsory Enlistment of the Convicted Person for Labor

Conditional release from places of deprivation of freedom with compulsory enlistment of the convicted person for labor may be applied in places determined by agencies executing the judgment to able-bodied persons who have reached majority and are serving a punishment in places of deprivation of freedom, except for convicted persons serving punishment in colonies and settlements for persons who have committed crimes through negligence, and also in colonies and settlements if further reform and reeducation of these persons is possible without isolation from society but in conditions of supervision over them.

Conditional release from places of deprivation of freedom with compulsory enlistment of the convicted person for labor may be applied to:

(1) persons sentenced for a term of up to ten years inclusive after they have actually served not less than one-third of the term of punishment assigned;

(2) persons sentenced for a term exceeding ten years after they have actually served not less than half of the assigned term of punishment;

(3) persons sentenced for crimes enumerated in Article 44, paragraph six, of the present Fundamental Principles after they have actually served not less than two thirds of the assigned term of punishment;

(4) persons enumerated in Article 44-1 of the present Fundamental Principles after they have actually served not less than three-fourths of the assigned term of punishment.

Conditional release from places of deprivation of freedom with compulsory enlistment of the convicted person for labor shall be applied by the court at the place where the convicted person is serving the punishment upon the joint recommendation of the agency executing the punishment and the supervisory commission attached to the executive committee of the local soviet of working people's deputies.

Conditional release from places of deprivation of freedom with compulsory enlistment of the convicted person for labor shall not be applied to:

(1) persons enumerated in Article 23-2, paragraph three, points 2 and 3, of the present Fundamental Principles;

(2) persons who systematically or maliciously violate the requirements of the regime for serving punishment.

If a conditionally released person evades work or systematically or maliciously violates labor discipline, public order, or the rules for residence established for him, he shall be sent by ruling of a court to serve deprivation of freedom assigned by the judgment. The time of evading work shall not be counted, but the time during which the conditionally released person worked may be counted by a court partially or wholly toward the term for serving punishment at a rate of a day for a day.

If a conditionally released person committed an intentional crime during the compulsory work term for which he is sentenced to deprivation of freedom, the court shall assign punishment to him according to the rules provided for by Article 36 of the present Fundamental Principles.

Article 45. Conditional Early Relief from Punishment and Replacement of Punishment by a Milder Punishment with Respect to Persons Who Have Committed a Crime When Under Eighteen Years of Age

Conditional early relief from punishment or replacement of the unserved part of the punishment by a milder punishment may be applied to persons sentenced to deprivation of freedom or correctional tasks for crimes committed when under eighteen years of age.

Conditional early relief from punishment or replacement of the unserved part of the punishment by a milder punishment may be applied to a convicted person for a crime committed when under eighteen years of age only in the event he has proved his reform by exemplary conduct and an honorable attitude toward labor and study.

Conditional early relief from punishment and replacement of the unserved part of the punishment by a milder punishment shall be applied by a court at the place where the convicted person is serving punishment upon the joint recommendation of the agency executing the punishment and a commission for cases of minors or supervisory commission attached to the executive committee of the local soviet of working people's deputies.

Conditional early release from punishment or replacement of the unserved part of punishment by a milder punishment may be applied to a convicted person for a crime committed when under eighteen years of age after not less than one-third of the assigned term of punishment actually has been served.

Conditional early relief from punishment or replacement of the unserved part of the punishment by a milder punishment may be applied after not less than half of the assigned term of punishment actually has been served to persons:

(1) sentenced to deprivation of freedom for a term of not less than five years for an intentional crime committed when under eighteen years of age;

(2) who have previously served punishment in places of deprivation of freedom for an intentional crime and who before the cancellation or removal of the conviction again committed an intentional crime when under eighteen years of age for which they have been sentenced to deprivation of freedom;

(3) who have committed an intentional crime when under eighteen years of age while serving a punishment in places of deprivation of freedom for which they have been sentenced to deprivation of freedom.

Conditional early relief from punishment or replacement of the punishment by a milder punishment may be applied after not less than two-thirds of the assigned term of punishment actually has been served to persons:

(1) previously sentenced to deprivation of freedom for an intentional crime for which conditional early relief from punishment or replacement of the unserved part of the punishment by a milder punishment was applied if these persons before attaining eighteen years of age and before the unserved term of punishment elapses again have committed an intentional crime for which they have been sentenced to deprivation of freedom;

(2) sentenced for a crime committed when under eighteen years of age: banditism; assault with intent to rob with a view to taking possession of state or social property or the personal property of citizens under aggravating circumstances; rape committed by a group of persons or entailing especially grave consequences, and also rape of a minor; infringement on the life of a police worker or a people's guard in connection with their official or social activity to protect public order under aggravating circumstances; especially malicious hooliganism; hijacking of an aircraft; stealing of a firearm, ammunition, or explosives by assault with intent to rob.

When replacing the unserved part of deprivation of freedom with correctional tasks, they shall be assigned within the limits of terms established by law for this type of punishment and should not exceed the unserved term of deprivation of freedom.

When applying conditional early relief from punishment or replacement of the unserved part of punishment by a milder punishment, the court may entrust to a specified collective of working people or a person, with their consent, the duty to supervise a person granted conditional early release during the unserved part of the term of punishment assigned by a court or a person for whom the unserved part of the punishment is replaced by a milder punishment, and to carry on educational work with him.

In the event that the person to whom conditional early relief was applied when under eighteen years of age committed a new intentional crime during the unserved part of the punishment for which he has been sentenced to deprivation of freedom, the court shall assign punishment to him according to the rules provided for by Article 36 of the present Fundamental Principles.

Article 46. Relief from Serving Punishment

Relief of a convicted person from serving punishment, and also mitigation of the punishment assigned, except relief from punishment or mitigation of punishment by way of amnesty or pardon, may be applied only by a court in the instances and in the procedure specified in a law.

Article 47. Cancellation of Conviction

There shall be deemed not to have a conviction:

(1) persons who have served punishment in a disciplinary battalion or have been released early therefrom, and also military servicemen who have served punishment in the form of confinement in a guardhouse instead of correctional tasks;

(2) persons conditionally sentenced if they do not commit a new crime during the probation period;

(2-1). persons conditionally sentenced to deprivation of freedom with compulsory enlistment for labor if they do not commit a new crime during the term of compulsory enlistment for labor or are not sent to a place of deprivation of freedom on the grounds provided for by law;

(2-2). persons sentenced to deprivation of freedom with the application of Article 39-1 of the present Fundamental Principles unless they commit a new crime during the term of deferral of execution of judgment and the judgment with respect to them has not been executed in the established procedure;

(3) persons sentenced to social censure, a fine, deprivation of the right to hold specified posts or to engage in a specified activity, or correctional tasks unless they commit a new crime within one year from the date of serving the punishment;

(4) persons sentenced to deprivation of freedom for a term of not more than three years, exile, or banishment unless they commit a new crime within three years from the date of serving punishment (basic and supplementary);

(5) persons sentenced to deprivation of freedom for a term of more than three years but not exceeding six years unless they commit a new crime within five years from the date of serving punishment (basic and supplementary);

(6) persons sentenced to deprivation of freedom for a term of more than six years but not exceeding ten years unless they commit a new crime within eight years from the date of serving punishment (basic or supplementary);

(7) persons sentenced to deprivation of freedom for a term exceeding ten years, and especially dangerous recidivists, unless they commit a new crime within eight years from the date of serving punishment (basic or supplementary) and if it is established by a court that the convicted person has been reformed and there is no need to consider him as having a conviction.

If a person sentenced to deprivation of freedom has proved his reform after serving his punishment by exemplary conduct and an honorable attitude toward labor, then upon the petition of social organizations the court may cancel his conviction before the terms specified in the present Article elapse.

If a person was granted early relief from punishment in the procedure established by law, the term for cancellation of the conviction shall be calculated by proceeding from the punishment actually served from the moment of being relieved from serving punishment (basic and supplementary).

If a person who has served punishment again commits a crime before the term for cancellation of conviction elapses, the running of the term for cancellation of conviction shall be interrupted. The term for cancellation of conviction for the first crime shall be calculated anew after the punishment for the subsequent crime has actually been served (basic and supplementary). In such instances the person shall be considered convicted of both crimes until the term for cancellation of conviction elapses for the gravest of them.

FUNDAMENTAL PRINCIPLES OF CRIMINAL PROCEDURE OF THE USSR AND UNION REPUBLICS

[Confirmed by Law of the USSR Supreme Soviet, December 25, 1958, as amended May 7, 1960, June 21, 1961, April 6, 1963, August 31, 1970, February 3, 1972, February 8, 1977. Vedomosti SSSR (1959), no. 1, item 15; (1960), no. 18, item 149; (1961), no. 26, item 270; (1963), no. 16, item 181; (1970), no. 36, item 362; (1972), no. 6, item 51; (1977), no. 7, item 120]

Section I. General Provisions

Article 1. Legislation on Criminal Procedure

The method of procedure in criminal cases shall be determined by the present Fundamental Principles and other laws of the USSR issued in accordance therewith and by the union republic codes of criminal procedure.

Article 2. Tasks of Criminal Procedure

The tasks of Soviet criminal procedure shall be the speedy and complete disclosure of crimes, exposure of the guilty persons, and ensuring the correct application of the law so that everyone who has committed a crime was subjected to just punishment and not a single innocent person was brought to criminal responsibility and convicted.

Criminal procedure should further the strengthening of socialist legality, the prevention and eradication of crimes, the nurturing of citizens in a spirit of undeviating execution of Soviet laws and respect for the rules of socialist community life.

Article 3. Duty to Initiate Criminal Case and Disclose a Crime

A court, procurator, investigator, and agency of inquiry shall be obliged within the limits of their competence to initiate a criminal case in every instance of discovering the indicia of a crime and to take all measures provided by law to establish the events of the crime and the persons guilty of committing the crime, and to punish them.

Article 4. Impermissibility of Prosecution as an Accused Other than on the Grounds and in the Procedure Established by Law

No one may be prosecuted as an accused other than on the grounds and in the procedure established by law.

Article 5. Circumstances Precluding a Proceeding in a Criminal Case

A criminal case may not be initiated, and a case initiated shall be subject to termination:

(1) for the absence of the occurrence of a crime;

(2) for the absence of the constituent elements of a crime in the act;

(3) upon the expiry of the periods of limitations;

(4) as a consequence of an act of amnesty, if it eliminates the application of punishment for the act committed, and also when individual persons have been pardoned;

(5) with respect to a person who has not attained, at the moment of committing a socially dangerous act, the age at whose attainment, according to law, criminal responsibility is possible;

(6) for reconciliation of the victim with the accused in the instances provided for by union republic legislation;

(7) for the absence of a complaint by the victim unless the case can be initiated other than through his complaint except for instances when by union republic legislation the procurator has been granted the right to initiate a case in the absence of a complaint of the victim;

(8) with respect to a deceased person, except for instances when a proceeding in a case is needed to rehabilitate the deceased person or to reopen a case in respect of other persons on the basis of newly discovered facts;

(9) with respect to a person concerning whom under the same accusation there is a judgment which has entered into legal force.

If the circumstances specified in points 1, 2, 3, and 4 of the present Article are discovered at a stage of judicial examination, the court shall bring the examination of the case to an end and decree a judgment of acquittal or a judgment of conviction with relief of the convicted person from punishment.

Termination of a case on the grounds specified in points 3 and 4 of the present Article shall not be permitted if the accused objects. In this event the proceeding in the case shall be continued in the usual procedure

Article 5-1. Termination of a Criminal Case and Bringing a Person to Administrative Responsibility, Transfer of Materials to a Comrades' Court or Commission for Cases of Minors, or Transfer of a Guilty Person on Suret

A proceeding in a criminal case may be terminated in the instances and procedure provided for by USSR and union republic legislation in connection with:

(1) bringing a person to administrative responsibility;

(2) transfer of the materials of the case for consideration of a comrades' court;

(3) transfer of the materials of a case for consideration of a commission for cases of minors;

(4) transfer of a person on surety to a social organization or collective of working people.

Article 6. Inviolability of the Person

No one may be subjected to arrest other than by decree of a court or with the sanction of a procurator.

A procurator shall be obliged to release immediately any person illegally deprived of freedom or confined under guard beyond the term provided for by law or a court judgment.

Article 7. Justice Shall Be Carried Out Only by a Court

Justice in criminal cases shall be carried out only by a court. No one may be deemed guilty of committing a crime or subjected to criminal punishment other than by the judgment of a court.

Article 8. Justice Shall be Carried Out on the Principle of Equality of Citizens Before the Law and Court

Justice in criminal cases shall be carried out on the principle of equality before the law and court of all citizens irrespective of their social, property, and official position, national or racial affiliation, or confession of faith.

Article 9. Participation of People's Assessors and Collegiality in the Consideration of Cases

Criminal cases in all courts shall be considered by judges and people's assessors elected in the established procedure.

Criminal cases in all courts of first instance shall be considered by a judge and two people's assessors.

People's assessors shall enjoy equal rights with the person presiding in the judicial session in deciding all questions arising during the consideration of the case and the decreeing of judgment.

Consideration of a case by way of cassation shall be carried out by courts composed of three members of the court, and by way of judicial supervision, composed of not less than three members of the court.

Article 10. Independence of Judges and Their Subordination Only to Law

When carrying out justice in criminal cases, judges and people's assessors shall be independent and subordinate only to law. Judges and people's assessors shall decide criminal cases on the basis of law, in accordance with a socialist legal consciousness, in conditions excluding outside pressure on the judges.

Article 11. Language in Which a Judicial Proceeding Shall be Conducted

A judicial proceeding shall be conducted in the language of the union or autonomous republic or autonomous region, and in the instances provided for by union and autonomous republic constitutions, in the language of the national area or of the majority of the local populace.

Persons participating in the case who do not have command of the language in which a judicial proceeding is being conducted shall be secured the right to make statements, give testimony, speak in court, and make petitions in their native language, and also to enjoy the services of an interpreter in the procedure established by law.

Investigative and judicial documents shall, in accordance with the procedure established by law, be handed over to the accused in a translation into his native language or in another language of which he has command.

Article 12. Publicity of Judicial Examination

The examination of cases in all courts shall be open except for instances when this is contrary to the interests of the protection of state secrecy.

A closed judicial examination shall, in addition, be permitted upon a reasoned ruling of a court in cases concerning the crimes of persons who have not attained sixteen years of age, in cases concerning sex crimes, and also in other cases with a view to preventing the disclosure of information concerning the intimate aspects of the life of persons participating in the case.

The judgments of courts in all instances shall be proclaimed publicly.

Article 13. Ensuring the Accused a Right to Defense

An accused shall have the right to defense.

An investigator, procurator, and court shall be obliged to ensure the accused the possibility to defend himself by the means and methods established by law against the accusation brought against him and to ensure the protection of his personal and property rights.

Article 14. Thorough, Complete, and Objective Analysis of the Facts of a Case

The court, procurator, investigator, and person conducting an inquiry shall be obliged to take all measures provided by law for the thorough, complete, and objective analysis of the facts of a case and to uncover facts both incriminating and vindicating the accused, and also aggravating or mitigating his guilt.

The court, procurator, investigator, and person conducting an inquiry shall not have the right to shift the duty of proof to the accused.

It shall be prohibited to seek the testimony of the accused by force, threat, or other illegal measures.

Article 15. Facts Subject to Proof in a Criminal Case

In a preliminary investigation and examination of a criminal case in court there shall be subject to proof:

(1) the occurrence of a crime (time, place, means, and other facts of the commission of a crime);

(2) the guilt of the accused in committing the crime;

(3) the facts influencing the degree and character of responsibility of the accused;

(4) the character and amount of damage caused by the crime.

Article 16. Evidence

Any factual data on the basis of which in the procedure determined by law agencies of inquiry, the investigator, or the court establish the existence or the absence of a socially dangerous act, the guilt of the person who committed the act, and other facts having significance for the correct decision of the case shall be evidence in a criminal case.

Such data shall be established by: testimony of a witness, testimony of the victim, testimony of a suspect; testimony of an accused, opinion of an expert, real evidence, and protocols of investigative and judicial actions, and other documents.

Article 17. Evaluation of Evidence

The court, procurator, investigator, and person conducting an inquiry shall evaluate evidence in accordance with their inner conviction based on a thorough, complete, and objective consideration of all the facts of the case in their totality, being guided by law and a socialist legal consciousness.

No evidence shall have a previously established force for the court, procurator, investigator, and person conducting the inquiry.

Article 18. Challenge of Judge, Procurator, and Other Participants of a Trial

A judge, people's assessor, procurator, investigator, person conducting an inquiry, secretary of the judicial session, expert, and interpreter may not take part in a proceeding in a criminal case and shall be subject to challenge if they are personally, directly or indirectly, concerned in the case.

Article 19. Supervision of the USSR Supreme Court, and Union and Autonomous Republic Supreme Courts Over Judicial Activity

The USSR Supreme Court shall exercise supervision over the judicial activity of USSR judicial agencies, and also union republic judicial agencies, within the limits established by law.

Union republic supreme courts and autonomous republic supreme courts shall exercise supervision over judicial activity of judicial agencies of the respective republics.

Article 20. Procuracy Supervision in a Criminal Proceeding

Supervision over the exact execution of the laws of the USSR and of the union and autonomous republics in a criminal proceeding shall be carried out by the USSR Procurator General both directly and through procurators subordinate to him.

The procurator shall be obliged at all stages of a criminal proceeding to take timely measures provided by law to eliminate any violations of the law, irrespective of from whom these violations emanate.

A procurator shall exercise his powers in a criminal proceeding independently of any agencies and officials whatever, being subordinate only to law and being guided by instructions of the USSR Procurator General.

Decrees of the procurator rendered in accordance with law shall be binding for execution by all institutions, enterprises, organizations, officials, and citizens.

Section II. Participants in the Trial, Their Rights and Duties

Article 21. Rights of the Accused

An accused shall have the right to: know of what he is accused and to give explanations concerning the accusation brought against him; give evidence; make petitions; acquaint himself upon completion of the preliminary investigation with all the materials of the case; have defense counsel; participate in the judicial examination in the court of first instance; make challenges; bring appeals against the actions and the decision of the investigator, procurator, and court.

The person brought to trial shall have the right to the last word.

Article 22. Participation of Defense Counsel in a Criminal Proceeding

A defense counsel shall be permitted to participate in a case from the moment of the accused is informed about the completion of the preliminary investigation and the accused is presented with the proceedings in the case in order to become acquainted with them. By decree of a procurator, a defense counsel may be permitted to participate in a case from the moment the accusation is presented.

Participation of defense counsel in a preliminary investigation and during judicial examination shall be obligatory in cases: of minors, of deaf, dumb, and blind persons, and other persons who by virtue of their physical or psychological defects can not themselves exercise their right to defense. In such instances the defense counsel shall be permitted to participate in the case from the moment the accusation is presented.

The participation of defense counsel shall be obligatory in cases of persons who do not have command of the language in which the judicial proceeding is conducted and also persons accused of committing crimes for which the death penalty may be assigned as a measure of punishment from the moment the accused is informed about the completion of the preliminary investigation and the accused is presented with the proceedings of the case in order to become acquainted with them.

Obligatory participation of defense counsel in a case also may take place in other instances determined by union republic legislation.

Advocates, representatives of trade unions, and other social organizations, and other persons to whom such right is granted by union republic legislation, shall be permitted as defense counsel.

Article 23. Duties and Rights of a Defense Counsel

Defense counsel shall be obliged to use all means and methods of defense specified in law with a view to eliciting the facts vindicating the accused or mitigating his responsibility and render necessary legal assistance to the accused.

From the moment of being permitted to participate in a case the defense counsel shall have the right: to meet with the accused; to acquaint himself with all materials of the case and copy out necessary information therefrom; present evidence; make petitions; participate in the judicial examination; make challenges; bring appeals against the actions and decisions of the investigator, procurator, and court. In addition, with the permission of the investigator, a defense counsel may be present during interrogations of the accused and during the performance of other investigative actions fulfilled upon the petitions of the accused or his defense counsel.

An advocate shall not have the right to refuse to assume the defense of an accused.

Article 24. Victim

A person to whom moral, physical, or financial harm has been caused by a crime shall be deemed a victim.

A citizen deemed a victim from a crime or his representative shall have the right to: give testimony in the case; present evidence; make petitions; acquaint himself with the materials of the case from the moment the preliminary investigation is completed; participate in the analysis of evidence at the judicial investigation; make challenges; bring appeals against the actions of the person conducting an inquiry, investigator, procurator, and court, and also bring appeals against a judgment or ruling of a court or decree of a people's judge.

In the instances provided for by union republic legislation, the victim shall have the right to support the accusation in the judicial examination personally or through his representative.

Article 25. Civil Plaintiff

A person that has suffered material loss from a crime shall have the right during a proceeding in a criminal case to bring a civil suit against the accused or persons bearing material responsibility for the actions of the accused, which shall be considered by the court jointly with the criminal case.

A civil plaintiff or his representative shall have the right to: present evidence; make petitions; participate in the judicial examination; request an agency of inquiry, investigator, and court to take measures to secure the suit filed by him; support the civil suit; acquaint himself with the materials of the case from the moment the preliminary investigation is completed; make challenges; bring appeals against the actions of the person conducting the inquiry, investigator, procurator, and court, and also bring appeals against the judgment or ruling of the court in that part affecting the civil suit.

Article 26. Civil Defendant

Parents, guardians, curators, or other persons, as well as institutions, enterprises, and organizations which by virtue of law bear material responsibility for a loss caused by the criminal actions of an accused, may be involved as civil defendants.

A civil defendant or his representative shall have the right to: oppose the suit brought; give explanations regarding the substance of the suit; present evidence; make petitions; acquaint himself with the materials of the case within the limits established by law; participate in the judicial examination; make challenges; bring appeals against the actions of the person conducting the inquiry, investigator, procurator, and court, as well as bring appeals against the judgment and ruling of the court in that part affecting the civil suit.

Article 27. Duty to Explain and Secure Rights of Persons Participating in a Case

The court, procurator, investigator, and person conducting an inquiry shall be obliged to explain to persons participating in a case their rights and to ensure the possibility of exercising such rights.

Section III. Inquiry and Preliminary Investigation

Article 28. Agencies of Preliminary Investigation

Preliminary investigation in criminal cases shall be performed by investigators of the procuracy, as well as by investigators of agencies for the protection of public order in cases concerning crimes, a list of which shall be established by USSR and union republic legislation, and by investigators of state security agencies in cases concerning crimes provided for by Articles: 1 (treason), 2 (espionage), 3 (terrorist act), 4 (terrorist act against a representative of a foreign state), 5 (sabotage), 6 (wrecking), 7 (anti-Soviet agitation and propaganda), 9 (organized activity directed toward the commission of especially dangerous crimes against the state, and also participation in an anti-Soviet organization), 10 (especially dangerous crimes against the state committed against another working people's state), 12 (disclosure of a state secret), 13 (loss of documents containing a state secret), 15 (smuggling), 16 (mass disorders), 20 (illegal exit abroad or illegal entry into the USSR), 21 (violation of international flight rules), 25 (violation of rules concerning currency transactions), 26 (that part relating to the failure to report crimes against the state provided for by Articles 1-6, 9), 27 (that part relating to concealment of crimes against the state provided for by Articles 1-6, 9, 15, and 25) of the Law on Criminal Responsibility for Crimes Against the State and Article 23(a), (b) and (c) (disclosure of a military secret or loss of documents containing a military secret) of the Law on Criminal Responsibility for Military Crimes.

A preliminary investigation shall be obligatory in cases concerning crimes against the state and military crimes, and also other crimes a list of which shall be established by USSR and union republic legislation.

Article 29. Inquiry

Police agencies and other institutions and organizations empowered by law, and also commanders of military units, formations, and heads of military institutions, shall be agencies of inquiry.

Agencies of inquiry shall be entrusted with the taking of necessary operational-search measures with a view to discovering the indicia of a crime and the persons who committed them.

If the indicia of a crime are present for which a preliminary investigation is obligatory, the agency of inquiry shall initiate a criminal case and, being guided by the rules of criminal procedure law, shall perform urgent investigative actions to establish and preserve the traces of the crime: view, search, seizure, examination, detention, and interrogation of suspects, and interrogation of victims and witnesses.

The agency of inquiry shall inform a procurator immediately about the discovery of the crime and the commencement of the inquiry.

In cases for which a preliminary investigation is not obligatory, the materials of the inquiry shall be the basis for consideration of the case in court. In such instances the agency of inquiry shall submit the materials of the inquiry to the procurator, with whose confirmation the case shall be sent for consideration in court.

Article 30. Powers of Investigator

When performing a preliminary investigation all decisions concerning the orientation of the investigation and the performance of investigative actions the investigator shall take independently, except for instances when obtaining the sanction of a procurator is provided for by law, and shall bear full responsibility for their lawful and timely execution.

If an investigator disagrees with instructions of a procurator concerning the prosecution of a person as an accused, the classification of the crime and the scope of the accusation, the referral of a case for bringing the accused to trial, or termination of the case, the investigator shall have the right to present the case to a superior procurator, setting forth his objections in writing. In this event the procurator either shall vacate the instructions of the lower procurator or shall hand over the investigation in this case to another investigator.

In cases investigated by him the investigator shall have the right to give commissions and instructions to agencies of inquiry concerning the performance of search and investigative actions and demand assistance from agencies of inquiry when performing individual investigative actions Such commissions and instructions of an investigator shall be obligatory for agencies of inquiry.

Decrees of an investigator rendered in accordance with the law in criminal cases which he is conducting shall be binding for execution by all institutions, enterprises, organizations, officials, and citizens.

Article 31. Supervision Over the Execution of Laws When Conducting an Inquiry or Preliminary Investigation

Supervision of the execution of laws when conducting an inquiry or preliminary investigation shall be exercised by the procurator in accordance with the Statute on Procuracy Supervision in the USSR.

Instructions of a procurator shall be given in writing and shall be binding upon the investigator or person performing the inquiry.

Article 32. Detention of a Suspect for Commission of a Crime

An agency of inquiry or an investigator shall have the right to detain a person suspected of committing a crime for which punishment in the form of deprivation of freedom may be assigned only if one of the following grounds is present:

(1) when such person is caught committing the crime or immediately after committing it;

(2) when eyewitnesses, including the victim, directly point out the particular person as having committed the crime;

(3) when obvious traces of the crime are discovered on the suspect or his clothing, with him, or at his dwelling.

If other data are present giving grounds to suspect a person of committing a crime, he may be detained only if such person attempts to flee or when he has no permanent place of residence or when the identity of the suspect has not been established;

A person detained on suspicion of committing a crime shall have the right to appeal against the actions of the person performing the inquiry, investigator, or procurator, to give explanations, and to make petitions.

An agency of inquiry or investigator shall be obliged to draw up a protocol concerning every instance of the detention of a person suspected of committing a crime, specifying the grounds and reasons for the detention and within twenty four hours to notify the procurator thereof. Within forty eight hours from the moment of receiving notification of the detention, the procurator shall be obliged to give sanction to confinement under guard or to release the detained person.

Article 33. Application of Measures of Restraint

If there exist sufficient grounds to suppose that an accused, while free, will hide himself from the investigation and court or hinder the establishment of the truth in the criminal case or engage in criminal activity, and also to ensure execution of a judgment, the person performing the inquiry, investigator, procurator, and court shall have the right to apply with respect to an accused one of the following measures of restraint; signed statement not to depart, personal surety or surety of social organizations, confinement under guard, or other measures of restraint which may be determined by union republic legislation.

In exceptional instances a measure of restraint may be applied with respect to a person suspected of committing a crime even before presentation of an accusation against him. In this event an accusation should be presented not later than ten days from the moment of the application of the measure of restraint. If an accusation has not been presented within this period, the measure of restraint shall be vacated.

A person confined under guard before an accusation is presented against him shall have the right to: appeal the actions of the person performing the inquiry, investigator, or procurator, give explanations, and make petitions.

Article 34. Confinement Under Guard

Confinement under guard as a measure of restraint shall be applied in cases concerning crimes for which punishment in the form of deprivation of freedom for a term exceeding one year is provided by law. In exceptional instances this measure of restraint may be applied in cases concerning crimes for which punishment in the form of deprivation of freedom for a term not exceeding one year is provided by law.

To persons accused of committing the most grave crimes, a list of which shall be established by law, confinement under guard may be applied only on grounds of the danger of the crime.

Confinement under guard during the investigation of a case may not be continued for more than two months. This term may be extended only in view of the special complexity of the case by the procurator of an autonomous republic, territory, region, autonomous region, national area or by the military procurator of a military district or fleet, for up to three months, and by a union republic procurator or the Chief Military Procurator, for up to six months from the date of confinement under guard. The term of confinement under guard may be further extended only in exceptional instances by the USSR Procurator General for a term, additionally, of not more than three months.

Article 35. Procedure for Conducting Search and for Seizure of Correspondence

A search may be performed by decree of an agency of inquiry or an investigator, and only with the sanction of the procurator.

In instances not permitting delay a search may be performed by an agency of inquiry or investigator without the sanction of a procurator, but with subsequent notification of the procurator within a twenty-four period about the search performed.

The impounding of correspondence and its seizure at postal and telegraph institutions may be carried out only with the sanction of the procurator or by decree of a court.

Search and seizure shall be performed in the presence of witnesses.

Section IV. Procedure for Cases in a Court of First Instance

Article 36. Bringing to Trial

When there are sufficient grounds for considering a case in a judicial session, the judge shall, without predetermining the question of guilt, render a decree to bring the accused to trial.

In cases concerning crimes of minors and concerning crimes for which the death penalty may be applied as a measure of punishment, and also in instances when the judge disagrees with the findings of the conclusion to indict, or if it is necessary to change the measure of restraint selected with respect to the accused, an administrative session of the court shall be held.

A court in administrative session shall render a ruling to bring the accused to trial or return the case for further investigation or terminate the proceeding in the case, and also decide the question of the measure of restraint. If the accused is brought to trial, the court in administrative session may exclude individual points of the accusation from the conclusion to indict or apply the criminal law to a less grave crime without changing the formulation of the accusation.

Article 37. Directness, Oral Nature, and Continuity of Judicial Examination

A court of first instance shall, when considering a case, be obliged to analyze directly the evidence in the case; interrogate the persons brought to trial, victims, witnesses, hear opinions of experts, view real evidence, and disclose protocols and other documents.

A judicial session for every case shall proceed without interruption except for time designated for rest. Consideration by the same judges of other cases before finishing the hearing of the case already begun shall not be permitted.

Article 38. Equality of Rights of Participants in Judicial Examination

An accuser, a person brought to trial, defense counsel, victim, and also a civil plaintiff, civil defendant, and their representatives shall enjoy equal rights in a judicial examination to present evidence, participate in the analysis of the evidence, and make petitions.

Article 39. Participation of the Person Brought to Trial in Judicial Examination

Cases in a session of a court of first instance shall be examined with the participation of the person brought to trial, whose appearance in court is mandatory. Examination of cases in the absence of the person brought to trial shall be permitted only in exceptional instances specially provided for by law.

Article 40. Participation of the Procurator in a Judicial Examination

A procurator shall support the state accusation before the court, take part in the analysis of the evidence, give an opinion on questions arising during the judicial examination, and present to the court his own views concerning the application of the criminal law and measures of punishment in respect of the person brought to trial.

A procurator shall, in supporting the accusation, be guided by the requirements of the law and his own inner conviction based on a consideration of all the facts of the case.

If as a result of the judicial examination a procurator is convinced that the data of the judicial investigation do not confirm the accusation brought against the person brought to trial, he shall be obliged to withdraw the accusation and set forth to the court the reasons for the withdrawal.

A procurator shall have the right to bring or to support a civil suit filed by a victim if the protection of state or social interests or the rights of citizens require this.

Article 41. Participation of Social Accusers or Defenders in Judicial Examination

Representatives of social organizations of working people may, by ruling of a court, be permitted to participate in the judicial examination of criminal cases as social accusers or defenders.

Article 42. Limits of Judicial Examination

Cases in court shall be examined only with respect to the accused and only pursuant to the accusation for which they have been brought to trial.

The modification of an accusation in court shall be permitted if this does not worsen the position of the person brought to trial and does not violate his right to defense. If a modification of accusation entails a violation of the right of the person brought to trial to defense, the court shall send the case for a new preliminary investigation.

Article 43. Judgment of the Court

The judgment of a court should be legal and well-founded.

The court should base the judgment only on that evidence which was considered at the judicial session.

The judgment of a court may be to convict or to acquit. A judgment to convict or a judgment to acquit should be reasoned by the court.

A judgment to convict may not be based on presuppositions and shall be decreed only on condition that the guilt of the person brought to trial in committing a crime was proved in the court of judicial examination. A court shall decree a judgment to convict without assigning punishment if at the moment of considering the case in court the act has lost social danger or the person who committed it has ceased to be socially dangerous.

A judgment to acquit shall be decreed in instances when the occurrence of a crime is not established, if the act of the person brought to trial does not contain the constituent elements of a crime, and also if the participation of the person brought to trial in the commission of the crime has not been proved.

The USSR Supreme Court and military tribunals shall render judgment in the name of the Union of Soviet Socialist Republics, and union republic courts, in the name of the union republic.

Section V. Procedure for Cases in Cassational and Supervisory Instances

Article 44. Right of Cassational Appeal and Protest of Judgment

A person brought to trial, his defense counsel and legal representative, and also a victim, shall have the right to appeal by way of cassation against the judgment of a court.

A procurator shall be obliged to protest by way of cassation each illegal or unfounded judgment.

A civil plaintiff, civil defendant, and their representatives shall have the right to appeal against a judgment in that part relating to the civil suit.

A person acquitted by a court shall have the right to appeal by way of cassation against a judgment to acquit in the part concerning the reasons and grounds of the acquittal.

The periods for bringing and the procedure for considering cassational appeals and protests, and also the procedure for appealing or protesting rulings and decrees of courts shall be determined by USSR and union republic legislation.

Judgments of the USSR Supreme Court and the union republic supreme courts shall not be subject to appeal or protest by way of cassation.

Article 45. Consideration of a Case by Cassational Appeal or Protest

When considering a case by way of cassation, a court shall verify the legality and well-foundedness of a judgment which exists in the case and materials additionally submitted. The court shall not be bound by the arguments of the cassational appeal or protest and shall verify the case in full with respect to all those convicted, including those who have not filed appeals and with respect to whom a cassational protest has not been brought.

As a result of considering a case by way of cassation, a court shall take one of the following decisions: to leave the judgment without change and the appeal or protest without satisfaction; to vacate the judgment to send the case for new consideration or new judicial consideration; vacate the judgment and terminate the case; change the judgment.

When considering a case by way of cassation, a procurator shall give an opinion on the legality and well-foundedness of the judgment.

The question of the participation of the convicted person in the session of the court which considers the case by way of cassation shall be decided by that court. A convicted person who appears at a judicial session shall, in all instances, be permitted to give explanations.

A defense counsel may participate in the session of a court of cassational instance.

Article 46. Impermissibility of Increasing Punishment for a Convicted Person or Applying to Him a Law for a Graver Crime in a Cassational Instance

When considering a case by way of cassation, a court may mitigate the punishment assigned by the court of first instance or apply a law for a less grave crime, but shall not have the right to increase a punishment nor to apply a law for a graver crime.

A judgment may be vacated in connection with the need to apply a law for a graver crime or for the mildness of punishment only in instances when a protest of the procurator has been brought on these grounds or the victim has filed an appeal.

Article 47. Vacating a Judgment to Acquit

A judgment to acquit may be vacated by way of cassation not otherwise than upon the protest of a procurator, the appeal of a victim, or the appeal of the person acquitted by the court.

Article 48. Review by Way of Judicial Supervision of Judgment, Ruling, of Decree of Court Which Has Entered into Legal Force

The review by way of judicial supervision of a judgment, ruling, or decree of a court which has entered into legal force shall be permitted only upon the protest of that procurator, chairman of the court, or their deputies to whom such right is granted by USSR and union republic legislation.

The USSR Procurator General, the Chairman of the USSR Supreme Court, their deputies, the Chief Military Procurator, and the Chairman of the Military Division of the USSR Supreme Court shall, in accordance with their competence, have the right to suspend, before deciding a case by way of judicial supervision, the execution of the judgment, ruling, or decree of any court of the USSR or union or autonomous republic being protested. The procurator or chairman of the union republic supreme court shall enjoy the same right with respect to a judgment, ruling, or decree of any union republic court or autonomous republic court therein being protested. If there is data testifying to an obvious violation of law, the said persons shall have the right simultaneously with obtaining a criminal case to suspend execution of the judgment, ruling, and decree for a period not exceeding three months until they are protested.

Review by way of judicial supervision of a judgment to convict or a ruling or decree for reasons of mildness of punishment or the need to apply a law for a graver crime to a convicted person, and also a judgment to acquit or a ruling of decree of a court to terminate a case, shall be permitted only within a year from their entry into legal force.

As a result of considering a case by way of supervision a court may: leave the protest without satisfaction; vacate the judgment and all subsequent judicial rulings and decrees and terminate the proceedings in the case or transfer it for new investigation or new judicial examination; vacate the cassational ruling, and also subsequent judicial rulings and decrees if such have been rendered, and transfer the case for new cassational consideration; vacate rulings and decrees rendered by way of supervision and leave in force, with or without change, the judgment of the court and cassational ruling; make changes in a judgment, ruling, or decree of a court.

When considering a case by way of judicial supervision, a court may mitigate the punishment assigned to the convicted person or apply a law for a less grave crime, but shall not have the right to increase a punishment nor to apply a law for a graver crime.

The procurator shall take part in the consideration of criminal cases by presidiums of the respective courts, who shall support the protest brought by him and give an opinion on the case being considered upon the protest of the chairman of the court or his deputy.

A court considering a case by way of judicial supervision shall, when necessary, have the right to summon the convicted person to the judicial session.

Article 49. Grounds for Vacating or Changing a Judgment by Way of Cassation or by Way of Supervision

The grounds for vacating or changing a judgment when considering a case by way of cassation or by way of judicial supervision shall be: bias or incompleteness of preliminary or judicial investigation; failure of the conclusions of the court to conform to the actual circumstances of the case set forth in the judgment; material violation of criminal procedure law; incorrect application of a criminal law; failure of punishment assigned by a court to conform to the gravity of a crime or the personality of the convicted person.

Article 50. Reopening of Cases for Newly Discovered Facts

A judgment which has entered into legal force may be vacated for newly discovered facts.

Review of a judgment to acquit shall be permitted only within the periods of limitation established by law for bringing to criminal responsibility and not later than one year from the date of discovering the new facts.

Article 51. Binding Nature of Instructions of Superior Courts

The instructions of a court considering a case by way of cassation or by way of supervision shall be binding during the additional investigation or during the second consideration of the case by a court.

A court considering a case by way of cassation or by way of judicial supervision shall not have the right to establish or to consider proved facts which have not been established in the judgment or rejected by it, and also shall not have the right to predetermine questions as to whether an accusation is proved or not proved, the reliability or unreliability of particular evidence, or the priority of some evidence over others, or the application by the court of first instance of a particular criminal law or measure of punishment.

When considering a case by way of judicial supervision, a court shall not, in vacating a cassational ruling, have the right to predetermine conclusions which might be made by the cassational instance when considering the case for a second time.

Article 52. Consideration of a Case by Court of First Instance After Initial Judgment is Vacated

After the initial judgment has been vacated, a case shall be subject to consideration in the ordinary procedure.

An increase of punishment or application of a law for a graver crime during the new consideration of a case by a court of first instance shall be permitted only on condition that the initial judgment was vacated for mildness of punishment or in connection with the need to apply a law for a graver crime upon the cassational protest of the procurator, the appeal of the victim, or by way of judicial supervision, and also if during the new investigation of a case after the judgment is vacated, facts are discovered which testify to the accused having committed a graver crime.

Section VI. Execution of Judgment

Article 53. Entry of Judgment into Legal Force and Bringing it into Execution

A judgment shall enter into legal force upon the expiry of the period for cassational appeal or protest unless it has been appealed or protested. If a cassational appeal or cassational protest is brought, the judgment shall, unless it is vacated, enter into legal force upon the consideration of the case by a superior court.

A judgment which is not subject to cassational appeal shall enter into legal force from the moment it is proclaimed.

A judgment to convict shall be executed upon its entry into legal force.

A judgment to acquit and a judgment relieving a person brought to trial from punishment shall be executed immediately upon proclamation of the judgment. If the person brought to trial is under guard, the court shall release him from being under guard in the room of the judicial session.

Supervision over the legality of execution of judgments shall be carried out by the procurator.

Article 54. Binding Nature of Judgment, Ruling, and Decree of a Court

A judgment, ruling, and decree of a court which has entered into legal force shall be binding upon all state and social institutions, enterprises, and organizations, officials, and citizens and shall be subject to execution throughout the territory of the USSR.

FUNDAMENTAL PRINCIPLES OF CORRECTIONAL LABOR LEGISLATION OF THE USSR AND UNION REPUBLICS

[Confirmed by Law of the USSR Supreme Soviet, July 11, 1969, as amended April 26, 1973, February 8, 1977, September 7, 1977, and December 16, 1977. Vedomosti SSSR (1969), no. 29, item 247; (1973), no. 18, item 229; (1977), no. 37, item 556; no. 51, item 772]

Section I. Correctional Labor Legislation of the USSR and Union Republics

Article 1. Tasks of Soviet Correctional Labor Legislation

Correctional labor legislation shall have as its task ensuring the execution of criminal punishment so that it is not merely a chastisement for the crime committed but also reforms and re-educates convicted persons in the spirit of an honorable attitude toward labor, exact execution of the laws, and respect for the rules of socialist community life, prevents the commission of new crimes both by convicted persons and other persons, and also promotes the eradication of criminality.

Article 2. Correctional Labor Legislation of the USSR and Union Republics

Correctional labor legislation of the USSR and union republics shall consist of the present Fundamental Principles determining the principles and establishing the general provisions for the execution and serving of criminal punishment assigned by a court, other laws of the USSR, and also correctional labor codes and other laws of the union republics.

The procedure and conditions for serving punishment and the application of measures of correctional labor pressure to persons sentenced to deprivation of freedom, exile, banishment, and correctional tasks without deprivation of freedom, and also the procedure for the activity of institutions and agencies executing judgments for these types of punishment and for the participation of the public in the reform and re-education of convicted persons shall be established by the Fundamental Principles of Correctional Labor Legislation of the USSR and Union Republics, other laws of the USSR, and also correctional labor codes and other laws of the union republics.

The procedure and conditions for serving punishment by persons sentenced to being sent to a disciplinary battalion shall be established by USSR legislation.

The procedure and conditions for executing and serving other types of criminal punishment shall be established by USSR legislation and union republic legislation.

Article 3. Application of Correctional Labor Legislation of the USSR and Union Republics

Correctional labor legislation of the USSR and the union republic on whose territory the convicted person is serving punishment shall be applied to persons sentenced to deprivation of freedom, exile, and correctional tasks without deprivation of freedom, and with regard to persons sentenced to other types of punishment, the correctional labor legislation of the USSR and also of the union republic at the place of conviction.

Article 4. Basis for Serving Punishment

Only a judgment of a court which has entered into legal force shall be the basis for serving criminal punishment and the application to convicted persons of measures of correctional labor pressure.

Section II. General Provisions for Executing Punishments in the Form of Deprivation of Freedom, Exile, Banishment, and Correctional Tasks Without Deprivation of Freedom

Article 5. Institutions and Agencies Executing Judgments of Courts for Deprivation of Freedom, Exile, Banishment, and Correctional Tasks Without Deprivation of Freedom

Judgments of courts for deprivation of freedom, exile, banishment, and correctional tasks without deprivation of freedom shall be executed by correctional labor institutions and agencies of the USSR Ministry of Internal Affairs and union republic ministries of internal affairs.

Correctional labor institutions shall be organized and liquidated by the USSR Ministry of Internal Affairs and union republic ministries of internal affairs.

Article 6. Places for Serving Punishment

Persons sentenced for the first time to deprivation of freedom shall serve punishment, as a rule, within the limits of the union republic on whose territory they resided prior to arrest or were convicted. In exceptional instances, with a view to more successful reform and re-education of convicted persons, they may be sent to serve punishment in the respective correctional labor institutions of another union republic.

Persons who previously have served punishment in the form of deprivation of freedom, who are convicted, and for whom punishment in the form of the death penalty has been replaced by deprivation of freedom by way of amnesty or pardon, convicted of especially dangerous crimes against the state, and also convicted foreigners or stateless persons, shall be sent to serve punishment in correctional labor institutions designated for the confinement of such categories of convicted persons irrespective of which union republic they resided in prior to arrest or were convicted.

Women sentenced to deprivation of freedom, persons requiring special care, and minors, in the absence of an appropriate correctional labor institution in the union republic where they resided prior to arrest or were convicted, may be sent to serve punishment in a correctional labor institution of another union republic.

A list of localities in which persons sentenced to exile serve punishment, and also a list of localities in which persons sentenced to banishment are prohibited to live shall be established by the USSR Council of Ministers and the union republic councils of ministers.

Persons sentenced to correctional tasks without deprivation of freedom shall serve punishment at their place of work or other places in the district of their residence.

Article 7. Basic Means of Reform and Re-education of Convicted Persons

The basic means of reform and re-education of convicted persons shall be: regime of serving punishment, socially useful labor, political-educational work, and general education and professional-technical training.

Means for reform and re-education should be applied taking into account the character and degree of social danger of the crime committed, the personality of the convicted person, and also the conduct of the convicted person and his attitude toward labor.

Article 8. Legal Status of Persons Serving Punishment in the Form of Deprivation of Freedom, Exile, Banishment, and Correctional Tasks Without Deprivation of Freedom

Persons serving punishment in the form of deprivation of freedom, exile, banishment, and correctional tasks without deprivation of freedom shall bear the duties and enjoy the rights established by legislation for citizens of the USSR with the limitations provided by legislation for convicted persons, and also arising from the judgment of the court and the regime established by the present Fundamental Principles and by union republic correctional labor codes for serving punishment of the particular type.

The legal status of foreigners and stateless persons serving punishment in the form of deprivation of freedom, exile, banishment, and correctional tasks without deprivation of freedom shall be determined by USSR legislation establishing the rights and duties of such persons while they are on the territory of the USSR, with the limitations provided by legislation for convicted persons, and also arising from the judgment of the court and the regime established by the present Fundamental Principles and union republic correctional labor codes for serving punishment of the particular type.

Article 9. Participation of the Public in the Reform and Re-education of Convicted Persons

The public shall participate in the reform and re-education of convicted persons, and also in effectuating social control over the activity of institutions and agencies executing the judgments of courts to deprivation of freedom, exile, banishment, and correctional tasks without deprivation of freedom.

The forms and procedure for public participation in the reform and re-education of convicted persons shall be established by union republic legislation.

Article 10. Procuracy Supervision Over the Execution of Punishment

Supervision over the exact observance of the laws when executing judgments to deprivation of freedom, exile, banishment, and correctional tasks without deprivation of freedom shall be effectuated by the USSR Procurator General and procurators subordinate to him in accordance with the Statute on Procuracy Supervision in the USSR. In effectuating supreme supervision over the observance of legality in the name of the state, the procurator shall be obliged to take timely measures for the prevention and elimination of any violations of the law, from wherever such violations emanate, and bring the guilty persons to responsibility.

The administration of correctional labor institutions and agencies executing judgments of courts for exile, banishment, and correctional tasks without deprivation of freedom shall be obliged to fulfill decrees and proposals of the procurator relative to the observance of rules for serving punishment established by USSR and union republic correctional labor legislation.

Section III. Procedure and Conditions for Execution of Punishment in the Form of Deprivation of Freedom

Article 11. Types of Correctional Labor Institutions

The correctional labor institutions executing punishment in the form of deprivation of freedom shall be: correctional labor colonies, prisons, and educational labor colonies.

Persons who have attained majority and are sentenced to deprivation of freedom shall serve punishment in a correctional labor colony or a prison, and minors under the age of eighteen years, in an educational labor colony.

Correctional labor colonies shall be the basic type of correctional labor institutions for the confinement of persons sentenced to deprivation of freedom who have attained majority.

The type of correctional labor institution with corresponding regime in which convicted persons shall serve punishment shall be determined by the court on the basis of Article 23 of the Fundamental Principles of Criminal Legislation of the USSR and Union Republics.

Article 12. Sending Persons Sentenced to Deprivation of Freedom to Serve Punishment

Persons sentenced to deprivation of freedom shall be sent to serve punishment not later than ten days from the date the judgment entered into legal force or from the date it was levied for execution. The procedure for sending persons sentenced to correctional labor institutions shall be determined by the USSR Ministry of Internal Affairs in accordance with Article 6 of the present Fundamental Principles.

If it is necessary to perform investigative actions in a case concerning a crime committed by another person, the person sentenced to deprivation of freedom, the punishment to be served in a correctional labor or educational labor colony, may be kept in an investigative solitary confinement cell or a prison with the sanction of the procurator of the region, territory, autonomous republic for a term of up to two months, with the sanction of the union republic procurator for a term up to four months, and with the sanction of the USSR Procurator General, for up to six months.

If a convicted person is brought to criminal responsibility in another case and a measure of restraint is selected in respect of him in the form of confinement under guard, the periods for confining him in an investigative solitary confinement cell shall be determined in accordance with Article 34 of the Fundamental Principles of Criminal Procedure of the USSR and Union Republics.

In exceptional instances, in the procedure established by union republic correctional labor codes, persons sentenced for the first time to deprivation of freedom for a crime which is not grave and who are assigned to serve punishment in correctional labor colonies of general regime may, with their consent, be left in a prison or investigative solitary confinement cell for work in municipal services.

Article 13. Separate Confinement of Persons Sentenced to Correctional Labor Institutions

Separate confinement shall be established in correctional labor institutions for: men and women; minors and adolescents.

Males sentenced for the first time to deprivation of freedom shall be confined separately from persons who have previously served deprivation of freedom and those sentenced for the first time for crimes which are not grave or sentenced for the first time for a term not exceeding three years for grave crimes, separately from persons sentenced for the first time to a term exceeding three years for grave crimes; females and minors sentenced to deprivation of freedom shall be confined separately in accordance with the rules provided by Articles 14 and 16 of the present Fundamental Principles. There shall be isolated from other convicted persons and also confined separately: persons sentenced for especially dangerous crimes against the state; especially dangerous recidivists; convicted persons for whom punishment in the form of the death penalty has been replaced by deprivation of freedom by way of pardon or amnesty. Convicted foreigners and stateless persons shall be confined, as a rule, separately from convicted citizens of the USSR. Convicted persons sent in accordance with a court judgment to colonies or settlements for persons who have committed a crime through negligence and convicted persons transferred in the procedure provided by Article 33 of the present Fundamental Principles to colonies and settlements shall be confined separately in different colonies and settlements.

Separate confinement for other categories of convicted persons also may be provided by union republic correctional labor codes.

The requirements for separate confinement of convicted persons established by the present Article shall not extend to therapeutic institutions of places of deprivation of freedom. The procedure for confinement of convicted persons in such therapeutic institutions shall be determined by the USSR Ministry of Internal Affairs by agreement with the Procuracy of the USSR.

Article 14. Correctional Labor Colonies

Correctional labor colonies shall be divided into colonies of general regime, reinforced regime, strict regime, special regime, colonies and settlements for persons who have committed crimes through negligence, and colonies and settlements.

Males sentenced to deprivation of freedom shall serve punishment in correctional labor colonies: general regime, persons sentenced for the first time for a crime which is not grave and sentenced for the first time for a term not exceeding three years for grave crimes; reinforced regime, persons sentenced for the first time for a term exceeding three years for grave crimes; strict regime, persons sentenced for especially dangerous crimes against the state or who have previously served punishment in the form of deprivation of freedom; special regime, persons deemed especially dangerous recidivists and convicted persons for whom punishment in the form of the death penalty has been replaced by deprivation of freedom by way of pardon or amnesty.

Females sentenced to deprivation of freedom shall serve punishment in correctional labor colonies or general and strict regimes. Females shall serve punishment in strict regime colonies who were sentenced for especially dangerous crimes against the state or deemed especially dangerous recidivists, and women for whom punishment in the form of the death penalty has been replaced by deprivation of freedom by way of pardon or amnesty.

Persons sentenced for the first time to deprivation of freedom for a term not exceeding five years for crimes committed through negligence shall serve punishment in colonies or settlements for persons who committed crimes through negligence, and persons who have firmly embarked upon the path to reform and transferred to such colonies in the procedure provided for by Article 33 of the present Fundamental Principles from general, reinforced, and strict regime colonies shall serve punishment in colonies and settlements.

Article 15. Prisons

There shall serve punishment in prisons:

especially dangerous recidivists sentenced to deprivation of freedom in the form of confinement in prison, persons under eighteen years of age who have committed especially dangerous crimes against the state, and persons who upon attaining eighteen years of age have committed other grave crimes and been sentenced for these to deprivation of freedom for a term exceeding five years;

persons transferred from correctional labor colonies on the grounds provided for by Article 34 of the present Fundamental Principles.

Persons left in prison in the procedure established by Article 12 of the present Fundamental Principles for work in municipal services also shall serve punishment in prisons.

Two types of regime, general and strict, shall be established in prisons.

Persons sentenced for the first time to confinement in prison and persons transferred from strict regime shall be confined in the general regime.

There shall be confined in the strict regime: persons who have previously served confinement in prison; persons sentenced to confinement in prison for crimes committed in places of deprivation of freedom; persons transferred from colonies in order to serve punishment in prison; persons transferred in the established procedure to strict regime as a sanction.

The term for confinement in strict regime shall be established within the limits of two to six months in the procedure determined by union republic correctional labor codes.

Pregnant women, and also women having nursing children with them, may not be confined in strict regime.

Article 16. Educational Labor Colonies

Educational labor colonies shall be divided into general regime and reinforced regime colonies.

Minors of the male sex sentenced for the first time to deprivation of freedom for crimes which are not grave or sentenced for the first time to a term not exceeding three years for grave crimes, and also all convicted minors of the female sex shall serve punishment in educational labor colonies of general regime; minors of the male sex who have previously served punishment in the form of deprivation of freedom, and also those sentenced to deprivation of freedom for a term exceeding three years for grave crimes, in colonies of reinforced regime.

Article 17. Serving by Convicted Persons of the Entire Term of Punishment in One Correctional Labor Institution

Persons sentenced to deprivation of freedom should serve the entire term of punishment, as a rule, in one correctional labor colony, prison, or educational labor colony.

The transfer of a convicted person to serve further punishment from one colony to another of the same type of regime or from one prison to another shall be permitted in the event of his illness or of a material change in the amount or character of the work fulfilled by the convicted persons, and also if there are other exceptional circumstances preventing the further confinement of the convicted person in the particular colony or prison. The procedure for the transfer of convicted persons shall be determined by the USSR Ministry of Internal Affairs by agreement with the Procuracy of the USSR.

A convicted person may be transferred from one colony to another colony of another type of regime, from a colony to a prison, and also from a prison to a colony, by a court on the grounds provided for by Articles 18, 33, and 34 of the present Fundamental Principles.

The transfer of a convicted person from a correctional labor institution to an investigative solitary confinement cell or prison shall be permitted:

in connection with the consideration of a case in court: by ruling of the court at the time the case is considered;

in connection with the performance of investigative actions in a case concerning a crime committed by another person: with the sanction of the procurator of the region, territory, or autonomous republic for a term of two months, with the sanction of a union republic procurator, for up to four months, and with the sanction of the USSR Procurator General, for up to six months.

Article 18. Transfer of Convicted Persons from Educational Labor Colonies to Correctional Labor Colonies

Convicted persons who have attained eighteen years of age shall be transferred from an educational labor colony to serve further punishment in a correctional labor colony: persons confined in an educational labor colony of general regime, to a correctional labor colony of general regime; persons confined in an educational labor colony of reinformed regime, to a correctional labor colony of general or reinforced regime, depending on the degree of social danger of the crime committed and the personality and conduct of the convicted person.

For the purpose of consolidating the results of reform and re-education or completing general education or professional-technical training, convicted persons who have attained eighteen years of age may be left, in the instances and in the procedure established by law, in an educational labor colony until the end of the term of punishment but not longer than until they attain twenty years of age.

The question of transfer to a correctional labor colony of a convicted person who has attained eighteen years of age shall be settled by a court in the procedure established by USSR and union republic legislation.

Article 19. Basic Requirements of the Regime in Places of Deprivation of Freedom

The basic requirements of the regime in places of deprivation of freedom shall be: obligatory isolation of convicted persons and constant supervision over them so that the possibility of their committing new crimes or other antisocial offenses is precluded; various conditions of confinement depending upon the character and degree of social danger of the crime committed and the personality and conduct of the convicted person.

Convicted persons shall wear a uniform design of clothing and shall be subjected to search. The correspondence of convicted persons shall be subject to censorship, and packages and parcels, to inspection.

Convicted persons serving punishment in correctional labor colonies of special regime shall be confined in cell-type premises and shall wear a special design of clothing.

A strictly regulated internal discipline shall be established in correctional labor institutions.

Convicted persons shall not be allowed to keep money or valuable articles with themselves nor articles prohibited for use in correctional labor institutions. Money and valuable articles discovered on convicted persons shall be seized and, as a rule, shall be converted to state revenue by a reasoned decree of the head of the correctional labor institutions which is sanctioned by a procurator.

Convicted persons shall be permitted in the procedure established by the present Fundamental Principles and the union republic correctional labor codes to acquire food products and basic necessities through noncash clearing accounts, have meetings, receive packages, parcels, printed matter, cash remittances, carry on correspondence, and send cash remittances to relatives.

Article 20. Peculiarities of the Regime in Correctional Labor Colonies and Settlements

In correctional labor colonies or settlements for persons who have committed crimes through negligence and in colonies and settlements, convicted persons shall:

be confined without guard but under supervision;

in the hours from rising to retreat, enjoy the freedom of movement within the limits of the entire territory of the colony;

with the authorization of the administration of the colony, may move about without supervision outside the territory of the colony, but within the limits of the region, territory, autonomous republic, or union republic not divided into regions, if this is necessary by virtue of the nature of the work they fulfill or in connection with training;

may wear clothing used in ordinary dress, have money and valuable articles with them, and use money without restrictions;

with the authorization of the administration of the colony, where there are housing conditions, may live in the colony with their families, acquire a dwelling house in accordance with prevailing legislation, and set up a home on the territory of the colony.

On condition of conscientious work and exemplary conduct of convicted persons who have served punishment in colonies and settlements for persons who have committed crimes through negligence and convicted persons who have served punishment in colonies and settlements where they were transferred in the procedure provided by Article 33 of the Fundamental Principles, the court upon the joint petition of the agency executing punishment and the supervisory commission attached to the executive committee of a local soviet of people's deputies may include the time they worked in colonies and settlements in their overall labor experience record.

Convicted males and females may be confined in a single colony or settlement irrespective of what type of colonies they were previously confined in.

Article 21. Peculiarities of the Regime in Prisons

Convicted persons shall be confined in prisons in common cells. When necessary, convicted persons may be confined in one-man cells by a reasoned decree of the head of the prison and with the consent of the procurator.

Convicted persons confined in a prison of general regime shall enjoy a daily walk of one hour in duration, and those confined in strict regime, of thirty minutes in duration.

Convicted persons left in accordance with Article 12 of the present Fundamental Principles in prison or investigative solitary confinement cells for work in municipal services shall use money, have meetings, receive packages, parcels, and printed matter according to the norms established for convicted persons confined in correctional labor colonies of general regime. Two lengthy meetings shall replace six brief meetings.

Article 22. Changing Conditions for Confinement of Persons Sentenced to Deprivation of Freedom While Serving Punishment

Depending on conduct and attitude toward labor, the conditions of confinement for convicted persons may be changed both within the limits of one correctional labor institution and by means of transfer to other correctional labor institutions.

The conditions of confinement for convicted persons within the limits of one correctional labor institution shall be changed by decree of the head of the correctional labor institution.

The conditions of confinement for convicted persons by means of transfer from one correctional labor colony to another colony of another type of regime, from a colony to a prison, or from prison to a colony shall be changed on the grounds established by Articles 33 and 34 of the present Fundamental Principles.

Article 23. Acquisition by Convicted Persons of Food Products and Basic Necessities

Convicted persons shall be permitted to acquire food products and basic necessities for money earned at places of deprivation of freedom, and convicted persons who are not capable of working, pregnant women, nursing mothers, and minors, also for money received through remittances. The amount of money allowed to be spent shall be determined by the union republic correctional labor codes in an amount not exceeding fifteen rubles per month, taking into account the type of correctional labor institution, the regime established therein, the term of punishment being served, conduct, attitude toward labor, character of the work fulfilled, and climatic conditions.

Article 24. Meetings of Persons Sentenced to Deprivation of Freedom with Relatives and Other Persons

Convicted persons shall be allowed meetings: short-term, up to four hours in duration, and long-term, up to three days in duration. Short-term meetings shall be allowed with relatives and other persons in the presence of a representative of a correctional labor institution. Long-term meetings shall be allowed with the right of joint cohabitation and only with close relatives.

Meetings shall be allowed during a year: in correctional labor colonies of general regime, three short-term and two long-term; reinforced regime, two short-term and two long-term; strict regime, two short-term and one long-term; special regime, one short-term and one long-term; in educational labor colonies of general regime, six short-term; reinforced regime, four short-term; prisons, two short-term for those confined in general regime; correctional labor colonies and settlements, without restriction.

A convicted person with good conduct and an honorable attitude toward labor in serving at least half the term of punishment may be allowed additionally during a year: in correctional labor colonies, one long-term meeting, and if the convicted person does not have close relatives, one short-term meeting; in correctional labor colonies of general regime when convicted persons have served one-quarter of the term of punishment, six short-term meetings; in colonies of reinforced regime where convicted persons have served one third of the term of punishment, two short-term meetings.

Article 24-1. Short-Term Leaves Beyond the Limits of Places of Deprivation of Freedom

Short-term leaves beyond the limits of places of deprivation of freedom for a term of not more than seven days may be authorized for convicted persons confined in correctional labor colonies of general regime or colonies and settlements for persons who committed crimes through negligence or colonies and settlements and educational labor colonies, not counting the time needed for round-trip travel (not exceeding five days) in connection with exceptional personal circumstances: death or grave illness of a close relative threatening the life of the ill person; accident causing significant material damage to the convicted person or his family.

Authorization for short-term leave shall be given by the head of the correctional labor institution by agreement with the procurator, taking into account the personality and conduct of the convicted person. The time during which the convicted person is outside the limits of the correctiona labor institution shall be counted toward the term of serving punishment. The cost of travel of the convicted person shall be paid by him personally or by his relatives. Earnings shall not be added to the account during the convicted person's time beyond the limits of the correctional labor institution.

The procedure for granting short term leaves to convicted persons beyond the limits of places of deprivation of freedom in connection with exceptional personal circumstances shall be determined by the USSR Ministr of Internal Affairs by agreement with the Procuracy of the USSR.

Article 25. Receipt of Packages and Parcels by Persons Sentenced to Deprivation of Freedom

Convicted persons confined in correctional labor colonies shall be permitted, upon serving half the term of punishment, to receive up to three packages or parcels per year.

Convicted persons serving punishment in educational labor colonies shall be permitted to receive up to six packages and parcels per year.

The number and weight of the packages and parcels shall be established depending on the type of regime of the colonies by the union republic correctional labor codes.

The receipt of packages and parcels shall not be allowed for convicted persons serving deprivation of freedom in prisons.

Irrespective of the type of regime assigned to them, convicted persons shall be allowed to receive not more than two packages of printed matter per year, and also to acquire without restriction literature through the book trade network.

The quantity of packages, parcels, and printed matter received by convicted persons shall not be restricted in correctional labor colonies and settlements.

Article 26. Correspondence of Persons Sentenced to Deprivation of Freedom

Convicted persons shall be permitted to receive letters without restriction as to quantity.

The number of letters which convicted persons may send shall be restricted by the following norms: in correctional labor colonies of reinforced regime, not more than three letters per month; of strict regime, not more than two letters; of special regime, one letter per month; in prisons: in general regime, one letter per month; in strict regime, one letter in two months.

Convicted persons serving punishment in correctional labor colonies of general regime, in correctional labor colonies and settlements, and educational labor colonies may send letters without restriction as to number.

Correspondence between convicted persons confined in places of deprivation of freedom who are not relatives shall be prohibited.

Convicted persons shall have the right to direct complaints, applications, and letters to state agencies, social organizations, and officials. Complaints, applications, and letters of convicted persons shall be sent by affiliation and shall be authorized in the procedure established by law.

Complaints, applications, and letters addressed to a procurator shall not be subject to inspection and shall be sent by affiliation within a twenty-four hour period.

Article 27. Labor of Persons Who are Deprived of Freedom

Each convicted person shall be obliged to work. The administration of correctional labor colonies shall be obliged to ensure that convicted persons are involved in socially useful labor, taking into account their capacity to work and, if possible, their specialization. Persons serving punishment in correctional labor colonies of special regime shall be used, as a rule, for heavy work.

Convicted persons shall be enlisted for labor, as a rule, at enterprises of correctional labor institutions.

The production and economic activity of correctional labor institutions should be subordinated to their basic task: reform and re-education of convicted persons.

Article 28. Labor Conditions of Persons Who are Deprived of Freedom

An eight-hour work day shall be established for persons serving punishment in correctional labor colonies and prisons; they shall be granted one day of rest weekly. Convicted persons shall be relieved from work on holidays in the procedure provided by labor legislation.

The length of the work day for convicted persons serving punishment in correctional labor colonies and settlements and in educational labor colonies, and also the weekly days of rest allowed them, shall be established on the general grounds in accordance with labor legislation.

Persons who are deprived of freedom shall not have the right to leave during the period of serving punishment.

The work time of convicted persons while they are serving punishment in the form of deprivation of freedom shall not be counted as labor experience except for the instances specially provided for in law.

The labor of convicted persons shall be organized with observance of the rules for labor protection and safety techniques established by labor legislation.

Persons who have lost the capacity to work while serving punishment shall, after their release from punishment, have the right to a pension and to compensation for harm in the instances and in the procedure established by USSR legislation.

Article 29. Payment of Labor of Persons Deprived of Freedom

The labor of persons deprived of freedom shall be paid in accordance with its quantity and quality according to norms and rates prevailing in the national economy. The earnings of convicted persons shall be calculated by taking into account the partial reimbursement by him of expenses for confinement in correctional labor institutions.

Persons serving punishment in correctional labor colonies and prisons shall reimburse, from earnings calculated for them, the cost of food and clothing, except for the cost of special clothing. After reimbursement of these expenses from the earnings calculated, withholdings shall be made according to writs of execution and other executory documents in the procedure provided for by union republic legislation. As an exception to this rule, alimony for minor children shall be calculated from the entire amoun earned by the convicted person, including that portion deducted in reimbursement of expenses for maintenance in correctional labor institutions and shall be withheld before reimbursement of such expenses.

In correctional labor colonies and prisons for the personal account of convicted persons who have not violated the regime and have fulfilled the work norms or established planned tasks at least ten per cent of their monthly earnings should be entered irrespective of all withholdings, and for the personal account of first and second group disabled persons who have not violated the regime, at least twenty-five per cent. In educationa labor colonies at least forty-five per cent of the monthly earnings should be entered in the personal account of convicted persons who have not violated the regime irrespective of all withholdings.

At least fifty per cent of the total amount of earnings should be paid to persons serving punishment in correctional labor colonies and settlements for persons who have committed crimes through negligence and in colonies and settlements, as well as to convicted females who are permitted to live outside the colony in accordance with Article 36 of the present Fundamental Principles irrespective of all withholdings.

The conditions and procedure for the payment of labor of persons deprived of freedom shall be determined by the USSR Council of Ministers.

Convicted persons may be enlisted for labor without payment in the procedure established by the present Fundamental Principles and union republic correctional labor codes only for work relating to the amenities of places of deprivation of freedom and territory adjacent thereto, and also to improve the cultural and domestic conditions of the convicted persons.

Article 30. Political-Educational Work with Persons Deprived of Freedom

Political-educational work shall be carried on with persons deprived of freedom directed toward educating them in the spirit of an honorable attitude toward labor, exact execution of the laws, and respect for the rules of socialist community life, an attitude of care toward socialist ownership, toward raising consciousness and their cultural level, and toward the development of useful initiative of convicted persons.

The participation of convicted persons in political-educational measures shall be encouraged and taken into account when determining the degree of their reform and re-education.

Article 31. General Education and Professional-Technical Training of Persons Deprived of Freedom

Compulsory eight-year general education for convicted persons shall be carried on in correctional labor institutions. Pupils shall be relieved of work in order to take examinations for the period provided by USSR and union republic labor legislation. Wages shall not be calculated for them during this period, and food shall be granted free of charge.

Compulsory professional-technical training shall be organized for convicted persons not having a specialization.

Convicted persons more than forty years old shall be enlisted for general education at their wish, and first and second group disabled persons, also for professional-technical training.

The organization of general education and professional-technical training for persons deprived of freedom shall be carried out in the procedure established by the USSR Council of Ministers.

Article 32. Amateur Organizations in Places of Deprivation of Freedom

With a view to developing the skills of collectivism in convicted persons serving punishment in places of deprivation of freedom and encouraging useful initiative, and also using the influence of the collective for the reform and re-education of convicted persons in correctional labor institutions, amateur organizations of convicted persons working under the direction of the administration of these institutions shall be created.

Types of amateur organizations and their work procedure shall be determined by union republic correctional labor codes.

Article 33. Measures of Incentive Applicable to Persons Deprived of Freedom

The following incentive measures may be applied to convicted persons for good conduct and an honorable attitude toward labor and study:

-- announcement of gratitude;

-- being placed on the board of production peredoviki;

-- awarding a certificate of merit;

-- bonus for the excellent work indicators;

-- permission to receive one package or parcel additionally per year;

-- granting one short-term or long-term meeting additionally per year;

-- permission to spend additional money in an amount of up to two rubles for the purchase of food products and basic necessities on holidays, and in educational labor colonies, in an amount of up to two rubles per month;

-- removal of a previously imposed sanction before time;

-- transfer in a correctional labor colony of special regime for convicted persons who have served at least one-third of the term of punishment from cell-type premises to ordinary living premises in the same colony;

-- increasing the walking time for convicted persons confined in a prison on general regime to up to two hours, and on strict regime, up to one hour.

The procedure for the application to convicted persons of incentive measures shall be established by union republic correctional labor codes.

Convicted persons who have firmly embarked on the path of reform may be recommended for transfer to serve further punishment in the procedure established by USSR and union republic legislation:

-- from prison to a correctional labor colony: upon serving at least half the term of prison confinement assigned by court judgment;

-- from a correctional labor colony of special regime to a colony of strict regime: upon serving at least half the term of punishment in the colony of special regime;

-- from correctional labor colonies of general, reinforced, and strict regime to a colony or settlement: upon serving at least half the term of punishment if conditional early release may be applied to them by law and upon serving at least two thirds of the term of punishment if conditional early release may not be applied to them by law;

-- from correctional labor colonies of general, reinforced, and strict regimes to a colony or settlement: upon serving at least one third of the term of punishment, and the convicted persons enumerated in Article 44, paragraph six, and Article 44-1 of the Fundamental Principles of Criminal Legislation of the USSR and Union Republics, respectively: upon serving at least half and two-thirds of the term of punishment assigned.

Convicted persons who have proved their reform by exemplary conduct and an honorable attitude toward labor and study may be recommended in the procedure established by law for conditional early release or for replacement of the unserved part of the punishment by a milder punishment.

Article 34. Penalties Applicable to Persons Deprived of Freedom

The following penalties may be applied to convicted persons for violation of the requirements of the regime of serving punishment:

-- warning or reprimand;

-- extra duty in cleaning the premises or territory of the place of deprivation of freedom;

-- depriving for one time convicted persons confined in educational labor colonies of visiting the cinema, a concert, or participating in sport games;

-- deprivation of a regular meeting;

-- deprivation of the right to receive a regular package or parcel and prohibiting for a period of up to one month the purchase of food products;

-- cancelling improved conditions for confinement provided for by Articles 23, 24, and 25 of the present Fundamental Principles;

-- installing convicted persons confined in correctional labor colonies in a punitive solitary confinement cell with or without bringing them out for work or study for a term of up to fifteen days, and persons confined in educational labor colonies, in a disciplinary solitary confinement cell for a term of up to ten days;

-- installing convicted persons confined in prisons in a cell without bringing them out for work or study for a term of up to fifteen days;

-- transfer of convicted persons confined in correctional labor colonies of general, reinforced, and strict regime in cell-type premises for a term of up to six months; in colonies of special regime, in one-person cells for a term of up to one year; and in prisons, on strict regime for the term established by Article 15 of the present Fundamental Principles; the transfer of convicted persons confined in ordinary dwelling premises of a colony of special regime, to cell-type premises in the same colony.

The regime provided for the confinement of convicted persons on strict regime in prison shall be established in cell-type premises of correctional labor colonies.

Females having nursing children with them, and females released from work because of pregnancy, shall not be installed in a punitive solitary confinement cell, a cell-type premise, nor, in a prison, in a cell or on strict regime.

The procedure for the application of penalties to convicted persons shall be established by union republic correctional labor codes.

Convicted persons who maliciously violate the requirements of the regime may be recommended for transfer in the procedure established by USSR and union republic legislation to serve punishment from colonies and settlements to a correctional labor colony of the same type of regime which was previously determined for them by a court, and persons convicted for crimes committed through negligence and sent to a colony or settlement for persons who have committed crimes through negligence, to a colony of general regime; convicted persons transferred from a colony of special regime to a colony of strict regime, to a colony of special regime; from a correctional labor colony, to a prison for a term not exceeding three years, serving the remaining term of punishment in the colony; from a correctional labor colony of general regime, to an educational labor colony of reinforced regime.

Penalties imposed should correspond to the gravity and character of the offense of the convicted person.

If in the course of a year from the date of serving a penalty the convicted person is not subjected to a new penalty, he shall be deemed as not having had a penalty.

Article 35. Material Responsibility of Persons Deprived of Freedom

Persons deprived of freedom shall bear material responsibility for material damage caused while serving punishment to the state in the amounts established by USSR and union republic legislation.

Damage shall be recovered by decree of the head of the correctional labor institution in the procedure established by union republic correctional labor codes.

After the release of the convicted person from punishment, the damage not compensated by him while serving punishment may be recovered by decision of a court in the procedure established by law.

If material damage is caused by a crime committed while serving punishment, the damage shall be recovered on the general grounds.

Article 36. Material-Domestic Provision for Persons Deprived of Freedom

Persons serving punishment in places of deprivation of freedom shall be provided the necessary housing and domestic conditions corresponding to the sanitary and hygiene rules.

Convicted persons shall be granted an individual sleeping place and bedding. They shall be provided with clothing, linen, and footwear according to the season and taking into account climatic conditions.

Convicted persons shall receive food ensuring the normal activity of the organism. Food norms shall be differentiated depending on the climatic conditions of the place where the correctional labor institution is locate the character of work fulfilled by convicted persons, and their attitude toward labor. Persons installed in a punitive or disciplinary solitary confinement cell, a cell, a cell-type premise, and also in a one-person cell in a colony of special regime, shall receive reduced rations of food.

Pregnant women, nursing mothers, minors, and also ill persons shall have improved living and domestic conditions and higher food norms shall be established. Upon the opinion of a medical commission such persons shall be permitted to receive additional food packages and parcels.

Convicted females who work conscientiously and observe the requirements of the regime may, by agreement with the supervisory commission, be permitted by the administration of a correctional labor institution to live outside the colony while released from work for pregnancy and birth, and also until the child attains two years of age. The procedure for convicted females to live outside the colony shall be determined by the unior republic correctional labor codes.

Food shall be granted free of charge to convicted persons released from work for illness, pregnant females, and nursing mothers for the period of their release from work. Minors, and also first and second group disabled persons, shall be granted food and clothing free of charge. The cost of food and clothing shall be recovered from convicted persons who maliciously evade work from assets which they have in their personal accounts.

Food norms and the material-domestic provision for persons deprived of freedom shall be established by the USSR Council of Ministers.

Article 37. Medical Service for Persons Deprived of Freedom

The necessary treatment institutions shall be organized at places of deprivation of freedom.

Prophylactic treatment and anti-epidemic work in places of deprivation of freedom shall be organized and carried out in accordance with public health legislation.

The procedure for rendering medical care to persons deprived of freedom, for the use of treatment institutions of public health agencies, and for recruiting medical personnel for this purpose shall be determined by the USSR Ministry of Internal Affairs and the USSR Ministry of Public Health.

When necessary, a children's home shall be organized attached to correctional labor colonies. Convicted persons may place their children in a children's home who are up to two years of age.

Article 38. Movement of Persons Deprived of Freedom Without Escort

In exceptional instances at correctional labor colonies convicted persons who are firmly on the path of reform and have served at least one-third of the term of punishment, and convicted persons to whom in accordance with law conditional early release does not apply and who have served at least two-thirds of the term of punishment, may be permitted to move about without escort beyond the limits of the colony if this is necessary by virtue of the character of work fulfilled by the convicted persons.

Convicted persons confined in educational labor colonies who are firmly on the path of reform and have served at least six months deprivation of freedom may be permitted to move about beyond the limits of the colony without being accompanied if this is necessary by virtue of the character of the work fulfilled by the convicted persons.

Movement without escort beyond the limits of the colony by especially dangerous recidivists, persons convicted for especially dangerous crimes against the state, convicted persons for whom punishment in the form of the death penalty has been replaced by deprivation of freedom by way of pardon or amnesty, and also convicted foreigners and stateless persons, shall not be permitted. The movement of other categories of convicted persons without escort also may be prohibited by the union republic correctional labor codes.

The movement of convicted persons without escort shall not be permitted in union republic capital cities, in frontier and resort localities, and also in other population centers determined by the USSR Ministry of Internal Affairs.

The procedure for granting convicted persons the right of movement without escort beyond the limits of a colony shall be established by the union republic correctional labor codes.

Article 39. Security Measures and Grounds for Using Weapons

The application of handcuffs or a strait jacket to persons deprived of freedom, if they show physical resistance to workers of correctional labor institutions, display unruly conduct or commit other coercive actions, shall be permitted with a view to averting their causing harm to those around them or to themselves.

If a person deprived of freedom commits an attack or other intentional action directly threatening the life of workers of correctional labor institutions or other persons, and also when escaping from under guard, the use of weapons shall be permitted as an exceptional measure if it is impossible to restrain the said actions by other measures. Weapons shall not be permitted in the event of the escape of females and minors.

The administration of a place of deprivation of freedom shall be obliged to inform the procurator immediately about each instance of the use of a weapon.

Section III-A. Procedure and Conditions for Executing Conditional Sentence to Deprivation of Freedom with Obligatory Enlistment of the Convicted Person to Labor and Conditional Release from Places of Deprivation of Freedom with Obligatory Enlistment of the Convicted Person to Labor

Article 39-1. Sending Convicted Persons to a Place of Obligatory Enlistment for Labor

Persons conditionally sentenced to deprivation of freedom with obligatory enlistment for labor who at the moment of the entry of the judgment into legal force are free shall travel at state expense to the place of work independently. In such instances the court which decreed the judgment shall send a regulation concerning execution of the judgment to the internal affairs agency at the place of residence of the convicted person. The internal affairs agency shall hand an order concerning travel to the place of work to the convicted person. The convicted person shall be obliged within three days from the date of receiving the order to depart for the place of work and to arrive there within the period necessary for travel specified in the travel order.

Persons conditionally sentenced to deprivation of freedom with obligatory enlistment for labor who at the moment of the entry of the judgment into legal force are under guard shall be sent to work in the procedure established for persons sentenced to deprivation of freedom. Such persons, and also persons conditionally released from places of deprivation of freedom with obligatory enlistment for labor, shall be subject to being released from under guard upon arrival at the place of work.

Persons who have committed crimes in complicity shall be sent to work, as a rule, at different enterprises.

If a convicted person avoids receiving a travel order to the place of work, fails to travel within the established period, or fails to appear at the place of work, the convicted person shall be detained by an internal affairs agency with the sanction of a procurator for a term of not more than 30 days in order to establish the reasons for the violation of the procedure for independent travel to the place of work. The internal affairs agency shall send the detained person to the place of work in the procedure established for persons sentenced to deprivation of freedom or, if there is data concerning the evasion of execution of the judgment, shall transfer the materials to the court at the place where the convicted person is detained in order to decide the question of sending him to a place of deprivation of freedom in accordance with the judgment.

Article 39-2. Duties and Rights of Persons Conditionally Sentenced and Conditionally Released, Responsibility of Such Persons for Violation of Labor Discipline and Public Order, and Rules for Registration and Supervision Over Them

Persons conditionally sentenced to deprivation of freedom with obligatory enlistment for labor and conditionally released from places of deprivation of freedom with obligatory enlistment for labor shall bear the duties and enjoy the rights established by legislation for citizens of the USSR, with the following limitations:

-- they shall be obliged to work where they are sent by agencies executing the judgment and, in the case of production need, may be transferred without their consent to other work, including work in another locality. Such persons shall be obliged to reside, as a rule, in specially designated dormitories; with good conduct, a conscientious attitude toward labor, and if their families are present, they may be permitted by decree of the head of the internal affairs agency to live with their families in dwelling space which they have rented;

-- they shall be prohibited during the period of the obligatory work term to leave the limits of the administrative district at their place of work without the special permission of the internal affairs agency exercising supervision. They shall be obliged to appear at the internal affairs agency from one to four times per month for registration. The periodicity of registration of a convicted person shall be established by decree of the head of the internal affairs agency exercising supervision over convicted persons.

In exceptional instances, by joint decision of the administration of an enterprise and internal affairs agency, and if there is exemplary conduct and an honorable attitude toward labor, persons conditionally sentenced to deprivation of freedom with obligatory enlistment for labor and conditionally released from places of deprivation of freedom with obligatory enlistment for labor shall be permitted to leave beyond the limits of the administrative district for a business trip, leave, or other important reasons.

A violation by convicted persons of labor discipline or the public order shall entail the application of measures of disciplinary or administrative responsibility in accordance with prevailing legislation.

Persons who have violated labor discipline, public order, or registration rules may, by decree of the head of an internal affairs agency, be prohibited for a term of up to six months from living outside a dormitory, from leaving the dormitory at an established time, or from staying in specified places.

The administration shall be obliged to notify the internal affairs agency immediately about the absence of a convicted person at work for more than three days for unknown reasons or the failure of such persons to return to the place of work.

A convicted person who has gone beyond the limits of the administrative district of his place of work without authorization shall be detained by the internal affairs agency with the sanction of the procurator for a term of not more than 30 days in order to establish the reasons for leaving without authorization. The internal affairs agency shall send the detained person to his place of work in the procedure established for persons sentenced to deprivation of freedom or, if there is data concerning the evasion of execution of judgment, shall transfer the materials to the court at the place where the convicted person is detained in order to decide the question of sending him to a place of deprivation of freedom in accordance with the judgment.

The exercise of supervision over the conduct of persons conditionally sentenced to deprivation of freedom with obligatory enlistment for labor and conditionally released from places of deprivation of freedom with obligatory enlistment for labor shall be entrusted to internal affairs agencies. The procedure for exercising supervision shall be established by the USSR Ministry of Internal Affairs by agreement with the Procuracy of the USSR.

Article 39-3. Labor of Persons Conditionally Sentenced and Conditionally Released, Dismissal from Work, and Transfer of Such Persons to Work in Another Locality

The administration of an enterprise at the place of work of persons conditionally sentenced to deprivation of freedom with obligatory enlistment for labor and conditionally released from places of deprivation of freedom with obligatory enlistment for labor shall be obliged to ensure that such persons are involved in socially useful labor taking into account, if possible, their specializations, to organize their professional training, and to create for them the necessary housing and domestic conditions.

The administrations of enterprises shall be prohibited from dismissing persons conditionally sentenced and conditionally released from work during the term of obligatory enlistment for labor except for instances of conditional early release from punishment, transfer to another enterprise, sending to a place of deprivation of freedom to serve punishment, or being deemed a first or second group disabled person in the established procedure.

The transfer of such persons to work in another locality may be effectuated by the administration only by agreement with the internal affairs agency exercising supervision.

Article 39-4. Political-Educational Work with Persons Conditionally Sentenced and Conditionally Released

Political-educational work shall be carried on with persons conditionally sentenced to deprivation of freedom with obligatory enlistment for labor and conditionally released from places of deprivation of freedom with obligatory enlistment for labor, directed toward educating them in the spirit of an honorable attitude toward labor, exact execution of the laws and respect for the rules of socialist community life, an attitude of care toward socialist ownership, raising consciousness and the cultural level, and the development of useful initiative.

The participation of convicted persons in political-educational measures shall be encouraged and shall be taken into account when determining the degree of their reform and re-education.

The administration and social organizations at the place of work of convicted persons and the agency executing the judgment shall carry on political-educational work with convicted persons.

Section IV. The Procedure and Conditions for Executing Punishment in the Form of Exile, Banishment, and Correctional Tasks Without Deprivation of Freedom

Article 40. Procedure and Conditions for Serving Exile

Persons sentenced to exile shall serve punishment in the locality specified for this purpose.

Persons sentenced to exile shall, not later than ten days after the date the judgment enters into legal force or from the date it is applied for execution, be sent at state expense to the place for serving punishment without an escort or under escort in the procedure established by union republic legislation. The time under escort when being sent to exile shall be subject to being counted toward the term of punishment at a rate of one day under escort for three days of exile.

The reform and re-education of persons serving exile shall be carried out on the basis of their being obligatorily enlisted for socially useful labor, taking into account their capacity to work, and of carrying on political-educational work with them. Exiled persons shall bear responsibility on the general grounds for evading socially useful labor.

Within the limits of the administrative district specified for residence, the exiled person shall select a place of residence at his own discretion. An exiled person shall have the right to leave the limits of the administrative district only in the instances provided by the union republic correctional labor codes.

The procedure for serving exile, responsibility for violation of the regime of exile, and also incentive measures applicable to exiled persons, shall be established by union republic correctional labor codes.

In the procedure established by law persons serving exile who have proved their reform by exemplary conduct and an honorable attitude toward labor may be recommended for conditional early release or for replacement of the unserved part of the punishment by a milder punishment.

Executive committees of local soviets of people's deputies shall, not later than fifteen days from the date exiled persons arrive at the place for serving punishment, provide work for them, taking into account their capacity to work and, if possible, their specialization, and also dwelling space and render them, when necessary, financial assistance until they commence work.

Orders of executive committees of local soviets of people's deputies concerning the arrangement of employment for exiled persons shall be binding upon the directors of enterprises, institutions, and organizations.

The labor of persons serving exile shall be regulated on the general grounds of labor legislation.

Article 41. Procedure and Conditions for Serving Banishment

Persons sentenced to banishment shall, not later than ten days from the date of entry of the judgment into legal force or from the date it is applied for execution, move away from their place of residence. The procedure for moving away convicted persons from their places of residence shall be established by the union republic correctional labor codes.

Banished persons shall select a place of work and a place of residence at their own discretion except for localities in which residence is prohibited for them by virtue of the court judgment.

In the procedure established by law, persons sentenced to banishment who have proved their reform by exemplary conduct and an honorable attitude toward labor may be recommended for conditional early release or for replacement of the unserved part of the punishment by a milder punishment.

Executive committees of local soviets of people's deputies shall render assistance to banished persons in the arranging of employment and obtaining living space.

The labor of persons serving banishment shall be regulated on the general grounds of labor legislation.

Article 42. Types of Correctional Tasks without Deprivation of Freedom and the Procedure for Serving Them

Correctional tasks without deprivation of freedom shall be served in accordance with the judgment of the court at the place of work of the convicted person or in other places determined by agencies executing this type of punishment but in the district of residence of the convicted person, taking into account his capacity to work and, if possible, his specialization. With respect to a minor, in addition, there shall be taken into account the need to ensure proper supervision over his conduct and for him to receive a production qualification.

Judgments for correctional tasks without deprivation of freedom shall be executed not later than ten days from the date of entry of the judgment into legal force or its being applied for execution.

The term for serving correctional tasks without deprivation of freedom shall be calculated in months and days during which the convicted person has worked and deductions have been made from his earnings. The time also shall be counted in this term during which the convicted person did not work for justifiable reasons and earnings were paid to him in accordance with law. Time of illness and time granted to care for a sick person, and also time for pregnancy or birth leave, shall be counted in the term for serving punishment.

Article 43. Organization of the Executing of Punishment in the Form of Correctional Tasks Without Deprivation of Freedom

The reform and re-education of persons serving correctional tasks without deprivation of freedom shall be carried out on the basis of their participation in socially useful labor. Control over the conduct of convicted persons and carrying on political-educational work with them shall be carried out by collectives of the enterprises, institutions, and organizations at the place where they are serving punishment.

Agencies executing this type of punishment shall send persons for work who were sentenced to correctional tasks in other places and, when necessary, shall render assistance in arranging employment for persons sentenced to correctional tasks at their place of work; exercise control over the correctness of making deductions from the earnings of convicted persons and the observance by the administrations of enterprises, institutions, and organizations of the conditions for serving punishment established by USSR and union republic correctional labor legislation; participate in carrying on politital-educational work with convicted persons; apply incentive measures and penalties to them.

With respect to convicted persons deemed not capable of working after the judgment is rendered, agencies executing this type of punishment shall initiate a petition to the court to replace correctional tasks without deprivation of freedom by another milder form of punishment.

Persons sentenced to correctional tasks without deprivation of freedom shall be obliged to observe the established procedure for serving punishment and to appear upon the summons of the agencies executing this type of punishment. In the event of the failure to fulfill this requirement without justifiable reasons, the convicted person may be subjected to being taken into custody.

Article 44. Conditions for Serving Correctional Tasks Without Deprivation of Freedom

Deductions shall be made from the earnings of persons sentenced to correctional tasks without deprivation of freedom for the revenue of the state during the term of serving punishment in amounts established by the judgment of the court. Deductions shall be made from the entire amount of earnings, without excluding taxes and other payments from such amounts, and also irrespective of whether claims exist against the convicted person under executory documents.

The dismissal of convicted persons from work at their own wish without the permission of agencies executing this type of punishment shall be prohibited during the term of serving correctional tasks without deprivation of freedom.

The time of serving correctional tasks without deprivation of freedom shall not be counted in the general and uninterrupted labor experience of the convicted person, an entry thereof being made in his labor book.

On condition of conscientious work and exemplary conduct while serving correctional tasks without deprivation of freedom, this time may be included in the general labor experience of the person who served the punishment on the basis of a court decision in the procedure established by union republic legislation.

Persons sentenced to correctional tasks without deprivation of freedom shall not be granted regular leave while serving punishment. The time of serving punishment shall not be included in the experience giving a right to leave nor to receive privileges or supplementary earnings.

Allowances to persons serving correctional tasks without deprivation of freedom for temporary incapacity to work, pregnancy, and birth shall be calculated in the earnings for which deductions are made assigned by a court judgment.

Article 45. Incentive Measures and Penalties Applicable to Persons Serving Correctional Tasks Without Deprivation of Freedom

Incentive measures and penalties shall be applied to persons serving correctional tasks without deprivation of freedom in accordance with labor legislation.

Convicted persons who have proved their reform by exemplary conduct and an honorable attitude toward labor and study may be recommended in the procedure established by law for conditional early release or for replacement of the unserved part of the punishment by a milder punishment.

In the event persons sentenced to correctional tasks without deprivation of freedom evade serving punishment, they may be warned by the agency executing this type of punishment. In the event of malicious evasion of convicted persons to serve punishment, a recommendation may be submitted to a court by the agency executing this type of punishment to replace the unserved term of correctional tasks without deprivation of freedom by punishment in the form of deprivation of freedom.

Section V. Grounds for Relief from Serving Punishment; Assistance to Persons Released from Places of Deprivation of Freedom; Observance and Supervision Over Them

Article 46. Grounds for Relief from Serving Punishment

Convicted persons shall be relieved from punishment upon serving the term of punishment and upon other grounds established by law. If the term of punishment in the form of deprivation of freedom ends on a day off or on a holiday, the convicted person shall be released on the day preceding the day off or the holiday.

Convicted persons who are ill with a chronic mental or other grave illness preventing further serving of punishment may be released by a court from further serving of punishment.

A person conditionally sentenced to deprivation of freedom with obligatory enlistment for labor or conditionally released from places of deprivation of freedom with obligatory enlistment for labor shall, in the event of being deemed a first or second group disabled person in the established procedure if the disability was received as a consequence of labor mutilation or professional disease, be released before time by a court from further serving punishment.

If a first or second group disability was received by a person specified in paragraph three of the present Article for reasons not connected with his production activity, the court may either release this person before time from further serving punishment or send him to serve deprivation of freedom.

The procedure for the release of the persons specified in paragraphs one, two, three, and four of the present Article from further serving punishment shall be determined by USSR and union republic legislation.

Article 46-1. Recommendation for Conditional Early Release from Punishment and for Replacement of Punishment by a Milder Punishment and for Conditional Release from Places of Deprivation of Freedom with Obligatory Enlistment for Labor

With respect to a convicted person to whom in accordance with Articles 44, 44-2, and 45 of the Fundamental Principles of Criminal Legislation of the USSR and Union Republics conditional early release from punishment or replacement of the unserved part of the punishment by a milder punishment or conditional release from places of deprivation of freedom with obligatory enlistment for labor may be applied, the agency executing punishment shall make, jointly with the agencies and social organizations specified in the enumerated Articles of the Fundamental Principles of Criminal Legislation, a recommendation to the court concerning conditional early release of a convicted person from punishment or replacement of the unserved part of the punishment by a milder punishment or concerning conditional release of the convicted person from places of deprivation of freedom with obligatory enlistment for labor.

Data describing the conduct of the convicted person, his attitude toward labor and study throughout the time of serving punishment should be contained in the recommendation. The personal file of the convicted person shall be sent to the court at the same time as the recommendation.

Article 47. Rendering Material Assistance to Persons Relieved from Punishment; Arranging Employment for Them

Persons released from places of deprivation of freedom shall be provided with passage free of charge to their place of residence or work, and also food products or money en route according to the established norms.

In the absence of necessary seasonal clothing, footwear, or the means for acquiring them, released persons shall be provided with clothing and footwear free of charge. A one-time cash allowance from a special fund may be issued to them.

Payment for the passage of persons released from places of deprivation of freedom, providing them with food, clothing, and footwear, and also issuing one-time cash allowances, shall be by correctional labor institutions in the procedure established by the USSR Council of Ministers.

Persons relieved from punishment should be provided with work, taking into account if possible their specialization, by the executive committees of local soviets of people's deputies not later than fifteen days from the date they apply for assistance in arranging employment. When necessary, dwelling space shall be granted to persons relieved from punishment.

Orders of executive committees of local soviets of people's deputies concerning the arrangement of employment of persons relieved from punishment shall be binding upon the directors of enterprises, institutions, and organizations.

Disabled persons and elderly persons shall, at their request, be subject to being accommodated in homes for the disabled and elderly. Minors not having parents shall, when necessary, be sent by commissions for cases of minors to boarding schools or transferred to guardianship.

Article 48. Observation Over Persons Conditionally Released Early from Serving Punishment

The observation of social organizations and collectives of working people shall be established over persons conditionally released early from serving punishment during the unserved part of the punishment and educational work shall be carried on with such persons.

The procedure for observation over persons conditionally released early from serving punishment shall be established by union republic legislation.

Article 49. Administrative Supervision Over Persons Released from Places of Deprivation of Freedom

The administrative supervision of police agencies shall be established for especially dangerous recidivists and persons who have served punishment for grave crimes and been released from places of deprivation of freedom if their conduct while serving punishment testifies to a persistent lack of desire to embark upon the path to reform and join in an honorable working life.

The grounds for establishing administrative supervision shall be:

-- with respect to especially dangerous recidivists: a judgment which has entered into legal force or a court ruling in which the particular person has been deemed an especially dangerous recidivist;

-- with respect to other persons serving punishment for grave crimes: the opinion of the administration of the correctional labor colony or prison and the supervisory commission concerning the need to establish administrative supervision.

The procedure for effectuating administrative supervision over persons released from places of deprivation of freedom shall be established by USSR and union republic legislation.

STATUTE ON PRELIMINARY CONFINEMENT UNDER GUARD

[Confirmed by Law of the USSR Supreme Soviet, July 11, 1969. Vedomosti SSSR (1969), no. 29, item 248]

Article 1. Preliminary Confinement

Preliminary confinement under guard in accordance with USSR and union republic criminal procedure legislation shall be a measure of restraint with respect to an accused, a person brought to trial, and also a suspect in connection with the commission of a crime, for which punishment in the form of deprivation of freedom may be assigned under the law.

The procedure for preliminary confinement under guard shall be determined by the present Statute, by other USSR legislation, and by union republic legislation.

The procedure for preliminary confinement shall also be extended to convicted persons confined under guard with respect to whom judgments have not entered into legal force.

Article 2. Tasks of the Statute on Preliminary Confinement

The Statute on Preliminary Confinement Under Guard shall, in accordance with Articles 33 and 34 of the Fundamental Principles of Criminal Procedure of the USSR and Union Republics, have as its task the establishment of rules for the confinement of persons in places of preliminary confinement with respect to whom confinement under guard has been selected as a measure of restraint so as to preclude the possibility of their hiding from investigation or the court, to obstruct the establishment of the truth in a criminal case or to engage in criminal activity, and also to ensure execution of the judgment.

Article 3. Grounds for Preliminary Confinement

The grounds for preliminary confinement under guard shall be a decree of an investigator or a decree of the person conducting the inquiry sanctioned by the procurator, the decree of a procurator, or the judgment or ruling of a court selecting confinement under guard as a measure of restraint rendered in accordance with criminal or criminal procedure legislation of the USSR and union republics.

Article 4. Places for Preliminary Confinement

Investigative solitary confinement cells shall be the places of preliminary confinement for confining persons with respect to whom confinement under guard is selected as a measure of restraint. In individual instances such persons may be confined in a prison, preliminary confinement cell, and also the guardhouse.

Persons confined under guard may be confined in a preliminary confinement cell for not more than three days. If the delivery of confined persons to an investigative solitary confinement cell is impossible because of distance or the absence of proper communication, a lengthier term of confinement in a preliminary confinement cell may be established by union republic legislation, but not more than 30 days. In such instances, and also when confined persons under guard are confined in a prison as a measure of restraint, the procedure for confining them shall be determined by the present Statute.

The procedure for confining persons confined under guard in a preliminary confinement cell for up to three days, and also in a guardhouse, shall be determined by USSR legislation.

If persons serving punishment in places of deprivation of freedom are brought to criminal responsibility for the commission of another crime and confinement under guard is selected as the measure of restraint in respect to them, they, by decree of the person or agency proceeding with the case, may be confined in a punitive solitary confinement cell of a correctional labor colony or in a disciplinary solitary confinement cell of an educational labor colony.

Article 5. Ensuring the Procedure for Confinement Under Guard in Places of Preliminary Confinement

Ensuring the procedure for the confinement under guard of persons in places of preliminary confinement shall be entrusted to the administration of places of preliminary confinement.

The administration of places of preliminary confinement shall carry out its activity in accordance with the present Statute and other USSR and union republic legislation.

Article 6. Legal Status of Persons Confined in Places of Preliminary Confinement.

Persons confined in places of preliminary confinement shall bear the duties and have the rights established by legislation for citizens of the USSR, with the limitations provided for by the present Statute and arising from the regime of confinement under guard.

The legal status of foreigners and stateless persons confined in places of preliminary confinement shall be determined by USSR legislation which provides for the rights and duties of such persons while on the territory of the USSR, with the limitations established by the present Statute and arising from the regime of confinement under guard.

Article 7. Basic Requirements of the Regime in Places of Preliminary Confinement

The basic requirements of the regime in places of preliminary confinement shall be: the isolation of persons confined under guard, constant supervision over them, and separate confinement in the procedure provided by Article 8 of the present Statute.

Persons confined under guard as a measure of restraint shall be subject to search, fingerprinting, and being photographed; articles found on them and also parcels or packages arriving for them shall be subject to inspection, and correspondence, to censorship. They shall be prohibited to have money and valuable articles with them, and also articles not authorized for being kept in places of preliminary confinement. Money seized from them during their stay in places of preliminary confinement shall be placed in personal accounts, and valuable articles and items shall be handed over for safekeeping; money and valuable articles acquired by nonlabor means or the source for receiving which has not been established shall be applied to the revenue of the state by a reasoned decree of the head of a place of preliminary confinement sanctioned by the procurator.

Persons confined under guard may be enlisted for labor only within the limits of the territory of the place of preliminary confinement with their consent and upon the authorization of the person or agency proceeding with the case. The conditions for payment for their labor shall be determined in the procedure established by the USSR Council of Ministers.

Article 8. Separate Confinement in Places of Preliminary Confinement

Persons confined under guard shall be confined in common cells. In exceptional instances upon the reasoned decree of the person or agency proceeding with the case or of the head of a place of preliminary confinement sanctioned by the procurator, they may be confined in one-man cells.

Persons confined under guard shall be placed in cells with observance of the following requirements of isolation:

males: separately from females;

minors: separately from adults. In exceptional instances with the sanction of the procurator, the confinement of adults shall be permitted in cells where minors are confined;

persons who have previously served punishment in places of deprivation of freedom: separately from persons not confined in places of deprivation of freedom;

persons accused or suspected of committing grave crimes: separately from other persons confined under guard;

persons accused or suspected of committing especially dangerous crimes against the state: separately, as a rule, from other persons confined under guard;

especially dangerous recidivists: separately from other persons confined under guard;

convicted persons: separately from other persons confined under guard and in accordance with the type of regime of correctional labor colony determined by court judgment;

foreigners and stateless persons: separately, as a rule, from other persons confined under guard.

Persons sentenced to the death penalty shall be confined in isolation from all other persons confined under guard.

Persons suspected or accused in one and the same case shall be confined separately if the person or agency proceeding with the case so instructs.

The procedure for placing persons confined under guard in treatment institutions of places of confinement shall be established by the USSR Ministry of Internal Affairs.

Article 9. Rights of Persons Confined Under Guard

Persons confined under guard shall have the right to:

enjoy a daily walk of one hour in length;

receive a parcel or package once per month of up to five kilograms in weight; receive cash remittances; purchase food products and basic necessities on account for an amount of up to ten rubles per month; use their own clothing and footwear;

have with them documents and records relating to the criminal case;

use table games and books from the library of the place of preliminary confinement;

make appeals and applications to state agencies, social organizations, and officials in the procedure established by Article 13 of the present Statute.

Females confined under guard shall have the right to have children up to two years of age with them. Pregnant women and women having children with them, and also minors, shall have a daily walk of up to two hours in length.

Persons serving punishment in places of deprivation of freedom shall, if confinement under guard is selected as a measure of restraint with respect to them in connection with a proceeding in another case, be confined in accordance with the rules established by the present Statute. The right to receive packages and parcels, and also to buy food products and basic necessities, shall be established by USSR and union republic legislation for the type of regime of correctional labor colony assigned them under the judgment, ruling, or decree of the court.

Article 10. Duties of Persons Confined Under Guard

Persons confined under guard shall be obliged to:

observe the procedure established in places of preliminary confinement;

fulfill the requirements of the administration;

regularly perform cell duty by assignment of the administration;

carefully treat inventory, equipment, and other property of places of preliminary confinement.

Article 11. Material-Domestic Provision and Medical Services for Persons Confined Under Guard

The necessary housing and domestic conditions corresponding to sanitary and hygiene rules shall be provided to persons confined under guard.

Persons confined under guard shall be granted food free of charge according to the established norms, an individual sleeping place, bedding, and other types of material-domestic provision. When necessary, clothing and footwear of the established form shall be issued to them.

Medical services, and also prophylactic treatment and anti-epidemic work in places of preliminary confinement shall be organized and carried out in accordance with public health legislation.

The procedure for rendering medical assistance to persons confined under guard, the use of treatment institutions of public health agencies, and the enlistment of their medical personnel for this purpose shall be determined by the USSR Ministry of Internal Affairs and the USSR Ministry of Public Health.

Article 12. Procedure for Allowing Meetings to Persons Confined Under Guard

Meetings with relatives or other persons may be allowed persons confined under guard by the administration of the place of preliminary confinement only with the authorization of the person or agency proceeding with the case. The duration of meetings shall be established as from one to two hours. The person or agency proceeding with the case may authorize a meeting, as a rule, not more than once a month.

From the moment defense counsel is permitted to take part in a case, confirmed by notification in writing from the person or agency proceeding with the case, persons confined under guard shall have the right to a meeting with defense counsel alone, without limitation as to the number of meetings or their duration.

Article 13. Correspondence of Persons Confined Under Guard and the Procedure for Sending Appeals, Applications, and Letters

Persons confined under guard may correspond with relatives and other citizens upon the authorization of the person or agency proceeding with the case.

Appeals, applications, and letters of persons confined under guard shall be reviewed by the administration of the place of preliminary confinement. Appeals, applications, and letters addressed to the procurator shall not be subject to inspection and shall be sent to the address within twenty four hours from the time they are submitted.

In accordance with criminal procedure legislation of the USSR and union republics, appeals against the action of the person conducting an inquiry or the investigator shall be sent by the administration of the place of preliminary confinement to the procurator not later than three days from the time they are submitted, and appeals against the action and decision of a procurator, to the superior procurator.

Other appeals, applications, and letters connected with the proceeding in a criminal case shall be sent not later than three days from the time they are submitted by the administration of the place of preliminary confinement to the person or agency proceeding with the case. They shall be reviewed by this person or agency and not later than three days from the time received shall be sent to the proper quarter. Appeals, applications, and letters containing information whose communication may hinder the establishment of the truth in a criminal case shall not be sent to the proper quarter, the person confined under guard being notified thereof and the procurator also informed.

Appeals, applications, and letters relating to questions not connected with the proceeding in the case shall be considered respectively by the administration of the place of preliminary confinement or shall be sent to the proper quarter in the procedure established by law.

Article 14. Incentive Measures Applicable to Persons Confined Under Guard

The following incentive measures may be applied by the administration of a place of preliminary confinement to persons confined under guard if their conduct is exemplary:

announcement of gratitude;

removal of a previously imposed penalty before time;

increasing the duration of walking.

Article 15. Penalties Applicable to Persons Confined Under Guard

The following penalties may be applied by the administration of a place of preliminary confinement to persons confined under guard who have violated the requirements of the regime:

warning or reprimand;

extra duty in cleaning the premises;

deprivation of the right for one month to buy food products and receive a regular package or parcel.

Persons confined under guard who maliciously violate the requirements of the regime may, by a reasoned decree of the head of the place of preliminary confinement, be installed in a cell for a term of up to ten days, and minors, for a term up to five days. Pregnant women and women having children with them shall not be subject to being installed in a cell.

Penalties applied to persons confined under guard should correspond to the gravity and character of the offense. The application of measures shall not be permitted which have as their purpose the infliction of physical suffering on or reducing human dignity of persons confined under guard.

Article 16. Material Responsibility of Persons Confined Under Guard

Persons confined under guard shall bear material responsibility for material damage caused during a stay in places of preliminary confinement to the state in amounts established by USSR and union republic legislation.

The damage shall be recovered by decree of the head of the place of preliminary confinement from cash amounts which the person confined under guard has in his personal account. Damage not compensated by him during the stay in the place of preliminary confinement may, if the said person is sentenced to punishment in the form of deprivation of freedom, be recovered by the administration of a correctional labor institution from assets deposited in the personal account of the convicted person.

In the event the measure of restraint is vacated or changed, the material damage not compensated by the person released from under guard may be recovered on the general grounds.

Article 17. Security Measures and Grounds for Using Weapons

The use of handcuffs or a strait jacket shall be permitted on persons confined under guard if they show physical resistance to workers of places of preliminary confinement, display riotous conduct, or commit other coercive actions, with a view to preventing them causing harm to persons around them or to themselves.

If a person confined under guard commits an attack or other intentional action directly threatening the life of workers of places of preliminary confinement or other persons, and also in the event of an escape from under guard, the use of weapons shall be permitted as an exceptional measure if other measures are impossible to restrain the said actions. The use of weapons shall not be permitted in the event of the escape of females and minors.

The administration of places of preliminary confinement shall be obliged to inform the procurator immediately about each instance of the use of a weapon.

Article 18. Grounds for Release of Persons Confined Under Guard as a Measure of Restraint

The grounds for the release of persons confined under guard shall be:

(1) vacating of the measure of restraint;

(2) change of the measure of restraint;

(3) expiry of the term of confinement under guard as a measure of restraint provided by law, if this term is not extended in the procedure established by law. The head of a place of preliminary confinement shall be obliged not later than seven days from the expiry of the term of confinement under guard of the confined person to notify in writing the person or agency proceeding in the case thereof, and also the procurator exercising supervision over the observance of legality in places of preliminary confinement.

Persons confined under guard shall be released by the head of the place of preliminary confinement on the basis of the decree of the person conducting the inquiry, the investigator, the procurator, or the judgment or ruling of a court. In the instance provided by point 3 of the present Article, confined persons shall be released by decree of the procurator exercising supervision over the observance of legality in places of preliminary confinement.

A decree, judgment, or ruling concerning the release of a person from under guard shall be subject to execution immediately upon receipt at the place of preliminary confinement.

Persons released from under guard shall be provided by the administration of the place of preliminary confinement with passage free of charge to their place of residence. When necessary, they shall be issued a cash allowance and clothing.

Article 19. Procuratorial Supervision Over the Observance of Legality in Places of Preliminary Confinement

Supervision over the observance of legality in places of preliminary confinement shall be exercised by the USSR Procurator General and procurators subordinate to him in accordance with legislation of procuracy supervision in the USSR.